CALIFORNIA REAL ESTATE PRINCIPLES

First Edition

All content, suggestions, ideas, concepts and conclusions presented in this book are subject to local, state and federal law; court cases revisions or any revisions of the same. Great care has been taken to provide the most accurate, up-to-date material, however all topics may be subject to revisions both legal and otherwise. The reader is urged to consult legal counsel regarding any points of law. This publication is not intended to be used a substitute for competent legal or accounting advice.

TABLE OF CONTENTS

CHAPTER 4 — Contracts

CHAPTER 5 — Agency

CHAPTER 6 — Conveyance and Escrow

CHAPTER 7 — Landlord and Tenant

CHAPTER 8 — Real Estate Finance

CHAPTER 9 — National Lending Practices

CALIFORNIA DEPARTMENT OF REAL ESTATE

What you will learn in this Chapter

- The structure and operations of the Department of Real Estate

- Types of licenses and requirements for obtaining them

- Continuing education requirements

- Violations of Real Estate Law

- California trade and professional organizations

1. Representing more than one party in a transaction without the knowledge or consent of all other parties is best described as:
    A. Divided Agency
    B. Collusion
    C. Commingling
    D. Conspiracy

2. To become truly successful in the real estate business, one should:
    A. Attain as high a level of academic education as possible
    B. Take as many courses in real estate as possible
    C. Educate oneself throughout one's career
    D. All of the above

3. How many classes are required of a broker candidate before he or she is eligible to sit for the state exam?
    A. 5
    B. 3
    C. 8
    D. None of the above

4. A broker persuades a Caucasian family to list their home for sale by telling them that non-white people are moving into the area, and that this may reduce property values. Such persuasion is considered all of the following, except:
    A. Blockbusting
    B. Encouragement of panic selling
    C. Legal but unethical
    D. Illegal conduct

5. Unlawful Conduct as set forth in the Commission's Regulations is best described as:
    A. Acts which are not grounds for disciplinary action by DRE
    B. Not an actual act, but a statement of duties imposed by law
    C. Specific acts and omissions, which violate existing law and are grounds for disciplinary action
    D. Acts which are set as guidelines

6. Commingling of funds is:
    A. Misappropriation and use of funds
    B. Mixing broker's funds with those of the principal
    C. More serious an offense than conversion
    D. All of the above

7. Who appoints the Real Estate Commissioner?
    A. Governor
    B. State Legislators
    C. California Association of Realtors
    D. Both A and B

INTRODUCTION

The purchase of real estate is one of the largest investments a person will make in his or her lifetime, and is no doubt a very big decision. The buyer of property places complete trust in his or her realtor, as the realtor is the industry professional who knows all the rules and regulations to keep the process on track and running smoothly. It is important for you, as a future realtor, to have a deep understanding of this process and provide guidance for all of your clients.

This book is an introduction to real estate, and provides you with a base knowledge of the rules, regulations, processes, laws and other important matters necessary to represent a client in a property transaction or transfer. By no means is this an exhaustive source of information. Throughout the book, you may see suggested websites or different codes. These are important resources for your benefit, as they further your understanding of real estate. Additionally, there are many other classes you can take to delve deeper into each of the subject areas to which you will be introduced.

As a realtor, you are expected to have knowledge of a variety of subjects. However, you are not expected to know everything. So, it is important for you to offer alternative resources, in the event that you are unable to fully supply your client with information. For example, you may know the current interest rates and the different programs for which your client may qualify. But, it is in your client's best interest to refer them to a mortgage broker for more specific information in these cases. It is common for realtors to form a working relationship with mortgage brokers, escrow officers and other real estate professionals to provide the best and most accurate information possible to clients.

As a student of real estate, this textbook is merely an initial resource for your learning. As you progress in your training, you should take advantage of all the resources available to you, to ensure a successful career.

HISTORY OF CALIFORNIA REAL ESTATE LAW

Real estate law in North America is an import from England. All laws pertaining to land and estates, though modified through time, derive from English common law which was itself heavily influenced by Germanic medieval habits and mores.

Legislation in California was compiled into a series of books called codes. Most California real estate licensing laws are contained in the Business and Professional Code, among the nation's first to be enacted (in 1917). Real estate licensing law is upheld by police power.

> **Police Power**
> The power of the state to enact laws to promote the order, safety, health and general welfare of the public.

The complete text of the California code, as well as information on bills pending before the legislature, can be found at www.leginfo.ca.gov. It is important to note that updates and changes to code are made yearly. So, keep current with yearly changes in legislation, through this website or through your local California Association of Realtors office.

California Department of Real Estate

The foremost objective of the California Department of Real Estate (DRE) is protecting the public interest with regard to the handling of real estate transactions and the subdivision of lands. The DRE serves as the government regulatory body, which oversees the real estate industry in California. The DRE uses real estate law and the regulations of the Real Estate Commissioner to enforce these rules.

Every state has a similar agency or department responsible for protecting its citizens and enforcing laws concerning real estate licensees.

STRUCTURE OF THE DEPARTMENT OF REAL ESTATE

The chief executive of the DRE is the Real Estate Commissioner, who is appointed by the state's Governor. The legislature must also approve the appointment of the Real Estate Commissioner, who is required to have been a practicing real estate broker for at least five years. If he or she has not been a practicing real estate broker for at least five years, he or she must have been involved in some form of real estate activity for five of the last ten years.

The Commissioner is empowered by law to issue regulations, to facilitate the administration and enforcement of Real Estate Law and Subdivided Lands Law. These regulations are known as the Regulations of the Real Estate Commissioner and have the force and effect of law. Other duties of the Real Estate Commissioner:

Duties of the Real Estate Commissioner:

- Issues rules and regulations, which have the force and effect of law and become part of the California Code of Regulations.
- Regulates the sale of subdivision and nonexempt franchises.
- Screens and qualifies applicants for licenses. Has the sole authority to issue, suspend and revoke all licenses.
- Determines the business policies of the Department of Real Estate
- Investigates complaints against licensees and non-licensees who engage in acts which require a real estate license. *The District Attorney prosecutes law violations in his or her own county.*
- Holds formal hearings within terms of the Administrative Procedure Act (using established legal procedures to discipline licensees). *The Commissioner cannot make the licensee pay damages; only the courts can do this.*
- If a buyer wins a civil judgment against a broker for fraud, the Commissioner may suspend or revoke the broker's license, but only after a hearing.
- Has the power to discipline a licensee who provides a falsified application or one who fails to reveal a prior criminal record.
- Uses the state Attorney General as legal advisor.

Real Estate Advisory Commission

The Commissioner then appoints a Real Estate Advisory Commission, comprised of ten members; six California real estate brokers and four non-licensed, public members. Unlike the Commissioner, advisory committee members are not compensated, although they may be reimbursed for some expenses.

The Commissioner and the Advisory Commission meet in public at least four times per year. At these meetings, they consult regarding policies of the DRE and help determine how the people of the State of California may best be served by it. They also strive to meet the needs of the industry they regulate. In enforcing the statutes of the Real Estate Law, the Commissioner has the authority, if supported by evidence obtained, to hold formal hearings to decide on any issues involving a licensee or a license applicant. The Commissioner also has the authority to issue Desist and Refrain Orders, to stop activities that are in violation of the Real Estate Law or the Subdivided Lands Law.

Operations of the Department of Real Estate

The money necessary to run the DRE is generated from fees charged for real estate licenses, subdivision public reports and other various permits issued by the DRE. The department has five district offices (Sacramento, Oakland, Fresno, Los Angeles and San Diego) from which the department's employees carry out their responsibilities as mandated by the Real Estate Law and Subdivided Lands Law.

While the DRE protects the public interest and increases consumer awareness, it also assists the real estate industry in expanding and upholding the standards of responsibility and professional ethics.

REAL ESTATE LICENSES

Any person wishing to engage in the real estate business on behalf of another for compensation, or in expectation of compensation, must hold a California real estate license, either as a **real estate broker** or a **real estate salesperson**.

A real estate salesperson, also called a **sales associate** or **associate licensee**, may act only under the control and supervision of the real estate broker of record (the broker by whom the salesperson is employed).

Listed below are some activities that require a real estate license:

- Buying, selling, soliciting or obtaining listings of, or negotiating the purchase, sale or exchange of: real property; business opportunities; or mineral, oil or gas properties.

- Collecting rents, leasing, managing and renting property, or negotiating the sale or exchange of leased real property, business opportunities, or mineral, oil or gas properties.

- Soliciting borrowers or lenders or negotiating loans on real property, business opportunities, or mineral, oil or gas properties.

- Buying or selling a promissory note secured by real property, business opportunities, or mineral, oil or gas properties.

The fine for an unlicensed person who receives an illegal commission from such a sale is $10,000 per individual and $50,000 per corporation.

Exceptions – persons that do not require a real estate license to conduct such sales:

- A Principal handling his or her own properties.

- An attorney-in-fact, acting under a power of attorney.

 Attorney-in-fact: A person who is authorized to perform certain acts for another under power of attorney. Powers of attorney may be limited to a specific act or acts, or may be general in nature.

- Attorney-at-law (lawyer) while performing duties as an attorney. *If the attorney charges a broker's fee a real estate license is required.*

- Trustee selling under a deed of trust.

- Resident property managers (or their employees) and hotel, motel and trailer park managers. *A full-service, off-site property manager must have a real estate license.*

- Anyone working under the direction of a court.

- A licensed securities broker or dealer involved in the sale, lease or exchange of a business opportunity.

- A corporation that performs any of the specified activities through one of its regular officers, who must receive no special compensation for so doing.

- Employees of lending institutions, pension trusts, credit unions or insurance companies, in connection with loans secured by liens on real property or business opportunities.

- Escrow agents collecting funds in connection with loans secured by liens on real property, when the funds are deposited in the escrow agent's trust account.

Real Estate Brokerage

A real estate brokerage is a business in which real estate license-related activities are performed under the supervision of a real estate broker. A real estate brokerage may consist of just one broker of record by himself/herself with no employees, or it may be large enough to have separate departments with numerous salespersons and administrative support staff, along with branch offices.

Either way, there must always be one broker of record, one under whose license the real estate activities are carried out.

Corporation. Provided that at least one officer is a licensed broker and designated the responsible broker-officer, a brokerage may be set up as a corporation.

CALIFORNIA
ASSOCIATION
OF REALTORS®

**BROKER/ASSOCIATE-LICENSEE/ASSISTANTS
THREE-PARTY AGREEMENT**
(C.A.R. Form TPA, Revised 10/04)

This Agreement, dated _____, is made by_____
_____ ("Broker"), and
_____ ("Associate-Licensee"), and
_____, ("Assistant").

In consideration for the covenants and representations contained in this Agreement, Broker, Associate-Licensee, and Assistant agree as follows:

1. **BROKER:** Broker represents that Broker is licensed as a real estate broker by the State of California, and is doing business as (firm name)_____,
a ☐ sole proprietorship, ☐ partnership, or ☐ corporation. Broker is a member of the_____
_____ Association(s) of REALTORS®, and a
subscriber to the _____ Multiple Listing Service(s).

2. **ASSOCIATE-LICENSEE:** Associate-Licensee represents that he/she is licensed by the State of California as a ☐ real estate broker, ☐ real estate salesperson, and has entered into a separate agreement with Assistant for the performance of services related to Associate-Licensee's real estate activity.

3. **ASSISTANT:** Assistant represents that he/she has entered into an agreement with Associate-Licensee for the performance of services related to Associate-Licensee's licensed real estate activity. Assistant represents that he/she ☐ does, ☐ does not, have a California real estate license.

4. **RELATIONSHIP AMONG THE PARTIES:** Associate-Licensee has entered into an independent contractor agreement with Broker to perform real estate licensed activity under the name and license of Broker. Assistant works for Associate-Licensee as specified under the terms of their separate written agreement. Other than as specified in this Agreement, Assistant has no other agreements with Broker for the performance of any acts specified in the separate agreement with Associate-Licensee.

5. **COMPLIANCE WITH REAL ESTATE LAW:** Broker, Associate-Licensee and Assistant each acknowledge that California real estate law imposes certain obligations on a broker with regard to supervision, employment and compensation of any person who acts on behalf of the broker in pursuit of real estate licensed activity. Accordingly, Broker, Associate-Licensee and Assistant all agree that the following terms contained in this paragraph are made solely for the purpose of compliance with the real estate law and that no other inference of employment between Broker and Associate-Licensee, Broker and Assistant, or Associate-Licensee and Assistant shall be drawn therefrom. Broker has the right to review and supervise the files and activities of Assistant, the right to recommend termination and, if necessary, to actually terminate the relationship between Associate-Licensee and Assistant as it relates to the performance of acts under Broker's license. If Assistant has a California real estate license, and performs licensed activity, Assistant's real estate license shall immediately be given to Broker. If Assistant is licensed as a real estate salesperson and performs licensed activity, then: **(i)** all compensation to Assistant for licensed activity shall be paid through Broker, and **(ii)** for the sole and limited purpose of complying with California real estate law, the Assistant shall be deemed employed by Broker.

6. **ASSISTANT COMPENSATION:** Associate-Licensee shall be solely responsible for compensation to Assistant under the terms of their agreement. If payment of compensation to Assistant must be made through Broker because Assistant has a California real estate license, then Associate-Licensee shall be responsible to Broker for such compensation and all administrative and other costs necessary to accommodate the relationship between Associate-Licensee and Assistant. Any compensation paid to Assistant, and all administrative and other necessary costs, shall be offset against any compensation due Associate-Licensee by Broker.

Broker's Initials (_____)(_____)
Associate-Licensee's Initials (_____)(_____)
Assistant's Initials (_____)(_____)

Reviewed by _____ Date _____

TPA REVISED 10/04 (PAGE 1 OF 3) Print Date

BROKER/ASSOCIATE-LICENSEE/ASSISTANT THREE-PARTY AGREEMENT (TPA PAGE 1 OF 3)

7. INSURANCE:

A. Automobile: Assistant shall maintain automobile insurance coverage for liability and property damage in the following amounts $_____ /$_____. Broker shall be named as an additional insured party on Assistant's policies. A copy of the endorsement showing the additional insured parties shall be provided to Broker.

B. Workers Compensation: Broker ☐ does, ☐ does not, carry workers' compensation insurance which covers Assistant. (If checked) ☐ Associate-Licensee agrees to carry workers' compensation insurance which covers Assistant.

(Workers' Compensation Advisory: Even though Assistant may be treated as an independent contractors for tax and other purposes, the California Labor and Workforce Development Agency may consider Assistant to be an employee for workers' compensation purposes. If Assistant is, or is considered to be an employee: **(i)** Broker or Associate-Licensee must obtain workers' compensation insurance for Assistant, and **(ii)** Broker or Associate Licensee, not Assistant, must bear the cost of workers' compensation insurance. Penalties for failure to carry workers' compensation include, among others, the issuance of stop-work orders and fines of up to $1,000 per agent, not to exceed $100,000 per company.)

C. Errors and Omissions: Broker ☐ does, ☐ does not, maintain errors and omissions insurance which covers the activities of Assistant.

D. All: Whether Broker carries workers compensation, errors and omissions, unemployment, liability or any other insurance which provides coverage for Assistant or Associate-Licensee, Broker does so in the exercise of Broker's business judgment, for the sole benefit of Broker, and all parties agree that, other than for compliance with California real estate law, no inference of employment between Broker and Associate-Licensee, Broker and Assistant, or Associate-Licensee and Assistant shall be drawn therefrom.

8. PROPRIETARY INFORMATION:
All files and documents pertaining to listings, leads and transactions are the property of Broker and shall be delivered to Broker by Assistant immediately upon request or termination of the relationship between either Broker and Associate-Licensee or Associate-Licensee and Assistant. Assistant shall not use to his/her own advantage, or the advantage of any other person, business, or entity, except as specifically agreed in writing, either during Assistant's association with Broker, or thereafter, any information gained for or from the business, or files of Broker. After termination, Assistant shall not solicit: **(i)** prospective or existing clients or customers based upon company-generated leads obtained during the time Associate-Licensee was affiliated with Broker: **(ii)** any principal with existing contractual obligations to Broker; or **(iii)** any principal with a contractual transactional obligation for which Broker is entitled to be compensated.

9. COMPLIANCE WITH APPLICABLE LAWS, RULES, REGULATIONS AND POLICIES:
Assistant agrees to comply with all local, state and federal laws and regulations and any office policy and procedures to which Associate-Licensee is subject as a result of engaging in real estate activity. If Assistant does not have a real estate license, Assistant shall not engage in any activity for which a real estate license is required. (Assistant may become more familiar with these limitations by reading the "DRE Guidelines for Unlicensed Assistants.")

10. INDEMNITY AND HOLD HARMLESS:
Assistant agrees, regardless of responsibility, to indemnify, defend and hold Broker harmless from all claims, disputes, litigation, judgments, awards, costs and attorney's fees arising from any action taken or omitted by Assistant, in connection with services rendered or to be rendered, pursuant to Assistant's agreement with Associate-Licensee.

11. DISPUTE RESOLUTION:

A. All Disputes: This Agreement shall govern all disputes and claims among Broker, Associate-Licensee, and Assistant or between Broker and Assistant, arising out of their relationship under this and any attached agreements, and applies even after termination of any relationship with Assistant.

B. Mediation: Mediation is recommended as a method of resolving disputes arising out of this Agreement between and among Broker, Associate-Licensee, and Assistant.

C. Arbitration: All disputes or claims between Broker, Associate-Licensee and Assistant which cannot be otherwise resolved, shall be decided by neutral, binding arbitration in accordance with substantive California law. The Federal Arbitration Act, Title 9, U.S. Code Section 1 et seq., shall govern this Agreement to arbitrate.

Broker's Initials (_____)(_____)
Associate-Licensee's Initials (_____)(_____)
Assistant's Initials (_____)(_____)

Reviewed by _____ Date _____

TPA REVISED 10/04 (PAGE 2 OF 3)

BROKER/ASSOCIATE-LICENSEE/ASSISTANT THREE-PARTY AGREEMENT (TPA PAGE 2 OF 3)

12. OTHER TERMS AND CONDITIONS AND ATTACHED SUPPLEMENTS:
☐ Broker and Associate-Licensee Independent Contractor Agreement (Such as C.A.R. Form ICA)
☐ Associate-Licensee and Assistant Agreement (Such as C.A.R. Form PAC)
☐ Broker Office Policy Manual (or, if checked, ☐ in Broker's office)
☐ DRE Guidelines for Unlicensed Assistants
☐ California Association of REALTORS® "Real Estate Licensing Chart"

_____
_____
_____
_____
_____
_____
_____

13. ATTORNEY FEES: In any action, proceeding, or arbitration between or among Broker, Associate-Licensee or Assistant, arising from or related to this Agreement, the prevailing Broker, Associate-Licensee or Assistant shall be entitled to reasonable attorney fees and costs.

14. ENTIRE AGREEMENT: All prior agreements between the parties concerning their relationship as Broker, Associate-Licensee, and Assistant are incorporated in this Agreement, which constitutes the entire contract. Its terms are intended by the parties as a final and complete expression of their agreement with respect to its subject matter, and may not be contradicted by evidence of any prior agreement or contemporaneous oral agreement. This Agreement may not be amended, modified, altered, or changed, except by a further agreement in writing executed by Broker, Associate-Licensee, and Assistant.

BROKER:

_____   _____
(Signature)   (Name Printed)

By _____
Its Broker/Office Manager (circle one)

_____   _____
(Address)   (City, State, Zip)

_____   _____
(Telephone)   (Fax)

_____
(E-mail)

ASSOCIATE-LICENSEE:

_____   _____
(Signature)   (Name Printed)

_____   _____
(Address)   (City, State, Zip)

_____   _____
(Telephone)   (Fax)

_____
(E-mail)

ASSISTANT:

_____   _____
(Signature)   (Name Printed)

_____   _____
(Address)   (City, State, Zip)

_____   _____
(Telephone)   (Fax)

_____
(E-mail)

THIS FORM HAS BEEN APPROVED BY THE CALIFORNIA ASSOCIATION OF REALTORS® (C.A.R.). NO REPRESENTATION IS MADE AS TO THE LEGAL VALIDITY OR ADEQUACY OF ANY PROVISION IN ANY SPECIFIC TRANSACTION. A REAL ESTATE BROKER IS THE PERSON QUALIFIED TO ADVISE ON REAL ESTATE TRANSACTIONS. IF YOU DESIRE LEGAL OR TAX ADVICE, CONSULT AN APPROPRIATE PROFESSIONAL.

This form is available for use by the entire real estate industry. It is not intended to identify the user as a REALTOR®. REALTOR® is a registered collective membership mark which may be used only by members of the NATIONAL ASSOCIATION OF REALTORS® who subscribe to its Code of Ethics.

Published and Distributed by:
REAL ESTATE BUSINESS SERVICES, INC.
a subsidiary of the California Association of REALTORS®
525 South Virgil Avenue, Los Angeles, California 90020

SURE TRAC
The System for Success®

Reviewed by _____ Date _____

TPA REVISED 10/04 (PAGE 3 OF 3)

BROKER/ASSOCIATE-LICENSEE/ASSISTANT THREE-PARTY AGREEMENT (TPA PAGE 3 OF 3)

The corporation must send to the DRE:

- The corporation license application and fee

- A Certificate of Status issued by the Secretary of State within 30 days prior to submission of the application

- A statement of the corporation's officers as filed with the Secretary of State

A salesperson may be an officer of the corporation, provided that the salesperson's supervising broker is a director and officer. Also, salespersons working for a corporate licensee may not, individually or collectively, own or control a majority of the outstanding stock of the corporation, directly or indirectly.

Partnership. For a brokerage to be established as a partnership, every partner who performs activities that require a real estate license must have an individual license. At least one broker partner must be licensed at each branch location. The partnership itself needs no separate license.

Fictitious Business Name Statement. Any brokerage, whether a partnership, corporation or an individual, may do business under a fictitious name. A fictitious business name statement must be filed with the county in which the business has its principal business address.

Commonly referred to as a DBA, the statement is good for five years from December 31 of the filing year. A copy of the fictitious business name statement must be sent to the DRE.

The business cards of the licensee should use exactly the same name that appears on the real estate license. Any change, such as a marital name change or nickname, will require the filing of a fictitious business name statement. The Commissioner may refuse the use of any name that is inappropriate or misleading.

License Inspection. At the brokerage's principal business address, the broker's license must be available for inspection by the Commissioner or the Commissioner's representative. If the broker has more than one place of business, the broker must apply for and obtain an additional license for each branch office. Any salesperson(s) working for the broker must also have their license(s) available for inspection by the Commissioner or the Commissioner's representative at the principal place of business.

Broker and Salesperson Relationships

For purposes of Real Estate Law a salesperson is always considered an employee of the broker. What this means is that the broker is responsible for all actions of the salesperson when the salesperson is conducting the business of real estate. With regard to compensation, taxes, etc., the salesperson may be regarded as either an independent contractor or an employee of the broker.

A salesperson's license is activated only after the employing broker's name has been submitted to the DRE. The employing broker and salesperson (or broker) are required by Real Estate Law to have a written agreement, outlining the duties of each of them and the compensation to be paid to the salesperson/broker. An example of a broker-salesperson contract is on the preceding pages.

Broker License Requirements

As stated previously, a real estate broker's license enables any individual who meets the requirements to establish a brokerage business in his/her name or, if so licensed, under a fictitious name.

There are four requirements to obtain a real estate broker's license in California.

Basic Requirements for Broker Applicants
• Applicant must be at least 18 years of age
• Applicant must have previous experience and/or education as required by law
• Applicant must be honest and truthful
• Applicant must pass the qualifying examination

California law requires either two years of real estate sales experience or a four-year degree from an accredited college. Applicants may submit a transcript from their college or university in lieu of the experience requirements. Additionally, the applicant must successfully pass the following eight (8) college-level courses:

Mandatory Courses:	**Elective Courses:**
• Real Estate Practice • Accounting or Real Estate Economics • Legal Aspects of Real Estate • Real Estate Appraisal • Real Estate Finance • Any three (3) of the courses listed in the right-hand column:	• Business Law • Escrow • Mortgage Loan Brokering and Lending • Real Estate Office Administration • Property Management • Advanced Legal Aspects of Real Estate • Advanced Real Estate Appraisal • Advanced Real Estate Finance

Real Estate Principles

If an applicant completes courses in both Accounting and Economics, only two courses from Group Six are required. More extensive licensing requirement information can be found at the DRE's web site, www.dre.ca.gov.

Applicants who are attorneys and current members of the Bar Association of any state in the United States are exempt from both the education and experience requirements for obtaining a broker's license.

Before a broker's license may be issued, the applicant must pass a written, qualifying examination. On its web site, the DRE provides a list of examination topics, to aid broker applicants in studying. Below is the current weighted distribution of the examination:

Real Estate Broker Licensing Exam	
	Content Weight
Land Use Controls and Regulations and Property Ownership	Approx. 15%
Agency Laws	Approx. 12%
Market Analysis and Valuation	Approx. 11%
Financing	Approx. 13%
Transfer of Property	Approx. 10%
Real Estate Practice and Mandated Disclosures	Approx. 27%
Contracts	Approx. 12%

Salesperson License Requirements

A real estate salesperson's license is issued to a person who wishes to engage in the real estate business but under the employment of a real estate broker. He/she must work under the supervision and control of a broker.

Much like the broker's license requirements, applicants for the real estate salesperson's license must also meet four requirements. The applicant must be at least 18 years old at the time the license is issued, be ethical and honest, pass a qualifying examination and meet educational requirements.

The applicant must successfully complete a college-level course in Real Estate Principles to be eligible to take the licensing examination. If the applicant passes the examination, he or she is issued a **conditional license**. In order to maintain this license while obtaining a four-year **regular license**, two additional courses must be completed within eighteen (18) months of receipt of the conditional license. It is mandatory that Real Estate Practice be one of those two courses.

Other choices include:

• Business Law	• Real Estate Appraisal
• Escrows	• Real Estate Economics
• General Accounting	• Real Estate Finance
• Legal Aspects of Real Estate	• Real Estate Office Administration
• Mortgage Loan Brokering and Lending	• Property Management

If the salesperson has not completed two additional courses within the eighteen-month period, the salesperson's license is suspended automatically.

However, once these courses have been completed, the DRE will issue the salesperson a full, four-year salesperson's license.

Here is the DRE's current weight distribution for the salesperson qualifying examination:

Real Estate Salesperson Licensing Exam	
	Content Weight
Land Use Controls and Regulations and Property Ownership	Approx. 18%
Agency Laws	Approx. 12%
Market Analysis and Valuation	Approx. 12%
Financing	Approx. 13%
Transfer of Property	Approx. 9%
Real Estate Practice and Mandated Disclosures	Approx. 24%
Contracts	Approx. 12%

Both licensing examinations consist of multiple-choice questions. The purpose of the written examination is to determine if the applicant has sufficient knowledge of the required topics. They also indicate whether the applicant can read and comprehend the English language.

Additionally, common real estate mathematics computations are a factor in the exam.

The salesperson's exam contains 150 questions. An applicant must correctly answer 70% of the questions (105 questions) to pass the exam. The salesperson's exam is taken in one 3 1/4 hour session.

The broker's exam has 200 questions and is conducted in one 1/2 hour morning session and one 2 1/2 hour evening session. Applicants must correctly answer 75% of the questions (150 questions) to pass the exam.

License Term and Renewal
The initial term for all California real estate licenses is four years. Generally speaking, a license may be renewed for an additional four years by successfully completing 45 course hours of continuing education (CE) within the four years during which the license was held, as well as paying the appropriate renewal fee.

Salesperson's First Renewal
Those salespersons renewing their original license for the first time must complete four separate three-hour DRE-approved CE courses, for a total of twelve (12) course hours. These courses must be in Ethics, Agency, Trust Fund Handling, and Fair Housing.

Broker's First Renewal
Brokers who will be renewing their original license must complete 45 clock hours of DRE-approved CE courses. The courses must include the following:

- Four separate three-hour classes (one in each of the following areas), for a total of twelve (12) hours:

  i. Ethics

  ii. Agency

  iii. Trust Fund Handling

  iv. Fair Housing

- A minimum of eighteen (18) hours of consumer protection courses

- Fifteen (15) clock hours related to either consumer protection or consumer service

Subsequent Renewals

After the initial renewal, all real estate licensees (brokers and salespersons) must complete forty-five (45) clock hours of DRE-approved CE, including the following:

- One six (6) hour survey course that covers the four mandatory study areas (ethics, agency, trust fund handling and fair housing)

- At least eighteen (18) hours of consumer protection courses

- The remaining twenty-one (21) hours must be related to either consumer protection or consumer service

If a licensee has not renewed their license by its expiration date, the licensee must immediately cease all real estate activity. For a licensee who is an employing broker, this mistake can be a profound one. Expiration of the broker's license will put *all* licensees who work for the employing broker (whether salespersons or brokers) on nonworking status.

Any license that is not renewed before its expiration date may be renewed up to two (2) years after that expiration date, upon application and payment of a late renewal fee. However, after this two-year period, an original application must be made.

V I O L A T I O N S   O F   R E A L   E S T A T E   L A W

California Real Estate Law specifies many activities that can result in suspension or revocation of a real estate license. In order to enhance the professionalism of the California real estate industry, and to protect members of the public when dealing with real estate agents, licensees are prohibited from committing unlawful conduct, which includes (but is not limited to) the following acts and omissions:

Fraud - the intentional deceit of material facts used to induce another party to enter into a contract to his or her detriment. Actual fraud includes the suppression of the truth or the concealment of material facts

Misrepresentation - making a false statement of facts without knowing whether they are true. A misrepresentation is a civil wrong that differs from criminal fraud in that it is not intentional. Nevertheless, misrepresentation is fraud

Puffing - making a statement that exaggerates a property's benefits. An agent should never misrepresent a material fact

Divided agency - acting for more than one party in a transaction without the knowledge and consent of all parties (also called *undisclosed dual agency*)

    i. If an agent informs and obtains consent from all principals, he or she may collect a commission from each principal

    ii. If an agent does not disclose his or her dual agency to both parties, the agent may be disciplined, may provide grounds for either party to rescind, and may not receive any commission

Commingling - occurs when a broker mixes his or her own money with the funds of his or her principals. Failure to deposit or place trust funds received into escrow, the hands of the principal, or a trust fund account by the next business day is commingling. The licensee can, however, place up to $200 into the trust account to cover account fees.

    i. Keeping the buyer's cash deposit in the broker's safe is commingling

    ii. A broker may hold an uncashed check with written instructions from the seller or the buyer

    iii. The opposite of commingling is segregation

Conversion - misappropriation of a client's funds. It is using a client's money as one's own (for example, to finance a vacation in Hawaii)

No Contract Copies - failing to give a copy of a listing or a deposit receipt to the person signing, after he or she has signed

Secret Profit - no compensation in any form may be received by the licensee without the knowledge of the principal. If a licensee is offered a secret profit, he or she has a duty to let the principal know of the profit, which can be constituted as a bribe. In addition, a broker may not allow others (friends and/or relatives) to make a secret profit with his or her knowledge. An agent who makes a secret profit violates the fiduciary relationship between principal and agent. All financial offers, whether legitimate or not, must be presented to the seller;

No listing termination date for any exclusive listing or other agreement;

Proceeding without principal's signature - no agreement to represent someone or receive compensation for the purchase, lease, rent, sale or exchange of a business opportunity or real property can be obtained without prior authorization

Willfully or repeatedly violating any provision of the Civil Code regarding real property transfer disclosures.

Similarly, for those licensees who solicit, negotiate or arrange a loan secured by real property, or the sale of a promissory note secured by real property, the following acts and/or omissions are prohibited by the Business and Profession Code:

Misrepresentation of lender/purchaser to borrower – deliberately leading the prospective borrower of a loan to be secured by real property (or an assignor/endorser of a promissory note secured by real property) to believe that there is an existing lender to make the loan or that there is a purchaser for the note. This is done for the purpose of inducing the borrower to use the services of the licensee;

Misrepresentation of borrower to lender/purchaser – making a false or deliberate misrepresentation to a prospective lender or purchaser of a loan, secured or collateralized by real property, about the borrower's ability to repay the proposed loan in accordance with the terms and conditions; or, withholding from the prospective lender, broker or purchaser of the loan any material information about the borrower;

Misrepresentation of expenses to borrower/lender – knowingly underestimating the probable closing costs in any communication with the prospective borrower or lender of a loan secured by real property, for the purpose of enticing either or both to enter into the loan transaction;

Misrepresentation of lien status – knowingly misrepresenting the priority of the security, as a lien against the real property securing the loan, to a prospective lender in the solicitation of the lender to make the loan;

Misrepresentation of service fee – knowingly misrepresenting, in any transaction with a prospective borrower or purchaser, that a specific service is free when the licensee knows or can reasonably presume that it is covered by a fee that will be charged as part of the transaction;

Misrepresentation of loan payments – knowingly misrepresenting to either a lender or assignee/endorsee of a lender of a loan secured directly or collaterally by a lien on real property about the amount and treatment of loan payments. This includes loan pay-offs, and the failure to account to the lender or assignee/endorsee of a lender as to the disposition of such payments;

No accountability of advance fee – when acting as a licensee in a transaction for the purpose of obtaining a loan (and in receipt of an advance fee from the borrower for this purpose) failure to account to the borrower for the disposition of the advance fee;

Misrepresentation of loan terms - knowingly making a false or misleading representation about the terms and conditions of a loan to be secured by a lien on real property when soliciting a borrower or negotiating the loan; and

Misrepresentation of security - knowingly making a false or misleading representation without a reasonable basis for believing its truth, when soliciting a lender or negotiating a loan to be secured by a lien on real property, about the market value of the securing real property, the nature and/or condition of the interior or exterior features of the securing real property, its size or the square footage of any improvements on the securing real property.

Enforcement of Real Estate Law

Now that you are familiar with acts that violate real estate law, you should know how the Real Estate Commissioner deals with these violations.

The Commissioner is mandated to investigate all written complaints brought forward against real estate licensees. This investigation may include a statement by the licensee, examination of the licensee's financial records, bank records, title company records and public records. Part of this investigation may include an informal hearing to determine the necessity for a formal hearing, in which all parties involved may be asked to attend.

Formal Hearing

If a formal hearing is necessary, an administrative law judge presides over the affair in accordance with the Administrative Procedure Act. The Commissioner now becomes the complainant and is represented by Commissioner's counsel. The person who originally brought the complaint becomes a witness, and the licensee becomes the respondent.

The licensee may appear with or without an attorney. The official accusation or statement of issues is served on the licensee and they are made aware of the rights of the accused. All testimony is taken under oath and other evidence may be presented. A record of the proceedings is made, and the hearing is conducted according to the rules of evidence.

The Commissioner has the authority to accept or reject the proposed decision or reduce the recommended penalty, and the respondent has the right of appeal to the courts.

Formal Hearing Outcome

If the charges are not proven by the evidence presented, the charges are dismissed. However, if they are proven, the license of the respondent is either **suspended** or **revoked**. If the license is revoked, one year must pass before the licensee may apply for reinstatement of the license.

Under certain circumstances, the Commissioner may decide to issue a **restricted license** to the licensee. Among other things, the restriction(s) imposed could:

- Limit the length of the license term

- Require employment by a particular real estate broker

- Contain some other condition, such as filing a surety bond for the protection of persons doing business with the licensee

A licensee holding a restricted license cannot renew the license unless and until the restriction is lifted. Only the Commissioner has the authority to suspend a restricted license without a hearing, pending final determination after a formal hearing.

More Penalties
Additionally, the Real Estate Commissioner has the discretion to order one or more of the following penalties for violation of the Real Estate Law:

- Payment of a fine

- Return of documents and other materials

- Education (requiring the offending licensee to successfully complete one or more classes)

- Reimbursement to the Real Estate Recovery Account Fund

Real Estate Funds

There are two (2) accounts that are maintained by the DRE: the Education and Research Fund and the Recovery Account Fund. The Education and Research Fund receives funds from proceeds of license and examination fees to promote real estate education and research at the University of California, other state colleges and community colleges.

The Recovery Account Fund receives funds from proceeds of license and examination fees in order to pay for damages and awards issued to those who have suffered financial loss because of the unlawful acts of a licensee during the course of a real estate transaction.

In order to qualify for these funds, plaintiffs must first obtain a judgment through arbitration (the previously discussed formal hearing) or in civil court against a licensee on the grounds of fraud, misrepresentation, deceit or conversion of trust funds. If, after reasonable effort, the judgment remains uncollectable, a claim may be filed with the Commissioner's office.

Payment Limits

For losses incurred after January 1980, the payment limits are as follows:

- $20,000 for each claimant in any one transaction

- $100,000 for multiple transactions for any one licensee

When a claim against a licensee is paid out of the recovery account fund, the licensee's license is automatically suspended until the licensee has repaid the fund and the legally-prevailing party.

| Licensee's license suspended until repayment of the recovery account is paid |

T R A D E   A S S O C I A T I O N S

A trade association is a voluntary, member organization of independent and competing entities who are engaged in the same industry or trade. Trade associations are usually created to identify and solve an industry's problems, promote its assets and enhance its service to the public at large.

NATIONAL ASSOCIATION OF REALTORS

The largest real estate trade association in the United States is the National Association of Realtors® (NAR), which is the national trade association for all state associations and local boards of Realtors. Its purpose is to unite the national real estate industry, by encouraging a professional code of conduct for its members and encouraging legislative action that is favorable to the real estate industry.

CALIFORNIA ASSOCIATION OF REALTORS® (CAR)
California's state organization of the NAR is the California Association of Realtors®. It is made up of approximately 130,000 members and roughly 200 local organizations, statewide and is the largest Realtor organization in the United States.
CAR's purposes include:

- To promote high standards and unite its members

- To encourage legislation for the benefit of the real estate industry

- To contribute to the economic growth and development of the state

- To safeguard the public

To accomplish these objectives, CAR offers a broad array of services and products to its members and affiliate members: standard forms, magazines, legislative advocacy, legal services, local government relations liaison services, and various other programs.

Only a licensee who is a member of NAR can be called a **Realtor**. No licensee may advertise himself or herself as a Realtor if not associated with CAR or NAR.

CAR can be found on the web at www.car.org.

NATIONAL ASSOCIATION OF REAL ESTATE BROKERS (NAREB)

NAREB is a trade association made up of mostly African-American real estate brokers. NAREB members are known as Realtists and have member boards in most states. The California Association of Real Estate Brokers (CAREB) was organized in 1955 and has eight membership boards. Realtists work for democracy in housing and more democratic housing in the communities they serve.

AMERICAN INSTITUTE OF REAL ESTATE APPRAISERS

This organization of real estate appraisers merged with the Society of Real Estate Appraisers in 1991 to form the Appraisal Institute. The professional designation of a member is **MAI**, Member of the Appraisal Institute.

CERTIFIED COMMERCIAL INVESTMENT MEMBER (CCIM)

A certified commercial investment member is a designated professional in the commercial real estate industry in the areas of: brokerage; leasing; financing; investment analysis; asset management and valuation.

INSTITUTE OF REAL ESTATE MANAGEMENT (IREM)

The Institute of Real Estate Management was created by the National Association of Realtors as a professional society for property managers and asset managers who have met certain criteria in education, experience and commitment to specific, ethical conduct.

The professional designation of Certified Property Manager is offered to individual members and Accredited Management Organizations for property management company members.

T E R M S   A N D   P H R A S E S

Broker/Salesperson Relationship Agreement - A written agreement required by the regulations of the Real Estate Commissioner, setting forth the material aspects of the relationship between a real estate broker and each salesperson and broker performing licensed activities in the name of that supervising broker

Advance Fees - A fee paid in advance of any services rendered. This fee is sometimes unlawfully charged, in connection with that illegal practice of obtaining a fee in advance for the advertising of property or businesses for sale, with no intent to obtain a buyer, by persons representing themselves as real estate licensees, or representatives of licensed real estate firms.

Appraiser - One qualified by education, training and experience who is hired to estimate the value of real and personal property based on experience, judgment, facts, and use of formal appraisal processes.

Attorney-in-fact - Person authorized to perform certain acts for another under a power of attorney. Powers of attorney may be limited to a specific act or acts, or may be general

Broker - A person employed for a fee by another to carry on any of the activities listed in the license law definition of a broker.

CAR - California Association of Realtors.

CCIM - Certified Commercial Investment Member.

Corporation - An entity established and treated by law as an individual or unit with rights and liabilities (or both), distinct and apart from those of the persons composing it. A corporation is a creature of law with certain powers and duties of a natural person. Since it was created by law it may continue for any length of time that the law prescribes.

CPM© - Certified Property Manager, a designation of the Institute of Real Estate Management.

Fraud - The intentional and successful employment of any cunning, deception, collusion, or artifice, used to circumvent, cheat or deceive another person, whereby that person acts upon it to the loss of property and to legal injury. (Actual Fraud - A deliberate misrepresentation or representation made in reckless disregard of its truth or its falsity, the suppression of truth, a promise made without the intention to perform it, or any other act intended to deceive.)

Lien - A form of encumbrance, which usually makes specific property security for the payment of a debt or discharge of an obligation. Examples include judgments, taxes, mortgages, deeds of trust, etc.

MAI - Member of the American Institute of Real Estate Appraisers

Misrepresentation - A false or misleading statement or assertion

NAR - National Association of Realtors

NAREB - National Association of Real Estate Brokers

Partnership - A voluntary association of two or more persons to carry on a business or venture on terms of mutual participation in profits and losses

Police power - The right of the State to enact laws and enforce them for the order, safety, health, morals and general welfare of the public

Real Estate Board - An organization whose members consist primarily of real estate brokers and salespersons

Realtist - A real estate broker holding active membership in a real estate board affiliated with the National Association of Real Estate Brokers

Realtor - A real estate broker holding active membership in a real estate board affiliated with the National Association of Realtors

1. If a licensee is guilty of conversion, he or she is someone who is:
   A. Misrepresenting
   B. Misappropriating the funds of client
   C. Commingling
   D. Failing to make a full disclosure of material facts

2. A real estate salesman went into a neighborhood to obtain listings of residential property. He made representations that, because of the entry into the neighborhood of minority groups, property values would be reduced (due to a decline in the quality of schools, coupled with an increase in the crime rate). These practices by the salesman are:
   A. Permissible, if the representations are true
   B. Unethical, but beyond the jurisdiction of the Real Estate Commissioner
   C. Grounds for disciplinary action
   D. Justified, if his activities do not decrease property values for neighboring properties

3. What is a REALTOR®?
   A. A specially-licensed real estate professional who acts as a point of contact between two or
      more people in negotiating the sale, purchase or rental of property.
   B. Any real estate broker or salesperson who assists buyers, sellers, landlords or tenants in
      any real estate transaction.
   C. A member of the National Association of Real Estate Brokers who specializes in residential
      properties.
   D. A real estate licensee who is a member of the National Association of REALTORS®.

4. The initial term of all California real estate licenses is:
   A. One year
   B. Two years
   C. Four years
   D. Six years

5. The majority of California laws relating to real property are created by which of the following?
   A. The State Constitution
   B. Legislative acts
   C. The Real Estate Commissioner
   D. The Business and Professions Code

6. Which of the following has a meaning most completely opposite of Commingle?
   A. Trust fund
   B. Conversion
   C. Segregate
   D. Mingle

7. Of the following, which is not a penalty that the Real Estate Commissioner is authorized to issue against an offending licensee?
   A. Reimbursing the Recovery Account Fund
   B. Paying a fine
   C. Serving jail time
   D. Attending specific real estate classes

8. Unlawful Conduct as set forth in the Commission's Regulations is best described as:
   A. Acts which are not grounds for disciplinary action by DRE
   B. Not an actual act but a statement of duties imposed by law
   C. Specific acts and omissions which do violate existing law and are grounds for disciplinary action
   D. Acts which are set as guidelines

9. Which of the following is not considered unethical conduct?
   A. Failing to disclose to a purchaser a direct or indirect ownership interest of the licensee in the property
   B. Failing to respond to reasonable inquiries of a principal as to the extent of efforts to market property listed with the licensee
   C. Making a modification to the terms of a contract previously signed by a party with out the knowledge and consent of the party
   D. Representing that a service is free, when in fact, it is covered by a fee to be charged as part of the transaction

10. What is the fine for a corporation, which receives an illegal commission?
    A. $100,000
    B. $50,000
    C. $25,000
    D. $10,000

11. The power of the state to enact laws in order to promote the order, safety, health and general welfare of the public.
    A. Eminent Domain
    B. Police Power
    C. Zoning
    D. None of the above

12. Making statement that exaggerates a property's benefits is called
    A. Puffing
    B. Misrepresentation
    C. Fraud
    D. Commingling

13. All broker candidates must be at least what age?
    A. 18
    B. 19
    C. 21
    D. 25

14. Acting for more than one party in a transaction without knowledge or consent of all parties thereto is best described as
    A. Divided Agency
    B. Collusion
    C. Commingling
    D. Conspiracy

15. To become truly successful in the real estate business, one should:
    A. Attain as high a level of academic education as possible
    B. Take as many courses in real estate as one can find
    C. Continually educate oneself throughout one's career
    D. All of the above

16. How many classes are required of a broker candidate before he or she is eligible to sit for the state exam?
    A. 5
    B. 3
    C. 8
    D. None of the above

17. A broker persuades a Caucasian family to list their home for sale by telling them that non white people are moving into the area and that this may reduce property values. Such persuasion is considered all of the following, except:
    A. Blockbusting
    B. Encouragement of panic selling
    C. Legal but unethical
    D. Illegal conduct

18. What is the experience requirement for becoming a real estate broker?
    A. Candidate must be a real estate agent for 2 years
    B. Candidate must have a 4-year degree
    C. Candidate must be a member of the California Bar Association.
    D. Any of the above.

19. Commingling of funds is:
    A. Misappropriating and using of funds
    B. Mixing the broker's funds with funds of the principal
    C. More serious of an offense than conversion
    D. All of the above

20. Who appoints the Real Estate Commissioner?
    A. Governor
    B. State Legislators
    C. California Association of Realtors
    D. Both A and B

CHAPTER

REAL PROPERTY IN CALIFORNIA

What you will learn in this Chapter

- Bundle of Rights

- A Definition of Real Property

- Types of Estates in Real Property

- Fixtures

- Trade Fixtures

- Methods used to Describe Land

1. Rights of possession, use, enjoyment, encumbrance and transfer are all
   characteristics of:
   A. Life Estate
   B. Bundle of Rights
   C. Deeded Rights
   D. Real Property

2. What are the two types of freehold estates?
   A. Fee Simple and Life Estate
   B. Absolute and Qualified
   C. Defeasible and Life Estate
   D. Fee Simple and Leasehold Estate

3. Property is considered:
   A. Anything that can be owned
   B. Real
   C. Personal
   D. All of the above

4. An example of real property is:
   A. Grain harvested from harvest
   B. Car
   C. The airspace immediately above the property
   D. Money

5. Which one of the following examples is not considered a fixture?
   A. Ceiling fan
   B. Space heater
   C. Custom made window coverings
   D. Dishwasher

6. Trade fixtures are considered:
   A. Personal property
   B. Real property
   C. Both A and B
   D. Neither A nor B

7. All of the following are descriptions of land EXCEPT:
   A. Lot, block and tract system
   B. Metes and bounds
   C. U.S. government section and township survey
   D. Encroachment

INTRODUCTION

Owning property, or ownership, is the basic concept for the subject of real estate. In this chapter we will examine the different types of ownership, or estates, that a person can have in property. We will also look at the different ways property can be transferred from one person to another, and the length of time of ownership. The concepts of owning, leasing and renting will become clear to you as they are differentiated and explained.

You will also learn the definition of real property and the difference between real and personal property. Fixtures and trade fixtures are other concepts, which will be differentiated and explained. The distinction between fixtures and trade fixtures is important, as the two are often confused with one another. Finally, we will discuss land descriptions, divisions and area.

BUNDLE OF RIGHTS

"Bundle of rights" is an ownership concept that describes a property owner's legal rights that attach to the ownership of real property. The bundle of rights includes the right to own, possess, use, enjoy, borrow against (encumber) and dispose of (transfer) real property.

> **Bundle of Rights**
> - **Possession**. The right to inhabit property.
> - **Enjoyment**. The right to keep others off the property to ensure a peaceful and quiet space.
> - **Use**. The right to utilize the property within the rules of the law.
> - **Transfer**. The right to dispose property through a legal will, as a gift or sale of property.
> - **Encumber**. The right to borrow money against the value of a property to use said property as security for the loan.

TYPES OF ESTATES IN REAL PROPERTY

An **estate** is ownership or interest in real property. Thus, real estate or real property means ownership. There are two types of estates in real property: freehold estate and less-than-freehold estate (or leasehold estate). The type of estate a person has in property determines the degree of ownership, or claim, the property owner has in his or her estate.

Estates In Land		
		Fee Simple Absolute
	Fee Simple-	Fee Simple Qualified/Fee Simple Defeasible
Freehold Estates -		
	Life Estate-	Estate In Reversion
		Estate In Remainder
		Estate for Years
		Estate for Period to Period
Leasehold Estate-		Estate at Will
		Estate at Sufferance

Freehold Estates

A *freehold estate* is the highest form of ownership. The term freehold stems from medieval England, where the landowner was free from the demands of his overlord and could use the land in any way he desired. A freehold estate may continue for an indefinite period, or be limited to a specific number of years. Additionally, although the freehold estate allows the owner the most freedom of use, this use may be limited.

There are two types of freehold estates: *fee simple estate* and *life estate*.

Fee Simple Estate

Fee simple estates allow the property owner to use the property now and for an indefinite number of years. It provides the owner with the largest bundle of rights of any type of estate. A fee simple estate may also be known as an *estate of inheritance* since it can be conveyed by a will.

A fee simple estate that holds no conditions or limitations is called a **Fee Simple Absolute**. This estate is generally transferred through a normal real estate transaction. If a fee simple estate is transferred with limitations, conditions or qualifications, it is referred to as a **Fee Simple Qualified** or **Fee Simple Defeasible**. Under the provisions of a fee simple qualified or defeasible estate, the interest in the property can be limited or taken away in the event of misuse of the property per any agreed upon conditions.

> **Example**
> Adam gives 420 acres of land to Peter, a developer, to build a new amusement park. Adam grants the gift with the condition that no trees are cut down in the development of the park. During construction, Adam learns that 100 acres had been stripped of all vegetation to allow for a parking garage. Since Peter broke the condition against Adam's wishes, Adam can take the property back and repossess it for his own use.

Life Estate

A *life estate* is an estate that is granted for a definite period of time. The owner of the property has the right to use and possess the property for the duration of his or her lifetime or the **measuring life** of another individual. Upon the death of the land-owner or specified individual, the estate will revert back to the original owner who made the life estate.

> **Measuring Life**
> A person's lifespan upon which the life estate duration is based. This may be the grantee of the life estate or a neutral third party.

A life estate is a type of freehold estate. As a result, the owner has all rights associated with fee ownership EXCEPT conveyance of the property by will. The owner may sell the property with the condition that the property reverts back to the original owner upon the death of the individual whose life measures the length of the estate.

Taxes and maintenance of the property are the sole responsibility of the holder of the life estate. The property may be rented out, encumbered or disposed of at his or her discretion. However, any interest in the property that extends beyond the life of the person on whom the life estate is measured will become invalid upon that individual's death.

Possession returns to the original owner of the property when the life estate ends and the original owner has a reversion. Sometimes the property will revert to a third party when the life estate ends and the owner does not have a reversion; this person holds a life estate in remainder during the existence of the life estate. This person is referred to as the **remainderman**.

Remainderman
The person a life estate reverts to upon the death of the current owner, not the original owner of the estate.

If a person should die before the individual whose life measures the life estate, then the estate will transfer to the holder's heirs for the duration of the measuring life.

Example:
Art grants a life estate to Pat for the duration of Pat's life with the provision that ownership of the property will revert back to Art upon Pat's death. Pat is the life tenant, with a life estate based on her life span. Art will hold an estate in reversion upon Pat's death.

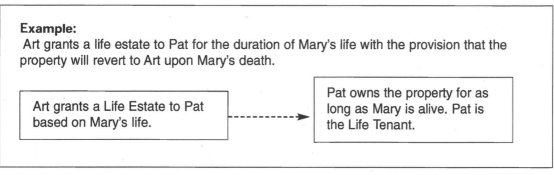

Art grants a Life Estate to Pat.

Pat owns the property for as long as Pat is alive. Pat is the Life Tenant.

Upon Pat's death the property reverts back to Art.

Example:
Art grants a life estate to Pat for the duration of Mary's life with the provision that the property will revert to Art upon Mary's death.

Art grants a Life Estate to Pat based on Mary's life.

Pat owns the property for as long as Mary is alive. Pat is the Life Tenant.

Example:
Art grants a life estate to Pat for the duration of Pat's life. Upon Pat's death the estate will go to Joe. Joe has an estate in remainder.

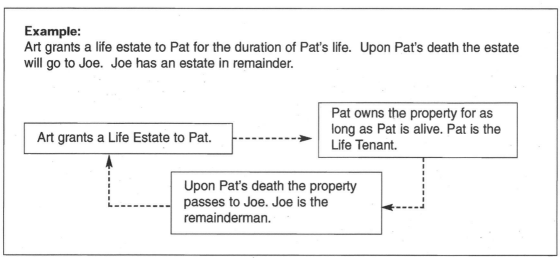

Art grants a Life Estate to Pat.

Pat owns the property for as long as Pat is alive. Pat is the Life Tenant.

Upon Pat's death the property passes to Joe. Joe is the remainderman.

Leasehold Estates

A *leasehold estate* (or less-than-freehold estate) contains fewer bundles of rights than a freehold estate. People who own this type of estate are called *renters* and *tenants*. The owner of a leasehold estate has exclusive right of possession of the land and everything attached to it during the duration of the lease. The lease will outline the conditions for use, duration of rental and occupancy of the property. The bundle of rights a tenant or renter holds with a leasehold includes the right of possession, use and enjoyment.

- The *tenant*, or *lessee*, is someone who acquires the use of property for a specific time period as outlined by the lease and holds the right of exclusive possession.

- The *landlord* or *lessor* is the person who owns the title to the property or reversion during the lease.

- The tenant will pay the landlord *rent* at predetermined time periods for use of the property.

A leasehold estate is a lease between a tenant, or lessee and a landlord, or lessor.

Leaseholds are considered personal property or chattel real. Tenants hold the right of possession and use of the property, yet it is not considered real property as they cannot encumber or convey the property and only hold possession of the property for the duration of the lease. There are four different types of leasehold estates. They are:

- **estate for years**
- **estate from period to period**
- **estate at will**
- **estate at sufferance**

Estate for Years

An *estate for years* is a lease agreement that will continue for a definite period of time, which is agreed upon in advance. The term of this type of lease can extend to 99 years. This term can be broken down into years, months, weeks or days. No notice is required from either party to vacate the property or terminate the agreement.

Estate from Period to Period

An *estate from period to period* is one that continues for a specified period of time such as week-to-week, month-to-month or year-to-year. This type of lease is automatically renewed for the same type of time period unless the tenant or landlord gives notice to vacate the property or terminate the lease agreement. Periodic tenancies generally have month-to-month terms and require one month's notice from either party to vacate or terminate the lease.

Estate at Will

An *estate at will* is a lease for an indeterminable amount of time with no express rent promised for the occupancy. This type of lease is uncommon.

Estate at Sufferance

An *estate at sufferance* occurs when a tenant remains on the land after the lease has run out. Additionally, an estate at sufferance may be formed when a tenant gives the landlord a notice to vacate but then does not leave the property by the specified time. In both instances the landlord has not given the tenant permission to stay on the property. This type of leasehold estate contains the fewest bundle of rights, making it the least desirable form of estate, as the landlord may start eviction proceedings at any time or the tenant may vacate the property with no notification required.

> **Leasehold Estates Include:**
> - Estate for years
> - Estate from period to period
> - Estate at will
> - Estate at sufferance

Written agreements are helpful in any leasehold situation. However, a written contract is required if the lease is going to last longer than one year. Written agreements or contracts help both parties avoid any misunderstandings regarding the property, terms of the lease or length of occupancy. A written contract is also required if a lease is going to end more than one year in the future, even if the lease term is less than one year.

Characteristics of Every Lease

- All leases are contracts whether they are in written or oral form. The landlord must sign all written contracts. Tenants, on the other hand, are not required to sign a written contract as occupancy is considered his or her acknowledgement of the lease and its terms.

- Contracts must have clear terms understood by both parties backed by **consideration** or a form of rent.

- Once written, a contract cannot be altered by oral means.

> **Characteristics of a lease:**
> - Landlords must sign all written contracts.
> - Possession by a tenant is considered his or her acknowledgement of a lease contract.
> - Contracts must be backed by some form of consideration (or a form of rent).
> - Once written, a contract cannot be altered by oral means.

R E A L   P R O P E R T Y

Property is anything that can be owned. **Real Property** refers to: land; any permanent fixtures attached to the land such as a house or building; anything appurtenant to the land such as an easement; or anything attached to the land such as trees. A broader way to think about real property is in spatial terms, such as land, airspace, mineral rights, water rights and fixtures. Ownership in real property can be defined as the bundle of rights. Generally speaking, real property is immovable.

Airspace
The airspace above a building to a specific height is considered real property. Homeowners, including condominium owners, may restrict the use of the airspace immediately above their property if it is being used in a disruptive way.

Minerals
Solid minerals contained in the ground are considered real property until taken out of the ground. Coal is an example. Once the coal is taken out of the ground, it becomes personal property. You will learn more about personal property later in this chapter.

Non-solid minerals such as oil and gas are not considered real property because of their fluid nature. The property owner has the right to drill for gas or oil on his or her own land, but it does not become property until it is reduced to possession after drilling.

Water Rights
Water is considered real property, but it cannot be owned. A property owner cannot dam surface water to collect it for his or her own use; nor can water be channeled for the benefit of any one person. Under the **Doctrine of Correlative User** the landowner may take a reasonable share of the ground water.

The different types of water rights include:
- Littoral: the rights of a property owner who owns a piece of land boarding a lake or ocean
- Surface: these rights outline rain runoff rights and regulations
- Riparian: rights to use rivers and streams bordering a piece of property, as defined in the Doctrine of Correlative Users
- Underground: a landowner's right to use percolating or underground water Right of Appropriation: allows the state to allocate non-riparian property owners to take surplus ground water for their own beneficial use. An example of this would be for agricultural production.

Permanent Attachments
Real property not only includes water rights, mineral rights and land itself. It also includes those items permanently attached to the ground itself. These include:

- Buildings or other structures resting on the land
- Growing plants attached to the ground with roots
- Items permanently fixed (referred to as fixtures) in or on a house or building

Growing plants such as trees, shrubs and vines are considered real property. Industrial crops are considered real property only until they are harvested for sale, severed, cut or mortgaged. Once these crops are harvested they become personal property.

Emblements are growing crops that are considered personal property and are an exception to the rule of growing crops as real property. Such crops may be owned by the landowner or by a tenant leasing land from a landlord. The crops themselves are considered personal property, while the land on which the crops are growing is NOT considered personal property. An example of this is a peach tree orchard. The peaches themselves are personal property to the grower; the trees themselves are real property attached to the land. Personal property will be further discussed in the next section.

Appurtenances

An appurtenance is anything used with the land for its benefit. An example is an ease-ment, which is the right-of-way to cross another person's property. Stock in a mutual water company is another type of appurtance. These appurtenant rights are sold with the land as they are considered real property.

Immovable by Law

Anything deemed immovable by law is also real property. A seller of real property can-not exclude an orchard growing on the property in the sale, as the orchard is real prop-erty. Any produce growing may be negotiated in the sale of the property, yet the trees are immovable by law and are therefore considered real property.

> **Real Property Includes:**
> - Land - including airspace, minerals, and water rights
> - Attachments to the land such as buildings and trees
> - Appurtenances such as easements
> - Objects immovable by law

Personal Property

Personal property is considered movable. Any property that is not considered real property is personal property. As briefly stated earlier in this chapter, items such as mature, harvested crops, furniture in a house, a cut tree used for lumber, automobiles, stocks or money are all considered personal property. Personal property is also known as **chattel**, as it is movable and transferred or sold using a bill of sale. When real property is sold, all personal property goes with the seller unless he or she has agreed to leave such personal property on the property or include it in the contract.

Real and personal property can change form from one to the other. An example of this is a tree. While it is growing and attached to the ground it is considered real property. When it is cut down or harvested for lumber it becomes personal property. When the lumber is used to build a house, it again becomes real property. If the house is torn down, and the lumber is recycled for different use, it again becomes personal property.

As discussed earlier, emblements (such as crops that are sold, mortgaged or harvest-ed) are considered personal property. The physical plant itself is not personal property; it is real property. The crop it yields is personal property.

> - Personal property is also called *chattel*
> - Property may change form from real to personal and back to real

F I X T U R E S

A fixture is real property that began as personal property. It has become real property because it was permanently attached to another real property. Examples of this include: a refrigerator, a ceiling fan, or custom-built shelves for a closet.

There are five tests to determine what are fixtures:

- Method of attachment or degree of permanence
- Adaptability

- Relationship of the parties
- Intention of the person who attached it
- Agreement between the parties.

As you can see, an easy way to remember these determinations is the acronym MARIA as is spelled by the first letter of each test. One important note to make is that cost is NOT a test for fixtures.

Method of Attachment
The greater the degree of attachment or permanence, the more likely the item is a fixture. For example, a ceiling fan wired into the electrical system of a home has a high degree of attachment and is considered real property.

Adaptability
The more an item is adapted to a specific room or place, the more likely it is a fixture. To revisit the ceiling fan example, the fan was purchased intentionally for one room in a home, with consideration of size, style and color. On the other hand, a floor fan plugged into a wall can be moved from one room to another. As the floor fan is not adapted for specific needs or purposes of a room, it is personal property – while the ceiling fan is *real* property.

Relationship of the Parties
Relationships between parties can be of the buyer-seller or landlord-tenant type. Courts can determine if an item is a fixture or not based on the relationship of the parties. If a seller of land attaches a fixture onto the land before a sale, the fixture will be considered real property and transfer to the new owner upon sale of the property.

Intention of the Person Attaching the Item
If a person intends to remove a piece of personal property upon the sale of said property, he or she should not attach it to the property itself. **This is the most important test of a fixture**. If a tenant purchased a ceiling fan for the bedroom of an apartment and informed the landlord she planned on removing and taking it with her upon moving, the ceiling fan will not be considered a fixture. It will instead be considered personal property.

Agreement between Parties
Parties should put their intentions into writing to avoid disputes between fixtures and personal property. This determines the intentions of each party more clearly.

Five Fixture Tests:
• Method of attachment
• Adaptability
• Relationship of the parties
• Intention of the person attaching the item
• Agreement between parties

T R A D E   F I X T U R E S

Trade fixtures are personal property affixed to real property for x use in a trade, business or craft. These fixtures can be removed, provided that their removal causes no damage to the real property. This is especially important when a tenant attaches his or her trade fixtures to a rented space.

Examples of Trade Fixtures:
- Built-in work benches
- Dividing screens or temporary walls
- Cash registers

DESCRIPTIONS OF LAND

Every piece of land is unique, as no other piece of land has exactly the same characteristics. Some pieces of land may look very similar to one another with like topography and features. Yet, the land's physical geographical positioning makes it unique in itself. Street names and addresses are used to describe areas of land or locations; but this is not an adequate distinction for all parcels of land. Rural areas cannot be adequately described by addresses, while currently developed areas are undergoing constant changes or reconstruction.

Today, legal descriptions of land are used to describe a specific property. These legal descriptions are required before a property is sold to a new owner or before a deed may be recorded. There are three methods to describe land. They are:

- Lot, block and tract system
- Metes and bounds
- U.S. government section and township survey

Lot, Block and Tract System

The lot, block and tract system is also called the subdivision system. The subdivision is mapped out with a **Plat Map** showing the divisions of tracts, blocks within the tracts and the lots within each block. Each deed to a property that uses a plat map description will contain the tract, the block and the lot number. This will be separate and unique to any other parcel of property. The tract is the largest area on a plat map, which can be broken down into blocks and then again into lots, which are the smallest portion on the map. Below is the Plat Map of 10304 S. Central Avenue in Los Angeles.

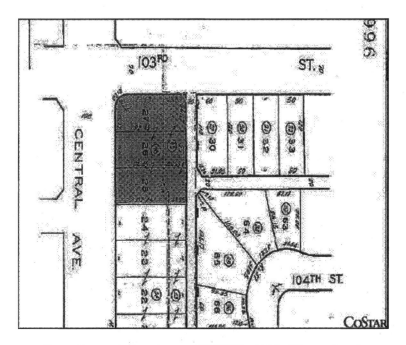

(http://www.jmkenv.com/UST/Site%207/Comp.htm)

Plat Maps are used to show the divisions within the lot, block and tract system.

Metes and Bounds

The *metes and bounds* measurement system is used when Lot, Block and Tract or U.S. government section and township survey are not practical, or would not work.. Metes and bounds are used mostly to describe complicated or irregular shaped properties. Metes and bounds describe property based on measurements between boundaries or landmarks. These measurements are based on the distance, direction or angle from a given point.

Metes most closely describe the distance or measurement between two given points, while bounds refer to the boundaries, or points, being referenced in the measurement between landmarks or monuments. Bounds can include both artificial and natural features. Examples of artificial bounds are roads, canals or stakes. Examples of natural bounds are rivers, streams, lakes, boulders, land formations and trees.

A metes and bounds description starts at a well-known landmark or point and follows the natural boundaries of the land to another landmark or point. The distance between the boundaries and back to the original starting point is measured to determine the metes and bounds.

Example of a Metes and Bounds Description:
Commencing from a point one-half mile upstream from Smith Bridge on Jones Creek, proceed northeast 500 feet to Spring Hill, then northwest to the large oak tree, then southwest to the large rock in the middle of Jones Creek, then along Jones Creek to the origin. (see map on the next page)

Be cautioned that metes-and-bounds surveys are liable to create problems. Since surveys were done as land was claimed, the result was often overlapping claims -- and lengthy court battles. Even today, land titles are more difficult to verify in areas surveyed by metes-&-bounds. A larger problem is that the boundary markers (oak tree, big rock, etc.) are eventually obliterated. The result is often an ambiguous boundary. One measure to avoid such ambiguity is to replace landmarks or boundary markers with exact compass directions and distances (also known as "Coordinate Geometry"). So, using coordinate geometry, the description above might be replaced with

Example:
Commencing from a point one-half mile upstream from Smith Bridge on Jones Creek, proceed N 45° E 500 feet, then N 50° W 324 feet, then S 35° W to Jones Creek, then along Jones Creek to the origin. (see map on the next page)

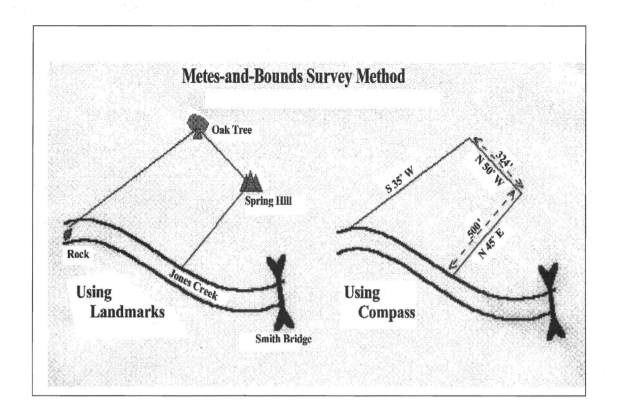

Metes-and-Bounds Survey Method

Oak Tree

Spring Hill

Rock

Jones Creek

Using
Landmarks

Smith Bridge

S 35° W

N 50° W

324'

N 45° E

500'

Using
Compass

The metes and bounds survey method is used when the township survey or lot, block and tract systems would not be sufficient survey methods. This occurs primarily in cases of irregularly-shaped plots of land, or land that is difficult to survey (such as wetlands or mountainous terrain).

U.S. Government Section and Township Survey

Most of the land in the US is described under the US government section and township survey. This system is used in 30 of the 50 states. A rational, rectangular survey, is called the Public Land Survey (PLS) system, which was enacted under the Northwest Land Ordinance of 1785.

The township survey system starts out with a coordinate system for a given area. **Principal meridians** form lines running north and south. **Baselines** are the lines that run east and west. Each baseline is given a name, so that each land parcel may be identified by that name.

- Meridians run north and south
- Baselines run east and west

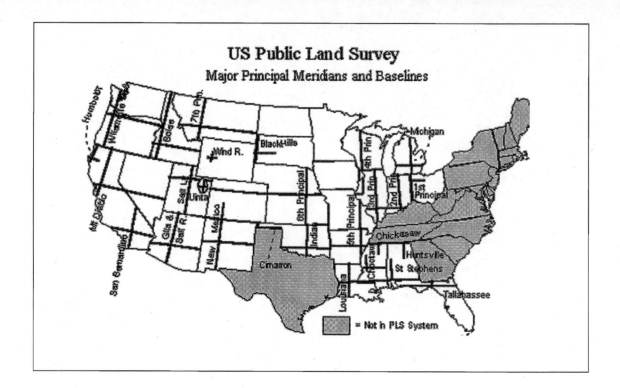

US Public Land Survey
Major Principal Meridians and Baselines

= Not in PLS System

California has three principal meridian / baseline pairs
- San Bernardino meridian (Southern California)
- Mount Diablo meridian (most of Northern California)
- Humboldt Meridian (Northwestern California)

The initial point is the intersection of the principal meridian and baseline. From this point, townships are marked off east/west and north/south. Each **township** is 6 miles on a side, or 36 square miles. Townships are designated on the east-west direction as being a certain number of Ranges east or west of the principal meridian. The township is also a certain number of townships north or south of the baseline. For example, the township that is just on the southeast corner of the initial point is Township 1 South, Range 1 East (usually abbreviated T. 1 S, R. 1 E). Another example: T. 4 S, R. 5 E would be the fourth township south of the baseline and five townships to the east.

- Range lines are every 6 miles east and west of the meridian
- Township lines are every 6 miles north and south of the base line

Each township was divided so that individuals could afford to purchase one **section**, or a portion of each section further divided (see graphic below). The township was divided into 36 sections of one square mile each. Each of the sections is numbered consecutively from 1 to 36, starting at the northeast corner and snaking around the rows, with 36 at the southeast corner.

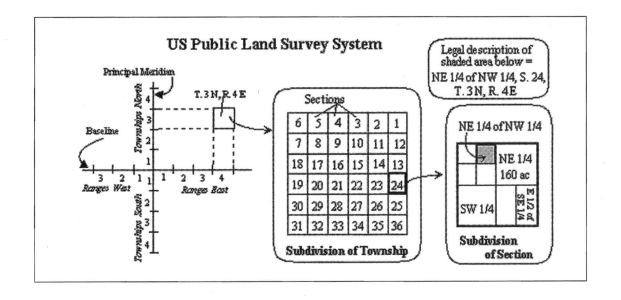

Chapter 2 **Sections can be broken down into halves, quarters or eighths, designated by a compass direction. If divided in half, we have either east/west halves, or north/south halves. If divided into quarters, we have the NE, NW, SW, and SE quarters. Quarters can be broken down further if necessary. For example, an eighth of a section might be designated by the NE quarter of the SE quarter. One section contains 640 acres, while a quarter section contains 160 acres.**

Property descriptions must include a township number, section number, and fraction of a section. So, a property description may read:

SW 1/2 of SE 1/4, Sect. 4, T. 87 N, R. 34 E, 6th Principal Meridian

The township survey system is not a flawless system. There are irregularities in certain geographic areas. Section and township lines are not always exactly north/south and east/west, and sections are sometimes less than a full square mile (in the event that the sections are less than a full square mile, they are called government lots). The irregularities of the township survey system arise from several different sources. The following are just a few possible reasons for irregularities:

- Meridians converge to the north, so as surveyors moved north, townships didn't match up with those further south. Often east-west correction lines were set up, along which townships were re-aligned. You'll notice this effect when driving north or south along a country road when you have to take a sudden turn right or left, then turn north/south again after a short distance.

- Surveying in difficult terrain where there are mountains or adverse weather conditions caused some lines to go astray. Once set up, however, the errors were kept, and these lines were never resurveyed or redrawn.

(http://www.sonoma.edu/users/f/freidel/remote/380packet3.htm)

S U M M A R Y

The bundle of rights are the rights or privileges associated with ownership of property. The number of rights associated with ownership, through the bundle of rights, is determined by the type of estate. Freehold estates are the highest form of property ownership and come with the most bundle of rights.

Freehold estates are considered real property. Leasehold estates contain fewer rights to the owner as a leasehold estate is considered personal property. Individuals holding a leasehold estate are tenants or renters. Real property is land and anything fixed to the land such as buildings, easements or trees. Real property is extended to airspace, mineral rights and water rights. Personal property is moveable. Examples of personal property include: harvested crops, cars, trees cut for lumber and stocks.

Another name for personal property is *chattel*. A fixture is real property that began as personal property. An example of this would be kitchen cabinets. The cabinets started out as lumber constructed into cabinets and then affixed into the kitchen, thus becoming part of the house and eventually becoming real property. Trade fixtures are considered fixtures, but retain their status as personal property because they are moved out when a tenant or business owner vacates. The trade fixture is legally moveable as long as no real property is damaged in the trade fixture's removal.

Legal descriptions are used to describe a specific piece of property. There are three methods to describe land: lot, block and tract; metes and bounds; and U.S. government section and township survey system. Before real property can be sold there must be a legal description of the land.

T E R M S   A N D   P H R A S E S

Appurtenance - Rights, privileges and improvements that belong to and pass with the transfer of real property but are not necessarily a part of the actual property

Base Line - A survey line running east and west (used as a reference when mapping land)

Bill of Sale - A written agreement used to transfer ownership of personal property

Bundle of Rights – An ownership concept describing all the legal rights that attach to the ownership of real property

Chattel – Personal property

Chattel Real – An item of personal property, which is connected to real estate (e.g., a lease or an easement)

Condition Precedent – A condition that requires something to occur before a transaction becomes absolute and enforceable (e.g., a sale that is contingent on the seller clearing up a mechanics lien)

Condition Subsequent – A condition which, if it occurs at some point in the future, can cause ownership of a property to revert back to the grantor (e.g., a requirement contained in a grant deed that restricts a buyer from consuming alcohol on the property)

Consideration – An exchange, usually rent, given to a lessor by a lessee in a leasehold estate

Doctrine of Correlative User – A doctrine which states that a property owner may use only a reasonable amount of the total underground water supply for his or her benefit

Emblements – Annual crops produced for sale. Emblements are considered personal property and belong to the grower whether he or she is the tenant or landlord

Estate –A legal interest in land; defines the nature, degree, extent and duration of a person's ownership in land or property

Estate in Fee – The most complete form of ownership in real property; a freehold estate that can be passed by descent or by will after the owner's death (also known as *estate of inheritance* or fee simple estate)

Estate of Inheritance – The most complete form of ownership in real property; a freehold estate that can be passed by descent or by will after the owner's death (also known as *estate in fee*)

Fee Simple Absolute – The most complete ownership recognized by law; an estate in fee with no restrictions on the land's use

Fee Simple Estate – The most complete form of ownership of real property; a freehold estate that can be passed by descent or by will after the owner's death (also known as *estate of inheritance*)

Fee Simple Defeasible / Qualified – An estate in which the holder has a fee simple title, subject to return to the grantor if a specified condition occurs

Fixture – Personal property that has become part of, or affixed to, real property

Freehold Estate – An estate in real property that continues for an indefinite period of time

Less-Than-Freehold Estate – A leasehold estate, or rental agreement, that exists for a definite period of time or successive periods of time until termination of the contract or lease

Life Estate – An estate that is measured by the life of the grantee or the life of another person dictating the length of the estate

Littoral – that which borders a lake, ocean or sea

Measuring Life - a person's lifespan on which the life estate duration is based The measuring life may be based on the lifespan of the grantee of the life estate or the lifespan of a neutral third party

Meridian – A survey line running north and south (used as a reference when mapping land)

Metes and Bounds – A survey method by which land is described by the distance and angle between landmarks or boundaries

Monument – A fixed landmark used in metes and bounds land description

Personal Property – Anything moveable that is not real property

Plat Map – A map of a town or subdivision showing the division of property into tracts, blocks and lots

Property – The rights or interests an individual has in something owned

Range – A land description used in the U.S. government survey system consisting of a strip of land located every six miles east and west of each principal meridian

Real Property – Land, fixtures on the land, appurtenances to the land or anything immovable by law

Riparian Rights – The rights of a landowner to reasonable use of the water flowing from his or her property when said property or land is located next to a natural watercourse

Section – 640 acres of land, considered 1/36th of a township. Each section measures one mile by one mile

Township – A surveyed area of land totaling 36 square miles, or six miles by six miles. Each township contains 36 individual sections of land

Trade Fixture – A fixture used for business that has been affixed onto rented or leased property. Trade fixtures are considered personal property as they may be removed from the real property as long as there is no damage to the real property at the end of a lease

C H A P T E R   Q U I Z

1. Possession, use, enjoyment, encumber and transfer are all characteristics of:
    A. Life Estate
    B. Bundle of Rights
    C. Deeded Rights
    D. Real Property

2. The concept under the bundle of rights that allows a land owner to use his or her property as collateral to secure a loan is:
    A. Transfer
    B. Reversion
    C. Mortgage
    D. Encumber

3. What does an estate refer to?
    A. Land
    B. Property
    C. Ownership
    D. Buildings

4. What are the two types of freehold estates?
    A. Fee Simple and Life Estate
    B. Absolute and Qualified
    c. Defeasible and Life Estate
    d. Fee Simple and Leasehold Estate

5. Which of the following conditions are characteristics of a Fee Simple Absolute Estate?
   A. Provides the owner with the most bundle of rights
   B. Holds no limitations or conditions
   C. Can be conveyed by a will
   D. All of the above

6. In reference to a life estate, a measuring life is:
   A. the life duration of the grantor of the life estate
   B. the life duration of the person on whose life the estate is based
   C. a life estate in reversion
   D. None of the above

7. All of the following characteristics are correct regarding a leasehold estate EXCEPT:
   A. The owner of a leasehold estate possesses more bundles of rights than a free hold estate.
   B. The owner of the leasehold has exclusive right of possession.
   C. The landlord holds title to the property.
   D. People holding a leasehold estate are referred to as tenants or renters.

8. Which of the following are considered the lowest form of estate?
   A. Fee Simple Defeasible
   B. Estate at Will
   C. Estate at Sufferance
   D. Estate in Reversion

9. All of the following are characteristics of a lease EXCEPT:
   A. Every lease is considered a contract whether it is written or oral.
   B. Tenants are required to sign all written contracts.
   C. All contracts are backed by some form of consideration.
   D. Written contracts may not be altered orally.

10. Property is considered:
    A. Anything that can be owned
    B. Real
    C. Personal
    D. All of the above

11. An example of real property is
    A. Grain harvested from harvest
    B. Car
    C. The airspace immediately above the property
    D. Money

12. Which of the following is NOT considered a water right for a property owner?
    A. Riparian
    B. Right of appropriation
    C. Littoral
    D. Emblement

13. Another term for personal property is:
    A. Chattel
    B. Appurtenance
    C. Fixture
    D. MARIA

14. Property can change from real to personal and back to real property.
    A. True
    B. False

15. Which one of the following examples is not considered a fixture?
    A. Ceiling fan
    B. Space heater
    C. Custom-made window coverings
    D. Dishwasher

16. Which one of the following is NOT considered a test of a fixture?
    A. Method of attachment
    B. Emblement
    C. Relationship between parties
    d. Adaptability

17. Trade fixtures are considered
    A. Personal property
    B. Real property
    C. Both A and B
    D. Neither A nor B

18. All of the following are descriptions of land EXCEPT
    A. Lot, block and tract system
    B. Metes and bounds
    C. U.S. government section and township survey
    D. Encroachment

19. Metes and bounds land descriptions are most commonly used when
    A. land is irregularly shaped and would be difficult to describe with any other system.
    B. developers divide up land into lots and record a plat map.
    C. using meridians and baselines.
    D. using a grid system.

20. A plot of land containing 36 square miles most likely describes
    A. 1 township
    B. 6 townships
    C. 36 sections
    D. Both A and C

3

TITLES
AND ESTATES

What you will learn in this Chapter

- History of land title in California

- Acknowledgement and Recording

- Ownership of real property

- Encumbrances

- Homestead declaration

- Marketability of title

- Title insurance

1. What concept carried over from Spanish law into modern day property ownership?
    A. Civil law
    B. Common law
    C. Community property
    D. None of the above

2. By law, all documents affecting the title to real property must be
    A. Acknowledged
    B. Recorded
    C. Both A and B
    D. Neither A nor B

3. Which of the following may own property in severalty?
    A. Corporations
    B. Trusts
    C. Individuals
    D. All of the above

4. Which of the following is NOT considered an encumbrance on real property?
    A. Lien
    B. Encroachment
    C. Homestead
    D. Easement

5. What is the maximum homestead exemption a person 65 years of age or older can declare on their residence?
    A. $150,000
    B. $75,000
    C. $50,000
    D. $85,000

6. A certificate of title will tell what about a property?
    A. Vesting
    B. Encumbrances
    C. Neither A nor B
    D. Both A and B

7. A standard title insurance policy will guard against all of the following except
    A. Federal tax liens
    B. Forgery
    C. Water Rights
    D. Fraud

INTRODUCTION

It is important when looking for property to understand some basic concepts such as how property can be transferred from one person to another. It is also useful to have an understanding of how a title can be held both individually and jointly. Most importantly, we need to know if the property is available or capable of being acquired.

This chapter will introduce you to land title, starting with a brief introduction of how we evolved to our current system of title, conveyance and laws regulating the transfer of title from one party to another. You will also be taught the different ways in which title can be held both individually and jointly. Once you have a firm grasp of how title can be held, you will be ready to move on to understanding the various limitations of the title to property, as well as some of the ways a buyer can protect him or herself against some of these limitations.

HISTORY OF LAND TITLE IN CALIFORNIA

We all know that the first people to live in California were Native Americans. They were here before the Spanish explorers and before Mexico began colonizing and governing California. In 1513, Spanish explorers (representing the King of Spain) advanced into California and claimed all the land that touched the Pacific Ocean. The King would make land grants to individuals for farming and ranching or make similar land grants to cities for their use. Cities did not actually need a formal grant from the King for the use of the land, however, as each city would automatically receive four leagues. Each league was roughly 4,440 acres; so each city was given a little more than 2/3 of what we now refer to as a township. The governing body of the city then decided who would be given property rights and ownership for land contained within the four leagues of the city. Authorities were given this power to grant ownership and transfer of land directly from the King, although there were very strict rules to follow when making these grants.

Moving on to the year 1822 when Mexico won its independence from Spain: Mexico had been colonizing California while a territory of Spain. Upon gaining their independence the Mexicans were able to take possession of California, as well. Under their rule, Mexican governors controlled all land grants, and then recorded the grants. The recording of the grants is known as Expedients. Expedients were a rough form of recording and did not provide a very accurate land description. This ultimately caused confusion and problems amongst landowners once California became a state.

California became a possession of the United States when the Treaty of Guadalupe Hidalgo ended the Mexican American War in 1848. Individuals who had land granted to them by the ruling Mexican governors (provided they could prove ownership of such lands) were able to retain their ownership and were given land patents by the United States government. While California was a territory of Spain and Mexico, civil law ruled land ownership. When California became a territory of the United States civil law ended and common law was adopted (one effect of which was that squatters claimed ownership rights to the newly-acquired territory). Common laws were created from the legislature and had to be followed as along with common law customs adopted from judicial decisions. One of the concepts that carried over from Spanish and Mexican rule was the concept of *community property*. Community property outlined how property acquired by a married couple during their marriage provided for dual ownership. According to community property laws, property could not be disposed of without the consent of both spouses.

REMEMBER:

- California, under Spanish and Mexican rule, utilized Civil Law regarding land ownership
- As part of the United States, California utilizes Common Law governing land ownership
- Community Property is used in California. Although it is not part of Common Law, it is part of Civil Law.

To resolve confusion caused from upholding the Mexican land grants as well as the squatters claims to land, the Board of Land Commissioners was formed. Appeals between disputing parties could be heard by the United States District Court, and sometimes followed by the Supreme Court, to decide who was the lawful owner. In most cases, the Mexican land grants were upheld.

ACKNOWLEDGMENT AND RECORDING

Recording is a system by which evidence of title or a person's interest in property was publicly written down for anyone to research or view. This protected people's rights from secret liens and conveyances, while also ensuring that their property could be freely transferred to another interested party. Recording is not required by law, but it is a helpful way to inform others of your interest in a title to real property.

All written documents affecting the title to real property must be acknowledged before they are considered legal. Acknowledgement occurs when the documents are signed in front of a notary or other public official. Acknowledgement of documents may occur anywhere in the state provided a proper official is present upon acknowledgement. The official or notary may not be related to the parties conducting the transaction or be part of the transaction itself. Upon acknowledgement, the documents can be recorded in the county recorder's office. Documents that may be recorded are all documents affecting the title or possession of real property.

Public officials who may take an acknowledgment include judges, court clerks and notary publics. The notary must place the necessary seal on the document(s) as required by the state of California. In addition to the required signatures, deeds must include the thumbprint of the grantor in order for the document to be considered legal.

Instruments that may be recorded:
- Deeds
- Loan Documents
- Agreements for Sale
- Option Agreements
- Deposit Receipts
- Commission Receipts
- Affidavits concerning any one of the above documents.

Documents must be recorded in the county where the property is located. All documents are filed in alphabetical order under the name of the interested party. The original document is not filed. Rather a copy of the document is put on file. All original documents are stamped with the date and time of the recording and then given back to the person or party who requested the original recording.

Recording serves as constructive notice to the public of all recordings regarding a property. Since law does not require recording, possession also serves as constructive notice to interested parties. It is the responsibility of any interested person or persons to inspect property if they are interested in purchasing the property. Just because a deed has not been recorded, which is not required by law, does not mean the property is vacant or unoccupied. Recording is still the best and most efficient way to protect one's interest in property, ensuring that the title is unquestioned.

It is possible that more than one party may claim ownership or rights to the same piece of property. When this happens the law of *'first in time, first in right'* applies. First in time, first in right means that the first person or party to record a deed to the property will be considered the lawful owner. If a property owner sold more than one person the same piece of land, the first person to record the deed with the county recorder will be considered the legal owner of the property. As we have already learned, possession serves as constructive notice. So, if more than one person purchased the same property it is the buyer's responsibility to inspect the property before making the purchase. This ensures that there is no occupant inhabiting the property.

There may be more than one recording regarding a piece of property. In such cases, the order of the recorded instrument will determine the order of importance or priority of the recording. Deeds, liens or encumbrances may be recorded against a property, and the date and time stamped on the recording will determine the priority of the document. There are, however, some exceptions to this rule. Certain liens such as tax liens and mechanics liens will take precedence over other liens - even if these liens are recorded after a deed.

As a general rule, the date of recording determines priority in the event a property owner should default on any payments and be forced to sell the property. As mentioned tax liens and mechanics liens are exempt from this recording order.

The Real Estate Fraud Prosecution Trust Fund has been set up in California to aid authorities in deterring, investigating and prosecuting real property fraud crimes. The money for this trust fund comes from optional recording fees ($2 per recording in California) that each county in California may elect to charge.

OWNERSHIP OF REAL PROPERTY

Title to property serves as tangible proof that there is an owner for a specific piece of property. Land, or real property, may be owned by an individual, a corporate entity or by the government. One single individual or a collective group of individuals may own real estate.

Real property owned by one person is known as *ownership in severalty*. This includes not only one single individual holding title to a piece of real estate, but also real property owned by corporations. Corporations hold title as ownership in severalty because of the nature of the entity. In a corporation partners are held responsible for all financial matters, this means if there is default on property, individual members of the corporation may be held liable for losses and damages. Corporations will hold title to property in severalty because of this. Ownership in severalty is also known as separate ownership and sole ownership. Individuals holding title to property this way are responsible for all burdens(such as taxes) and benefits (consideration, or rent, etc.) of ownership.

When several people own property together it is called *co-ownership* or *concurrent ownership*. There are four different types of concurrent ownership tenancy in common:

Types of Concurrent or Co-ownership
1. Tenancy in common
2. Joint tenancy
3. Community property
4. Tenancy in partnership

Tenancy in Common

Tenancy in common is created when individuals take possession of property specifically as tenants, if they are not married, or if no other method of title is specified.

Equal right of possession (also referred to as *undivided interest*) is the only element required of a tenancy in common. Equal right of possession means that each party has unrestricted use of the property even though one party may have a greater or lesser financial interest in the property. In an equal right of possession, none of the other tenants may exclude any one of the tenants from using the entire property, nor can a tenant claim exclusive right to any one part of the property.

Example of Tenancy in Common:
Fred, Angela and Gary hold title to a ski cabin as tenants in common. Fred and Angela both own 40% interest in the cabin while Gary owns 20% interest. Gary holds undivided interest in the cabin even though he holds lesser interest in the property. Fred and Angela cannot restrict Gary from any portion of the cabin despite his lesser interest in the property.

In the above example, Fred, Angela and Gary are all responsible for a proportionate amount of expenses incurred by the property such as taxes, repairs, loan payments, insurance and other costs. Because Fred and Angela own 40% each, they are each responsible for 40% of the expenses. Because he owns 20% interest, Gary will be responsible for the remaining 20% of expenses. If the three should find themselves in disagreement they may file a partition action, which requests help from a court to help settle the dispute or decide the fate of the investment.

Each tenant in a tenancy in common may dispose of their interest by will or sale of the interest. Alternatively, they may encumber their own individual interest. The sale, will or encumbrance of the individual interest will not adversely affect the interest of the other tenants. Any person purchasing the share being sold, or any heir receiving property through a will becomes a tenant in common with the other tenants.

Joint Tenancy

Joint tenancy is a distinctive type of co-ownership due to its right of survivorship and four unities. The *four unities* are conditions that must be met for a joint tenancy to occur. The four conditions, or unities, are: Time, Title, Interest and Possession.

Joint tenancy utilizes right of survivorship, which outlines what happens to each co-owner's share of the property upon his or her death. When one co-owner dies, his or her share of the property will become the property of the surviving owner or owners. The property will not be given to heirs or be disposed of by a will. Surviving heirs are, however, entitled to any profits that may be made from the property. In addition, any debts incurred by the deceased co-owner against the property will not pass onto the surviving partners.

Example:
Amy and Adam own a house as joint tenants. Adam dies and the house now becomes Amy's property in severalty despite the fact that Adam has heirs who will be receiving other monetary gifts from his will. Because Amy and Adam are joint tenants, the right of survivorship grants Amy the entire property. Before his death, Adam had borrowed money against his interest in the house to finance a trip; but he had not paid off the loan in full upon the time of his death. This debt will not pass onto Amy when she receives Adam's interest in the house.

The four unities must occur for a joint tenancy to occur. If one of the four unities is broken, then the joint tenancy is dissolved and usually becomes a tenancy in common. Let's examine the four unities:

- **Unity of Time** – All parties must enter into the joint tenancy at the same time.
- **Unity of Title** – All parties entering into the joint tenancy must take title on the same deed
- **Unity of Interest** – All parties entering into the joint tenancy must have undivided interest or equal ownership in the property
- **Unity of Possession** – All parties entering into the joint tenancy have equal right of possession.

Joint Tenancy's Four Unities

1. Unity of Time
2. Unity of Title
3. Unity of Interest
4. Unity of Possession

Co-owners may borrow money against their interest in the property. As we saw in the earlier example of Amy and Adam, if one of the parties borrows money against his or her interest, then dies before paying the entire loan back, the debt will not pass onto the surviving owner or owners.

Co-owners may sell their interest in the property. When this happens, the individual purchasing the interest will not be entering into the joint tenancy, as there would be no unity of time or title. Thus, all four unities would not have occurred. The new co-owner would then be considered a tenant in common.

Community Property

California is one of only nine community property states. It is important to understand which states have community property laws, particularly if any property is purchased by individuals in a marriage. The nine states with community property laws are: Arizona, California, Idaho, Louisiana, Nevada, New Mexico, Texas, Washington and Wisconsin.

Community property refers to a husband and wife owning property together. All property acquired after a marriage is considered community property. The exception to this rule applies only when a property is a separate property. Separate property includes: any property owned by either spouse before entering into marriage; any property purchased from separate funds during a marriage; or any property willed or gifted to one of the spouses during the marriage.

Community and separate property can become confusing, and it is important to understand the distinctions between the two. We know what separate property is, and how it is acquired. But, what about the less obvious areas of separate and community property? For example, either spouse is able to purchase separate property with his or her own money. However, it is important to understand what each spouse can claim as his or her own money while in the marriage.

For example, wages are considered community property, while personal investments or savings prior to marriage are considered separate money. Monetary gifts or income from separate property are also considered separate money. If one spouse chooses to purchase property from these separate money funds, the property will be considered separate property. If one spouse chooses to purchase separate property (such as an investment property) with separate money and needs additional income to correct a negative cash flow, he or she is not allowed to use community money. Commingling of community money with separate property is not lawful in states that adhere to community property laws.

Community Property / Money	Separate Property / Money
<ul><li>All property acquired during a marriage</li><li>Wages earned while married.</li><li>Money earned from community property investments or investment properties</li></ul>	<ul><li>Property acquired before marriage</li><li>Property inherited or gifted individually</li><li>Real Estate Finance</li><li>Property acquired from separate money</li><li>Money earned from separate property</li></ul>

Community property can be a confusing concept to grasp. There are certain situations where both spouses must give consent, in the form of a signature, to the conveyance or encumbrance of property, and there are certain situations when only one spouse can make decisions for both. Additionally if one spouse used his or her own money, that is money derived from inheritance, savings before the marriage occurred or money earned from separately owned property, which was owned before marriage, property may be purchased and sold as a single person. Lets look at some examples to hopefully simplify this concept.

Example 1
Paul and Julie are a married couple in California, and own a home together. Paul wants to purchase a new boat, but needs to encumber the home for the collateral in order to purchase the boat. Paul cannot encumber the home without the consent of Julie. When it comes time for the loan, both Paul and Julie must sign all loan documents acknowledging that their home is encumbered for the purposes of purchasing the boat. This keeps both spouses safe, as one spouse will not be able to pull equity money out of the home to make frivolous purchases.

Example 2
Paul and Julie are a married couple. Julie wishes to purchase a home but Paul is in military service and is not able to sign any of the documents. California law allows Julie to purchase a home, as community property, without the consent or presence of Paul, however either Julie or Paul wishes to sell the home, both spouses must sign all documents related to the property transfer.

Example 3
Paul and Julie are a married couple. Paul owns an apartment complex that he has had for many years before getting married, generating income that is not considered community income, but personal income. Paul wishes to purchase a cabin in the mountains for vacationing and future rental income. He is able to make this purchase, and take title in severalty, or as a single person as he used his own money, not community funds, to purchase the home. If he ever wishes to sell the cabin, he may do so without Julies consent as it is not considered community property.

Community property laws allow each spouse to will half of the interest in their community property. When there is no will in place, the surviving spouse will inherit the entire property. Wills are important so that each spouse can make sure their interest in the property is left to the person they choose. Separate property is treated a bit differently. Upon the death of an individual holding separate property with no will in place, half the property will be given to the surviving spouse, and half to the child. If there is more than one child, one-third of the property will go the surviving spouse and two-thirds will be given to the children.

One final type of community property is quasi-community property. Quasi-community property refers to any California real estate acquired by a married person not living in the state of California. Additionally, any California property acquired in exchange for a property located anywhere else by a married person is considered quasi-community property.

Tenancy in Partnership
Partnerships are formed between two or more people to conduct business for profit. Property can be owned by members in a partnership for such business purposes. Members of a partnership may own property individually as a tenancy in partnership. Each partnership has the right of possession of the property owned together. The death of a partner will dissolve the partnership; thus prompting the sale of the property. The dissolution of the partnership or business can also prompt the sale of the property. When a property is sold, all creditors are paid and profits are disbursed to all partners.

	Tenancy in Common	Joint Tenancy	Community Property	Tenancy in Partnership
Parties	Any number	Any number	Spouses only	Any number
Time	Any time	Same time	Same time	Any time
Title	Separate titles to each person holding an interest	Only one title	Only one title	Only one title
Interest	Separate, undivided interest	Equal, undivided interest	Equal, undivided interest	Equal, undivided interest
Possession	Equal right for each person	Equal right for each person	Equal right for each person	Equal right except for personal property
Conveyance	Each person can separately convey his or her interest	Each person can separately convey his or her interest, but it creates tenancy in common to that sold share	Must be sold jointly between both spouses	Each partner must agree to the sale jointly
Deceased Share on Death	Passes by will	Passes to surviving joint tenants	Half of the property passes to the surviving spouse, half passes by will	Passes to surviving partners; deceased heirs have rights to the deceased share of the profits
New Owner of Partial Interest	Tenant in Common	Tenant in Common	Tenant in Common, no community interest	Tenant in Common
Creditor Sale	Sale of individual tenant's interest unaffecting other tenants interests	Creates tenancy in common as to that interest	Entire property may be sold to satisfy a debt of either spouse	Entire property may be sold to satisfy the debt on one partner

E N C U M B R A N C E S

An *encumbrance* is a limitation on real property imposed by someone who is not the owner of the property. Encumbrances can be identified because they will affect the fee simple title to real estate or the use of the property. A property that has an encumbrance will not be able to be sold until the encumbrance is cleared. An encumbrance is most often a legal obligation against the title of the property, though not all encumbrances are bad however. Some encumbrances require property in certain developments or zoned areas to maintain a certain standard of property improvements for the good of the entire community. The end result is a more attractive community in which to live.

Encumbrances may affect the marketable title to property. A title free of any liens or encumbrances is one an informed buyer is likely to accept. When a title has a debt against it, this is referred to as a 'cloud on the title'. Property with a cloud on the title is less attractive to sell, often causing the property owner to sell below market value. In extreme cases, it may even prevent the property owner from selling the property at all.

There are two types of encumbrances: money and non-money encumbrances. *Money encumbrances* are also called *liens*, or debt against the title of the property. Liens form a legal obligation to repay a debt that was secured by real property. These liens may be voluntarily or involuntarily acquired.

Non-money encumbrances are limitations on the use of the property. The different types of liens are mortgages and trust deeds, tax liens, mechanics liens, judgments, attachments and special assessments. Easements, building restrictions or codes, zoning requirements and encroachments are all considered non-money encumbrances (or physical restrictions) placed on property.

Two Types of Encumbrances
- Non-money encumbrances: such as easements, building restrictions, zoning requirements and encroachments
- Money encumbrances: restrictions or liens such as mortgages and trust deeds, tax liens, mechanics liens, judgments, attachments and special assessments

Liens encumber property for a debt secured against the property. General liens apply to all property owned by the debtor, while specific liens attach only to one specific property. Some examples of general and specific liens are mechanics liens, court judgments, and trust deeds, or mortgages. Mechanics liens and trust deeds are specific liens that attach only to the property being financed (trust deed) or improved (mechanics lien), while a court judgment is a general lien that attaches to all property owned.

Liens are not always a negative thing. A loan secured against property, lines of credit, mortgages and trust deeds and other financial advances to be used to make improvements to a property or to purchase desired items such as a car, boat or additional property are all examples of positive results of a lien. Such liens are *voluntary liens*, meaning that the property owner agreed to the lien. Liens such as mechanics liens, tax liens or judgments are *involuntary liens*, meaning that the property owner did not willingly seek these liens. Rather, they were imposed upon the owner.

Mechanics liens will secure a payment for any services performed, materials consumed or work done to on improve a property. Any party or supplier who contributes to the improvement of a property is eligible to file a mechanics lien to ensure payment for services rendered. Professionals who are eligible to file a mechanics lien are:

- Contractors
- Subcontractors
- Architects
- Engineers
- Surveyors
- Material Suppliers
- Machinists
- Equipment Lessors
- Truckers
- Laborers or Workers

Professionals who indirectly supply materials or sub-contractors not working directly for the property owner can utilize the mechanics lien to ensure they are paid for services they render to a contractor who is working for the property owner. If the property owner pays the contractor or builder, but does not pay the material supplier or subcontractors working through the contractor, these professionals have the option of filing a mechanics lien to receive payment. Sometimes the property owner will pay the contractor in full for the job performed, and the contractor will in turn fail to pay the subcontractor or suppliers. In this situation, the homeowner will be held liable for the money still owed to the subcontractors and suppliers. One way a homeowner can prevent this situation is by requiring the contractor to obtain a *payment bond*. A payment bond is a form of insurance where the issuing company will compensate the property owner if a contractor does not follow through with all agreed upon obligations. The bonding company will see to it that all parties receive payment. This relieves the property owner from liability in the event the contractor fails to pay all other subcontractors and suppliers.

The enforcement of a mechanics lien results in foreclosure on a property. Once the property has been sold through judicial sale, all lien holders are paid from the proceeds and any funds left over after the sale of the property are returned to the property owner. All mechanics liens must be enforced within 90 days of filing. Lien holders may grant an extension to the property owner, but only for a period of not more than one year after the work has been completed.

Anyone filing a mechanics lien must be sure to follow the procedures to make sure the lien is valid. All mechanics liens must be verified and recorded.

The following is a list of steps that must be taken to initiate a valid mechanics lien:

1. **Preliminary Notice**: A written notice is given to the property owner within 20 days of when work first begins or when materials are delivered. This serves as notice to the property owner that if they fail to pay for any materials or labor, a lien may be filed. The Preliminary notice may be hand delivered or mailed (via first class registered mail or certified mail) to the property owner, general contractor or construction lender.

2. **Starting Time**: Begins upon construction on a project and determines when the preliminary notice must given.

3. **Completion Time**: When the project is completed, when the property owner begins to use the new improvement, when the work has been accepted or when construction has been stopped for 60 days

4. **Notice of Completion**: An owner may file a notice of completion with the county recorder 10 days after the project has been finished. Once this notice is filed, contractors have 60 days to file a mechanics lien; all others have 30 days to file their mechanics liens. If the owner does not file a notice of completion, all parties filing a mechanics lien have 90 days to file.

5. **Foreclosure Action**: After a mechanics lien is filed, the person filing the lien has 90 days to bring foreclosure action against the property owner. If the person who filed the lien does not bring action against the property owner within the 90-day period, the lien filer will lose the right to foreclose on the property and will not be compensated for the work performed.

Time Line
1. Materials are delivered or work begins on the project
2. Preliminary 20-day notice is given
3. Work has been completed
4. Notice of completion is recorded*
5. Lien Recorded
6. Foreclosure Action Recorded
7. Service of Process
8. Court Decision

* The property owner does not always file notice of completion. It is important to understand the difference in timeframe between when a completion is filed and when one is not.

The order in which a lien will be paid upon foreclosure is determined by the order (by date) of when a lien was filed. This order will be followed only if there is more than one lien against a property. Mechanics liens are the exception to this rule, as a mechanics lien takes priority over all other liens - including trust deeds. A trust deed may be recorded months ahead of any mechanics lien; however, the mechanics lien will be the first to be paid in full upon foreclosure.

If a property owner did not authorize any work to be done, but a contractor begin working in spite of this, the property owner may file a notice of non-responsibility. This notice must be recorded with the county recorder and posted on the property where the work is taking place. This will relieve the property owner from any responsibility to pay for unauthorized work.

The notice of non-responsibility must be filed within 10 days of any construction or work beginning on the property and must include the following: a property description; name, address and property interest of the person giving notice (usually the owner); and a statement of non-responsibility.

Tax liens and special assessments When a property owner fails to pay property taxes, the amount of the unpaid tax becomes a lien against the property. If there is a utility project or local improvement levied against the property owner which is not paid by the agreed upon time, this amount also becomes a lien. Special assessments and local taxes are *specific liens* attaching only to one specific piece of property, while any government tax will become a *general lien* attaching to all property owned.

Attachments and Judgments An attachment occurs when the court orders a freeze on personal or real property that has been awarded to another in a lawsuit. A judgment is the decision of the judge in a court case. The losing party has the right to appeal the judgment to a higher court to reverse the decision. However, once a judgment becomes final, this judgment becomes a lien. A court judgment is a general lien. This general lien will also be applied to all property - including property acquired after the judgment has been made. A writ of execution may be requested from the lien holder to pay off a lien. A *writ of execution* is a court order directing an officer of the court to satisfy a judgment out of the debtor's property. A portion of the property will be sold to raise the funds to pay off the lien or debt. The property to be sold may include the nonexempt property or exempt property, subject to the judge's discretion.

Lis Pendens: *Lis Pendens* is a cloud on a title of a property pending litigation. A lis pendens will prevent the sale or transfer of a property until litigation is completed and judgment rendered.

Easements An easement is the right to use someone else's land for a specific purpose. Easements are sometimes called right of way. An easement is a *non-posessory interest*, meaning that the person benefiting from the easement does not own the land. The property owner giving the easement is known as the servient tenement and the person receiving the right to use the easement is known as the *dominant tenement.*

Easements are useful in that they allow an individual to access property or landmarks not accessible from a main road, or from one's own property. For example, Joe owns a house on a lot that is not accessible from any main street. In order to get to his house, Joe must utilize 30 feet of his neighbor's driveway to reach his own property. The 30 feet of his neighbor's driveway is the easement. Again, it is important to note that Joe does not own any portion of his neighbor's driveway, but is allowed to use it to gain access to his own property. When Joe sells his home, the person buying the house will also have access to the easement. Easements are appurtenant and are automatically sold with the property of the dominant tenement. You will remember appurtenances to the land, whether it is an easement, fixture or stock in a mutual water company, will be transferred with the property. The seller will not retain ownership rights.

Easements don't only benefit persons owning property. Easements can allow access to streams, lakes, camping sites or other recreational areas requiring the crossing of someone else's land. For example, a canoe outfitter regularly takes his patrons to Millers Landing to launch a 36-mile canoe trip downriver. In order to access Millers Landing, the canoe outfitter must cross 40 yards of private land. An easement will allow the canoe outfitter to legally cross the land in both directions. Without this easement, Millers Landing would be inaccessible to everyone except its landowner.

Easements in Gross are easements that benefit public utilities. This type of easement is not appurtenant to one property. If or when a utility company needs to cross private land to reach a utility pole, transformer or any other structure, they will be allowed access due to easement in gross. This type of easement is similar to a license. However, unlike a license, an easement in gross cannot be terminated.

RECORDING REQUESTED BY

AND WHEN RECORDED MAIL TO

NAME

ADDRESS

CITY
STATE & ZIP

APN NO.

HOMESTEAD DECLARATION

I, _____

do hereby certify and declare as follows:

(1) I hereby claim as a declared homestead the premises located in the City of _____

County of _____, State of California, commonly known as

(Street Address)_____,

and more particularly described as follows: (Give complete legal description)

(2) I am the declared homestead owner of the above declared homestead.

(3) I own the following interest in the above declared homestead:

(4) The above declared homestead is (strike inapplicable clause) my principal dwelling / the principal dwelling of my

spouse, and (strike inapplicable clause) I am / my spouse is currently residing on that declared homestead.

(5) The facts stated in this Declaration are true as of my personal knowledge.

Dated_____   _____

STATE OF CALIFORNIA
COUNTY OF _____) SS

On _____ before me, _____ personally appeared
_____ personally known to me (or proved to me on the basis of satisfactory
evidence) to be the person(s) whose name(s) is/are subscribed to the within instrument, and acknowledged to me that he/she/they executed the same in
his/her/their authorized capacity(ies), and that by his/her/their signature(s) on the instrument the person(s) or the entity upon behalf of which the person(s)
acted, executed the instrument.

WITNESS my hand and official seal.

Signature_____

HMSTEAD.DOC

Form No. 1490 EAGLE (6/98)
CLTA Homeowner's Policy of Title Insurance (6/2/98)

Policy of Title Insurance

ISSUED BY

First American Title Insurance Company
EAGLE Protection Owner's Policy
FOR A ONE-TO-FOUR FAMILY RESIDENCE

OWNER'S COVERAGE STATEMENT

This Policy insures You against actual loss, including any costs, attorneys' fees and expenses provided under the Policy, resulting from the Covered Risks set forth below, if the Land is an improved residential lot on which there is located a one-to-four family residence and each insured named in Schedule A is a Natural Person.

Your insurance is effective on the Policy Date. This policy covers Your actual loss from any risk described under Covered Risks if the event creating the risk exists on the Policy Date or, to the extent expressly stated, after the Policy Date.

Your insurance is limited by all of the following:

- The Policy Amount shown in Schedule A
- For Covered Risk 14, 15, 16 and 18, Your Deductible Amount and Our Maximum Dollar Limit of Liability shown in Schedule A
- Exceptions in Schedule B
- Our Duty To Defend Against Legal Actions
- Exclusions on page 2
- Conditions on page 2 and 3.

COVERED RISKS

The Covered Risks are:

1. Someone else owns an interest in Your Title.

2. Someone else has rights affecting Your Title arising out of leases, contracts, or options.

3. Someone else claims to have rights affecting Your Title arising out of forgery or impersonation.

4. Someone else has an easement on the Land.

5. Someone else has a right to limit Your use of the Land.

6. Your Title is defective.

7. Any of Covered Risks 1 through 6 occurring after the Policy Date.

8. Someone else has a lien on Your Title, including a:

   a. Mortgage;

   b. judgment, state or federal tax lien, or special assessment;

   c. charge by a homeowner's or condominium association; or

   d. lien, occurring before or after the Policy Date, for labor and material furnished before the Policy Date.

9. Someone else has an encumbrance on Your Title.

10. Someone else claims to have rights affecting Your Title arising out of fraud, duress, incompetency or incapacity.

11. You do not have both actual vehicular and pedestrian access to and from the Land, based upon a legal right.

12. You are forced to correct or remove an existing violation of any covenant, condition or restriction affecting the Land, even if the covenant, condition or restriction is excepted in Schedule B.

13. Your Title is lost or taken because of a violation of any covenant, condition or restriction, which occurred before You acquired Your Title, even if the covenant, condition or restriction is excepted in Schedule B.

14. Because of an existing violation of a subdivision law or regulation affecting the Land:

   a. You are unable to obtain a building permit;

   b. You are forced to correct or remove the violation; or

   c. someone else has a legal right to, and does, refuse to perform a contract to purchase the Land, lease it or make a Mortgage loan on it.

   The amount of Your insurance for this Covered Risk is subject to Your Deductible Amount and Our Maximum Dollar Limit of Liability shown in Schedule A.

15. You are forced to remove or remedy Your existing structures, or any part of them — other than boundary walls or fences — because any portion was built without obtaining a building permit from the proper government office. The amount of Your insurance for this Covered Risk is subject to Your Deductible Amount and Our Maximum Dollar Limit of Liability shown in Schedule A.

16. You are forced to remove or remedy Your existing structures, or any part of them, because they violate an existing zoning law or zoning regulation. If You are required to remedy any portion of Your existing structures, the amount of Your insurance for this Covered Risk is subject to Your Deductible Amount and Our Maximum Dollar Limit of Liability shown in Schedule A.

17. You cannot use the Land because use as a single-family residence violates an existing zoning law or zoning regulation.

18. You are forced to remove Your existing structures because they encroach onto Your neighbor's Land. If the encroaching structures are boundary walls or fences, the amount of Your insurance for this Covered Risk is subject to Your Deductible Amount and Our Maximum Dollar Limit of Liability shown in Schedule A.

19. Someone else has a legal right to, and does, refuse to perform a contract to purchase the Land, lease it or make a Mortgage loan on it because Your neighbor's existing structures encroach onto the Land.

20. You are forced to remove Your existing structures because they encroach onto an easement or over a building set-back line, even if the easement or building set-back line is excepted in Schedule B.

21. Your existing structures are damaged because of the exercise of a right to maintain or use any easement affecting the Land, even if the easement is excepted in Schedule B.

22. Your existing improvements (or a replacement or modification made to them after the Policy Date), including lawns, shrubbery or trees, are damaged because of the future exercise of a right to use the surface of the Land for the extraction or development of minerals, water or any other substance, even if those rights are excepted or reserved from the description of the Land or excepted in Schedule B.

23. Someone else tries to enforce a discriminatory covenant, condition or restriction that they claim affects Your Title which is based upon race, color, religion, sex, handicap, familial status, or national origin.

24. A taxing authority assesses supplemental real estate taxes not previously assessed against the Land for any period before the Policy Date because of construction or a change of ownership or use that occurred before the Policy Date.

25. Your neighbor builds any structures after the Policy Date — other than boundary walls or fences — which encroach onto the Land.

26. Your Title is unmarketable, which allows someone else to refuse to perform a contract to purchase the Land, lease it or make a Mortgage loan on it.

27. A document upon which Your Title is based is invalid because it was not properly signed, sealed, acknowledged, delivered or recorded.

28. The residence with the address shown in Schedule A is not located on the Land at the Policy Date.

29. The map, if any, attached to this Policy does not show the correct location of the Land according to the Public Records.

OUR DUTY TO DEFEND AGAINST LEGAL ACTIONS

We will defend Your Title in any legal action only to the part of the action which is based on a Covered Risk and which is not excepted or excluded from coverage in this Policy. We will pay the costs, attorneys' fees, and expenses We incur in that defense.

We will not pay for any part of the legal action which is not based on a Covered Risk or which is excepted or excluded from coverage in this Policy.

We can end Our duty to defend Your Title under paragraph 4 of the Conditions.

This Policy is not complete without Schedules A and B.

CEO

EXCLUSIONS

In addition to the Exceptions in Schedule B, You are not insured against loss, costs, attorneys' fees, and expenses resulting from:

1. Governmental police power, and the existence or violation of any law or government regulation. This includes ordinances, laws and regulations concerning:
   a. building
   b. zoning
   c. land use
   d. improvements on the Land
   e. land division
   f. environmental protection

   This Exclusion does not apply to violations or the enforcement of these matters if notice of the violation or enforcement appears in the Public Records at the Policy Date.
   This Exclusion does not limit the coverage described in Covered Risk 14, 15, 16, 17 or 24.

2. The failure of Your existing structures, or any part of them, to be constructed in accordance with applicable building codes. This Exclusion does not apply to violations of building codes if notice of the violation appears in the Public Records at the Policy Date.

3. The right to take the Land by condemning it, unless:
   a. a notice of exercising the right appears in the Public Records at the Policy Date; or
   b. the taking happened before the Policy Date and is binding on You if You bought the Land without Knowing of the taking.

4. Risks:
   a. that are created, allowed, or agreed to by You, whether or not they appear in the Public Records;
   b. that are Known to You at the Policy Date, but not to Us, unless they appear in the Public Records at the Policy Date;
   c. that result in no loss to You; or
   d. that first occur after the Policy Date - this does not limit the coverage described in Covered Risk 7, 8.d, 22, 23, 24 or 25.

5. Failure to pay value for Your Title.

6. Lack of a right:
   a. to any Land outside the area specifically described and referred to in paragraph 3 of Schedule A; and
   b. in streets, alleys, or waterways that touch the Land.

   This Exclusion does not limit the coverage described in Covered Risk 11 or 18.

CONDITIONS

1. DEFINITIONS:

a. **Easement** - the right of someone else to use the Land for a special purpose.

b. **Known** - things about which You have actual knowledge. The words "Know" and "Knowing" have the same meaning as Known.

c. **Land** - the Land or condominium unit described in paragraph 3 of Schedule A and any improvements on the Land which are real property.

d. **Mortgage** - a mortgage, deed of trust, trust deed or other security instrument.

e. **Natural Person** - a human being, not a commercial or legal organization or entity. Natural Person includes a trustee of a Trust even if the trustee is not a human being.

f. **Policy Date** - the date and time shown in Schedule A. If the insured named in Schedule A first acquires the interest shown in Schedule A by an instrument recorded in the Public Records later than the date and time shown in Schedule A, the Policy Date is the date and time the instrument is recorded.

g. **Public Records** - records that give constructive notice of matters affecting Your Title, according to the state statutes where the Land is located.

h. **Title** - the ownership of Your interest in the Land, as shown in Schedule A.

i. **Trust** - a living trust established by a human being for estate planning.

j. **We/Our/Us** - First American Title Insurance Company.

k. **You/Your** - the insured named in Schedule A and also those identified in paragraph 2.b. of these Conditions.

2. CONTINUATION OF COVERAGE:

a. This Policy insures You forever, even after You no longer have Your Title. You cannot assign this Policy to anyone else.

b. This Policy also insures:
   (1) anyone who inherits Your Title because of Your death;
   (2) Your spouse who receives Your Title because of dissolution of Your marriage;
   (3) the trustee or successor trustee of a Trust to whom You transfer Your Title after the Policy Date; or
   (4) the beneficiaries of Your Trust upon Your death.

c. We may assert against the insureds identified in paragraph 2.b. any rights and defenses that We have against any previous insured under this Policy.

3. HOW TO MAKE A CLAIM

a. Prompt Notice Of Your Claim
   (1) As soon as You Know of anything that might be covered by this Policy, You must notify Us promptly in writing.
   (2) Send Your notice to First American Title Insurance Company, 114 East Fifth Street, Santa Ana, California, 92701, Attention: Claims Department. Please include the Policy number shown in Schedule A, and the county and state where the Land is located. Please enclose a copy of Your policy, if available.
   (3) If You do not give Us prompt notice, Your coverage will be reduced or ended, but only to the extent Your failure affects Our ability to resolve the claim or defend You.

b. Proof Of Your Loss
   (1) We may require You to give Us a written statement signed by You describing Your loss which includes:
       (a) the basis of Your claim;
       (b) the Covered Risks which resulted in Your loss;
       (c) the dollar amount of Your loss; and
       (d) the method You used to compute the amount of Your loss.
   (2) We may require You to make available to Us records, checks, letters, contracts, insurance policies and other papers which relate to Your claim. We may make copies of these papers.
   (3) We may require You to answer questions about Your claim under oath.
   (4) If You fail or refuse to give Us a statement of loss, answer Our questions under oath, or make available to Us the papers We request, Your coverage will be reduced or ended, but only to the extent Your failure or refusal affects Our ability to resolve the claim or defend You.

4. OUR CHOICES WHEN WE LEARN OF A CLAIM

a. After We receive Your notice, or otherwise learn, of a claim that is covered by this Policy, Our choices include one or more of the following:
   (1) Pay the claim;
   (2) Negotiate a settlement;
   (3) Bring or defend a legal action related to the claim;
   (4) Pay You the amount required by this Policy;
   (5) End the coverage of this Policy for the claim by paying You Your actual loss resulting from the Covered Risk, and those costs, attorneys' fees and expenses incurred up to that time which We are obligated to pay;
   (6) End the coverage described in Covered Risk 14, 15, 16 or 18 by paying You the amount of Your insurance then in force for the particular Covered Risk, and those costs, attorneys' fees and expenses incurred up to that time which We are obligated to pay;
   (7) End all coverage of this Policy by paying You the Policy Amount then in force and all those costs, attorneys' fees and expenses incurred up to that time which We are obligated to pay;
   (8) Take other appropriate action.

b. When We choose the options in paragraphs 4.a. (5), (6) or (7), all Our obligations for the claim end, including Our obligation to defend, or continue to defend, any legal action.

c. Even if We do not think that the Policy covers the claim, We may choose one or more of the options above. By doing so, We do not give up any rights.

5. HANDLING A CLAIM OR LEGAL ACTION

a. You must cooperate with Us in handling any claim or legal action and give Us all relevant information.

b. If You fail or refuse to cooperate with Us, Your coverage will be reduced or ended, but only to the extent Your failure or refusal affects Our ability to resolve the claim or defend You.

c. We are required to repay You only for those settlement costs, attorneys' fees and expenses that We approve in advance.

d. We have the right to choose the attorney when We bring or defend a legal action on Your behalf. We can appeal any decision to the highest level. We do not have to pay Your claim until the legal action is finally decided.

e. Whether or not We agree there is coverage, We can defend a legal action, or take other appropriate action under this Policy. By doing so, We do not give up any rights.

6. LIMITATION OF OUR LIABILITY

a. After subtracting Your Deductible Amount if it applies, We will pay no more than the least of:

(1) Your actual loss,

(2) Our Maximum Dollar Limit of Liability then in force for the particular Covered Risk, for claims covered only under Covered Risk 14, 15, 16 or 18, or

(3) the Policy Amount then in force,

and any costs, attorneys' fees and expenses which We are obligated to pay under this Policy.

b. (1) If We remove the cause of the claim with reasonable diligence after receiving notice of it, all Our obligations for the claim end, including any obligation for loss You had while We were removing the cause of the claim.

(2) Regardless of 6.b. (1) above, if You cannot use the Land because of a claim covered by this Policy:

(a) You may rent a reasonably equivalent substitute residence and We will repay You for the actual rent You pay, until the earlier of:

(1) the cause of the claim is removed; or

(2) We pay You the amount required by this Policy. If Your claim is covered only under Covered Risk 14, 15, 16 or 18, that payment is the amount of Your insurance then in force for the particular Covered Risk.

(b) We will pay reasonable costs You pay to relocate any personal property You have the right to remove from the Land, including transportation of that personal property for up to twenty-five (25) miles from the Land, and repair of any damage to that personal property because of the relocation. The amount We will pay You under this paragraph is limited to the value of the personal property before You relocate it.

c. All payments We make under this Policy reduce the Policy Amount, except for costs, attorneys' fees and expenses. All payments we make for claims which are covered only under Covered Risk 14, 15, 16 or 18 also reduce Our Maximum Dollar Limit of Liability for the particular Covered Risk, except for costs, attorneys' fees and expenses.

d. If We issue, or have issued, a policy to the owner of a Mortgage on Your Title and We have not given You any coverage against the Mortgage, then:

(1) We have the right to pay any amount due You under this Policy to the owner of the Mortgage to reduce the amount of the Mortgage, and any amount paid shall be treated as a payment to You under this Policy, including under paragraph 4.a.of these Conditions;

(2) Any amount paid to the owner of the Mortgage shall be subtracted from the Policy Amount of this Policy; and

(3) If Your claim is covered only under Covered Risk 14, 15, 16 or 18, any amount paid to the owner of the Mortgage shall also be subtracted from Our Maximum Dollar Limit of Liability for the particular Covered Risk.

e. If You do anything to affect any right of recovery You may have against someone else, We can subtract from Our liability the amount by which You reduced the value of that right.

7. TRANSFER OF YOUR RIGHTS TO US

a. When We settle Your claim, We have all the rights You have against any person or property related to the claim. You must transfer these rights to Us when We ask, and You must not do anything to affect these rights. You must let Us use Your name in enforcing these rights.

b. We will not be liable to You if We do not pursue these rights or if We do not recover any amount that might be recoverable.

c. We will pay any money We collect from enforcing these rights in the following order

(1) to Us for the costs, attorneys' fees and expenses We paid to enforce these rights;

(2) to You for Your loss that You have not already collected;

(3) to Us for any money We paid out under this Policy on account of Your claim; and

(4) to You whatever is left.

d. If You have rights under contracts (such as indemnities, guaranties, bonds or other policies of insurance) to recover all or part of Your loss, then We have all of those rights, even if those contracts provide that those obligated have all of Your rights under this Policy.

8. ENTIRE CONTRACT

This Policy, with any endorsements, is the entire contract between You and Us. To determine the meaning of any part of this Policy, You must read the entire Policy. Any changes to this Policy must be agreed to in writing by Us. Any claim You make against Us must be made under this Policy and is subject to its terms.

9. INCREASED POLICY AMOUNT

The Policy Amount will increase by ten percent (10%) of the Policy Amount shown in Schedule A each year for the first five years following the policy date shown in Schedule A, up to one hundred fifty percent (150%) of the Policy Amount shown in Schedule A. The increase each year will happen on the anniversary of the policy date shown in Schedule A.

10. SEVERABILITY

If any part of this Policy is held to be legally unenforceable, both You and We can still enforce the rest of this Policy.

11. ARBITRATION

a. If permitted in the state where the Land is located, You or We may demand arbitration.

b. The arbitration shall be binding on both You and Us. The arbitration shall decide any matter in dispute between You and Us.

c. The arbitration award may be entered as a judgment in the proper court.

d. The arbitration shall be under the Title Insurance Arbitration Rules of the American Arbitration Association. You may choose current Rules or Rules in existence on the Policy Date.

e. The law used in the arbitration is the law of the place where the Land is located.

f. You can get a copy of the Rules from Us.

SHORT FORM EXPANDED COVERAGE RESIDENTIAL LOAN POLICY
ONE-TO-FOUR FAMILY
Issued by
Blank Title Insurance Company

SCHEDULE A

Policy Number: Lo   an Number:
[File Number:]
Amount of Insurance: $ [Premium: $]

Mortgage Amount: M   ortgage Date:

Date of Policy: a.m./p.m. or the date of recording of the insured mortgage, whichever is later

Name of Insured:

Name of Borrower(s):

Street Address:
County and State:

      The estate or interest in the land identified in this Schedule A and which is encumbered by the insured mortgage is fee simple and is, at Date of Policy, vested in the borrower(s) shown in the insured mortgage and named above.

      The land referred to in this policy is described as set forth in the insured mortgage.

      This policy consists of [one] page(s), [including the reverse side hereof,] unless an addendum is attached and indicated below:

      _____ Addendum attached

      [The following state statutes are made part of Schedule B, relating to the ALTA 8.1 Environmental Protection Lien Endorsement:_____]

[Witness clause optional]

BLANK TITLE INSURANCE COMPANY

BY: _____
        PRESIDENT

BY: _____
        SECRETARY

[bracketed material optional–alternative paragraphs: one must be used]

SUBJECT TO THE EXCEPTIONS FROM COVERAGE CONTAINED IN SCHEDULE B BELOW, AND ANY ADDENDUM ATTACHED HERETO, BLANK TITLE INSURANCE COMPANY, A _____ CORPORATION, HEREIN CALLED THE "COMPANY," HEREBY INSURES THE INSURED IN ACCORDANCE WITH AND SUBJECT TO THE TERMS, EXCLUSIONS, CONDITIONS AND STIPULATIONS SET FORTH IN THE AMERICAN LAND TITLE ASSOCIATION EXPANDED COVERAGE RESIDENTIAL LOAN POLICY (10- __-01), ALL OF WHICH ARE INCORPORATED HEREIN. ALL REFERENCES TO SCHEDULES A AND B SHALL REFER TO SCHEDULES A AND B OF THIS POLICY.

SCHEDULE B

EXCEPTIONS FROM COVERAGE

Except to the extent of the coverage provided in the Endorsements listed after item 27 [28] of COVERED RISKS, This policy does not insure against loss or damage (and the Company will not pay costs, attorneys' fees or expenses) which arise by reason of:

1. Those taxes and special assessments, which become due or payable subsequent to Date of Policy. (This does not limit the coverage provided in items 8 (e) or 26 of COVERED RISKS)
2. Covenants, conditions and restrictions, if any, appearing in the public records. (This does not limit the coverage provided in items 5, 6, 8(b), or 23 of COVERED RISKS)
3. Any easements or servitudes appearing in the public records. (This does not limit the coverage provided in item 8(b) of COVERED RISKS)
4. Any lease, grant, exception or reservation of minerals or mineral rights appearing in the public records. (This does not limit the coverage provided in item 8(b) or 21 of COVERED RISKS)

NOTICES, WHERE SENT: All notices required to be given the Company and any statement in writing required to be furnished the Company shall include the number of this policy and shall be addressed to the Company at
_____

ADDENDUM TO SHORT FORM EXPANDED COVERAGE RESIDENTIAL LOAN POLICY

Addendum to Policy Number: _____ [File Number: _____]

SCHEDULE B (Continued)

IN ADDITION TO THE MATTERS SET FORTH ON SCHEDULE B OF THE POLICY TO WHICH THIS ADDENDUM IS ATTACHED, THIS POLICY DOES NOT INSURE AGAINST LOSS OR DAMAGE BY REASON OF THE FOLLOWING:

Creation of an Easement Requires:
- Contract
- Express Grant from the property owner
- Express Reservation
- Implied Grant / Reservation
- Necessity
- Prescription

Contract An easement created by a contract is one where the property owner (servient tenement) grants use to cross his or her property to another individual (dominant tenement). The person receiving the easement may not need to own property adjacent to the granting property owner, depending on the type of easement that is created.

Express Grant An easement is created through express grant when the servient tenement grants an easement by deed to the person who will benefit from the easement (the dominant tenement).

Express Reservation An easement is created through express reservation when the dominant tenement sells his or her property to another but reserves the easement rights in the deed for use by the new property owner.

Implied Grant / Reservation This occurs when an easement is created through an implication of law. No formal mention of such easement need be made in the deed. However, due to the proximity of one piece of property to another, an easement may be necessary and obvious.

Necessity An easement is created through necessity when there is no other way to reach a land locked property. If or when an alternative way on or off the property is created, the easement will automatically be terminated. An example of this is when city blocks are drawn and interior lots with no street access are created. The person purchasing the interior lot will need to cross the neighbor's property to reach his or her own. Usually this is done by utilizing the neighbor's driveway as an easement.

Prescription An easement is created through prescription when open and notorious use of someone else's land has occurred continuously for five or more years. The person using the land against the property owners will, however, must have a valid reason for crossing the land.

There are Eight Ways to Terminate an Easement:
1. Express agreement between both parties
2. Lawsuit
3. Abandonment
4. Estoppel
5. Merger of the easement between the dominant and servient tenements
6. Destruction of the servient tenement
7. Adverse possession
8. Excessive use

Express Agreement Express agreement terminates an easement when the dominant tenement surrenders the use of the servient tenement's land through a *quitclaim deed*. A quitclaim deed transfers property with no warranty.

Lawsuit Quiet title action, or court proceedings to establish title to property, *(NOTE: Define)* to terminate an easement can be brought upon the dominant tenement by the servient tenement.

Abandonment If an easement created through prescription is not used for a continuous period of five years, the easement will be terminated.

Estoppel Occurs when the easement is not being used, if the dominant tenement implies that the easement is no longer necessary, or if the servient tenement utilizes the land based on recommendations made by the dominant tenement.

Merger of the Easement Occurs when the dominant tenement purchases the property containing the easement from the servient tenement.

Destruction of the Servient Tenement For example: there is a hallway owned by the servient tenement in a condominium used by the dominant tenement. The servient tenement decides to remodel and take out the hallway to put in a new room. As the servient tenement has destroyed the easement, the easement is terminated.

Adverse Possession Occurs when the servient tenement performs all the actions necessary for adverse possession, ultimately taking the easement rights away from the dominant tenement.

Excessive Use If the dominant tenement uses the easement more frequently than originally intended, or uses it for a different purpose than originally stated in an agreement, the easement will terminate.

Restrictions Restrictions are limitations placed on a certain property or group of properties in a certain area. Zoning laws, development or building restrictions and building requirements are all considered restrictions. Private individuals, developers or the government may place these restrictions on a property. Private restrictions are placed on a property by a previous owner, creating a restriction for a single property or development only. Alternatively, zoning laws are created by the government and designed to benefit the public in a large area consisting of multiple properties.

A restriction is placed in the deed at the time of sale or may be created during the planning of a subdivision.

Restrictions are placed on property to insure the conformity or unity of an area. For example, if a subdivision is known for its view, a restriction of house heights or number of stories in a condominium building may be placed to ensure every unit or property has an optimal view. Because restrictions dictate what people can do on or with their own personal property, it is a form of encumbrance, but it is usually done for the benefit of an area.

When there is more than one restriction in place for a given area, the stricter regulations, rules, zoning ordinances or restrictions will be the one(s) that must be followed.

Restrictions are also called C.C & R.'s or covenants, conditions and restrictions. A covenant is a promise to either engage in, or abstain from a certain action. Breach of a covenant will most often result in monetary penalties. An example of a covenant is when a property owner purchases a plot of land with the agreement that it will only be used for raising agricultural crops, rather than development of a subdivision.

A condition is very similar to a covenant. However, if a condition is not met, the penalty is to surrender the property to the original owner or grantor. There are two types of conditions. The first is *condition subsequent* ,where a restriction is placed in the deed regarding a property. If this condition is violated, the property will revert back to the original grantor. The second type is *condition precedent* wherein certain actions or events must take place before a property may pass to its new owner.

Encroachments An encroachment is an improvement on real property that crosses adjacent property lines. An example is a privacy fence that crosses property lines and extends up six inches into the neighbor's back yard. By law, the owner of the property encroached upon has three years to remove the improvement. Examples of encroachments are fences, walls, trees, shrubs, buildings or drives.

If the encroachment fulfills the requirements for an easement by prescription or adverse possession, the owner of the improvement may earn the right to use the encroached-upon land. In the above example, if the fence crosses six inches into the neighbor's lot, and its existence was not contested for five years, the owner of the fence has full right to use the encroached-upon land.

> **Examples of Encroachments**
> - Fences
> - Walls
> - Buildings
> - Trees / Shrubs
> - Drives or Walkways

H O M E S T E A D   D E C L A R A T I O N

We learned earlier in this chapter that a lien may be attached to a property to satisfy a debt against the property owner. If the lien is not satisfied, foreclosure may occur against the homeowner or property owner. A *homestead exemption* is a recorded document protecting a certain amount of a homeowner's investment. This protection will guard against foreclosure from certain creditors as well as judgments rendered against the property owner. It is important to note that a property that has been homesteaded is not protected against trust deeds, mechanic's liens or other liens recorded prior to the homestead declaration.

California allows the head of household to homestead $75,000 of a home's value to be protected against creditors. Persons 65 years of age or older or persons with a mental or physical disability are entitled to $150,000 homestead exemption. All other individuals falling outside of the above mentioned parameters are entitled to a $50,000 homestead exemption.

Each homeowner may file only one homestead. If a homeowner owns more than one property, only one property may be homesteaded at a time. If the homeowner chooses to terminate the homestead on one property in favor of another, an abandonment of homestead must be filed on the property where the homestead will be terminated and only then may a new homestead be filed for the newly-favored property. Sale of a property will automatically terminate a homestead on that property.

MARKETABILITY OF TITLE

When a person is ready to sell property, it is important that they have a marketable title to the property. This does not mean that the title is perfect (in what sense?), but it does mean that a person likely and willing to purchase the property would be confident of no challenge to the title or purchase of property. A chain of title will reveal the actual owner of the property. This chain of title can be found in the county recorder's office in the county where the property can be found. The chain of title is the original basis to establish marketable title.

> A marketable title is on that a person is likely to accept in confidence that it will be free and clear of any challenge of ownership.

In times before accurate record keeping,, abstractors were used to research a property to determine the current or lawful owner. The abstractor would search all available documents to trace any conveyances or ownership changes and put together an abstract of title listing such information. A prospective buyer would then consult the abstract of title to ensure that none of the previous property owners had a legal claim to the property.

These days, records are organized such that any person can go into the county recorders office and conduct a title search for themselves. Since records are kept in a title plant and will provide any interested party with information regarding the certificate of title. A certificate of title will detail how the property is currently vested to the owner as well as outline any encumbrances attached to the title. Title insurance is also used now to guarantee the title to real property. This is important in that it protects any interested parties against loss in the case of an unmarketable title.

TITLE INSURANCE

Title insurance is used to guarantee a marketable title against risk. Properties maintain value as long as they are capable of being sold. When the property cannot be sold due to a cloud on the title, the value of the property decreases.

Due to the high demand of property and the value associated with it, land or property may be bought and sold several times during the documented periods. Marriage rights associated with community property, joint tenancy and property legally willed to an heir create complications in freely selling or buying property. How are we to be sure the property being sold is being sold by its rightful owner?

Records are kept regarding change of ownership for each piece of property in a given county. Any interested person can search the chain of title (researching all owners of a specific property) for as the time that records have been kept. This chain of title search reveals the abstract of title, (a record of each time a property has changed ownership), as well as prior owners. Abstract of title is used (along with an attorney's opinion of title) to determine any claims of ownership on a property. Although it is a very good way of ensuring there is a marketable title, the process can be very time consuming.

The chain of title, abstract of title and an attorney's opinion of title are good resources in determining who is the lawful owner of a property. In some cases, however, they may be faulty methods, as in cases of fraud or forgery. In cases such as this, a marketable title may be contested. The last thing a new property owner wants to worry about is whether or not the title to his or her property will be contested. Title insurance companies may help guard against recorded and unrecorded risks that may affect the marketable title to property.

There are two different types of title insurance: the standard policy and the extended policy.

Two Types of Title Insurance
• Standard Policy
• Extended Policy

A *standard policy* of title insurance protects against matters of record already on file with the county recorders office. It also protects against matters that would not be on record, such as forgery, fraud, impersonation or the failure of a competent party to create or enter into a contract. In addition, a standard policy will protect against federal tax liens and any expenses incurred in legally defending the title to a property. The standard policy will NOT protect against the following:

- Title defects either known to the policyholder at the time of insurance or shown in a survey
- Rights or claims of people in physical possession of the property, even those rights or claims that would not show up in public record
- Easements and liens not shown in public record
- Changes in land use dictated by zoning laws
- Water rights
- Mining claims
- Reservations

The California Land Title Association (CLTA) is an association of California title companies that provides all members with a standard form for insurance. Note that this form is only used by those who choose to take out a standard policy. Those individuals who choose extended coverage will fill out a different form.

For an additional cost, most risks not covered in a standard policy can be covered in an extended policy. The American Land Title Association (ALTA) offers a policy known as the A.L.T.A. Owner's Policy, which covers the same items as in the standard policy, In addition, the policy protects the insured against the claims of people who may be in physical possession of the property, but have no recorded interest, marketability of title, water rights, mining claims, recorded easements and liens, rights or claims discovered from a proper survey and reservations in patents. Lenders, as well as property owners, usually take out this type of policy to protect their investment.

S U M M A R Y
_____

In this chapter we studied the concept of holding title and its beginnings. The idea of separate or concurrent ownership was broken down into: different types of vesting of a title; when each type of concurrent ownership is appropriate; and the regulations or limitations on each vesting method. Upon understanding the different types of vesting, we studied the various limitations on title. Challenges to title, liens or other encumbrances may create a situation where the title is not marketable and thus must be cleared before the property can be sold to an interested party. Finally, we analyzed the different ways in which property owners can protect themselves from a monetary encumbrance through a homestead declaration as well as ways in which how consumers can protect themselves from challenges to title on a new property by taking out a title insurance policy.

T E R M S   A N D   P H R A S E S

A.L.T.A. (American Land Title Association) Owner's Policy- a policy of extended title insurance, which can be purchased by either a lender or buyer

Abstract of Title - A full summary of all consecutive grants, conveyances, wills, records and judicial proceedings affecting title to a specific parcel of real estate

Abstractor – Historically, a person who searches out any issues affecting the title to real property and summarizes the information in a findings report.

Acknowledgment - A formal declaration to a public official or notary stating that a person has voluntarily signed an instrument.

Actual Notice - Knowledge acquired on the basis of actual observance(as opposed to Constructive Notice)

California Land Title Association - A trade organization consisting of the state's title companies

Chain of Title - The recorded history of matters such as conveyances, liens and encumbrances affecting title to a parcel of real estate

Condition Precedent - Requires that a certain event, or condition occur before title can pass to a new owner

Condition Subsequent - A restriction on future use of a property, placed in a deed at the time of conveyance

Constructive Notice - Recording of a deed or possession of property

Conveyance - The written transfer of title to land from one person to another

Declaration of Homestead - a recorded document that protects a homeowner from foreclosure by certain judgment creditors

Dominant Tenement - The property that benefits from an easement.

Easement - The right to use another's land for a specified purpose (also referred to as a right-of-way)

Easement in Gross - An easement that is not appurtenant to any one parcel (e.g., public utilities)

Encroachment - The placement of permanent improvements on adjacent property owned by another

Expedients - Land grants recorded by the Mexican government in California

Extended Policy - An extended title insurance policy

Guarantee of Title- An assurance that a title to property is clear

Instrument - A written legal document setting forth the rights and liabilities of the parties involved

Judgment - The final legal decision of a judge in a court of law regarding the legal rights of parties to disputes

License - Permission to use a property, which may be revoked at any time

Lien - A claim on the property of another for payment of a debt

Lis Pendens - A recorded notice that indicates pending litigation affecting title on a property. Lis pendens will prevent a conveyance or any other transfer of ownership until the lawsuit is settled and the lis pendens removed

Marketable Title - a clear salable title that is reasonably free from risk of litigation over possible defects.

Partition Action - A court action to divide a property held by co-owners.

Patents - Deeds used by the U.S. government when confirming or transferring ownership to private parties.

Servient Tenement - The property that is burdened by an easement.

Severalty - Ownership of real property by only one person or entity.

Standard Policy - A policy of title insurance covering only matters of record.

Title - Evidence of land ownership.

Title Insurance - An insurance policy that protects the insured against loss or damage due to defects in the property's title.

Title Plant - The storage facility or a title company in which complete title records of properties in its area are housed.

Treaty of Guadalupe Hidalgo - Ended the war with Mexico in 1848, granting possession of California to the United States.

Undivided Interest - That interest a co-owner has in property, which carries with it the right to possession and use of the whole property, along with the co-owners.

Vested - The different methods of holding title.

1. What concept carried over from Spanish law into modern day property ownership?
    A. Civil law
    B. Common law
    C. Community property
    D. None of the above

2. By law, all documents affecting the title to real property must be (A):
    A. Acknowledged
    B. Recorded
    C. Both A and B
    D. Neither A nor B

3. Which of the following officials is NOT considered a public official who may take an acknowledgment?
    A. Judge
    B. County Clerk
    C. County Treasurer
    D. Notary Public

4. Which of the following may own property in severalty?
    A. Corporations
    B. Trusts
    C. Individuals
    D. All of the above.

5. Which of the following is not a type of concurrent ownership?
    A. Co-ownership
    B. Joint tenancy
    C. Tenancy in common
    D. Community Property

6. Which of the following is a characteristic of Tenancy in Common?
    A. Right of survivorship
    B. Equal, undivided interest
    C. Equal right of possession
    D. All parties must take title to the property at the same time.

7. Parties in a joint tenancy may dispose of their property in which of the following ways?
    A. Will
    B. Right of survivorship
    C. Sale
    D. Both B and C

8. Which one of the following is not one of the four unities of a Joint Tenancy?
    A. Unity of Time
    B. Unity of Survivorship
    C. Unity of Title
    D. Unity of Interest

9. Which of the following is true regarding community property?
   A. Community property may be sold with only one spouse's consent.
   B. Community property may be encumbered with only one spouse's consent.
   C. Community property may be purchased with only one spouse's consent.
   D. Separate property may be purchased with money earned from wages.

10. Which of the following is correct regarding community property?
    A. With no will in place, the surviving spouse inherits all of the deceased spouse's
       interest.
    B. Property cannot be willed to living heirs
    C. With no will in place, the surviving children inherit the deceased's interest half
       of the property
    D. None of the above is correct.

11. Which of the following is NOT considered an encumbrance on real property?
    A. Liens
    B. Encroachments
    C. Homestead
    D. Easement

12. Which of the following is considered a money-restricted encumbrance?
    A. Encroachment
    B. Judgment
    C. Easement
    D. None of the above.

13. Which of the following steps is not necessary to initiate a valid mechanics lien?
    A. Preliminary Notice
    B. Starting Time
    C. Completion Notice
    D. Adverse Possession

14. In a foreclosure situation, which of the following determines the order of lien
    payment?
    A. The date each lien was recorded always determines the order of
       reimbursement.
    B. The amount of money owed (with the most expensive lien taking priority and
       the least expensive lien as the last to be paid).
    C. The date each lien was recorded (from the first recorded to the most recent
       recorded) ,with the exception of mechanics liens, which are always paid first.
    D. The most recent lien recorded will be the first lien to be paid from a judgment
       to the oldest recorded lien to be paid last.

15. The continuous, notorious use of another persons land for a period of five or more
    years is an example of what kind of easement?
    A. Prescription
    B. Express Grant
    C. Contract
    D. Necessity

16. All of the following are examples of encroachments EXCEPT
    A. Buildings
    B. Easements
    C. Fences and walls
    D. Hedges, trees or other vegetation crossing boundary lines

17. What is the maximum homestead exemption a person 65 years of age or older can declare on their residence?
    A. $150,000
    B. $75,000
    C. $50,000
    D. $85,000

18. A certificate of title will reveal what about a property?
    A. Vesting
    B. Encumbrances
    C. Neither A nor B
    D. Both A and B

19. A standard title insurance policy will guard against all of the following EXCEPT
    A. Federal tax liens
    B. Forgery
    C. Water rights
    D. Fraud

20. The American Land Title Association (A.T.L.A.) provides an extended title insurance policy which guards against which of the following?
    A. Water rights
    B. Mining claims
    C. Unrecorded liens
    D. All of the above

CONTRACTS

What you will learn in this Chapter

- General Information regarding Contracts

- Elements of a Valid Contract

- Statute of Fraud(s)

- Performance of Contracts

- Discharge of Contracts

- Remedies to Breach of Contract

- Statute of Limitations

- Elements of Real Estate Contracts

1. Failure to perform a contract is also known as:
    A. A rescission
    B. A breach
    C. A novation
    D. A reformation

2. How long is the Statute of Limitations for an action based on a written real estate contract?
    A. Unlimited
    B. Two years
    C. Four years
    D. Twenty years

3. A well-drafted real estate purchase contract will include which of the following provisions?:
    A. The buyer's possession of the property
    B. The financing terms
    C. Proration of property expenses
    D. All of the above

4. According to the Statute of Frauds, all contracts for the sale of real estate must be :
    A. Originated by a real estate broker
    B. On preprinted forms
    C. Made in writing
    D. Accompanied by earnest money deposits

5. Which of the following parties is bound by an option to purchase?
    A. Buyer only
    B. Seller only
    C. Neither buyer nor seller
    D. Both buyer and seller

6. A contract that has not been performed is called a (n)
    A. Executory contract
    B. Executed contract
    C. Unilateral contract
    D. Bilateral contract

7. Which of the following are basic elements of a valid contract?
    A. Sufficient consideration
    B. Lawful purpose
    C. Competent parties
    D. All of the above

INTRODUCTION

The real estate industry would not be what it is today without the Law of Contracts. Nearly every transaction in the industry involves at least one contract; so, one must be familiar with the creation of contracts, as well as how they operate and are enforced.

WHAT IS A CONTRACT?

A contract is a binding agreement between two or more parties to perform or not perform an action. It is not necessarily a twenty-page legal document, written in single-space and printed on 8 1/2 x 14 paper. A contract may be a concert ticket, a library card or an oral agreement by parties.

Classes of Contracts
There are four basic ways to classify contracts:
- Express or implied
- Unilateral or bilateral
- Executory or executed and
- (Either) valid, voidable, void or unenforceable

Express or Implied Contracts

An *express contract* is expressed in words, either verbally or in writing. An implied contract is one that has not been put into words; but the agreement between parties is been implied by their actions.

Implied Contract Example
If you buy a ticket at the local multiplex theater,
you give your money to the ticket booth assistant,
with the expectation that when you walk inside and
they turn the lights off and the projector on,
management will show you the film for which you paid.

Bilateral or Unilateral Contracts
A *bilateral contract* is one in which each party promises to do some act in exchange for the other party or parties who are also doing a specific action for them (i.e., *a promise for a promise*). A *unilateral contract* is an agreement in which one party agrees to do (or not do) something in return for performance. This type of contract is not a promise.

Example
An open listing is a good example of a unilateral contract. A seller promises to pay the broker a commission if the broker sells his house. The broker is not obligated to find a buyer to buy the house; but, if the broker does find a buyer, the seller is obligated to pay the broker a commission.

Executory or Executed Contracts

An *executory contract* is one in which some=act specified in the contract has yet to be completed. An *executed contract* is one in which a performance or action has been fully completed executed. In an executed contract, all parties have fulfilled their contractual obligations or promises. Most contracts begin as executory and end as executed.

EITHER..............OR	
Express Written or oral	Implied Conducted by the parties
Bilateral A promise by one party in exchange for a promise by another party	Unilateral A promise by one party in exchange for an act by another party
Executory Performance or action not yet fully performed	Executed Performance or action fully performed

Valid, Void, Voidable or Unenforceable Contracts

The fourth classification of contracts is the 'V class.' Well... three Vs and a U. A contract may either be valid, void, voidable or unenforceable. A *valid contract* is one in which all the legal requirements for contract formation has been met. We will discuss these legal requirements later in this chapter.

The benefit of a valid contract is if one party does not fulfill their side of the contract (or *breaches* the contract), the injured party may sue in court to force the other party to fulfill their promise.

A *void contract* is a contract that does not contain all the legal elements of contract formation (which will be addressed in the next section). In the eyes of the law, a void contract does not exist and is therefore unenforceable. Thus, no court in the land will determine whether Joey Two Thumbs owes Nicky The Nose money for collecting protection money, since the action of collecting protection money is illegal.

When a contract is **voidable**, one of the parties may reject it because there is a **deficiency** (defect) in the contract that injures him or her. The injured party may proceed with the contract, but also has the option to **disaffirm** it (have the court terminate the contract).

Last, but not least, some contracts are **unenforceable (unable to be legally enforced),** even if they are not void or voidable. For example, a valid contract becomes unenforceable when the statute of limitations expires.

Remember Joey Two Thumbs and Nicky The Nose? We know that the contract between them is void because it was an agreement to perform an illegal action. Because that the action is illegal, any court in the land would (a) rule that the contract is unenforceable and (b) tell the bailiff to lock up both of them for breaking the law!

TYPE OF CONTRACT	LEGAL EFFECT	EXAMPLE
VALID or ENFORCEABLE	Binding and enforceable	An agreement that meets all requirements of a contract
VOID	No contract at all	An agreement for which there is no lawful purpose
VOIDABLE	Valid unless rejected by the injured party	A defect in the agreement hurts one of the parties
UNENFORCEABLE	Neither party may sue for performance	A contract that is no longer valid, as the statute of limitations has expired

B A S I C   E L E M E N T S   O F   V A L I D   C O N T R A C T S

There are four necessary elements of any valid contract:
- Capable parties
- Mutual consent
- Lawful purpose
- Sufficient consideration

Capable Parties

In the United States, everyone (including aliens) has the capacity to contract with another; everyone that is, EXCEPT: (1) minors, (2) incompetents and (3) convicts.

(1) Minors

A **minor** is defined as a person under the age of 18. A minor may not employ (hire) a broker.

Exception: A minor who is married or in the Armed Forces is considered emancipated, and therefore, capable of entering into a contract.

A minor may acquire real property by gift or inheritance. A minor may also purchase real property through a guardian, providing court approval has been given.

(2) Incompetents

According to United States Civil Code, someone who is "entirely without understanding" is **incompetent** and cannot enter into a contract. Once a court has determined that an individual is incompetent, any contract into which they enter is void.

(3) Convicts

A **convict** is a person serving a sentence in a state or federal prison. During their time of incarceration, they lose their right to contract, with certain exceptions.

Aliens (non-residents of the United States of America) may purchase, own, hold or transfer real property in California, regardless of whether they are U.S. citizens.

Mutual Consent

In order for a contract to be binding, all parties to the agreement must consent to the terms. This is commonly referred to as a "meeting of the minds." Mutual consent is normally achieved through **offer and acceptance**. One party offers something in the agreement, which is accepted by the other party or parties.

Offer
Formation of a contract begins when one person (the **offeror**) makes an offer to another person (the **offeree**). The offer must:

- Be communicated to the offeree
- Have certain and definite terms

In the communication of the offer, the intent to contract must be objective (i.e., expressed in word or deed) rather than subjective (i.e., without expression in word or deed). If something is said or done that a reasonable person could interpret as an objective expression of intent to form a contract, that expression may be considered a legally binding offer.

> **EXAMPLE**
> Suppose that A buys a motorcycle for $15,000 from B. After it breaks down three times in one week, A says to B, "I'm so sick of this bike that I'd sell this hunk of steel for $10."
> Hearing this, B takes out his wallet and hands A ten dollars.

In this case, A is not required to sell B the motorcycle. His statement was not intended to be a contract and no reasonable person would take it as such.

B would observe A's tone of voice, assess the situation and make a determination that the statement was not a serious one.

An offer must also communicate certain and definite terms. These include basic terms such as the subject matter, the time of performance and the price. These terms must be defined and stated. If too many items are left vague, the offer will not be considered binding.

Acceptance
To meet the definition of mutual consent, the offer in question must be accepted by the offeree. Once the offer is accepted, a contract is formed and the parties are legally bound. Following are the four requirements necessary to express acceptance:

1. An offer can only be accepted by an offeree
2. An acceptance must be communicated to the offeror (through word or deed)
3. An acceptance must be made in the manner specified in the offer or contract
4. An acceptance must not alter the terms of the offer

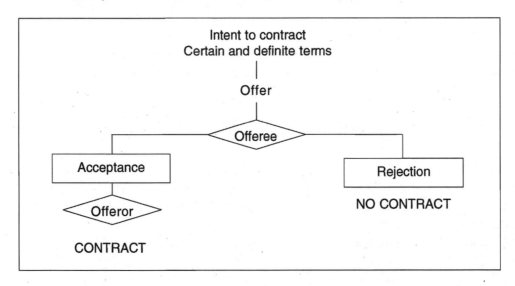

> *Silence cannot be considered an acceptance of an offer. In turn, no party can be forced to express rejection of an offer.*

If the terms of an offer are modified by the offeree and presented to the original offeror, this constitutes a rejection of the offer and is known as a counter offer. In a counter offer situation, the original offeree becomes the offeror.

Legality (Lawful Object)

The formation and operation of a contract must be legal. *A contract that requires a party to break the law is void.* A contract's objectives and considerations must also be legal.

The objective is the element or action in the contract that parties are required to perform or not perform. If the contract consists of a single objective that is unlawful (either wholly or in part), the entire contract is void. Similarly, if the contract consists of many objectives, only those that are lawful will be considered valid.

Sufficient Consideration (Compensation)

Each contract requires sufficient consideration (or compensation). Such considerations can be any item of value. **Consideration** can be defined as anything given or promised by one party to induce another party to enter into a contract. Consideration may include money, a promise, property, or the promise to abstain from a particular action. Illegal services or acts may not be an element of consideration.

In rare situations, contracts require that consideration be adequate in order for the contract to be enforceable.

An example of consideration is rent that a tenant pays a landlord in exchange for an apartment. The contract a tenant signs clearly spells out how much rent will be paid per month. If a tenant fails to pay this rent, he or she will be evicted from the property, as failure to pay rent is a breach of contract.

Writing

In addition to the four elements of a valid contract, a fifth element is dictated by the Statute of Frauds. This dictates that enforceable real estate contracts must be in writing.

STATUTE OF FRAUDS

Each state has a section of its civil code that requires certain contracts to be in writing and signed by all required parties entering into the contract. It is important to note that not all parties entering into a contract must sign the contract. On certain occasions the simple act of taking possession of property is acknowledgement enough. In California this provision is called the *statute of frauds*. Based on Old English common law, this statute provides guidelines to prevent against fraud and perjury. In California the statute of frauds is contained in California Civil Code Sections 1619 – 1633.

Let's examine which contracts must be in writing:

The statute of frauds applies to any agreement that will be carried out within one or more years after the time of the agreement. The statute of frauds also applies to any sale totaling $500 or more. This includes the sale of personal property as well as real property. Following are some of the contracts pertaining to real property that fall within the statute:

- An agreement to answer for the debt, default or nonperformance of another (a guaranty)

- An agreement for the exchange, sale or interest in real property
- An agency agreement authorizing an agent to procure, introduce or find a buyer or seller (or lessee or lessor, for a lease more than one year), if the agent will receive compensation (for example, a listing agreement)
- An agency agreement authorizing an agent to purchase or sell real property or lease it for more than one year (e.g., a power of attorney)
- An agreement by a purchaser of real property to assume an existing loan, unless the assumption of that debt by the purchaser is specifically provided for in the conveyance of the property (known as an assumption agreement)
- A lease of real property that will expire more than one year after it is signed

Performance of contracts

When one party to a contract meets his or her obligation of the contract, the other party must also meet their contractual obligation. If one party fails to uphold their obligation, a breach has occurred, and the other party is then released from their contractual obligation.

EXAMPLE

Joe contracts with Morgan to build Joe's house for $250,000. Morgan doesn't build the house; so, Joe does not owe Morgan any money.

There are times when a contract's performance is not so obvious. For example, suppose Morgan does build the house for Joe, but Joe feels that Morgan did not do the job well?

The answer to this dilemma depends on whether there has been *substantial performance* or there has been a *material breach*. If Morgan hasn't fulfilled every detail of the contract, but has carried out its key objectives, this may be considered substantial performance. In this situation, Joe would be obligated to complete his part of the contract (pay Morgan $250,000), though he could sue Morgan for damages caused by the unfulfilled elements of the contract.

On the other hand, if Morgan fails to complete some important portion of the contract, (such as not putting a roof on the house), Morgan will have committed a material breach. If Morgan commits a material breach, Joe is relieved of his contractual obligations. This is known as discharge of contract.

DISCHARGE OF CONTRACTS

A **discharge** of contract means that one has fulfilled one's duties as outlined by the contract. There is more than one way to discharge a contract.

Full Performance
Full performance is the ideal way to discharge a contract. In full performance, all parties to the contract have performed their obligations completely and fully.

Mutual Rescission
The parties may agree to rescind, or cancel, the contract by mutual agreement. This happens when one of the parties to an uncompleted contract agrees to excuse the other party from their obligations.

Assignment

Assigning a contract means transferring one party's interest in a contract to another party. Most contracts are assignable. Exceptions occur in cases where contracts call for the personal services of the **assignor** or when there is a clause specifically prohibiting an **assignment**.

Listing agreements, for example, are not assignable because they require the personal services of the listing agent.

The assignor also remains liable to execute the contract if the **assignee** does not execute his or her end of the contract.

Breach

As discussed earlier, material breach is one method of discharging a contract. Breach occurs when one of the parties does not perform all or part of their obligation(s) as outlined in the contract. The non-breached party (the party injured by the breach) is entitled to legal restitution.

HOW TO DISCHAREGE CONTRACTS	
Full Performance	Preferred method; contract is completed
Mutual Rescission	Parties agree to disagree
Assignment	One party gets someone else to fulfill obligation
Breach	One party doesn't perform

BREACH OF CONTRACT REMEDIES

There are four basic remedies to a breached contract:
1. Acceptance of breach
2. Sue for dollar damages (monetary remedies)
3. Sue for equitable remedies (non-monetary remedies)
4. Non-judicial remedies.

Acceptance of Breach

The first remedy for breach of contract is to accept the breach. A primary reason for the injured party not to pursue legal action is that he or she believes that the recoverable damages do not justify the expense of litigation. When the injured party believes that the other party does not have enough assets to satisfy a judgment, we may refer to the uninjured party as **judgment-proof**.

Monetary Remedies

If the victim of a breach of contract is unwilling to accept the breach, he or she may pursue an action for monetary (dollar) damages. There are three types of monetary damages:

1. Liquidated dollar damage
2. Actual dollar damage
3. Punitive dollar damage

Liquidated Damages (Predetermined Amount)

This form of dollar damage is a specific amount that has been agreed upon, usually in a clause within the contract. This amount is to be paid by the party who has breached the contract. This remedy is typically used when it is either impractical or difficult to repair the actual damage.

In most cases, purchase agreements call for the forfeiture of earnest money deposits as liquidated damages in the event that the buyer defaults. Earnest money is the deposit a buyer will offer a seller to purchase property. It is often times a good faith deposit showing the seller that the buyer is in fact interested in purchasing the property, and prevents the property from being sold to another interested party. In the case of residential purchase agreements, the law limits the amount of liquidated damages to a maximum of three percent (3%) of the sales price.

These damages are usually split equally (50/50) between the seller and the listing agent. If the contract states that the deposit is the sole remedy for the seller, he or she may not keep the deposit as liquidated damages and may sue for further damages.

With regard to construction projects, a per-day charge is usually assessed as liquidated damages in the event of a delay in construction completion.

Actual Damages (Actual Loss)

This form of dollar damage is usually referenced in a clause within the contract and provides that the actual amount of loss go to the injured party in the event that one party breaks the contract.

> If a seller or a real estate licensee willfully or through negligence fails to comply with a disclosure requirement, he or she will be liable for any actual damages suffered by the buyer.

Punitive Damages (Additional Awards)

These damages (in addition to compensatory damages) are awarded by courts in an effort to punish the wrongdoer. Though awarded by courts for intentional and outrageous acts, excessive punitive damages will not be upheld by the courts.

Typically, real estate contracts do not allow punitive damages as punishment of those who create a breach.

Equitable Remedies

Equitable remedies, or non-dollar damages, are determined by the courts. The courts base these remedies on ethical considerations. Unilateral rescission, specific performance, injunction, reformation and declaratory relief are some forms of equitable remedies (and will be covered later in this chapter).

Unilateral Rescission

This remedy is available to a party when they enter into a contract based on duress, fraud, menace, mistake, or undue influence. The rescission must (1) be made promptly and (2) return everything of value received from the offending party.

CALIFORNIA
ASSOCIATION
OF REALTORS®

**BROKER/ASSOCIATE-LICENSEE/ASSISTANTS
THREE-PARTY AGREEMENT**
(C.A.R. Form TPA, Revised 10/04)

This Agreement, dated _____, is made by_____
_____ ("Broker"), and
_____ ("Associate-Licensee"), and
_____, ("Assistant").

In consideration for the covenants and representations contained in this Agreement, Broker, Associate-Licensee, and Assistant agree as follows:

1. **BROKER:** Broker represents that Broker is licensed as a real estate broker by the State of California, and is doing business as (firm name)_____, a ☐ sole proprietorship, ☐ partnership, or ☐ corporation. Broker is a member of the_____ _____ Association(s) of REALTORS®, and a subscriber to the _____ Multiple Listing Service(s).

2. **ASSOCIATE-LICENSEE:** Associate-Licensee represents that he/she is licensed by the State of California as a ☐ real estate broker, ☐ real estate salesperson, and has entered into a separate agreement with Assistant for the performance of services related to Associate-Licensee's real estate activity.

3. **ASSISTANT:** Assistant represents that he/she has entered into an agreement with Associate-Licensee for the performance of services related to Associate-Licensee's licensed real estate activity. Assistant represents that he/she ☐ does, ☐ does not, have a California real estate license.

4. **RELATIONSHIP AMONG THE PARTIES:** Associate-Licensee has entered into an independent contractor agreement with Broker to perform real estate licensed activity under the name and license of Broker. Assistant works for Associate-Licensee as specified under the terms of their separate written agreement. Other than as specified in this Agreement, Assistant has no other agreements with Broker for the performance of any acts specified in the separate agreement with Associate-Licensee.

5. **COMPLIANCE WITH REAL ESTATE LAW:** Broker, Associate-Licensee and Assistant each acknowledge that California real estate law imposes certain obligations on a broker with regard to supervision, employment and compensation of any person who acts on behalf of the broker in pursuit of real estate licensed activity. Accordingly, Broker, Associate-Licensee and Assistant all agree that the following terms contained in this paragraph are made solely for the purpose of compliance with the real estate law and that no other inference of employment between Broker and Associate-Licensee, Broker and Assistant, or Associate-Licensee and Assistant shall be drawn therefrom. Broker has the right to review and supervise the files and activities of Assistant, the right to recommend termination and, if necessary, to actually terminate the relationship between Associate-Licensee and Assistant as it relates to the performance of acts under Broker's license. If Assistant has a California real estate license, and performs licensed activity, Assistant's real estate license shall immediately be given to Broker. If Assistant is licensed as a real estate salesperson and performs licensed activity, then: **(i)** all compensation to Assistant for licensed activity shall be paid through Broker, and **(ii)** for the sole and limited purpose of complying with California real estate law, the Assistant shall be deemed employed by Broker.

6. **ASSISTANT COMPENSATION:** Associate-Licensee shall be solely responsible for compensation to Assistant under the terms of their agreement. If payment of compensation to Assistant must be made through Broker because Assistant has a California real estate license, then Associate-Licensee shall be responsible to Broker for such compensation and all administrative and other costs necessary to accommodate the relationship between Associate-Licensee and Assistant. Any compensation paid to Assistant, and all administrative and other necessary costs, shall be offset against any compensation due Associate-Licensee by Broker.

Broker's Initials (_____)(_____)
Associate-Licensee's Initials (_____)(_____)
Assistant's Initials (_____)(_____)

Reviewed by _____ Date _____

EQUAL HOUSING
OPPORTUNITY

TPA REVISED 10/04 (PAGE 1 OF 3) Print Date

7. **INSURANCE:**
   A. **Automobile:** Assistant shall maintain automobile insurance coverage for liability and property damage in the following amounts $_____/$_____. Broker shall be named as an additional insured party on Assistant's policies. A copy of the endorsement showing the additional insured parties shall be provided to Broker.
   B. **Workers Compensation:** Broker ☐ does, ☐ does not, carry workers' compensation insurance which covers Assistant. (If checked) ☐ Associate-Licensee agrees to carry workers' compensation insurance which covers Assistant.
   (Workers' Compensation Advisory: Even though Assistant may be treated as an independent contractors for tax and other purposes, the California Labor and Workforce Development Agency may consider Assistant to be an employee for workers' compensation purposes. If Assistant is, or is considered to be an employee: (i) Broker or Associate-Licensee must obtain workers' compensation insurance for Assistant, and (ii) Broker or Associate Licensee, not Assistant, must bear the cost of workers' compensation insurance. Penalties for failure to carry workers' compensation include, among others, the issuance of stop-work orders and fines of up to $1,000 per agent, not to exceed $100,000 per company.)
   C. **Errors and Omissions:** Broker ☐ does, ☐ does not, maintain errors and omissions insurance which covers the activities of Assistant.
   D. **All:** Whether Broker carries workers compensation, errors and omissions, unemployment, liability or any other insurance which provides coverage for Assistant or Associate-Licensee, Broker does so in the exercise of Broker's business judgment, for the sole benefit of Broker, and all parties agree that, other than for compliance with California real estate law, no inference of employment between Broker and Associate-Licensee, Broker and Assistant, or Associate-Licensee and Assistant shall be drawn therefrom.

8. **PROPRIETARY INFORMATION:** All files and documents pertaining to listings, leads and transactions are the property of Broker and shall be delivered to Broker by Assistant immediately upon request or termination of the relationship between either Broker and Associate-Licensee or Associate-Licensee and Assistant. Assistant shall not use to his/her own advantage, or the advantage of any other person, business, or entity, except as specifically agreed in writing, either during Assistant's association with Broker, or thereafter, any information gained for or from the business, or files of Broker. After termination, Assistant shall not solicit: (i) prospective or existing clients or customers based upon company-generated leads obtained during the time Associate-Licensee was affiliated with Broker; (ii) any principal with existing contractual obligations to Broker; or (iii) any principal with a contractual transactional obligation for which Broker is entitled to be compensated.

9. **COMPLIANCE WITH APPLICABLE LAWS, RULES, REGULATIONS AND POLICIES:** Assistant agrees to comply with all local, state and federal laws and regulations and any office policy and procedures to which Associate-Licensee is subject as a result of engaging in real estate activity. If Assistant does not have a real estate license, Assistant shall not engage in any activity for which a real estate license is required. (Assistant may become more familiar with these limitations by reading the "DRE Guidelines for Unlicensed Assistants.")

10. **INDEMNITY AND HOLD HARMLESS:** Assistant agrees, regardless of responsibility, to indemnify, defend and hold Broker harmless from all claims, disputes, litigation, judgments, awards, costs and attorney's fees arising from any action taken or omitted by Assistant, in connection with services rendered or to be rendered, pursuant to Assistant's agreement with Associate-Licensee.

11. **DISPUTE RESOLUTION:**
    A. **All Disputes:** This Agreement shall govern all disputes and claims among Broker, Associate-Licensee, and Assistant or between Broker and Assistant, arising out of their relationship under this and any attached agreements, and applies even after termination of any relationship with Assistant.
    B. **Mediation:** Mediation is recommended as a method of resolving disputes arising out of this Agreement between and among Broker, Associate-Licensee, and Assistant.
    C. **Arbitration:** All disputes or claims between Broker, Associate-Licensee and Assistant which cannot be otherwise resolved, shall be decided by neutral, binding arbitration in accordance with substantive California law. The Federal Arbitration Act, Title 9, U.S. Code Section 1, et seq., shall govern this Agreement to arbitrate.

Broker's Initials (_____)(_____)
Associate-Licensee's Initials (_____)(_____)
Assistant's Initials (_____)(_____)

Reviewed by _____ Date _____

TPA REVISED 10/04 (PAGE 2 OF 3)

BROKER/ASSOCIATE-LICENSEE/ASSISTANT THREE-PARTY AGREEMENT (TPA PAGE 2 OF 3)

12. OTHER TERMS AND CONDITIONS AND ATTACHED SUPPLEMENTS:
- ☐ Broker and Associate-Licensee Independent Contractor Agreement (Such as C.A.R. Form ICA)
- ☐ Associate-Licensee and Assistant Agreement (Such as C.A.R. Form PAC)
- ☐ Broker Office Policy Manual (or, if checked, ☐ in Broker's office)
- ☐ DRE Guidelines for Unlicensed Assistants
- ☐ California Association of REALTORS® "Real Estate Licensing Chart"

_____
_____
_____
_____
_____

13. ATTORNEY FEES: In any action, proceeding, or arbitration between or among Broker, Associate-Licensee or Assistant, arising from or related to this Agreement, the prevailing Broker, Associate-Licensee or Assistant shall be entitled to reasonable attorney fees and costs.

14. ENTIRE AGREEMENT: All prior agreements between the parties concerning their relationship as Broker, Associate-Licensee, and Assistant are incorporated in this Agreement, which constitutes the entire contract. Its terms are intended by the parties as a final and complete expression of their agreement with respect to its subject matter, and may not be contradicted by evidence of any prior agreement or contemporaneous oral agreement. This Agreement may not be amended, modified, altered, or changed, except by a further agreement in writing executed by Broker, Associate-Licensee, and Assistant.

BROKER:

_____   _____
(Signature)   (Name Printed)

By_____
Its Broker/Office Manager (circle one)

_____   _____
(Address)   (City, State, Zip)

_____   _____
(Telephone)   (Fax)

_____
(E-mail)

ASSOCIATE-LICENSEE:

_____   _____
(Signature)   (Name Printed)

_____   _____
(Address)   (City, State, Zip)

_____   _____
(Telephone)   (Fax)

_____
(E-mail)

ASSISTANT:

_____   _____
(Signature)   (Name Printed)

_____   _____
(Address)   (City, State, Zip)

_____   _____
(Telephone)   (Fax)

_____
(E-mail)

SURE TRAC
The System for Success®

Published and Distributed by:
REAL ESTATE BUSINESS SERVICES, INC.
a subsidiary of the California Association of REALTORS®
525 South Virgil Avenue, Los Angeles, California 90020

Reviewed by _____ Date _____

TPA REVISED 10/04 (PAGE 3 OF 3)

BROKER/ASSOCIATE-LICENSEE/ASSISTANT THREE-PARTY AGREEMENT (TPA PAGE 3 OF 3)

CONFIRMATION REAL ESTATE AGENCY RELATIONSHIPS

CALIFORNIA ASSOCIATION OF REALTORS®

(As required by the Civil Code)

(C.A.R. Form AC-6, Revised 1987)

Subject Property Address _____

The following agency relationship(s) is/are hereby confirmed for this transaction:

LISTING AGENT: _____

is the agent of (check one):
- ❑ the Seller exclusively; or
- ❑ both the Buyer and Seller

SELLING AGENT: _____

(if not the same as Listing Agent)

is the agent of (check one):
- ❑ the Buyer exclusively; or
- ❑ the Seller exclusively; or
- ❑ both the Buyer and Seller

I/WE ACKNOWLEDGE RECEIPT OF A COPY OF THIS CONFIRMATION.

Seller _____ Date _____   Buyer _____ Date _____

Seller _____ Date _____   Buyer _____ Date _____

Listing Agent _____ By _____ Date _____
       (Please Print)   (Associate Licensee or Broker-Signature)

Selling Agent _____ By _____ Date _____
       (Please Print)   (Associate Licensee or Broker-Signature)

A REAL ESTATE BROKER IS QUALIFIED TO ADVISE ON REAL ESTATE. IF YOU DESIRE LEGAL ADVICE, CONSULT YOUR ATTORNEY.

This form is available for use by the entire real estate industry. It is not intended to identify the user as a REALTOR®. REALTOR® is a registered collective membership mark which may be used only by members of the NATIONAL ASSOCIATION OF REALTORS® who subscribe to its Code of Ethics.

The copyright laws of the United States (17 U.S. Code) forbid the unauthorized reproduction of this form by any means, including facsimile or computerized formats.

Copyright © 1987-1997, CALIFORNIA ASSOCIATION OF REALTORS®

SURE TRAC
The System for Success®

Published and Distributed by:
REAL ESTATE BUSINESS SERVICES, INC.
a subsidiary of the California Association of REALTORS®
525 South Virgil Avenue, Los Angeles, California 90020

Reviewed by _____ Date _____

EQUAL HOUSING OPPORTUNITY

CONFIRMATION REAL ESTATE AGENCY RELATIONSHIPS (AC-6 PAGE 1 OF 1) REVISED 1987

CALIFORNIA ASSOCIATION OF REALTORS®

DISCLOSURE REGARDING
REAL ESTATE AGENCY RELATIONSHIPS
(As required by the Civil Code)
(C.A.R. Form AD, Revised 10/04)

When you enter into a discussion with a real estate agent regarding a real estate transaction, you should from the outset understand what type of agency relationship or representation you wish to have with the agent in the transaction.

SELLER'S AGENT
A Seller's agent under a listing agreement with the Seller acts as the agent for the Seller only. A Seller's agent or a subagent of that agent has the following affirmative obligations:
To the Seller:
A Fiduciary duty of utmost care, integrity, honesty, and loyalty in dealings with the Seller.
To the Buyer and the Seller:
(a) Diligent exercise of reasonable skill and care in performance of the agent's duties.
(b) A duty of honest and fair dealing and good faith.
(c) A duty to disclose all facts known to the agent materially affecting the value or desirability of the property that are not known to, or within the diligent attention and observation of, the parties.

An agent is not obligated to reveal to either party any confidential information obtained from the other party that does not involve the affirmative duties set forth above.

BUYER'S AGENT
A selling agent can, with a Buyer's consent, agree to act as agent for the Buyer only. In these situations, the agent is not the Seller's agent, even if by agreement the agent may receive compensation for services rendered, either in full or in part from the Seller. An agent acting only for a Buyer has the following affirmative obligations:
To the Buyer:
A fiduciary duty of utmost care, integrity, honesty, and loyalty in dealings with the Buyer.
To the Buyer and the Seller:
(a) Diligent exercise of reasonable skill and care in performance of the agent's duties.
(b) A duty of honest and fair dealing and good faith.
(c) A duty to disclose all facts known to the agent materially affecting the value or desirability of the property that are not known to, or within the diligent attention and observation of, the parties.

An agent is not obligated to reveal to either party any confidential information obtained from the other party that does not involve the affirmative duties set forth above.

AGENT REPRESENTING BOTH SELLER AND BUYER
A real estate agent, either acting directly or through one or more associate licensees, can legally be the agent of both the Seller and the Buyer in a transaction, but only with the knowledge and consent of both the Seller and the Buyer.

In a dual agency situation, the agent has the following affirmative obligations to both the Seller and the Buyer:
(a) A fiduciary duty of utmost care, integrity, honesty and loyalty in the dealings with either the Seller or the Buyer.
(b) Other duties to the Seller and the Buyer as stated above in their respective sections.

In representing both Seller and Buyer, the agent may not, without the express permission of the respective party, disclose to the other party that the Seller will accept a price less than the listing price or that the Buyer will pay a price greater than the price offered.

The above duties of the agent in a real estate transaction do not relieve a Seller or Buyer from the responsibility to protect his or her own interests. You should carefully read all agreements to assure that they adequately express your understanding of the transaction. A real estate agent is a person qualified to advise about real estate. If legal or tax advice is desired, consult a competent professional.

Throughout your real property transaction you may receive more than one disclosure form, depending upon the number of agents assisting in the transaction. The law requires each agent with whom you have more than a casual relationship to present you with this disclosure form. You should read its contents each time it is presented to you, considering the relationship between you and the real estate agent in your specific transaction.

This disclosure form includes the provisions of Sections 2079.13 to 2079.24, inclusive, of the Civil Code set forth on the reverse hereof. Read it carefully.

I/WE ACKNOWLEDGE RECEIPT OF A COPY OF THIS DISCLOSURE AND THE PORTIONS OF THE CIVIL CODE PRINTED ON THE BACK (OR A SEPARATE PAGE).

BUYER/SELLER _____ Date _____ Time _____ AM/PM

BUYER/SELLER _____ Date _____ Time _____ AM/PM

AGENT _____ By _____ Date _____
(Please Print)   (Associate-Licensee or Broker Signature)

THIS FORM SHALL BE PROVIDED AND ACKNOWLEDGED AS FOLLOWS (Civil Code § 2079.14):
• When the listing brokerage company also represents Buyer, the Listing Agent shall have one AD form signed by Seller and one signed by Buyer.
• When Buyer and Seller are represented by different brokerage companies, the Listing Agent shall have one AD form signed by Seller and the Buyer's Agent shall have one AD form signed by Buyer and one AD form signed by Seller.

The System for Success®

Published and Distributed by:
REAL ESTATE BUSINESS SERVICES, INC.
a subsidiary of the California Association of REALTORS®
525 South Virgil Avenue, Los Angeles, California 90020

Reviewed by _____ Date _____

EQUAL HOUSING OPPORTUNITY

AD REVISED 10/04 (PAGE 1 OF 1) PRINT DATE

DISCLOSURE REGARDING REAL ESTATE AGENCY RELATIONSHIPS (AD PAGE 1 OF 1)

CIVIL CODE SECTIONS 2079.13 THROUGH 2079.24 (2079.16 APPEARS ON THE FRONT)

2079.13 As used in Sections 2079.14 to 2079.24, inclusive, the following terms have the following meanings: **(a)** "Agent" means a person acting under provisions of title 9 (commencing with Section 2295) in a real property transaction, and includes a person who is licensed as a real estate broker under Chapter 3 (commencing with Section 10130) of Part 1 of Division 4 of the Business and Professions Code, and under whose license a listing is executed or an offer to purchase is obtained. **(b)** "Associate licensee" means a person who is licensed as a real broker or salesperson under Chapter 3 (commencing with Section 10130) of Part 1 of Division 4 of the Business and Professions Code and who is either licensed under a broker or has entered into a written contract with a broker to act as the broker's agent in connection with acts requiring a real estate license and to function under the broker's supervision in the capacity of an associate licensee. The agent in the real property transaction bears responsibility for his or her associate licensees who perform as agents of the agent. When an associate licensee owes a duty to any principal, or to any buyer or seller who is not a principal, in a real property transaction, that duty is equivalent to the duty owed to that party by the broker for whom the associate licensee functions. **(c)** "Buyer" means a transferee in a real property transaction, and includes a person who executes an offer to purchase real property from a seller through an agent, or who seeks the services of an agent in more than a casual, transitory, or preliminary manner, with the object of entering into a real property transaction. "Buyer" includes vendee or lessee. **(d)** "Dual agent" means an agent acting, either directly or through an associate licensee, as agent for both the seller and the buyer in a real property transaction. **(e)** "Listing agreement" means a contract between an owner of real property and an agent, by which the agent has been authorized to sell the real property or to find or obtain a buyer. **(f)** "Listing agent" means a person who has obtained a listing of real property to act as an agent for compensation. **(g)** "Listing price" is the amount expressed in dollars specified in the listing for which the seller is willing to sell the real property through the listing agent. **(h)** "Offering price" is the amount expressed in dollars specified in an offer to purchase for which the buyer is willing to buy the real property. **(i)** "Offer to purchase" means a written contract executed by a buyer acting through a selling agent which becomes the contract for the sale of the real property upon acceptance by the seller. **(j)** "Real property" means any estate specified by subdivision (1) or (2) of Section 761 in property which constitutes or is improved with one to four dwelling units, any leasehold in this type of property exceeding one year's duration, and mobilehomes, when offered for sale or sold through an agent pursuant to the authority contained in Section 10131.6 of the Business and Professions Code. **(k)** "Real property transaction" means a transaction for the sale of real property in which an agent is employed by one or more of the principals to act in that transaction, and includes a listing or an offer to purchase. **(l)** "Sell," "sale," or "sold" refers to a transaction for the transfer of real property from the seller to the buyer, and includes exchanges of real property between the seller and buyer, transactions for the creation of a real property sales contract within the meaning of Section 2985, and transactions for the creation of a leasehold exceeding one year's duration. **(m)** "Seller" means the transferor in a real property transaction, and includes an owner who lists real property with an agent, whether or not a transfer results, or who receives an offer to purchase real property of which he or she is the owner from an agent on behalf of another. "Seller" includes both a vendor and a lessor. **(n)** "Selling agent" means a listing agent who acts alone, or an agent who acts in cooperation with a listing agent, and who sells or finds and obtains a buyer for the real property, or an agent who locates property for a buyer or who finds a buyer for a property for which no listing exists and presents an offer to purchase to the seller. **(o)** "Subagent" means a person to whom an agent delegates agency powers as provided in Article 5 (commencing with Section 2349) of Chapter 1 of Title 9. However, "subagent" does not include an associate licensee who is acting under the supervision of an agent in a real property transaction.

2079.14 Listing agents and selling agents shall provide the seller and buyer in a real property transaction with a copy of the disclosure form specified in Section 2079.16, and, except as provided in subdivision (c), shall obtain a signed acknowledgement of receipt from that seller or buyer, except as provided in this section or Section 2079.15, as follows: **(a)** The listing agent, if any, shall provide the disclosure form to the seller prior to entering into the listing agreement. **(b)** The selling agent shall provide the disclosure form to the seller as soon as practicable prior to presenting the seller with an offer to purchase, unless the selling agent previously provided the seller with a copy of the disclosure form pursuant to subdivision (a). **(c)** Where the selling agent does not deal on a face-to-face basis with the seller, the disclosure form prepared by the selling agent may be furnished to the seller (and acknowledgement of receipt obtained for the selling agent from the seller) by the listing agent, or the selling agent may deliver the disclosure form by certified mail addressed to the seller at his or her last known address, in which case no signed acknowledgement of receipt is required. **(d)** The selling agent shall provide the disclosure form to the buyer as soon as practicable prior to execution of the buyer's offer to purchase, except that if the offer to purchase is not prepared by the selling agent, the selling agent shall present the disclosure form to the buyer not later than the next business day after the selling agent receives the offer to purchase from the buyer.

2079.15 In any circumstance in which the seller or buyer refuses to sign an acknowledgement of receipt pursuant to Section 2079.14, the agent, or an associate licensee acting for an agent, shall set forth, sign, and date a written declaration of the facts of the refusal.

2079.17 (a) As soon as practicable, the selling agent shall disclose to the buyer and seller whether the selling agent is acting in the real property transaction exclusively as the buyer's agent, exclusively as the seller's agent, or as a dual agent representing both the buyer and the seller. This relationship shall be confirmed in the contract to purchase and sell real property or in a separate writing executed or acknowledged by the seller, the buyer, and the selling agent prior to or coincident with execution of that contract by the buyer and the seller, respectively. **(b)** As soon as practicable, the listing agent shall disclose to the seller whether the listing agent is acting in the real property transaction exclusively as the seller's agent, or as a dual agent representing both the buyer and seller. This relationship shall be confirmed in the contract to purchase and sell real property or in a separate writing executed or acknowledged by the seller and the listing agent prior to or coincident with the execution of that contract by the seller.
(c) The confirmation required by subdivisions (a) and (b) shall be in the following form.

_____(DO NOT COMPLETE. SAMPLE ONLY)_____ is the agent of (check one): ☐ the seller exclusively; or ☐ both the buyer and seller.
(Name of Listing Agent)

_____(DO NOT COMPLETE. SAMPLE ONLY)_____ is the agent of (check one): ☐ the buyer exclusively; or ☐ the seller exclusively; or
(Name of Selling Agent if not the same as the Listing Agent) ☐ both the buyer and seller.

(d) The disclosures and confirmation required by this section shall be in addition to the disclosure required by Section 2079.14.

2079.18 No selling agent in a real property transaction may act as an agent for the buyer only, when the selling agent is also acting as the listing agent in the transaction.

2079.19 The payment of compensation or the obligation to pay compensation to an agent by the seller or buyer is not necessarily determinative of a particular agency relationship between an agent and the seller or buyer. A listing agent and a selling agent may agree to share any compensation or commission paid, or any right to any compensation or commission for which an obligation arises as the result of a real estate transaction, and the terms of any such agreement shall not necessarily be determinative of a particular relationship.

2079.20 Nothing in this article prevents an agent from selecting, as a condition of the agent's employment, a specific form of agency relationship not specifically prohibited by this article if the requirements of Section 2079.14 and Section 2079.17 are complied with.

2079.21 A dual agent shall not disclose to the buyer that the seller is willing to sell the property at a price less than the listing price, without the express written consent of the seller. A dual agent shall not disclose to the seller that the buyer is willing to pay a price greater than the offering price, without the express written consent of the buyer. This section does not alter in any way the duty or responsibility of a dual agent to any principal with respect to confidential information other than price.

2079.22 Nothing in this article precludes a listing agent from also being a selling agent, and the combination of these functions in one agent does not, of itself, make that agent a dual agent.

2079.23 A contract between the principal and agent may be modified or altered to change the agency relationship at any time before the performance of the act which is the object of the agency with the written consent of the parties to the agency relationship.

2079.24 Nothing in this article shall be construed to either diminish the duty of disclosure owed buyers and sellers by agents and their associate licensees, subagents, and employees or to relieve agents and their associate licensees, subagents, and employees from liability for their conduct in connection with acts governed by this article or for any breach of a fiduciary duty or a duty of disclosure.

(AD BACKER)

92

**CALIFORNIA
RESIDENTIAL PURCHASE AGREEMENT
AND JOINT ESCROW INSTRUCTIONS**
For Use With Single Family Residential Property — Attached or Detached
(C.A.R. Form RPA-CA, Revised 10/02)

Date _____, at _____, California.
1. **OFFER:**
   A. **THIS IS AN OFFER FROM** _____ ("Buyer").
   B. **THE REAL PROPERTY TO BE ACQUIRED** is described as _____
   _____, Assessor's Parcel No. _____, situated in
   _____, County of _____, California, ("Property").
   C. **THE PURCHASE PRICE** offered is _____
   _____ Dollars $ _____
   D. **CLOSE OF ESCROW** shall occur on _____ (date)(or ☐ _____ **Days** After Acceptance).
2. **FINANCE TERMS:** Obtaining the loans below **is a contingency** of this Agreement unless: (i) either 2K or 2L is checked below; or
   (ii) otherwise agreed in writing. Buyer shall act diligently and in good faith to obtain the designated loans. Obtaining deposit, down
   payment and closing costs **is not a contingency.** Buyer represents that funds will be good when deposited with Escrow Holder.
   A. **INITIAL DEPOSIT:** Buyer has given a deposit in the amount of . . . .$ _____
   to the agent submitting the offer (or to ☐ _____), by personal check
   (or ☐ _____), made payable to _____
   which shall be held uncashed until Acceptance and then deposited within **3 business days** after
   Acceptance (or ☐ _____), with
   Escrow Holder, (or ☐ into Broker's trust account).
   B. **INCREASED DEPOSIT:** Buyer shall deposit with Escrow Holder an increased deposit in the amount of . . .$ _____
   within _____ **Days** After Acceptance, or ☐ _____.
   C. **FIRST LOAN IN THE AMOUNT OF** . . . .$ _____
   (1) NEW First Deed of Trust in favor of lender, encumbering the Property, securing a note payable at
   maximum interest of _____% fixed rate, or _____% initial adjustable rate with a maximum
   interest rate of _____%, balance due in _____ years, amortized over _____ years. Buyer
   shall pay loan fees/points not to exceed _____. (These terms apply whether the designated loan
   is conventional, FHA or VA.)
   (2) ☐ FHA ☐ VA: (The following terms only apply to the FHA or VA loan that is checked.)
   Seller shall pay _____% discount points. Seller shall pay other fees not allowed to be paid by Buyer,
   ☐ not to exceed $_____. Seller shall pay the cost of lender required Repairs (including
   those for wood destroying pest) not otherwise provided for in this Agreement, ☐ not to exceed $
   _____. (Actual loan amount may increase if mortgage insurance premiums, funding fees or
   closing costs are financed.)
   D. **ADDITIONAL FINANCING TERMS:** ☐ Seller financing (C.A.R. Form SFA); ☐ secondary financing, ...$ _____
   (C.A.R. Form PAA, paragraph 4A); ☐ assumed financing (C.A.R. Form PAA, paragraph 4B)
   _____
   _____
   E. **BALANCE OF PURCHASE PRICE** (not including costs of obtaining loans and other closing costs) in the amount of . . .$ _____
   to be deposited with Escrow Holder within sufficient time to close escrow.
   F. **PURCHASE PRICE (TOTAL):** . . . .$ _____
   G. **LOAN APPLICATIONS:** Within **7 (or ☐ _____) Days** After Acceptance, Buyer shall provide Seller a letter from lender or
   mortgage loan broker stating that, based on a review of Buyer's written application and credit report, Buyer is prequalified or
   preapproved for the NEW loan specified in 2C above.
   H. **VERIFICATION OF DOWN PAYMENT AND CLOSING COSTS:** Buyer (or Buyer's lender or loan broker pursuant to 2G) shall, within
   7 (or ☐ _____) Days After Acceptance, provide Seller written verification of Buyer's down payment and closing costs.
   I. **LOAN CONTINGENCY REMOVAL:** (i) Within **17 (or ☐ _____) Days** After Acceptance, Buyer shall, as specified in paragraph
   14, remove the loan contingency or cancel this Agreement; **OR** (ii) (if checked) ☐ the loan contingency shall remain in effect
   until the designated loans are funded.
   J. **APPRAISAL CONTINGENCY AND REMOVAL:** This Agreement is (**OR,** if checked, ☐ is NOT) contingent upon the Property
   appraising at no less than the specified purchase price. If there is a loan contingency, at the time the loan contingency is
   removed (or, if checked, ☐ within **17 (or _____) Days** After Acceptance), Buyer shall, as specified in paragraph 14B(3), remove
   the appraisal contingency or cancel this Agreement. If there is no loan contingency, Buyer shall, as specified in paragraph
   14B(3), remove the appraisal contingency within **17 (or _____) Days** After Acceptance.
   K. ☐ **NO LOAN CONTINGENCY** (If checked): Obtaining any loan in paragraphs 2C, 2D or elsewhere in this Agreement is NOT a
   contingency of this Agreement. If Buyer does not obtain the loan and as a result Buyer does not purchase the Property, Seller
   may be entitled to Buyer's deposit or other legal remedies.
   L. ☐ **ALL CASH OFFER** (If checked): No loan is needed to purchase the Property. Buyer shall, within **7 (or ☐ _____) Days** After Acceptance,
   provide Seller written verification of sufficient funds to close this transaction.
3. **CLOSING AND OCCUPANCY:**
   A. Buyer intends (or ☐ does not intend) to occupy the Property as Buyer's primary residence.
   B. **Seller-occupied or vacant property:** Occupancy shall be delivered to Buyer at _____ AM/PM, ☐ on the date of Close Of
   Escrow; ☐ on _____; or ☐ no later than _____ **Days** After Close Of Escrow. (C.A.R. Form PAA, paragraph 2.) If
   transfer of title and occupancy do not occur at the same time, Buyer and Seller are advised to: (i) enter into a written occupancy
   agreement; and (ii) consult with their insurance and legal advisors.

RPA-CA REVISED 10/02 (PAGE 1 OF 8) Print Date

Buyer's Initials (_____)(_____)
Seller's Initials (_____)(_____)

Reviewed by _____ Date _____

EQUAL HOUSING
OPPORTUNITY

CALIFORNIA RESIDENTIAL PURCHASE AGREEMENT (RPA-CA PAGE 1 OF 8)

Property Address: _____ Date: _____

C. **Tenant-occupied property: (i) Property shall be vacant** at least 5 (or ☐ _____) **Days** Prior to Close Of Escrow, unless otherwise agreed in writing. **Note to Seller: If you are unable to deliver Property vacant in accordance with rent control and other applicable Law, you may be in breach of this Agreement.**
OR (ii) (if checked) ☐ **Tenant to remain in possession.** The attached addendum is incorporated into this Agreement (C.A.R. Form PAA, paragraph 3.);
OR (iii) (if checked) ☐ **This Agreement is contingent** upon Buyer and Seller entering into a written agreement regarding occupancy of the Property within the time specified in paragraph 14B(1). If no written agreement is reached within this time, either Buyer or Seller may cancel this Agreement in writing.

D. At Close Of Escrow, Seller assigns to Buyer any assignable warranty rights for items included in the sale and shall provide any available Copies of such warranties. Brokers cannot and will not determine the assignability of any warranties.

E. At Close Of Escrow, unless otherwise agreed in writing, Seller shall provide keys and/or means to operate all locks, mailboxes, security systems, alarms and garage door openers. If Property is a condominium or located in a common interest subdivision, Buyer may be required to pay a deposit to the Homeowners' Association ("HOA") to obtain keys to accessible HOA facilities.

4. **ALLOCATION OF COSTS** (If checked): Unless otherwise specified here, this paragraph only determines who is to pay for the report, inspection, test or service mentioned. If not specified here or elsewhere in this Agreement, the determination of who is to pay for any work recommended or identified by any such report, inspection, test or service shall be by the method specified in paragraph 14B(2).

   A. **WOOD DESTROYING PEST INSPECTION:**
      (1) ☐ Buyer ☐ Seller shall pay for an inspection and report for wood destroying pests and organisms ("Report") which shall be prepared by _____, a registered structural pest control company. The Report shall cover the accessible areas of the main building and attached structures and, if checked: ☐ detached garages and carports, ☐ detached decks, ☐ the following other structures or areas _____. The Report shall not include roof coverings. If Property is a condominium or located in a common interest subdivision, the Report shall include only the separate interest and any exclusive-use areas being transferred and shall not include common areas, unless otherwise agreed. Water tests of shower pans on upper level units may not be performed without consent of the owners of property below the shower.
      OR (2) ☐ (If checked) The attached addendum (C.A.R. Form WPA) regarding wood destroying pest inspection and allocation of cost is incorporated into this Agreement.

   B. **OTHER INSPECTIONS AND REPORTS:**
      (1) ☐ Buyer ☐ Seller shall pay to have septic or private sewage disposal systems inspected _____.
      (2) ☐ Buyer ☐ Seller shall pay to have domestic wells tested for water potability and productivity _____.
      (3) ☐ Buyer ☐ Seller shall pay for a natural hazard zone disclosure report prepared by _____.
      (4) ☐ Buyer ☐ Seller shall pay for the following inspection or report _____.
      (5) ☐ Buyer ☐ Seller shall pay for the following inspection or report _____.

   C. **GOVERNMENT REQUIREMENTS AND RETROFIT:**
      (1) ☐ Buyer ☐ Seller shall pay for smoke detector installation and/or water heater bracing, if required by Law. Prior to Close Of Escrow, Seller shall provide Buyer a written statement of compliance in accordance with state and local Law, unless exempt.
      (2) ☐ Buyer ☐ Seller shall pay the cost of compliance with any other minimum mandatory government retrofit standards, inspections and reports if required as a condition of closing escrow under any Law. _____.

   D. **ESCROW AND TITLE:**
      (1) ☐ Buyer ☐ Seller shall pay escrow fee _____.
          Escrow Holder shall be _____.
      (2) ☐ Buyer ☐ Seller shall pay for **owner's** title insurance policy specified in paragraph 12E _____.
          Owner's title policy to be issued by _____.
          (Buyer shall pay for any title insurance policy insuring Buyer's **lender**, unless otherwise agreed in writing.)

   E. **OTHER COSTS:**
      (1) ☐ Buyer ☐ Seller shall pay County transfer tax or transfer fee _____.
      (2) ☐ Buyer ☐ Seller shall pay City transfer tax or transfer fee _____.
      (3) ☐ Buyer ☐ Seller shall pay HOA transfer fee _____.
      (4) ☐ Buyer ☐ Seller shall pay HOA document preparation fees _____.
      (5) ☐ Buyer ☐ Seller shall pay the cost, not to exceed $ _____, of a one-year home warranty plan, issued by _____,
          with the following optional coverage: _____.
      (6) ☐ Buyer ☐ Seller shall pay for _____.
      (7) ☐ Buyer ☐ Seller shall pay for _____.

5. **STATUTORY DISCLOSURES (INCLUDING LEAD-BASED PAINT HAZARD DISCLOSURES) AND CANCELLATION RIGHTS:**
   A. (1) Seller shall, within the time specified in paragraph 14A, deliver to Buyer, if required by Law: (i) Federal Lead-Based Paint Disclosures and pamphlet ("Lead Disclosures"); and (ii) disclosures or notices required by sections 1102 et. seq. and 1103 et. seq. of the California Civil Code ("Statutory Disclosures"). Statutory Disclosures include, but are not limited to, a Real Estate Transfer Disclosure Statement ("TDS"), Natural Hazard Disclosure Statement ("NHD"), notice or actual knowledge of release of illegal controlled substance, notice of special tax and/or assessments (or, if allowed, substantially equivalent notice regarding the Mello-Roos Community Facilities Act and Improvement Bond Act of 1915) and, if Seller has actual knowledge, an industrial use and military ordnance location disclosure (C.A.R. Form SSD).
      (2) Buyer shall, within the time specified in paragraph 14B(1), return Signed Copies of the Statutory and Lead Disclosures to Seller.
      (3) In the event Seller, prior to Close Of Escrow, becomes aware of adverse conditions materially affecting the Property, or any material inaccuracy in disclosures, information or representations previously provided to Buyer of which Buyer is otherwise unaware, Seller shall promptly provide a subsequent or amended disclosure or notice, in writing, covering those items. **However, a subsequent or amended disclosure shall not be required for conditions and material inaccuracies disclosed in reports ordered and paid for by Buyer.**

Buyer's Initials (_____)(_____)
Seller's Initials (_____)(_____)

Reviewed by _____ Date _____

CALIFORNIA RESIDENTIAL PURCHASE AGREEMENT (RPA-CA PAGE 2 OF 8)

(4) If any disclosure or notice specified in 5A(1), or subsequent or amended disclosure or notice is delivered to Buyer after the offer is Signed, Buyer shall have the right to cancel this Agreement within **3 Days** After delivery in person, or **5 Days** After delivery by deposit in the mail, by giving written notice of cancellation to Seller or Seller's agent. (Lead Disclosures sent by mail must be sent certified mail or better.)

(5) Note to Buyer and Seller: Waiver of Statutory and Lead Disclosures is prohibited by Law.

B. **NATURAL AND ENVIRONMENTAL HAZARDS:** Within the time specified in paragraph 14A, Seller shall, if required by Law: **(i)** deliver to Buyer earthquake guides (and questionnaire) and environmental hazards booklet; **(ii)** even if exempt from the obligation to provide a NHD, disclose if the Property is located in a Special Flood Hazard Area; Potential Flooding (Inundation) Area; Very High Fire Hazard Zone; State Fire Responsibility Area; Earthquake Fault Zone; Seismic Hazard Zone; and **(iii)** disclose any other zone as required by Law and provide any other information required for those zones.

C. **DATA BASE DISCLOSURE: NOTICE:** The California Department of Justice, sheriff's departments, police departments serving jurisdictions of 200,000 or more and many other local law enforcement authorities maintain for public access a data base of the locations of persons required to register pursuant to paragraph (1) of subdivision (a) of Section 290.4 of the Penal Code. The data base is updated on a quarterly basis and a source of information about the presence of these individuals in any neighborhood. The Department of Justice also maintains a Sex Offender Identification Line through which inquiries about individuals may be made. This is a "900" telephone service. Callers must have specific information about individuals they are checking. Information regarding neighborhoods is not available through the "900" telephone service.

6. CONDOMINIUM/PLANNED UNIT DEVELOPMENT DISCLOSURES:

A. **SELLER HAS: 7 (or ☐ _____) Days** After Acceptance to disclose to Buyer whether the Property is a condominium, or is located in a planned unit development or other common interest subdivision (C.A.R. Form SSD).

B. If the Property is a condominium or is located in a planned unit development or other common interest subdivision, Seller has **3 (or ☐ _____) Days** After Acceptance to request from the HOA (C.A.R. Form HOA): **(i)** Copies of any documents required by Law; **(ii)** disclosure of any pending or anticipated claim or litigation by or against the HOA; **(iii)** a statement containing the location and number of designated parking and storage spaces; **(iv)** Copies of the most recent 12 months of HOA minutes for regular and special meetings; and **(v)** the names and contact information of all HOAs governing the Property (collectively, "CI Disclosures"). Seller shall itemize and deliver to Buyer all CI Disclosures received from the HOA and any CI Disclosures in Seller's possession. Buyer's approval of CI Disclosures is a contingency of this Agreement as specified in paragraph 14B(3).

7. CONDITIONS AFFECTING PROPERTY:

A. Unless otherwise agreed: **(i)** the Property is sold **(a)** in its **PRESENT physical condition as of the date of Acceptance and (b) subject to Buyer's Investigation rights; (ii)** the Property, including pool, spa, landscaping and grounds, is to be maintained in substantially the same condition as on the date of Acceptance; and **(iii)** all debris and personal property not included in the sale shall be removed by Close Of Escrow.

B. **SELLER SHALL,** within the time specified in paragraph 14A, **DISCLOSE KNOWN MATERIAL FACTS AND DEFECTS** affecting the Property, including known insurance claims within the past five years, **AND MAKE OTHER DISCLOSURES REQUIRED BY LAW (C.A.R. Form SSD).**

C. **NOTE TO BUYER:** You are strongly advised to conduct investigations of the entire Property in order to determine its present condition since Seller may not be aware of all defects affecting the Property or other factors that you consider important. Property improvements may not be built according to code, in compliance with current Law, or have had permits issued.

D. **NOTE TO SELLER:** Buyer has the right to inspect the Property and, as specified in paragraph 14B, based upon information discovered in those inspections: **(i)** cancel this Agreement; or **(ii)** request that you make Repairs or take other action.

8. ITEMS INCLUDED AND EXCLUDED:

A. **NOTE TO BUYER AND SELLER:** Items listed as included or excluded in the MLS, flyers or marketing materials are **not** included in the purchase price or excluded from the sale unless specified in 8B or C.

B. **ITEMS INCLUDED IN SALE:**

(1) All EXISTING fixtures and fittings that are attached to the Property;

(2) Existing electrical, mechanical, lighting, plumbing and heating fixtures, ceiling fans, fireplace inserts, gas logs and grates, solar systems, built-in appliances, window and door screens, awnings, shutters, window coverings, attached floor coverings, television antennas, satellite dishes, private integrated telephone systems, air coolers/conditioners, pool/spa equipment, garage door openers/remote controls, mailbox, in-ground landscaping, trees/shrubs, water softeners, water purifiers, security systems/alarms; and

(3) The following items: _____
_____

(4) Seller represents that all items included in the purchase price, unless otherwise specified, are owned by Seller.

(5) All items included shall be transferred free of liens and without Seller warranty.

C. **ITEMS EXCLUDED FROM SALE:** _____
_____

9. BUYER'S INVESTIGATION OF PROPERTY AND MATTERS AFFECTING PROPERTY:

A. Buyer's acceptance of the condition of, and any other matter affecting the Property, is a contingency of this Agreement as specified in this paragraph and paragraph 14B. Within the time specified in paragraph 14B(1), Buyer shall have the right, at Buyer's expense unless otherwise agreed, to conduct inspections, investigations, tests, surveys and other studies ("Buyer Investigations"), including, but not limited to, the right to: **(i)** inspect for lead-based paint and other lead-based paint hazards; **(ii)** inspect for wood destroying pests and organisms; **(iii)** review the registered sex offender database; **(iv)** confirm the insurability of Buyer and the Property; and **(v)** satisfy Buyer as to any matter specified in the attached Buyer's Inspection Advisory (C.A.R. Form BIA). Without Seller's prior written consent, Buyer shall neither make nor cause to be made: **(i)** invasive or destructive Buyer Investigations; or **(ii)** inspections by any governmental building or zoning inspector or government employee, unless required by Law.

B. Buyer shall complete Buyer Investigations and, as specified in paragraph 14B, remove the contingency or cancel this Agreement. Buyer shall give Seller, at no cost, complete Copies of all Buyer Investigation reports obtained by Buyer. Seller shall make the Property available for all Buyer Investigations. Seller shall have water, gas, electricity and all operable pilot lights on for Buyer's Investigations and through the date possession is made available to Buyer.

Buyer's Initials (_____)(_____)
Seller's Initials (_____)(_____)

RPA-CA REVISED 10/02 (PAGE 3 OF 8)

Reviewed by _____ Date _____

CALIFORNIA RESIDENTIAL PURCHASE AGREEMENT (RPA-CA PAGE 3 OF 8)

Property Address: _____ Date: _____

10. **REPAIRS:** Repairs shall be completed prior to final verification of condition unless otherwise agreed in writing. Repairs to be performed at Seller's expense may be performed by Seller or through others, provided that the work complies with applicable Law, including governmental permit, inspection and approval requirements. Repairs shall be performed in a good, skillful manner with materials of quality and appearance comparable to existing materials. It is understood that exact restoration of appearance or cosmetic items following all Repairs may not be possible. Seller shall: **(i)** obtain receipts for Repairs performed by others; **(ii)** prepare a written statement indicating the Repairs performed by Seller and the date of such Repairs; and **(iii)** provide Copies of receipts and statements to Buyer prior to final verification of condition.

11. **BUYER INDEMNITY AND SELLER PROTECTION FOR ENTRY UPON PROPERTY:** Buyer shall: **(i)** keep the Property free and clear of liens; **(ii)** Repair all damage arising from Buyer Investigations; and **(iii)** indemnify and hold Seller harmless from all resulting liability, claims, demands, damages and costs. Buyer shall carry, or Buyer shall require anyone acting on Buyer's behalf to carry, policies of liability, workers' compensation and other applicable insurance, defending and protecting Seller from liability for any injuries to persons or property occurring during any Buyer Investigations or work done on the Property at Buyer's direction prior to Close Of Escrow. Seller is advised that certain protections may be afforded Seller by recording a "Notice of Non-responsibility" (C.A.R. Form NNR) for Buyer Investigations and work done on the Property at Buyer's direction. Buyer's obligations under this paragraph shall survive the termination of this Agreement.

12. **TITLE AND VESTING:**
   A. Within the time specified in paragraph 14, Buyer shall be provided a current preliminary (title) report, which is only an offer by the title insurer to issue a policy of title insurance and may not contain every item affecting title. Buyer's review of the preliminary report and any other matters which may affect title are a contingency of this Agreement as specified in paragraph 14B.
   B. Title is taken in its present condition subject to all encumbrances, easements, covenants, conditions, restrictions, rights and other matters, whether of record or not, as of the date of Acceptance except: **(i)** monetary liens of record unless Buyer is assuming those obligations or taking the Property subject to those obligations; and **(ii)** those matters which Seller has agreed to remove in writing.
   C. Within the time specified in paragraph 14A, Seller has a duty to disclose to Buyer all matters known to Seller affecting title, whether of record or not.
   D. At Close Of Escrow, Buyer shall receive a grant deed conveying title (or, for stock cooperative or long-term lease, an assignment of stock certificate or of Seller's leasehold interest), including oil, mineral and water rights if currently owned by Seller. Title shall vest as designated in Buyer's supplemental escrow instructions. THE MANNER OF TAKING TITLE MAY HAVE SIGNIFICANT LEGAL AND TAX CONSEQUENCES. CONSULT AN APPROPRIATE PROFESSIONAL.
   E. Buyer shall receive a CLTA/ALTA Homeowner's Policy of Title Insurance. A title company, at Buyer's request, can provide information about the availability, desirability, coverage, and cost of various title insurance coverages and endorsements. If Buyer desires title coverage other than that required by this paragraph, Buyer shall instruct Escrow Holder in writing and pay any increase in cost.

13. **SALE OF BUYER'S PROPERTY:**
   A. This Agreement is NOT contingent upon the sale of any property owned by Buyer.
   OR B. ☐ (If checked): The attached addendum (C.A.R. Form COP) regarding the contingency for the sale of property owned by Buyer is incorporated into this Agreement.

14. **TIME PERIODS; REMOVAL OF CONTINGENCIES; CANCELLATION RIGHTS: The following time periods may only be extended, altered, modified or changed by mutual written agreement. Any removal of contingencies or cancellation under this paragraph must be in writing (C.A.R. Form CR).**
   A. SELLER HAS: 7 (or ☐ _____) Days After Acceptance to deliver to Buyer all reports, disclosures and information for which Seller is responsible under paragraphs 4, 5A and B, 6A, 7B and 12.
   B. (1) BUYER HAS: 17 (or ☐ _____) Days After Acceptance, unless otherwise agreed in writing, to:
      (i) complete all Buyer Investigations; approve all disclosures, reports and other applicable information, which Buyer receives from Seller; and approve all matters affecting the Property (including lead-based paint and lead-based paint hazards as well as other information specified in paragraph 5 and insurability of Buyer and the Property); and
      (ii) return to Seller Signed Copies of Statutory and Lead Disclosures delivered by Seller in accordance with paragraph 5A.
      (2) Within the time specified in 14B(1), Buyer may request that Seller make repairs or take any other action regarding the Property (C.A.R. Form RR). Seller has no obligation to agree to or respond to Buyer's requests.
      (3) By the end of the time specified in 14B(1) (or 2I for loan contingency or 2J for appraisal contingency), Buyer shall, in writing, remove the applicable contingency (C.A.R. Form CR) or cancel this Agreement. However, if **(i)** government-mandated inspections/ reports required as a condition of closing; or **(ii)** Common Interest Disclosures pursuant to paragraph 6B are not made within the time specified in 14A, then Buyer has **5 (or ☐ _____) Days** After receipt of any such items, or the time specified in 14B(1), whichever is later, to remove the applicable contingency or cancel this Agreement in writing.
   C. CONTINUATION OF CONTINGENCY OR CONTRACTUAL OBLIGATION; SELLER RIGHT TO CANCEL:
      (1) Seller right to Cancel; Buyer Contingencies: Seller, after first giving Buyer a Notice to Buyer to Perform (as specified below), may cancel this Agreement in writing and authorize return of Buyer's deposit if, by the time specified in this Agreement, Buyer does not remove in writing the applicable contingency or cancel this Agreement. Once all contingencies have been removed, failure of either Buyer or Seller to close escrow on time may be a breach of this Agreement.
      (2) Continuation of Contingency: Even after the expiration of the time specified in 14B, Buyer retains the right to make requests to Seller, remove in writing the applicable contingency or cancel this Agreement until Seller cancels pursuant to 14C(1). Once Seller receives Buyer's written removal of all contingencies, Seller may not cancel this Agreement pursuant to 14C(1).
      (3) Seller right to Cancel; Buyer Contract Obligations: Seller, after first giving Buyer a Notice to Buyer to Perform (as specified below), may cancel this Agreement in writing and authorize return of Buyer's deposit for any of the following reasons: **(i)** if Buyer fails to deposit funds as required by 2A or 2B; **(ii)** if the funds deposited pursuant to 2A or 2B are not good when deposited; **(iii)** if Buyer fails to provide a letter as required by 2G; **(iv)** if Buyer fails to provide verification as required by 2H or 2L; **(v)** if Seller reasonably disapproves of the verification provided by 2H or 2L; **(vi)** if Buyer fails to return Statutory and Lead Disclosures as required by paragraph 5A(2); or **(vii)** if Buyer fails to sign or initial a separate liquidated damage form for an increased deposit as required by paragraph 16. **Seller is not required to give Buyer a Notice to Perform regarding Close of Escrow.**
      (4) Notice To Buyer To Perform: The Notice to Buyer to Perform (C.A.R. Form NBP) shall: **(i)** be in writing; **(ii)** be signed by Seller; and **(iii)** give Buyer at least **24 (or ☐ _____)** hours (or until the time specified in the applicable paragraph, whichever occurs last) to take the applicable action. A Notice to Buyer to Perform may not be given any earlier than **2 Days** Prior to the expiration of the applicable time for Buyer to remove a contingency or cancel this Agreement or meet a 14C(3) obligation.

Buyer's Initials (_____)(_____)
Seller's Initials (_____)(_____)

RPA-CA REVISED 10/02 (PAGE 4 OF 8)

Reviewed by _____ Date _____

CALIFORNIA RESIDENTIAL PURCHASE AGREEMENT (RPA-CA PAGE 4 OF 8)

D. EFFECT OF BUYER'S REMOVAL OF CONTINGENCIES : If Buyer removes, in writing, any contingency or cancellation rights, unless otherwise specified in a separate written agreement between Buyer and Seller, Buyer shall conclusively be deemed to have: **(i)** completed all Buyer Investigations, and review of reports and other applicable information and disclosures pertaining to that contingency or cancellation right; **(ii)** elected to proceed with the transaction; and **(iii)** assumed all liability, responsibility and expense for Repairs or corrections pertaining to that contingency or cancellation right, or for inability to obtain financing.

E. EFFECT OF CANCELLATION ON DEPOSITS: If Buyer or Seller gives written notice of cancellation pursuant to rights duly exercised under the terms of this Agreement, Buyer and Seller agree to Sign mutual instructions to cancel the sale and escrow and release deposits to the party entitled to the funds, less fees and costs incurred by that party. Fees and costs may be payable to service providers and vendors for services and products provided during escrow. **Release of funds will require mutual, Signed release instructions from Buyer and Seller, judicial decision or arbitration award. A party may be subject to a civil penalty of up to $1,000 for refusal to sign such instructions if no good faith dispute exists as to who is entitled to the deposited funds (Civil Code §1057.3).**

15. FINAL VERIFICATION OF CONDITION: Buyer shall have the right to make a final inspection of the Property within **5 (or _____) Days** Prior to Close Of Escrow, NOT AS A CONTINGENCY OF THE SALE, but solely to confirm: (i) the Property is maintained pursuant to paragraph 7A; (ii) Repairs have been completed as agreed; and (iii) Seller has complied with Seller's other obligations under this Agreement.

16. LIQUIDATED DAMAGES: If Buyer fails to complete this purchase because of Buyer's default, Seller shall retain, as liquidated damages, the deposit actually paid. If the Property is a dwelling with no more than four units, one of which Buyer intends to occupy, then the amount retained shall be no more than 3% of the purchase price. Any excess shall be returned to Buyer. Release of funds will require mutual, Signed release instructions from both Buyer and Seller, judicial decision or arbitration award.
BUYER AND SELLER SHALL SIGN A SEPARATE LIQUIDATED DAMAGES PROVISION FOR ANY INCREASED DEPOSIT. (C.A.R. FORM RID)

Buyer's Initials _____ / _____	Seller's Initials _____ / _____

17. DISPUTE RESOLUTION:

A. MEDIATION: Buyer and Seller agree to mediate any dispute or claim arising between them out of this Agreement, or any resulting transaction, before resorting to arbitration or court action. Paragraphs 17B(2) and (3) below apply whether or not the Arbitration provision is initialed. Mediation fees, if any, shall be divided equally among the parties involved. If, for any dispute or claim to which this paragraph applies, any party commences an action without first attempting to resolve the matter through mediation, or refuses to mediate after a request has been made, then that party shall not be entitled to recover attorney fees, even if they would otherwise be available to that party in any such action. THIS MEDIATION PROVISION APPLIES WHETHER OR NOT THE ARBITRATION PROVISION IS INITIALED.

B. ARBITRATION OF DISPUTES: (1) Buyer and Seller agree that any dispute or claim in Law or equity arising between them out of this Agreement or any resulting transaction, which is not settled through mediation, shall be decided by neutral, binding arbitration, including and subject to paragraphs 17B(2) and (3) below. The arbitrator shall be a retired judge or justice, or an attorney with at least 5 years of residential real estate Law experience, unless the parties mutually agree to a different arbitrator, who shall render an award in accordance with substantive California Law. The parties shall have the right to discovery in accordance with California Code of Civil Procedure §1283.05. In all other respects, the arbitration shall be conducted in accordance with Title 9 of Part III of the California Code of Civil Procedure. Judgment upon the award of the arbitrator(s) may be entered into any court having jurisdiction. Interpretation of this agreement to arbitrate shall be governed by the Federal Arbitration Act.
(2) EXCLUSIONS FROM MEDIATION AND ARBITRATION: The following matters are excluded from mediation and arbitration: (i) a judicial or non-judicial foreclosure or other action or proceeding to enforce a deed of trust, mortgage or installment land sale contract as defined in California Civil Code §2985; (ii) an unlawful detainer action; (iii) the filing or enforcement of a mechanic's lien; and (iv) any matter that is within the jurisdiction of a probate, small claims or bankruptcy court. The filing of a court action to enable the recording of a notice of pending action, for order of attachment, receivership, injunction, or other provisional remedies, shall not constitute a waiver of the mediation and arbitration provisions.
(3) BROKERS: Buyer and Seller agree to mediate and arbitrate disputes or claims involving either or both Brokers, consistent with 17A and B, provided either or both Brokers shall have agreed to such mediation or arbitration prior to, or within a reasonable time after, the dispute or claim is presented to Brokers. Any election by either or both Brokers to participate in mediation or arbitration shall not result in Brokers being deemed parties to the Agreement.

"NOTICE: BY INITIALING IN THE SPACE BELOW YOU ARE AGREEING TO HAVE ANY DISPUTE ARISING OUT OF THE MATTERS INCLUDED IN THE 'ARBITRATION OF DISPUTES' PROVISION DECIDED BY NEUTRAL ARBITRATION AS PROVIDED BY CALIFORNIA LAW AND YOU ARE GIVING UP ANY RIGHTS YOU MIGHT POSSESS TO HAVE THE DISPUTE LITIGATED IN A COURT OR JURY TRIAL. BY INITIALING IN THE SPACE BELOW YOU ARE GIVING UP YOUR JUDICIAL RIGHTS TO DISCOVERY AND APPEAL, UNLESS THOSE RIGHTS ARE SPECIFICALLY INCLUDED IN THE 'ARBITRATION OF DISPUTES' PROVISION. IF YOU REFUSE TO SUBMIT TO ARBITRATION AFTER AGREEING TO THIS PROVISION, YOU MAY BE COMPELLED TO ARBITRATE UNDER THE AUTHORITY OF THE CALIFORNIA CODE OF CIVIL PROCEDURE. YOUR AGREEMENT TO THIS ARBITRATION PROVISION IS VOLUNTARY."
"WE HAVE READ AND UNDERSTAND THE FOREGOING AND AGREE TO SUBMIT DISPUTES ARISING OUT OF THE MATTERS INCLUDED IN THE 'ARBITRATION OF DISPUTES' PROVISION TO NEUTRAL ARBITRATION."

Buyer's Initials _____ / _____	Seller's Initials _____ / _____

Buyer's Initials (_____)(_____)
Seller's Initials (_____)(_____)
Reviewed by _____ Date _____

RPA-CA REVISED 10/02 (PAGE 5 OF 8)

EQUAL HOUSING OPPORTUNITY

CALIFORNIA RESIDENTIAL PURCHASE AGREEMENT (RPA-CA PAGE 5 OF 8)

Property Address: _____ Date: _____

18. **PRORATIONS OF PROPERTY TAXES AND OTHER ITEMS:** Unless otherwise agreed in writing, the following items shall be PAID CURRENT and prorated between Buyer and Seller as of Close Of Escrow: real property taxes and assessments, interest, rents, HOA regular, special, and emergency dues and assessments imposed prior to Close Of Escrow, premiums on insurance assumed by Buyer, payments on bonds and assessments assumed by Buyer, and payments on Mello-Roos and other Special Assessment District bonds and assessments that are now a lien. The following items shall be assumed by Buyer WITHOUT CREDIT toward the purchase price: prorated payments on Mello-Roos and other Special Assessment District bonds and assessments and HOA special assessments that are now a lien but not yet due. Property will be reassessed upon change of ownership. Any supplemental tax bills shall be paid as follows: **(i)** for periods after Close Of Escrow, by Buyer; and **(ii)** for periods prior to Close Of Escrow, by Seller. TAX BILLS ISSUED AFTER CLOSE OF ESCROW SHALL BE HANDLED DIRECTLY BETWEEN BUYER AND SELLER. Prorations shall be made based on a 30-day month.

19. **WITHHOLDING TAXES:** Seller and Buyer agree to execute any instrument, affidavit, statement or instruction reasonably necessary to comply with federal (FIRPTA) and California withholding Law, if required (C.A.R. Forms AS and AB).

20. **MULTIPLE LISTING SERVICE ("MLS"):** Brokers are authorized to report to the MLS a pending sale and, upon Close Of Escrow, the terms of this transaction to be published and disseminated to persons and entities authorized to use the information on terms approved by the MLS.

21. **EQUAL HOUSING OPPORTUNITY:** The Property is sold in compliance with federal, state and local anti-discrimination Laws.

22. **ATTORNEY FEES:** In any action, proceeding, or arbitration between Buyer and Seller arising out of this Agreement, the prevailing Buyer or Seller shall be entitled to reasonable attorney fees and costs from the non-prevailing Buyer or Seller, except as provided in paragraph 17A.

23. **SELECTION OF SERVICE PROVIDERS:** If Brokers refer Buyer or Seller to persons, vendors, or service or product providers ("Providers"), Brokers do not guarantee the performance of any Providers. Buyer and Seller may select ANY Providers of their own choosing.

24. **TIME OF ESSENCE; ENTIRE CONTRACT; CHANGES:** Time is of the essence. All understandings between the parties are incorporated in this Agreement. Its terms are intended by the parties as a final, complete and exclusive expression of their Agreement with respect to its subject matter, and may not be contradicted by evidence of any prior agreement or contemporaneous oral agreement. If any provision of this Agreement is held to be ineffective or invalid, the remaining provisions will nevertheless be given full force and effect. **Neither this Agreement nor any provision in it may be extended, amended, modified, altered or changed, except in writing Signed by Buyer and Seller.**

25. **OTHER TERMS AND CONDITIONS,** including attached supplements:
    A. ☑ Buyer's Inspection Advisory (C.A.R. Form BIA) _____
    B. ☐ Purchase Agreement Addendum (C.A.R. Form PAA paragraph numbers _____) _____
    C. ☐ Statewide Buyer and Seller Advisory (C.A.R. Form SBSA) _____
    D. _____

26. **DEFINITIONS:** As used in this Agreement:
    A. **"Acceptance"** means the time the offer or final counter offer is accepted in writing by a party and is delivered to and personally received by the other party or that party's authorized agent in accordance with the terms of this offer or a final counter offer.
    B. **"Agreement"** means the terms and conditions of this accepted California Residential Purchase Agreement and any accepted counter offers and addenda.
    C. **"C.A.R. Form"** means the specific form referenced or another comparable form agreed to by the parties.
    D. **"Close Of Escrow"** means the date the grant deed, or other evidence of transfer of title, is recorded. If the scheduled close of escrow falls on a Saturday, Sunday or legal holiday, then close of escrow shall be the next business day after the scheduled close of escrow date.
    E. **"Copy"** means copy by any means including photocopy, NCR, facsimile and electronic.
    F. **"Days"** means calendar days, unless otherwise required by Law.
    G. **"Days After"** means the specified number of calendar days after the occurrence of the event specified, not counting the calendar date on which the specified event occurs, and ending at 11:59PM on the final day.
    H. **"Days Prior"** means the specified number of calendar days before the occurrence of the event specified, not counting the calendar date on which the specified event is scheduled to occur.
    I. **"Electronic Copy"** or **"Electronic Signature"** means, as applicable, an electronic copy or signature complying with California Law. Buyer and Seller agree that electronic means will not be used by either party to modify or alter the content or integrity of this Agreement without the knowledge and consent of the other.
    J. **"Law"** means any law, code, statute, ordinance, regulation, rule or order, which is adopted by a controlling city, county, state or federal legislative, judicial or executive body or agency.
    K. **"Notice to Buyer to Perform"** means a document (C.A.R. Form NBP), which shall be in writing and Signed by Seller and shall give Buyer at least 24 hours **(or as otherwise specified in paragraph 14C(4))** to remove a contingency or perform as applicable.
    L. **"Repairs"** means any repairs (including pest control), alterations, replacements, modifications or retrofitting of the Property provided for under this Agreement.
    M. **"Signed"** means either a handwritten or electronic signature on an original document, Copy or any counterpart.
    N. **Singular and Plural** terms each include the other, when appropriate.

Buyer's Initials (_____)(_____)
Seller's Initials (_____)(_____)

RPA-CA REVISED 10/02 (PAGE 6 OF 8)

Reviewed by _____ Date _____

CALIFORNIA RESIDENTIAL PURCHASE AGREEMENT (RPA-CA PAGE 6 OF 8)

Property Address: _____ Date: _____

27. AGENCY:

    A. DISCLOSURE: Buyer and Seller each acknowledge prior receipt of C.A.R. Form AD "Disclosure Regarding Real Estate Agency Relationships."

    B. POTENTIALLY COMPETING BUYERS AND SELLERS: Buyer and Seller each acknowledge receipt of a disclosure of the possibility of multiple representation by the Broker representing that principal. This disclosure may be part of a listing agreement, buyer-broker agreement or separate document (C.A.R. Form DA). Buyer understands that Broker representing Buyer may also represent other potential buyers, who may consider, make offers on or ultimately acquire the Property. Seller understands that Broker representing Seller may also represent other sellers with competing properties of interest to this Buyer.

    C. CONFIRMATION: The following agency relationships are hereby confirmed for this transaction:
Listing Agent _____ (Print Firm Name) is the agent of (check one): ☐ the Seller exclusively; or ☐ both the Buyer and Seller.
Selling Agent _____ (Print Firm Name) (if not same as Listing Agent) is the agent of (check one): ☐ the Buyer exclusively; or ☐ the Seller exclusively; or ☐ both the Buyer and Seller. Real Estate Brokers are not parties to the Agreement between Buyer and Seller.

28. JOINT ESCROW INSTRUCTIONS TO ESCROW HOLDER:

    A. The following paragraphs, or applicable portions thereof, of this Agreement constitute the joint escrow instructions of Buyer and Seller to Escrow Holder, which Escrow Holder is to use along with any related counter offers and addenda, and any additional mutual instructions to close the escrow: 1, 2, 4, 12, 13B, 14E, 18, 19, 24, 25B and C, 26, 28, 29, 32A, 33 and paragraph D of the section titled Real Estate Brokers on page 8. If a Copy of the separate compensation agreement(s) provided for in paragraph 29 or 32A, or paragraph D of the section titled Real Estate Brokers on page 8 is deposited with Escrow Holder by Broker, Escrow Holder shall accept such agreement(s) and pay out from Buyer's or Seller's funds, or both, as applicable, the Broker's compensation provided for in such agreement(s). The terms and conditions of this Agreement not set forth in the specified paragraphs are additional matters for the information of Escrow Holder, but about which Escrow Holder need not be concerned. Buyer and Seller will receive Escrow Holder's general provisions directly from Escrow Holder and will execute such provisions upon Escrow Holder's request. To the extent the general provisions are inconsistent or conflict with this Agreement, the general provisions will control as to the duties and obligations of Escrow Holder only. Buyer and Seller will execute additional instructions, documents and forms provided by Escrow Holder that are reasonably necessary to close the escrow.

    B. A Copy of this Agreement shall be delivered to Escrow Holder within **3** business days after Acceptance (or ☐ _____). Buyer and Seller authorize Escrow Holder to accept and rely on Copies and Signatures as defined in this Agreement as originals, to open escrow and for other purposes of escrow. The validity of this Agreement as between Buyer and Seller is not affected by whether or when Escrow Holder Signs this Agreement.

    C. Brokers are a party to the escrow for the sole purpose of compensation pursuant to paragraphs 29, 32A and paragraph D of the section titled Real Estate Brokers on page 8. Buyer and Seller irrevocably assign to Brokers compensation specified in paragraphs 29 and 32A, respectively, and irrevocably instruct Escrow Holder to disburse those funds to Brokers at Close Of Escrow or pursuant to any other mutually executed cancellation agreement. Compensation instructions can be amended or revoked only with the written consent of Brokers. Escrow Holder shall immediately notify Brokers: **(i)** if Buyer's initial or any additional deposit is not made pursuant to this Agreement, or is not good at time of deposit with Escrow Holder; or **(ii)** if Buyer and Seller instruct Escrow Holder to cancel escrow.

    D. A Copy of any amendment that affects any paragraph of this Agreement for which Escrow Holder is responsible shall be delivered to Escrow Holder within **2** business days after mutual execution of the amendment.

29. BROKER COMPENSATION FROM BUYER: If applicable, upon Close Of Escrow, **Buyer** agrees to pay compensation to Broker as specified in a separate written agreement between Buyer and Broker.

30. TERMS AND CONDITIONS OF OFFER:

This is an offer to purchase the Property on the above terms and conditions. All paragraphs with spaces for initials by Buyer and Seller are incorporated in this Agreement only if initialed by all parties. If at least one but not all parties initial, a counter offer is required until agreement is reached. Seller has the right to continue to offer the Property for sale and to accept any other offer at any time prior to notification of Acceptance. Buyer has read and acknowledges receipt of a Copy of the offer and agrees to the above confirmation of agency relationships. If this offer is accepted and Buyer subsequently defaults, Buyer may be responsible for payment of Brokers' compensation. This Agreement and any supplement, addendum or modification, including any Copy, may be Signed in two or more counterparts, all of which shall constitute one and the same writing.

Buyer's Initials (_____)(_____)
Seller's Initials (_____)(_____)

Reviewed by _____ Date _____

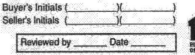

CALIFORNIA RESIDENTIAL PURCHASE AGREEMENT (RPA-CA PAGE 7 OF 8)

Property Address: _____ Date: _____

31. EXPIRATION OF OFFER: This offer shall be deemed revoked and the deposit shall be returned unless the offer is Signed by Seller and a Copy of the Signed offer is personally received by Buyer, or by _____ who is authorized to receive it by 5:00 PM on the third calendar day after this offer is signed by Buyer (or, if checked, ☐ by _____ (date), at _____ AM/PM).

Date _____ Date _____

BUYER _____ BUYER _____

(Print name) _____ (Print name) _____

(Address) _____

32. BROKER COMPENSATION FROM SELLER:
    A. Upon Close Of Escrow, Seller agrees to pay compensation to Broker as specified in a separate written agreement between Seller and Broker.
    B. If escrow does not close, compensation is payable as specified in that separate written agreement.

33. ACCEPTANCE OF OFFER: Seller warrants that Seller is the owner of the Property, or has the authority to execute this Agreement. Seller accepts the above offer, agrees to sell the Property on the above terms and conditions, and agrees to the above confirmation of agency relationships. Seller has read and acknowledges receipt of a Copy of this Agreement, and authorizes Broker to deliver a Signed Copy to Buyer.
    ☐ (If checked) **SUBJECT TO ATTACHED COUNTER OFFER, DATED** _____

Date _____ Date _____

SELLER _____ SELLER _____

(Print name) _____ (Print name) _____

(Address) _____

(___/___) **CONFIRMATION OF ACCEPTANCE:** A Copy of Signed Acceptance was personally received by Buyer or Buyer's authorized (Initials) agent on (date) _____ at _____ AM/PM. A binding Agreement is created when a Copy of Signed Acceptance is personally received by Buyer or Buyer's authorized agent whether or not confirmed in this document. Completion of this confirmation is not legally required in order to create a binding Agreement; it is solely intended to evidence the date that Confirmation of Acceptance has occurred.

REAL ESTATE BROKERS:
A. Real Estate Brokers are not parties to the Agreement between Buyer and Seller.
B. Agency relationships are confirmed as stated in paragraph 27.
C. If specified in paragraph 2A, Agent who submitted the offer for Buyer acknowledges receipt of deposit.
D. COOPERATING BROKER COMPENSATION: Listing Broker agrees to pay Cooperating Broker (**Selling Firm**) and Cooperating Broker agrees to accept, out of Listing Broker's proceeds in escrow: **(i)** the amount specified in the MLS, provided Cooperating Broker is a Participant of the MLS in which the Property is offered for sale or a reciprocal MLS; or **(ii)** ☐ (if checked) the amount specified in a separate written agreement (C.A.R. Form CBC) between Listing Broker and Cooperating Broker.

Real Estate Broker (Selling Firm) _____
By _____ Date _____
Address _____ City _____ State _____ Zip _____
Telephone _____ Fax _____ E-mail _____

Real Estate Broker (Listing Firm) _____
By _____ Date _____
Address _____ City _____ State _____ Zip _____
Telephone _____ Fax _____ E-mail _____

ESCROW HOLDER ACKNOWLEDGMENT:
Escrow Holder acknowledges receipt of a Copy of this Agreement, (if checked, ☐ a deposit in the amount of $ _____), counter offer numbers _____ and _____, and agrees to act as Escrow Holder subject to paragraph 28 of this Agreement, any supplemental escrow instructions and the terms of Escrow Holder's general provisions.

Escrow Holder is advised that the date of Confirmation of Acceptance of the Agreement as between Buyer and Seller is _____

Escrow Holder _____
By _____ Escrow # _____
Address _____ Date _____
Phone/Fax/E-mail _____
Escrow Holder is licensed by the California Department of ☐ Corporations, ☐ Insurance, ☐ Real Estate. License # _____

(___/___) **REJECTION OF OFFER:** No counter offer is being made. This offer was reviewed and rejected by Seller on (Seller's Initials) _____ (Date)

 Published by the California Association of REALTORS®

The System for Success®

 EQUAL HOUSING OPPORTUNITY

RPA-CA REVISED 10/02 (PAGE 8 OF 8)

Reviewed by _____ Date _____

CALIFORNIA RESIDENTIAL PURCHASE AGREEMENT (RPA-CA PAGE 8 OF 8)

Each state has laws that limit the amount of time within which legal action may be taken. Below are the real estate activities and the time limits by which they must be filed in order to be considered enforceable.

Personal Property - 90 Days

An individual has 90 days to recover personal property, especially property left at a hotel, motel or boarding house.

Injury – One Year

An individual has one year to file an action for libel, slander, injury or death caused by the neglect of another. There is also a one-year stuate of limitations for filing an action against a banking institution for payment of a forged check.

Oral Contracts - Two Years
An individual has two years to settle a dispute resulting from an oral contract.

Fraud and Trespassing - Three Years

An individual has three years to file a lawsuit relating to fraud. The time period begins upon discovery of the fraud. Likewise, there is a three year statue for filing an action for trespassing on real property, encroachment or attachment.

Written Instruments - Four Years

An individual has four years to settle a dispute over a written contract, such as a real estate sales contract.

Title to Property - Five Years

An individual has five years to take action in an effort to recover title to real property (adverse possession, tax sale, escheat, easement by prescription)

Judgment - Ten Years

An individual has ten years to take action based on a court judgment. The time period begins upon the judgment award date.

Abstract of Judgment (General, Involuntary Lien) - Recording an abstract of a judgment creates a lien on all of the debtor's property in the county where it is recorded. A judgment is a general, involuntary, equitable lien on both real and personal property owned by the debtor. Judgment liens normally continue for ten years from the date of entry of the judgment or decree and can be renewed for an additional 10 years.

Injunction (Restrict) – An injunction is a court order to stop (restrict) a party from committing an act such as violating private restrictions. An injunction is a permanent order, while a restraining order is temporary.

Writ of Execution (Court Order To Sell) – A writ of execution is a court order forcing the sale of the debtor's property to satisfy a judgment. The Sheriff's Sale is the usual method in California of forcing someone to sell property to pay off a judgment. In a Sheriff's Sale, the county sheriff (or other local authority) secures and sells the real or personal property of the debtor to satisfy the lien.

The State of California controls lien and attachment laws; cities and counties do not.

Agency Contracts

Agency is defined as the authority to act for a principal (client) in a specified capacity for a stated period of time.

An **agent** is the person authorized to represent their principal in business dealings with third parties. This places the agent in a position of good faith towards the principal and creates a **fiduciary relationship.**

The Statute of Frauds dictates that a contract that authorizes an agent to find a purchaser or lessee (in cases of more than one year) of real property be made in writing. This agreement, which is basically an employment contract, is called a **listing agreement.**

In addition, the California Real Estate Law requires that the employment agreement between a real estate broker and a salesperson be in writing. Let's examine this agreement first.

Broker – Salesperson Employment Contract

Brokers must have a written agreement with each licensed member of the sales staff. This employment agreement is also required of salespeople who are themselves brokers (known
as associate brokers), but who are working under another broker's license.

All parties must retain a copy of this contract for a period of three years from the date of termination.

For purposes of the Real Estate Law and the Civil Code, the real estate salesperson is an employee of the real estate broker under whom they are licensed. If the broker is a corporation, the salesperson is an agent of the corporation, and not of the supervising, qualifying broker in their individual capacity, but rather in the capacity of the corporation.

Additionally, salespersons are usually independent contractors of the broker for purposes of state and federal income tax reporting (and sometimes for certain other purposes such as Workers' Compensation Insurance coverage). See, for example, Unemployment Insurance Code Section 650 and 26 U.S.C. Section 3508.

Salespersons are agents and employees of the broker for purposes of dealing with the public but may be independent contractors for the purposes of income tax reporting and certain other matters.

All of the details of this broker-salesperson association (including supervision, duties and compensation) must be delineated in the contract and adhered to in practice.

Now let's take a look at agents and agency agreements.

Types of Agents

GENERAL AGENT

A general agent has the authority to perform all necessary acts for the principal within a specified area. For example, a property manager who has authority to rent or lease, collect rents, hire and fire personnel and make repairs and/or improvements would most likely be a general agent.

SPECIAL AGENT

While a general agent has broad powers to act for his or her principal, a special agent is limited to those acts specifically set forth in the agency agreement. For example, a real estate licensee is normally the special agent of an owner. The agent usually has no power to contractually bind the owner to an agreement.

POWER OF ATTORNEY

Power of attorney is a written agreement whereby a principal appoints an agent to act in his or her place. This person is known as an attorney in fact, not to be confused with an attorney at law.

There are two categories of power of attorney:

1. General power of attorney
2. Special power of attorney

General Power of Attorney

A *general power of attorney* allows the person so authorized to perform any act that the principal could perform. Thus, the person authorized to act on behalf of the principal is called the *general attorney in fact.*

The specific powers conferred to the general attorney in fact must be laid out in writing, duly acknowledged and recorded with the county recorder's office, in the county where the property is located for the agency to take effect.

Special Power of Attorney

A *special power of attorney* allows the person so authorized to perform only a specific act (e.g., to sell the property). The person thus authorized to act on behalf of the principal is call the *special attorney in fact.* A listing agent, as a special attorney in fact, is usually authorized to find a ready, willing and able buyer.

Death of either party, or an acknowledged declaration from the principal, may bring about a revocation of the power of attorney.

In order to be valid, the power of attorney must be recorded in the county where the property is located.

Single Versus Dual Agency

In a *single agency*, an agent represents only one principal. Each principal in a transaction may be represented by a different broker.

In a *dual agency*, the same agent represents both principals in the same transaction. A dual agency may be created when a real estate broker works as the subagent of a seller (perhaps through a multiple listing service), while also acting as the buyer's agent.

Any agent who acts on behalf of both parties to a transaction is required by law to inform both parties and obtain their written consent to the dual representation. If this does not happen, the agent faces suspension or even revocation of their real estate license. A party acting without knowledge of the dual agency may ask the court to rescind any contract that results.

Agency Creation

The agreement between principal and agent that forms the basis of the agency may arise in the following ways: agreement, ratification or estoppel.

AGREEMENT

A broker has a duty to both know and understand the agency relationship being constructed.

The broker must be certain that the employment agreement with the principal (known as the listing) is in a correct form and is constructed in a fair manner.

An agency agreement must be in writing for the agent to enforce a commission claim based upon a breach of contract.

If you remember, earlier in this chapter, we mentioned that an agreement between parties may be express or implied. A real estate agency is generally created by express written contract.

a. A unilateral contract occurs when the principal promises to pay a com mission while the broker makes no promises.

b. A bilateral contract is created when the broker promises to use 'due dili gence.' Due diligence is defined as a broker doing everything his or her power to find a ready, will and able buyer for the seller and the principal promises to pay the broker a commission for their work.

Elements of an Agency Agreement

An agency agreement/listing typically includes:

1. The names of the parties
2. Effective identification of the property
3. Terms and conditions of the anticipated sale lease or loan
4. The amount of commission or other compensation to be paid
5. The expiration date of the agency (an exclusive listing must include a definite, specified date of final and complete termination.)
6. Signatures of the parties to the listing

In addition, a listing concerning the sale of residential property consisting of one to four units, or a mobile home, must contain (immediately before the commission clause) a statement (in ten point boldface type or larger) that commission amounts are negotiable between seller and broker and are not set by law. The exact wording to be used is found in the California Business and Professions Code Section 10147.5.

Types of Listing Agreements

Below are the four kinds of listing agreements most commonly used:

- The open listing
- The exclusive agency listing
- The exclusive right to sell listing
- The net listing

OPEN LISTING

An *open listing* is the least restrictive of the four principal kinds of listing agreements. It is distinguishable by the fact that the owner retains the right to revoke the listing at any time, sell the property him or herself, or list the property with another broker. An open listing is also called a *nonexclusive listing.*

Open listings will usually generate questions regarding a real estate broker's claim to a commission for the simple reason that the sale of the property by either the owner or any subsequently hired agent could defeat the original broker's right to a commission.

EXCLUSIVE AGENCY

An *exclusive agency* is an agreement by which the owner agrees to employ a particular real estate broker to solicit prospective buyers, tenants/lessees, or lenders.

Under an exclusive agency listing, the broker's right to a commission is protected against other brokers for the duration of the listing agreement. Also, the broker is usually still entitled to a commission if the owner sells directly to a buyer who was introduced into the process by the broker. This applies even if the sale occurs after the termination date of the agreement.

Under an exclusive agency agreement, the owner retains the right to sell, encumber or rent/lease the property on their own. Should that be the case, the owner may terminate the agency agreement leaving the broker with no claim to a commission or other compensation.

EXCLUSIVE RIGHT TO SELL

An *exclusive right to sell listing* affords a real estate broker the highest degree of protection by making him or her the sole agent for the sale of the property. The broker is entitled to a commission, provided that the property is sold during the listing period. This occurs regardless of who procures the buyer.

Under an exclusive right to sell agreement, the owner sells the property himself, thereby relinquishing both the right to list the property with other agents and the right to defeat the broker's claim for a commission. An exclusive right to sell listing may also be used in a rental or loan transaction.

NET LISTING

A *net listing* is one, which presupposes that the seller will realize certain net proceeds. Any sum received over and above the seller's net becomes the real estate broker's commission.

EXAMPLE

Sally Seller enters into a net listing with Bonnie Broker for a $300,000 net. If the net proceeds of the sale are $300,000 or less, Bonnie will receive no commission. On the other hand, if the net proceeds of the sale are $325,000, Bonnie is entitled to a commission of $25,000.

This type of listing has more to do with the type of compensation than whether the listing is exclusive or not.

Receipt of Deposits

Most listing agreements authorize the broker to accept a deposit. In such cases, the following caveats apply:

    a. A deposit never belongs to the broker
    b. A broker cannot hold uncashed checks unless directed to do so
    c. If a broker is not authorized in the listing agreement, the broker becomes the buyer's agent for deposits

RATIFICATION

Ratification is defined as affirming a prior act that was not legally binding. The affirmation gives the act legal effect. This occurs when an unauthorized agent acts and the principal affirms the action only later, thus giving authority retroactively.

A principal may become bound by ratifying acts of an agent who acted beyond his or her authority, or a person who acted as an agent without any authority. When a person authorizes an agent to act for him or her after the agent has already done so, the action is called ratification.

ESTOPPEL (STOP, PREVENT)

Another way to form an agency by operation of law is by estoppel.

Estoppel means that a person is prohibited by virtue of his or her own past actions (e.g., a waiver) from claiming a right that would work to the detriment of another person who relied on the past actions. Estoppel often works in conjunction with a waiver.

The idea is that if a principal has knowledge that a person is acting on his or her own behalf and takes no steps to correct the representation; the principal cannot later say that the agent took action without his or her consent. The principal may be barred from denying the agency based on the doctrine of estoppel.

This kind of agency creation is also called an *ostensible* (or implied) agency.

Estoppel prevents inconsistencies and is seldom possible in real estate dealings, since a written contract is needed.

Laws of Agency

Whenever one person represents another in a business transaction, the Law of Agency applies. The Law of Agency is found in the California Civil Code and defines an agent's duties and responsibilities. Further, since the broker is a licensed real estate agent, he or she must comply with the laws and regulations of the California Department of Real Estate.

ACTUAL AGENCY (BY AGREEMENT)

Actual agency occurs when a principal intentionally confers upon the agent (or allows the agent to believe) that he or she possesses certain authority.

OSTENSIBLE AGENCY (QUASI/APPARENT)

As discussed previously, ostensible agency occurs when a principal causes or allows third persons to believe that the agent possesses authority to act on a principal's behalf. A principal is liable to third persons that have, in good faith, relied upon the ostensible authority of the agent to their detriment.

An agency relationship can result from the conduct of the parties even when there is no express employment agreement and regardless of the source of compensation.

Warranty of Authority

As an agent, the broker warrants that he or she has the authority to represent another person.

If there is a written listing between the seller and the broker, the broker has an expressed warranty of authority. A broker gives implied warranty of authority to act for a seller merely by showing the seller's property.

When a broker has no listing contract and offers to sell a property to a buyer who relies on the fact that the agent has certain authority, the broker could be liable for this misrepresentation.

Fiduciary Duties of an Agent

The California Civil Code boils the laws of agency down to a couple of basic rules applying to the licensed agent.

The agent:

- Must inform his or her client(s) of all facts pertaining to the handling of the client's case (and thus put a client's interest above the interests of self or others)
- May not gain any monetary interest in the transaction without a client's prior knowledge and consent.

As a reminder, the real estate agent owes a definite duty of fiduciary relationship to his or her principal. They may not obtain any advantage over the principal by the slightest misrepresentation, concealment, duress, or adverse pressure of any kind.

To expand on the above basic rules, the agent:

- Cannot use a confidential relationship for his or her own benefit, nor use the position of trust to take advantage of the principal (e.g., no secret profits)
- Must disclose all material facts to the principal, including existence of an imminent offer
- Must submit all offers received prior to the closing of the sale
- Must use reasonable care and skill
- Must obey the lawful instructions of his principal, or otherwise be liable for damages
- May not act for two principals in negotiations with each other without the knowledge and consent of both parties
- May not give legal advice on any subject (best left to CPAs and attorneys)

Agent's Duties to Third Parties

Both the principal and agent owe certain duties to third persons. Both must:

- Disclose all material facts and defects affecting the desirability of the property
- Inspect the property and reveal its condition to the potential buyer

In addition, the agent must not make a secret profit at the expense of a third person, and must be careful when puffing, or exaggerating, the benefits of a property. Even in some situations where an agent honestly believes that representations to the potential buyer are nothing more than puffing or sales talk, a problem may develop if the impression made upon the buyer is that the representation in question is one of fact.

In general, an agent will be liable to third persons for any tort or other action that the agent performs. The agent is liable for the following:

- Injury to the victim's property or person.

Negligence and fraudulent misrepresentation:

a. May be in the form of a statement made recklessly and carelessly without sufficient knowledge to justify the statement
b. May be from the agent's silence or from known material facts that the broker should disclose, whether asked or not. If the principal supplies the agent with false information and the agent repeats this information, the agent is not liable for damages and is entitled to a full commission, even if the potential buyer rescinds.

An *As Is Clause* in a deposit receipt does not relieve an agent of the duty to disclose material facts.

In the area of disclosing the death or cause of death of a prior occupant, the agent is not required to do so unless a direct inquiry is made. Brokers must strive to balance the principle of full disclosure against the right to privacy. An occupant's death from AIDS or AIDS-related illness, or any other contagious disease, is a highly emotional issue.

Casually disclosing that an occupant or former occupant died, or is dying, from AIDS might very well be in violation of that person's civil rights and might expose the broker to civil or criminal penalties. By law, sellers, brokers and landlords have no liability for failure to disclose a prior occupant's death or its cause after three years have passed since the death.

Principal's Duties to the Agent

The principal owes a commission to the broker when:

1. The broker initiates a valid binding contract upon terms and conditions agree able to the principal. If the seller and buyer later rescind, the broker still earns a commission based on the listing contract

2. The broker is the *procuring cause*, or the person who initiated the sale

3. They produce a ready, willing and able buyer for the property, as described in the listing

"Ready and willing" means that the buyer is willing to enter into a binding purchase contract. "Able" means that the buyer is financially able to purchase the property.

Termination of Agency

The agency relationship between a seller and a real estate broker can be terminated by a few different means.

ACTS OF THE PARTIES

When both parties have fulfilled their duties of the agreement, the agency relationship is terminated - even if the duties were fulfilled before the specified termination date in the listing.

MUTUAL AGREEMENT TO TERMINATE

If both parties agree to terminate, it is considered termination by mutual agreement.

UNILATERAL CANCELLATION

The seller or agent may terminate the agency unilaterally, but he or she might be liable for damages to the other party. If the seller revokes the listing before it expires, they may be liable for expenses incurred by the listing agent on a commission, provided that there is a ready, willing and able buyer.

EXPIRATION OF THE TERM OF THE LISTING AGREEMENT

Exclusive Agency Listing Agreements and Exclusive Authorization and Right to Sell Listing Agreements have definite termination dates. These listings will end automatically upon the stated date if not terminated in some other way before that date.

An open listing doesn't require a termination date because it can be terminated at any time.

EXTINCTION / DESTRUCTION OF THE SUBJECT

If the property is destroyed or damaged by certain causes, such as fire or earthquake, the listing agreement is terminated.

DEATH OR INCAPACITY OF THE PRINCIPAL OR THE AGENT

If either the agent or seller is incapable of fulfilling the agency agreement because of death or incapacity, the agreement is terminated.

Disclosure of Agency Relationship

According to the Agency Disclosure Law of January 1, 1988, the first thing a broker must do is establish their relationship with the principal.

Both the listing broker and the selling broker must declare in writing, as soon as possible, who it is they represent. They may represent either:

1. The seller (listing agent)

2. The buyer (selling agent, or cooperating agent)

3. Both the seller and buyer (dual agency)

This type of law, which differs from state to state, profoundly affects the way brokers represent their clients and the way the industry is perceived by the public.

Real Estate Contracts

PURCHASE CONTRACT AND DEPOSIT FOR RECEIPT

Since most offers to purchase real property include a money deposit (also known as *earnest money*), the contract of sale, or *purchase agreement*, is also a receipt of the deposit and is known as a *deposit receipt*. Again, a purchase agreement, contract of sale and a deposit receipt **are all the same thing**.

The earnest money is collected as consideration (from the prospective buyer on behalf of the seller) by the agent for the deposit receipt contract.

If a *liquidated damage clause* is initialed by both parties, and the buyer later defaults on the transaction, the seller may keep the deposit (totaling up to 3% of the purchase price). The deposit would then be split equally (50/50) between the seller and the listing broker, unless stated otherwise in the deposit receipt. Deposits are always the property of the seller, never the broker.

Since the prospective buyer is making the offer to the owner to purchase the property, the prospective buyer is considered the offeror and the owner is the offeree.

- The deposit receipt is both an offer to purchase a specific property on certain terms and conditions and a deposit of consideration for the same property.
- When acceptance is communicated, this becomes a binding contract on both the buyer(s) and the seller(s) part.
- After a contract is signed, an agent should always give a copy to every involved parties

ELEMENTS OF THE DEPOSIT RECEIPT

Initial Offer

This part of the deposit receipt must express the offeror's willingness to enter into the contract, as well as:

- Be communicated to the offeree (owner)
- Manifest contractual intention
- Be definite and certain in its terms
- Have all the characteristics of a contract

Acceptance

Every deposit receipt requires that the offeree (seller) communicate their acceptance of the buyer's terms to the offeror (buyer). The acceptance should also meet the following standards:

- The offeree (seller) must have knowledge of the offer
- Acceptance must be absolute and unqualified. Any modification by the offeree becomes a counter offer
- It must be within the time limits specified, or within a reasonable period if no time limit is specified
- It must be expressed or communicated. Silence ordinarily cannot be considered acceptance

- It must be in the manner specified in the offer. If not specified in that manner, it may be specified by any reasonable, usual mode

- Once accepted, the death or insanity of either party will not terminate the contract. The contract is valid and heirs can be bound to the contract terms

- Even conflicting offers must be submitted to the seller

Termination of an Offer

Before acceptance, an offer may be terminated in one of the following ways:

- **Revocation:** The offeror may withdraw their offer anytime before the offeree has communicated acceptance. An offeror is not required to wait for the period specified in the offer before withdrawing said offer

- **Lapse of time:** The offeree does not accept an offer within the prescribed period or reasonable time (if a time is not prescribed)

- **Rejection by the offeree:** Any unequivocal rejection ends the offer. Generally, oral bargaining in the form of suggested changes is not usually considered rejection

- **Death or insanity:** Whether it is of the offeror or the offeree

- **Supervening illegality:** The proposed contract becomes illegal before acceptance

Contingencies and Conditions

Contingencies or *conditions* are provisions by which all parties are released from any obligations of a contract if the stated condition fails to materialize.

If a contingency falls through, the contract is voidable by the offeror.

If the buyer wants to make any condition or act subject to a specified contingency, the clause should be preceded with any of the following: "offer subject to," "offer contingent upon" or "offer conditioned upon."

For example, an offer may be contingent on the buyer obtaining successful financing or subject to the successful sale of another property. With any contingency or condition, all reasonable efforts must be made to fulfill the contingency or condition.

Covenants are considered promises between the parties to a contract. If a party breaks a contractual promise, the party may be liable for damages.

COUNTEROFER AND THE PURCHASE AGREEMENT ADDENDUM

When the original offer is rejected, a new offer is called a *counter offer*. The counter offer must contain a clause that states that all the conditions of the original deposit receipt are accepted - with the exception of the list of new terms. Those new terms can be listed on a purchase agreement addendum.

A Purchase Agreement Addendum is a form that is used as an addendum to a purchase agreement, another offer form or the counteroffer form. Only the paragraphs that are checked are included in the addendum as part of the contract.

There are generally five separate topics that are relevant to the transaction:

- The cancellation of prior sale offers
- Court confirmation of various court procedures (probate, guardianship, bankruptcy, etc.)
- Tenant-occupied properties
- Secured lenders and lien holders
- Assumed or junior financing

It is always preferable to start a new deposit receipt if there have been too many counter offers or too many changes in the offer.

OPTION

An **option** is a unilateral contract in which the optionor (owner) gives the optionee (prospective buyer) a right to purchase or lease real property upon specific terms within a specified time in exchange for actual consideration. In short, an option is a contract to make a contract.

Here are the characteristics of an option:

- As with all real estate contracts, it must be in writing
- It can be in the form of an exclusive right to purchase or lease, or in the form of the privilege of first right of refusal to purchase or lease
- The owner (optionor) cannot sell or lease to another party during the option period
- Actual consideration must pass from optionee to the owner
    1. Consideration may be made in the form of cash, check, promissory note or another thing of value
    2. If the consideration is an unsecured promissory note, the option cannot be assigned without consent of the optionor (owner)
- The owner (optionor) retains consideration whether the option is exercised or not
- The buyer (optionee) is not obligated to purchase or lease the property
- The optionee may also secure another buyer during the option term. Thus, all rights and interests may be transferred without the consent of the optionor, unless stated otherwise.

Agents Holding Options

If a listing broker takes an option on the listed property, they have put themselves in the dual position of agent and principal. This creates a conflict of interest. When exercising an option, the broker must:

- Advise every prospective buyer that he or she is acting as a principal and not as the owner's agent
- Reveal all facts to the owner (including any anticipated profit) and obtain the owner's written approval

RIGHT OF FIRST REFUSAL

The difference between an option and a *right of first refusal* is that the prospective buyer is not given the absolute right to purchase (option). Rather, he or she is given only the right to match an offer from a third party.

This right is generally given only when the owner is willing to sell the property. If this right has been given before the owner can sell, the owner must offer the property to the holder of the right of first refusal at the price and terms that the owner wishes to accept from a buyer. The holder of this right loses the right if they do not meet the price and terms of the offer within a certain time period.

There is a possibility that a tenant who holds the right of first refusal may be at a disadvantage if the prospective buyer offers consideration in a form other than cash.

S U M M A R Y

Understanding contracts, their creation, enforcement and their general legal nature is very important for you as a real estate agent. As an agent you will have to deal with contracts with every property transfer and you must know how to execute these contracts accurately the first time to avoid any complications with the transaction, not to mention unhappy clients.

It is important to understand the different types of contracts and how they are formed as some contracts may have clauses allowing one or more party to be dismissed from any obligation, if the contract is created legally. Additionally it is important for you to understand who is eligible to enter into a contract, or who cannot.

With the amount of paperwork and contracts that are involved in each transaction it is imperative for a real estate agent to understand these contracts so the property transfer goes as smoothly as possible, the client is satisfied with your performance, and perhaps most importantly you receive your compensation for a job well done.

T E R M S   A N D   P H R A S E S

Abstract of Judgment - This is a summary of money judgment. The summary is usually prepared so that it may be recorded, and thereby creates a lien on real and/or personal property owned by the debtor.

As Is Clause - A provision in a deposit receipt stating that the buyer accepts the property in its present condition

Assignee - A person or entity receiving the assignment

Assignment - The act of transferring an interest in property or some right to another party

Assignor - A person or entity that has made an assignment of rights or property

Bilateral Contract - A contract in which the consideration given by each party is a promise (i.e., a promise for a promise)

Breach - The violation of or failure to perform an obligation, either by omission or commission (the breaking of a law or failure of duty)

Condition - A provision in an agreement or deed that makes wherein the parties' rights and obligations depend on the occurrence (or nonoccurrence) of a particular event (also called a contingency clause)

Consideration - Something of value given by one party to another in return for entering into a contract.

Contract - An agreement to perform or not perform do a certain action. A contract must have four essential elements: parties capable of contracting, consent of the parties, a lawful object, and consideration. A contract for sale of real property must also be in writing and signed by the party or parties to be charged with performance.
Convict - A person who has been convicted of a felony and sent to prison. (in the United States, convicts do not have a right to contract while incarcerated)

Counter Offer - A response to an offer to enter into a contract, which changes some of the terms of the original offer. It is a rejection of the original offer and does not create a binding contract unless accepted by the original offeror.

Covenant - In a deed or lease, a guarantee or promise, whether express or implied.

Deposit - Money that is offered as an indication of good faith regarding the future performance of a contract to purchase(also called earnest money)

Deposit Receipt - The document used for a prospective real estate buyer's offer to a seller, which also serves as the buyer's receipt for the deposit. If the seller accepts the buyer's offer, the deposit receipt becomes their contract(also called a contract of sale or purchase and sale agreement or purchase agreement)

Disaffirm - To refuse confirmation; to annul, as a judicial decision

Earnest Money - See Deposit

Emancipated - A minor who is (or has been) married, is on active duty in the armed forces or has a declaration of emancipation from a court (an emancipated minor has the legal capacity to contract)

Estoppel - A doctrine that prevents a person from asserting rights or positions that are inconsistent with his or her earlier actions or statements

Exclusive Agency Listing - A listing agreement that entitles the broker to a commission if anyone other than the seller finds a buyer for the property during the listing term

Exclusive Right to Sell Listing - A listing under which only one broker may sell a property and is entitled to a commission even if the owner sells the property directly to any party

Executed Contract - A contract in which all parties have completely met their contractual obligations

Executory Contract - A contract in which an action remains to be performed by one or both of the parties

Express Contract - One in which the agreement is in words (either written or spoken)

Fiduciary Relationship - A relationship of trust and confidence, in which one party owes the other (or both parties owe each other) loyalty and a higher standard of good faith than they owe to third parties(for example, a husband and a wife are fiduciaries in relation to each other)

Full Performance - Full performance is when both parties in a contract have fulfilled their specific duties.

Implied Contract - One in which some of the terms are not expressed in words (either written or spoken)

Incompetent - Someone incapable of managing his or her own affairs by reason of age, disease, weakness of mind, or other mental defect or cause.

Injunction - An equitable remedy (in the form of a court order) compelling a party to commit or refrain from committing a specific act. Injunction is also available as a remedy for harm for which there is no adequate remedy in law. Thus, it is used to prevent a future harmful action, rather than to compensate for an injury that has already occurred. It may also be used to provide relief from harm for which an award of money damages is not a satisfactory solution or for which a monetary value is impossible to calculate. An individual who violates an injunction is subject to penalty for contempt.

Liquidated Damages Clause - A clause in a purchase agreement that sets a sum that the parties to a contract agree in advance will serve as compensation in the event of a breach

Material Breach - A breach serious enough to destroy the value of the contract and to give a basis for an action for breach of contract

Minor - A person under 18 years of age

Mutual Rescission - Termination of uncompleted contract: a means of terminating an uncompleted contract in which each party agrees to release the other party from obligation

Net Listing - A listing under which the broker that sells the property retains as compensation the amount of the sale price in excess of a specified sum

Offer and acceptance - Two major requirements of a contract forming mutual consent (combined with capacity and valuable consideration)

Offeree - One who receives an offer (the seller)

Offeror - A person or entity who makes a specific proposal to another (the offeree) to enter into a contract (the buyer)

Open Listing - A listing that does not preclude the use of multiple brokers or a direct sale by the owner and requires no commission paid to a broker (also called a nonexclusive listing).

Option - A contract giving one party the right, but not the obligation to perform an action

Procuring Cause - The broker who sets in motion a continuous series of events that lead to the sale, lease or financing of a property

Purchase Agreement - A contract in which a seller promises to convey title to real property to a buyer in exchange for the purchase price. (also called purchase and sale agreement or contract of sale) See Deposit Receipt

Ratification - The later approval or confirmation of an act that was not authorized when it was initially performed

Right of First Refusal - The right to first opportunity to purchase property at the same terms offered by a third party or at predetermined terms upon the owner's decision to sell. (also called preemptive right)

Statute of Frauds - A state law, based on an old English statute, requiring certain contracts to be in writing and signed before they will be enforceable by law (e.g., contracts for the sale of real property, contracts not to be performed within one year)

Substantial Performance - That degree of performance of a contract which, while not equal to full and complete performance, is so nearly equivalent that it would be unreasonable to deny the contractor the payment agreed upon in the contract. This is subject to the owner's right to recover whatever damages he has suffered by reason of the contractor's failure to render full and complete performance.

Unenforceable - A contract that cannot be legally enforced by the courts (such as contracts with minors and those containing fraud)

Unilateral Contract - A contract in which only one party makes a promise to perform or not perform an action

Valid Contract - One that has force, or binding force; legally sufficient and authorized by law

Void Contract - One that has no force or no effect

Voidable Contract - A contract that is capable of being adjudged void, but is not void unless action is taken to make it so

Writ of Execution - An order directing the sheriff to seize property to satisfy a judgment

C H A P T E R   Q U I Z
_____

1. An option to purchase a specific vacant lot:
    a. Can never be assigned
    b. Can always be assigned
    c. Can be assigned if purchased for cash
    d. Can be assigned unless prohibited by contract

2. A broker must maintain listing agreement copies for:
   a. Two years
   b. Three years
   c. Four years
   d. Six years

3. To be entitled to a commission, a broker must show that they were the procuring cause of the sale or lease of a property under all of the following types of listings EXCEPT:
   a. Exclusive agency
   b. Exclusive right to sell
   c. Open listing
   d. Nonexclusive listing

4. In her capacity as an agent, a real estate licensee is liable to third parties for:
   a. Her own torts
   b. A tort committed by her principal
   c. A written contract made in the name of her principal
   d. Actions committed by a duly appointed sub-agent

5. An exclusive right to sell listing:
   a. Must contain a termination date
   b. Must be in writing if the broker wants to be successful in suing for a commission
   c. Must be kept by the broker for at least three years
   d. All of the above are correct statements

6. A voidable contract is a contract that:
   a. Contains all of the legal essentials required for its existence
   b. Has no legal effect because it is not an actual contract
   c. Is valid and enforceable on its face, but may be rejected by one of the parties
   d. Was valid at the time that it was signed, but for some reason cannot be proven or sued upon by either or both parties

7. Under the Statute of Frauds, all contracts for the sale of real estate must be in writing. The principal reason for this statute is to:
   a. Protect the public from fraud resulting from unrecorded deeds
   b. Prevent the buyer from defrauding the seller
   c. Protect the buyer's rights
   d. Prevent fraudulent proof of a fictitious oral contract

8. The broker who most qualifies for a commission is the one who:
   a. Gave the offer to the seller
   b. Received the offer from the buyer
   c. Received the acceptance of an offer
   d. Communicated the acceptance to the buyer

9. An offer to fully perform a purchase contract is known as:
   a. A condition
   b. A deposit
   c. A tender
   d. A covenant

10. A remedy in court compelling a vendor to execute a deed in pursuance of a valid written contract is known as:)
    a. Specific performance
    b. Foreclosure
    c. Execution
    d. Equity of redemption

11. Failure to perform a contract is also known as:
    a. A rescission
    b. A breach
    c. A notation
    d. A reformation

12. How long is the Statute of Limitations for an action based on a written real estate contract?
    a. Unlimited
    b. Two years
    c. Four years
    d. Twenty years

13. A well-drafted real estate purchase contract will include which of the following provisions?
    a. The buyer's possession of the property
    b. The financing terms
    c. Proration of property expenses
    d. All of the above

14. According to the Statute of Frauds, all contracts for the sale of real estate must be :
    a. Originated by a real estate broker
    b. On preprinted forms
    c. Made in writing
    d. Accompanied by earnest money deposits

15. Which of the following parties is bound by an option to purchase?
    a. Buyer only
    b. Seller only
    c. Neither buyer nor seller
    d. Both buyer and seller

16. A contract that has not been performed is called a(n)
    a. Executory contract
    b. Executed contract
    c. Unilateral contract
    d. Bilateral contract

17. Which of the following are basic elements of a valid contract?
    a. Sufficient consideration
    b. Lawful purpose
    c. Competent parties
    D. All of the above

18. Due diligence is the promise a broker makes to whom?
     a. The salesperson working for the broker.
     b. The principal
     c. The third party
     d. None of the above.

19. All of the following are types of listing agreements EXCEPT
     a. Open listing
     b. Net listing
     c. Private listing
     d. Exclusive agency listing

20. A broker may be accused of fraud or misrepresentation when which of the following occurs?
     a. Silence regarding known defects or problems with the property.
     b. Knowingly passing on false information regarding the property
     c. Recklessly making assumptions, and then passing them on as fact
     d. All of the above.

5

AGENCY

What you will learn in this Chapter

- The definition of 'agency'
- Special distinctions of a general agency
- Creating an agency relationship
- Dual and ostensible agencies
- Agency disclosure and confirmation
- Agency Confirmation
- Multiple listing service
- Cooperating brokers
- Agent's authority
- Duties of an agent to the principal
- Duties / Liabilities of an agent to the buyer or third party
- Duties of a Principal to Agent (or rights of an agent)
- Cancellation of agency
- Real estate transfer disclosure statement

1. What word best describes an agent's responsibility to the client?
   A. Fiduciary
   B. Authority
   C. Exclusive
   D. Estoppel

2. Which of the following is NOT a way to create an agency?
   A. Agreement
   B. Contract
   C. Ratification
   D. Estoppel

3. An agent can place their listings on what service to allow all members to view an available listing?
   A. Commingling
   B. Open listing service
   C. Multiple Listing Service
   D. Net listing service

4. Which of the following duties is NOT considered a duty owed to the principal by the agent?
   A. Fiduciary
   B. Flexibility
   C. Full disclosure
   D. Loyalty

5. What percentage of the state license fee is contributed to the Recovery Account?
   A. 2%
   B. 5%
   C. 7%
   D. 10%

6. When is an agent's commission earned?
   A. Upon entering into the listing agreement
   B. Upon posting the listing on the Multiple Listing Service
   C. When the listing contract expires
   D. When the agent finds a ready, willing and able buyer who meets all of the sellers' terms

7. Commission rates are determined by
   A. Real estate commission
   B. State legislature
   C. Brokers
   D. Sellers

INTRODUCTION

In real estate, the duty of a licensee is to represent his or her client. When a licensee forms a working relationship with a client, this is called an agency. In this chapter, we will examine the different types of agency relationships between agent, seller and buyer. We will discover who represents whom in these relationships. We will also examine the law as it pertains to the obligations and responsibilities owed by a broker to a client. Licensees are not the only party responsible for their actions; the client also has obligations the licensee.

It is important for licensees to understand agency. When a licensee fulfills all duties outlined by the contract, or listing agreement, he or she will receive the agreed-upon compensation for their work. A licensee must also understand all the laws of agency to ensure the licensee is operating legally. This is crucial, as this knowledge helps to avoid any damages that may be caused by the licensee's actions. Licensees are held liable for any damages they may cause for either their client or any third party involved in the real estate transaction.

Agency is one of the most important concepts in real estate. The following chapter will provide you with a basic understanding of agency.

AGENCY

When a potential seller of real estate requests representation from a real estate agent, an agency is formed. An agency consists of three parties: the agent, the principal and a third party. The broker is the agent, the seller is the principal and the third party is the potential buyer. For example, if Bill is a real estate agent representing Jane who is selling her home, Bill is the Agent, Jane is the Principal and the buyer or potential buyers are the third party.

The agent has a responsibility to act in the best interest of the principal. Fiduciary responsibility and loyalty are given to the principal by the agent, while remaining fair and truthful with all third parties. These basic responsibilities are defined in the laws of agency and bind the agent, principal and third party in a legal relationship. The law of agency defines the duties of an agent and is found in the California Civil Code.

> California Civil Code (law of agency) basic duties for an agent:
> - An agent must reveal to the principal all facts pertaining to the handling of the client's case. An agent must put the client's interest before those of anyone else.
> - An agent may not collect a commission or any other form of compensation in the transaction without the client's prior knowledge and consent.

There are many different agency relationships that can be established. The primary agency relationship is between the broker and the principal who is also the seller. In any real estate transaction, the agent is defined as the broker, while any salesperson working with a principal is an agent of the broker, while the broker is the agent of the principal. There are also separate brokers representing the buyer in an agency capacity. The buyer's broker will also have salespersons working as agents. As you can see, there are many different layers in an agency agreement. So, it is important to understand both who represents whom, and the responsibility the parties owe to one another. The seller has an agency agreement with the broker. The buyer has an agency agreement with a separate broker, all of whom must work together professionally, disclosing all necessary information regarding the property in question.

In an agency, some of the responsibilities entrusted to the broker may be delegated to a salesperson or office assistant, provided that these duties do not require licensure on the part of said assistant. An example of this would be filing documents or typing a sales brochure. Other delegated activities that are part of the sales process may require the consent of the principal. Every person aiding the broker in representing the principal is referred to as a subagent. Cooperating brokers are agents who work for one broker while trying to sell property that is already listed by another broker. A cooperating broker is usually entitled to a share of the commission from the listing agent, provided the listing agent has disclosed this share to the principal.

Remember:
- The agent is the listing broker
- The principal is the seller employing the broker
- The third party is any potential buyer
- A salesperson is an agent of the listing broker
- All agents of the broker may be considered subagents of the principal
- Cooperating brokers are agents trying to sell another broker's listing

SPECIAL DISTINCTIONS OF A GENERAL AGENCY

A traditional agency is relatively simple to understand. An agent represents a principal in dealing with a third party. But what happens when an agent is buying property? Are they allowed to represent themselves? It is important to understand the different dynamics involved in an agency relationship when the agent represents himself or herself as a principal. There are three situations that present themselves in these cases: the broker may act as a principal; there may be an employer-employee relationship; or an independent contractor may provide services.

Agents Acting On Their Own Behalf
There may be times when you, as an agent, desire to purchase property for yourself. Given that you are a real estate professional, you don't need to utilize a real estate agent. The state of California allows you to act on your own behalf as a principal provided you are ethical and closely follow the letter of the law. To be an ethical and lawful agent, you must fully disclose your position as a principal in the transaction. You must also make all parties involved aware of the legal effect of the contract into which they are entering.

A situation involving a broker acting on his or her own behalf will occur when he or she: takes an option to buy one of their listings; takes a net listing; or becomes personally involved in a sale in some way. The broker is also required to fully disclose his or her involvement in the transaction. A full disclosure means revealing all facts that would likely affect the judgment of the principal in giving consent to an agent to enter into the particular transaction on the specified terms. The broker must alert the principal to all interests he or she has in the property. The broker must also reveal any other facts that may have an influence on the transaction's desirability from the viewpoint of the principal.

Example:

You are the agent representing Ben and Carrie, who wish to sell their home in San Diego. You have been looking for a larger home and discover that the house that Ben and Carrie are selling would be perfect. You immediately disclose to Ben and Carrie that you wish to make an offer and will be acting on your own behalf as a principal. This creates a situation where Ben and Carrie are no longer in an agency relationship and are not represented by an agent.

The above transaction will be conducted at *Arms Length*, which means all of the parties are acting in their own self-interest and are under no undue influence or pressure from the other parties. You, as an agent, must also be very careful when taking an option on one of your own listings. Full disclosure in this situation not only involves presenting all information regarding the prospect of a sale to someone else; but disclosing any profits made in the transaction, as well.

Independent Contractor vs. Employer-Employee Relationship
There are two main differences between the employer-employee and independent contractor relationship. The first difference is the amount of control the principal extends over an agent. The second difference is the manner in which the agent is compensated.

In an employer-employee relationship, the agent is considered an employee of the principal. Thus, the agent works under the control and direct supervision of the principal. There may be set hours that the agent must work, along with guidelines. In contrast, an independent contractor holds a contract with the principal. The agent is responsible for results based on the employment contract he or she has made with the principal. The agent does not work under the supervision of the principal and can decide how to obtain the desired results as long as he or she works within the letter of the law.

In a real estate transaction the generally desired outcome is to find a ready, wiling and able buyer for a specific piece of property. Upon finding the buyer, the agent is entitled to receive the previously agreed-upon commission for his or her efforts. This brings us to the other important difference between the employer-employee and independent contractor relationship:

An employer will pay his or her employee for a job in the form of a salary, from which taxes may be deducted and the employee may also receive other benefits from the employer. On the other hand, an independent contractor will receive a lump sum upon satisfactory completion of the job. This is usually a commission; agreed upon in advance and paid when a ready, willing and able buyer is found.

Lets look at this from another angle. By analyzing the relationship between salesperson and broker. The salesperson is the employee of the broker and therefore directly represents the broker when dealing with all clients. As a result, the broker is responsible for the actions of the salesperson. The salesperson will most likely receive a portion of the commission that the broker receives (rather than a salary) upon the successful sale of a property. However, the law will always treat the salesperson as an employee of the broker.

- A principal holds an employment contract with the broker, who is sometimes called the listing agent.
- Salespersons are agents of the broker and act as an independent contractor when dealing with the principal.
- Real estate law considers a salesperson an employee of the broker (employer-employee relationship). Yet, brokers generally treat the salesperson as an independent contractor for compensation, tax and work assignment purposes.

CREATING AN AGENCY RELATIONSHIP

An agency is created in one of three ways: by **agreement**, **ratification** or **estoppel**.

Agreement
An agreement may be express or implied. Written, express agreements are most commonly used in California; but there are other types of agreements that may be used, as well.

An express agreement is a contract between the agent and principal. This type of agreement must be in writing. An agent is authorized by the listing agreement (the contract) to act on behalf of the principal by all lawful means.

An express agreement may be unilateral or bilateral depending on the promises the agent and principal make to one another. A unilateral contract is created when the principal promises to pay the agent a commission for finding a ready, willing and able buyer who meets all terms of the contract. The agent makes no promises to the principal in a unilateral contract. Contrarily, in a bilateral contract, the principal makes a promise to the agent to pay him or her a commission for finding a ready, willing and able buyer. In turn, the agent promises the principal that the agent will use due diligence in finding the buyer.

Remember:
- An express agreement is the most common way to establish an agency relationship in California
- Express agreements are usually in writing (to comply with the statute of frauds)
- Agreements may be bilateral or unilateral

Ratification
An agency relationship may be formed "after-the-fact." This mean an agent acted beyond his or her authority, which was later, affirmed by the principal. The affirmation by the principal creates a legal agency, entitling the principal to a commission. If an

agency agreement is formed by ratification, it must be in writing to be considered a valid contract. This is important because a contract must be valid for the agent to receive his or her commission.

Example: Susan is trying to sell her home on her own, but is open to the idea of having an agent assist her in the sale. At this time, Susan does not have an agency agreement with a broker. Herbert, a broker, lives in the same neighborhood as Susan, and does not realize Susan is selling her home as she has not advertised, or placed a 'for sale' sign in her yard. Still Herbert is very familiar with the size, layout and amenities of Susan's home. One day Herbert receives a call from a prospective client describing the type of home for which he is looking. He immediately considers of Susan's home. Herbert calls Susan to see if he can show her home to his client and she agrees. Herbert's client loves Susan's home and make a generous offer. Herbert presents it to Susan and she accepts, offering to pay him a commission on the sale of the home.

In the above example, an agency by ratification was created, because Susan accepted the offer and agreed to pay a commission..

Estoppel

Estoppel is created when a person claims to be represented by an agent, when in actuality, no agency agreement exists.. A third party interested in the property may choose to deal directly with the agent who they believe represents the seller. If a seller allows a buyer to believe an agent is representing them, and the buyer utilizes this agent to see the property and make an offer, the seller cannot deny the agency and is thereby bound by the actions of the agent.

An agency can be created in one of three ways:
- Agreement
- Ratification
- Estoppel

DUAL AGENCY

A licensee may be the agent for both the seller and the buyer, provided the licensee has informed both parties of this agreement and gained the parties' written consent to the dual agency. In the next section we will discuss *disclosure* and *confirmation*. Dual agency is tricky for a licensee, as they are responsible to two different principles with opposing interests. The licensee must act fairly and honestly in disclosing all facts to both parties. As long as the licensee discloses all facts and acts fairly when dealing with both parties, dual agency is allowed by law.

A licensee who functions as a dual agent in a transaction may not disclose any price information to either the buyer or seller, as it may influence the acceptance of an offer. As the agent for both principles, this would violate the rule regarding fair and honest dealing. Any agent found to be in violation of the law while acting as a dual agent may have his or her license suspended or revoked.

AGENCY DISCLOSURE

In an agency, there is a traditional principal(represented by the listing agent) and a buyer (represented by another agent). The buyer is sometimes called the client or third party. The agent representing the buyer is also called the selling agent. It is important for all parties to understand the roles and responsibilities of the individual agents as well as who is representing each party. Fiduciary responsibility binds the listing agent's responsibility to the seller and under law; the selling agent is considered a subagent of the listing agent (and thus is bound to the seller). So where does that leave the buyer? In these cases, the buyer is representing him or herself.

Lets make sure there is no confusion with terms to which you will be exposed.

The client is the seller, also called the principal. The listing broker has a contract with the seller and is an agent of the seller. The buyer is the customer, and needs to be aware that he or she is representing him or herself (though he receives services benefiting another). Sometimes the buyer is also referred to as the third party.

In California, the law requires that details of all agency relationships must be disclosed to all parties when dealing with property consisting of one to four units. This law went into effect on January 1, 1988. A written document which discloses who is being represented by the agent, as well as all interests and relationships between the parties, must be given to both the buyer and the seller as soon as possible.

The following disclosures must be made:
• The listing agent must disclose to the seller the nature of the relationship before the seller signs the listing agreement
• By the selling agent (who may be both the selling agent and listing agent) to the buyer before the buyer makes any offer to purchase the property
• By the selling agent to the seller (only if different from the listing agent) before an offer to purchase is accepted

In agency disclosure, there are a few possible scenarios. An agent may be either the seller's agent, the buyer's agent or a dual agent (in cases where both the client and customer have a relationship established with the broker). If an agent is the seller's agent, he or she may also function as the buyer's agent. If the agent is a listing agent, he or she may function as a dual agent; but, the listing agent cannot be the buyer's agent only. An agent always owes fiduciary responsibility to the seller or client - even if the agent is working in a dual agency capacity. A dual agent may never tell the buyer what the seller's bottom line is. As mentioned earlier, in a dual agency situation, the buyer is basically representing him or herself. However, the agent has a responsibility to treat the buyer fairly and honestly, by disclosing all facts and information known about a certain property.

Agency disclosure is one of the most important elements in making a real estate transaction. It ensures that every party knows who is representing whom. All parties can be confident that their interests are being protected and that they have a knowledgeable professional acting on their behalf in all transactions pertaining to a specific property.

The law requires agency disclosure between the realtor and the client. Every licensee must understand the process and be able to explain it to any prospective client or customer. An agent's misunderstanding regarding disclosure is not an excuse for damages resulting from his or her actions, and he or she will be held accountable for any such damages.

CALIFORNIA ASSOCIATION OF REALTORS®

DISCLOSURE REGARDING REAL ESTATE AGENCY RELATIONSHIPS
(As required by the Civil Code)
(C.A.R. Form AD, Revised 10/04)

When you enter into a discussion with a real estate agent regarding a real estate transaction, you should from the outset understand what type of agency relationship or representation you wish to have with the agent in the transaction.

SELLER'S AGENT
A Seller's agent under a listing agreement with the Seller acts as the agent for the Seller only. A Seller's agent or a subagent of that agent has the following affirmative obligations:
To the Seller:
    A Fiduciary duty of utmost care, integrity, honesty, and loyalty in dealings with the Seller.
To the Buyer and the Seller:
    (a) Diligent exercise of reasonable skill and care in performance of the agent's duties.
    (b) A duty of honest and fair dealing and good faith.
    (c) A duty to disclose all facts known to the agent materially affecting the value or desirability of the property that are not known to, or within the diligent attention and observation of, the parties.

An agent is not obligated to reveal to either party any confidential information obtained from the other party that does not involve the affirmative duties set forth above.

BUYER'S AGENT
A selling agent can, with a Buyer's consent, agree to act as agent for the Buyer only. In these situations, the agent is not the Seller's agent, even if by agreement the agent may receive compensation for services rendered, either in full or in part from the Seller. An agent acting only for a Buyer has the following affirmative obligations:
To the Buyer:
    A fiduciary duty of utmost care, integrity, honesty, and loyalty in dealings with the Buyer.
To the Buyer and the Seller:
    (a) Diligent exercise of reasonable skill and care in performance of the agent's duties.
    (b) A duty of honest and fair dealing and good faith.
    (c) A duty to disclose all facts known to the agent materially affecting the value or desirability of the property that are not known to, or within the diligent attention and observation of, the parties.

An agent is not obligated to reveal to either party any confidential information obtained from the other party that does not involve the affirmative duties set forth above.

AGENT REPRESENTING BOTH SELLER AND BUYER
A real estate agent, either acting directly or through one or more associate licensees, can legally be the agent of both the Seller and the Buyer in a transaction, but only with the knowledge and consent of both the Seller and the Buyer.

In a dual agency situation, the agent has the following affirmative obligations to both the Seller and the Buyer:
    (a) A fiduciary duty of utmost care, integrity, honesty and loyalty in the dealings with either the Seller or the Buyer.
    (b) Other duties to the Seller and the Buyer as stated above in their respective sections.

In representing both Seller and Buyer, the agent may not, without the express permission of the respective party, disclose to the other party that the Seller will accept a price less than the listing price or that the Buyer will pay a price greater than the price offered.

The above duties of the agent in a real estate transaction do not relieve a Seller or Buyer from the responsibility to protect his or her own interests. You should carefully read all agreements to assure that they adequately express your understanding of the transaction. A real estate agent is a person qualified to advise about real estate. If legal or tax advice is desired, consult a competent professional.

Throughout your real property transaction you may receive more than one disclosure form, depending upon the number of agents assisting in the transaction. The law requires each agent with whom you have more than a casual relationship to present you with this disclosure form. You should read its contents each time it is presented to you, considering the relationship between you and the real estate agent in your specific transaction.

This disclosure form includes the provisions of Sections 2079.13 to 2079.24, inclusive, of the Civil Code set forth on the reverse hereof. Read it carefully.

I/WE ACKNOWLEDGE RECEIPT OF A COPY OF THIS DISCLOSURE AND THE PORTIONS OF THE CIVIL CODE PRINTED ON THE BACK (OR A SEPARATE PAGE).

BUYER/SELLER _____ Date _____ Time _____ AM/PM

BUYER/SELLER _____ Date _____ Time _____ AM/PM

AGENT _____ By _____ Date _____
    (Please Print)   (Associate-Licensee or Broker Signature)

THIS FORM SHALL BE PROVIDED AND ACKNOWLEDGED AS FOLLOWS (Civil Code § 2079.14):
- When the listing brokerage company also represents Buyer, the Listing Agent shall have one AD form signed by Seller and one signed by Buyer.
- When Buyer and Seller are represented by different brokerage companies, the Listing Agent shall have one AD form signed by Seller and the Buyer's Agent shall have one AD form signed by Buyer and one AD form signed by Seller.

The System for Success®

Published and Distributed by:
REAL ESTATE BUSINESS SERVICES, INC.
a subsidiary of the California Association of REALTORS®
525 South Virgil Avenue, Los Angeles, California 90020

Reviewed by _____ Date _____

EQUAL HOUSING OPPORTUNITY

AD REVISED 10/04 (PAGE 1 OF 1) PRINT DATE

DISCLOSURE REGARDING REAL ESTATE AGENCY RELATIONSHIPS (AD PAGE 1 OF 1)

CIVIL CODE SECTIONS 2079.13 THROUGH 2079.24 (2079.16 APPEARS ON THE FRONT)

2079.13 As used in Sections 2079.14 to 2079.24, inclusive, the following terms have the following meanings:
(a) "Agent" means a person acting under provisions of title 9 (commencing with Section 2295) in a real property transaction, and includes a person who is licensed as a real estate broker under Chapter 3 (commencing with Section 10130) of Part 1 of Division 4 of the Business and Professions Code, and under whose license a listing is executed or an offer to purchase is obtained. **(b)** "Associate licensee" means a person who is licensed as a real broker or salesperson under Chapter 3 (commencing with Section 10130) of Part 1 of Division 4 of the Business and Professions Code and who is either licensed under a broker or has entered into a written contract with a broker to act as the broker's agent in connection with acts requiring a real estate license and to function under the broker's supervision in the capacity of an associate licensee. The agent in the real property transaction bears responsibility for his or her associate licensees who perform as agents of the agent. When an associate licensee owes a duty to any principal, or to any buyer or seller who is not a principal, in a real property transaction, that duty is equivalent to the duty owed to that party by the broker for whom the associate licensee functions. **(c)** "Buyer" means a transferee in a real property transaction, and includes a person who executes an offer to purchase real property from a seller through an agent, or who seeks the services of an agent in more than a casual, transitory, or preliminary manner, with the object of entering into a real property transaction. "Buyer" includes vendee or lessee. **(d)** "Dual agent" means an agent acting, either directly or through an associate licensee, as agent for both the seller and the buyer in a real property transaction. **(e)** "Listing agreement" means a contract between an owner of real property and an agent, by which the agent has been authorized to sell the real property or to find or obtain a buyer. **(f)** "Listing agent" means a person who has obtained a listing of real property to act as an agent for compensation. **(g)** "Listing price" is the amount expressed in dollars specified in the listing for which the seller is willing to sell the real property through the listing agent. **(h)** "Offering price" is the amount expressed in dollars specified in an offer to purchase for which the buyer is willing to buy the real property. **(i)** "Offer to purchase" means a written contract executed by a buyer acting through a selling agent which becomes the contract for the sale of the real property upon acceptance by the seller. **(j)** "Real property" means any estate specified by subdivision (1) or (2) of Section 761 in property which constitutes or is improved with one to four dwelling units, any leasehold in this type of property exceeding one year's duration, and mobilehomes, when offered for sale or sold through an agent pursuant to the authority contained in Section 10131.6 of the Business and Professions Code. **(k)** "Real property transaction" means a transaction for the sale of real property in which an agent is employed by one or more of the principals to act in that transaction, and includes a listing or an offer to purchase. **(l)** "Sell," "sale," or "sold" refers to a transaction for the transfer of real property from the seller to the buyer, and includes exchanges of real property between the seller and buyer, transactions for the creation of a real property sales contract within the meaning of Section 2985, and transactions for the creation of a leasehold exceeding one year's duration. **(m)** "Seller" means the transferor in a real property transaction, and includes an owner who lists real property with an agent, whether or not a transfer results, or who receives an offer to purchase real property of which he or she is the owner from an agent on behalf of another. "Seller" includes both a vendor and a lessor. **(n)** "Selling agent" means a listing agent who acts alone, or an agent who acts in cooperation with a listing agent, and who sells or finds and obtains a buyer for the real property, or an agent who locates property for a buyer or who finds a buyer for a property for which no listing exists and presents an offer to purchase to the seller. **(o)** "Subagent" means a person to whom an agent delegates agency powers as provided in Article 5 (commencing with Section 2349) of Chapter 1 of Title 9. However, "subagent" does not include an associate licensee who is acting under the supervision of an agent in a real property transaction.

2079.14 Listing agents and selling agents shall provide the seller and buyer in a real property transaction with a copy of the disclosure form specified in Section 2079.16, and, except as provided in subdivision (c), shall obtain a signed acknowledgement of receipt from that seller or buyer, except as provided in this section or Section 2079.15, as follows: **(a)** The listing agent, if any, shall provide the disclosure form to the seller prior to entering into the listing agreement. **(b)** The selling agent shall provide the disclosure form to the seller as soon as practicable prior to presenting the seller with an offer to purchase, unless the selling agent previously provided the seller with a copy of the disclosure form pursuant to subdivision (a). **(c)** Where the selling agent does not deal on a face-to-face basis with the seller, the disclosure form prepared by the selling agent may be furnished to the seller (and acknowledgement of receipt obtained for the selling agent from the seller) by the listing agent, or the selling agent may deliver the disclosure form by certified mail addressed to the seller at his or her last known address, in which case no signed acknowledgement of receipt is required. **(d)** The selling agent shall provide the disclosure form to the buyer as soon as practicable prior to execution of the buyer's offer to purchase, except that if the offer to purchase is not prepared by the selling agent, the selling agent shall present the disclosure form to the buyer not later than the next business day after the selling agent receives the offer to purchase from the buyer.

2079.15 In any circumstance in which the seller or buyer refuses to sign an acknowledgement of receipt pursuant to Section 2079.14, the agent, or an associate licensee acting for an agent, shall set forth, sign, and date a written declaration of the facts of the refusal.

2079.17 **(a)** As soon as practicable, the selling agent shall disclose to the buyer and seller whether the selling agent is acting in the real property transaction exclusively as the buyer's agent, exclusively as the seller's agent, or as a dual agent representing both the buyer and the seller. This relationship shall be confirmed in the contract to purchase and sell real property or in a separate writing executed or acknowledged by the seller, the buyer, and the selling agent prior to or coincident with execution of that contract by the buyer and the seller, respectively. **(b)** As soon as practicable, the listing agent shall disclose to the seller whether the listing agent is acting in the real property transaction exclusively as the seller's agent, or as a dual agent representing both the buyer and seller. This relationship shall be confirmed in the contract to purchase and sell real property or in a separate writing executed or acknowledged by the seller and the listing agent prior to or coincident with the execution of that contract by the seller.
(c) The confirmation required by subdivisions (a) and (b) shall be in the following form.

(d) The disclosures and confirmation required by this section shall be in addition to the disclosure required by Section 2079.14.

2079.18 No selling agent in a real property transaction may act as an agent for the buyer only, when the selling agent is also acting as the listing agent in the transaction.

2079.19 The payment of compensation or the obligation to pay compensation to an agent by the seller or buyer is not necessarily determinative of a particular agency relationship between an agent and the seller or buyer. A listing agent and a selling agent may agree to share any compensation or commission paid, or any right to any compensation or commission for which an obligation arises as the result of a real estate transaction, and the terms of any such agreement shall not necessarily be determinative of a particular relationship.

2079.20 Nothing in this article prevents an agent from selecting, as a condition of the agent's employment, a specific form of agency relationship not specifically prohibited by this article if the requirements of Section 2079.14 and Section 2079.17 are complied with.

2079.21 A dual agent shall not disclose to the buyer that the seller is willing to sell the property at a price less than the listing price, without the express written consent of the seller. A dual agent shall not disclose to the seller that the buyer is willing to pay a price greater than the offering price, without the express written consent of the buyer. This section does not alter in any way the duty or responsibility of a dual agent to any principal with respect to confidential information other than price.

2079.22 Nothing in this article precludes a listing agent from also being a selling agent, and the combination of these functions in one agent does not, of itself, make that agent a dual agent.

2079.23 A contract between the principal and agent may be modified or altered to change the agency relationship at any time before the performance of the act which is the object of the agency with the written consent of the parties to the agency relationship.

2079.24 Nothing in this article shall be construed to either diminish the duty of disclosure owed buyers and sellers by agents and their associate licensees, subagents, and employees or to relieve agents and their associate licensees, subagents, and employees from liability for their conduct in connection with acts governed by this article or for any breach of a fiduciary duty or a duty of disclosure.

(AD BACKER)

CALIFORNIA ASSOCIATION OF REALTORS®

CONFIRMATION REAL ESTATE AGENCY RELATIONSHIPS
(As required by the Civil Code)
(C.A.R. Form AC-6, Revised 1987)

Subject Property Address _____

The following agency relationship(s) is/are hereby confirmed for this transaction:

LISTING AGENT: _____

is the agent of (check one):
- ❏ the Seller exclusively; or
- ❏ both the Buyer and Seller

SELLING AGENT: _____

(if not the same as Listing Agent)
is the agent of (check one):
- ❏ the Buyer exclusively; or
- ❏ the Seller exclusively; or
- ❏ both the Buyer and Seller

I/WE ACKNOWLEDGE RECEIPT OF A COPY OF THIS CONFIRMATION.

Seller _____ Date _____ Buyer _____ Date _____

Seller _____ Date _____ Buyer _____ Date _____

Listing Agent _____ By _____ Date _____
(Please Print)   (Associate Licensee or Broker-Signature)

Selling Agent _____ By _____ Date _____
(Please Print)   (Associate Licensee or Broker-Signature)

A REAL ESTATE BROKER IS QUALIFIED TO ADVISE ON REAL ESTATE. IF YOU DESIRE LEGAL ADVICE, CONSULT YOUR ATTORNEY.

This form is available for use by the entire real estate industry. It is not intended to identify the user as a REALTOR®. REALTOR® is a registered collective membership mark which may be used only by members of the NATIONAL ASSOCIATION OF REALTORS® who subscribe to its Code of Ethics.

The copyright laws of the United States (17 U.S. Code) forbid the unauthorized reproduction of this form by any means, including facsimile or computerized formats.
Copyright © 1987-1997, CALIFORNIA ASSOCIATION OF REALTORS®

SURE TRAC
The System for Success®

Published and Distributed by:
REAL ESTATE BUSINESS SERVICES, INC.
a subsidiary of the California Association of REALTORS®
525 South Virgil Avenue, Los Angeles, California 90020

Reviewed by _____ Date _____

EQUAL HOUSING OPPORTUNITY

CONFIRMATION REAL ESTATE AGENCY RELATIONSHIPS (AC-6 PAGE 1 OF 1) REVISED 1987

CALIFORNIA
ASSOCIATION
OF REALTORS®

**MANUFACTURED HOME AND MOBILEHOME:
TRANSFER DISCLOSURE STATEMENT**

(C.A.R. Form MHTDS, Revised 10/99)

THIS DISCLOSURE STATEMENT CONCERNS THE MANUFACTURED HOME OR MOBILEHOME (HEREAFTER REFERRED TO AS "HOME") LOCATED AT _____ IN THE CITY OF _____ COUNTY OF _____, STATE OF CALIFORNIA, DESCRIBED AS _____

| Year | Make | Serial #(s) | HCD Decal # or Equivalent |

THIS STATEMENT IS A DISCLOSURE OF THE CONDITION OF THE ABOVE-DESCRIBED HOME IN COMPLIANCE WITH SUBDIVISION (b) OF SECTION 1102 OF THE CIVIL CODE AND SECTIONS 18025 AND 18046 OF THE HEALTH AND SAFETY CODE AS OF _____.

DATE

IT IS NOT A WARRANTY OF ANY KIND BY THE LAWFUL OWNER OF THE MANUFACTURED HOME OR MOBILEHOME WHO OFFERS THE HOME FOR SALE (HEREAFTER THE SELLER), OR ANY AGENT(S) REPRESENTING ANY PRINCIPAL(S) IN THIS TRANSACTION, AND IS NOT A SUBSTITUTE FOR ANY INSPECTIONS OR WARRANTIES THE PRINCIPAL(S) MAY WISH TO OBTAIN. AN "AGENT" MEANS ANY DEALER OR SALESPERSON LICENSED PURSUANT TO PART 2 (COMMENCING WITH SECTION 18000) OF THE HEALTH AND SAFETY CODE, OR A REAL ESTATE BROKER OR SALESPERSON LICENSED PURSUANT TO DIVISION 4 (COMMENCING WITH SECTION 10000) OF DIVISION 13 OF THE BUSINESS AND PROFESSIONS CODE.

COORDINATION WITH OTHER DISCLOSURES & INFORMATION

This Manufactured Home and Mobilehome Transfer Disclosure Statement is made pursuant to Article 1.5 (commencing with Section 1102) of Chapter 2 of Title 4 of Part 4 of Division 2 of the Civil Code. Other statutes require disclosures, or other information may be important to the prospective buyer, depending upon the details of the particular transaction (including, but not limited to, the condition of the park in which the manufactured home or mobilehome will be located, disclosures required or information provided by the Mobilehome Residency Law, Section 798 of the Civil Code et seq.; the mobilehome park rental agreement or lease; the mobilehome park rules and regulations; and park and lot inspection reports, if any, completed by the state or a local enforcement agency). **Substituted Disclosures:** The following disclosures have or will be made in connection with this transfer, and are intended to satisfy the disclosure obligations of this form, where the subject matter is the same:

☐ Home inspection reports completed pursuant to the contract of sale or receipt for deposit.

☐ Additional inspection reports or disclosures: _____
_____

II

SELLER'S INFORMATION

The Seller discloses the following information with the knowledge that even though this is not a warranty, prospective buyers may rely on this information in deciding whether, and on what terms, to purchase the subject Home. Seller hereby authorizes any agent(s), as defined in Section 18046 of the Health and Safety Code, representing any principal(s) in this transaction to provide a copy of this statement to any person or entity in connection with any actual or anticipated sale of the Home.

THE FOLLOWING ARE REPRESENTATIONS MADE BY THE SELLER(S) AND ARE NOT THE REPRESENTATIONS OF THE AGENT(S), IF ANY, AS DEFINED IN SECTION 18046 OF THE HEALTH AND SAFETY CODE. THIS INFORMATION IS A DISCLOSURE AND IS NOT INTENDED TO BE PART OF ANY CONTRACT BETWEEN THE BUYER AND THE SELLER.

Seller ☐ is ☐ is not occupying the Home.

A. The subject Home includes the items checked below which are being sold with the Home (read across):

☐ Range	☐ Oven	☐ Microwave
☐ Dishwasher	☐ Trash Compactor	☐ Garbage Disposal
☐ Burglar Alarm	☐ Smoke Detectors	☐ Fire Alarm
☐ TV Antenna	☐ Satellite Dish	☐ Intercom
☐ Central Heating	☐ Central Air Conditioning	☐ Wall/Window Air Conditioning
☐ Evaporative Cooler(s)	☐ Sump Pump	☐ Water Softener

(Continued on page 2)

Buyer and Seller acknowledge receipt of copy of this page, which constitutes Page 1 of _____ Pages.
Buyer's Initials (_____) (_____)   Seller's Initials (_____) (_____)

Buyer's Initials (_____)(_____)
Seller's Initials (_____)(_____)

| Reviewed by _____ Date _____ |

EQUAL HOUSING OPPORTUNITY

MHTDS REVISED 10/99 (PAGE 1 OF 3) Print Date

MANUFACTURED HOME TRANSFER DISCLOSURE STATEMENT (MHTDS PAGE 1 OF 3)

Home Address: _____ Date: _____

- ☐ Porch Decking
- ☐ Private Sauna
- ☐ Private Hot Tub
- ☐ Solar/Spa Heater
- ☐ Electric Water Heater
- ☐ Carport Awning
- ☐ Automatic Garage Door Opener(s)*
- ☐ Window Secure Bars
- ☐ Earthquake Resistant Bracing System

- ☐ Porch Awning
- ☐ Private Spa
- ☐ Hot Tub Locking Cover*
- ☐ Gas Water Heater
- ☐ Water Heater Anchored, Braced, or Strapped*
- ☐ Attached Garage
- ☐ # Remote Controls _____
- ☐ Bedroom Window Quick Release Mechanism*
- ☐ Washer/Dryer Hookups

- ☐ Gazebo
- ☐ Spa Locking Safety Cover*
- ☐ Gas/Spa Heater
- ☐ Solar Water Heater
- ☐ Bottled Propane
- ☐ Detached Garage

- ☐ Window Screens
- ☐ Rain Gutters

Exhaust Fan(s) in _____ 220 Volt Wiring in _____
Fireplace(s) in _____ Gas Starter(s) _____
Roof(s) and type(s) _____ Roof Age (Approximate) _____
Other: _____

*If there is an automatic garage door opener or safety cover listed above, it may not be in compliance with the safety standards relating to automatic reversing devices as set forth in Chapter 12.5 (commencing with Section 19890) of Part 3 of Division 13 of the Health and Safety Code, or with the pool safety standards of Article 2.5 (commencing with Section 115920) of Chapter 5 of Part 10 of Division 104 of the Health and Safety Code. The water heater may not be anchored, braced, strapped or secured in accordance with Section 19211 of the Health and Safety Code. Window security bars may not have quick-release mechanisms in compliance with the 1995 edition of the California Building Standards Code.

Are there, to the best of your (Seller's) knowledge, any of the above that are not in operating condition? ☐ Yes ☐ No. If yes, then describe. (Attach additional sheets if necessary): _____
_____

B. Are you (the Seller) aware of any significant defects/malfunctions in any of the following in connection with the Home? ☐ Yes ☐ No. If yes, check appropriate space(s) below:

☐ Interior Walls, ☐ Ceilings, ☐ Floors, ☐ Exterior Walls, ☐ Insulation, ☐ Roof(s), ☐ Windows, ☐ Doors, ☐ Home Electrical Systems, ☐ Plumbing, ☐ Porch or Deck, ☐ Porch Steps & Railings, ☐ Other Steps & Railings, ☐ Porch Awning, ☐ Carport Awning. ☐ Other Awnings, ☐ Skirting, ☐ Home Foundation or Support System, ☐ Other Structural Components (Describe: _____
_____
_____)

If any of the above is checked, explain. (Attach additional sheets if necessary) _____
_____

C. Are you (the Seller) aware of any of the following:
1. Substances, materials, or products which may be an environmental hazard, such as, but not limited to, asbestos, formaldehyde, radon gas, lead-based paint, or chemical storage tanks on the subject home interior or exterior.......... ☐ Yes ☐ No
2. Room additions, structural modifications, or other alterations or repairs made without necessary permits .... ☐ Yes ☐ No
3. Room additions, structural modifications, or other alterations or repairs not in compliance with applicable codes......... ☐ Yes ☐ No
4. Any settling from slippage, sliding or problems with leveling of the home or the foundation or support system........... ☐ Yes ☐ No
5. Drainage or grading problems with the home, space or lot.. ☐ Yes ☐ No
6. Damage to the home or accessory structures being sold with the home from fire, flood, earthquake, or landslides........ ☐ Yes ☐ No
7. Any notices of abatement or citations against the home or accessory structures being sold with the home.......... ☐ Yes ☐ No
8. Any lawsuits by or against the seller threatening to or affecting the home or the accessory structures being sold with the home, including any lawsuits alleging any defect or deficiency in the home or accessories sold with the home....... ☐ Yes ☐ No
9. Neighborhood noise problems or other nuisances .... ☐ Yes ☐ No
10. Any encroachment, easement, nonconforming use or violation of setback requirements with the home, accessory structures being sold with the home, or space .... ☐ Yes ☐ No

If the answer to any of these is yes, explain. (Attach additional sheets if necessary): _____
_____
_____

Seller certifies that the information herein is true and correct to the best of the Seller's knowledge as of the date signed by the Seller.

Seller _____ Date _____

Seller _____ Date _____

Buyer's Initials (_____)(_____)
Seller's Initials (_____)(_____)

MHTDS REVISED 10/99 (PAGE 2 OF 3)

Reviewed by _____ Date _____

MANUFACTURED HOME TRANSFER DISCLOSURE STATEMENT (MHTDS PAGE 2 OF 3)

Property Address: _____ Date: _____

III
AGENT'S INSPECTION DISCLOSURE
(To be completed only if the Seller is represented by an Agent in this transaction.)

THE UNDERSIGNED, BASED ON THE ABOVE INQUIRY OF THE SELLER(S) AS TO THE CONDITION OF THE HOME AND BASED ON A REASONABLY COMPETENT AND DILIGENT VISUAL INSPECTION OF THE ACCESSIBLE AREAS OF THE HOME IN CONJUNCTION WITH THAT INQUIRY, STATES THE FOLLOWING:

☐ Agent notes no items for disclosure.
☐ Agent notes the following items: _____
_____
_____
_____

Agent
Representing Seller _____ By _____ Date _____
           (Please Print)   (Signature)

IV
AGENT'S INSPECTION DISCLOSURE
(To be completed only if the agent who has obtained the offer is other than the Agent above.)

THE UNDERSIGNED, BASED ON A REASONABLY COMPETENT AND DILIGENT VISUAL INSPECTION OF THE ACCESSIBLE AREAS OF THE HOME, STATES THE FOLLOWING:

☐ Agent notes no items for disclosure.
☐ Agent notes the following items: _____
_____
_____
_____

Agent
Representing Buyer _____ By _____ Date _____
           (Please Print)   (Signature)

V

BUYER(S) AND SELLER(S) MAY WISH TO OBTAIN PROFESSIONAL ADVICE AND/OR INSPECTIONS OF THE HOME AND TO PROVIDE FOR APPROPRIATE PROVISIONS IN A CONTRACT BETWEEN THE BUYER(S) AND SELLER(S) WITH RESPECT TO ANY ADVICE/INSPECTIONS/DEFECTS.

I/WE ACKNOWLEDGE RECEIPT OF A COPY OF THIS STATEMENT.

Seller _____ Date _____   Buyer _____ Date _____

Seller _____ Date _____   Buyer _____ Date _____

Agent
Representing Seller _____ By _____ Date _____
           (Please Print)   (Signature)

Agent
Representing Buyer _____ By _____ Date _____
           (Please Print)   (Signature)

VI

SECTION 1102.3a OF THE CIVIL CODE PROVIDES A PROSPECTIVE BUYER WITH THE RIGHT TO RESCIND THE PURCHASE OF THE MANUFACTURED HOME OR MOBILEHOME FOR AT LEAST THREE DAYS AFTER DELIVERY OF THIS DISCLOSURE, IF DELIVERY OCCURS AFTER THE SIGNING OF AN OFFER TO PURCHASE. IF YOU WISH TO RESCIND THE CONTRACT, YOU MUST ACT WITHIN THE PRESCRIBED PERIOD.

A MANUFACTURED HOME OR MOBILEHOME DEALER OR A REAL ESTATE BROKER IS QUALIFIED TO PROVIDE ADVICE ON THE SALE OF A MANUFACTURED HOME OR MOBILEHOME. IF YOU DESIRE LEGAL ADVICE, CONSULT YOUR ATTORNEY.

SURE TRAC
The System for Success®

Published and Distributed by:
REAL ESTATE BUSINESS SERVICES, INC.
a subsidiary of the California Association of REALTORS®
525 South Virgil Avenue, Los Angeles, California 90020

MHTDS REVISED 10/99 (PAGE 3 OF 3)

Reviewed by _____ Date _____

EQUAL HOUSING OPPORTUNITY

MANUFACTURED HOME TRANSFER DISCLOSURE STATEMENT (MHTDS PAGE 3 OF 3)

Agency Confirmation

The selling agent's relationship must be confirmed in writing in the purchase contract (or in a separate document acknowledged by the buyer, seller and selling agent) before or at the time of execution of the purchase contract.

Just as the selling agent has to confirm his or her relationship, the listing agent must do the same. It must be in writing on either the purchase contract or a separate document acknowledged by the buyer, seller and listing agent.

O S T E N S I B L E   A G E N C Y

We know from earlier in this chapter that there are three ways to establish an agency agreement with a client. The most obvious way to do this is with an express contract, usually in writing with the consent of both parties. Although this is the most common way to establish agency in California, an agent must be very careful, because he or she can establish an agency through his or her actions. Ostensible agency is similar to estoppel. An agent may establish an agency with a customer by his or her actions. When or if this happens, the agent must be very careful to follow the laws of disclosure and agency very closely.

A selling agent is always responsible to his or her client. He or she must conduct all negotiations in the best interest of the seller with care, honesty, loyalty and integrity. Additionally, the agent must be fair and honest by fully disclosing any information regarding the transaction or property to all involved parties. As you can see, it is difficult for an agent to honor the fiduciary responsibility to the seller while meeting all obligations owed to the buyer.

Because of the principle of estoppel, the principal may not deny the agent from establishing a dual agency with the buyer. This means that the agent must act very carefully and be mindful of all of his or her actions in order to avoid any misunderstands, or give the impression of implied agency. If the agent is also aiding the buyer, the agent must avoid violating the agency they have established with the seller. Agents must not make statements disclosing the seller's bottom line or guarantee that an offer will be accepted based on their knowledge of the seller(s).

It may be confusing to understand all the aspects of agency. You may not quite understand how an agent can represent the seller but still aid the buyer without establishing an ostensible (implied) agency relationship with the buyer as well. If an agent does not wish to become the buyers agent, but wishes to fulfill their duty of honest and fair dealing with the buyer, he or she may show a buyer properties, explain any amenities that come with the property, and keep the buyer abreast to the condition and status of the property. An agent may also complete the purchase contract making sure that the buyer's terms are correctly inserted into the contract, and deliver it to the seller. Additionally an agent may alert a buyer to different options they have with regard to financing, legal services, inspections and title companies available to aid in completion of a transaction. While the broker is allowed to conduct all of the above tasks for a buyer, he or she needs to carefully monitor his or her conduct so as not to establish an implied agency .

> **Remember:**
> Agents must be very mindful of their conduct because it is easy to establish an implied agency with a buyer in the course of fulfilling duties requiring fair dealing and full disclosure.

The multiple listing service (MLS) is an organization of real estate professionals that receives information on available property listings and then publishes this list of available properties to all members. Listings of properties are submitted to the MLS and a computerized list is generated for its members. This process benefits both the sellers and buyers. The sellers benefit because many more agents will see their properties, increasing the likelihood of bringing in qualified buyers for the available property. Buyers benefit from the MLS because they have a wider choice of suitable properties from which to select. These properties may be preferable to those properties represented by the brokerage or firm with whom they are working.

Remember!

The MLS benefits both buyers and sellers. It increases the visibility of the seller's listing (thus recruiting more qualified buyers), while providing buyers with more options when conducting their home search.

Sellers have the option of listing their property with the MLS. By doing so, they provide valuable information to other brokers or agents searching for property for qualified buyers of their own. The information listed in the MLS posting will inform other agents of the asking price of the property, list any amenities the property may include, provide a legal description of the property and alert the broker or agent as to when and how the property may be shown. In addition to this information, the MLS posting will also reveal the commission that the listing agent will receive upon sale of the property. Brokers or agents who find a ready, willing and able buyer based on an MLS listing are entitled to a portion of the commission generated from a sale.

At times, disputes may arise from MLS postings. More than one agent may show the same client the same property listed on the MLS. If this buyer is ready, willing and able to purchase the property and ultimately makes an offer, there may be a dispute between the agents as to who earned the commission on the sale. The law dictates that the agent who actually wrote the offer is entitled to the commission. All other brokers and agents, whether they had prior knowledge of one another, are **not** entitled to a share in the commission because they were not able to bring the client to the point of sale, when an offer is made.

COOPERATING AGENTS AND BROKERS

Cooperating agents are agents who assist the listing agent in the sale of a piece of property. A cooperating agent may also be an agent who is trying to sell a piece of property currently listed with another agent. Cooperating agents are entitled to a share of the commission that the listing agent makes at the close of escrow. Cooperating agents are sometimes referred to as subagents of the listing agent.

Sellers authorize their agent to cooperate with other brokers in showing the seller's property. This does not authorize the listing agent to designate a subagent; but it does allow brokers to show each other's listings as posted on the MLS. The listing agent may offer subagency to the cooperating broker with the permission of the principal.

The cooperating agent may choose to accept or decline this offer, but any offers made in this capacity must be made in writing. If a cooperating broker chooses to become a subagent of the listing broker, the cooperating broker becomes an agent of the principal and thereby owes fiduciary responsibility to the seller. The cooperating agent may choose to represent the buyer or seller, provided that disclosure is made to all parties. This is important because all parties must have knowledge of who is representing them. Depending on the licensee's choice, he or she must make sure that his or her actions are indicative of the decision as to whom they chose to represent. The licensee must also keep in mind that there are legal consequences, conflict of loyalty and real estate laws to consider in making this choice.

If the cooperating agent decides to serve as agent of the buyer, the buyer becomes the principal and the seller becomes the third party. When making an offer on a piece of property, the buyer must sign confirmation of agency forms. This confirms the agency relationship he or she has with the cooperating agent. At this point, the cooperating agent owes fiduciary responsibility to the buyer, and must act in the best interest of the buyer, who is now a client.

The Orange County Association of Realtors defines subagency in the rule.

7.12 Unilateral Contractual Offer; Subagency Optional.

In filing a property with the MLS, the broker participant makes a blanket, unilateral contractual offer of compensation to the other MLS broker participants for their services in selling the property. A broker participant must specify some compensation to be paid to either a buyer's agent or a subagent. The offer of compensation must be stated in one or more of the following ways:

    (1) a percentage of the gross selling price
    (2) a definite dollar amount

At the broker participant's option, a broker participant may limit his or her offer of compensation to buyer's agents only, to subagents only, or both the buyer's agent and subagents. Any such limitations must be specified on the property data form as well as the MLS. The amount of compensation offered to buyer's agents or subagents may be the same or different; but the amount must be clearly specified on the property data profile sheet. Broker participants wishing to offer subagency to the other MLS participants must specify this on the property data profile sheet and on the MLS. If this is not done, the offer of compensation does not constitute an offer of subagency.

A G E N T ' S   A U T H O R I T Y

When an agent enters into a listing agreement with the principal, the client authorizes the agent to act on his or her behalf to find a ready, willing and able buyer. This does not mean that the agent has total authority; as there are certain restrictions by which the agent must abide. Lets look now at some of the restrictions that an agent may face when representing a principal.

(www.//leginfo.ca.gov California law – civil code, agency)

1. A principal is not responsible for the acts of the agent if said acts are beyond | the agent's actual authority. If the principal has not given the agent actual or ostensible authority to commit the act, a third party cannot hold the principal responsible for any adverse result of those actions.

2. An agent may have authority under a power of attorney, allowing him or her to conduct certain business for a principal. Both the special power of attorney and the general power of attorney authorize the agent to perform certain specific duties. However, a general power of attorney also allows the agent to transact all business of the principal. The agent is functioning as attorney in fact.

3. A broker cannot accept a deposit from a buyer unless specifically authorized to do so in the listing agreement. When an agent does so without authorization from the seller, he or she is acting as an agent of the buyer and not as an agent of the seller. Any misappropriation of these funds by the broker will result in loss to the buyer as opposed to the seller. However, most listing agreements do allow the agent to receive the buyer's deposit on behalf of the seller. This authority given to the agent also applies to any subagents, unless the subagent is already working as an agent of the buyer.

4. An agent may not return a buyer's deposit after the seller accepts the buyer's unless the seller has given consent.

5. The acceptance of a check as an earnest money deposit must be disclosed to the seller at the time the offer is presented. This does not apply if the earnest money deposit is in the form of cash or a promissory note. If the buyer instructs the agent to hold the check until the offer is accepted, this fact must also be disclosed to the seller when the offer is presented.

6. An agent who puts a client's money in his or her own personal bank account is guilty of *commingling*. Checks must be deposited into a trust account or a neutral escrow account by the next business day after they have been received. If an agent spends a client's money, the agent is guilty of *conversion*.

DUTIES OF AN AGENT TO THE PRINCIPAL

There are several duties an agent owes the principal. Perhaps the most important of them is loyalty. An agent will act as the fiduciary (a person in whom power is entrusted on behalf of someone else). An agent's first duty in a transaction is to consider the interests of the principal. The agent may or may not benefit financially from this fiduciary relationship. If there is a previously agreed upon commission, the agent will receive payment for his or her actions. If the agent is working on no commission, he or she must still abide by the duties of fiduciary in dealings with the principal. As a fiduciary, the agent is bound by law to show good faith, loyalty and honesty to the principal.

Another duty an agent has to the principal is to make full disclosure of all facts concerning the transaction. Agents should bring qualified buyers to view the property and assess their intentions in buying the property. The agent must then reveal to the principal any information disclosed by the buyer. These may include: time frame, financial situations or other important information that would affect the seller's decision to accept or reject potential offers from that particular customer. This is, at times, in direct conflict with the agent's interests, as an agent often benefits from the sale of a property (for instance, in the form of a commission). If the agent finds qualified buyers with restrictions such as timeframe or other sensitive areas, which would give the seller an advantage in the bargaining process, the buyer may try to find other properties. This leaves the agent to find a new, qualified buyer, which may prolong the earning of a commission.

Other disclosures that must be made to the seller pertain to the possible conflict of interest between the agent and the principal. This includes any personal relationships an agent may have with a potential customer. For example, the broker may be interested in purchasing the principal's property, or may have a personal relationship with the possible buyer. This information must be disclosed to the seller. Secret profit is not allowed in any real estate transaction. Secret profit would occur if full disclosure was not made. An agent's failure to fully disclose all material facts to the principal will be considered a violation of the law.

Most listing agreements authorize the agent to accept deposits on behalf of the principal. Agents need to be certain that they have the authorization to perform such actions. If an agent accepts a deposit on behalf of the principal, but was not authorized by the seller to do so, the agent becomes the buyer's agent. .Agents must also obtain permission from the principal before accepting a postdated check as a deposit. Deposits never belong to the agent. Such monies should always be placed into a separate account (earmarked for earnest money deposits).

Example of Agency Disclosure

Broker Aaron is the listing agent for Mr. and Mrs. Smith. Aaron discovers that the home the Smith's are selling would be perfect for his family. Aaron knows that if he finds a ready, willing and able buyer, he may make a commission.

Is Aaron allowed by law to make an offer on the Smith house?

Yes. However, Aaron must disclose to the Smiths his interest in the property. He must also reveal that he will be representing himself as a principal and that he stands to earn a commission upon the close of escrow.

The agent also owes obedience to the principal. Agents usually work in an unrestricted fashion (yet still within the letter of the law) to find a ready, willing and able buyer. However, there are certain perimeters an agent must observe, which constitute obedience toward the principal. For instance, an agent must consult with the seller regarding days or times when a principal may show the property for sale. The seller should not sacrifice his or her privacy and should be aware of the times when the home will be open to potential buyers for viewing. The principal will agree upon days or times to have the home ready for showing, and the agent must comply with the seller's schedule.

Duties of an Agent to the Principal:
- Fiduciary
- Loyalty
- Good Faith
- Honesty
- Obedience
- Full Disclosure

The main goal an agent has in any listing agreement is to find a qualified ready, willing and able buyer for the listed property. Upon finding a buyer who has both the financing secured at the time of closing and a proper purchase contract, the agent's duties are complete. If the buyer makes an offer that differs from the seller's original requirements, the seller has the option to either accept or reject the changes or stipulations. If the changes are accepted, a new contract is created. Upon mutual acceptance of the contract, the agent's obligations are complete and he or she may be eligible for the previously agreed-upon commission.

It is important to note that if there is any sub-agent in the transaction, said subagent owes the principal the same duties as the agent. The subagent owes the agent these same duties, as well. If the subagent acts improperly, the agent is held responsible for these improper actions. However, if the principal authorized the subagent to act in a specific way, the principal would share in the liability of any damages caused by the subagent's actions.

DUTIES OF AN AGENT TO THE BUYER OR THIRD PARTY

An agent must, without exception, disclose all material facts to the customer or third party. Even if instructed not to disclose these material facts by the principal, the agent is legally responsible for full disclosure. Material facts regarding a property include information regarding the structure or defects in the property. An agent may be held responsible for any misrepresentation made regarding the property.

Civil Code Section 1710.2. Material Facts Provision:

A material fact can be anything that affects the value or desirability of the subject property. Because this is such a broad definition, the legislature and courts have created their own interpretations of what the prospective purchaser must know about a property. Of course, conspicuous physical defects must be revealed; but, it is not always easy to determine what other facts must be revealed.
It is not necessary, for instance, to reveal a death on the premises if it occurred more than three years before an offer to purchase or lease the property is made. Nevertheless, the agent handling such a property may not make a misrepresentation if asked a direct question by the buyer, which might reveal the fact of death. The agent, however, need not reveal that an occupant of the property was afflicted with, or died from, AIDS.

An agent has a duty to act with honesty and fairness when dealing with all third parties. Accidentally blurring the truth, or blatantly misrepresenting a property is a violation of the law. Agents must be very careful not to misrepresent any material facts to third parties; as the agent is liable in such cases and may have to pay monetary damages to the third party or place their license in jeopardy as a result of their misconduct. An agent is protected, however, from any misrepresentation made by the principal. For example, if a principal does not tell the agent that there is a leak in the roof, and the agent then does not disclose this to the customer, the agent cannot be held responsible for the principal's misrepresentation.

There are three types of misrepresentation: innocent misrepresentation, negligent misrepresentation and fraudulent misrepresentation.

- Innocent misrepresentations are statements made regarding property that are not known to be false at the time they are made. Agents are not held liable for mis representations of this nature, though the injured party may elect to cancel the purchase contract.

- Negligent misrepresentations are statements made with no material facts to back them up. For example, an agent may tell a prospective buyer that the roof was newly installed five years ago when he or she has no real knowledge of the age of the roof. In such cases, an agent may be held liable for such statements.

- Fraudulent misrepresentations are false statements made by the agent despite the fact that the truth is known.

Puffing is also a form of misrepresentation to which an agent must be careful not to fall prey. An agent may make a false statement regarding a property if he or she believes it will aid in selling the property. An agent may be held responsible for any damages caused as a result of these statements.

An 'as is' clause in a contract does not eliminate the broker's responsibility of disclosure to the buyer. Even if a contract contains an 'as is' clause the broker must disclose all material facts to the buyer(s) just as if there were no 'as is' clause in place. The broker may be held liable for damages suffered due to a withholding of facts regarding the property.

The court case of *Easton v. Strassburger* (1984) expanded the agent's duty of full disclosure to third parties. This case dealt with a home built over a landfill. The agent noticed that there were uneven floors on the property. The verdict in this case not only made it mandatory for an agent to disclose any defects in the property that they could visually identify; it also required sellers to disclose to the agent any defects that could not be identified through a casual visual inspection. As a result of this case, agents are now required to make a competent inspection of a property and disclose their findings to all third parties.

When advertising property, agents must be careful not to make statements, which may lead customers to believe that the agent's opinions are fact. For example, an agent whose advertisement for homes in a new neighborhood claims the neighborhood is in the best school district in the city must be able to back up this claim with raw data (such as standardized test scores comparing the performance of students in its own and other school districts). If there is no data present to back up such claims, an agent may be held liable for his or her statements.

Agents are not only responsible for their own misrepresentation; they are also responsible for any misrepresentations made by their principal. The principal is responsible for his or her own actions, the acts of an agent or subagent on behalf of the principal, and torts committed by an agent who is an employee of the principal. Principles utilizing an independent contractor, however, are not held responsible for the actions of the contractor.

A recovery account was set up in California to aid those victims of fraud or misrepresentation in real estate. The account is designed for those who cannot collect from a licensee after a court judgment. The recovered account allows individuals to collect up to $20,000 per transaction and $100,000 per licensee. The money for the recovery fund comes from license fees collected from each licensee's license fee (currently 5% of the total fee) is placed in the recovery account for damage restitution. Recovery against a licensee will result in immediate suspension of his or her license. The license is reinstated when the licensee repays the recovery account in full (plus any interest that may have accrued).

Five percent of every licensee's license fee is placed in a recovery account designed to protect individuals from fraud or misrepresentation.

DUTIES OF A PRINCIPAL AGENT (RIGHTS OF AN AGENT)

Once an agent has fulfilled the contractual obligations of a listing, he or she is entitled to the agreed-upon commission. Fulfilling these obligations means finding a ready, willing and able buyer who meets all of the seller's requirements. In addition a written offer, signed by both parties, must be produced.

In a situation where there are many different brokers showing potential customers the same property, the agent receiving compensation must be the broker who procured the sale of the home. The procuring broker is the one who presented the qualified buyer to the seller and wrote the accepted offer.

Commissions are usually paid as a percentage of the selling price of the property. This also applies to rental properties where the commission is a percentage of the rental fee for those properties compensating the manager in this way. Commissions are earned when the agent both procures a ready, willing and able buyer who meets all the qualifications set forth by the seller as well as when the seller has accepted a purchase contract. This includes all counter offers or changes to the original purchase contract. All negotiations must be complete and acceptable to the seller.

Commissions are earned when:
- The agent finds a ready, willing and able buyer who meets all of the seller's terms (including the asking price of the seller)
- An offer has been made and a contract has been secured that meets all terms of the seller.

In an agency agreement, if the seller decides to cancel the agency, he or she is allowed, but may be held liable for any or all of the agent's commission. If the seller maintains an open listing and a broker other than the listing broker procures the sale of the home, the procuring broker, rather than the listing agent, will receive a commission. If the listing broker utilizes an exclusive authorization and right-to-sell listing agreement, that broker will make a commission regardless of which agent actually sells the home. Brokers generally work with each other in the sale of homes. If there are two brokers involved in the sale of a property, the commission is usually split between the listing broker and the broker who procured the sale.

A principle owes his or her agent the duty of care. This means that the principal may not sabotage the agent in securing a ready, willing and able buyer for the property For instance, the principal may not make a private deal with the person the agent has secured to buy the property (cutting the agent out of the process). When a broker produces a buyer who meets all of the seller's terms, a commission is earned by the broker.

Commissions are not set by law. Rather, commissions are a negotiable amount agreed upon by the listing agent and the principal. California does not regulate the maximum or minimum amount a broker may charge a principal. Instead, it is left to the individual agent to decide.

CANCELLATION OF AGENCY

Both the agent and the principal have the authority to cancel the agency agreement at any time without the consent of the other party. The canceling party must be careful, however, as they will be responsible for any damages the other party suffers as a result of the cancellation. Additionally, all third parties or customers that are involved in a potential transaction must be made aware that the agency has been cancelled.

Ways to cancel an agency:
- Full performance of the agency agreement
- Expiration of the term of the agency agreement
- Destruction of the property
- Agreement between both the principal and agent
- Death of the principal or agent
- Through operation of the law (such as bankruptcy)
- Incapacity of the agent to act as such or incapacity of the principal to enter into a contract.

REAL ESTATE TRANSFER DISCLOSURE STATEMENT

Beginning January 1, 1987 the California State Legislature required all sellers of property consisting of one to four units to supply the buyer with a real estate transfer disclosure statement. This statement tells the exactly buyer what the seller knows about the condition of a property. All current defects or potential problems that could affect the value of the property (as well as the future value of the property) must be mentioned in the transfer disclosure statement. This statement must be given to all potential buyers before an offer is presented. Otherwise, the buyer has the right to rescind the offer within three business days.

SUMMARY

An agency relationship establishes the authority of a licensee or agent as a special agent or general agent to act on behalf of the principal or client in dealing with third parties. The agent is authorized by the principal to lawfully find a ready, willing and able buyer for the listing held by the agent. The listing agreement allows the agent to accept deposits on the listing; but, any special circumstances (such as post-dated checks) must be cleared with the principal. Otherwise, the agent becomes an agent of the buyer, or third party. Listing agreements also authorize the agent to split any commission with cooperating agents or brokers.

Agents may be an employee or independent contractor of the principal. Usually, brokers are considered independent contractors who are working for the agent to achieve a desired end result. Any salesperson working for the broker is considered, by law, an employee of the broker, yet the salesperson is compensated as if they were an independent contractor. Independent contractors are generally paid in one lump sum (such as a commission), while employees are most often paid with a salary (and, perhaps, additional benefits).

Agents list their properties with the Multiple Listing Service (MLS) to increase their listing's visibility in the marketplace. The MLS is an association of real estate agents who place properties for sale in one central database (searchable by other MLS members). When a cooperating broker sells an agent's listing, the commission is usually split between the cooperating broker and agent.

Single agents will represent only their principal in a real estate transaction; while dual agents will represent both parties the buyer and the seller. All agents are required to provide written disclosure statements to their clients to delineate who is representing whom in the transaction. Agents who represent their principals do so by power of attorney. This power grants them authority to act on behalf of the principal.

Agents owe fiduciary responsibility to the client and are therefore required, by law, to fully disclose all facts regarding a property to a client. This includes any facts the agent discovers regarding the intention of the customer, as well as any conflict of interest and options the agent may decide to exercise. Agents are prohibited by law from making any secret profit. Full disclosure will prevent such secret profit. In addition to fiduciary responsibility to the principal, agents must also make full disclosure regarding material facts to all third parties. It is the duty of both agents and third parties to inspect the property to determine its condition.

Agencies are established in one of three ways: *agreement, ratification* or *estoppel.* Most agency agreements in California are written, express agreements. Agents are bound to these contracts and may be held liable for severing the agency agreement. The same is true for the principal --if the principal severs the agency agreement, he or she may be liable for some or all of the agent's commission. In the state of California, third parties who have suffered damages from an agent's misconduct may be compensated from a recovery account. This account is funded by licensee fees. If a licensee has caused a third party to collect from the recovery account, that licensee's license will be suspended. The licensee will also be required to re pay the money to the recovery account.

T E R M S   A N D   P H R A S E S

Actual Authority - the authority of an agent, specified in the agency agreement.

Agency - a relationship in which one party (the principal) authorizes another party (the agent) to act as the principal's representative in dealing with third parties or customers in a real estate transaction

Agency Confirmation Form - a written document acknowledged by the seller, buyer, selling agent or listing agent at the time a written contract is executed.

Agency Disclosure Form - a written document that explains both the various relationships of all parties involved in a residential property sale as well as whom the agent is representing in the transaction.

Agent - a person acting on behalf of the principal when dealing with a third party in a real estate transaction

Apparent Authority – an agent who appears to have authority despite the fact that he or she actually has none.

Associate Licensee - a licensee employed by a broker

Attorney in Fact - a competent person with no personal connection to the transaction authorized by another to act in his or her place

Bilateral Contract - contract where each party has a separate obligation to perform as provided in the contract

Commingling - depositing a client's funds into a broker's personal account

Compensation - the payment for having fulfilled all obligations of an agency agreement, (usually in the form of a commission on the sale of a property)

Conflict of Interest - actions or interests an agent has in property that must be disclosed to the principal. (e.g., dual representation or personal relationships with the third party in a sale, for example)

Cooperating Brokers - agents working in concert to sell property listed for sale by another agent

Cooperating Split - the cooperating broker's share of the commission the listing broker receives from the sale of a property

Dual Agency - an agent who represents both parties in a real estate transaction

Due Diligence - acting with the appropriate degree of skill and care in fulfilling one's responsibilities under an agency or other contractual relationship

Duty of Care - the promise of a principal not to interfere with the agent's prospective economic advantage in finding a ready, willing and able buyer (for instance, by conducting separate negotiations with the third party unknown to the agent

Employer and Employee - an agency agreement where the agent, or salesperson, works as an employee of the principal (broker), or the employer

Equal Dignities Rule - an express agency agreement established by action, rather than in writing (i.e., not in word, but in deed). Agencies which permit an agent to establish agency in this way must establish a written contract to the principal

Estoppel - a legal doctrine preventing a person from denying something to be true or a fact which is contrary to previous statements made by that same person

Exclusive Agency Listing - a listing with an agent which prevents the principal from listing the same property with other agents during the same time period

Exclusive Authorization and Right-to-Sell Listing - a type of listing in which the broker is entitled to a commission (generally split between the listing broker and the cooperating broker), regardless of who sells the property. This is the most common listing agreement in California.

Express Agreement - an agreement established by an act acknowledged by both parties.

Fiduciary - a type of relationship that implies trust or confidence between parties

Full Disclosure – revilement of all material facts to parties involved in a real estate transaction

General Agent - an agent granted authority to carry out several transactions for one client

General Power of Attorney – authorization of an agent to conduct all of the business dealings of the principal

Good Faith and Honesty - the fulfillment of an agent's duties in fairly representing a principal's interest(s)

Implied Agency – an action of a principal that causes a third party to rely on the representation of an agency relationship

Independent Contractor - a person (employed by another) with nearly complete freedom to accomplish the purpose of the employment (usually, the employment agreement between principals and listing agents)

Inherent Authority - the authority of an agent to perform activities that are not specifically mentioned in the agency agreement yet are necessary or customary to carry out an authorized act

Loyalty – an important duty of an agent to reassure the principal that the agent is acting in his or her best interest in any real estate matters (and thus placing them above all other third parties in a negotiation or transaction)

Multiple Listing Clause - the clause in a listing agreement [usually part of an exclusive authorization and right-to-sell listing, and taken by a member of a multiple-listing service (MLS)], which provides that a property will be made available through the MLS to participating brokers, (and in accordance with MLS rules)

Multiple Listing Service (MLS) - an organization of real estate agents which provides for a pool of listings for the sharing of commissions on transactions involving more than one agent

Net Listing - a listing agreement which provides that the agent may retain (as compensation for his or her services) all sums received over and above a net price supplied to the owner of a property

Obedience - an agent's duty to the principal to follow all wishes and guidelines set forth by the principal regarding a listing agreement. (and in which the principal cannot obstruct the agent's activities, but may offer general direction)

Open Listing – a nonexclusive listing and right given by a property owner to a real estate agent to secure a purchaser,. Note that more than one agent may be given such authorization, but only the first to either procure a ready, willing, and able buyer or an offer acceptable to the seller will be entitled to compensation

Option Listing – grants the broker the right to purchase the property that is listed

Ostensible Agency - holding out an agency relationship on which another relies

Power of Attorney - a written instrument that authorizes an agent to act in the capacity of the principal and provides authority to carry out all business dealings of the principal (in contrast to special power of attorney which provides authority to carry out only a specific act or acts).

Principal - the employer of an agent and one of the parties to a transaction

Procuring Cause - the cause of a series of events that lead directly to an intended objective (in a real estate transaction, the procuring cause is the agent who first procures a ready, willing, and able buyer)

Prospective Economic Advantage - the idea that an agent stands to gain compensation from finding a ready, willing and able buyer who meets the seller's terms

Puffing - exaggerated comments or opinions not made as representations of fact, and thus not grounds for misrepresentation

Ratification - the adoption or approval of an act by the person on whose behalf it was performed (as when a principal ratifies conduct of an agent that was not previously authorized)

Ready, Willing, and Able Buyer - a buyer who wants and is prepared to purchase property, and is able to finance the purchase at an agreed-upon price and terms

Real Estate Transfer Disclosure Statement - a written statement, which the seller is required to give the buyer, regarding details of the mechanical and structural condition of a property

Reasonable Care and Skill - a duty owed by an agent to a principal in carrying out the tasks dictated by an agency agreement (a duty owed even if representing a principal at no cost)

Recovery Account - state fund, financed by real estate license fees, intended to help compensate victims of real estate licensee fraud, misrepresentation, deceit, or conversion of trust funds, in the event that a court-ordered judgment cannot be collected from the party committing the fraud

Red Flag - that which would warn a reasonably observant person of a potential problem and thus require further investigation

Safety Clause - provision that protects a listing broker's commission in the event that a property is sold within a stated period to someone who was first brought to the property during the term of the listing by another agent.

Secret Profit - any compensation an agent stands to gain without the principal's knowledge (and is not allowed by the law of disclosure)

Single Agency - representation of only one party to a transaction (e.g., a seller's agent or buyer's agent)

Special Agent – an agent appointed to carry out only one single act or transaction.

Special Power of Attorney - power granted an agent the power to carry out a specific act or acts

Subagent - an agent of a person who is already acting as agent for the principal

Third Party - a person who may be affected by the terms of an agreement but who is not a party to the agreement itself

Tort - a negligent or intentional wrongful act arising from breach of duty created by law and not by contract

Unilateral Contract – a contract wherein only one party has an obligation under agreement of a contract

C H A P T E R   Q U I Z

1. What term best describes an agent's responsibility to the client?
   A. Fiduciary
   B. Authority
   C. Exclusive
   D. Estoppel

2. A broker who takes an option on his or her own listing is conducting the transaction:
   A. As a third party
   B. As a subagent
   C. Through power of attorney
   D. At arms length

3. An agent who represents both the buyer and the seller has what type of agency?
   A. Dual Agency
   B. Estoppel
   C. Ratification
   D. Flexibility

4. The listing agent must fully disclose all facts to
   A. The buyer
   B. The seller
   C. Both the buyer and seller
   D. Neither the buyer nor seller

5. Ostensible agency is most closely related to
   A. Ratification
   B. Agreement
   C. Estoppel
   D. None of the above

6. Which of the following is NOT a way to create an agency?
   A. Agreement
   B. Contract
   C. Ratification
   D. Estoppel

7. Agents can place their listings on what service to allow all its members to see the available listing?
   A. Commingling
   B. Open Listing Service
   C. Multiple Listing Service
   D. Net Listing Service

8. Brokers who show clients properties found on the Multiple Listing Service are referred to as:
   A. Cooperating Brokers
   B. Principals
   C. Clients
   D. Sellers

9. When a broker accepts a deposit from a buyer without permission from the seller, the broker is acting as
   A. The seller's agent
   B. The buyer's agent
   C. Both the buyer's and seller's agent
   D. Neither the buyer's nor seller's agent

10. Which of the following is not one of the types of misrepresentation?
   A. Innocent
   B. Negligent
   C. Fraudulent
   D. Blatant

11. Puffing is a form of
   A. Misrepresentation
   B. Tort
   C. Agreement
   D. Listing

12. Which of the following duties is NOT considered a duty owed to the principal by the agent?
   A. Fiduciary
   B. Flexibility
   C. Full Disclosure
   D. Loyalty

13. What percentage of the state license fee is contributed to the California Recovery Account?
   A. 2%
   B. 5%
   C. 7%
   D. 10%

14. Is a broker who takes an option on his or her own listing eligible to make a commission on the transaction?
    A. Yes, provided the agent fully discloses his intentions or interest in the property to the sellers
    B. Yes, disclosure is not required, as it is the broker's listing
    C. Yes, as long as the seller agrees to the commission
    D. No

15. Which of the following would cancel an agency?
    A. Full performance
    B. Destruction of the property
    C. Death of the principal or agent
    D. All of the above

16. If an agent cancels an agency agreement, causing damages for the principal, is the agent responsible for these damages?
    A. Yes, but only if damages exceed $1,000
    B. Yes, but only if damages exceed $1,500
    C. Yes, regardless of the dollar amount of damage
    D. No

17. When is an agent's commission earned?
    A. Upon entering into the listing agreement
    B. Upon posting the listing to the Multiple Listing Service
    C. When the listing contract expires
    D. When the agent finds a ready, willing and able buyer who meets all of the seller's terms

18. The promise of a principal not to interfere with an agent's prospective economic advantage in finding a ready, willing and able buyer by having separate negotiations with the third party behind the agent's back best is described as which of the following?
    A. Duty of care
    B. Loyalty
    C. Obedience
    D. Commingling

19. When is a seller required by law to deliver the Real Estate Transfer Disclosure Statement to a buyer?
    A. When the buyer views the home for the first time
    B. At the close of escrow
    C. Before a purchase contract or offer is made
    D. When a purchase contract or offer is made

20. Commission rates are determined by
    A. Real estate commissions
    B. State legislature
    C. Brokers
    D. Seller

6

CONVEYANCE AND ESCROW

What you will learn in this Chapter

- Acquisition and conveyance of real estate

- Definition, rules and procedures of Escrow

- Rules for termination of an escrow

- Rights and obligations of parties to a transaction

- Relationship between escrow holder and real estate agent

- Designation of an escrow holder

- RESPA (Real Estate Settlement Procedures Act)

1. A person who dies without a will in place is said to have died
    A. Quitclaim
    B. Intestate
    C. Probate
    D. Succession

2. All of the following are correct statements regarding a valid escrow except
    A. Escrow is mandatory in California
    B. Escrow agents primarily serve as a communication vessel between parties
    C. Escrow agents act as a neutral party
    D. Escrow instructions are outlined in the purchase contract

3. Which of the following statements is correct?
    A. An escrow agent may not make any changes to the escrow instructions
    B. Escrow opens upon the signing of the purchase contract or escrow instructions and delivery of the purchase contract to the escrow agent
    C. Escrow agents may council or mediate any disputes between principals
    D. Escrow agents may not give legal advice to the principals

4. In what ways may an escrow be terminated?
    A. By full performance
    B. By a written agreement between both principals
    C. By request of the escrow agent
    D. Both A and B

5. When may a real estate agent receive his or her commission?
    A. Upon finding a ready, willing and able buyer
    B. When the purchase agreement is signed
    C. At the close of escrow
    D. At the open of escrow

6. Who is entitled to receive a copy of the escrow instructions?
    A. Any interested party, as escrow information is considered public domain
    B. The buyer only
    C. The seller only
    D. Only the principals who sign the document

7. Who determines which escrow company to use in a transaction?
    A. The seller's broker
    B. The buyer's broker
    C. The seller
    D. Both the buyer and seller

INTRODUCTION

It is important to understand the different methods of transferring property from one party to another. We understand the concept of purchasing an available property from a willing seller, but what about other methods of property transfer? For instance, what if you have a property you would like to give as a gift, or leave to a loved one upon your death? Or what happens if you acquire property through means other than as a sale or a gift? Is this legal?

In this chapter we will examine the different ways to convey, or transfer, property from one party to another. We will examine not only willing property transfers, but also those transfers, which were compelled by foreclosure or some other judgment.

In this chapter, we will also learn about escrow. California utilizes escrow agents in the transfer of property from one individual to another to ensure that contracts are upheld and executed exactly as intended. The escrow agent acts as a third party between the buyer and seller and performs a series of actions to complete a transaction to its close.

ACQUISITION AND CONVEYANCE OF REAL ESTATE

To acquire property means to purchase a home or other piece of real estate. Conveyance of real estate is defined as selling or transferring one's interest in property to another. A monetary exchange is not always required to convey real property, as we will see in this chapter. There are five ways that property may be purchased or sold. They are: will; accession; succession; occupancy and transfer.

A *will* is an instrument that will dispose of both personal and real property upon the death of the property owner. Real property transferred by a will is also referred to as a devise, while personal property that is transferred in the same manner is called a bequest or legacy. The person who makes the will is called the *testator* and upon death is said to have died *testate*. Those persons who don't have a will in place upon their death are said to have died *intestate*.

There are two separate types of wills: the witnessed will and the holographic will. A witnessed will is a formal will prepared by an attorney under the guidance of the testator, and signed by three people: the testator and two witnesses.

The holographic will is less formal than the witnessed will, but equally legal. The holographic will is handwritten signed and dated by the testator. It is important that the holographic will be completely handwritten (i.e., with no printing or type) to be considered valid. Both types of wills may be altered or changed before the creator of the will dies through a document called a *codicil*.

A person chosen, or named in the will to administer the will upon the testator's death is called an *executor*. The executor is chosen by the testator to represent him or her and ensure that the terms of the will are carried out. If the testator does not name an executor in the will, the courts will appoint an administrator to fulfill the wishes of the deceased.

Upon the death of the testator, the court disposes of the deceased's property through a process called *probate*. Probate determines which debtors will receive money, whether or not heirs have a legal claim to real or personal property, while aiding in the transfer of property from the deceased to his or her heirs. If there is a will, the probate court will authorize the administrator or executor to carry out the will's instructions.

If there are no heirs to the deceased's property and no will has been left to determine how to dispose of the property, probate may authorize the exclusive right to publicly auction or sell the property within 90 days. There are rules, however, on how the property may be sold. The first bid on the property must total at least 90% of the property's appraised value. All subsequent bids on the property must total 10% of the first $10,000 (or $1,000), plus 5% of the remaining balance. Once the representative accepts an offer, this offer must be approved through the court. Like any other funds from the estate, the real estate professional's commission is subject to approval by the court before such funds can be paid to the broker. For example, if a property being sold probate is appraised at $140,000, the first bid must total at least $126,000. This would be the minimum bid, of course the initial bid could be higher, however it is an auction where people go to find cheap property and most likely would follow the rules set forth by the real estate commission regarding property transfer at public auctions making an initial bid at the minimum price. The second bid on the property must total at least $132,800.

Explanation of Probate:

- First bid = 90% of the appraised value of the property = $140,000 x 90% = $126,000
- Second bid = 10% of the first $10,000 = $1,000
  5% of the remaining value = $126,000 - $10,000 = $116,000 x 5% = $5,800
- Answer = $126,000 + $5,800 + $1000 = $132,800

The probate court must approve any commission(s) paid to real estate professionals who aid in the sale of a home. The probate court must also approve of any fees to be collected by attorneys, and any outstanding taxes or debts the property owner owes. After all fees are paid from the sale of the property, the probate court will distribute any funds to heirs or devisees of the deceased.

The appointed representative of the will -- whether the executor or administrator -- must make sure that several steps are taken when fulfilling the wishes of the deceased as outlined by the will. The will's executor must provide a notice to any creditors upon the decedent's death so that they may collect any monies owed to them. The executor must take an inventory of all personal or real property to be disposed of by the will. This includes conducting an appraisal of the estate.

Upon collecting all information regarding debts owed to creditors and assessing the inventory of the will, the executor prepares a report for the probate court, listing all liabilities and assets. The final step the executor must take is to disburse all proceeds per the probate court's instructions.

In order to encourage people to make a will, the California Bar Association has created two separate forms, both available to the public. These forms of will are called the California Statutory Will. The first type of will allows the testator's property to be willed to any devisee. There are places on this form for witnesses to sign the will, thus making it legal .

The second type of statutory will establishes a trust for all property until the testator's youngest child turns 21 years old. The property placed in trust is managed by a trustee and may be utilized to support or educate the children) before age 21 (when they will legally obtain the property placed in the trust). For more information regarding the California Statutory Will, contact the California Bar Association.

Accession refers to the buildup of property, either by natural or man-made forces. Regardless of whether additions to the property are man-made or natural, they will extend the owner's title to include all new additions. The ways accession can occur are by accretion, construction or reliction.

Accession is the gradual buildup of soil; so gradual that a property owner most likely will not notice the change right away. The accession usually occurs when a property is adjacent to a moving body of water, such as a river or stream. The accumulation of new soil is also called *alluvium*. A vivid example of this is a delta, where a river meets a major body of water. Soil can erode just as easily as it can be accumulated. Moving water may wash away soil, creating erosion and depleting the area of some property. Floods can also rapidly change the landscape, by washing away large amounts of property adjacent to a river, depositing it downstream and possibly increasing the amount of property owned by a neighbor.

Construction may add fixtures to the land (improving its value) or personal property may be affixed to the land. Improvements may also occur by accident if an improvement is placed where it is not meant to be placed. An example of this is a walkway, which crosses a property line into a neighbor's property, thereby creating an encroachment. The person responsible for the misplaced improvement may also be responsible for any loss or damage that the misplaced "improvement" causes to the adjacent property.

Reliction is the third way by which property may be accumulated. Reliction occurs when water begins to permanently recede, exposing the land underneath the water and adjacent to the property. This now becomes part of the adjacent property, increasing the square footage of that lot or property.

Succession

As we mentioned earlier, a person who dies without a will is said to have died intestate. In a situation such as this, the deceased's property will pass to any of his or her heirs, according to the laws of the state. In California, if a married person dies intestate, all community property will pass to the surviving spouse. If a married person with only one child dies intestate and has separate property, half of it will pass to the remaining spouse; the other half to the child. In a situation when there is more than one child, the surviving spouse will receive one third of the property while the children will split the remaining two thirds.

Occupancy

It is possible to acquire property by simply living on it for a specific time period, without the current owner's permission. There are three ways to acquire property by occupancy: adverse possession; prescription; and abandonment.

| **Three Ways to Acquire Property through Occupancy:** |
| 1. Adverse Possession |
| 2. Prescription |
| 3. Abandonment |

Adverse Possession

Adverse possession requires that five steps be followed in order to acquire property. The five steps are:

1. Any person occupying property must do so openly and notoriously. This means that they cannot hide (from anyone, especially the rightful property owner) the fact that they are utilizing or living on the property.

2. Any person occupying property must do so without permission.

3. Any person occupying property must claim title to the land through occupancy or through color of title. In cases of color of title, it will appear as if the land has been conveyed to the occupant. Color of title will also document the legal boundaries of the property.

4. Any person making a claim to the land must occupy the property uninterruptedly for a period of five years.

5. Any person occupying the land must have paid all taxes for the property for five continuous years.

Example of Occupancy:
Jordan owns a house next to an empty lot (which is owned by Robert). Robert currently lives in another city and does not have plans to develop the property he owns next to Jordan's house. Tired of seeing a dirt lot next to his own, Jordan decides to seed grass, and care for the property. He utilizes the lot for entertaining guests and other outdoor activities.

Jordan pays taxes on the lot and, after doing so for years, he decides to install a pool in Robert's lot, as well as erect a fence separating the lot from Jordan's own home. After six years, Robert decides to sell his lot, because he had no plans to ever build a home there. Upon beginning this process, he finds the fence, pool and well-manicured lot. When he takes legal action against Jordan, the court finds Jordan as the rightful owner of the property, given that he acquired it through adverse possession.

Prescription

Prescription occurs when a property will not be owned as in adverse possession; rather, the occupant will have created an easement for him or herself. Prescription is created in the same way as adverse possession, the difference being, that the person notoriously utilizing the easement is not paying any property taxes. There must be exclusive use of the land for at least five years for this to occur. Just as we learned in Chapter Three, an easement may be lost if the dominant tenement does not use the property for a period of five years.

RECORDING REQUESTED BY:

When Recorded Mail Document and Tax Statement To:

Escrow No.
Title Order No.
APN:

SPACE ABOVE THIS LINE FOR RECORDER'S USE

GRANT DEED

The undersigned grantor(s) declare(s)
Documentary transfer tax is $_____ City tax $ _____
   [   ] computed on full value of property conveyed, or
   [   ] computed on full value less value of liens or encumbrances remaining at time of sale,
   [   ] Unincorporated Area   City of _____

FOR A VALUABLE CONSIDERATION, receipt of which is hereby acknowledged,

hereby GRANT(S) to

the following described real property in the City of
County of

State of California:

DATED: _____

STATE OF CALIFORNIA
COUNTY OF _____
ON _____ before me,
_____ personally appeared
_____

personally known to me (or proved to me on the basis of satisfactory evidence) to be the person(s) whose name(s) is/are subscribed to the within instrument and acknowledged to me that he/she/they executed the same in his/her/their authorized capacity(ies), and that by his/her/their signature(s) on the instrument the person(s), or the entity upon behalf of which the person(s) acted, executed the instrument.

Witness my hand and official seal.

Signature _____

MAIL TAX STATEMENT AS DIRECTED ABOVE

GRANT DEED

NOTE SECURED BY DEED OF TRUST

INSTALLMENT — INTEREST EXTRA

$_____ _____, California,_____, 19___

In installments as herein stated, for value received, I promise to pay to

or order at _____

the sum of _____ DOLLARS,

with interest from _____ on unpaid principal at the rate of

_____ per cent per annum, payable _____

_____; principal payable in installments of

_____ Dollars

or more on the _____ day of each _____ month, beginning on the

_____ day of _____, 19_____ _____

_____

_____

_____ and continuing until said principal and interest have been paid.

In the event of any default in the payment of any installment of principal or interest as herein provided all sums so due including interest, shall bear interest at the rate set forth above but such unpaid interest so compounded shall not exceed an amount equal to simple interest on the unpaid principal at the maximum rate permitted by law. In the event of any default in the payment of any installment of principal or interest when due the whole sum of principal and interest shall become immediately due at the option of the holder of this note. Principal and interest payable in lawful money of the United States. If action be instituted on this note I promise to pay such sum as the Court may fix as attorney's fees. This note is secured by a Deed of Trust to PROVIDENT TITLE COMPANY, a California corporation.

_____   _____

_____   _____

0-18

IMPORTANT! WHEN PAID DO NOT DESTROY THIS NOTE OR THE DEED OF TRUST. SURRENDER BOTH TO PROVIDENT TITLE COMPANY WITH SIGNED REQUEST FOR FULL RECONVEYANCE.

INTEREST ACCRUAL DATE OF THIS NOTE IS HEREBY ADJUSTED SO THAT INTEREST IS TO ACCRUE FROM _____, 19___

ON THIS _____ day of _____, 19___ FOR VALUE RECEIVED, the undersigned hereby sells, assigns and transfers to _____ The within note and the Deed of Trust Recorded in Book _____ Page _____ of Official Records in the _____ County Recorder's Office.

DATE DUE			DATE DUE			AMOUNT PAID	CREDITED ON		BALANCE OF PRINCIPAL UNPAID
M	D	Y	M	D	Y		INT.	PRIN.	

SPACE ABOVE THIS LINE FOR RECORDER'S USE

QUITCLAIM DEED

The undersigned grantor(s) declare(s)
Documentary transfer tax is $ _____ City tax $ _____

[   ] computed on full value of property conveyed, or
[   ] computed on full value less value of liens or encumbrances remaining at time of sale,
[   ] Unincorporated Area   City of _____

FOR A VALUABLE CONSIDERATION, receipt of which is hereby acknowledged,

hereby remises, releases and quitclaims to

the following described real property in the City of
County of   **State of California:**

DATED: _____   _____

STATE OF CALIFORNIA
COUNTY OF _____
ON _____ before me,   _____
_____ personally appeared
_____

personally known to me (or proved to me on the
basis of satisfactory evidence) to be the person(s)
whose name(s) is/are subscribed to the within
instrument and acknowledged to me that he/she/they
executed the same in his/her/their authorized
capacity(ies), and that by his/her/their signature(s) on
the instrument the person(s), or the entity upon
behalf of which the person(s) acted, executed the
instrument.

Witness my hand and official seal.

Signature _____

MAIL TAX STATEMENT AS DIRECTED ABOVE

QUITCLAIM DEED

160

Abandonment

Abandonment is when a tenant leaves a property that had been leased. Upon abandonment the property, the landlord or lessor has the right to repossess the property and do with it whatever he or she pleases. Abandonment happens when the lessee stops paying rent, moves all of his or her belongings off the premises, and makes no signs that indicate re-entry to the property will take occur.

Transfer

Property can be transferred from one party to another by a sale or by an operation of the law. Sale refers to a transaction between a buyer and seller, while operation of the law indicates that there was a foreclosure or other legal transfer from one party to another. Property may be transferred by the following methods: private grant, public grant, public dedication, and operation of the law.

Four methods to transfer property

1. Private Grant
2. Public Grant
3. Public Dedication
4. Operation of the law

Private Grant

There are seven different kinds of deeds: gift deed; grant deed; trust deed; quitclaim deed; warranty deed; sheriff's deed and reconveyance deed.

Gift deeds are used to give property to a close friend or family member. In the transfer of property, there is usually some form of consideration or payment received. In a gift deed the consideration (written into the contract) is love and affection. It is important to note that a gift deed may not be used to hide property or dispose of property in an effort to avoid creditors or taxes.

Grant deed is the instrument used to transfer property through the sale of a home or other real estate. The grant deed carries two implied guarantees or warranties: the first is that the grantor, or person selling the property, has not conveyed the title of the property to any other party. The second is that the grantor promises the grantee, or the buyer of the property, that there are no encumbrances (other than those already disclosed).

Two Implied Warranties of a Grant Deed:

1. Grantor has only conveyed the property's title to one party, the grantee
2. The property has no undisclosed encumbrances

There are several requirements that must be met to create a valid grant deed. They are:

1. The grant deed must be in writing.
2. The grantor and grantee must be identified in the deed.
3. The grantor must be considered competent (of legal age and mentally able to make and carry through with the decision) to convey the property.

4. The grantee must be a real, living person. Title cannot be transferred to a fictional person or entity.
5. There must be an adequate property description of the real estate to be conveyed.
6. The words "grant" or "convey" must be used to indicate the intention to grant property to the grantee.
7. The grantor must sign the deed. The grantee, however, does not have to sign the deed, as acceptance of it is considered sufficient.
8. The deed must be delivered and accepted by the grantee.

In a grant deed, the grantor promises to surrender any rights to the property that may have been acquired during ownership. All rights (including mineral rights) will transfer to the new owner after title is acquired.

As we previously learned in this book, deeds or conveyance of title from one person to another must be acknowledged in order for a deed to be recorded. Recordation of the deed is the same as delivering the deed (which is one of the criteria for a deed's validity). To be acknowledged, the deed must be signed before a notary public so there is a witness that the signature of the grantor is original and valid (this helps to avoid fraud). If a deed is recorded, it does not have to be delivered, as recordation is considered constructive notice. Recording the deed will also serve to protect the chain of title to the property, which benefits future conveyance of the property and is necessary for title insurance to be issued.

A grantee must accept the deed before it is considered effective. If the grantor records the deed and the grantee takes possession of the property, this is considered acceptance by the grantee (as possession, much like recordation) is considered constructive notice. It is important that deeds be recorded, in order to prevent any other person from making a claim to the land (particularly if the grantor granted the property to more than one individual). If this is the case, the first party to record the deed is considered the rightful owner of the property. If more than one person received a grant deed for the same property, and no recordation has been filed, the first person taking possession of the property will be considered the lawful owner (so long as possession is taken before any deeds are recorded).

There are some elements that need NOT appear to create a valid grant deed, These include:

1. Acknowledgement
2. Competent grantee (as the grantee may be a minor of any age or mentally incompetent)
3. Legal description of the property
4. Recordation of the property
5. Date of grant deed
6. Signature of the grantee
7. Notation of the consideration

Trust deeds are security instruments used by lending institutions who are using the property itself as collateral for the promissory note. There are three parties to consider in a trust deed situation: the trustor (or person borrowing money to purchase the property); the beneficiary (or person making the loan); and the trustee (or neutral third party who holds the deed until the note has been paid in full). While the trustee does hold title to the property, he or she is not the owner of the property. The only authority the trustee has while holding "bare legal title" is to foreclose if the trustor fails to make payments on the promissory note.

A *Quitclaim deed* transfers property with no guarantee of a clear title. Oftentimes, a husband or wife will use this type of deed to transfer interest in a property to their spouse. This type of deed is also useful to clear a cloud on the title.

A *warranty deed* transfers property from one party to another with the guarantee that the title is clear. This type of deed is rarely used, because title insurance companies now insure the title to property.

A *sheriff's deed* is given to the purchaser of property in a foreclosure sale. A foreclosure sale occurs when there is a court order for the property to be sold in an effort to satisfy a debt on the property.

A *reconveyance deed* conveys property back to a borrower upon payment of a note in full.

At the time the note is paid off, the trustee who holds the trust note will issue a reconveyance deed, which acknowledges that the note was paid in full.

Public Grant
Public grant is a grant in which private parties receive title to land from the government. An example of this is when the government was offering 160 acres of land in the Homestead Act in an effort to entice people to move west build and improve the land and plant crops in that area. Upon fulfilling all the necessary requirements to receive a plot of land through the Homestead Act, the landowner receives (as proof of ownership) a patent deed from the government.

Public Dedication
There are three ways in which property may be acquired through public dedication: common law dedication, deed and statutory dedication. Public dedication occurs when private land is intended for public use.

- Common law dedication implies public use through the actions of the property owner, with no official transfer.
- A deed will formally convey property intended for public use. In this type of public dedication, no consideration is needed.
- Statutory dedication occurs when an owner follows procedures outlined in the Subdivision Map Act. This dedication can be used to dedicate privately owned public areas, to the public. One example is a park.

> Three Types of Public Dedication:
>
> 1. Common Law Dedication
> 2. Statutory Dedication
> 3. Deed

Operation of Law
Property can be transferred through a court judgment, such as a foreclosure. This type of transfer is usually not voluntary and is done to satisfy a debt incurred by the property owner. There are seven reasons the court may get involved in a transfer:

1. Partition action, (when the court settles a dispute between co-owners of property), such as community property owned between a husband and wife.

2. An execution sale occurs when the court forces the sale of a property to satisfy a judgment against the property owner.

3. Quiet title action is used to clear a cloud on the title.

4. Foreclosure action will occur when the borrower defaults on a loan. The property is then sold to pay the note, which was secured by the trust deed. This is the only time when the trustee has any authority in holding bare legal title.

5. Bankruptcy occurs when a property must be sold to satisfy debts to creditors. If the property has been homesteaded, either $50,000, $75,000 or $100,000 of the home may be protected (depending on age, head of household status or mental stability). However, if there are debts in excess of these amounts, the property will not be protected.

6. Eminent domain is the term, which describes a government takeover of private property in the interest of the public good. The government will pay the property owner a fair price for the property. An example of this is when a piece of land is required to make room for a freeway.

7. If a person dies intestate, and no heirs come forth to claim the property, it will escheat to the state after five years.

E S C R O W

Escrow is the "in-between" time, beginning when a purchase agreement is accepted and signed, and ending when the buyer takes possession of the property. During escrow, all documents that need to be collected, processed or distributed (as well as the necessary disbursement of funds) will be completed, . The person or company assigned to carry out all instructions provided to them by the principals (outlined in the purchase contract) is called the escrow holder.

Escrow may involve more than just the sale of real property. Escrow agents are typically used in situations such as leasing of real property, sale of personal property, securities, loans or mobile homes. As in the sale of real property, the escrow agent must follow the instructions as laid out by the principals.

The escrow agent must follow instructions outlined in the purchase contract. Once escrow is opened, both parties must agree to any changes made. In other words, the buyer or seller alone cannot change escrow instructions without the approval of the other party. The two parties involved in the transaction are usually, but not always, a buyer and a seller.

California does not require escrow agents or that escrow be utilized in a real estate transaction. The decision to use an escrow agent is completely up to the principals involved in the transaction. It is advisable to go into escrow, however, because any mistakes -whether innocent or intentional regarding the terms of the contract -could be costly to one or both parties, as they initiate litigation or challenges to the property transfer.

The main job of the escrow agent is to provide a line of communication between all parties involved in a sale. An escrow agent's duties go far beyond just communication between the buyer and the seller. The escrow agent must communicate with both of the brokers and sales agents involved in the transaction, the lender, and any service companies called in (such as inspectors, plumbers, appraisers and pest control companies). Thus, it is important that the escrow agent be a neutral third party who is not otherwise involved in the transaction.

In order for an escrow to be valid it must include the following:

- Binding contract
- Conditional delivery

Escrow Agent's Main Duties:

- Disburse funds as outlined in the purchase contract
- Communicate between all parties involved in the transaction

A binding contract is the first step of an escrow opening. This contract can be created in a number of different forms, though a purchase contract is the usual type. The following are all examples of a binding contract, capable of opening escrow:

1. Purchase contract
2. Agreement of sale
3. An option
4. An exchange agreement
5. Any legally binding document

The California Association of Realtors has created a single form, thus combining both the escrow instructions and the purchase agreement into one contract. This form creates a uniform contract for all realtors across California, making this process easier and less redundant than it might be otherwise.

The second step for escrow is *conditional delivery* of instruments of transfer to the escrow agent. These instruments include:

1. Money
2. Loan Documents
3. Deed transferring title
4. Other required paperwork

This 4-step process is called a conditional delivery, as all terms of the contract or additional escrow instructions must still be carried out. These contract items include the disbursement of all necessary funds, the signing and delivery of the trust deed to the escrow agent to hold until close of escrow, the signing of the note by the buyer, as well as any other terms requested by either party. Shortly before closing of escrow, a buyer will receive the grant deed to the property, while the seller will receive any monies from the purchase.

E S C R O W   R U L E S

As mentioned earlier in this chapter, the only parties allowed to make changes to escrow instructions are the principals, the buyer and seller. The escrow agent must follow the instructions or changes made in the purchase contract by the principals to the letter. Just as the escrow agent has no authority to make any changes to an escrow, neither does the broker. In addition, no changes may be made by one principal without the agreement and acknowledgement of the other.

Remember!
An escrow agent is a neutral third party; thus, he or she may not make changes to the escrow instructions at any time.

All escrow agents must observe the following rules:

1. All actions of the escrow agent must be under the direction or approval of the principals. This means and requires that the principals must fully under stand both the purchase contract and all its binding obligations. The pur chase contract will serve as the instructions for the escrow agent.

2. An escrow agent must not function as a mediator between the principals in the event of a disagreement between the principals. It is the escrow agent's responsibility to voice any concerns or objections of any one principal, while remaining a neu|tral party.

3. Escrow agents may not give legal advice regarding matters, which would require an attorney.

4. An escrow agent must remain a neutral third party, as he or she is a dual agent to both principals. This means that no favoritism may be given to one principal over another. The agent is only allowed to abide by the instructions contained in the purchase contract or escrow instructions.

5. Escrow is open when both parties sign the purchase contract (or escrow instructions). Upon signature, these instructions are delivered to the escrow agent.

6. Escrow instructions must instruct the agent regarding which funds or documents may be accepted as payment in the transaction.

7. An escrow agent may not have a negative balance in the trust account.

8. If there are discrepancies between the escrow instructions and the purchase agreement, the signed escrow instructions will take precedence over the purchase agreement.

9. The escrow agent must remain neutral at all times and in all dealings during an open escrow.

10. Documents must be recorded in a timely manner and copies of each document distributed to all parties.

11. An escrow agent must be trustworthy.

12. The escrow agent must hold all information regarding the escrow in confidence (unless the principals give written permission to release that information to outside interested parties).

13. Escrow records must be maintained on a daily basis.

14. All information previously undisclosed to the principals by any broker, sales agent or other party must be disclosed by the escrow agent. Both principals must sign any changes this may create in the purchase agreement.

15. Any exchange of funds in the form of a check must have already been approved by a bank before the exchange of money is considered official.

16. A careful audit is required of all funds before the close of escrow is allowed.

17. Escrow must close in a timely manner.

E S C R O W   P R O C E D U R E S

Once a purchase agreement is signed to indicate agreement to its, escrow may be opened. Escrow begins when the selling agent deposits the earnest money into an escrow account, which must occur within three days of the purchase agreement being signed. The escrow agent must also receive the signed purchase contract to begin escrow.

Some details of the purchase contract, or questions on which parties must come to agreement, include: Have all inspections been made? Who will pay for these inspections? Have all disclosures been made? If the broker is making a commission, has the amount of commission been made clear? Is the seller going to pay for this entire commission? It is a good idea to use a checklist to make sure all points have been considered, discussed and agreed upon.

Each party in an escrow has a responsibility. The parties involved in an escrow are the buyer, the seller and the escrow company or agent. The real estate broker is not considered a party to the escrow, although he or she will have a responsibility toward all other parties in the escrow. Each party must understand their responsibilities, which include:

Buyer's Responsibilities:
- Sign escrow instructions or purchase agreement
- Analyze the bill of sale (to become familiar as to which items of personal property will be conveyed separate of the purchase agreement)
- Acquire hazard insurance
- Review the preliminary report of the property and its encumbrances, if any, that appear on record
- Deposit all necessary funds to cover any deposits or other costs associated with the transaction (such as the earnest money deposit)
- Review the property inspection reports (to which an approval must be given by the buyer to move forward towards closing)
- Produce all copies of any documents that might affect the escrow
- Review all loan documents

Seller's Responsibilities:

- Sign escrow instructions
- Provide a release on any mortgage or encumbrance to be paid
- Include seller's deed, title insurance policy or any other document affecting title
- Produce copies of any document that might affect the escrow
- Provide the present loan status on the property
- Produce executed deed on the property
- Produce any existing insurance policies, which may be assumed by the buyer
- Provide any subordination agreements as required by the contract
- Provide any current tenant information (if the property being purchased is a rental)
- Provide any additional documentation necessary for escrow to close
- Produce bill of sale for all personal property items not included in the purchase agreement

Real Estate Broker's Responsibilities:

- Deliver signed copies of the purchase agreement to all parties in the escrow
- Deliver and explain all escrow instructions to all parties
- Review preliminary report and explain it, in detail, to the buyer
- Provide escrow officer with necessary seller's payment coupons (for current loans against the property), the grant deed or any additional documents required for escrow.
- Provide all disclosure reports
- Suggest to the buyers that he or she consult an attorney to figure out how to take title of the property
- Advise the seller to maintain the property as agreed in the purchase agreement, as well as continue to make all loan payments
- Assist buyer in obtaining all property inspection reports
- Assist the seller in finding the necessary companies to conduct all pest reports, and then ensure all necessary corrections are made
- Make sure each party delivers the required money into escrow (as detailed in the escrow instructions)
- Assist buyer in obtaining loans
- Provide any assistance needed by all parties to help close escrow

Most of the closing costs between buyer and seller are negotiable. Typically the buyer will pay for the following: credit report; loan origination; note and deed of trust; appraisal; lender's title insurance; applicable assumption fees; notary; recording; new hazard insurance premiums; FHA mortgage insurance, and prorated expenses agreed upon in the purchase contract. Sellers generally pay for: pest inspections; repairs; VA transaction charges; taxes; prorated items; notary fees for documents prepared for the seller only; loan payoff; prepayment penalties, if applicable, and the beneficiary statement. Again, these costs are all negotiable. The purchase agreement or escrow instructions will direct the escrow agent as to the party from whom to collect fees to cover these costs.

Escrow instructions, once prepared, will be computer-generated. Each party must sign the instructions, with the seller's instructions containing information regarding the broker's commission. The instructions will most likely contain the following information and instructions:

1. Purchase price
2. Terms – whether the transaction will be in cash, loan assumption or new loan, as well as other agreements regarding the financial transaction
3. Vesting or title
4. Recorded issues (such as who will be responsible for any encumbrance at the time of sale)
5. Closing or time of escrow
6. Inspections
7. Prorations (all fees that may be prorated are based on a 30-day month, 360-day year)
8. Possession – the date the buyer moves in is not always considered the close of escrow. In some transactions the buyer will remain on the property after selling it, and renting from the new owner.
9. Documents
10. Disbursement – a final distribution of all necessary funds at the end of escrow.

The escrow officer will request a preliminary report, or *title search* of all records regarding the property in escrow. This information includes all previous owners and any liens or encumbrances the property may have against it. If the title search reveals no liens or encumbrances, escrow may be closed. Any existing liens or encumbrances must be paid before the title may be transferred from the seller to the buyer. The buyer, upon inspecting the document, must sign the preliminary report.

It is not uncommon for property to be conveyed before the trust deed or mortgage is paid in full. When this happens, the escrow agent must contact the existing lending institution to receive a *beneficiary statement*, which reflects the current payoff. This is necessary for closing, as the lender will receive a disbursement from the transaction to pay the current note on the property.

Lenders require a fire insurance policy on all property, including property currently in escrow. It is the escrow agent's responsibility, as well as the buyer's, to have a fire insurance policy in effect or that the seller's old policy is transferred. The escrow agent will hold and deliver the necessary policy during escrow.

In California, the escrow agent receives all loan documents regarding the property and completes them as necessary. The buyer then reviews the documents and signs them, for the escrow agent, who delivers them back to the lending institution. The escrow agent takes care of these documents, because he or she is in charge of disbursement of the funds before closing.

Reports regarding pest control, structural condition or other issues whose disclosure is required in the transaction are held in escrow. These documents may need review by the buyer or seller. As a result, they are held in escrow until needed. The reports will be held in escrow until close, when the escrow agent may be required to deliver a report to a particular party.

One of the most important jobs of the escrow agent is the *audit* of any files upon close of escrow. Each file in the transaction must be audited to ensure the accounting is accurate and that all funds have been disbursed in accordance with the escrow instructions. These closing statements are accompanied by a cash reconciliation statement.

Escrow instructions will contain instructions about *prorations*, decided upon by the buyer and seller. Most often, the prorated items are taxes, interest on the note, fire insurance premiums and rental income. The escrow agent will determine the debits and credits of both the buyer and seller as directed by each. After this, the buyer will be required to make the down payment (plus all closing costs) to the escrow officer. At this time, the buyer will also sign the loan, sending the appropriate funds to escrow for disbursement. Escrow can now be closed.

Items that may be prorated:
- Taxes
- Interest
- Fire insurance premiums
- Rental income

All documents can be recorded by the escrow agent upon doing a final check of title. First, there is a preliminary report to inspect the title on the property, followed by a final check on the title. Once the title check is finished, the escrow agent may record all necessary documents, including: the trust deed, the grant deed or the option.

Finally, escrow may close. *Closing* occurs when the closing statement is delivered to both the buyer and the seller. Additionally, all monies will now be disbursed to the appropriate parties, along with any recorded documents. The seller of the property will receive his or her check (less any commissions, fees, payoffs or other costs required to be deducted from the amount due). Completing the closing occurs when the buyer receives a grant deed to the property. As mentioned before, closing does not necessarily mean the seller vacates the property or that the buyer is moving in to the property. For example, the seller may choose to rent the property from the buyer for a certain amount of time, thus preventing the buyer from moving into the property right at closing. So, closing simply means that the transaction is complete. These details would be worked out in the purchase agreement and escrow instructions.

TERMINATION OF ESCROW

Escrow can be terminated in one of two ways. The first way escrow is terminated is by carrying out all instructions, disbursing all funds, and recording and delivering all documents to the involved parties. This is called *full performance of escrow*. The second way escrow can be terminated is by mutual agreement between the principals. One principal may not decide to terminate escrow without the consent of the other, with the mutual decision made in writing.

> **Ways to terminate escrow:**
>   1. Full performance
>   2. Mutual decision between both principals in writing

RIGHTS AND OBLIGATIONS OF EACH PARTY TO AN ESCROW

The parties involved in an escrow include the buyer, seller and escrow agent. Real estate agents are not a party to the escrow process unless they are making a personal purchase and thus representing themselves as a private agent. Real estate agents will not receive their commission until escrow has closed. It is important to point out again that the escrow agent is a neutral third party, and thus may not favor one principal over another. Additionally it is important to note that the escrow agent can only act as directed by the principals.

> **Parties involved in an escrow:**
>   • Buyer
>   • Seller
>   • Escrow Agent

An escrow agent or company may be: a real estate broker; bank; savings and loan institution; Escrow Company; title insurance company or an attorney. Real estate agents may only act as escrow agents if they are the buyer's or seller's broker.

The escrow agent holds *limited agency,* in that he or she must act as agent to both the buyer and seller. We say the agency is limited because the escrow agent does not hold any authority or power outside of the instructions provided by his or her principals. Escrow agents must treat both principles equally, showing no partiality, and should keep this in mind during the entire escrow period.

Each year, the escrow company must submit a report to the real estate commissioner outlining the escrow company's operation. This report must be prepared by a CPA. In addition to this report, an additional audit must be prepared for the Commissioner of Corporations.

The Commission of Corporations must license all escrow companies. Corporations are the only entities that are eligible to be licensed. Individuals cannot hold license as an escrow company. There are, however, exemptions to licensure by the Commission of Corporations. Real estate brokers, banks, savings and loan institutions, attorney's and title insurance companies are exempt from licensure. All escrow companies must be bonded, to protect against loss of escrow funds.

Each party signing the escrow instructions or purchase agreement must be given a copy of the document. Additionally, only those involved in the escrow may be given information regarding the escrow. Blank escrow documents (to be filled in after-the-fact) are not legally allowable documents. Any changes or alterations to the escrow must be initialed by all parties involved.

RELATIONSHIP OF THE ESCROW HOLDER AND REAL ESTATE AGENT

A real estate broker is not considered a party to the escrow, but that does not mean that he or she is not an important part of the process. It is necessary for the broker and escrow agent to keep the lines of communication open to ensure all agreements made in the escrow instructions are carried out correctly. An escrow agent should check with the broker on a routine basis to ensure all information is correct and then report the progress of the escrow to the broker. This allows the broker to keep his or her clients informed about the process.

REAL ESTATE SETTLEMENT PROCEDURES ACT (RESPA)

The Real Estate Settlement Procedures Act (RESPA) requires that lenders providing certain federal mortgage loans make certain disclosures. The act pertains only to private homes consisting of 1-4 units. Loans that fall under this type of jurisdiction are: loans made by a lender who is FDIC insured; any federal agencies such as the FHA (Federal Housing Authority) or VA (Department of Veteran Affairs); or loans made in the secondary mortgage market (such as Ginnie Mae).

Lenders are required to supply each applicant with a special information booklet, prepared by the Department of Housing and Urban Development along with an estimate of closing costs. If more than one applicant is applying for a loan, only one set of materials is required. By law, lenders must send out the special information booklet within 3 days from receipt of a loan application. Almost all lenders fall under RESPA. Private parties will be exempt from these rules and regulations. Violators of RESPA may be fined up to $10,000 and face imprisonment for one year.

> **Remember!**
> Almost all lender fall under RESPA, with the exception of private lenders

Designating the Escrow Holder

Once the buyer and seller have agreed to the terms of the purchase agreement, signed the purchase agreement, and made out the earnest money deposits, escrow may be opened. Who will serve as the escrow agent or company? What laws dictate how an escrow company is chosen? In California, the escrow agent is chosen by the buyer and seller. Real estate agents may suggest an escrow agent to use if the buyer and seller do not have one in mind. Just as we learned earlier in this chapter, escrow agents are not allowed to pay referral fees to brokers for this service, as the service is based on a professional working relationship.

SUMMARY

Title can be acquired or transferred from one person to another in a number of different ways. As a real estate professional, it is important to understand all the different methods of property transfer. Whether through a will, gift, foreclosure or traditional purchase there are steps to follow. Property may also be acquired by natural forces or means.

Moving water depositing a significant amount of particles may build up a person's property or may erode property away. Property may be created when it is permanently uncovered from receding water.

To complete a transaction, an escrow officer is usually used to carry out the escrow instructions (which can also be the purchase agreement, if applicable). The escrow agent must be a neutral third party, who is following the instructions as agreed upon by both the buyer and the seller. These instructions may be altered only if both the buyer and seller mutually agree and sign off on the changes. An escrow agent cannot make any changes to the instructions, or favor one party over another. Each party in an escrow knows what is required of them, and the escrow officer can carry out the escrow procedures based on these responsibilities. After all instructions have been carried out, and money disbursed, escrow can close.

T E R M S   A N D   P H R A S E S

Abstract of title – A summary of all recorded transfers, conveyances, legal proceedings, (and any other facts relied on as evidence of title) to show continuity of ownership and indicate any possible impairment to title

Accession – The process of manufactured or natural improvements or additions to property

Accretion – The deposit of soil onto land adjacent to rivers, lakes or streams

Acknowledgment – A formal declaration, made before an authorized person (such as a notary public), by a person who has executed a written instrument, which states that the execution of the instrument is the person's own act. Any documents to be recorded require acknowledgment.

Administrator – A personal representative of the estate of a decedent, appointed by the probate court

Adverse Possession – Acquiring title to real property by open, notorious occupation of the
land, against the intentions of the rightful owner. A person acquiring property through adverse possession must live on or use the property for a period of five years and pay all taxes on the property.

After Acquired Title – Title that is acquired by a grantor only after a conveyance to a grantee. The deed to the grantee becomes effective at the time the grantor actually receives title.

Alienate – To sell ones interest in real property or to transfer ownership to another individual

Alluvial Deposit – Sedimentary particles that make up soil (such as sand) or soil that is carried by moving water and deposited on land

Alluvium – The buildup of land as a result of accretion

Avulsion – Erosion, or washing away of soil, due to moving water

Beneficiary Statement – The amount of the existing loan on property and the condition of the debt as it relates to the trust deed.

Binding Contract – A document that legally binds two parties to carry out specific actions or agreements

Bequest – To leave personal property to another through a will

Certificate of Title – A document noting the owner of a specific piece of property, as well as any encumbrances the property may have against it

Chain of Title – A complete history of all conveyances and encumbrances affecting property, and showing its history as far back as the records go

Closing Escrow – The portion of the escrow period when delivery of documents and disbursement of all funds is done – making the escrow complete

Codicil – The act of making a change to a will before the testator's death

Conditional Delivery – delivering all documents of transfer to the escrow agent for the processing and transmittal of necessary documents or funds in order to complete the escrow

Convey – Transfer of ownership to real property

Devise – Gifting property to another individual through the use of a will

Erosion – Wearing away of land through natural forces, such as wind and moving water.

Escrow – The process by which a neutral third party will carry out all instructions of the purchase agreement or escrow instructions between the time an offer is made and the buyer's taking possession of the property. Escrow occurs when all necessary documents are processed, transmitted and funds are disbursed.

Escrow Agent – The neutral third party who carries out the instructions of an escrow, or holds money and other items of value in trust during the transfer of real property or other goods

Escrow Instructions – The purchase agreement or written set of instructions signed by the principles, and which the escrow agent must follow, outlining all processes necessary for the real property exchange, transfer or purchase to close.

Executor – The person named in the will as the administrator of the will

Gift Deed – The instrument used to give a gift of property to a close friend or relative

Grant Deed – Written instrument used to transfer real property (must contain a granting clause)

Grantee – The person receiving property

Grantor – The person transferring property

Holographic Will – A handwritten will, with no print or typewritten components, written and signed by the testator

Instrument – A document in real estate

Interpleader – A court preceding that may be brought by a party (such as an escrow agent) who holds property for another party, for the purpose of deciding who among the claimants is legally entitled to the property.

Intestate – A person who dies without a will

Legacy – Giving a gift of personal property through a will

Love and Affection – The consideration used when making a gift deed.

Patent Deed – A deed given by the government to private individuals as evidence of title transfer for land that has been given to a private person from the government.

Preliminary Title Report – The initial report a title company will issue regarding property that lists any leans or encumbrances that may affect the marketability of the property.

Principal – A person involved in transfer of real estate, usually authorizing another person to act on his or her behalf in the transaction

Private Grant – Granting private property to another person

Proration – Division of closing costs or other expenses by the buyer or seller, incurred when selling property

Public Dedication – Private land that is intended to be used publicly may be transferred or acquired in this way

Public Grant – Transfer of title from the government to a private person

Quitclaim Deed – A deed transferring ownership of property from the grantor to the grantee, with no warranties regarding a clear title

Reconveyance Deed – The document that transfers the title of property from the trustee back to the borrower when a note for real estate is paid in full

Reliction – Increasing in property by the permanent receding of water adjacent to the property

Settlement Statement – A document provided to both the buyer and seller in a real estate transaction that indicates all profit or expenses of the transaction

Sheriff's Deed – The deed given to a buyer when purchasing property that is being sold by a court order, or foreclosure, or to satisfy the debts of the outgoing property owner

Succession – Transfer of a person's interest in property under the laws of descent

Testator – The person creating a will for him or herself

Trust Deed – Deed issued to the trustor (or borrower), conveying title to a trustee on behalf of the lender. The trustee holds bare legal title to the property, meaning the trustee can only convey the property to satisfy a debt on that property

Warranty Deed – Deed used to transfer property with the guarantee of a clear and marketable title

Will – A written instrument either by the testator or by another person, whereby the testator makes a disposition of his real and personal property to take effect upon the testator's death

Witnessed Will – A will prepared by someone other than the testator, usually an attorney, and signed by the testator and two witnesses

C H A P T E R   Q U I Z

1. A person who dies without a will is said to have died
    A. Quitclaim
    B. Intestate
    C. Probate
    D. Succession

2. Which of the following is not a way to acquire property through occupancy?
    A. Adverse possession
    B. Abandonment
    C. Accession
    D. Prescription

3. Which of the following in necessary to make a valid grant deed?
    A. Property description
    B. Legal description of the property
    C. Recordation
    D. Signature of the grantee

4. All of the following are correct regarding a valid escrow except
    A. Escrow is mandatory in California
    B. Escrow agents are primarily a communication vessel between all parties
    C. The buyer and seller may select the escrow officer to be used.
    D. Escrow instructions are outlined in the purchase contract

5. An example of a binding contract capable of opening escrow is
    A. Purchase contract
    B. Option
    C. Exchange agreement
    D. All of the above

6. Which of the following statements is NOT correct?
    A. An escrow agent may not make changes to the escrow instructions
    B. Escrow is opened when the purchase contract or escrow instructions are signed and delivered to the escrow agent
    C. Escrow agents may council or mediate any disputes between principals
    D. Escrow agents may not give legal advice to the principal

7. When may an escrow agent disburse funds?
   A. As soon as thee agent receives the check
   B. Only after all checks clear
   C. This is not a function of the escrow agent
   D. None of the above

8. In what ways may an escrow be terminated?
   A. Full performance
   B. A written agreement between both principals
   C. By request from the escrow agent
   D. Both A and B

9. When may a real estate agent receive his or her commission?
   A. Upon finding a ready, willing and able buyer
   B. When the purchase agreement is signed
   C. At the close of escrow
   D. At the open of escrow

10. Who is entitled to receive copies of the signed escrow documents?
    A. Any interested party; as this information is considered public domain
    B. The buyer only
    C. The seller only
    D. Only the principles signing the document

11. Who determines what escrow company to use?
    A. The seller's broker
    B. The buyer's broker
    C. The seller
    D. Both the buyer and seller

12. Which of the following are considered parties in an escrow?
    A. Buyer
    B. Escrow Agent
    C. Real Estate Agent
    D. Both A and B

13. Which of the following is exempt from the Real Estate Settlement Procedures Act?
    A. Federal backed loans
    B. Private loans
    C. Secondary mortgage market
    D. VA loans.

14. What items might be prorated in escrow?
    A. Property taxes
    B. Fire insurance premiums
    C. Rental income
    D. All of the above

15. Which of the following is not considered one of the responsibilities of the buyer?
    A. Signing escrow instructions
    B. Making repairs based on inspections made to the property
    C. Acquiring hazard insurance
    D. Reviewing and signing all loan documents

16. A seller would most likely pay for which of the following?
    A. Credit reports, loan origination fees and lenders title insurance
    B. Credit reports, brokers commissions and appraisal fees
    C. Brokers commissions, beneficiary statement, and fees in a VA transaction
    D. Fees in a VA transaction, beneficiary and hazard insurance

17. Which of the following items will NOT be contained in the escrow instructions?
    A. Credit report
    B. Purchase price
    C. Vesting
    D. Prorations

18. Who holds the reports from the home inspections?
    A. Real estate broker
    B. Seller
    C. Escrow agent
    D. Inspection agency preparing the report

19. When does the buyer receive the grant deed to the property?
    A. At closing
    B. When the loan is signed
    C. When the purchase agreement is signed
    D. 30-days after closing

20. How many title reports are prepared during escrow?
    A. 1
    B. 2
    C. 3
    D. 4

7

LANDLORD AND TENANT

What you will learn in this Chapter

- Leaseholds and leasehold estates

- How a lease is created

- Security deposits

- Payment of rent

- Responsibilities and rights of tenants and landlords

- Transfer and termination of a lease

- Discrimination

1. If a lease has been terminated, yet a landlord continues to accept rent payments from a tenant, the tenancy is now considered
    A. An estate at will
    B. An estate from period to period
    C. Periodic tenancy
    D. All of the above

2. Payment, or rent, is also called:
    A. Consideration
    B. Lease assignment
    C. Covenant
    D. Fees

3. Which best describes a percentage lease?
    A. The percent of fair market value a tenant is willing to pay.
    B. A percentage of gross monthly profits that a tenant pays to the landlord.
    C. The percent of open market value a landlord charges for rent.
    D. The amount of rent a tenant pays plus a percentage of utilities and other costs shared with the landlord.

4. How many times a year may a tenant make necessary repairs to a rental property, and deduct the amount from rent?
    A. 1
    B. 2
    C. 3
    D. 4

5. To whom may a landlord refuse to rent?
    A. Tenants with children
    B. Tenants based on their race
    C. Tenants based on their religion
    D. None of the above

6. Which of the following statements is true?
    A. In a sublease situation, the original tenant subleasing the apartment to a secondary tenant will forfeit his or her interest in the lease.
    B. An assignment of a lease allows the original tenant to return to the property after a set period of time.
    C. The tenant subleasing from the original tenant is responsible to the landlord
    D. An assignment of a lease relieves the original tenant from all contractual obligations and transfers responsibility to the new tenant.

7. A lease may be terminated by which of the following methods?
    A. Expiration of the lease
    B. Destruction of the property
    C. Eviction
    D. All of the above

We already know the difference between a freehold estate and a less-than-freehold estate. The freehold estate, as you will recall, is in effect when an individual owns property. The less-than-freehold estate, or leasehold estate, is when a tenant rents property from a landlord. Both freehold and leasehold estates have a bundle of rights associated with them. However, the freehold estate owner enjoys more rights than the leasehold estate owner. Freehold estates are considered real property, while leasehold estates are considered personal property (or chattel real). The owner has an estate in real property, but does not own the property. He or she only has an interest in the use of the property.

This chapter will introduce you to the different types of leasehold estates. It will also teach you about the different requirements or terms a lease may contain that will govern the actions of both landlord and tenant. We will cover the responsibilities of all parties in the lease, as well as how to terminate a lease, and what happens when a lease is terminated. Finally we will cover discrimination with regard to leasing property to another individual.

T H E   L E A S E H O L D

A lease is a contract between two parties that describes the transfer of interest in property from the owner (landlord) to the person interested in utilizing or inhabiting the property (the tenant). It is important to understand that the lease only transfers the right to use the property, it does not transfer ownership. This is sometimes confusing for people, as the leasehold is considered an estate in property. A lease may allow a person to live on the property, or it may allow a person to use the property (for instance, in leasing agricultural land to a farmer). A leasehold may also transfer rights to a person to mine minerals from within the earth.

All leases must contain or mention:

- The owner of real property (called **landlord** or **lessor**)
- The person using the land for a specific time period (called **tenant** or **lessee**)
- Some form of consideration for the use of the land (usually this is in the form of **rent**)

The leasehold or less-than-freehold estate is considered personal property, or chattel real. Real property is, generally, any property or portion of the property that is immovable. A leasehold is created through a contract, or a moveable document. While the tenant in a leasehold agreement does not enjoy all the bundle of rights, he or she still possesses the right of use and the right to quiet possession of the property.

Types of Leasehold Estates

There are different types of leaseholds. These are *estate for years, estate from period to period, estate at will* and *estate at sufferance*. The main difference between these types of leaseholds is the duration of the tenancy. If the duration of the tenancy is over one year, a lease is required. For tenancy duration of less than one year, either a written or verbal agreement may be used.

Types of Leaseholds:

- Estate for years
- Estate from period to period
- Estate at will
- Estate at sufferance

An *estate for years* is a lease created between a landlord and tenant and valid only for a specific amount of time. This type of lease may last for several years, as its name indicates. However, an estate for years may also last only months, weeks or even days. Because both the landlord and tenant know when the lease expires, no notice is required at the end of the lease period.

This type of estate is attractive to tenants who are looking for long term housing or rental space, because the rental price will usually stay the same for that specific duration. Landlords like this type of lease, because they can find tenants who will occupy the space for an extended period of time. This prevents the landlord from continually filling vacancies.

Additionally when this lease is up, there are no automatic extensions or renewals of the lease. If the tenant and landlord mutually agree to renew the tenancy, another estate for years is formed. Some contracts or leases will have an option for the tenant to form a month-to-month contract. Such a contract is not considered an estate for years; rather, it is an estate from period to period.

An *estate from period to period* is also referred to as a *periodic tenancy*. This type of tenancy occurs when a tenant pays his or her rent at the end of a lease, and the landlord accepts the payment. The lease automatically extends for the duration for which the tenant paid. As long as the landlord accepts payment, the lease is renewed. To terminate this type of rental agreement, a notice must be given by one party to the other. If the tenant plans to vacate the space, he or she must notify the landlord prior to leaving. If the landlord does not wish to renew the tenant's contract, the landlord must give notice to the tenant that the lease will not be renewed.

Periodic tenancy is generally a month-to-month contract. Because most leases require the tenant to pay rent once each month; by paying the additional month of rent, the contract will be extended for any additional months for which rent is paid. Periodic tenancies are not always month-to-month leases, though that is the most common form.

An *estate at will* requires no rental agreement or contract between the landlord and tenant. Either party may terminate the contract at will without the others consent. However, if the contract if terminated, a 30-day notice must be given by the party who chooses to terminate the contract. This type of tenancy is uncommon in California.

An *estate at sufferance* is created when a tenant does not vacate a property at the end of a lease agreement, and so remains in possession of the property. The tenant will remain in control of the property against the wishes, or without the consent of the landlord. Additionally, if a tenant gives notice to vacate, yet never leaves and does not pay rent, an estate at sufferance is created. The landlord may give notice of termination of the lease at any time. This type of instability makes the estate at sufferance the least desirable type, or lowest form of tenancy. If the tenant pays rent, and the landlord accepts the payment, it is no longer an estate at sufferance. Rather, it is a periodic tenancy.

The agreement between the landlord (or lessor) and tenant (or lessee) is called a lease. The lease will outline all terms of the tenancy, including: the rent amount; beginning and ending dates of the tenancy; and any restrictions or rules a tenant must observe.

In California, any lease for a period of more than one year must be made in writing. This lease must be signed by the landlord, but do not have to be signed by the tenant. When a tenant takes possession of the property, he or she is acknowledging the terms of the lease, and is therefore not required to sign the contract. Although the tenant is not required to sign the lease, it is a good idea for both parties to carefully read the lease, to understand all its terms. It is also wise for both parties to sign the lease, to avoid any misunderstanding, which may arise in the future. The right of the landlord to reclaim the property being leased is called *reversionary rights.*

All leases must contain: the name of the parties; description of the property involved; period of time or duration the lease will last; and the required, monthly rent or consideration. An easy way to remember these requirements is with the four P's:

> Lease Requirements (or, the Four Ps)
> - Parties
> - Property
> - Period (of time)
> - Payment (rent)

All leases should clearly identify the landlord, the tenant and any additional persons occupying the property. These people are known as the *parties*, though leases will usually use the terms lessee and lessor to identify the parties involved in the tenancy.

Leases must clearly describe the property that will be occupied as well as any restrictions or allowable uses the tenant must observe in leasing the property.

Every lease will specify a time period during which the lease will be valid. This should indicate the start and end date of the lease. If there is no duration mentioned in the lease the consideration or payment is used to indicate the length of time for which the lease is intended valid. For example, if rent has been paid for 3 months, the lease is considered to be valid for three months.

There are a few exceptions to the duration of lease time that can be offered. For instance, a lease time for property located within a city may only be leased for a maximum for 99 years. Property leased outside of a city or town (for instance, agricultural land) may only be leased for 51 years.

Each lease must specify the consideration or payment (also called rent) required for a lessee to take and retain possession of a property. The rent (as well as the schedule for payment of rent) will be specified in the lease. For example, if a tenant moves into an apartment building in the middle of a month, rent may be due on that date each month. Alternatively, the first and last months of rent may be prorated, with rent due on the first day of each month. Advance payments, penalties on late payments and other issues regarding consideration will also be covered in this part of the lease.

Leases may be altered or changed as long as both parties acknowledge the change. If the lease is for less then one year in duration, and is made verbally, the contract may be altered orally. If the lease is for more than one year in duration, the lease must be made in writing, and any changes to this contract must also be made in writing. It is important to remember that leases are legal, binding contracts and all persons entering into the lease must be of legal competence for such a contract to be valid. As we have seen with the four Ps, each lease must specify the terms of the contract.

SECURITY DEPOSITS

Landlords will usually require a security deposit to be paid at the beginning of the lease and held until the tenant vacates the property. This security deposit may be used to cover any damage caused by the tenant, as well as any routine costs and repairs needed after the tenant vacates the unit. Such costs include repainting or cleaning. While not every landlord requires a security deposit (nor is there a minimum deposit a landlord must accept), the state has set maximums on the amount of security deposit a landlord is allowed to collect from a tenant. For unfurnished properties, a landlord may lawfully collect up to two months rent, for furnished properties a landlord can collect up to three months rent.

Tenants are entitled to a refunded deposit, less repairs and routine maintenance, within three weeks of vacating a property. The landlord must include an itemized list of all work performed, as well as the cost of each of the services, and provide a check for the remaining balance of the renter's deposit. Any landlord who does not provide this documentation to the tenant or a landlord who keeps any amount of the deposit in bad faith is subject to a $600 fine (and is also liable for any loss suffered by the tenant). Landlords must prove that all claims made to the security deposit are valid and must defend them if challenged. The law will accept a tenant's challenge and award the full security deposit if the landlord cannot prove the validity of each claim.

Tenants should always inspect property before they move in or occupy the space. They should document any defects or damages to the property before taking possession. By inspecting the property before moving in and filling out the statement of property condition, a tenant will protect their security deposit from being used to fix prior damage to the unit or property. The statement of property condition also helps avoid disputes between the tenant and landlord upon termination of the contract. The statement will outline which damages were already present, as well as any damages for which the tenant will be held financially responsible.

If a landlord sells a rental property, currently occupied by tenants during a tenants lease term, the security deposit made by the renter will be transferred to the new owner. The new owner must be aware of each tenant's security deposit, so that the necessary accounting and documentation may be prepared for any existing tenants upon the termination of their leases.

Nonresidential property has different rules governing its security deposits. There are no limits or restriction on how much money a landlord may collect as security deposit on this type of property. As a result, a landlord may collect as much as he or she considers necessary to protect his or her own interest in the property. When a tenant vacates a property, the landlord may take up to 60 days to return the tenant's security deposit (less any charges made against it for repairs or routine maintenance). Landlords of non-residential property are not required to provide a written statement of charges made to the security deposit.

RESIDENTIAL LEASE OR
MONTH-TO-MONTH RENTAL AGREEMENT
(C.A.R. Form LR, Revised 10/04)

_____ ("Landlord") and
_____ ("Tenant") agree as follows:

1. **PROPERTY:**
   A. Landlord rents to Tenant and Tenant rents from Landlord, the real property and improvements described as: _____
      _____ ("Premises").
   B. The Premises are for the sole use as a personal residence by the following named person(s) only: _____
      _____.
   C. The following personal property, maintained pursuant to paragraph 11, is included: _____
      _____ or ☐ (if checked) the personal property on the attached addendum.

2. **TERM:** The term begins on (date) _____ ("Commencement Date"), **(Check A or B):**
   ☐ **A. Month-to-Month:** and continues as a month-to-month tenancy. Tenant may terminate the tenancy by giving written notice
      at least 30 days prior to the intended termination date. Landlord may terminate the tenancy by giving written notice as
      provided by law. Such notices may be given on any date.
   ☐ **B. Lease:** and shall terminate on (date) _____ at _____ ☐ AM/ ☐ PM.
      Tenant shall vacate the Premises upon termination of the Agreement, unless: **(i)** Landlord and Tenant have extended this
      agreement in writing or signed a new agreement; **(ii)** mandated by local rent control law; or **(iii)** Landlord accepts Rent from
      Tenant (other than past due Rent), in which case a month-to-month tenancy shall be created which either party may
      terminate as specified in paragraph 2A. Rent shall be at a rate agreed to by Landlord and Tenant, or as allowed by law. All
      other terms and conditions of this Agreement shall remain in full force and effect.

3. **RENT:** "Rent" shall mean all monetary obligations of Tenant to Landlord under the terms of the Agreement, except security deposit.
   A. Tenant agrees to pay $ _____ per month for the term of the Agreement.
   B. Rent is payable in advance on the **1st (or** ☐ _____ **) day** of each calendar month, and is delinquent on the next day.
   C. If Commencement Date falls on any day other than the day Rent is payable under paragraph 3B, and Tenant has paid one full
      month's Rent in advance of Commencement Date, Rent for the second calendar month shall be prorated based on a 30-day
      period.
   D. PAYMENT: Rent shall be paid by ☐ personal check, ☐ money order, ☐ cashier's check, or ☐ other _____, to (name)
      _____ (phone) _____ at (address)
      _____, (or at any other location
      subsequently specified by Landlord in writing to Tenant) between the hours of _____ and _____ on the following days
      _____. If any payment is returned for non-sufficient funds ("NSF") or
      because tenant stops payment, then, after that: (i) Landlord may, in writing, require Tenant to pay Rent in cash for three months
      and (ii) all future Rent shall be paid by ☐ money order, or ☐ cashier's check.

4. **SECURITY DEPOSIT:**
   A. Tenant agrees to pay $ _____ as a security deposit. Security deposit will be
      ☐ transferred to and held by the Owner of the Premises, or ☐ held in Owner's Broker's trust account.
   B. All or any portion of the security deposit may be used, as reasonably necessary, to: **(i)** cure Tenant's default in payment of Rent (which
      includes Late Charges, NSF fees or other sums due); **(ii)** repair damage, excluding ordinary wear and tear, caused by Tenant or by a
      guest or licensee of Tenant; **(iii)** clean Premises, if necessary, upon termination of the tenancy; and **(iv)** replace or return personal
      property or appurtenances. **SECURITY DEPOSIT SHALL NOT BE USED BY TENANT IN LIEU OF PAYMENT OF LAST
      MONTH'S RENT.** If all or any portion of the security deposit is used during the tenancy, Tenant agrees to reinstate the total security
      deposit within five days after written notice is delivered to Tenant. Within 21 days after Tenant vacates the Premises, Landlord shall:
      (1) furnish Tenant an itemized statement indicating the amount of any security deposit received and the basis for its
      disposition and supporting documentation as required by California Civil Code § 1950.5(g); and **(2)** return any remaining
      portion of the security deposit to Tenant.
   C. **Security deposit will not be returned until all Tenants have vacated the Premises. Any security deposit returned by
      check shall be made out to all Tenants named on this Agreement, or as subsequently modified.**
   D. No interest will be paid on security deposit unless required by local law.
   E. If the security deposit is held by Owner, Tenant agrees not to hold Broker responsible for its return. If the security deposit is held
      in Owner's Broker's trust account, **and** Broker's authority is terminated before expiration of this Agreement, **and** security deposit
      is released to someone other than Tenant, **then** Broker shall notify Tenant, in writing, where and to whom security deposit has
      been released. Once Tenant has been provided such notice, Tenant agrees not to hold Broker responsible for the security
      deposit.

5. **MOVE-IN COSTS RECEIVED/DUE:** Move-in funds made payable to _____
   shall be paid by ☐ personal check, ☐ money order, or ☐ cashier's check.

Category	Total Due	Payment Received	Balance Due	Date Due
Rent from _____ to _____ (date)				
*Security Deposit				
Other _____				
Other _____				
Total				

*The maximum amount Landlord may receive as security deposit, however designated, cannot exceed two months' Rent for
unfurnished premises, or three months' Rent for furnished premises.

Tenant's Initials (_____)(_____)
Landlord's Initials (_____)(_____)

Reviewed by _____ Date _____

LR REVISED 10/04 (PAGE 1 OF 6) Print Date

RESIDENTIAL LEASE OR MONTH-TO-MONTH RENTAL AGREEMENT (LR PAGE 1 OF 6)

Premises: _____ Date: _____

6. LATE CHARGE; RETURNED CHECKS:

   A. Tenant acknowledges either late payment of Rent or issuance of a returned check may cause Landlord to incur costs and expenses, the exact amounts of which are extremely difficult and impractical to determine. These costs may include, but are not limited to, processing, enforcement and accounting expenses, and late charges imposed on Landlord. If any installment of Rent due from Tenant is not received by Landlord within 5 (or ☐ _____) **calendar days** after the date due, or if a check is returned, Tenant shall pay to Landlord, respectively, an additional sum of $ _____ or _____ % of the Rent due as a Late Charge and $25.00 as a NSF fee for the first returned check and $35.00 as a NSF fee for each additional returned check, either or both of which shall be deemed additional Rent.

   B. Landlord and Tenant agree that these charges represent a fair and reasonable estimate of the costs Landlord may incur by reason of Tenant's late or NSF payment. Any Late Charge or NSF fee due shall be paid with the current installment of Rent. Landlord's acceptance of any Late Charge or NSF fee shall not constitute a waiver as to any default of Tenant. Landlord's right to collect a Late Charge or NSF fee shall not be deemed an extension of the date Rent is due under paragraph 3 or prevent Landlord from exercising any other rights and remedies under this Agreement and as provided by law.

7. PARKING: (Check A or B)

   ☐ **A.** Parking is permitted as follows: _____
_____
The right to parking ☐ is ☐ is not included in the Rent charged pursuant to paragraph 3. If not included in the Rent, the parking rental fee shall be an additional $ _____ per month. Parking space(s) are to be used for parking properly licensed and operable motor vehicles, except for trailers, boats, campers, buses or trucks (other than pick-up trucks). Tenant shall park in assigned space(s) only. Parking space(s) are to be kept clean. Vehicles leaking oil, gas or other motor vehicle fluids shall not be parked on the Premises. Mechanical work or storage of inoperable vehicles is not permitted in parking space(s) or elsewhere on the Premises.

   OR ☐ **B.** Parking is not permitted on the Premises.

8. STORAGE: (Check A or B)

   ☐ **A.** Storage is permitted as follows: _____
The right to storage space ☐ is, ☐ is not included in the Rent charged pursuant to paragraph 3. If not included in the Rent, storage space fee shall be an additional $ _____ per month. Tenant shall store only personal property Tenant owns, and shall not store property claimed by another or in which another has any right, title or interest. Tenant shall not store any improperly packaged food or perishable goods, flammable materials, explosives, hazardous waste or other inherently dangerous material, or illegal substances.

   OR ☐ **B.** Storage is not permitted on the Premises.

9. UTILITIES: Tenant agrees to pay for all utilities and services, and the following charges: _____
except _____, which shall be paid for by Landlord. If any utilities are not separately metered, Tenant shall pay Tenant's proportional share, as reasonably determined and directed by Landlord. If utilities are separately metered, Tenant shall place utilities in Tenant's name as of the Commencement Date. Landlord is only responsible for installing and maintaining one usable telephone jack and one telephone line to the Premises. Tenant shall pay any cost for conversion from existing utilities service provider.

10. CONDITION OF PREMISES: Tenant has examined Premises and, if any, all furniture, furnishings, appliances, landscaping and fixtures, including smoke detector(s).

   (Check all that apply:)

   ☐ **A.** Tenant acknowledges these items are clean and in operable condition, with the following exceptions: _____
_____

   ☐ **B.** Tenant's acknowledgment of the condition of these items is contained in an attached statement of condition (C.A.R. Form MIMO).

   ☐ **C.** Tenant will provide Landlord a list of items that are damaged or not in operable condition within 3 (or ☐ _____) days after Commencement Date, not as a contingency of this Agreement but rather as an acknowledgment of the condition of the Premises.

   ☐ **D.** Other: _____

11. MAINTENANCE:

   A. Tenant shall properly use, operate and safeguard Premises, including if applicable, any landscaping, furniture, furnishings and appliances, and all mechanical, electrical, gas and plumbing fixtures, and keep them and the Premises clean, sanitary and well ventilated. Tenant shall be responsible for checking and maintaining all smoke detectors and any additional phone lines beyond the one line and jack that Landlord shall provide and maintain. Tenant shall immediately notify Landlord, in writing, of any problem, malfunction or damage. Tenant shall be charged for all repairs or replacements caused by Tenant, pets, guests or licensees of Tenant, excluding ordinary wear and tear. Tenant shall be charged for all damage to Premises as a result of failure to report a problem in a timely manner. Tenant shall be charged for repair of drain blockages or stoppages, unless caused by defective plumbing parts or tree roots invading sewer lines.

   B. ☐ Landlord ☐ Tenant shall water the garden, landscaping, trees and shrubs, except: _____
_____

   C. ☐ Landlord ☐ Tenant shall maintain the garden, landscaping, trees and shrubs, except: _____
_____

   D. ☐ Landlord ☐ Tenant shall maintain _____

   E. Tenant's failure to maintain any item for which Tenant is responsible shall give Landlord the right to hire someone to perform such maintenance and charge Tenant to cover the cost of such maintenance.

   F. The following items of personal property are included in the Premises without warranty and Landlord will not maintain, repair or replace them: _____

Tenant's Initials (_____)(_____)
Landlord's Initials (_____)(_____)

LR REVISED 10/04 (PAGE 2 OF 6)

Reviewed by _____ Date _____

RESIDENTIAL LEASE OR MONTH-TO-MONTH RENTAL AGREEMENT (LR PAGE 2 OF 6)

12. **NEIGHBORHOOD CONDITIONS:** Tenant is advised to satisfy him or herself as to neighborhood or area conditions, including schools, proximity and adequacy of law enforcement, crime statistics, proximity of registered felons or offenders, fire protection, other governmental services, availability, adequacy and cost of any speed-wired, wireless internet connections or other telecommunications or other technology services and installations, proximity to commercial, industrial or agricultural activities, existing and proposed transportation, construction and development that may affect noise, view, or traffic, airport noise, noise or odor from any source, wild and domestic animals, other nuisances, hazards, or circumstances, cemeteries, facilities and condition of common areas, conditions and influences of significance to certain cultures and/or religions, and personal needs, requirements and preferences of Tenant.

13. **PETS:** Unless otherwise provided in California Civil Code § 54.2, no animal or pet shall be kept on or about the Premises without Landlord's prior written consent, except: _____ .

14. **RULES/REGULATIONS:**
   A. Tenant agrees to comply with all Landlord rules and regulations that are at any time posted on the Premises or delivered to Tenant. Tenant shall not, and shall ensure that guests and licensees of Tenant shall not, disturb, annoy, endanger or interfere with other tenants of the building or neighbors, or use the Premises for any unlawful purposes, including, but not limited to, using, manufacturing, selling, storing or transporting illicit drugs or other contraband, or violate any law or ordinance, or commit a waste or nuisance on or about the Premises.
   B. **(If applicable, check one)**
      ☐ **1.** Landlord shall provide Tenant with a copy of the rules and regulations within _____ days
      or _____ .
      OR ☐ 2. Tenant has been provided with, and acknowledges receipt of, a copy of the rules and regulations.

15. ☐ **(If checked) CONDOMINIUM; PLANNED UNIT DEVELOPMENT:**
   A. The Premises is a unit in a condominium, planned unit development, common interest subdivision or other development governed by a homeowners' association ("HOA"). The name of the HOA is _____. Tenant agrees to comply with all HOA covenants, conditions and restrictions, bylaws, rules and regulations and decisions. Landlord shall provide Tenant copies of rules and regulations, if any. Tenant shall reimburse Landlord for any fines or charges imposed by HOA or other authorities, due to any violation by Tenant, or the guests or licensees of Tenant.
   B. **(Check one)**
      ☐ **1.** Landlord shall provide Tenant with a copy of the HOA rules and regulations within _____ days
      or _____ .
      OR ☐ 2. Tenant has been provided with, and acknowledges receipt of, a copy of the HOA rules and regulations.

16. **ALTERATIONS; REPAIRS:** Unless otherwise specified by law or paragraph 27C, without Landlord's prior written consent, (i) Tenant shall not make any repairs, alterations or improvements in or about the Premises including: painting, wallpapering, adding or changing locks, installing antenna or satellite dish(es), placing signs, displays or exhibits, or using screws, fastening devices, large nails or adhesive materials; (ii) Landlord shall not be responsible for the costs of alterations or repairs made by Tenant; (iii) Tenant shall not deduct from Rent the costs of any repairs, alterations or improvements; and (iv) any deduction made by Tenant shall be considered unpaid Rent.

17. **KEYS; LOCKS:**
   A. Tenant acknowledges receipt of (or Tenant will receive ☐ prior to the Commencement Date, or ☐ _____):
      ☐ _____ key(s) to Premises,   ☐ _____ remote control device(s) for garage door/gate opener(s),
      ☐ _____ key(s) to mailbox,   ☐ _____ ,
      ☐ _____ key(s) to common area(s),   ☐ _____ .
   B. Tenant acknowledges that locks to the Premises ☐ have, ☐ have not, been re-keyed.
   C. If Tenant re-keys existing locks or opening devices, Tenant shall immediately deliver copies of all keys to Landlord. Tenant shall pay all costs and charges related to loss of any keys or opening devices. Tenant may not remove locks, even if installed by Tenant.

18. **ENTRY:**
   A. Tenant shall make Premises available to Landlord or Landlord's representative for the purpose of entering to make necessary or agreed repairs, decorations, alterations, or improvements, or to supply necessary or agreed services, or to show Premises to prospective or actual purchasers, tenants, mortgagees, lenders, appraisers, or contractors.
   B. Landlord and Tenant agree that 24-hour written notice shall be reasonable and sufficient notice, except as follows. 48-hour written notice is required to conduct an inspection of the Premises prior to the Tenant moving out, unless the Tenant waives the right to such notice. Notice may be given orally to show the Premises to actual or prospective purchasers provided Tenant has been notified in writing within 120 days preceding the oral notice that the Premises are for sale and that oral notice may be given to show the Premises. No notice is required: (i) to enter in case of an emergency; (ii) if the Tenant is present and consents at the time of entry or (iii) if the Tenant has abandoned or surrendered the Premises. No written notice is required if Landlord and Tenant orally agree to an entry for agreed services or repairs if the date and time of entry are within one week of the oral agreement.
   C. ☐ (If checked) Tenant authorizes the use of a keysafe/lockbox to allow entry into the Premises and agrees to sign a keysafe/lockbox addendum (C.A.R. Form KLA).

19. **SIGNS:** Tenant authorizes Landlord to place FOR SALE/LEASE signs on the Premises.

20. **ASSIGNMENT; SUBLETTING:** Tenant shall not sublet all or any part of Premises, or assign or transfer this Agreement or any interest in it, without Landlord's prior written consent. Unless such consent is obtained, any assignment, transfer or subletting of Premises or this Agreement or tenancy, by voluntary act of Tenant, operation of law or otherwise, shall, at the option of Landlord, terminate this Agreement. Any proposed assignee, transferee or sublessee shall submit to Landlord an application and credit information for Landlord's approval and, if approved, sign a separate written agreement with Landlord and Tenant. Landlord's consent to any one assignment, transfer or sublease, shall not be construed as consent to any subsequent assignment, transfer or sublease and does not release Tenant of Tenant's obligations under this Agreement.

21. **JOINT AND INDIVIDUAL OBLIGATIONS:** If there is more than one Tenant, each one shall be individually and completely responsible for the performance of all obligations of Tenant under this Agreement, jointly with every other Tenant, and individually, whether or not in possession.

Tenant's Initials (_____)(_____)
Landlord's Initials (_____)(_____)

Reviewed by _____ Date _____

LR REVISED 10/04 (PAGE 3 OF 6)

RESIDENTIAL LEASE OR MONTH-TO-MONTH RENTAL AGREEMENT (LR PAGE 3 OF 6)

Premises: _____ Date: _____

22. ☐ **LEAD-BASED PAINT (If checked):** Premises was constructed prior to 1978. In accordance with federal law, Landlord gives and Tenant acknowledges receipt of the disclosures on the attached form (C.A.R. Form FLD) and a federally approved lead pamphlet.

23. ☐ **MILITARY ORDNANCE DISCLOSURE:** (If applicable and known to Landlord) Premises is located within one mile of an area once used for military training, and may contain potentially explosive munitions.

24. ☐ **PERIODIC PEST CONTROL:** Landlord has entered into a contract for periodic pest control treatment of the Premises and shall give Tenant a copy of the notice originally given to Landlord by the pest control company.

25. **DATABASE DISCLOSURE: NOTICE:** The California Department of Justice, sheriff's departments, police departments serving jurisdictions of 200,000 or more, and many other local law enforcement authorities maintain for public access a database of the locations of persons required to register pursuant to paragraph (1) of subdivision (a) of Section 290.4 of the Penal Code. The data base is updated on a quarterly basis and a source of information about the presence of these individuals in any neighborhood. The Department of Justice also maintains a Sex Offender Identification Line through which inquiries about individuals may be made. This is a "900" telephone service. Callers must have specific information about individuals they are checking. Information regarding neighborhoods is not available through the "900" telephone service.

26. **POSSESSION:**
   A. Tenant is not in possession of the premises. If Landlord is unable to deliver possession of Premises on Commencement Date, such Date shall be extended to the date on which possession is made available to Tenant. If Landlord is unable to deliver possession within 5 (or ☐ _____) **calendar days** after agreed Commencement Date, Tenant may terminate this Agreement by giving written notice to Landlord, and shall be refunded all Rent and security deposit paid. Possession is deemed terminated when Tenant has returned all keys to the Premises to Landlord.
   B. ☐ Tenant is already in possession of the Premises.

27. **TENANT'S OBLIGATIONS UPON VACATING PREMISES:**
   A. Upon termination of the Agreement, Tenant shall: **(i)** give Landlord all copies of all keys or opening devices to Premises, including any common areas; **(ii)** vacate and surrender Premises to Landlord, empty of all persons; **(iii)** vacate any/all parking and/or storage space; **(iv)** clean and deliver Premises, as specified in paragraph C below, to Landlord in the same condition as referenced in paragraph 10; **(v)** remove all debris; **(vi)** give written notice to Landlord of Tenant's forwarding address; and **(vii)** _____
   B. All alterations/improvements made by or caused to be made by Tenant, with or without Landlord's consent, become the property of Landlord upon termination. Landlord may charge Tenant for restoration of the Premises to the condition it was in prior to any alterations/improvements.
   C. **Right to Pre-Move-Out Inspection and Repairs as follows: (i)** After giving or receiving notice of termination of a tenancy (C.A.R. Form NTT), or before the end of a lease, Tenant has the right to request that an inspection of the Premises take place prior to termination of the lease or rental (C.A.R. Form NRI). If Tenant requests such an inspection, Tenant shall be given an opportunity to remedy identified deficiencies prior to termination, consistent with the terms of this Agreement. **(ii)** Any repairs or alterations made to the Premises as a result of this inspection (collectively, "Repairs") shall be made at Tenant's expense. Repairs may be performed by Tenant or through others who have adequate insurance and licenses and are approved by Landlord. The work shall comply with applicable law, including governmental permit, inspection and approval requirements. Repairs shall be performed in a good, skillful manner with materials of quality and appearance comparable to existing materials. It is understood that exact restoration of appearance or cosmetic items following all Repairs may not be possible. **(iii)** Tenant shall: **(a)** obtain receipts for Repairs performed by others; **(b)** prepare a written statement indicating the Repairs performed by Tenant and the date of such Repairs; and **(c)** provide copies of receipts and statements to Landlord prior to termination. Paragraph 27C does not apply when the tenancy is terminated pursuant to California Code of Civil Procedure § 1161(2), (3) or (4).

28. **BREACH OF CONTRACT; EARLY TERMINATION:** In addition to any obligations established by paragraph 27, in the event of termination by Tenant prior to completion of the original term of the Agreement, Tenant shall also be responsible for lost Rent, rental commissions, advertising expenses and painting costs necessary to ready Premises for re-rental. Landlord may withhold any such amounts from Tenant's security deposit.

29. **TEMPORARY RELOCATION:** Subject to local law, Tenant agrees, upon demand of Landlord, to temporarily vacate Premises for a reasonable period, to allow for fumigation (or other methods) to control wood destroying pests or organisms, or other repairs to Premises. Tenant agrees to comply with all instructions and requirements necessary to prepare Premises to accommodate pest control, fumigation or other work, including bagging or storage of food and medicine, and removal of perishables and valuables. Tenant shall only be entitled to a credit of Rent equal to the per diem Rent for the period of time Tenant is required to vacate Premises.

30. **DAMAGE TO PREMISES:** If, by no fault of Tenant, Premises are totally or partially damaged or destroyed by fire, earthquake, accident or other casualty that render Premises totally or partially uninhabitable, either Landlord or Tenant may terminate this Agreement by giving the other written notice. Rent shall be abated as of the date Premises become totally or partially uninhabitable. The abated amount shall be the current monthly Rent prorated on a 30-day period. If the Agreement is not terminated, Landlord shall promptly repair the damage, and Rent shall be reduced based on the extent to which the damage interferes with Tenant's reasonable use of Premises. If damage occurs as a result of an act of Tenant or Tenant's guests, only Landlord shall have the right of termination, and no reduction in Rent shall be made.

31. **INSURANCE:** Tenant's or guest's personal property and vehicles are not insured by Landlord, manager or, if applicable, HOA, against loss or damage due to fire, theft, vandalism, rain, water, criminal or negligent acts of others, or any other cause. **Tenant is advised to carry Tenant's own insurance (renter's insurance) to protect Tenant from any such loss or damage.** Tenant shall comply with any requirement imposed on Tenant by Landlord's insurer to avoid: **(i)** an increase in Landlord's insurance premium (or Tenant shall pay for the increase in premium); or **(ii)** loss of insurance.

32. **WATERBEDS:** Tenant shall not use or have waterbeds on the Premises unless: **(i)** Tenant obtains a valid waterbed insurance policy; **(ii)** Tenant increases the security deposit in an amount equal to one-half of one month's Rent; and **(iii)** the bed conforms to the floor load capacity of Premises.

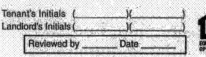

Tenant's Initials (_____)(_____)
Landlord's Initials (_____)(_____)

Reviewed by _____ Date _____

EQUAL HOUSING OPPORTUNITY

RESIDENTIAL LEASE OR MONTH-TO-MONTH RENTAL AGREEMENT (LR PAGE 4 OF 6)

Premises: _____ Date: _____

33. **WAIVER:** The waiver of any breach shall not be construed as a continuing waiver of the same or any subsequent breach.

34. **NOTICE:** Notices may be served at the following address, or at any other location subsequently designated:
Landlord: _____ Tenant: _____
_____ _____
_____ _____

35. **TENANT ESTOPPEL CERTIFICATE:** Tenant shall execute and return a tenant estoppel certificate delivered to Tenant by Landlord or Landlord's agent within 3 days after its receipt. Failure to comply with this requirement shall be deemed Tenant's acknowledgment that the tenant estoppel certificate is true and correct, and may be relied upon by a lender or purchaser.

36. **TENANT REPRESENTATIONS; CREDIT:** Tenant warrants that all statements in Tenant's rental application are accurate. Tenant authorizes Landlord and Broker(s) to obtain Tenant's credit report periodically during the tenancy in connection with the modification or enforcement of this Agreement. Landlord may cancel this Agreement: (i) before occupancy begins; (ii) upon disapproval of the credit report(s); or (iii) at any time, upon discovering that information in Tenant's application is false. A negative credit report reflecting on Tenant's record may be submitted to a credit reporting agency if Tenant fails to fulfill the terms of payment and other obligations under this Agreement.

37. **MEDIATION:**
   A. Consistent with paragraphs B and C below, Landlord and Tenant agree to mediate any dispute or claim arising between them out of this Agreement, or any resulting transaction, before resorting to court action. Mediation fees, if any, shall be divided equally among the parties involved. If, for any dispute or claim to which this paragraph applies, any party commences an action without first attempting to resolve the matter through mediation, or refuses to mediate after a request has been made, then that party shall not be entitled to recover attorney fees, even if they would otherwise be available to that party in any such action.
   B. The following matters are excluded from mediation: (i) an unlawful detainer action; (ii) the filing or enforcement of a mechanic's lien; and (iii) any matter within the jurisdiction of a probate, small claims or bankruptcy court. The filing of a court action to enable the recording of a notice of pending action, for order of attachment, receivership, injunction, or other provisional remedies, shall not constitute a waiver of the mediation provision.
   C. Landlord and Tenant agree to mediate disputes or claims involving Listing Agent, Leasing Agent or property manager ("Broker"), provided Broker shall have agreed to such mediation prior to, or within a reasonable time after, the dispute or claim is presented to such Broker. Any election by Broker to participate in mediation shall not result in Broker being deemed a party to this Agreement.

38. **ATTORNEY FEES:** In any action or proceeding arising out of this Agreement, the prevailing party between Landlord and Tenant shall be entitled to reasonable attorney fees and costs, except as provided in paragraph 37A.

39. **C.A.R. FORM:** C.A.R. Form means the specific form referenced or another comparable from agreed to by the parties.

40. **OTHER TERMS AND CONDITIONS;SUPPLEMENTS:** _____
_____

The following ATTACHED supplements are incorporated in this Agreement: ☐ Keysafe/Lockbox Addendum (C.A.R. Form KLA); ☐ Interpreter/Translator Agreement (C.A.R. Form ITA); ☐ Lead-Based Paint and Lead-Based Paint Hazards Disclosure (C.A.R. Form FLD)

41. **TIME OF ESSENCE; ENTIRE CONTRACT; CHANGES:** Time is of the essence. All understandings between the parties are incorporated in this Agreement. Its terms are intended by the parties as a final, complete and exclusive expression of their Agreement with respect to its subject matter, and may not be contradicted by evidence of any prior agreement or contemporaneous oral agreement. If any provision of this Agreement is held to be ineffective or invalid, the remaining provisions will nevertheless be given full force and effect. Neither this Agreement nor any provision in it may be extended, amended, modified, altered or changed except in writing. This Agreement is subject to California landlord-tenant law and shall incorporate all changes required by amendment or successors to such law. This Agreement and any supplement, addendum or modification, including any copy, may be signed in two or more counterparts, all of which shall constitute one and the same writing.

42. **AGENCY:**
   A. **CONFIRMATION:** The following agency relationship(s) are hereby confirmed for this transaction:
   Listing Agent: (Print firm name) _____ is the agent of (check one): ☐ the Landlord exclusively; or ☐ both the Landlord and Tenant.
   Leasing Agent: (Print firm name) _____ (if not same as Listing Agent) is the agent of (check one): ☐ the Tenant exclusively; or ☐ the Landlord exclusively; or ☐ both the Tenant and Landlord.
   B. **DISCLOSURE:** ☐ (If checked): The term of this lease exceeds one year. A disclosure regarding real estate agency relationships (C.A.R. Form AD) has been provided to Landlord and Tenant, who each acknowledge its receipt.

43. ☐ **TENANT COMPENSATION TO BROKER:** Upon execution of this Agreement, Tenant agrees to pay compensation to Broker as specified in a separate written agreement between Tenant and Broker.

44. ☐ **INTERPRETER/TRANSLATOR:** The terms of this Agreement have been interpreted for Tenant into the following language: _____. Landlord and Tenant acknowledge receipt of the attached interpretor/translator agreement (C.A.R. Form ITA).

45. **FOREIGN LANGUAGE NEGOTIATION:** If this Agreement has been negotiated by Landlord and Tenant primarily in Spanish, Chinese, Tagalog, Korean or Vietnamese. Pursuant to the California Civil Code Tenant shall be provided a translation of this Agreement in the language used for the negotiation.

Tenant's Initials (_____)(_____)
Landlord's Initials (_____)(_____)

Reviewed by _____ Date _____

RESIDENTIAL LEASE OR MONTH-TO-MONTH RENTAL AGREEMENT (LR PAGE 5 OF 6)

Premises: _____ Date: _____

Landlord and Tenant acknowledge and agree Brokers: **(a)** do not guarantee the condition of the Premises; **(b)** cannot verify representations made by others; **(c)** cannot provide legal or tax advice; **(d)** will not provide other advice or information that exceeds the knowledge, education or experience required to obtain a real estate license. Furthermore, if Brokers are not also acting as Landlord in this Agreement, Brokers: **(e)** do not decide what rental rate a Tenant should pay or Landlord should accept; and **(f)** do not decide upon the length or other terms of tenancy. Landlord and Tenant agree that they will seek legal, tax, insurance and other desired assistance from appropriate professionals.

Tenant   Date
Address _____ City _____ State _____ Zip _____
Telephone _____ Fax _____ E-mail_____
Tenant _____ Date _____
Address _____ City _____ State _____ Zip _____
Telephone _____ Fax _____ E-mail_____

46. ☐ **GUARANTEE:** In consideration of the execution of the Agreement by and between Landlord and Tenant and for valuable consideration, receipt of which is hereby acknowledged, the undersigned ("Guarantor") does hereby: **(i)** guarantee unconditionally to Landlord and Landlord's agents, successors and assigns, the prompt payment of Rent or other sums that become due pursuant to this Agreement, including any and all court costs and attorney fees included in enforcing the Agreement; **(ii)** consent to any changes, modifications or alterations of any term in this Agreement agreed to by Landlord and Tenant; and **(iii)** waive any right to require Landlord and/or Landlord's agents to proceed against Tenant for any default occurring under this Agreement before seeking to enforce this Guarantee.

Guarantor (Print Name) _____
Guarantor _____ Date _____
Address _____ City _____ State _____ Zip _____
Telephone _____ Fax _____ E-mail_____

47. OWNER COMPENSATION TO BROKER: Upon execution of this Agreement, Owner agrees to pay compensation to Broker as specified in a separate written agreement between Owner and Broker (C.A.R. Form LCA).

48. RECEIPT: If specified in paragraph 5, Landlord or Broker, acknowledges receipt of move-in funds.

Landlord _____ Date _____
(Owner or Agent with authority to enter into this Agreement)
Landlord _____ Date _____
(Owner or Agent with authority to enter into this Agreement)
Landlord Address _____ City _____ State _____ Zip _____
Telephone _____ Fax _____ E-mail_____

REAL ESTATE BROKERS:
A. Real estate brokers who are not also Landlord under the Agreement are not parties to the Agreement between Landlord and Tenant.
B. Agency relationships are confirmed in paragraph 42.
C. **COOPERATING BROKER COMPENSATION:** Listing Broker agrees to pay Cooperating Broker (Leasing Firm) and Cooperating Broker agrees to accept: **(i)** the amount specified in the MLS, provided Cooperating Broker is a Participant of the MLS in which the Property is offered for sale or a reciprocal MLS; or **(ii)** ☐ (if checked) the amount specified in a separate written agreement between Listing Broker and Cooperating Broker.

Real Estate Broker (Leasing Firm) _____
By (Agent) _____ Date _____
Address _____ City _____ State _____ Zip _____
Telephone _____ Fax _____ E-mail_____

Real Estate Broker (Leasing Firm) _____
By (Agent) _____ Date _____
Address _____ City _____ State _____ Zip _____
Telephone _____ Fax _____ E-mail_____

Published and Distributed by:
REAL ESTATE BUSINESS SERVICES, INC.
a subsidiary of the California Association of REALTORS®
525 South Virgil Avenue, Los Angeles, California 90020

Reviewed by _____ Date _____

LR REVISED 10/04 (PAGE 6 OF 6)

RESIDENTIAL LEASE OR MONTH-TO-MONTH RENTAL AGREEMENT (LR PAGE 6 OF 6)

NOTICE TO PAY RENT OR QUIT

(C.A.R. Form PRQ, Revised 4/03)

To: _____ ("Tenant")
_____ (Street Address)
_____ (Street Address), (Unit/Apartment #)
_____, ____ _____ (City), (State) (Zip Code) ("Premises").

Other notice address if different from Premises above: _____
_____.

Notice to the above-named person(s) and any other occupants of the above-referenced Premises:

WITHIN 3 (OR ☐ _____ (BUT NOT LESS THAN 3)) DAYS from service of this Notice you are required to either:

1.   Pay rent for the Premises in the following amount, which is past due, to _____
_____ (Name) _____ (Phone)
at _____
_____ (Address)
between the hours of _____ on the following days: _____.

Past Due Rent: $ _____ for the period _____ to _____
                 $ _____ for the period _____ to _____
                 $ _____ for the period _____ to _____
Total Due: $ _____

OR 2.   Vacate the Premises and surrender possession.

If you do not pay the past due amount or give up possession by the required time, a legal action will be filed seeking not only damages and possession, but also a statutory damage penalty of up to $600.00 (California Code of Civil Procedure § 1174). Landlord declares a forfeiture of the lease if past due rent is not paid and you continue to occupy the Premises. As required by law, you are hereby notified that a negative credit report reflecting on your credit record may be submitted to a credit reporting agency if you fail to pay your rent.

Landlord _____ Date _____
(Owner or Agent)
Address _____ City _____ State _____ Zip _____
Telephone _____ Fax _____ E-mail _____

(Keep a copy for your records.)

This Notice was served by:

1.   ☐   **Personal service.** A copy of the Notice was personally delivered to the above named Tenant.

2.   ☐   **Substituted service.** A copy of the Notice was left with a person of suitable age and discretion at the Tenant's residence or usual place of business and a copy was mailed to the Tenant at Tenant's residence.

3.   ☐   **Post and mail.** A copy of the Notice was affixed to a conspicuous place on the Premises and a copy was mailed to the Tenant at the Premises.

Published by the
California Association of REALTORS®

PRQ REVISED 4/03 (PAGE 1 OF 1)   Print Date

Reviewed by _____ Date _____

NOTICE TO PAY RENT OR QUIT (PRQ PAGE 1 OF 1)

Security Deposit Quick Guideline:

Residential:
- Landlord must return a tenant's deposit within three weeks of the tenant's vacating the property
- Landlord must supply a written statement of damages or routine maintenance costs deducted from the security deposit
- Landlord may only collect a security deposit equal to: two months rent for unfurnished units; three months rent for furnished units

Nonresidential:
- Landlord may collect any amount of security deposit
- Landlord must return security deposit to the tenant within 60 days of tenant's vacating the property
- Landlord is not required to provide a written statement of damages or routine maintenance paid for with the security deposit upon returning the remainder to the tenant

P A Y M E N T   O F   R E N T

Rent is the consideration or payment a tenant will give a landlord for property inhabited or used during the length of a tenancy. Generally, rent is a monetary payment between landlord and tenant. However, it need not always be an exchange of money. Sometimes, an exchange of goods or services performed may be used as a form of consideration.

There are four different types of rent payments:

1. Gross lease
2. Net lease
3. Graduated lease
4. Percentage lease

In a *gross lease*, a tenant pays a landlord a fixed amount of money per month. The landlord will use this amount to pay utility bills, taxes, mortgages or other expenses incurred by the building or property. Generally a landlord will consider these costs before setting the price of rent, to ensure all rental expenses are covered.

The *net lease* is similar to the gross lease, with the exception that the tenant pays expenses incurred by the landlord. A set monthly rent is agreed upon, and each month the tenant must pay for additional expenses (such as repairs, taxes or other costs that may be billed monthly, or a single occurrence during the duration of the tenancy).

In a *graduated lease* the base rent or monthly charge varies from month to month, unlike the fixed amount of monthly rent associated with gross and net leases. One factor causing fluctuations in a graduated lease may be the time of year for which the lease is in place and the corresponding energy costs associated with that season. For example, utility bills go up in winter, due to the cooler weather and cost of heating the unit.

A *percentage lease* might be used by a landlord who owns commercial space that is rented to a retail business. In a percentage lease, rent is based on a percentage of the tenant's gross profits.

Landlords must take into account several different factors when determining rent they will charge for a specific piece of property. Landlords, of course, need to cover all of their costs of maintenance, repairs, utilities, taxes and any additional mortgage payment if applicable. The landlord also wants to ensure a little extra income for him or herself. After all, most people invest in an income property to make money. The amount of money a landlord asks in rent from a tenant is usually called the *contract rent*. Contract rent is not the same as *economic rent* (which is how much rent a specific property could bring). For example, let's say you have been living in the same apartment building for 10 years. Your rent has most likely increased while you have lived there. However, you are most likely not paying what your new neighbor across the hall is paying. Your rent is contract rent, kept low due to a few different factors (such as rent control). Your neighbor's rent is closer to economic rent (if not right at economic rent), as they are new to the building.

Remember!

Contract Rent is the amount of rent a landlord is currently charging or receiving for a property, **Economic Rent** is the amount of rent a landlord could charge for a specific property in an open market.

RESPONSIBILITIES AND RIGHTS OF A TENANT

In a lease, a tenant is expected to perform certain tasks, and is guaranteed certain rights in return. Provided tenants obey all guidelines as outlined in the contract, and remain in good standing regarding the payment of rent, the tenant is entitled to peaceful enjoyment and possession of the property. The right of possession by the tenant is guaranteed by the covenant of quiet enjoyment, implied by law and granted by the landlord. Quiet enjoyment refers to the tenant's right not to be interfered with by the landlord. That is, a landlord may not enter the property and disrupt a tenant's possessions or use of the property, unless eviction proceedings against that tenant have begun.

In addition to quiet enjoyment a tenant has the right to live in a safe, healthy environment. If there is something that threatens this environment, the landlord must make any necessary repairs to rectify the threat. If the landlord does not make the necessary repairs, the tenant may use up to one months rent to make the necessary repairs, subtracting that cost from the next payment of rent. Tenants are allowed by law to make these repairs and deduct said expenses from his or her rent only twice in a 12-month period, with no retaliation from the landlord. Landlords may not retaliate by raising the rent to offset the cost of the repair for a period of 180 days. Additionally, a landlord may not evict a tenant who uses rent to make necessary repairs to a rental property.

Responsibilities of a Tenant:
- Pay rent on time
- Provide a 30 day notice before ending a periodic tenancy
- Not to interfere with the rights of other tenants.

A tenant must pay his or her rent on time. If the tenant does not do so, a landlord may begin the eviction process. Rent is usually due at the beginning of each month, unless stated differently in the rental agreement. In some cases, a partial month of tenancy may result in the proration of rent.

In a periodic tenancy, tenants are required to provide the landlord with a 30-day notice before terminating the tenancy. Usually periodic tenancies are month-to-month situations, where the tenant gives a one-month notice to vacate. This allows the landlord to find a replacement tenant to occupy the space currently held by the vacating tenant. This allows the landlord to avoid losing any income the property would otherwise generate.

Tenants are not allowed to interfere with the rights of other tenants. For example, they may not create an excessive amount of noise late in the evening, keeping neighbors awake. Apartment complexes often have rules or set hours for use of common recreational rooms or areas such as pool or Jacuzzi, as well as restricted hours when onsite laundry facilities may be used. These rules are intended to keep noise levels low in the evening, for the benefit of all tenants.

Improvements made by tenants, sometimes called tenant improvements, must be approved by the landlord before a tenant alters a unit. Many times, a landlord will agree to theses improvements, but require the tenant to change the unit back to its original condition upon vacating. An example of this is paint. If a tenant wants to repaint the original color of an apartment, he or she can usually do so, but he or she must paint the unit back to its original color before moving out, or pay to have it repainted.

RIGHTS AND RESPONSIBILITIES OF A LANDLORD

Just as a tenant has certain rights and responsibilities, so too does the landlord. The landlord makes a promise to the tenant for the quiet enjoyment of the property in exchange for rent. The landlord also agrees to give up possessory rights to the property during the tenancy, with a few exceptions. For example, the landlord may enter the property under the following circumstances:

1. An emergency
2. Pursuance of a court order
3. To perform necessary, agreed upon repairs
4. To show the property to prospective new tenants
5. When the property has been abandoned.

In the event that the landlord must enter onto his or her property, he or she must give the tenant sufficient notice. A 24-hour notice is usually considered adequate; though each rental agreement may contain different time advances for notification.

In addition to granting the tenant quiet enjoyment of the property, a landlord also guarantees to the tenant that all health and safety codes are being met. This means not only within the unit itself, but also the hallways, common areas of the building and any recreational areas. It is landlord's responsibility to adequately maintain and repair such areas in the appropriate manner.

Landlords must be very careful not to discriminate when renting their property to another individual. Both state and federal law prevent discrimination based on race, color, religion, creed, national origin, sex, marital status, presence or absence of children, or physical handicap.

Landlords must provide a tenant with a 30-day notice when terminating a month-to-month periodic tenancy (just as the tenant must do if vacating the property). If the termination of the tenancy is unjust, the tenant may have legal recourse.

Security deposits, as mentioned earlier in this chapter, must be refunded within 3 weeks of the tenant's vacating a property. This refund check must be accompanied by an itemized list of all deductions made from the security deposit. Any landlord who does not refund a tenant's deposit within the 3-week period will be subject to a $600 fine, and may also be held liable for any damages , which may have occurred.

Landlords are bound to all established building standards and requirements. These established standards (also referred to as codes) insure the safety of the tenants. Even if a contract does not directly state this, such a standard is implied under the warranty of habitability. This warranty prevents rental property from being rented if it is considered untenantable. An untenantable dwelling is one that has any of the following characteristics:

- Damaged floors, railings or stairways
- Inadequate or dirty trash collection areas
- Damaged, or missing hot and cold water, fixtures or proper sewage disposal
- Inadequate weatherproofing
- Damaged or inadequate heating system
- Dirty conditions or infested with pests at the inception of the lease
- Inadequate or non-functional plumbing or gas lines
- Wiring that is not up to code

As mentioned earlier, landlords are not allowed to penalize tenants for complaining about inadequate living conditions nor may they penalize them for remedying such a situation. Unjust eviction or increased rents, as a result of a tenant's fixing any of the problems with the unit (especially those that make the unit untenantable) is strictly prohibited.

Responsibilities of a landlord:

- Protect the health and safety of tenants by ensuring the unit is tenantable
- Give 24-hours notice before entering the property for any reason
- Return deposits within 21 days
- Give a 30-day notice when terminating a month-to-month tenancy
- Must not engage in discriminatory renting practices against any parties

T R A N S F E R R I N G   A   L E A S E

Jennifer is a young professional just graduating from UCLA. She had signed a year-long lease during her last semester of school and had planned on finding a job in Los Angeles upon completing her schooling. Two weeks before graduation ceremonies, she receives a job offer in Sacramento that she could not turn down. She accepts the position to begin one month following her graduation. What happens to Jennifer's lease? She agreed to an entire year, but she has only been there for half the time period to which she committed. Is she allowed to break the lease, or must she tell her new employer that she is not able to accept the job based on her lease agreement?

As you can see from the above example, there are situations when we need to exit a lease early. But, is this possible? The answer is "yes", and there are two different ways to do so. A tenant may transfer his or her interest in a lease by assignment or subleasing.

> **Remember**
>
> There are two ways to transfer a lease
> - Assignment
> - Subleasing

In assignment of a lease, the current tenant of a property transfers his or her entire interest in a lease to another tenant. The original tenant is no longer responsible to the landlord, and can walk away from the lease in good standing. The new tenant is completely responsible to the landlord and will occupy the property for the duration of the original lease. Assignment of a lease is the best option for someone like Jennifer. She plans on moving away from Los Angeles, not returning. So, she needs to transfer her complete interest in the lease to another separate person for the duration of the lease.

In subleasing, the current tenant transfers only some interest in the lease. The original tenant is still responsible to the landlord, and the subleasing tenant is responsible to the original tenant. Subleasing would be ideal for those people who are leaving for a short while, but plan on returning to a property and want to keep their interest in the lease.

Andrew lives in a very desirable beachfront apartment and enjoys rent control. He has lived there for several years and pays well under what the apartment could bring on the open market. He decides to take a short-term job in New York City, which would take him away from California for 5 months. Realizing that he cannot afford to pay rent in two places, but not willing to give up his beachfront apartment, he decides to sublease his California apartment to his friend Tammy. Tammy is now responsible to Andrew, and must pay him the monthly rent, which Andrew will, in turn, pay to the landlord. When Andrew returns to California from New York City, Tammy will have to vacate the property, and the sublease will be terminated.

TERMINATION OF A LEASE

A lease may be terminated for a number of reasons. The duration of the lease may have expired, and the tenant can choose to: sign a new lease; be on a periodic tenancy month to month; or choose to find a new place to rent. A lease may also be terminated because one party did not meet one or more of the contractual obligations of the lease.

A lease can be set up for a number of different time frames; but the majority of us are most familiar with a year lease agreement to rent an apartment. Once that year is over, the lease is expired. The lease will state a termination date that meets the expectations of both parties. For example, a 30-day notice might be expected if the tenant does not plan on extending the lease. Termination of a lease by expiration is considered *bilateral termination* because both parties are aware of and agree to the termination. Additionally both parties are aware of all options a vailable (such as periodic tenancy, a new lease or complete termination of a lessee / lessor relationship).

Leases may also be unilaterally terminated. This happens when one party violates the terms of the contract and the other party decides to terminate the lease, whether is the lease is due to expire or not. The party who terminates the lease does not have to obtain the other parties permission to terminate.

Tenants may terminate a lease when:

- The landlord has violated the duty to repair a unit, or has failed to keep the unit habitable
- The landlord has violated the tenants right to quiet enjoyment
- The landlord violates a condition of the lease
- The landlord has evicted the tenant
- The property has been destroyed
- The government has operated the power of eminent domain and taken the property

Landlords may terminate a lease when:

- Tenants use the unit for purposes unauthorized by the lease agreement
- The tenant breaches the contract of the lease
- The tenant abandons the property
- The property has been destroyed

Abandonment happens when a tenant simply vacates a property with no notice. If the tenant has been away from the property, rent has been delinquent for at least 14 days and/or the landlord believes that the tenant is not going to return to the property, the landlord may establish abandonment by giving written notice. The tenant must respond to the notice within 18 days of receipt, to deny the fact that he or she intends to abandon the property. If abandonment has been established, the landlord will reclaim the property.

Eviction happens when the landlord legally removes the tenant from the premises for violating one or more terms of the contract or lease agreement. Eviction commonly happens when rent is not paid for a certain period of time, yet the tenant remains in possession of the property. If the tenant fails to pay rent, the landlord may begin eviction proceedings by giving the tenant a three-day notice in writing. This notice is called three-day notice to pay rent or quit, where the tenant is given the option to either pay the rent or move out within three days.

If the tenant fails to respond to the three-day notice, the landlord may file an unlawful detainer in a municipal court. The unlawful detainer is a document that lists all charges against the tenant, to which the tenant must respond within five days. If the tenant fails to respond to the unlawful detainer, a hearing will be set. The landlord may choose to sue the tenant for all rent owed. Alternatively, the landlord can request an order of eviction from the court. If the landlord sues the tenant, this does not constitute an eviction, and the tenant may retain possession of the unit currently being rented.

Just because a landlord has filed an unlawful detainer does not mean that the tenant has no rights. A tenant may defeat the unlawful detainer if:

- The landlord's facts are not true
- If the landlord files an unlawful detainer in retaliation to a tenant's improvements or corrections to a unit that have been charged to the landlord
- If the landlord's action is arbitrary
- If property notice was not given
- Other violations occur in the process of the eviction procedures.

If the tenant does not answer the lawsuit brought by the landlord, or the court finds in favor of the landlord, a writ of possession is granted. A writ of possession authorizes the sheriff (of the county where the property is located) to serve an eviction notice to the tenant. After five days have passed since delivery of the eviction, the landlord may physically move the tenant's possessions into a storage locker; with the tenant paying for the cost of storage. After 30 days have passed, a public auction to sell the tenant's stored belongings may be held. Any profits made from this auction may be used to pay for the storage of the belongings, as well as any sale costs. Any remaining amount is returned to the tenant.

DISCRIMINATION

Tenants in California have a number of state and federal laws that protect against discrimination in renting property. The Unruh Civil Rights Act, Fair Housing and Employment Act, Rumford Fair Housing Act and the Fair Housing Administration Act are all designed to keep landlords from unfairly discriminating against tenants. Under these acts, it is illegal for a landlord to discriminate against a prospective tenant based on sex, race, religion, marital status, the presence or absence of children, physical disability, national origin, ancestry or age.

Not only do these laws protect against discrimination of people seeking rental of property; it also protects current tenants from unjust eviction, rent increases or the landlord's withholding of any necessary or agreed upon service. Any tenant who feels that they have been unjustly discriminated against should take their grievance to the state Department of Fair Employment and Housing. The U.S. Department of Housing and Urban Development (USHUD) also handles claims or complaints from tenants against landlords. Those persons who feel as if they have been discriminated against can also seek justice in a court of law. If a landlord is found guilty, he or she may be responsible for damages suffered by the tenant.

Landlords may not discriminate based on:
- Sex
- Race
- Religion
- Marital status
- Presence or absence of Children
- Physical disability
- National origin
- Ancestry
- Age

S U M M A R Y

In this chapter you learned that a lease is a document or contract that transfers interest in property from the lessor to the lessee (or the landlord to the tenant). This contract is often times referred to as a less-than-freehold estate. A less than freehold estate is considered personal property, not real property. The tenant has the right to possess the property, but cannot convey it to an interested party. There are different types of leases appropriate to situations such as time of tenancy or notification to vacate property.

Landlords promise tenants that a property will be habitable, clean and safe during their tenancy. The law also implies that the landlord will grant the tenant a right to quiet enjoyment. This means that the landlord will not enter the property without first giving notice to the tenant. Sufficient notice is usually considered 24-hours. Tenants are allowed, by law, to make any necessary repairs to a property if the landlord is not able or has not completed such repairs in a timely fashion. These improvements or repairs may be deducted from the next months rent, so long as the repair or improvement does not exceed the dollar amount of one months rent. A tenant is allowed by law to do this twice during the course of one year. Landlords are not allowed to retaliate against a tenant for making such repairs through eviction or the raising of rent for a period of 180 days.

Landlords can use eviction as a way to get rid of problematic tenants provided they utilize all appropriate and legal channels of eviction. If a tenant fails to pay rent, a landlord may post a three days or quit notice, alerting the tenant that they must either pay rent in three days, or remove themselves from the property. If the three days to pay or quit is ignored, a landlord may file an unlawful detainer with the court. As a last resort, a landlord may file a *writ of possession*, allowing the sheriff to physically remove a tenant from the property.

Finally, we learned that discrimination is not tolerated in rental situations. There are several state and federal agencies in place, designed to protect the rights and interests of renters or prospective renters. Any person who feels that they have been discriminated against may file a complaint with the appropriate agency or file a case in a court of law.

T E R M S   A N D   P H R A S E S

Abandonment – Forfeiting property through non-use (generally acknowledged by removing belongings from the premises)

Assignee – Person or party to whom a lease is assigned or, in some cases, transferred

Assignment – To transfer the entire interest in a lease from the original lessee to the new lessee (who is sometimes called the assignee)

Chattel real – Another name for personal property (leases are considered such personal property, or chattel real)

Contract rent – The amount of rental income a landlord will receive from a tenant's rent as agreed upon in the rental contract

Constructive eviction – The interference of a landlord to tenants agreed upon use of property by entering property and making unwarranted alterations or changes to the property, thus preventing the intended use

Covenant of quiet enjoyment – The promise a landlord makes to a tenant, implied by law, not to interfere in the possession or use of leased property

Covenant to repair – Legally implied responsibility of the landlord to make necessary repairs to leased properties

Demise – The conveyance of real estate to a person for use during a set period of time. A lease will demise property to the tenant for the duration of the contract

Economic rent – The amount of rent for which a property could expect to be rented for in the current market if the property were vacant and available to be rented

Escalator clause – Provisions in a lease which allow for increases in rent based on increases in the consumer price index

Estate at sufferance – Tenancy created when one is in wrongful possession of property (even if the initial possession was lawful)

Estate at will – Tenancy where the lease may be ended unilaterally by either party. There is no official termination of the estate; however, one party must give the other party 30-days notice of termination

Estate for years – Tenancy with a definite end date (must be renegotiated upon its termination)

Estate from period to period – Tenancy that will automatically be renewed at the end of each period by the landlord's acceptance of rent. This type of tenancy does not require renegotiation at the end of the term, and is usually called a month-to-month tenancy, or periodic tenancy

Eviction –The process by which a landlord legally removes a tenant from a property for some breach in the contract or lease agreement

Fair Employment and Housing Act (FEHA) – A California civil code preventing discrimination against tenants based on marital status, race, color, religion, sex, national origin or ancestry

Fair Housing Amendments Act of 1988 - A federal law preventing landlords from discriminating against physical handicap, familial status and age of tenants

Graduated payment lease – Lease requiring periodic increase in rent

Gross lease – A lease in which the landlord pays for the operating expenses on a property (which may include taxes, maintenance and repairs)

Holdover tenancy – A tenancy where the tenant remains in possession of the property after the lease term has ended

Landlord – The lessor or property owner who rents property to another individual

Lease – An agreement between the landlord and tenant (lessor and lessee) allowing the tenant possession of property for a specific amount of time. The lease may be written or verbal depending on the duration of the contract.

Lease assignment – The action wherein a tenant transfers his or her interest in the leasehold to another interested tenant. The transfer of lease is permanent, and the original tenant has no responsibilities to the landlord.

Lease option – A lease wherein the landlord gives the current tenant the option to purchase the property within a certain time period

Lessee – The tenant or person leasing property from another individual

Lessor – The Landlord or person leasing property to another individual

Less-than-freehold – Another name for a lease or the interest a lessee has in property when leasing from another

Net lease – A lease where the tenant will pay all expenses (such as taxes, maintenance and repairs) in addition to monthly rent.

Notice to pay or quit – The notice a landlord will supply to a prospective tenant providing them three days to pay rent or vacate the premises

Percentage lease – A lease where the tenant will pay the landlord a percentage of gross sales as rental consideration

Periodic tenancy – The same as a tenancy from period to period. This type of tenancy is valid for a set time period, but is automatically renewed upon the landlord's acceptance of rent.

Rent – The consideration a tenant will pay the landlord for use of a property

Rent control – The imposition by local government to control prices that landlords charge for rental property

Residential rental property – Property where 80% or more of the profits come from residential units

Retaliatory eviction – The process by which a landlord will either evict a tenant for making unauthorized repairs (made to keep the unit within health or safety codes) or evict a tenant as a response to complaints made by the tenant.

Reversionary right – The right of possession in which rental property returns to the landlord upon termination of a lease

Right of entry – The right of a landlord to enter into the rental property to make necessary repairs or to check on the safety and wellbeing of a tenant

Sandwich lease – A lease created when a tenant subleases his or her interest to another tenant for a short period of time. The original lessee is responsible to the landlord, and the new tenant is responsible to the original lessee. Thus, the original lessee is "sandwiched" between the new lessee and the landlord.

Security deposit – The amount a tenant pays a landlord at the beginning of the tenancy. This money is to be held in an account to make necessary or routine repairs once the tenant vacates the property. If the entire deposit is not used in repairs, the landlord must return any remaining amount to the tenant within 21 days of the tenant's vacating the premises, accompanied by an itemized statement of how the deposit was utilized.

Sublease – The process by which a lessee transfers his or her interest to another lessee. The new lessee is responsible to the original lessee, while the original lessee is responsible to the landlord.

Surrender – The process by which a tenant voluntarily gives up control of a property

Tenant – The person leasing property from a landlord (also called a lessee)

Unlawful detainer –The papers filed in a court of law against a tenant in unlawful possession of a property

Unruh Civil Rights Act – California civil code making it unlawful to discriminate against tenants based on sex, race, color, religion, ancestry or national origin

Untenantable dwelling – Property lacking necessary utilities, or one that is in poor condition causing it to fall under the minimum property standards, making it uninhabitable for tenants.

Warranty of habitability – A legal implication whereby landlords must maintain certain standards of minimal housing to keep buildings up to code.

Writ of possession – Court order directing the sheriff to physically remove a tenant from the premises.

CHAPTER QUIZ

1. Upon termination of a lease, if the landlord accepts payment of rent from a tenant, the tenancy is now considered?
    - A. Estate at will
    - B. Estate from period to period
    - C. Periodic tenancy
    - D. All of the above.

2. Payment, or rent, is also called
    - A. Consideration
    - B. Lease assignment
    - C. Covenant
    - D. Fee

3, Which is considered the least desirable type of leasehold estate?
    - A. Estate for years
    - B. Estate from period to period
    - C. Estate at will
    - D. Estate at sufferance

4. How long a duration must a lease be before it must be in writing?
    A. 3 months
    B. 6 months
    C. 1 year
    D. 2 years

5. When is a tenant required to sign a lease?
    A. Only when its duration is longer than one year
    B. For contracts lasting 6 months or longer
    C. A tenant must always sign the lease
    D. Tenants are not required to sign any lease.

6. What form of least transfer relieves the current tenant of all responsibility?
    A. Assignment
    B. Subleasing
    C. Bilateral
    D. Unilateral

7. How many days must a landlord give a tenant before terminating a month-to-month tenancy?
    A. 29
    B. 30
    C. 31
    D. 32

8. A lease is considered which of the following
    A. Chattel Real
    B. Real Property
    C. Personal Property
    D. Both A and C

9. Which of the following is NOT considered on of the four P's of a lease requirement?
    A. Property
    B. Parties
    C. Proprietor
    D. Payment of rent

10. If there is a dispute between the landlord and tenant regarding a security deposit from a residential rental, which must defend or justify the claim?
    A. The landlord must prove that all charges taken out of the security deposit are valid and appropriate, the tenant is assumed to be correct otherwise.
    B. The tenant must prove that the landlord took too much out of the security deposit by providing proof of prior damages paid for by the current security deposit.
    C. Neither the landlord nor tenant must prove their claim; the contract and statement of condition filled out upon moving in will determine what damages need to be charged to the current deposit.
    D. A third party mediator will decide who is in the right and make a determination accordingly.

11. What is the maximum-security deposit a landlord may charge on a furnished residential apartment?
    A. The greater of $1,000 or one month of rent.
    B. Two month's of rent.
    C. Three month's of rent
    D. None of the above.

12. Which one of the following characteristics does NOT describe a non-residential security deposit?
    A. Return the remainder of the tenant's security deposit within 60 days.
    B. Landlord must provide an itemized statement of charges taken out of the security deposit.
    C. Landlord does not have to provide an itemized statement of charges taken out of the deposit.
    D. Landlord can charge an unlimited security deposit.

13. Which of the following terms is different?
    A. Rent
    B. Consideration
    C. Fee
    D. Payment

14. Which best describes a percentage lease?
    A. The percent of fair market value a tenant is willing to pay.
    B. A percentage of monthly gross profits a tenant pays to the landlord.
    C. The percent of open market value a landlord charges for property.
    D. The amount of rent a tenant pays plus a percentage of the utilities and other costs shared with the landlord.

15. How many times a year may a tenant make necessary repairs to a rental property and then deduct the amount from the rent?
    A. 1
    B. 2
    C. 3
    D. 4

16. Which statement is true?
    A. A landlord may immediately raise a tenant's rent to offset the cost of repairs performed or paid for by the tenant.
    B. A landlord may evict a tenant for making or paying for necessary repairs to a rental unit.
    C. A landlord may not raise rent on a tenant who paid or made a necessary repair.
    D. A landlord may raise a tenant's rent 180 days after making or paying for a necessary repair.

17. Who may a landlord refuse to rent to?
    A. Tenants with children
    B. Tenants based on their race
    C. Tenants based on their religion
    D. None of the above.

18. Which of the following statements is true?
    A. In a sublease situation, the original tenant subleasing the apartment to a secondary tenant will forfeit his or her interest in the lease.
    B. An assignment of a lease allows the original tenant to return to the property after a set period of time.
    C. The tenant subleasing from the original tenant is responsible to the landlord
    D. An assignment of a lease relieves the original tenant from all contractual obligations and transfers responsibility to the new tenant.

19. A lease may be terminated by which of the following methods?
   A. Expiration of the lease
   B. Destruction of the property
   C. Eviction
   D. All of the above

20. Which of the following is not a state or federal law protecting tenants from discrimination?
   A. Fair Housing Amendment Act
   B. Costa-Hawkins Rental Housing Act
   C. Unruh Civil Rights Act
   D. Fair Housing and Employment Act

REAL
ESTATE
FINANCE

What you will learn in this Chapter

- The Lending Process
- Promissory Note Versus Trust Deeds
- Trust Deeds and Mortgages
- Transfer of Property by Borrower
- Special Clauses in Financing Instruments
- Junior Trust Deeds
- Balloon Payment Loans
- Foreclosure
- Other Types of Loans
- Alternative Financing
- Short Pay

1. Which one of the following characteristics is not found in a partially amortized note?
   A. Interest only payments
   B. Partial payment of principal; full payment of interest
   C. Balloon payment
   D. Periodic fixed payments

2. In a trust deed, who holds the original deed to the property until the promissory note is paid in full?
   A. The trustor
   B. The trustee
   C. The lender
   D. Both A and B

3. A deficiency judgment is allowed in which of the following situations?
   A. A buyer purchases a property with a purchase money loan, then defaults on the loan, resulting in foreclosure
   B. A buyer purchases a property by assuming an existing loan, and then defaults on the loan, resulting in a judicial foreclosure
   C. Both A and B
   D. Neither A nor B

4. Which best describes the subject to clause?
   A. A buyer takes over an existing loan from the seller without the lenders knowledge. The seller, or original owner, is responsible for the loan and may be held liable for any deficiency judgments.
   B. The borrower is subject to a credit check before being approved for a loan.
   C. The borrower is subject to a loan based on the inspection and appraisal of the property of interest.
   D. The buyer takes over the existing loan with the knowledge and approval of the lender.

5. If a seller finances a junior trust deed to the buyer of his or her property, what options do the sellers have regarding the loan?
   A. They may carry the note until it is paid in full
   B. They may sell the note at a discounted rate to a mortgage broker
   C. They may force the buyer into paying the note back sooner because they need the money for a new car.
   D. Both A and B

6. In a trustee's sale, which of the following parties does not require notification when the notice of default is recorded?
   A. Trustor
   B. Junior lien holders
   C. Beneficiary
   D. State Controller

7. Sellers who finance a buyer with a wrap around loan typically do which of the following?
   A. Carry back a note on the property
   B. Charge the buyer a higher interest rate than they currently pay on the original trust deed
   C. Collect the money directly from the buyer for the AITD
   D. Require a high down payment from the buyer

INTRODUCTION

Home ownership is one of the largest (if not the largest) investments a person can make. Since very few people can afford to purchase a home with cash, the vast majority of homeowners are currently paying on a mortgage (or trust deed, as they are called in California). So, it is important for you, the real estate agent, to understand how financing works, and provide advice to your clients accordingly. By knowing what programs are available to your client, and providing them with advice and guidance to speak with a mortgage broker, homeownership becomes a more realistic goal than many thought possible.

In this chapter, we will learn about real estate financing and how it operates. We will look at the different programs and options people have when financing a home and how those financing options function. Real estate finance has evolved far beyond obtaining a loan at a local bank; yet, it is often just as simple as that. Pay close attention to terms or concepts to which you are introduced, as most ideas in real estate finance are related to each other in some fashion.

THE LENDING PROCESS

When a person obtains a loan, they use the property they wish to purchase as collateral to secure the loan. Lenders require collateral on loans of this size to ensure they will be repaid in full. If the borrower defaults on the loan, the house can be sold to pay the note's remaining balance.

The loan itself is called a note. A person who wishes to obtain a loan signs a document called a *promissory note*. The promissory note is an intention to pay back the loan in the installments agreed upon with the lender. The promissory note itself is the evidence of debt and is held by the lender until the entire amount of the note is paid.

Most of us are familiar with the term *mortgage*. We take out a mortgage when we purchase a home. California uses trust deeds, which are essentially the same as a mortgage. A trust deed is the security for the note. Usually there is a neutral third party, called a trustee, who holds bare legal title (though he or she has no rights or interest in the property), until the note is paid in full. Once the note is paid in full, the trustee reconveys the deed from the lender to the trustor. The borrower takes possession of the home, but must make all payments on time. Otherwise, the home may be sold in order to satisfy the debt against it.

A person is said to be *leveraging* when he or she is using an investor's money to purchase property for him or herself. By leveraging money, a homeowner can risk very little of their personal money invested in the purchase of a home. However, they may take possession of the property immediately. This is a clear advantage for a person who has the means to make a monthly payment on property, but does not have a large sum to pay for the property at once. An investor will also benefit from interest earned on the loan that is given to the property owner.

Remember
A homeowner secures a note from a lending institution by promising to use the property being purchased as collateral against the note. If the homeowner fails to pay back the note, the property may be sold to satisfy any debt against the property.

As mentioned earlier, a promissory note is the written document that a borrower signs, stating to the lending institution that he or she will repay the entire amount of the loan. The promissory note is held by the lender. A lender will use the property itself as security or collateral for the note. Promissory notes are often referred to simply as 'notes'. So, when you see that term used by itself, you will know it means.

The borrower is the maker of the note, as he or she is 'making' a personal promise to repay the loan in full. The lender is referred to as the holder of the note.

Promissory notes are secured by trust deeds, which are held by a trustee or third party. The trustee holds bare legal title, which means that they have the authority to sell the property in the event that the lender forecloses on the borrower. Outside of this authority, the trustee has no rights or interest in the property. More on trust deeds will be covered later in this chapter.

There are four different types of notes: straight; partially amortized; full amortized and adjustable rate. The difference between these types of notes is the manner in which they are repaid. Some notes, such as the **straight note**, require only the payment of interest each month, followed by a large payment against the principal at the end of the note. In **fully amortized** notes, both the principal and interest are being paid throughout the life of the loan. Payments will remain the same from the beginning to end, with the loan being paid in full at the end of the note term. A **partially amortized** note is a combination of both straight note and fully amortized note. Partially amortized notes allow the borrower to pay on both the interest and principal, but with only a portion of the principal covered with this monthly payment. In addition, a balloon payment is required at a specific time, or at the end of a certain term, to cover the remaining balance of the principal. A balloon payment is a lump sum of money, larger than that of a regular monthly payment. Finally, an **adjustable rate** note fluctuates in accordance with market conditions. When interest rates drop, interest on the note will reflect this drop, in the form of a lower monthly payment. When interest rates rise, the note will also reflect this change by charging the lender a higher rate (thus, increasing the monthly payment).

Four Types of Promissory Notes:

1. Straight note – equal monthly payments sufficient to cover the interest only, with the principal due at the end of the note
2. Fully amortized note – equal monthly payments of both interest and principal
3. Partially amortized note – equal monthly payments for a certain term, followed by a balloon payment (required to cover the difference between the percentage of principal paid and the per centage of principal owed for that term)
4. Adjustable rate – monthly payments vary because interest rates may change, depending on market conditions

Promissory notes are considered *negotiable instruments*, as they are a promise to pay money to another party. You might compare it to a personal check. When you write a personal check, you are promising the party receiving the check that there is money in your account. You are further promising that they may deduct the amount that you are authorizing, in payment for a good or service. With the check, we are telling our bank to allow the merchant or person to deduct a specific amount of money from your account. Additionally, if endorsed, a promissory note may be transferred to another party, much the same as if you endorse a personal check made payable to one party, and pass it on to a third party. A promissory note, accurately prepared, can even be used as cash.

All negotiable instruments must be in written form, promising to pay a specific sum of money back to the holder of the note. The note is considered a legal contract that can only be made between two competent, legal parties. The note must be signed by the borrower and delivered to the lender. Promissory notes are voluntary, with both parties entering into the agreement for mutual benefit. The person making the note will be able to secure and take possession of property, while the holder of the note will make a profit on the return of the note. Promissory notes are paid either at specific intervals, or on demand. If a lender calls the note, the borrower must be able to repay the entire sum of the loan. Otherwise, the property may be sold to satisfy the debt.

The holder of the note may also sell the promissory note to another individual, or even give it away. The person buying the note, or receiving it will be the individual who is paid monthly payments on the property. As long as the promissory note is prepared correctly, it is very easy for it to change hands quickly. The person now holding the note is called the *assignee* or *transferee*, depending on the conditions the original holder has in place upon giving or selling the note to another individual. The new holder of the note becomes the *holder in due course*.

A holder in due course is someone who takes on a note, but receives more benefits than the original holder of the note (provided the note was prepared properly and is considered a transferable instrument). When the note is transferred to another person as holder in due course, this fact must be clearly written on the note. A holder in due course takes the promissory note in good faith and without notice that anyone else may have claim on the note .

> **A holder in due course takes a note:**
> - In good faith
> - For Value
> - Without notice of defense.

The reason that a holder in due course is in a favorable position over the original holder of the note is because the new holder is protected from defenses the maker (borrower) may bring against the note. If a court case is brought, the maker cannot use any of the following defenses against the holder in due course:

1. The maker cannot claim that he or she never received the promised funds or property
   in exchange for the note.
2. The maker cannot claim that the note has already been paid in full unless marked
   accordingly on the note (in this case, the note would never have been sold or transferred to the assignee).
3. Cancellation

4. Setoff (the difference of what is owed on the note and what is owed to the holder of the note)
5. Fraud

Any of the above defenses may be used by the maker of the note against the original holder of the note. However, none of these may be used against the new assignee if it is written on the note and he or she takes the note as holder in due course.. This does not mean that the maker of the promissory note is without defense. There are certain defenses that may be made by the maker against the original holder or the holder in due course. These defenses are:

- Incapable maker (whether a minor or not mentally competent to enter into a contract)
- Forgery (if the maker did not actually sign the note)
- Changes to the note of which the maker was not aware
- The note is connected to an illegal act

In any of these situations, the maker has a valid defense against any holder of the note.

PROMISSORY NOTES VERSUS TRUST DEEDS

Many people confuse the trust deed with the promissory note, as it is an easy mistake to make. It is important that we clearly understand the differences between the two. Remember that a trust deed is evidence of a debt. Trust deeds are used when a person finances a home. The trust deed is given to the lender to hold until the debt is paid in full.

The promissory note is the promise to repay the lender. Trust deeds do not make this promise. The trust deed is the security for the promissory note. A trust deed cannot exist without the note; however, a note can exist without a trust deed. Let's say, for example, that you want to purchase a car. You have saved enough for the down payment, but don't have the entire amount needed to purchase the car. When financed through a bank or dealership, you sign a promissory note, pledging to make payments on the car until it is paid in full. There is no trust deed involved. If you choose to finance a home, there is a trust deed (to secure the loan), or the loan itself, or the promissory note. If there are discrepancies between the note and the trust deed, the instructions in the note take precedence.

Remember
- Trust deeds are the security for a promissory note
- Trust deeds cannot exist without a promissory note
- The instructions in a note take precedence over a trust deed

TRUST DEEDS AND MORTGAGES

The terms mortgage and trust deed are oftentimes used synonymously, though this is a mistake. Mortgages and trust deeds basically function in the same way. They secure a note so that the buyer or borrower may obtain property and use it (per the mortgage or trust deed) as security for the note. However, there are distinct differences between mortgages and trust deeds, as you will see in this section.

Trust Deed

California is one of only 15 states that use trust deeds as security for a promissory note. As we have learned, if a borrower defaults on a loan, the lender may instruct the trustee to foreclose the property in an effort to raise the necessary funds to pay for the promissory note. Foreclosing on a trust deed generally takes less than four months. We will examine this in detail later in this chapter.

In a previous chapter, we learned about liens, and how they attach to property. There are liens that are voluntarily and liens that are involuntarily. A trust deed is a voluntary lien assumed by the homeowner. Once the trust deed is recorded, a lien is placed on the property, securing the note.

Under the *power of sale clause*, the lender gives the trustee the right to sell the property in the event the homeowner defaults on the note. The power of sale clause allows the trustee to foreclose, sell and then convey the property to a new buyer, using the proceeds of the sale to repay the promissory note. Additionally, if the person who purchased the property intended it for rental, the lender may take possession of the property and collect any rents the property may bring in.

Trust deeds may be difficult to understand if you are unfamiliar with the terminology used to describe a trust deed. So, let's make sure you are clear on the different parties involved in a trust deed and the names by which those parties are commonly referred.

Financial institutions or private investors lending money are referred to as either the *lender or beneficiary*. This person or institution will receive monthly payments on the promissory note. The lender holds both the trust deed to the property and the promissory note.

The person wishing to purchase a home and makes the promissory note is called the *borrower or trustor*. The trustor approaches the lender and requests a trust deed in the amount of the difference between the down payment and the purchase price of a property. The trustor is allowed to take possession of the property, but does not take possession of the title until the note is paid in full. The trustor does, however, hold equitable title in the property immediately

The neutral third party who holds bare legal title is known as the *trustee*. The trustee is responsible for reconveyance of the property's deed upon paying off the promissory note, or foreclosing on the property (if the homeowner defaults on their loan). Bare legal title refers to either the reconveyance or foreclosure. The trustee does not have any rights to the property and can only recconvey the deed or foreclose on the property when instructed to do so by the lender.

> **Remember!**
> - Beneficiary = the lender
> - Trustor = the borrower
> - Trustee = the neutral third party holding bare legal title to the property

The biggest difference between a mortgage and a trust deed is the conveyance of title to a trustee. As mentioned above, the trustee holds bare legal title to the property. The trustor basically owns the property; but he or she does not hold the deed to the property until the promissory note is paid in full.

Trust

The trust will allow the trustee to either foreclose on the property or reconvey the deed back to the trustor at the time the promissory note is paid in full. The trustee acts on the directions given him or her by the beneficiary. If the property is to be foreclosed, the beneficiary will direct the trustee to do so. If the note has been paid in full, the beneficiary signs the note and instructs the trustee to deliver it to the trustor. To illustrate the extent of power a trustee has, the trustee usually does not know that reconveyance or foreclosure is happening - until it is required by the borrower.

When a note is paid in full, the trustee will receive the original note and trust deed from thelender. The trustee is instructed to record the conveyance (along with any fees associated with the recording of the deed) within 21 days of receiving the original note and deed. The reconveyance deed given to the trustor is recorded, to give public notice that the note against the property has been paid in full.

The original trust deed must be signed by the borrower, so that it may be recorded in the county where the property is located. The purpose of recording the trust deed is to publicly announce that there is a lien on the property (in the event the property might be sold or transferred to another individual before the promissory note is paid in full). After the trust deed is recorded, it goes back to the lender, who will hold the trust deed for the life of the loan.

In the event that a trustor defaults on his or her loan obligation, the beneficiary has the option to request a trustee's sale or a judicial foreclosure. Either action may be chosen to dispose of the property and receive the necessary funds to repay the note and all fees. However, there is a 4-year statute of limitations on judicial foreclosure. The power of sale in a trust deed never expires, and the property can be sold at any time to satisfy the debt. The trustee's sale is made possible via the trust instrument (the deed itself). To initiate the trustee's sale, the beneficiary must notify the trustee of the reason for default by filing a declaration of default. The beneficiary must attach the original note and trust deed in the declaration of default.

There are a few guidelines that must be followed for a notice of default to be valid. For instance, the first statement of the notice must be printed in bold type. The notice must also clearly state that the entire amount of the note is due upon the sale as the result of default. Otherwise, the amount cannot be collected upon sale of the property. The statement must also be in Spanish if either the trustor requests, or if the note and trust deed were negotiated in Spanish.

The notice of default must be sent via certified or registered mail. Recipients of the are: the trustor; junior lien holders; State Controller, if necessary; all parties who have filed a request for notice with the county recorder's office; and any successor in interest to the trustor. In the event that there are other parties involved (other than the original trustor), the notice must be published in a newspaper of general circulation once each week for four weeks.

If there has been a notice of default filed against a trustor, the trustor can reinstate the note. The trustor may only do so if all overdue payments have been made prior to five businesses before the date of sale. A notice of trustee sale will be given, no later than three months after the notice of default, and the trustor has until five days before this sale to clear the overdue payments on the note. If the trustor cannot, or has not, made the necessary payments, the sale will happen as scheduled.

——— SPACE ABOVE THIS LINE FOR RECORDER'S USE ———

THIS FORM FURNISHED BY PROVIDENT TITLE COMPANY

Title Order No. _____

Escrow or Loan No. _____

LONG FORM ALL-INCLUSIVE DEED OF TRUST
AND ASSIGNMENT OF RENTS

This All-inclusive Deed of Trust, made this_____ day of, _____ between
_____,
_____,

herein called Trustor, whose address is_____
_____(number and street)_____(city)_____(state)_____(zip)

PROVIDENT TITLE COMPANY, A California corporation, herein called Trustee, and _____
_____
_____ herein called Beneficiary.

Witnesseth: That Trustor irrevocably Grants, Transfers and Assigns to Trustee in Trust, With Power of Sale, that property in _____
_____ County, California described as:

TOGETHER WITH the rents, issues and profits thereof, SUBJECT, HOWEVER, to the right, power and authority hereinafter given to and conferred upon Beneficiary to collect and apply such rents, issues and profits.

For the Purpose of Securing:

1.   Performance of each agreement of Trustor herein contained.   2. Payment of the indebtedness evidenced by one all-inclusive purchase money promissory note of even date herewith, and any extension or renewal thereof, in the principal sum of $ _____ executed by Trustor in favor of Beneficiary or order.

Underlying Obligations:

This is an all inclusive purchase money deed of trust, securing an all-inclusive purchase money promissory note in the original principal amount of _____
Dollars ($_____) (the "Note") which includes within such amount the unpaid balance of the following:

(a)   A promissory note in the original principal sum of _____ Dollars
($_____) in favor of_____ as
Payee, secured by a deed of trust recorded_____, 19___ as Document No. _____ in Book_____ Page_____
Official Records of _____ County,   California, and

(b)   A promissory note in the original principal sum of _____ Dollars
($_____) in favor of_____
as Payee, secured by a deed of trust recorded_____, 19___ as Document No. _____ in Book_____ Page
_____ Official Records of _____ County, California.

(The Promissory Notes secured by such deeds of trust are hereinafter called the "Underlying Notes").

To Protect the Security of This Deed of Trust, Trustor Agrees:

(1) To keep said property in good condition and repair; not to remove or demolish any building thereon; to complete or restore promptly and in good and workmanlike manner any building which may be constructed, damaged or destroyed thereon and to pay when due all claims for labor performed and materials furnished therefor; to comply with all laws affecting said property or requiring any alterations or improvements to be made thereon; not to commit or permit waste thereof; not to commit, suffer or permit any act upon said property in violation of law; to cultivate, irrigate, fertilize, fumigate, prune and do all other acts which from the character or use of said property may be reasonably necessary, the specific enumerations herein not excluding the general.

(2) To provide, maintain and deliver to Beneficiary fire, vandalism and malicious mischief insurance satisfactory to and with loss payable to Beneficiary. The amount collected under any fire or other insurance policy may be applied by Beneficiary upon any indebtedness secured hereby and in such order as Beneficiary may determine, or at option of Beneficiary the entire amount so collected or any part thereof may be released to Trustor. Such application or release shall not cure or waive any default or notice of default hereunder or invalidate any act done pursuant to such notice. The provisions hereof are subject to the mutual agreements of the parties as below set forth.

(3) To appear in and defend any action or proceeding purporting to affect the security hereof or the rights or powers of Beneficiary or Trustee; and to pay all costs and expenses, including cost of evidence of title and attorney's fees in a reasonable sum, in any such action or proceeding in which Beneficiary or Trustee may appear, and in any suit brought by Beneficiary to foreclose this Deed of Trust.

(4) To pay; at least ten days before delinquency all taxes and assessments affecting said property, including assessments on appurtenant water stock; subject to the mutual agreements of the parties as below set forth, to pay when due, all incumbrances, charges and liens, with interest, on said property or any part thereof, which appear to be prior or superior hereto; all costs, fees and expenses of this Trust.

0-13

Should Trustor fail to make any payment or to do any act as herein provided, then Beneficiary or Trustee, but without obligation so to do and without notice to or demand upon Trustor and without releasing Trustor from any obligation hereof, may: make or do the same in such manner and to such extent as either may deem necessary to protect the security hereof, Beneficiary or Trustee being authorized to enter upon said property for such purposes; appear in and defend any action or proceeding purporting to affect the security hereof or the rights or powers of Beneficiary or Trustee; pay, purchase, contest or compromise any incumbrance, charge or lien which in the judgment of either appears to be prior or superior hereto; and, in exercising any such powers, pay necessary expenses, employ counsel and pay his reasonable fees.

(5) To pay immediately and without demand all sums so expended by Beneficiary or Trustee, with interest from date of expenditure at the amount allowed by law in effect at the date hereof, and to pay for any statement provided for by law in effect at the date hereof regarding the obligation secured hereby any amount demanded by the Beneficiary not to exceed the maximum allowed by law at the time when said statement is demanded.

(6) That any award of damages in connection with any condemnation for public use of or injury to said property or any part thereof is hereby assigned and shall be paid to Beneficiary who may apply or release such moneys received by him in the same manner and with the same effect as above provided for disposition of proceeds of fire or other insurance. The provisions hereof are subject to the mutual agreements of the parties as below set forth.

(7) That by accepting payment of any sum secured hereby after its due date, Beneficiary does not waive his right either to require prompt payment when due of all other sums so secured or to declare default for failure so to pay.

(8) That at any time or from time to time, without liability therefor and without notice, upon written request of Beneficiary and presentation of this Deed and said note for endorsement, and without affecting the personal liability of any person for payment of the indebtedness secured hereby, Trustee may: reconvey any part of said property; consent to the making of any map or plat thereof; join in granting any easement thereon; or join in any extension agreement or any agreement subordinating the lien or charge hereof.

(9) That upon written request of the Beneficiary stating that all sums secured hereby have been paid, and upon surrender of this Deed and said note to Trustee for cancellation and retention and upon payment of its fees, Trustee shall reconvey, without warranty, the property then held hereunder. The recitals in such reconveyance of any matters or facts shall be conclusive proof of the truthfulness thereof. The grantee in such reconveyance may be described as "The person or persons legally entitled thereto." Five years after issuance of such full reconveyance, Trustee may destroy said note and this Deed unless directed in such request to retain them).

(10) That as additional security, Trustor hereby gives to and confers upon Beneficiary the right, power and authority, during the continuance of these Trusts, to collect the rents, issues and profits of said property, reserving unto Trustor the right, prior to any default by Trustor in payment of any indebtedness secured hereby or in performance of any agreement hereunder, to collect and retain such rents, issues and profits as they become due and payable. Upon any such default, Beneficiary may at any time without notice, either in person, by agent, or by a receiver to be appointed by a court, and without regard to the adequacy of any security for the indebtedness hereby secured, enter upon and take possession of said property or any part thereof, in his own name sue for or otherwise collect such rents, issues and profits, including those past due and unpaid, and apply the same, less costs and expenses of operation and collection, including reasonable attorney's fees, upon any indebtedness secured hereby, and in such order as Beneficiary may determine. The entering upon and taking possession of said property, the collection of such rents, issues and profits and the application thereof as aforesaid, shall not cure or waive any default or notice of default hereunder or invalidate any act done pursuant to such notice.

(11) That upon default by Trustor in payment of any indebtedness secured hereby or in performance of any agreement hereunder, Beneficiary may declare all sums secured hereby immediately due and payable by delivery to Trustee of written declaration of default and demand for sale and of written notice of default and of election to cause to be sold said property, which notice Trustee shall cause to be filed for record. Beneficiary also shall deposit with Trustee this Deed, said note and all documents evidencing expenditures secured hereby.

After the lapse of such time as may then be required by law following the recordation of said notice of default, and notice of sale having been given as then required by law, Trustee, without demand on Trustor, shall sell said property at the time and place fixed by it in said notice of sale, either as a whole or in separate parcels, and in such order as it may be determined, at public auction to the highest bidder for cash in lawful money of the United States, payable at time of sale. Trustee may postpone sale of all or any portion of said property by public announcement at such time and place of sale, and from time to time thereafter may postpone such sale by public announcement at the time fixed by the preceding postponement. Trustee shall deliver to such purchaser its deed conveying the property so sold, but without any covenant or warranty, express or implied. The recitals in such deed of any matters or facts shall be conclusive proof of the truthfulness thereof. Any person, including Trustor, Trustee, or Beneficiary as hereinafter defined, may purchase at such sale.

After deducting all costs, fees and expenses of Trustee and of this Trust, including cost of evidence of title in connection with sale, Trustee shall apply the proceeds of sale to payment of: all sums expended under the terms hereof, not then repaid, with accrued interest at the amount allowed by law in effect at the date hereof; all other sums then secured hereby; and the remainder, if any, to the person or persons legally entitled thereto.

(12) Beneficiary, or any successor in ownership of any indebtedness secured hereby, may from time to time, by instrument in writing, substitute a successor or successors to any Trustee named herein or acting hereunder, which instrument, executed by the Beneficiary and duly acknowledged and recorded in the office of the recorder of the county or counties where said property is situated, shall be conclusive proof of proper substitution of such successor Trustee or Trustees, who shall, without conveyance from the Trustee predecessor, succeed to all its title, estate, powers and duties. Said instrument must contain the name of the original Trustor, Trustee and Beneficiary hereunder, the book and page where this Deed is recorded and the name and address of the new Trustee.

(13) That this Deed applies to, inures to the benefit of, and binds all parties hereto, their heirs, legatees, devisees, administrators, executors, successors and assigns. The term Beneficiary shall mean the owner and holder, including pledgees, of the note secured hereby, whether or not named as Beneficiary herein. In this Deed, whenever the context so requires, the masculine gender includes the feminine and/or neuter, and the singular includes the plural.

(14) That Trustee accepts this Trust when this Deed, duly executed and acknowledged, is made a public record as provided by law. Trustee is not obligated to notify any party hereto of pending sale under any other Deed of Trust or of any action or proceeding in which Trustor, Beneficiary or Trustee shall be a party unless brought by Trustee.

The Undersigned Trustor requests that a copy of any Notice of Default and of any Notice of Sale hereunder be mailed to him at his address hereinbefore set forth.

Trustor and Beneficiary Mutually Agree:

(A) By Beneficiary's acceptance of this All-Inclusive Purchase Money Deed of Trust, Beneficiary covenants and agrees that provided Trustor is not delinquent or in default under the terms of the Note secured hereby, Beneficiary shall pay all installments of principal and interest which shall hereafter become due pursuant to the provisions of the Underlying Note(s) as and when the same become due and payable. In the event Trustor shall be delinquent or in default under the terms of the Note secured hereby, Beneficiary shall not be obligated to make any payments required by the terms of the Underlying Note(s) until such delinquency or default is cured. In the event Beneficiary fails to timely pay any installment of principal or interest on the Underlying Note(s) at the time when Trustor is not delinquent or in default under the terms of the Note secured hereby, Trustor may, at Trustor's option make such payments directly to the holder of such Underlying Note(s), in which event Trustor shall be entitled to a credit against the next installment(s) of principal and interest due under the terms of the Note secured hereby equal to the amount so paid and including, without limitation, any penalty, charges and expenses paid by Trustor to the holder of the Underlying Note(s) on account of Beneficiary's failing to make such payment. The obligation of Beneficiary hereunder shall terminate upon the earliest of (i) foreclosure of the lien of this All-Inclusive Purchase Money Deed of Trust, or (ii) cancellation of the Note secured hereby and reconveyance of this All-Inclusive Purchase Money Deed of Trust.

Should Trustor be delinquent or in default under the terms of the Note secured hereby and if Beneficiary consequently incurs any penalties, charges, or other expenses on account of the Underlying Note(s) during the period of such delinquency or default, the amount of such penalties, charges and expenses shall be immediately added to the principal amount of the Note secured hereby and shall be immediately payable by Trustor to Beneficiary.

If at any time the unpaid balance of the Note secured hereby, accrued interest thereon, and all other sums due pursuant to the terms thereof and all sums advanced by beneficiary pursuant to the terms of this Deed of Trust, is equal to or less than the unpaid principal balance of the Underlying Note(s) and accrued interest thereon, the Note secured hereby, at the option of Beneficiary, shall be cancelled and said property shall be reconveyed from the lien of this Deed of Trust.

(B) Trustor and Beneficiary agree that in the event the proceeds of any condemnation award or settlement in lieu thereof, or the proceeds of any casualty insurance covering destructible improvements located upon said property, are applied by the holder of the Underlying Note(s) in reduction of the unpaid principal amount thereof, the unpaid balance of the Note secured hereby shall be reduced by an equivalent amount which shall be deemed applied to the last sums due under the Note.

(C) At such times as the Note secured hereby becomes all due and payable, the amount of principal and interest then payable to Beneficiary thereunder shall be reduced by the then unpaid balance of principal and interest due on the Underlying Note(s).

(D) Any demand hereunder delivered by Beneficiary to Trustee for the foreclosure of the lien of this Deed of Trust may be not more than the sum of the following amounts:

(i) The difference between the then unpaid balance of principal and interest on the Note secured hereby and the then unpaid balance of principal and interest on the Underlying Note(s); plus

(ii) The aggregate of all amounts theretofore paid by Beneficiary pursuant to the terms of this Deed of Trust prior to the date of such foreclosure sale, for taxes and assessments, insurance premiums, delinquency charges, foreclosure costs, and any other sums advanced by Beneficiary pursuant to the terms of this Deed of Trust, to the extent the same were not previously repaid by Trustor to Beneficiary; plus

(iii) The costs of foreclosure hereunder; plus attorneys fees and costs incurred by Beneficiary in enforcing this Deed of Trust or the Note secured hereby as permitted by law.

(E) Notwithstanding any provision to the contrary herein contained, in the event of a Trustee's sale in furtherance of the foreclosure of this Deed of Trust, the balance then due on the Note secured hereby, for the purpose of Beneficiary's demand, shall be reduced, as aforesaid, by the unpaid balance, if any, of principal and interest then due on the Underlying Note(s), satisfactory evidence of which unpaid balances must be submitted to Trustee prior to such sale. The Trustee may rely on any statements received from Beneficiary in this regard and such statements shall be deemed binding and conclusive as between Beneficiary and Trustor, on the one hand, and the Trustee, on the other hand, to the extent of such reliance.

Signature of Trustor

_____   _____

_____   _____

Signature of Beneficiary

_____   _____

_____   _____

STAPLE APPROPRIATE ACKNOWLEDGEMENTS HERE

(THIS DEED OF TRUST IS APPROPRIATE FOR USE ONLY IN CERTAIN TRANSACTIONS. PRIOR TO THE EXECUTION OF THIS DEED OF TRUST, THE PARTIES SHOULD CONSULT THEIR ATTORNEYS WITH RESPECT TO ITS SUITABILITY FOR THEIR PURPOSE.)

Title Order No. _____   Escrow or Loan No. _____

Long Form All-Inclusive Purchase Money Deed of Trust With Power of Sale

Provident Title Company
AS TRUSTEE

———DO NOT RECORD———

FOR RECONVEYANCE OR FORECLOSURE SEND TO THE NEAREST

OFFICE OF PROVIDENT TITLE COMPANY

REQUEST FOR FULL RECONVEYANCE

To be used only when note has been paid.

Dated _____

TO PROVIDENT TITLE COMPANY, Trustee:

The Undersigned is the legal owner and holder of all indebtedness secured by the within Deed of Trust. All sums secured by said Deed of Trust have been fully paid and satisfied, and you are hereby requested and directed, on payment to you of any sums owing to you under the terms of said Deed of Trust, to cancel all evidences of indebtedness secured by said Deed of Trust, delivered to you herewith together with the said Deed of Trust, and to reconvey, without warranty, to the parties designated by the terms of said Deed of Trust, the estate now held by you under the same.

MAIL RECONVEYANCE TO:

_____   _____

_____   _____

_____   (By) _____

_____   (By) _____

Do not lose or destroy this Deed of Trust OR THE NOTE which it secures.
Both must be delivered to the Trustee for cancellation before reconveyance will be made.

REQUEST FOR FULL RECONVEYANCE

A Full Reconveyance will be issued only when original note or notes, together with the Deed of Trust securing payment thereof, are surrendered to the Trustee for cancellation, accompanied by this Request signed by all owners of the note or notes, together with the reconveyance fee.

Date _____ , 19 _____

The undersigned Beneficiary is the legal owner and holder of the _____ promissory

note _____ for the total sum of $ _____ and all other indebtedness secured by

Deed of Trust dated _____ , 19 ___ executed by _____

_____ , Trustor, to _____

_____ , Trustee, and recorded _____ , 19 _____

as Instrument No. _____ , in Book _____ Page _____

of Official Records in the office of the Recorder of _____ County, State of California. You are notified hereby that said note or notes and all other indebtedness secured by said Deed of Trust have been fully paid, and said note or notes and the said Deed of Trust the herewith surrendered to you for cancellation. You are therefore requested, upon payment to you of all sums owing to you under the terms of said Deed of Trust, to reconvey, without warranty to the "person or persons legally entitled thereto," the estate now held by you and acquired through said Deed of Trust.

Mail recorded reconveyance to: _____

_____   _____

_____   _____

_____   _____

0-57

218

CALIFORNIA
ASSOCIATION
OF REALTORS®

SELLER FINANCING ADDENDUM AND DISCLOSURE
(California Civil Code §§2956-2967)
(C.A.R. Form SFA, Revised 10/02)

This is an addendum to the ☐ California Residential Purchase Agreement, ☐ Counter Offer, or ☐ Other _____
_____ ("Agreement"), dated _____
On property known as _____ ("Property"),
between _____ ("Buyer"),
and _____ ("Seller").
Seller agrees to extend credit to Buyer as follows:

1. **PRINCIPAL; INTEREST; PAYMENT; MATURITY TERMS:** ☐ Principal amount $ _____, interest at _____ %
   per annum, payable at approximately $ _____ per ☐ month, ☐ year, or ☐ other _____,
   remaining principal balance due in _____ years.
2. **LOAN APPLICATION; CREDIT REPORT:** Within 5 (or ☐ _____) **Days** After Acceptance: **(a)** Buyer shall provide Seller a completed
   loan application on a form acceptable to Seller (such as a FNMA/FHLMC Uniform Residential Loan Application for residential one to four
   unit properties); and **(b)** Buyer authorizes Seller and/or Agent to obtain, at Buyer's expense, a copy of Buyer's credit report. Buyer shall
   provide any supporting documentation reasonably requested by Seller. Seller, after first giving Buyer a Notice to Buyer to Perform, may
   cancel this Agreement in writing and authorize return of Buyer's deposit if Buyer fails to provide such documents within that time, or if
   Seller disapproves any above item within 5 (or ☐ _____) **Days** After receipt of each item.
3. **CREDIT DOCUMENTS:** This extension of credit by Seller will be evidenced by: ☐ Note and deed of trust; ☐ All-inclusive
   note and deed of trust; ☐ Installment land sale contract; ☐ Lease/option (when parties intend transfer of equitable title);
   OR ☐ Other (specify) _____
**THE FOLLOWING TERMS APPLY ONLY IF CHECKED. SELLER IS ADVISED TO READ ALL TERMS, EVEN THOSE NOT
CHECKED, TO UNDERSTAND WHAT IS OR IS NOT INCLUDED, AND, IF NOT INCLUDED, THE CONSEQUENCES THEREOF.**
4. ☐ **LATE CHARGE:** If any payment is not made within _____ **Days** After it is due, a late charge of either $ _____,
   or _____ % of the installment due, may be charged to Buyer. **NOTE:** On single family residences that Buyer intends to occupy,
   California Civil Code §2954.4(a) limits the late charge to no more than 6% of the total installment payment due and requires a
   grace period of no less than 10 days.
5. ☐ **BALLOON PAYMENT:** The extension of credit will provide for a balloon payment, in the amount of $ _____,
   plus any accrued interest, which is due on _____ (date).
6. ☐ **PREPAYMENT:** If all or part of this extension of credit is paid early, Seller may charge a prepayment penalty as follows (if
   applicable): _____. Caution: California Civil Code
   §2954.9 contains limitations on prepayment penalties for residential one-to-four unit properties.
7. ☐ **DUE ON SALE:** If any interest in the Property is sold or otherwise transferred, Seller has the option to require immediate
   payment of the entire unpaid principal balance, plus any accrued interest.
8.* ☐ **REQUEST FOR COPY OF NOTICE OF DEFAULT:** A request for a copy of Notice of Default as defined in California Civil
   Code §2924b will be recorded. **If Not,** Seller is advised to consider recording a Request for Notice of Default.
9.* ☐ **REQUEST FOR NOTICE OF DELINQUENCY:** A request for Notice of Delinquency, as defined in California Civil Code §2924e,
   to be signed and paid for by Buyer, will be made to senior lienholders. **If not,** Seller is advised to consider making a Request for
   Notice of Delinquency. Seller is advised to check with senior lienholders to verify whether they will honor this request.
10.* ☐ **TAX SERVICE:**
   A. If property taxes on the Property become delinquent, tax service will be arranged to report to Seller. **If not,** Seller is
      advised to consider retaining a tax service, or to otherwise determine that property taxes are paid.
   B. ☐ Buyer, ☐ Seller, shall be responsible for the initial and continued retention of, and payment for, such tax service.
11. ☐ **TITLE INSURANCE:** Title insurance coverage will be provided to **both** Seller and Buyer, insuring their respective interests
   in the Property. **If not,** Buyer and Seller are advised to consider securing such title insurance coverage.
12. ☐ **HAZARD INSURANCE:**
   A. The parties' escrow holder or insurance carrier will be directed to include a loss payee endorsement, adding Seller to
      the Property insurance policy. **If not,** Seller is advised to secure such an endorsement, or acquire a separate
      insurance policy.
   B. Property insurance **does not** include earthquake or flood insurance coverage, unless checked:
      ☐ Earthquake insurance will be obtained; ☐ Flood insurance will be obtained.
13. ☐ **PROCEEDS TO BUYER:** Buyer will receive cash proceeds at the close of the sale transaction. The amount received will be
   approximately $ _____, from _____ (indicate source of
   proceeds). Buyer represents that the purpose of such disbursement is as follows: _____
14. ☐ **NEGATIVE AMORTIZATION; DEFERRED INTEREST:** Negative amortization results when Buyer's periodic payments are
   less than the amount of interest earned on the obligation. Deferred interest also results when the obligation does not
   require periodic payments for a period of time. In either case, interest is not payable as it accrues. This accrued interest
   will have to be paid by Buyer at a later time, and may result in Buyer owing more on the obligation than at its origination.
   The credit being extended to Buyer by Seller will provide for negative amortization or deferred interest as indicated below.
   (Check A, B, or C. CHECK ONE ONLY.)
   ☐ **A.** All negative amortization or deferred interest shall be added to the principal _____
      (e.g., annually, monthly, etc.), and thereafter shall bear interest at the rate specified in the credit documents (compound interest);
   OR ☐ **B.** All deferred interest shall be due and payable, along with principal, at maturity;
   OR ☐ **C.** Other _____

*(For Paragraphs 8-10) In order to receive timely and continued notification, Seller is advised to record appropriate notices and/or to
notify appropriate parties of any change in Seller's address.

SFA REVISED 10/02 (PAGE 1 OF 3) Print Date

Buyer's Initials (_____)(_____)
Seller's Initials (_____)(_____)

Reviewed by _____ Date _____

EQUAL HOUSING
OPPORTUNITY

SELLER FINANCING ADDENDUM AND DISCLOSURE (SFA PAGE 1 OF 3)

Property Address: _____ Date: _____

15. ☐ **ALL-INCLUSIVE DEED OF TRUST; INSTALLMENT LAND SALE CONTRACT:** This transaction involves the use of an all-inclusive (or wraparound) deed of trust or an installment land sale contract. That deed of trust or contract shall provide as follows:
    A. In the event of an acceleration of any senior encumbrance, the responsibility for payment, or for legal defense is: _____
    _____ ; OR ☐ **Is not** specified in the credit or security documents.
    B. In the event of the prepayment of a senior encumbrance, the responsibilities and rights of Buyer and Seller regarding refinancing, prepayment penalties, and any prepayment discounts are: _____ ;
    OR ☐ **Are not** specified in the documents evidencing credit.
    C. Buyer will make periodic payments to _____ (Seller,
    collection agent, or any neutral third party), who will be responsible for disbursing payments to the payee(s) on the senior encumbrance(s) and to Seller. **NOTE:** The Parties are advised to designate a neutral third party for these purposes.
16. ☐ **TAX IDENTIFICATION NUMBERS.** Buyer and Seller shall each provide to each other their Social Security Numbers or Taxpayer Identification Numbers.
17. ☐ **OTHER CREDIT TERMS** _____
18. ☐ **RECORDING:** The documents evidencing credit (paragraph 3) will be recorded with the county recorder where the Property is located. **If not,** Buyer and Seller are advised that their respective interests in the Property may be jeopardized by intervening liens, judgments, encumbrances, or subsequent transfers.
19. ☐ **JUNIOR FINANCING:** There will be additional financing, secured by the Property, junior to this Seller financing. Explain: _____
    _____
20. **SENIOR LOANS AND ENCUMBRANCES:** The following information is provided on loans and/or encumbrances that will be **senior** to Seller financing. **NOTE:** The following are estimates, unless otherwise marked with an asterisk (*). If checked: ☐ A separate sheet with information on additional senior loans/encumbrances is attached

		1st	2nd
A.	Original Balance	$ _____	$ _____
B.	Current Balance	$ _____	$ _____
C.	Periodic Payment (e.g. $100/month):	$ _____	$ _____ /
	Including Impounds of:	$ _____	$ _____ /
D.	Interest Rate (per annum)	_____ %	_____ %
E.	Fixed or Variable Rate:	_____	_____
	If Variable Rate: Lifetime Cap (Ceiling)	_____	_____
	Indicator (Underlying Index)	_____	_____
	Margins	_____	_____
F.	Maturity Date	_____	_____
G.	Amount of Balloon Payment	$ _____	$ _____
H.	Date Balloon Payment Due	_____	_____
I.	Potential for Negative Amortization? (Yes, No, or Unknown)	_____	_____
J.	Due on Sale? (Yes, No, or Unknown)	_____	_____
K.	Pre-payment penalty? (Yes, No, or Unknown)	_____	_____
L.	Are payments current? (Yes, No, or Unknown)	_____	_____

21. **BUYER'S CREDITWORTHINESS:** (CHECK EITHER A OR B. Do not check both.) In addition to the loan application, credit report and other information requested under paragraph 2:
    A. ☐ No other disclosure concerning Buyer's creditworthiness has been made to Seller;
OR **B.** ☐ The following representations concerning Buyer's creditworthiness are made by Buyer(s) to Seller.

Borrower	**Co-Borrower**
1. Occupation _____	1. Occupation _____
2. Employer _____	2. Employer _____
3. Length of Employment _____	3. Length of Employment _____
4. Monthly Gross Income _____	4. Monthly Gross Income _____
5. Other _____	5. Other _____

22. **ADDED, DELETED OR SUBSTITUTED BUYERS:** The addition, deletion or substitution of any person or entity under this Agreement or to title prior to close of escrow shall require Seller's written consent. Seller may grant or withhold consent in Seller's sole discretion. Any additional or substituted person or entity shall, if requested by Seller, submit to Seller the same documentation as required for the original named Buyer. Seller and/or Brokers may obtain a credit report, at Buyer's expense, on any such person or entity.

Buyer's Initials (_____)(_____)
Seller's Initials (_____)(_____)

Copyright © 1997-2003, CALIFORNIA ASSOCIATION OF REALTORS®, INC.
SFA REVISED 10/02 (PAGE 2 OF 3)

Reviewed by _____ Date _____

SELLER FINANCING ADDENDUM AND DISCLOSURE (SFA PAGE 2 OF 3)

Property Address: _____ Date: _____

23. **CAUTION:**
   A. If the Seller financing requires a balloon payment, Seller shall give Buyer written notice, according to the terms of Civil Code §2966, at least 90 and not more than 150 days before the balloon payment is due if the transaction is for the purchase of a dwelling for not more than four families.
   B. If **any** obligation secured by the Property calls for a balloon payment, Seller and Buyer are aware that refinancing of the balloon payment at maturity may be difficult or impossible, depending on conditions in the conventional mortgage marketplace at that time. There are no assurances that new financing or a loan extension will be available when the balloon prepayment, or any prepayment, is due.
   C. If **any** of the existing or proposed loans or extensions of credit would require refinancing as a result of a lack of full amortization, such refinancing might be difficult or impossible in the conventional mortgage marketplace.
   D. In the event of default by Buyer: (1) Seller may have to reinstate and/or make monthly payments on any and all senior encumbrances (including real property taxes) in order to protect Seller's secured interest; (2) Seller's rights are generally limited to foreclosure on the Property, pursuant to California Code of Civil Procedure §580b; and (3) the Property may lack sufficient equity to protect Seller's interests if the Property decreases in value.

If this three-page Addendum and Disclosure is used in a transaction for the purchase of a dwelling for not more than four families, it shall be prepared by an Arranger of Credit as defined in California Civil Code §2957(a). (The Arranger of Credit is usually the agent who obtained the offer.)

Arranger of Credit - (Print Firm Name) _____ By _____ Date _____

Address _____ City _____ State _____ Zip _____

Phone _____ Fax _____

BUYER AND SELLER ACKNOWLEDGE AND AGREE THAT BROKERS: (A) WILL NOT PROVIDE LEGAL OR TAX ADVICE; (B) WILL NOT PROVIDE OTHER ADVICE OR INFORMATION THAT EXCEEDS THE KNOWLEDGE, EDUCATION AND EXPERIENCE REQUIRED TO OBTAIN A REAL ESTATE LICENSE; OR (C) HAVE NOT AND WILL NOT VERIFY ANY INFORMATION PROVIDED BY EITHER BUYER OR SELLER. BUYER AND SELLER AGREE THAT THEY WILL SEEK LEGAL, TAX AND OTHER DESIRED ASSISTANCE FROM APPROPRIATE PROFESSIONALS. BUYER AND SELLER ACKNOWLEDGE THAT THE INFORMATION EACH HAS PROVIDED TO THE ARRANGER OF CREDIT FOR INCLUSION IN THIS DISCLOSURE FORM IS ACCURATE. BUYER AND SELLER FURTHER ACKNOWLEDGE THAT EACH HAS RECEIVED A COMPLETED COPY OF THIS DISCLOSURE FORM.

Buyer _____ Date _____
(signature)

Address _____ City _____ State _____ Zip _____
Phone _____ Fax _____ E-mail _____

Buyer _____ Date _____
(signature)

Address _____ City _____ State _____ Zip _____
Phone _____ Fax _____ E-mail _____

Seller _____ Date _____
(signature)

Address _____ City _____ State _____ Zip _____
Phone _____ Fax _____ E-mail _____

Seller _____ Date _____
(signature)

Address _____ City _____ State _____ Zip _____
Phone _____ Fax _____ E-mail _____

THIS FORM HAS BEEN APPROVED BY THE CALIFORNIA ASSOCIATION OF REALTORS® (C.A.R.). NO REPRESENTATION IS MADE AS TO THE LEGAL VALIDITY OR ADEQUACY OF ANY PROVISION IN ANY SPECIFIC TRANSACTION. A REAL ESTATE BROKER IS THE PERSON QUALIFIED TO ADVISE ON REAL ESTATE TRANSACTIONS. IF YOU DESIRE LEGAL OR TAX ADVICE, CONSULT AN APPROPRIATE PROFESSIONAL.

This form is available for use by the entire real estate industry. It is not intended to identify the user as a REALTOR®. REALTOR® is a registered collective membership mark which may be used only by members of the NATIONAL ASSOCIATION OF REALTORS® who subscribe to its Code of Ethics.

SURE TRAC
The System for Success™

Published by the
California Association of REALTORS®

Reviewed by _____ Date _____

EQUAL HOUSING OPPORTUNITY

SFA REVISED 10/02 (PAGE 3 OF 3)

SELLER FINANCING ADDENDUM AND DISCLOSURE (SFA PAGE 3 OF 3)

ALL INCLUSIVE PURCHASE MONEY PROMISSORY NOTE SECURED BY LONG FORM
ALL-INCLUSIVE PURCHASE MONEY DEED OF TRUST
(INSTALLMENT NOTE, INTEREST INCLUDED)

$ _____ _____, California, _____, 19____

In installments as herein stated, for value received, I/We ("Maker") promise to pay to_____

("Payee") or order, at _____

the principal sum of _____ DOLLARS, with interest

from _____ on unpaid principal at the rate of

_____ per cent per annum; principal and interest payable in installments of _____

or more on the _____ day of each _____ month, beginning

on the _____ day of _____ 19_____, and continuing until said principal and

interest have been paid.

Each installment shall be applied first on the interest then due and the remainder on principal; and interest shall thereupon cease upon the principal so credited.

The total principal amount of this Note includes the unpaid principal balance of the promissory note(s) ("Underlying Note(s)") secured by Deed(s) of Trust, more particularly described as follows:

1. (A) PROMISSORY NOTE:

Maker:_____

Payee:_____

Original Amount:_____

Date:_____

(B) DEED OF TRUST:

Beneficiary:_____

Original Amount:_____

Recordation Date:_____

Document No. _____ Book _____ Page_____

Place of Recordation: _____, County, California

2. (A) PROMISSORY NOTE:

Maker:_____

Payee:_____

Original Amount:_____

Date:_____

(B) DEED OF TRUST:

Beneficiary:_____

Original Amount:_____

Recordation Date:_____

Document No. _____ Book _____ Page _____

Place of Recordation: _____, County, California

By Payee's acceptance of this Note, Payee covenants and agrees that, provided Maker is not delinquent or in default under the terms of this Note, Payee shall pay all installments of principal and interest which shall hereafter become due pursuant to the provisions of the Underlying Note(s) as and when the same become due and payable. In the event Maker shall be delinquent or in default under the terms of this Note, Payee shall not be obligated to make any payments required by the terms of the Underlying Note(s) until such delinquency or default is cured. In the event Payee fails to timely pay any installment of principal or interest on the Underlying Note(s) at the time when Maker is not delinquent or in default hereunder, Maker may, at Maker's option, make such payments directly to the holder of such Underlying Note(s), in which event Maker shall be entitled to a credit against the next installment(s) of principal and interest due under the terms of this Note equal to the amount so paid and including, without limitation, any penalty, charges and expenses paid by Maker to the holder of the Underlying Note(s) on account of Payee failing to make such payment. The obligations of Payee hereunder shall terminate upon the earliest of (i) foreclosure of the lien of the All-Inclusive Purchase Money Deed of Trust securing this Note, or (ii) cancellation of this Note and reconveyance of the All-Inclusive Purchase Money Deed of Trust securing same.

Should Maker be delinquent or in default under the terms of this Note, and Payee consequently incurs any penalties, charges or other expenses on account of the Underlying Note(s) during the period of such delinquency or default, the amount of such penalties, charges and expenses shall be immediately added to the principal amount of this Note and shall be immediately payable by Maker to Payee.

Notwithstanding anything to the contrary herein contained, the right of Maker to prepay all or any portion of the principal of this Note is limited to the same extent as any limitation exists in the right to prepay the principal of the Underlying Note(s). If any prepayments of principal of this Note shall, by reason of the application of any portion thereof by Payee to the prepayment of principal of the Underlying Note(s), constitute such prepayment for which the holders of the Underlying Note(s) are entitled to receive a prepayment penalty or consideration, the amount of such prepayment penalty or consideration shall be paid by Maker to Payee upon demand, and any such amount shall not reduce the unpaid balance of principal or interest hereunder.

At any time when the total of the unpaid principal balance of this Note, accrued interest thereon, all other sums due pursuant to the terms hereof, and all sums advanced by Payee pursuant to the terms of the All-Inclusive Purchase Money Deed of Trust securing this Note, is equal to or less than the unpaid balance of principal and interest then due under the terms of the Underlying Note(s), Payee, at his option, shall cancel this Note and deliver same to Maker and execute a request for full reconveyance of the Deed of Trust securing this Note.

Should default be made by Maker in payment of any installments of principal, interest, or any other sums due hereunder, the whole sum of principal, interest and all other sums due from Maker hereunder, after first deducting

222

therefrom all sums then due under the terms of the Underlying Note(s), shall become immediately due at the option of the holder of this Note. Principal, interest and all other sums due hereunder payable in lawful money of the United States. If action be instituted of this Note, I/we promise to pay such sums as the Court may fix as attorney's fees. This Note is secured by a LONG FORM ALL-INCLUSIVE PURCHASE MONEY DEED OF TRUST to PROVIDENT TITLE COMPANY, a California corporation, as Trustee.

_____   _____
(Maker)   (Maker)

The undersigned hereby accept(s) the foregoing All-Inclusive Purchase Money Promissory Note and agree(s) to perform each and all of the terms thereof on the part of Payee to be performed.

Executed as of the date and place first above written.

_____   _____
(Payee)   (Payee)

(THIS NOTE IS FOR USE ONLY IN PURCHASE MONEY TRANSACTIONS. IT IS RECOMMENDED THAT, PRIOR TO THE EXECUTION OF THIS NOTE, THE PARTIES CONSULT WITH THEIR ATTORNEYS WITH RESPECT THERETO.)

THIS FORM FURNISHED BY **PROVIDENT TITLE COMPANY**

DO NOT DESTROY THIS NOTE

Requirements for a trustee's sale:

- Written notice of default including the amount delinquent must be issued via certified mail
- A notice of trustee's sale must be issued within three months of the notice of default
- Trustor may reinstate the note if all payments are made within five days of the trustee's sale
- Notice of the trustee's sale must run in a general circulation paper once each week for four weeks
- All sales are final; and there is no right of redemption
- There is no deficiency judgment allowed in a trustee's sale
- An unlawful detainer must be used to evict any previous property owner who refuses to vacate the property

Upon sale of the property, the beneficiary will accept payments in the form of cash or cashier's check. Any other forms of payment must be mentioned as optional payment methods in the notice of trustee sale. When selling the property at a trustee sale, the purchaser takes possession immediately. The trustor who was in default has no right of redemption after the sale is final. This is distinctly different from a judicial foreclosure.

If, after a trustee's sale the former owner refuses to give up possession of the property, the new owner must obtain an unlawful detainer. An unlawful detainer is a court order, prompting the sheriff to evict the present occupant. It is a risk that the bidder must factor into the process if purchasing property at a trustee sale.

With no right of redemption, the lender's risk in the promissory note is minimized. If the borrower defaults, the lender is usually paid in full with the proceeds from the trustee's sale. This is true despite the fact that a power of sale prohibits a deficiency judgment. In a deficiency judgment, the lender may seek a personal judgment against the trustor for any amount or fees not covered by the sale of the property.

Once a trustor pays off his or her promissory note in full, the lender delivers the original trust deed and note to the trustee. The trustee is directed to issue a deed of reconveyance to the trustor, and to record this reconveyance with the county recorder's office. The original deed and trust may be delivered to the trustor with a written request from the trustor for the original deed. It is important that the lender remembers to clear the title to the trustor's property. If the lender does not clear the title, he or she may be subject to civil and criminal penalties. A trustee is obligated to carry out all reconveyances and recordings, or the trustee may be penalized.

Upon the trustor paying off the note in full, the trustee will:

- Receive the original trust deed and note from the lender, and sign these documents
- Issue a deed of reconveyance to the trustor
- Clear the title to the property of all encumbrances related to the trust deed
- Record the reconveyance at the county recorder's office

Mortgage

A mortgage is similar to a trust, in that it is an instrument that secures \payment of a debt. In our situation, the property itself is the security for the promissory note (evidenced by the presence of a mortgage). The mortgage will create a lien on the property. If the property owner (or mortgager) defaults on the note, the mortgagee (or lender), may utilize a judicial foreclosure, which is court ordered. There is another method of foreclosure called a power-of-sale provision, which functions much like the trustee's sale in a trust.

In a judicial foreclosure, the court will order the property to be sold to satisfy the debt against it. The sale must occur in the county where the property or majority of the property is located. The property is sold in a manner similar to public auction; that is, t property will go to the highest bidder. A sheriff or court-appointed commissioner will oversee the sale to ensure the sale is carried out properly. Just as in a trustee's sale, proper notice is required before conducting a judicial foreclosure.

The person who places the highest bid is required to place a deposit on the property, with full payment due within 10 days of the sale. The deposit for a property selling for more than $5,000.00 is the greater of either $5,000.00 or 10% of the selling bid. Any bidder who chooses to make a deposit, with the full amount due later is also responsible for any interest that may accrue on the property during that time. In the event that the person who won the bid defaults on payment the property sale will be held again. Those people who successfully win the bid, but are not able to pay for the property, may be held liable for any costs of the original sale, plus attorney fees, interest and the difference, if any, between the original bid and the new bid. Sale may also be postponed if there are no satisfactory bids.

If the sale was a success, and the bidder paid the full amount she or he bid for the property, the commissioner or sheriff will issue the purchaser a certificate of sale. The new property owner should record this document immediately to both protect their interest in the property, and prevent claims made as such.

Once the property is sold, proceeds from the sale will be used to pay off the note on the house. Once the note is paid, any remaining proceeds will be distributed to any lien holders in order of priority (i.e., the order in which the lien was recorded). If there is any money remaining from the sale of the property once all debts against it have been paid, the remaining proceeds will be given to the mortgagor. The best case scenario is when all debts have been paid and the mortgagor receives the remaining amount, though this is not always the case. In some situations, the proceeds of the sale will not be sufficient to pay off the mortgagee. At that time, the mortgagee may seek a deficiency judgment against the mortgagor for the remaining debt. A mortgagee may NOT seek a deficiency judgment against a mortgagor if the mortgagee was the original seller of the property to the mortgagor. Also, a mortgagor may not seek a deficiency judgment if the loan was used to pay all or part of the purchase price of an owner-occupied residential dwelling consisting of no more than four units.

The mortgagee can reinstate the mortgage if he or she makes all delinquent payments plus any costs incurred during the foreclosure proceedings.

Judicial foreclosures are very time consuming. First, it takes many months before the sale is held. At that time, the person who purchases the property receives only a certificate of sale. The purchaser does not take possession of the property at this time, as that occurs only after the statutory *redemption period*. The statutory redemption period is the amount of time following the sale of a property when the former owner's heirs or successors may buy back the property. This redemption period must be taken into account by the purchaser of the property when making a bid. In fact, there is a chance the purchaser will never take possession of the property.

Steps in a Judicial Foreclosure:

- Court orders the sheriff or commissioner to sell the property
- Judicial sale is held, and creditors may seek a deficiency judgment in the event the sale does not raise enough money to cover the debt against the property
- Certificate of sale is issued to the purchaser of the property
- Redemption period must be satisfied before purchaser takes possession of the property

The old rule regarding the redemption period (for mortgages that were assumed before July 1, 1983) allowed junior lien holders to also buy back the property. The stipulation was that junior lien holders had to act within 3 months of the sale of the property if the proceeds of the sale were enough to cover all costs and interest. The redemption period for all others with an interest in the property is one year, unless the mortgagee waives his or her right to this time period, or is prohibited from obtaining a deficiency judgment. Since this is the old rule for mortgages made prior to July 1, 1983, it is advisable to consult an attorney for all foreclosures made after this time.

T R U S T   D E E D   V S .   M O R T G A G E

The major differences between a trust deed and mortgage are:
- Number of parties involved in the process
- Statute of Limitations
- Remedies available upon default
- Conveyance of the title
- Reinstatement period
- Deficiency judgment
- Redemption period
- Procedure following satisfaction of the debt

The trust deed offers lenders a bit more security in their investment. The trust deed allows the lender a faster and cheaper way to get their money back, in the event the trustor defaults on the note. There is also no guarantee that there will be bidders at a foreclosure sale. In such cases, the lender will be forced to purchase the property back from the owner. This is an undesirable scenario for any lender.

T R A N S F E R   O F   P R O P E R T Y   B Y   T H E   B O R R O W E R

It is possible for a seller to sell a property, and have the new buyer assume the existing loan on the property. When the buyer takes over the current loan, he or she is responsible for making all payments and installments on the loan. In addition to the assumption of a loan, the buyer may also purchase property subject to an existing loan.

In loan assumption, the original borrower does not completely dissolve his or her responsibilities to the loan. The buyer of the property will take over the responsibilities of the original loan, making the buyer primarily liable in the case of default. However, the original borrower retains secondary liability for the loan. Because the new borrower takes over the original loan with the approval of the lender, all loan assumptions must be approved by the lender.

The original borrower will never be required to make another payment, nor will they be responsible for any deficiency judgments. If the new owner defaults, the property may be foreclosed. This means that the new owner must vacate the property, and their credit will be adversely affected. In addition, the original owner or original borrower's credit will also be adversely affected.

A seller may sell a home, with the buyer agreeing to purchase the property subject to the existing loan. This means that the buyer will take possession of the property and make all payments on the note. However, the original owner, or the person selling the property will remain responsible for the loan. If the buyer of the property should happen to default on the property, the home will be sold to satisfy the debt to the lender. The original borrower's credit will be adversely affected by this action.

In the event that a purchaser defaults on a loan that is considered a hard money loan, the original borrower may be held liable in the form of a deficiency judgment. A hard money loan is one where the funds were made to get cash for unspecified purchases. A purchase money loan is for specific purchases, such as a car or a house. For those people receiving a loan specifically to purchase property, exemption from a deficiency judgment applies. If a deficiency judgment is allowed, the original owner may be responsible for the difference between the amount for which the home was sold, as well as any remaining, unpaid balance of the loan.

Example
Adam purchased a home with a first trust deed 15 years ago, and recently refinanced his home to put in a pool and new landscaping. The original loan was a purchase money loan, while the second loan was a hard money loan. Adam found out he was being transferred to Texas by his company, and needed to sell his home. He sold his home subject to the existing loans to Alex. Alex was a first time homeowner, and quickly found himself in over his head. Alex defaulted on the loan. The property was foreclosed and Adam was found liable for the second loan. When Adam sold the property to Alex, he should have requested a substitution of liability from the lender, to relieve himself of any responsibility for the loan.

When assuming an existing loan:

- New buyer is primarily responsible for the loan
- Original buyer is secondarily liable for the loan
- In the event of default, no deficiency judgment is allowed
- Both the original and new buyer's credit will be adversely affected

When purchasing a home subject to an existing loan:

- Original buyer remains responsible for the loan
- New buyer takes possession and makes all payments on the loan
- Deficiency judgments are allowed on hard money loans
- Both original and new buyers may be held liable for the deficiency judgment, and their credit may be adversely affected in the event of default on the loan

Lenders take a risk each time they make a loan to a borrower for any purpose. This is especially true when the loan is made for the purchase of property (due to the amount that must be borrowed). As we have seen in this chapter, there are ways for a lender to retrieve monies that have been lent; but there are situations where the lender may not be repaid in full, due to the type of loan granted. For a lender to protect themselves, they will usually include a specific clause or requirement in the loan.

Special Clauses:
- Acceleration
- Alienation or due-on-sale
- Assumption
- Subordination
- Subject to
- Prepayment
- Or more

A lender will use the *acceleration clause* if payment of the entire note is required in certain circumstances. Examples of times when a lender might call the note are: in the event of default for taxes; insurance or payment of the note; or, if the buyer decides to sell the property.

Just as the acceleration clause requires that the entire amount of the loan be paid in certain circumstances, the *due-on-sale* or *alienation clause* demands that the entire amount of the note be paid in the event that a property owner transfers ownership to another individual. A lender will typically do this to protect themselves from unqualified borrowers assuming the original loan, thus protecting the lender's interest from default.

As we just discussed in the section above, the *assumption clause* allows the buyer to take over an existing loan from the seller with knowledge and approval of the lender. The new buyer assumes primary responsibility for this loan, while the original borrower holds secondary responsibility for the loan.

In the event that a borrower defaults on a loan, the lender or creditors are paid from the sale of the property in the order in which the liens were recorded against the property. Trust deeds are considered liens, and will be paid accordingly. There are certain circumstances in which there may be more than one trust deed on a property with subsequent deeds recorded after the first. A *subordination clause* will change the priority of these trust deeds, or any other financial instrument. If a note is recorded, and an additional note is recorded after the original but is considered higher priority than the original, a subordination clause will allow the second note to be paid first in the event of default. The most common example of when this might occur when land is purchased for future construction, requiring separate financing at the time of building. The lender who is financing the development of the land would naturally prefer to be first in line in the event of default. The lender would use the subordination clause to position the later-recorded trust deed ahead of any previously recorded deeds.

Just as the assumption clause was discussed in the previous section, the *subject to clause* was also discussed. The difference between the assumption and subject to clause is in the assumption clause; the lender is made aware of and approves the new buyer's taking over the loan. In the subject to clause, the lender is **not** made aware of any changes in property ownership, leaving the original owner responsible for the loan. The subject to clause also allows for deficiency judgments for any hard money loans, meaning that the original owner may be liable for a new buyer's default on a loan.

Common sense dictates that if a loan is paid off early, there is less interest paid on the note. This is good for consumers, but bad for banks. In these cases, banks lose a portion of their return on the investment. To prevent this, banks may attach a *prepayment clause*, which basically penalizes the consumer if the note is paid in full before the loan period expires. If a borrower has the means to pay off a note early, he or she may pay a penalty on the loan, to help the lender recover some of the interest lost as a result of the early payoff. The good news for consumers is that banks are limited as to the amount they can charge for this prepayment clause. On residential property, the prepayment penalty may not exceed six months interest. A borrower may prepay up to 20% of the loan amount in any 12-month period, with no penalty charge. On any payment over 20%, a prepayment penalty may be applied. Different rules and regulations apply to non-residential properties.

The final clause in financing instruments is the or more clause, which is the opposite of the prepayment clause. The or more clause allows a borrower to pay off a loan early with no penalty, by making one lump payment or higher monthly payments.

J U N I O R   T R U S T   D E E D S

California is known, nationwide, for having one of the most expensive housing markets. Properties appreciate very quickly, leaving lucky homeowners with quite a bit of equity in their house. For first time homebuyers, this creates a challenge. The challenge is trying to save enough money for a down payment while securing a loan large enough to cover the purchase price of the home. Oftentimes, the amount of the down payment plus the loan will not cover the entire cost of the house. In such cases, the homeowner needs to take a second trust deed. These secondary loans or trust deeds are called *junior trust deeds*. A junior trust deed is recorded after the first deed, and is secured by taking out a second deed on the home. There are three ways to obtain a junior trust deed: seller financing; outside financing; and home equity loans.

| **Three ways to obtain a junior trust deed:** |
| 1. Seller financing |
| 2. Outside financing |
| 3. Home equity loans |

When a buyer finds that he or she is not able to afford a home by paying only the down payment plus the first trust deed, they must seek alternative financing. One way for a seller to obtain the necessary funds through a junior trust deed is by *seller financing*. Seller financing occurs when the seller of the property makes a secondary loan to the buyer, and records this loan only after the first trust deed is recorded. In these cases, the seller becomes the lender and will receive either a monthly or another installment payment to satisfy the debt. The act of the seller making a junior trust deed is sometimes referred to as "carrying back".

The loan a seller provides to a buyer is considered a purchase money loan, as it is intended for one purpose (that is, to cover any funds needed for the purchase of the property). It not only works in favor of the buyer, but also in favor of the seller. If the seller has sold his or her home for a an amount substantially more than originally purchased (and thus stands to make a large gain), the seller can use some of this additional money as part of the junior trust deed - to avoid a large tax liability. The seller is at an advantage because he or she can accept monthly payments and avoid paying capital gains on a large sum of money.

The idea of a seller financing a portion of the loan may be a bit confusing. After all, financial professionals are educated and are presumed to know more about interest rates, payment schedules and the technical aspects of a loan. The second trust deed that a seller may provide to a buyer must be negotiated between both the buyer and seller. There are no banks involved; it is simply an agreement between the two parties. The buyer and seller agree upon the interest rate, how the loan will be paid, whether it will be in monthly installments, quarterly, etc., with no payments at all, or with a large lump sum due after a specific amount of time. In addition, the buyer and seller decide if the loan will be a straight note, partially amortized or fully amortized. After all terms of the loan have been discussed and agreed upon, instructions will be carried through the escrow process.

Once a seller makes a secondary trust deed to a buyer, the seller is not bound to the loan until it is paid off. If the seller chooses to sell the secondary trust deed, he or she may sell it to an investor or to a mortgage broker. The mortgage broker will purchase the note and junior trust deed at a discounted rate. This means that the loan will be sold for less than the buyer owes the original seller. The advantage to the seller is that he or she will be repaid immediately, even if they are not receiving the full amount of the loan.

> *Example*
> *Deborah wishes to sell her home and puts it on the market for $400,000. Because of the neighborhood and economic conditions, the home sells fast for the asking price. The buyer offers a 10% down payment, or $40,000, and secures a new first loan for $320,000. Deborah agrees to make a loan to the buyer in the amount of $40,000 (so the transaction will go through, and Deborah will be able to move into her new home). Immediately after escrow closes and Deborah moves into her new home, she finds that her monthly payment is quite a bit harder to make than she originally thought. She chooses to sell the loan and junior trust deed to a mortgage broker, to cash out and use the money to make her own home payments. She finds an investor willing to purchase the loan at a 10% discount. This means that she immediately receives $36,000 for the loan (which is $4,000 less than made originally). However, it also means she will be able to make her monthly payment with no problem.*

There are, of course, disclosure statements that must be signed by the buyer and seller, in a transaction where the seller provides a junior trust deed. These disclosures are required by law, and provide both the buyer and seller with all the appropriate information to make an educated decision regarding this type of financing. The disclosure statements will allow the seller to see if the buyer is financially able to make the payment, and his or her credit rating. This is very important information for the seller to determine if the loan is feasible, and if it will be paid back in a timely manner. The buyer can see which loans are currently taking precedence over the junior trust deed that would possibly be created. A real estate professional can be used to arrange credit, to ensure all laws regarding the transaction have been followed.

If the seller is not in a position to make the second trust deed to a buyer, there are a few other options available to the buyer to secure the additional funds needed to purchase the property. The buyer can attempt to obtain *outside financing* through more traditional sources, such as mortgage banker, traditional bank or outside investor.

This second trust deed is considered a purchase money loan and will be sent to escrow for disbursement upon closing. The trust deeds will be recorded sequentially (first trust deed recorded first; and the second loan backed by a second or third trust deed).

The third way to obtain a junior trust deed is to secure, if possible, a *home equity loan*. A home equity loan is equal to the amount of equity, or value, a home has - above the amount owed on the loan against the home. If there is positive equity in the home, a homeowner may apply for a loan to withdraw money as a cash loan for any purpose. Some reasons for this withdrawal are: to make improvements to the home, take a vacation, purchase a vehicle, etc.

A smart lender is careful not to make home equity loans to unqualified persons or against a property that may not appreciate and/or may actually lose money in the long term. A lender also does not usually loan 100% of the difference between the money owed on the loan against the home and the determined value of the home. Typically, 80 – 90% of the equity in the home is loaned. This is to protect the lender from losing money, in the event the property depreciates in value.

Home equity loans are considered hard money loans and are naturally secured by a deed of trust. As you might remember, a hard money loan leaves the homeowner open to the possibility of a deficiency judgment in a judicial foreclosure.

> *Example:*
> *Emily has a home worth $150,000, with a first loan of $75,000. She wishes to take out a home equity loan of $65,000 to build a guesthouse and pool. When Emily began looking for a lender who she found that she could not secure a loan of that amount because its total was more than 80% of her equity in the home. The largest loan she could secure was $60,000 as $60,000 is 80% of the $75,000 of equity she has in her home.*

B A L L O O N   P A Y M E N T   L O A N S

A balloon payment is an installment payment, or a final payment that is substantially more than other payments, resulting in the complete payoff of a debt. A balloon payment will be made when a loan is not fully amortized during the term of the loan, thus requiring a large payment to completely satisfy the principle amount of the loan.

A balloon payment may happen on first trust deeds of over $30,000, second trust deeds of over $20,000 or a seller is rescinding a junior trust deed upon selling his or her home to a qualified buyer. These balloon payments are discussed at the onset of the loan; so, the consumer is aware of the obligation. Still, laws require a lender to notify the borrower of this obligation. This must be done between 90 – 150 days before the payment is actually due. Balloon payments are utilized on hard money loans, not for purchase money loans. As you might recall, a purchase money loan is specifically made to finance property, where a hard money loan is made in exchange for cash for any purpose.

Junior trust deeds may also have balloon payments for a hard money loan of under $20,000. For those junior trust deeds of less than three years, a final balloon payment maybe required, but the amount of the balloon payment must not exceed twice the amount of the smallest installment payment.

Facts regarding balloon payments:

- Utilized on hard money loans
- First trust deed of $30,000 or more, and a junior trust deed of $20,000 or more
- Junior trust deeds under $20,000 must have a term of less than three years, with a restricted balloon payment of no more than twice the smallest installment payment
- Lender must give 90 – 150 day's notice before the payment is due

FORECLOSURE

Foreclosure is the unfortunate event that happens when a borrower is unable to repay his or her loan to a lender, and falls behind on payments. If the payments have been delinquent for an extended period, the lender is able to foreclose on the property. Remember, the property itself is used as security or collateral for the promissory note as evidenced by the trust deed. So, the lender is able to sell the property to repay the debt against it. This not only pays back the lender for the promissory note against the property, but also pays other liens encumbered by the property.

Trust deeds can be foreclosed by a trustee's sale or through judicial action as determined by the courts. Mortgages, however, require judicial foreclosures. Since California primarily uses trust deeds, we will focus our attention on the trustee's sale in this section, while also highlighting judicial foreclosure.

In a deed of trust, you will remember, there are three parties involved. These parties are the lender, the borrower (or trustor) and the trustee (or third party holding bare legal title to the property). The trustee is the one called upon in the event of foreclosure. The trustee will conduct a *trustee's sale*, which is the most common way to foreclose on property utilizing a trust deed. The trustee is given the power of sale by the buyer when the buyer signs the trust deed at closing. A trustee's sale is the fastest way for property to be foreclosed, as there is no right of redemption after the sale, and deficiency judgments are not allowed against the trustor.

There is a process that must be followed in the trustee's sale. Notification must be given to the trustor in default, and all interested parties and then a formal sale must be held. There is a certain amount of time between the notification and sale called the *statutory reinstatement period*, when the trustor may repay the debt against the property and reinstate the loan. Not only can the trustor make the necessary payment to satisfy the debt; but any person holding a junior lien against the property may also reinstate the loan. The reinstatement period runs from the notification period until five days before the sale. Once the reinstatement period has expired, the trustor may still redeem the property by paying off the entire loan for the house, including all interest, fees and costs associated with the trustee's sale.

A lender generally does not begin foreclosure proceedings once a trustor is late or misses one payment. There is generally a grace period of 10 – 15 days for the trustor to make the payment and continue paying the note in good standing with the lender. One of the most important things to highlight about a foreclosure is that the lender does not want the property; he or she just wants to ensure they receive payment for the loan that was granted for the property to be purchased. In the event that the trustor simply cannot keep up with the payments, the lender has no choice but to foreclose. To begin foreclosure proceedings, the lender will deliver the original trust deed and note to the trustee and instruct the trustee to prepare a notice of default.

The *notice of default* must be recorded in the county recorder's office and then sent by certified mail to the trustor within 10 days after recording the notice of default. The recording with the county recorder's office must occur at least three months before the trustee's sales is held. In addition to sending a copy of the notice to the trustor, a copy of the notice of default must be sent to the trustor's successors or those with interest in the property, in addition to any junior lien holders, the State Controller and all parties requesting a copy of the notice. Anyone interested in a specific deed of trust can fill out a request for notice with the county recorder's office, and will be notified when or if a notice of default has been sent to the trustor.

The notice of default must state in **bold letters**, all caps, and as the first sentence that the property is in foreclosure due to the buyer's delinquency in payment. This is important, because if the notice of default is improperly prepared, a trustor may win a court case against the lender - even if payments have not been made.

Notice of default:

- Must be recorded in the country recorder's office in the county where the property is located
- First sentence of the notice must be in bold, all caps, stating the foreclosure is due to delinquent payment of the loan
- The notice of default must be delivered to the trustor, the trustor's successors, junior lien holders, the State Controller and any other interested party requesting the notice
- Notice of default begins the 3 month period until the trustee can record the trustee's sale

Once the notice of default has been recorded in the county recorder's office of the county where the property is located, the trustee must wait three months before taking any further action. During these three months, the trustor may repay the debt and reinstate the note on the property. After three months have expired, the trustee may then record a notice of trustee's sale.

The notice of trustee's sale must be published in a newspaper of general circulation where the property is located, so that the general public is made aware of the sale. The notice must run once each week for 20 days, with no more than 7 days between notices. The notice of trustee's sale must also contain a property description. Finally, the notice of trustee's sale must be posted in a public place - also in the area in which the property is located.

As mentioned, the reinstatement period will be valid until five days before the trustee's sale. Once this period has expired, the trustor is required to pay off the entire loan, along with all costs and interest, in order to take possession of the property.

Trustee's sale:

Must be recorded in the county recorder's office in the county where the property is located3 months after the notice of default

- Must be posted in a public place
- Must be printed in a newspaper of general circulation once each week for 20 days, with no more than 7 days separating each notice
- Redemption period ends 5 days before the sale

The sale will be conducted, auction-style, in the county where the property is located. People can make a bid on the property; but, until the bidding is over and finalized, the trustor may pay the entire amount owed on the loan (including all costs to cover interest, fees and cost of the sale). If this takes place before bidding is over, the sale will end, with the trustor as official owner of the property. If this does not happen, the person who makes the highest bid will become the new owner of the property.

The auction is open to any person wishing to make a bid on the property, though all bids must be paid in cash or cashiers check. The primary lien holder or the lender may credit the bid for the amount the trustor still owes on the note. In this case, the trustor will not have to pay the money, because they hold the lien on the property. This is not attractive to a lender. They would rather get their money back than own several properties they cannot use or do not wish to own.

Once a person successfully makes a bid and makes payment for their bid on the property; they will receive a trustee's deed to the property. The original trustor no longer has any rights or interest in the property and must vacate it. If the original trustor does not vacate the property, an unlawful detainer will be filed and the sheriff will legally remove the old trustor and his or her belongings from the property.

The proceeds from a trustee sale will first be applied to any costs or fees associated with the sale. After all fees associated with the sale are paid, the beneficiary will be paid the amount owed on the original loan for the property. After the beneficiary is paid, any junior lien holders will be paid. This will happen in the order in which the liens were recorded. Last in line for any money from the proceeds of the sale are the debtor or old trustor. After all debts have been satisfied, any remaining money is rightfully returned to the debtor.

The person who wins the bid on a property must understand that they are responsible for certain liens on that property, which may not have been paid off from the proceeds of the trustee sale. These liens include federal tax liens and real property taxes. Additionally, junior lien holders who stand to be repaid from the proceeds of a sale should attend the sale and ensure that the bid is high enough for the liens to be paid with the sale's proceeds. If the bids are relatively low, and it does not look like the liens will be paid, the trustor should make his or her own bid, to drive up the price of the property and thereby insuring payment to him or herself.

Trustee Sale Procedure:

1. Lender notifies the trustee of the foreclosure proceedings and delivers the original note and trust deed to the trustee
2. Trustee records the notice of default, and notifies the trustor and all other parties requiring notification
3. Reinstatement period begins after recording of the notice of default
4. Notice of the trustee's sale is recorded three months after recording the notice of default, is in place for three weeks
5. Sale is held
6. Trustee's deed is given to the highest bidder at the sale. All sales must be made in cash or cashier's check

A *Judicial foreclosure* may be used to foreclose on a property, in lieu of a trustee's sale. However, the process takes much longer than the three months and 21 days of a trustee's sale. In a judicial foreclosure, the trustee is not a part of the foreclosure process. Rather, a court proceeding takes place and a judge will determine who is in the wrong. The judge will also determine if there is to be a sale to repay any debts against the property. While this process generally takes longer than a trustee's sale, it might be appealing to a beneficiary, because in a judicial foreclosure, the beneficiary may seek a deficiency judgment against the trustor. Deficiency judgments are not allowed in a trustee's sale. A deficiency judgment seeks a personal payment from the trustor for all debts not covered in the sale of the property.

A Judicial foreclosure utilizes a court appointed commissioner or the sheriff to conduct the sale and ensure that all aspects of the sale are handled. The sheriff or commissioner will ensure the trustor vacates the property. In a judicial foreclosure, the person winning the bid for the property does not take possession of the property until the redemption period has expired; and – even then - only if no successors have come forward to pay the debt on the property. A judicial foreclosure takes more time, and is more risky, but allows for deficiency judgments to receive all monies owed to them.

O T H E R   T Y P E S   O F   L O A N S

In addition to the loans we have already discussed, there are a number of other loans available to persons wishing to purchase property.
These loans include:

- Open-ended loan
- Swing loan
- Blanket loan
- Package loan
- Wrap around loan
- Unsecured loan

An *open-ended loan* is structured in such a way that additional funds may be borrowed against the first trust deed, without any additional trust deeds needed. This is commonly used by developers of property who purchase land first, and then build houses, condominiums or apartments on that same land. The open-ended loan is an important one, because the original loan is always preserved as the priority claim in the event of foreclosure. A subordination clause is not necessary for lenders to ensure their loan gets paid first when the same loan stays open for additional funds.

Sometimes people will opt for a *swing loan* to withdraw money against the equity of a home they are trying to sell. This happens when another home is purchased as a replacement for the home being sold but the original home is not yet sold. The home-owner may take out a temporary loan against the equity in the home to be sold, use that money to purchase another home, and then pay back the loan upon sale of the old, or original house.

While developers might choose an open-ended loan when purchasing property and then building homes on it, they may also wish to utilize a *blanket loan*. The blanket loan encompasses more than one parcel of property. Builders might be attracted to this loan when building a new development of condominiums or homes to be sold to consumers at a later date. The blanket loan will usually contain a release clause releasing individual houses or properties one at a time upon their sale, so that they are no longer covered under the blanket loan.

Loans are secured by the property themselves, ensuring repayment to the lender by the borrower. Usually, the property itself is sufficient to secure the loan; but, some-times, more than property is required to secure a loan. Loans of this type are called package loans. The *package loan* utilizes not only the property or buildings as collater-al, but also the fixtures attached to the property and/or any personal property (such as a vehicle) necessary to secure the loan.

Wrap around loans are another way to finance property. Sometimes these loans are called an all-inclusive trust deed (AITD). A wrap around loan usually consists of both the existing note held by the seller, and the new loan secured by the buyer. The new loan "wraps around" the existing loan, and one payment is made to cover both loans. One loan consumes all the present encumbrances of the property plus the amount of the new loan.

Because this is not a blanket loan or open-ended loan, there is a hierarchy which makes the AITD subordinate to any previously recorded trust deed on the property. If the property should be foreclosed, any previous trust deeds must be paid first (even though the wrap-around loan is making the payments for these loans). One difference regarding the AITD loan versus other financing is that, with an AITD loan, the buyer receives the title to the property at closing. Usually an AITD is utilized when a seller and buyer are both financing a property. In a traditional loan assumption or when the seller carries back a note on the property, the buyer takes a loan to cover the cost of the existing loan plus the difference in the sale price of the home. The seller benefits from this situation, because he or she receives the full price for the home. The buyer generally benefits through a lower down payment, and also does not have to endure the traditional qualifying process to obtain the loan.

The AITD includes the unpaid principal balance of the existing loan plus the amount of the new loan being made by the seller to the buyer. The seller continues to make pay-ments on the loan they have taken out from their financial institution, while the buyer makes payments to the seller for the AITD. Of course payment from the buyer will be enough to cover the original loan plus a higher interest rate to the seller. This is in con-cert with the additional money borrowed from the seller to cover the difference between the original trust deed and the selling price of the property.

While this type of loan seems like a great idea for a buyer, there are situations when it simply does not work out as well. If a seller needs to cash out of a loan for the purchase of another property, or for any other reason, they are not able to do so with an AITD loan. The seller is obligated to repay the entire original note to the lender that is wrapped around by the loan they have provided to the buyer. Some loans contain a *due on sale clause*, meaning the seller would not be able to wrap around a loan to the existing loan, as the original loan must be paid off when the home is sold. If there is no due on sale clause, the lender may have to approve the wrap around loan, and there are some cases when the buyer may not qualify (for example, because of their credit score or debt to asset ratio). In a market with high interest rates, an AITD may not be the best choice, because the buyer ends up paying a much higher rate than the current market demands for the wrap around loan. This higher rate is, however, financially attractive to the seller.

The buyer typically does not make payments directly to the seller, although in theory that is what is happening. Instead, the buyer will usually make payments to a collection company, which will then distribute the money to the appropriate parties. The original lender will receive a monthly payment, while the seller will receive the amount predetermined by the contract. This is done to protect the buyer from mismanagement on the seller's behalf and to ensure that the original note is being paid according to the promissory note's terms and conditions. This protects all parties involved, and ensures that this type of financing remains feasible and functional.

Wrap around loan / All-inclusive trust deed:

- Seller finances the buyer, by providing a loan encompassing all payments to the first or subsequent trust deeds
- Buyer's payment to the seller includes the payment on the original loan, plus the higher interest rate, as well as the difference between the principal owed on the first note and the amount of the sale price of the home
- Wrap around loan is subordinate to the original loan
- Buyer takes the title to the home
- Buyer makes payments to a collection company ensuring that all funds are distributed to the appropriate parties

---

The *unsecured loan* is a promissory note that does not have any collateral to secure the payment of the note. The lender is taking a risk in making this type of loan, as the only way to receive payment for the note in the event of default is through court action.

A L T E R N A T I V E   F I N A N C I N G

Alternative financing describes the different programs available to consumers. Whereas in the past, only one type of loan was available to those attempting to purchase a home; there are now many different types of programs available to match the individual needs of homebuyers. Depending on market conditions, a consumer's credit or a down payment that is feasible, one
or more of these types of loans are usually ideal to help a consumer achieve the goal of home ownership.

The programs available to consumers include:

- Graduated Payment Adjustable Mortgage
- Contact of Sale
- Shared Appreciation Mortgage
- Variable / Adjustable Rate Mortgage (ARM)
- Rollover Mortgage
- Reverse Annuity Mortgage

The *Graduated Payment Adjustable Mortgage* (also known as a *flexible rate mortgage*) is a loan that defers part of the principal until the end of the loan. The payments for the first few years will be lower than the payments for the final few years, allowing people who anticipate making more money at their job in the future to purchase property now, and thus defer some of the principal until a later time. Both interest and principal will be paid down with each payment; but, the amount of principal being paid is adjusted from the beginning of the loan to the end of the loan.

Contract of sale is a unique financing option, because the seller of the property remains the legal owner of that property until the buyer has made his or her final payment. For those who are familiar with a traditional car note (where the bank or finance company legally owns the car until the note has been paid in full), this concept is similar. This type of financing may be attractive for buyers with below average credit or those in a very tight money market.

The buyer (sometimes referred to as the vendee) will receive possession of the property and may use the property as intended at the time of purchase. Additionally, the buyer holds equitable title, while the seller (or vendor) holds legal title to the property. A contract of sale is very similar to the AITD or wrap around loan. The vendor continues to pay the original note on the property while the vendee pays the vendor for the property itself. The main difference between these two properties is that those who finance with a wrap around loan will take the title to a property immediately, while those who finance with contract of sale will only receive equitable title, as the legal title remains with the vendor.

A *shared appreciation mortgage* allows the buyer to enjoy more attractive loan terms, by sharing the appreciation in the home with the lender. The lender will use their share of this appreciation as security for the loan. The lender and buyer must mutually agree to these terms for the life of the loan.

Variable rate mortgage / adjustable rate mortgages (ARM) fluctuate with changes in market interest rates. When interest rates rise, interest on the loan will reflect the increase, and thus increase the amount of each monthly payment. Correspondingly, a decrease in market interest rates will have the opposite effect, decreasing the monthly payment of the note. In addition to the amount of the monthly payment, the term and monthly payment of the loan may change.

Sometimes a note is renegotiated after many years, to adjust the interest rate and monthly payment based to keep with market conditions. This loan is called a *rollover mortgage*. Typically, a rollover mortgage is reviewed or renegotiated every five years.

Reverse Annuity mortgages are basically the opposite of a traditional home loan. Most people seek a loan to purchase property; however, a reverse annuity mortgage takes a property that has been owned for many years (and may even be paid off), and begins drawing money against the equity in the home. This is attractive to retirees, who may have been living in their home for several years and are living on a fixed income. When they find that this fixed income does not meet their standard of living, they may begin drawing a monthly payment against their home.

Generally, this money does not have to be paid off until the person dies or chooses to sell the property. At this time, the debt to the bank is paid, and any remaining monies are paid to the seller (or the seller's estate or family in the event of death).

S H O R T   P A Y

Sometimes a trustor owes more money on his or her home than the home is actually worth. It is hard to imagine this situation in California, since property values appreciate so much and so fast. Yet, it is a possibility. When this occurs, the lender may allow the buyer to sell the property at market value and walk away from the debt, even if the market value of the property is less than the loan amount.

The process described above is called *short payoff*. A short payoff may seem undesirable to a lender, as they do not receive the entire loan amount in return. However, in some cases a short payoff is better than the alternative. Many lenders will use either a foreclosure (to send the property to a trustee's sale) or judicial foreclosure (to sell the property through a court order) as an alternative. This will generally, though not always, bring in the amount owed on the loan, The trustee's sale and judicial foreclosure also may not bring in enough money to pay off the loan, or the home may not sell at all. The buyer may back out of the sale due to lack of funds; or, there may be no bidders on the property. In this case, the lender purchases the property for the amount owed on the note. This is not attractive to the lender; as they would much rather sell the property to earn their money back. By taking a short payoff versus acquiring the property, the lender may see a return of some of their money. The advantage to that is that the lender does not have to worry about paying for the trustee's sale, court proceedings, interest and fees associated with these proceedings, or perhaps be stuck with a property that they do not want.

Short Payoff:
- Allows a borrower to sell their home at market value, less what is owed on the loan to avoid foreclosure and further financial hardships
- Attractive to a lender because they receive some of their initial investment back, and does not have to tie up additional monies in a judicial foreclosure, trustee's sale or ownership of property worth less than the original investment

S U M M A R Y

As we have seen in this chapter, homeownership is feasible for more people nowadays, due to the different financing options available. Homes may be purchased by making a promissory note to a lender, securing the note by using the property as collateral (as evidenced by the trust deed or mortgage). By assuming a trust deed or mortgage, the lender is assured of recouping their initial investment through monthly payments on the loan, or by selling the property to cover the debt against it.

After examining promissory notes, trust deeds and mortgages, we took a look at how property could be transferred from the seller to the buyer. A person who has taken out a loan out on a home, and has not paid the note in full may transfer this loan responsibility to another individual who wishes to purchase the property or assume the debt. This is done by the buyer assuming the debt, or by the seller carrying back a note for the buyer. In either case, if the buyer defaults on the loan, the original borrower may suffer. He or she may have his or her credit adversely affected or may be held liable for any hard money loans against the property in a default judgment.

There are special clauses in financing which describe the hierarchy (or importance) of trust deeds or by requiring action on a loan in the event ownership changes. Additionally, junior trust deeds may be used to secure additional funding, in the event that the first trust deed and down payment are not sufficient to cover the selling price of the home.

Alternative financing is intended for those people who may have special situations or circumstances that make a traditional real estate loan impossible or unattractive. These loan programs allow rates, payments and terms of the loan to fluctuate with the needs of the borrower. Additionally, balloon payments may be utilized, allowing a low monthly payment and a large installment due at the end of the loan. This is attractive for those people who foresee higher incomes in the future, but are only able to make a smaller payment now.

Finally, this chapter discusses foreclosure and the process of what happens to property when an owner defaults. Trustee's sales, judicial foreclosures and short payoffs are all options a lender or borrower has to remedy default on a loan. The lender can use any of these options to recover their investment in the property; while the borrower may find a short payoff attractive to escape from a poor financial situation and protect his or her credit.

Real estate finance is very in-depth and by no means does this chapter cover everything there is to know. For further understanding of a complicated, yet very important concept, it is in your best interest to take a real estate finance course.

T E R M S   A N D   P H R A S E S

Acceleration Clause – A condition of a loan that states that the entire payment for the loan is due in certain circumstances (such as upon sale of the property).

Adjustable Rate Mortgage (ARM) – A loan with a flexible interest rate that increases or decreases with market interest rate changes.

Agreement of Sale – A financing option in which the seller finances the property for the buyer, without giving up legal title to the property. The s receives possession of the property, but does not receive the title to the property until the loan is paid in full.

Alienation Clause – A condition of a loan that allows the lender to require full payment of the loan in the event the property is going to be sold.

Assignment of Rents – Agreement between the property owner and the holder of a trust deed or loan on the property. In this case, the holder has the right to collect rents from any tenants occupying the property, as security for the loan. The holder of the loan will only receive this right if the property owner defaults on the note.

Assumption Clause – A financing option where the buyer takes over the existing loan on a property and is thereby liable for the note. The seller still remains secondarily liable in the event the buyer defaults on the loan. The buyer can only take over the existing loan if approved by the lender.

Balloon Payment – A note requiring a large payment at the end of its term to cover the debt in full. This is used when only a small percentage of the principal is being covered by each of the monthly payments

Beneficiary – The lender or financial institution that provides a loan to the borrower.

Blanket Loan – A loan covering several properties whereby each individual property can be released by paying a specific amount on the loan.

Collateral – An object of value that is pledged as security for the purchase of another object of value. In real estate, collateral is the property that is pledged as security for the note as evidenced by the trust deed.

Contract of Sale – A financing option where the seller finances the property for the buyer, but does not give up legal title to the property. The buyer receives possession of the property, but does not receive the title to the property until the loan is paid in full.

Default – Failure by the trustor to pay the monthly or installment payments on the promissory note for the property purchased.

Deficiency Judgment – A court ruling against a borrower for the balance of debt owed on property after foreclosure and sale of the property. Deficiency judgments can only be imposed on hard money loans involved in a judicial foreclosure.

Equitable Title – Interest in property held by a trustor or vendee before the entire loan has been paid off.

Equity – The value in a property (or the appreciated value of the property over what is owed on the loan) after all the debts have been paid off,.

Foreclosure – The procedure a lender may take to legally sell property in default (done through court action or by a trustee's sale).

Foreclosure Sale – Sale that occurs when property is being foreclosed on to satisfy a debt against it.

Fully Amortized Note – A note where the installment payments pay both the interest and principal in equal amounts until the debt is paid off in full.

Grace Period – The amount of time a lender will allow a borrower to be late on a loan installment payment. During this time, the loan is not considered to be in default and no action is taken against the borrower.

Graduated Payment Adjustable Mortgage – A financing option where the loan install-ment payment gradually increases during the life of the loan, until it eventually levels off

Hard Money Loan – A type of trust deed or loan given in exchange for cash. The borrower can utilize the money for any purpose; it need not be used to purchase property.

Holder – The party to whom the promissory note is made payable (usually the lender).

Holder in Due Course – A person who has obtained a negotiable instrument (such as a check, promissory note or any other legal tender document) in the ordinary course of business, before it is due, in good faith, for value, and without knowledge that it has been previously dishonored.

Home Equity Loan – A loan made to a homeowner against the equity built up in their home (generally will not exceed 80 – 90% of the equity in the home)

Hypothecation – The process by which a borrower may use a property as collateral for a loan, yet still remain in possession of the property

Interest – The cost a lender will charge when lending money to a borrower.

Judicial Foreclosure – Foreclosure by court action.

Junior Trust Deed – A trust deed that is recorded after the first trust deed. The junior trust deed is considered less important (or of lesser priority) than the trust deed that was recorded first.

Land Contract – A financing option in which the seller finances the property for the buyer, but does not give up legal title to the property. The buyer receives possession of the property, but does not receive its title until the loan is paid in full.

Legal Title – Title to property that is complete, with no encumbrances. This title may be held by a trustee in a trust deed, to be reconveyed to the trustor when the note is paid in full.

Maker – The borrower who requests funds from a lender. The borrower will make a promissory note and become liable for the debt against him or her. Usually, the promissory note is accompanied by the trust deed in a real estate purchase.

Mortgage – Legal document pledging property as security for a debt.

Mortgagee - The lender loaning the money for the purchase of real estate.

Mortgagor – The borrower requesting a loan to purchase real estate.

Naked Legal Title – The title allowing a trustee to reconvey title to property upon satisfactory payment of a debt, or foreclosure (in the event of default). This title does not grant any ownership privileges to the property.

Negotiable Instrument – Any written document that may be transferred by endorsement or delivery from one party to another.

Notice of Default – A written notice given to the borrower, informing them that they are delinquent on payment of the loan.

Notice of Trustee's Sale – Notice published regarding a trustee's sale to dispose of property in an effort to satisfy a debt against it.

Novation – The substitution of a new obligation for an old one.

Open Ended Loan – A financing option whereby the borrower is allowed to request additional funds secured by one, existing trust deed.

Or More Clause – A clause in a note that allows a borrower to pay off the funds early, incurring no penalties.

Package Loan – A financing option where a loan can be secured not only by property, but by personal property or the fixtures attached to that property

Partially Amortized Installment Note – A loan that will require a balloon payment at the end. The installment payments will cover the interest and part of the principal amount, but will not be sufficient to fully pay the principal at the end of the loan term, making a balloon payment necessary.

Pledge – Transferring property to a lender as security for a loan. In this situation, the lender will take possession of the property.

Power of Sale – The clause in a loan that allows the lender to sell a property in the event that a borrower defaults on the loan.

Prepayment Clause –A clause in a loan that penalizes a borrower from paying the loan back early. In the event the loan is paid off early, a percentage of the loan may be collected as penalty.

Principal – The amount of a loan, not including the interest.

Promissory Note – The written promise a borrower makes to a lender pledging to pay back the loan. This promissory note is the evidence of debt.

Purchase Money Loan – A loan made specifically for the purchase of real estate.

Reconveyance Deed –The deed used to transfer property from a lender back to the borrower, once the loan is paid in full.

Reinstate – To reactivate a loan after any default debt is paid.

Release Clause – A provision found in blanket loans that allows the release of certain properties after partial payment of the loan is made.

Request for Notice – The notice sent to all parties that have an interest, or that have requested notice, that a loan is in default.

Reverse Annuity Mortgage – A financing option that allows a person to borrow money against the equity in his or her home. This type of loan is attractive to retired people on a fixed income who own their home as a means to supplement their income. The loan will not have to be paid off until a later date (such as upon death of the homeowner, or when the home is sold).

Rollover Mortgage – A financing option that allows the rewriting of a new loan at the termination of a prior one.

Second Trust Deed – A junior trust deed, or evidence of a debt that is recorded after the original trust deed.

Security – The collateral used to secure a loan.

Shared Appreciation Mortgage – A financing option where the borrower and lender agree to share a percentage of the appreciation of a home as security for the loan.

Sheriff's Deed – The deed given by a court to the successful bidder at a foreclosure sale.

Soldier's and Sailor's Relief Act – A federal law protecting service men and women from foreclosure while serving in the military.

Statutory – Laws created by legislation, rather than by a court judgment.

Straight Note – A financing option where payments of only the interest on a loan are made during the term of the note with a large lump sum due at the end of the note (to pay off the principal). Straight notes may also be set up where there are no payments required until the end of the loan when both the interest and principal are due.

Subject-To Clause – A buyer takes over an existing loan, and makes payments on it; yet is not responsible for the loan itself.

Subordination Clause – A clause in a loan that allows a subsequent loan, or a loan recorded later to take precedence.

Swing Loan – A short-term loan allowing the seller of property to purchase another property to replace the one being sold. Upon the sale of the first property, the loan will be called.

Trust Deed – A document where the title to property (bare legal title) will pass to a third party (called a trustee) as security for the debt.

Trustee's Deed – The deed given to the successful bidder at a trustee's sale.

Trustee's Sale –The sale of property, after foreclosure, to satisfy the debt against a property.

Trustee – Holds bare legal title to property where there is a deed of trust.

Trustor – The borrower in a trust deed.

Usury – The act of lending money and charging an interest rate more than what is allowed by law.

Variable Rate Mortgage – A loan with a flexible interest rate that increases or decreases when market interest rates change.

Vendee – The buyer utilizing a contract of sale.

Vendor – The seller utilizing a contract of sale.

Wrap Around Loan – A financing option in which a new loan is placed in a secondary position. The new loan includes both the unpaid principal balance of the first loan as well as whatever sums are loaned by the lender. Wrap around loans are sometimes called all-inclusive trust deeds.

C H A P T E R   Q U I Z

1. When a person signs a promissory note to purchase property, they generally use what as security?
   A. Trust Deed
   B. Collateral
   C. Leverage
   D. Both A and B

2. Which of the following is not considered a promissory note?
   A. Adjustable
   B. Full Reconveyance
   C. Straight note
   D. Amortized

3. Which one of the following characteristics is not found in a partially amortized note?
   A. Interest only payments
   B. Partial payment of principal, full payment of interest
   C. Balloon payment
   D. Periodic fixed payments

4. Which of the following parties in a trust holds the trust deed?
   A. Trustee
   B. Beneficiary
   C. Trustor
   D. None of the above.

5. In a trust deed, who holds the original deed to the property before the promissory note is paid in full?
   A. The trustor
   B. The trustee
   C. The lender
   D. Both A and B

6. How many days does the trustor have to reinstate the promissory note before the date of the trustee's sale?
   A. 10 days
   B. 7 days
   C. 5 days
   D. 3 days

7. A judicial foreclosure is used in which of the following situations?
   A. Trust deeds
   B. Mortgages
   C. Both A and B
   D. Neither A nor B

8. What is the redemption period?
   A. The time in which junior lien holders or the mortgagee's successors may repurchase a property after a foreclosure sale.
   B. The act of seeking a personal judgment against the person defaulting on the promissory note.
   C. The time by which a bidder must pay the amount in full for the property he or she is purchasing.
   D. The time between the notice of sale and the actual sale of the foreclosed property.

9. A deficiency judgment is allowed in which of the following situations?
   A. A buyer purchases a property with a purchase money loan and then defaults on the loan, resulting in foreclosure.
   B. A buyer purchases a property by assuming an existing loan and then defaults on the loan, resulting in a judicial foreclosure.
   C. Both A and B
   D. Neither A nor B

10. Which of the following is NOT a special clause in financial instruments?
    A. Acceleration
    B. Subordination
    C. Or more
    D. Redemption

11. Which best describes the "subject-to" clause?
    A. A buyer takes over the existing loan from the seller without the lender's knowledge. The seller, or original owner, is responsible for the loan and may be held liable for any deficiency judgments.
    B. The borrower is subject to a credit check before being approved for a loan.
    C. The borrower is subject to a loan based on the inspection and appraisal of the property of interest.
    D. The buyer takes over the existing loan with the knowledge and approval of the lender.

12. If a seller finances a junior trust deed to the buyer of his or her property, what options does the buyer have regarding the loan?
    A. They may carry the note until it is paid in full.
    B. They may sell the note at a discounted rate to a mortgage broker.
    C. They may force the buyer into paying the note back earlier than originally planned, because they need the money for a new car.
    D. Both A & B

13. Louise wishes to obtain a home equity loan to remodel her living room and have money to go back to school. Her home is worth $120,000 and she currently has a first loan of $75,000. She wishes to pull out $25,000 to accomplish both her remodeling project and tuition. Will a lender be willing to do this for Louise?
    A. Yes. Louise has plenty of equity in her home for this loan.
    B. No. Louise cannot take out money for any purpose other than the purchase of property.
    C. No. Louise does not have enough equity in her home for this size of a loan.
    D. None of the above.

14. Balloon payments
    A. Are used on hard money loans.
    B. Require a large final payment to completely repay the debt.
    C. Require a 90 – 150 day notice from the lender to the borrower that the payment is forthcoming.
    D. All of the above.

15. In a trustee's sale, which of the following parties does not require notification when the notice of default is recorded?
    A. Trustor.
    B. Junior lien holders
    C. Beneficiary
    D. State Controller

16. How many days does the trustor have to repay the debt to reinstate the note on a foreclosed property?
    A. 10 days
    B. 7 days
    C. 5 days
    D. 0 days, as he or she may redeem property until the date of the sale.

17. Sellers who finance a buyer with a wrap around loan typically do which of the following?
    A. Carry back a note on the property
    B. Charge the buyer a higher interest rate than they currently pay on the original trust deed.
    C. Collect the money directly from the buyer for the AITD.
    D. Require a high down payment from the buyer.

18. Which of the following loans allow individual properties to be released from the responsibilities of the loan, provided there is a sufficient payment?
    A. Blanket loan
    B. Wrap around loan
    C. Open-ended loan
    D. Unsecured loan

19. Which of the following mortgage types best describe a loan similar to the wrap around loan or all-inclusive trust deed?
    A. Graduated payment adjustable mortgage
    B. Rollover mortgage
    C. Shared appreciation mortgage
    D. Contract of Sale

20. What is the term for selling a property at market value, below what is owed on the loan?
    A. Short Pay
    B. Walk away
    C. Foreclosure
    D. Trustee's sale

NATIONAL LENDING PRACTICES

What you will learn in this Chapter

- Importance of real estate finance

- Government agencies and other federal participation in real estate finance

- The money mortgage market

- RESPA – Real Estate Settlement Procedures Act

- Regulation Z – the Truth in Lending Act

- Equal Credit Opportunity Act

- Personal property secured transactions

1. Which one of the following methods is NOT used by the Fed to regulate the nation's money supply?
    A. Reserving requirements
    B. Opening market operations
    C. Selling loans on the secondary mortgage market
    D. Changing the discount rate

2. What conditions caused the restructuring of real estate finance and mortgage options available to consumers?
    A. Disintermediation
    B. High interest rates
    C. Short money supply
    D. All of the above

3. Which of the following institutions are considered non-institutional lenders?
    A. Credit Unions
    B. Insurance Companies
    C. Mortgage Companies
    D. Commercial Banks

4. Who or what funds Cal-Vet loans?
    A. Voter-approved bonds
    B. Outside funding
    C. California Department of Veteran Affairs
    D. Traditional banks and mortgage companies

5. When must the special information booklet and the good-faith estimate of closing costs be delivered to the borrower by the lender?
    A. No more than 2 days after receiving the loan application
    B. No more than 3 days after receiving the loan application
    C. No more than 5 days after receiving the loan application
    D. No more than 7 days after receiving the loan application

6. Which of the following is NOT protected from discrimination under the Equal Credit Opportunity Act?
    A. Sex
    B. Color
    C. Religion
    D. Sexual Orientation

7. How many days does a buyer have to rescind a loan under the truth in lending act?
    A. 1
    B. 3
    C. 5
    D. 10

INTRODUCTION

In the previous chapter, we examined all the different ways a person can finance real estate, the types of loans available, and the different options for repayment of these loans. In this chapter, we will focus on government-controlled programs and institutions which keep our real estate financial institutions healthy, honest and efficient. We will learn about the overall real estate financial system, followed by which government agencies have their hand in setting policy and aiding borrower's secure loans while protecting the lender's investment. We will learn about the different mortgage markets, and the primary players in each market, followed by the different government agencies and the programs they offer the borrower. Finally, we will end the chapter with an exploration of consumer rights.

IMPORTANCE OF REAL ESTATE FINANCE

Real estate finance is important to understand, as it is a major force in the drive of our country's financial system. The main source of funding for loans in real estate comes from savings accounts held in savings banks, commercial banks, credit unions and mutual savings banks (otherwise known as financial intermediaries). When negative forces affect the economy, customers are quick to withdraw funds from their savings accounts and invest it in alternate ways that generate higher returns. The act of customers withdrawing money from their savings accounts is called *disintermediation*. With less money to lend, banks are forced to charge higher interest rates, to make up for the losses incurred by this disintermediation. At higher interest rates, it becomes very expensive for prospective homebuyers to finance a home, creating even larger problem for banks. When less money is available from lenders to consumers, interest rates go up. This makes homes even more expensive to purchase, thus decreasing the number of people who are able to do so. Such trends have often caused severe downward spirals in the economy.

> Disintermediation is the process by which depositors remove money from their traditional savings account and seek alternative investment opportunities, to gain a higher rate of return. Usually, these alternative investment opportunities are uninsured (unlike a savings account).

Given this scenario, banks had to find alternative methods of financing homes or making money available to people who were interested in purchasing property. Deregulation was the answer. With deregulation, banks were no longer restricted in their lending activities by federal law, and were allowed to compete freely. Lending institutions now needed to make funds available for consumers. With deregulation and alternative mortgage avenues, banks have developed programs that allow consumers to once again afford to borrow money to purchase property.

Traditionally, loans were fixed rate loans but, these loans did not always meet the needs of the consumer. New programs were developed to make loans more accessible to new consumers and other types of borrowers.

Variable rate mortgages were designed so that lenders could offer loans at a lower interest rate to consumers. In this way, the customer was able to secure a loan, and the bank was able to make the loan. With a variable rate mortgage, the lender is not tied to the initial interest rate. Rather, the interest rate now changes with the national interest rate. So, if the national interest rate goes up, the loan will reflect the increase, and the lender is not stuck with an unprofitable loan. Similarly, if the national rate goes down, payment on the note will go down, as well.

What was happening at this time in history was an acknowledgment that traditional real estate financing tools were not sufficient to satisfy changing market conditions. With less money available in savings accounts, higher interest rates, and fewer consumers able to make such high payments, new financing tools had to be developed. These tools would have to be sufficient to tailor a mortgage to the specific consumer's needs and financial situation. In a stable real estate finance market, the general economy becomes stronger and, thus, less volatile.

GOVERNMENT AGENCIES IN REAL ESTATE FINANCE

In the late 1980's, Congress sought to reform the banking system in the United States. This reform was necessary due to rampant greed and corruption within the banking industry. What resulted, however, was an alphabet soup of new boards, corporations, and other administrations that protected the investor and borrower from what was, otherwise, a broken system.

First, Congress passed the Financial Institutions Reform, Recovery and Enforcement Act (FIRREA), which reformed the industry as a whole. The first group under FIRREA was developed to oversee savings and loan institutions. This group was called the Office of Thrift Supervision (OTS) and Housing Finance Board. Second, the Federal Deposit Insurance Corporation (FDIC) was created to insure those depositors using federally-chartered banks. Each depositor in an FDIC-insured lending institution is insured up to $100,000 per account. Additionally, the FDIC supervises the Savings Association Insurance Fund (SAIF), which collects premiums to produce the money needed to insure accounts at savings banks, as well as the Resolution Trust Corporation (RTC).

The Financial Institutions Reform, Recovery and Enforcement Act did not stop there; additional agencies were also formed. The purpose of these agencies was to fix the current state of the banking crisis in this country and to regulate the industry for the future.

Remember!
• FIRREA stands for Financial Institutions Reform, Recovery and Enforcement Act and reformed the entire financial industry
• There are two groups under the FIRREA: FDIC and OTS
• FDIC stands for Federal Deposit Insurance Corporation, and insures individual depositors at federally-chartered banks
• OTS stands for Office of Thrift Supervision

As you can already see, there are numerous agencies in charge of regulating or overseeing one or more financial institutions and its reform. The Department of Housing and Urban Development (HUD) was developed as an all-encompassing organization to bring one authority for these agencies, some that already existed and some that were being newly formed.

Savings banks allow consumers to open a savings account in which to deposit their money and draw interest on these deposits. These savings banks will use these deposits for loans to homebuyers, charging an interest rate (higher than that being paid to the depositor) to the borrower. This allows the depositor to see a return on his or her investment. Banks may borrow money from Federal Home Loan Banks, to make additional loans to homebuyers above the deposits they currently hold in their bank. Savings banks that are allowed to take loans from the Federal Home Loan Banks must meet all qualifications as outlined in the qualified thrift lender guidelines (QTL). Banks which do not meet these guidelines may not borrow funds from a Federal Home Loan Bank. The Federal Housing Finance Board (FHFB) supervises the mortgage lending practices of the twelve regional Federal Home Loan Banks. The Federal Housing Finance Board also has the authority to close any banks that may be in financial trouble and transfer management of that bank to the Resolution Trust Corporation.

We know that the FDIC insures individual depositors up to $100,000 for accounts held in federally-chartered banks. But, what about insurance on mortgages that banks extend to homebuyers? The Federal Housing Administration (FHA) was set up to insure loans made by all approved providers. Loan providers who either hold loans or sell them using the secondary mortgage market are insured through the FHA, making a homebuyer's mortgage funds guaranteed.

Remember!

- FHFB stands for Federal Housing Finance Board, which supervises the 12 Federal Home Loan Banks in charge of making loans to savings banks for the purpose of providing mortgage loans to home buyers
- FHFB also has the power to close banks that are in financial trouble, sending them to the Resolution Trust Corporation
- FHA stands for the Federal Housing Administration, which insures mortgage loans made by approved providers

The Federal Reserve Bank System (commonly referred to as the Fed) serves is the central bank of the nation. The Fed is made up of 12 Federal Reserve Banks throughout the country. The Fed develops national monetary policy, and the 12 Federal Reserve banks aid in applying the policy. The Fed's main purpose is to create economic growth and stability. This is accomplished through regulating both the money supply and credit extended to federally-chartered banks.

The Fed uses three techniques to regulate the money supply and accomplish its goal of stimulating economic growth and stability. With these techniques, the Fed is able to control the behavior of both lenders and borrowers by controlling the federal money supply and interest rates. The three techniques the Fed uses are: reserve requirements; discount rate; and open market operations.

The reserve requirement is the amount of money the Fed requires its member banks to have in reserve. This money may not be used to make loans. The amount of money in question is based on the percentage of deposits that may not be used. As this requirement is raised or lowered, the amount of money released into circulation in the form of loans goes up or down, accordingly. When the Fed raises the reserve requirement, each bank has less money to lend its customers. With a higher reserve requirement comes a higher interest rate. This is done so that banks will make the same return on smaller investments as one would on a larger investment. Additionally, when the Fed raises the reserve requirement, there will be fewer people borrowing or spending money, as high interest rates discourage borrowing. When the reserve requirement is lowered, the opposite scenario occurs. Lower reserve requirements mean more money to lend out at a lower interest rate. This encourages increased borrowing and spending by consumers.

The discount rate is the interest rate a bank must pay to the Fed for the privilege of borrowing money. Just as you and I must pay interest on borrowed money; banks must also pay interest on money borrowed from the Fed. When the discount rate is lowered, banks can borrow more money from the Fed, increasing available monies for loans. When the discount rate is raised, banks less money is available for loans.

Open market operations describe(s) the Fed's activity in buying and/or selling government securities. There is a direct coloration between the amount of credit available banks have to lend to consumers. When the Fed buys securities, it puts more money in circulation, allowing banks to increase the number of loans to make to consumers. When the Fed sells securities, it restricts the amount of money in circulation, decreasing the amount of money available for consumer lending. This is the most common way the Fed controls the economy.

Remember!
- The Fed stands for the Federal Reserve Bank System, which operates as the central bank for the nation.
- The Fed controls the money supply, to keep our economy healthy through economic growth and stability
- The Fed will use reserve requirements, discount rates and open market operations to control the behaviors of lenders and consumers and to accomplish the Fed's goal of a strong, stable economy

THE MONEY MORTGAGE MARKET

The mortgage market consists of the primary and secondary mortgage markets. Under each of the primary and secondary markets there are subdivisions. These subdivisions determine where the money comes from and the type of lenders that provide funds for consumers. As mentioned briefly earlier in the chapter, the main source of money for real estate loans comes from individual savings accounts held in banks and savings institutions.

Primary Mortgage Market
In the Primary mortgage market, lenders make loans directly to the consumer. These are purchase loans made in the form of a trust deed for the lender to purchase property. Both institutional and non-institutional lenders can make these purchase money loans in the primary money market.

Primary Money Mortgage Market:
- Made up of institutional and non-institutional lenders
- Loans are made directly to the consumers
- Provides purchase money loans in the form of a trust deed.

Institutional Lenders

Institutional lenders are conventional lenders, and are perhaps the financial institutions we first think of when we need to borrow money for a home. Institutional lenders include: savings banks; commercial banks; mutual savings banks, credit unions and insurance companies. These lenders can provide money for loans by using the money of those investors who maintain a savings account. The lender can then, transfer that money to others who wish to borrow funds for a property purchase (or any other purchase, for that matter). The process by which the financial institution takes the depositor's money and transfers it to the borrower is called *intermediation*.

Institutional lenders include:
- Savings Banks
- Commercial Banks
- Mutual Savings Banks
- Credit Unions
- Insurance Companies

Savings banks are financial institutions that use money in an individual's savings account to make loans in the form of trust deeds. Because savings banks are based primarily on savings accounts held by private individuals, and because most mortgages are made from personal savings accounts, savings banks are the main source for home loans. Savings banks are made up of both state- and federally-chartered institutions, and make it very simple for people to place excess money into a savings account to earn interest.

Commercial banks are the most versatile of all lenders. They make home loans, equity loans, business loans and other short-term loans. Commercial banks make quite a few construction loans, as they are short term and are paid off as soon as the property is sold. Commercial banks also lend money for traditional trust deeds, though not on the same scale as savings banks.

Mutual savings banks allow the depositors to share in the profits of the entire bank once all formal expenses; reserves and contributions to the surplus have been made. This means that the depositor will not only make money from the money they have deposited in the bank, but they will also draw interest on all funds the bank handles, once all bank obligations have been met. Mutual savings banks are uncommon in California.

Credit unions were developed for members who hold the same occupation (e.g., educators) to deposit their savings. These banks offer their members some benefits that a traditional bank or savings institution cannot offer, such as higher paid interest rates on deposits and lower interest rates on loans.

Insurance companies are not thought of as traditional lenders when it comes to real estate. Yet, they are able to provide funds for the purchase of property. Insurance companies will not generally provide a home loan to an individual; but they provide large-scale loans to developers who are building several properties at a time, or commercial properties that require a high dollar loan or investment. Additionally, insurance companies participate in the secondary mortgage market. This means they will buy or sell government issued loans. This information will be examined later in this chapter

Non-Institutional Lenders

Non-institutional lenders are a separate group, different from institutional lenders. When we think of obtaining a loan for property, we typically think of one or more of the traditional lenders. Non-institutional lenders (with the exception of mortgage companies) do not usually come to mind. Some non-institutional lenders we will study are: mortgage companies; non-financial institutions; and private individuals.

> **Non-Institutional Lenders:**
> - Mortgage Companies
> - Non-Financial Lenders
> - Private Individuals

The process by which *mortgage companies* lend may be a bit confusing for consumers who are trying to secure a loan to purchase property. Does a mortgage company make the loan itself? Do they just do the legwork for the buyer, to find the best options from a number of available lenders? In actuality, a mortgage company does both. Some mortgage companies actually use their own money to extend purchase loans in the form of trust deeds, while others simply find a lender who satisfies all the needs of the borrower. Usually, when a mortgage company makes a loan to a borrower, this loan is sold to an investor. Again, this is not as clear as a traditional bank, which makes loans to borrowers who, in turn, make payments to the bank for the term of the loan.

When a mortgage company does not use their own money, but uses funding from a commercial bank with the intentions to sell the loan to an investor, the mortgage company is *warehousing the mortgage*. By doing this, the mortgage company will make a profit, and use those profits to make additional loans. They mortgage company then sells those loans to investors, as well.

Because of the nature of the mortgage company being a warehousing entity, they usually secure loans made by a government institution. These loan types are generally FHA or VA loans. The advantage in making such loans is that they are easily sold in the secondary mortgage market. Mortgage companies also seek conventional loans, which have advance purchase commitments. Clearly, the biggest role of the mortgage companies is to originate, service, then sell the loans, moving on to the next client as soon as possible.

> Mortgage Companies:
> - Make mortgages using their own money, and then sell those mortgages to investors
> - Act as an intermediary between lenders and borrowers
> - Usually secure conventional or VA loans so they can be easily sold into the secondary mortgage market

There are procedures that must be followed to insure that loans made by a mortgage broker are ultimately sold in the secondary mortgage market. In order for loans to be sold in the secondary mortgage market, the applicant must follow the following procedures:

- A loan application must be filled out by the customer
- A credit report of the loan applicant must be ordered
- The property involved must be appraised
- The full application package must be presented to the lender. The full package includes: the application form; the borrower's financial statement; property appraisal report; and a copy of the sales agreement
- The investor decides whether or not to accept the application
- Approval, if accepted, will then be sent to the mortgage company
- Loan funds are sent to escrow once all conditions of the loan are met
- After closing, all documents are sold to the interested investor, while the mortgage broker will continue to service the loan. This means that the borrower of funds will send payments directly to the mortgage broker. The mortgage broker keeps track of the loan status for the life of the loan.

Non-financial institutions include people or organizations who are not part of a traditional lending institution, but have money to invest. Non-financial institutions include: universities; pension funds; and title companies; trust departments of banks, or mortgage investment companies.

As we saw in the previous chapter on real estate finance, *private individuals* sometimes finance the home they are selling to the buyer. A private investor can also go through a mortgage broker, who will find a borrower in need of funds. This type of loan is usually a short-term loan. This is one way for a private individual to provide money to borrowers, while gaining a large return on their investment. However, there is another method for gaining a larger return on investment. Individuals can form a Real Estate Investment Trust (REIT) where each person contributes a small amount of money to a larger, collective pool. This creates a large resource of funds. A REIT requires 100 investors or more.

Secondary Mortgage Market
The initial lender of a real estate loan may be in full contact with the borrower issuing periodic statements of payments made, principal paid, balance remaining and other correspondence deemed necessary. Though the original lender may still be in contact with the borrower, there is a good chance that the original lender has sold the loan to another investor. Even if the lender has sold the promissory note, he or she will continue to service the loan until it has been paid in full.

The sale of real estate promissory notes makes up the secondary mortgage market. This provides investors with an additional opportunity to invest money in the secondary mortgage market, when they may have otherwise sought out different investment opportunities. In this section, we will review the federal agencies involved in the largest portion of the secondary mortgage market. These agencies are the Federal National Mortgage Association (Fannie Mae), Government National Mortgage Association (Ginnie Mae), Federal Home Loan Mortgage Corporation (Freddie Mac), and the Office of Federal Housing Enterprise Oversight (OFHEO).

Secondary Mortgage Market:
- Federal National Mortgage Association (Fannie Mae)
- Government National Mortgage Association (Ginnie Mae)
- Federal Home Loan Mortgage Corporation (Freddie Mac)
- Office of Federal Housing Enterprise Oversight (OFHEO)

Fannie Mae (www.fanniemae.com) was created in 1938, to serve as a secondary market for FHA-insured and VA-guaranteed loans. In later years, Fannie Mae's authority was expanded to allow them to offer conventional loans, as well. Fannie Mae currently buys properties financed through FHA, VA, graduated payment mortgages, adjustable-rate mortgages and conventional fixed rate first (and some second) mortgages for properties consisting of 1-4 units.

Loans meeting Fannie Mae's criteria are conforming loans. The dollar amount is limited to $333,700 per single-family residences; though higher limits exist for states outside of California.

Fannie Mae buys a group of mortgages from a lender in exchange for mortgage-backed securities that represent undivided interest in the group of loans. The lender may choose to keep these loans, or sell them into the secondary mortgage market. Fannie Mae guarantees the payment of both interest and principal of these loans to the holder of the note, whether the note holder is the original lender or an investor.

In 1968, Fannie Mae was divided into a corporation owned by private investors called Ginnie Mae. Fannie Mae today issues its own stock and obtains its capital from its functions of buying, selling and investing.

Ginnie Mae (www.hud.gov/funcgnma) offers people high yielding, risk-free, guaranteed securities. Ginnie Mae does not buy securities as Fannie Mae does. Rather, it guarantees securities already issued by FHA-approved home lenders. Investors who purchase the FHA loans in the secondary mortgage market are guaranteed to receive their investment back including interest (less any fees charged by Ginnie Mae). This means that if an investor purchases a loan, and the borrower is late on a payment, Ginnie Mae will make the payment to the investor who holds the note. This assures the investor that he or she will always be paid on time.

Freddie Mac (www.freddiemac.com) was created in 1970, due to a shortage of mortgage funds available to consumers. Freddie Mac will buy loans and then sell them into the secondary mortgage market to provide additional funds for borrowers and investors. Freddie Mac is restricted to the same $333,700 as Fannie Mae. Freddie Mac also issues stock to the general public, much like Fannie Mae.

The **Office of Federal Housing Enterprise Oversight** (OFHEO) (www.ofheo.gov) makes legislative recommendations designed to enhance Fannie Mae and Freddie Mac programs. OFHEO conducts audits of Fannie Mae and Freddie Mac, in which the OFHEO can make recommendations to the legislature when these programs are under consideration.

MORTGAGE LOAN DISCLOSURE STATEMENT
(BORROWER)
(As required by the Business and Professions Code §10241
and Title 10, California Administrative Code, §2840)

_____
(Name of Broker/Arranger of Credit)

_____
(Business Address of Broker)

I. SUMMARY OF LOAN TERMS
- A. PRINCIPAL AMOUNT .... $ _____
- B. ESTIMATED DEDUCTIONS FROM PRINCIPAL AMOUNT
  - 1. Costs and Expenses (See Paragraph III-A) .... $ _____
  - *2. Broker Commission/Organization Fee (See Paragraph III-B) ..... $ _____
  - 3. Lender Origination Fee/Discounts (See Paragraph III-B) .... $ _____
  - 4. Additional compensation will/may be received from lender not deducted from loan proceeds.
    □ YES $ _____ (if known) or □ NO
  - 5. Amount to be Paid on Authorization of Borrower (See Paragraph III) .... $ _____
- C. ESTIMATED CASH PAYABLE TO BORROWER (A less B) .... $ _____

II. GENERAL INFORMATION ABOUT LOAN
- A. If this loan is made, Borrower will be required to pay the principal and interest at _____ % per year, payable as follows: _____ _____ payments of $ _____
  (number of payments)   (monthly/quarterly/annually)
  and a **FINAL/BALLOON** payment of $ _____ to pay off the loan in full.

  NOTICE TO BORROWER: IF YOU DO NOT HAVE THE FUNDS TO PAY THE BALLOON PAYMENT WHEN IT COMES DUE, YOU MAY HAVE TO OBTAIN A NEW LOAN AGAINST YOUR PROPERTY TO MAKE THE BALLOON PAYMENT. IN THAT CASE, YOU MAY AGAIN HAVE TO PAY COMMISSIONS, FEES AND EXPENSES FOR THE ARRANGING OF THE NEW LOAN. IN ADDITION, IF YOU ARE UNABLE TO MAKE THE MONTHLY PAYMENTS OR THE BALLOON PAYMENT, YOU MAY LOSE THE PROPERTY AND ALL OF YOUR EQUITY THROUGH FORECLOSURE. KEEP THIS IN MIND IN DECIDING UPON THE AMOUNT AND TERMS OF THIS LOAN.

- B. This loan will be evidenced by a promissory note and secured by a deed of trust on property identified as (street address or legal description):

  _____
  _____

- C. 1. Liens presently against this property (do not include loan being applied for)

Nature of Lien	Priority	Lienholder's Name	Amount Owing
_____	_____	_____	_____
_____	_____	_____	_____
_____	_____	_____	_____

  2. Liens that will remain against this property after the loan being applied for is made or arranged (include loan being applied for):

Nature of Lien	Priority	Lienholder's Name	Amount Owing
_____	_____	_____	_____
_____	_____	_____	_____
_____	_____	_____	_____

  NOTICE TO BORROWER: Be sure that you state the amount of all liens as accurately as possible. If you contract with the broker to arrange this loan, but it cannot be arranged because you did not state these liens correctly, you may be liable to pay commissions, fees and expenses even though you do not obtain the loan.

MS REVISED 10/2000 (PAGE 1 OF 3) Print Date

Borrower acknowledges receipt of copy of this page.

Borrower's Initials (_____)(_____)

Reviewed by _____ Date _____

MORTGAGE LOAN DISCLOSURE STATEMENT (MS PAGE 1 OF 3)

Property Address: _____ Date: _____

D. If Borrower pays all or part of the loan principal before it is due, a PREPAYMENT PENALTY computed as follows may be charged:
_____
_____
_____

E. Late Charges: ☐ YES, see loan documents or ☐ NO
F. The purchase of credit life or credit disability insurance by a borrower is not required as a condition of making this loan.
G. Is the real property which will secure the requested loan an "owner-occupied dwelling?" ☐ YES _____ or ☐ NO _____
   (Borrower initial opposite YES or NO)

An "owner-occupied dwelling" means a single dwelling unit in a condominium or cooperative or residential building of four or fewer separate dwelling units, one of which will be owned and occupied by a signatory to the mortgage or deed of trust for this loan within 90 days of the signing of the mortgage or deed of trust.

III. DEDUCTIONS FROM LOAN PROCEEDS
A. Estimated Maximum Costs and Expenses of Arranging the Loan to be Paid Out of Loan Principal:

	PAYABLE TO Broker	Others
1. Appraisal fee	_____	_____
2. Escrow fee	_____	_____
3. Title insurance policy	_____	_____
4. Notary fees	_____	_____
5. Recording fees	_____	_____
6. Credit investigation fees	_____	_____
7. Other costs and expenses:		
_____	_____	_____
_____	_____	_____
Total Costs and Expenses	$ _____	

*B. Compensation .... $ _____
   1. Brokerage Commission/Origination Fee .... $ _____
   2. Lender Origination Fee/Discounts .... $ _____
C. Estimated Payment to be Made out of Loan Principal on Authorization of Borrower

	PAYABLE TO Broker	Others
1. Fire or other hazard insurance premiums	_____	_____
2. Credit life or disability insurance premiums (see Paragraph II-F)	_____	_____
3. Beneficiary statement fees	_____	_____
4. Reconveyance and similar fees	_____	_____
5. Discharge of existing liens against property:		
_____	_____	_____
_____	_____	_____
6. Other:		
_____	_____	_____
_____	_____	_____
Total to be Paid on Authorization of Borrower	$ _____	

If this loan is secured by a first deed of trust on dwellings in a principal amount of less than $30,000 or secured by a junior lien on dwellings in a principal amount of less than $20,000, the undersigned licensee certifies that the loan will be made in compliance with Article 7 of Chapter 3 of the Real Estate Law.

*This loan **may / will / will not** (delete two) be made wholly or in part from broker-controlled funds as defined in Section 10241(j) of the Business and Professions Code.

MS REVISED 10/2000 (PAGE 2 OF 3) Print Date

Borrower acknowledges receipt of copy of this page.
Borrower's Initials (_____)(_____)

Reviewed by _____ Date _____

MORTGAGE LOAN DISCLOSURE STATEMENT (MS PAGE 2 OF 3)

Property Address: _____ Date: _____

*NOTICE TO BORROWER: This disclosure statement may be used if the Broker is acting as an agent in arranging the loan by a third person or if the loan will be made with funds owned or controlled by the broker. If the Broker indicates in the above statement that the loan "may" be made out of Broker-controlled funds, the Broker must notify the borrower prior to the close of escrow if the funds to be received by the Borrower are in fact Broker-controlled funds.

_____   _____
Name of Broker   Broker Representative

_____   _____
License Number   License Number

_____ OR _____
Signature of Broker   Signature

The Department of Real Estate License Information phone number is _____.

<u>**NOTICE TO BORROWER:**</u>

DO NOT SIGN THIS STATEMENT UNTIL YOU HAVE READ AND UNDERSTAND ALL OF THE INFORMATION IN IT. ALL PARTS OF THE FORM MUST BE COMPLETED BEFORE YOU SIGN.

Borrower hereby acknowledges the receipt of a copy of this statement.

DATED _____

_____
(Borrower)

_____
(Borrower)

<u>Broker Review</u>: Signature of Real Estate Broker after review of this statement.

DATED _____

_____
Real Estate Broker or Assistant Pursuant to Section 2725

Published and Distributed by:
REAL ESTATE BUSINESS SERVICES, INC.
a subsidiary of the California Association of REALTORS®
525 South Virgil Avenue, Los Angeles, California 90020

MS REVISED 10/2000 (PAGE 3 OF 3) Print Date

Reviewed by _____ Date _____

MORTGAGE LOAN DISCLOSURE STATEMENT (MS PAGE 3 OF 3)

Overview
Fannie Mae:
- Issues stock to general public
- Issues mortgage-backed securities

Ginnie Mae:
- Guarantees securities issued by FHA approved lenders

Freddie Mac:
- Issues stock to general public
- Buys and sells conventional loans

Office of Federal Housing Enterprise Oversight:
- Conducts audits of Fannie Mae and Freddie Mac
- Makes legislative recommendations

Real Property Loan Law

It is important to have knowledge of the laws governing real estate finance (also known as real estate loan law). Any person in California who negotiates a loan must have a real estate license. All facts must be disclosed by the lender, to ensure that there are no surprises for the borrower (such as a high balloon payment at the end of the loan or large expense to secure the loan).

Due to abuses in the system, legislators and regulators passed laws governing the amount of commissions a broker may receive on both first and second trust deeds. The law only applies to loans that are under a set amount. For first trust deeds, the note amount must be under $30,000. For second trust deeds, the note amount must be under $20,000.

A mortgage loan disclosure statement must be provided to the borrower. This statement contains all disclosures regarding the loan the borrower is interested in acquiring. This disclosure statement must be signed by the prospective borrower before the borrower signs any loan documents.

In addition to the amounts that qualify a loan as a real estate loan law, real estate mortgage brokers are limited to the amount of commission they can charge for these loans. The allowable commission is based on whether the loan is a first trust deed or second trust deed, as well as the number of years for which the loan is set up. The box below describes the commission amounts that mortgage brokers are allowed to charge for each type of loan.

Real Property Loan Law:

First Trust Deed:
- Trust deeds of less than $30,000 fall under the loan law
- For loans lasting less than 3 years, the maximum amount of commission that may be charged is 5%
- For loans lasting 3 years or more, the maximum amount of commission that may be charged is 10%

Second Trust Deed:
- Trust deeds of less than $20,000 fall under the loan law
- For loans lasting less than 2 years, the maximum amount of commission that may be charged is 5%
- For loans lasting at least 2 years, but less than three years, the maximum amount of commission that may be charged is 10%
- For loans lasting three years or more, the maximum amount of commission that maybe charged is 15%

It is important to note that for first trust deeds of $30,000 or more and second trust deeds of $20,000 or more; there is no commission cap. In other words, mortgage brokers may charge as much as they want for these loans.

FEDERAL PARTICIPATION IN REAL ESTATE FINANCE

Most people try diligently to save enough money to someday purchase a home. For some, this task is easy, because they can quickly save the down payment and qualify for a necessary loan. For others, it is difficult to save the down payment, pay their existing bills, and maintain a sufficient credit rating to be considered for a loan. For some, obtaining manageable financing is simply out of reach, even if they have a decent income. For people who find that purchasing a home is simply out of their reach, the government has set up two federal agencies that participate in real estate financing. These agencies make it possible for people to purchase a home using government-backed loans. The two federal agencies are the Federal Housing Administration (FHA) and the Veterans Administration (VA). In addition to these federal programs, California has a state program called the California Farm and Home Purchase Program, or Cal-Vet.

Federal Agencies:
- Federal Housing Administration (or FHA)
- Veterans Administration (or VA)

State Agency:
- California Farm and Home Purchase Program (or Cal-Vet)

Federal Housing Administration

The Federal Housing Administration (www.hud.gov) was created to insure loans made by approved lending institutions (such as banks or mortgage companies). The loans made must follow all FHA guidelines. If they do, the loans will be insured against default in the event that the borrower is unable to pay the note. In the event of default, the FHA will pay cash to the lender up to the established limit of the insurance. In addition, the lender may foreclose on the borrower. This is a way for lenders to ensure that they will recoup their investment in the case of default, beyond just a foreclosure sale.

The FHA has been around since 1934, rewriting the history of real estate finance. Since this time, there have been changes to the regulations; but it is important for you as a real estate professional to be aware of how this program works and the different changes made to the administration over time. Mortgage brokers will be a good resource for you to learn more about current changes.

The lender's investment remains protected in a FHA insured loan, due to the Mutual Mortgage Insurance policy. The borrower is charged a fee for this policy, insuring the investment will be sound. The FHA is able to fund its program through premiums on the Mutual Mortgage Insurance. Borrowers have an option to pay for the insurance in cash, or the amount of the premium may be financed in the loan. This premium must be paid at the close of escrow. A secondary premium is collected each month, if the property is a single-family residence.

The FHA also offers a graduated payment mortgage (GPM). The GPM is ideal for those borrowers who anticipate an increase in their income, but may not currently have the money for a down payment, or can only budget a limited payment. For the first five years, the borrower will pay only a percent of the interest. The remaining interest will be added to the principal. After five years, the loan will be recalculated and the payments adjusted accordingly. After the fifth year, and recalculation of the payment, the payments will remain the same until the note is paid in full.

Consumers wishing to apply for an FHA loan apply directly to an approved lender, rather than the Federal Housing Administration. The lender is then responsible for processing the application and submitting it to the FHA directly. Any borrower may apply for an FHA loan; and there are no restrictions or caps on qualifications

Overview:

- FHA insures loans
- Borrowers apply directly to approved lenders, who process the application and submit it to the FHA
- Borrowers pay Mutual Mortgage Insurance
- FHA offers the Graduated Payment Mortgage for clients anticipating an increase in income, but who currently have budget restrictions.

Department of Veteran Affairs

The department of Veteran Affairs started out as the Servicemen's Readjustment Act of 1944, and helped enlisted service men and women transition back to civilian life. As time went by, the act was expanded to include service men and women from later wars, their spouses and widows of service men and women, provided they remained unmarried. Today, the Department of Veteran Affairs (simply called the VA) authorizes first and second trust deeds for up to 25% of a property's value. The VA will guarantee payment of the remaining value of the mortgage debt, up to a certain maximum amount. This program does not cost the borrower any money. What the VA guarantees the lender is that they will pay the lender's net loss up to the amount of money guaranteed. This value will decrease over time, as the loan value is repaid.

People eligible for the VA guaranteed loan are service men and women who have served in the military and were not dishonorably discharged. The spouses of these men and women as well as members of the Army Reserve or the National Guard (as long as they have served for six years or more) are also eligible for the VA-guaranteed loan.

The lender will screen applicants, verify their veteran status and process the loan if the candidate meets all qualifications. The Department of Veteran Affairs does not need to approve any applications. Interested candidates request a Certificate of Eligibility from their VA office before filling out the loan application. This certificate will indicate the amount of loan guarantee or their veteran's entitlement.

VA loans may be used for the purchase of property, construction, repairs to a property or improvements to a property. The loan must be used for property consisting of one to four units, or a condominium. Residential complexes with more than four units will not qualify for a VA-guaranteed loan.

The loan guarantee amount is based on the size of the loan. The maximum guarantee is 60% of the loan (or $50,750 whichever is the lesser amount). A veteran is only able to use this loan once in his or her lifetime. If a veteran only uses a portion of their entitlement, they may use the remaining portion on a separate loan at a later date. There are, however, certain exceptions to this rule. For example: if a veteran has sold the property, and the VA-guaranteed loan is paid in full; if the Department of Veteran's Affairs is released from the original loan; if any losses suffered by the Department of Veteran's Affairs is paid in full; or, if the property is transferred to another veteran with loan guarantee benefits. In these cases, the veteran is entitled to increase the loan guarantee amount to its full amount.

If a veteran decides to sell his or her home, the VA requires a release from personal liability to the government to be signed prior to the sale of the home. If this release is not completed, the veteran will remain responsible for the property. Additionally, the release should be included as a condition of the sale. The VA can release the veteran from liability in the event of a foreclosure, provided there has been no fraud or bad faith by the veteran.

The VA must issue a certificate of reasonable value to the purchaser before signing the contract of sale. Otherwise, there should be a clause in the sale contract stating that: if the certificate of reasonable values is less than the purchase price, the buyer may either proceed with the purchasing property, or withdraw the offer. The certificate of reasonable value amount is determined by VA-recommended appraisers.

There are several different loan types available to veterans wishing to utilize a VA-guaranteed loan. The loans available are: fixed-term; adjustable rate mortgage; growing equity mortgage, and graduated payment mortgage.

VA – guaranteed loan types:
• Fixed-term
• Adjustable-rate mortgage
• Growing equity mortgage
• Graduated payment mortgage

Fixed term loans are fully amortized to no more than 30 years and 32 days.

Adjustable-rate mortgages (ARM) are adjusted based on the Treasury's securities index. This causes the loan payment amount to fluctuate, depending on the volatility of interest rates. Today, this loan is not available to veterans; however any veteran who obtained this type of loan before 1995 may still be utilizing an ARM loan.

Growing equity mortgage (GEM) is connected to an index that increases the amount of payments. The increase of the payment goes directly toward the principal balance. The GEM is a way to pay off a mortgage early, while building equity in a home more quickly.

Graduated payment mortgage (GPM) allows the borrower to make a lower monthly payment for the first five years (or the equivalent of only 7% interest), regardless of interest rates. After five years, the payment will go up and shall remain at the same level for the life of the loan. Any interest not being covered in the first five years will automatically be added to the principal balance of the loan.

Interest rates are not negotiable on VA-guaranteed loans. If the payment is too large for the borrower to make, the lender may suggest a graduated payment mortgage, to allow for lower payments in the beginning of the note.

Mobile homes fall under a separate category. A mobile home must measure at least 400 square feet to qualify as a property for purchase with a VA-guaranteed loan. Single-wide mobile homes have a maximum financing term of 15 years and 32 days. Double-wide mobile homes have a maximum financing term of 20 years and 32 days.

VA-guaranteed loans do not require a down payment, provided that the estimate of reasonable value does not exceed the VA loan guarantee. The lender, on the other hand, may require a down payment of his or her own. This is negotiated directly with the lender. If the purchase price of a property is more than the reasonable value, a VA guaranteed loan may still be used, as long as the buyer pays the difference between the reasonable value and the purchase price in cash at closing.

In the event that a veteran has a difficult time paying the loan, and defaults for a period of three months, a notice of default is given to the Department of Veteran Affairs, alerting them to the situation. The VA will then aid the veteran in making the necessary payments, and counsel him or her on how to keep on track with future payments.

Overview:

- VA loans provide a guarantee to the lender that they will receive the loan guarantee amount based on the selling price of the home
- Lenders fill out all applications and submit them to the Department of Veteran's Affairs
- An approved VA appraiser must be used to arrive at the amount of the certificate of reasonable value
- There are 4 different loan types that may be used: fixed-term loans; adjustable-rate mortgage; growing equity mortgage, and graduated payment mortgage
- VA guaranteed loans for property consisting of 1-4 units (or condominiums) may be financed for up to 30 years and 32 days
- Single-wide mobile homes may be financed for up to 15 years and 32 days, while double-wide mobile homes may be financed for up to 20 years and 32 days
- There is no down payment required for a VA-guaranteed loan

California Veterans Farm and Home Purchase Program
California Veterans Farm and Home Purchase Program, or Cal-Vet (www.ns.net/cadva.) is a full service lender for veterans. Cal-Vet authorizes, processes, funds and services all loans they administer. The program was developed in 1921, to assist veterans in purchasing both homes and farms. There are no outside funds involved in the Cal-Vet programs; all the money that is used for these loans come from voter-approved bonds, issued by the legislature.

The California Department of Veteran Affairs will buy a property from its seller, and sell the property to an interested, qualified veteran. The title will remain with the California Department of Veteran Affairs until the note has been paid in full, though the borrower may take possession of the property immediately. Veterans may use the Cal-Vet program to purchase an existing home or farm, finance a land purchase to build a new home, remodel a home purchased as-is or make home improvements.

Veterans eligible for the Cal-Vet program must be purchasing a property in California, and must also be a California resident. They may not have taken a previous benefit from another state and must have served at least 90 days active service duty. Those veterans not serving at least 90 days on active duty must have been honorably discharged in order to qualify. In addition to the above criteria, each veteran must have served at lease one day in one of the following periods:

World War I	April 6, 1917 through November 11, 1918
World War II	December 7, 1941 through December 31, 1946
Korean Conflict	June 27, 1950 through January 31, 1955
Vietnam War	August 5, 1964 through May 7, 1975
Persian Gulf War	August 2, 1990 through present

Unmarried spouses of those veterans who were killed, or who have died by other means are also eligible for benefits. The Cal-Vet system occasionally experiences shortages of funds for all applicants. In this event, there is a hierarchy of preference given to applicants, which is as follows:

1. Wounded or disabled veterans
2. Former prisoners of war and unmarried spouses of prisoners or war or those missing in action
3. Vietnam War veterans and Native American veterans applying for loans on reservation or trust land
4. All other eligible candidates

There is a maximum amount of money available to each applicant for a VA-guaranteed loan. The maximum amount of money available to purchase a home is $250,000, with a $70,000 lending limit for a mobile home and a $300,000 lending limit for the purchase of a farm. These loans require a down payment of 5% of the selling price. All applicants wishing to participate in a Cal-Vet loan must have applied for the loan before the purchase of property was made.

Overview:
- Cal-Vet loans are funded, serviced, processed and authorized in-house
- Eligibility requirements state that veterans must have served active duty for 90 days (or have been honorably discharged), and have also served at least one day during an active war or conflict
- Maximum loan amount for a home is $250,000, with a $70,000 lending limit for a mobile home and $300,000 lending limit for a farm

	FHA	VA	Cal-Vet
Type of Property	Dwellings consisting of one to four units	Dwellings consisting of one to four units	One-unit dwellings or farms
Borrower Eligibility	All U.S. Residents	U.S. Veterans	California Veterans
Maximum Loan Amount	$121,296 - $219,849	None, but a loan based on maximum entitlement would be $203,000, including the funding fee.	$70,000 – Mobile home $250,000 – home $300,000 - Farm
Maximum Purchase Price	None	None	None
Down Payment	At least 3% of acquisition cost	At the discretion of the lender	5%
Discount points	Yes	Yes	No
Type of loan	Variety of fixed and variable-rate loans	Fixed rate; GEM; GPM	Variable rate; others possible
Interest Rate	Negotiated	Negotiated	Set by Cal-Vet; can change annually
Maximum Loan Term	30 years; 35 years for new construction; less for mobile homes	30 years; less for mobile homes	30 years
Prepayment Penalty	None	None	None
Secondary Financing	Not at time of sale	Not at time of sale	Yes

REAL ESTATE SETTLEMENT PROCEDURES ACT – RESPA

The Real Estate Settlement Procedures Act (RESPA) requires that lenders make certain disclosures to borrowers utilizing a federal mortgage loan or loan program. Any sale of property using these loans, with property that consists of one to 4 units must supply the appropriate disclosures. The federal mortgage loan or loan program includes the following:

- A loan made by a lender insured by FDIC or another federal agency
- A loan financed through a federal agency such as the Federal Housing Administration (FHA) or through the Department of Veteran's Affairs (VA)
- Sold in the secondary mortgage market to Fannie Mae, Ginnie Mae or Freddie Mac

Lenders are required to supply every applicant with all disclosures and material. If there is more than one person applying for a loan, each applicant must receive his or her own copy of all disclosures. The lender must send the applicants all material no later than three days after the application has been received. The following information must be supplied to the applicants:

- A copy of the special information booklet
- A good-faith estimate of the closing costs

A copy of the real estate settlement statement must also be supplied to the borrower no later than one day after closing on the property. The settlement statement lists all charges to the buyer and seller, and accompanied by the real estate transaction. Real estate settlement statements were covered in the escrow chapter.

REGULATION Z – THE TRUTH IN LENDING ACT

The Federal Reserve Board created the Truth in Lending Act (simply called Regulation Z), which requires creditors to disclose various credit terms to the borrower. This allows the borrower to make an informed decision between the different creditors and/or sources of available credit.

Creditors are those who extend credit or make loans to borrowers (more than 25 times each year for non-secured loans; 5 times each year for those loans requiring real property as security for the loan). A written arrangement, outlining payment amount, timing and other terms of the loan is required. A creditor is allowed to charge interest on the loan, provided that the interest on the loan is payable in four installments and that there is written agreement to these terms. It is important to note that the person arranging credit is not the creditor. Rather, the institution, or actual person making the loan, is the creditor. For example, a loan officer at Wells Fargo Bank is not a creditor; Wells Fargo Bank is the creditor.

There are certain transactions that are exempt from the Truth in Lending Act. These transactions are commercial, agricultural or business loans. Loans made for more than $25,000 are exempt from Regulation Z, unless it is a purchase money loan (where the loan must be secured by real or personal property) and the borrower plans to use the property as his or her primary place of residence. Any loans made to purchase, maintain or improve a rental property fall under different regulations and rules. If this rental property will be owner-occupied within one year the following rules apply:

- Loans made to acquire rental property consisting of one or more units are considered business loans, and are regulated as such

- Loans made to improve or maintain a property consisting of four or more units are also considered business loans and are regulated as such

Any loans acquired for the purpose of purchasing, maintaining or improving a rental property, which will not be owner occupied will always, be considered a business loan.

Customers who have decided not to go ahead with the purchase of a property may cancel the loan. This is known as the *right to rescind*. A borrower has three days to cancel any loan involving a security interest in the borrower's principal residence. The three-day period will end at midnight on the third business day. The following events must occur for the borrower to rescind:

- Use of the transaction
- Borrower has received the truth in lending disclosure statement
- Borrower has received notice of the right to rescind

The right to rescind does not apply to the following situations:

- Refinancing a loan secured by property which is not occupied by the owner
- Residential purchase money, first mortgage, or trust deed loans
- Borrower refinances a loan, and no new funds are advanced to the borrower

In emergency situations the right to rescind may be waived so that the lender can fund the borrower's loan as fast as possible. Such situations may occur when closing needs to happen at a specific time for the purchase contract to be accepted.

There are certain disclosures required by Regulation Z. All disclosures must be grouped together, with the information set off by a box apart from the rest of the information on the loan. A different type style, bold type, or a different color background is also required, so that the disclosures will clearly stand out. These disclosures must be made before the transaction is completed (which is generally before closing). Usually, this disclosure statement will be delivered to the borrower at the same time as the loan commitment information is sent. This is normally after the loan has been approved, but before the loan has been funded.

The required disclosures pertain to financial information. It is necessary to state: the name of the creditor; the description of the security interest; the amount of money to be financed; the finance charge associated with the loan; the annual percentage rate; the total amount of the payments, and the total sales price. The borrower must be informed of any prepayment penalties, rebates or late payment charges, so that there are no surprise charges associated with an early payoff or a late payment. When insurance is not a requirement of the loan, and the borrower wishes to obtain insurance on the item to be purchased, the borrower must sign a request for insurance. When a signature is not required, the borrower's initials must be placed on the document.

Five most important disclosures:
- Amount to be financed
- Finance charge
- Annual percentage rate
- Total amount of the payments
- Total sales price (for any credit sales)

As we learned in another chapter, loans may be assumable when the borrower wishes to sell the property to another buyer. A borrower in a residential mortgage transaction must be informed of whether or not this is possible with their loan. This should be included in the disclosure statement.

Regulation Z also governs the types of advertisements that may be made for loans. In any advertisement, the ad must state the annual percentage rate of the loan, along with its payment terms. Specific information regarding the different forms of adjustable rate loans must also be included in the advertisement.

EQUAL CREDIT OPPORTUNITY ACT

The Equal Credit Opportunity Act (www.lawdog.com/equal2/ec1.htm) protects people from discrimination when applying for a loan. Under this act, no person may be discriminated based on their sex, religion, race, color, age, marital status, national origin or on the grounds of receiving public funds from welfare. Every buyer is assured that they will be treated fairly, without discrimination, when going through the loan application process for a home or for other credit.

Equal Opportunity Credit Act Guidelines:

- Borrowers are not required to answer questions regarding birth control practices or methods or whether they plan on starting a family

- Borrowers may be asked if they are married, however a lender is not allowed to ask if a borrower is divorced or widowed

- Borrowers must be notified within 30 days if they qualify for the loan for which they applied. If the borrower is denied for the loan, the lender must supply the reason(s) for the denial of the loan

- Borrowers are not required to reveal any information regarding receipt of child support or alimony. Those borrowers who must pay child support or alimony may be asked about it, as it pertains directly to the borrower's income versus obligations. Such obligations may be a determining factor in whether a borrower can make the necessary payment on a loan

- Borrowers who have a poor credit rating due to sharing a joint account with another person may provide information showing that the delinquent account is through the fault of another person, and not their own

PERSONAL PROPERTY SECURED TRANSACTIONS

You will remember that personal property is distinctly separated from real property. Personal property are things of value that may be moved. Examples include: jewelry, cars, money, boats and other such valuable items. Often, to purchase such items, a loan is necessary. When a consumer does not have enough money to purchase their dream car, or take a European cruise, they must secure a loan - just as if they were purchasing a home. When purchasing a home, the trust deed secures the home. When purchasing a high dollar item of personal property, the security agreement secures the loan for the car, boat or other desired good.

When placing an item of personal property as the security agreement to secure a loan to purchase another item, people usually attach a financing statement to the security agreement. This protects the item that is placed as security for the loan. The reason for doing this is so the item securing the loan will not be sold in the event that the loan defaults. A security interest is "perfected" (protected) when it is has been attached to a financing statement and recorded in the office of the Secretary of State in Sacramento.

The financing statement is the only form used to record a debt. It will contain all details of the agreement, as well as all obligations. Once the security agreement is protected, or perfected, the security interest is protected from other creditors to whom the debtor may owe money.

> Security interest "attaches" when:
> - An agreement between two parties has been reached
> - The item has been given value
> - The debtor has acquired rights in the form of collateral

SUMMARY

In this chapter, we examined real estate finance beyond the lender and borrower relationship. We learned about the different federal and state agencies that play a role in keeping real estate finance ethical and feasible for borrowers. We also learned of the different federal and state agencies which aid in guaranteeing and insuring loans to keep a lender's investment safe while helping the borrower to secure the loan they need to purchase property. We outlined special programs for those persons serving in the military, as well as the requirements of such programs. Finally, we examined the borrower's right to be informed and protected against discrimination. Real estate finance is a very technical, oftentimes confusing, topic to examine. Be sure to reference the various web sites listed in this chapter, for additional information on the different programs or agencies that provide assistance to borrowers and lenders.

TERMS AND PHRASES

Adjustable Rate Mortgage (ARM) – A type of loan, which allows its interest rate to fluctuate with market conditions. When the national interest rate goes up, so does the interest rate on the note (and vice versa). Payment of the note will fluctuate with changes in the interest rate.

Deregulation – Policy that now allows financial institutions to shed old restraints and restrictions that made it difficult for them to compete freely for profits in the marketplace

Disintermediation – The process by which depositors take money out of their savings accounts and invest it in a higher-yield, riskier investment

Financial Intermediary –A financial institution, which collects funds through deposits and then lends those funds to other people in an effort to earn return via interest. Banks and credit unions are an example of this type of institution

Financing Statement – A recorded instrument giving notice to the public of the security interest, thus protecting the interest of the secured party in the collateral

Intermediation – Transferring capital from those persons who deposit or invest funds to those persons wishing to borrow money.

Mortgage Loan Disclosure Statement – required statement given to a buyer informing him or her of all charges or fees related to a particular loan.

Real Estate Investment Trust (REIT) –A group of at least 100 individuals who individually invest a small amount of money and pool it together to buy real estate.

Security Agreement – device used to secure a loan to purchase personal property.

Tight Money – condition in which there is a limited supply of money; high demand creates high interest rates.

Variable Rate Mortgage (VRM) – A mortgage in which the interest rates may vary, depending on the national interest rate. The rate will alter the amount of each monthly payment on a note.

Warehousing – Assembling a number of loans into a package before selling them to an investor.

CHAPTER QUIZ

1. Which federal agency insures loans made by approved provider banks?
   A. Federal Deposit Insurance Corporation (FDIC)
   B. Federal Housing Administration (FHA)
   C. Savings Association Insurance Fund (SAIF)
   D. Federal Reserve Bank System (Fed)

2. Which one of the following methods is NOT used by the Fed to regulate the nation's money supply?
   A. Reserve requirements
   B. Open market operations
   C. Sell loans on the secondary mortgage market
   D. Change the discount rate

3. What conditions caused the restructuring of real estate finance and mortgage options available to consumers?
   A. Disintermediation
   B. High interest rates
   C. Short money supply
   D. All of the above

4. Which of the following institutions are considered non-institutional lenders?
   A. Credit Unions
   B. Insurance Company
   C. Mortgage Company
   D. Commercial Banks

5. From where does the majority of real estate loan funding come?
   A. Personal savings accounts
   B. Mortgage companies
   C. Insurance companies
   D. Non-financial institutions

6. What is the minimum number of investors required for an REIT?
   A. 100
   B. 75
   C. 125
   D. 50

7. What is the primary function of a mortgage company?
   A. Originate loans with its own money
   B. Connect borrowers with lenders who can provide the necessary funds or programs for their loan needs.
   C. Service loans they have originated or sold.
   D. All of the above

8. Which primary participant in the secondary mortgage market guarantees investors that they will receive payment for the security they hold by making late payments for the borrower, if necessary?
    A. Ginnie Mae
    B. Fannie Mae
    C. Freddie Mac
    D. Office of Federal Housing Enterprise Oversight

9. When must the Mortgage Loan Disclosure Statement be signed by the borrower?
    A. After all loan documents have been reviewed and signed
    B. After loan documents have been reviewed, but before they are signed
    C. Before any loan document is presented to the borrower
    D. None of the above

10. A mortgage broker providing a second trust deed worth $17,000, with a term of two years, may charge the borrower what percent in commission?
    A. 5%
    B. 7%
    C. 10%
    D. 15%

11. What is the purpose of a FHA loan?
    A. To guarantee the loan
    B. To insure the loan
    C. Both A and B
    D. Neither A nor B

12. Who funds Cal-Vet loans?
    A. Voter-approved bonds
    B. Outside funding
    C. California Department of Veteran Affairs
    D. Traditional banks and mortgage companies

13. Under a VA-guaranteed loan, for how long may a traditional single-family dwelling be financed?
    A. 25 years.
    B. 20 years
    C. 35 years
    D. 30 years

14. Which one of the following loan types is not allowed when using a VA-guaranteed loan?
    A. Fixed-term
    B. Seller financed loan
    C. Adjustable-rate mortgage
    D. Graduated payment mortgage

15. When must the special information booklet and the good-faith estimate of closing costs be delivered to the borrower by the lender?
    A. No later than 2 days after receiving the loan application
    B. No later than 3 days after receiving the loan application
    C. No later than 5 days after receiving the loan application
    D. No later than 7 days after receiving the loan application

16. Which one of the following is NOT protected from discrimination under the Equal Credit Opportunity Act?
    A. Sex
    B. Color
    C. Religion
    D. Sexual Orientation

17. What document must be filed when protecting interest by creating a security interest?
    A. Financing statement
    B. Disclosure
    C. Investment Trust
    D. Intermediation

18. Under the truth in lending act, how many days does a buyer have to rescind a loan?
    A. 1
    B. 3
    C. 5
    D. 10

19. How many loans in which there must be a security interest placed on the borrower's primary place of residence must a lender make in one year to be considered a creditor?
    A. 5
    B. 10
    C. 20
    D. 25

20. Which of the following is NOT considered one of the five most important disclosures under the truth in lending act?
    A. Annual percentage rate
    B. Finance charge
    C. Total amount of payments
    D. Right to rescind

APPRAISAL

What you will learn in this Chapter

- Definition

- Value

- Forces Influencing Value

- The Appraisal Process

- Reconciliation

- Obtaining an Appraisal License

1. Which one of the following is not considered a reason for obtaining an appraisal of property?
   A. Taxation
   B. Insurance
   C. Financing and credit
   D. Fair market value

2. Which one of the following terms best describes the statement "the price a property would bring if freely offered in an open market with both a willing seller and buyer?"
   A. Market value
   B. Utility value
   C. Market price
   D. Objective value

3. A development where all the homes are constructed in a similar architectural style, of similar age and built out of similar materials, to keep the value of the homes high, best describes the principle of
   A. Contribution
   B. Conformity
   C. Balance
   D. Highest and best use

4. Which of the following is NOT one of the three appraisal techniques to determine the value of a property?
   A. Sales comparison approach
   B. Cost approach
   C. Square foot method
   D. Income capitalization approach

5. An appraiser is required to take continuing education classes every
   A. Year
   B. 2 years
   C. 3 years
   D. 4 years

6. Which of the following are considered examples of physical deterioration?
   A. Termite damage
   B. Damage from severe weather
   C. Damage from normal wear and tear
   D. All of the above

7. Which of the following is NOT an appraisal report form?
   A. Short form
   B. Final conclusion
   C. Letter form
   D. Narrative

INTRODUCTION

If you have ever looked for property, whether a home, an income property (such as a duplex or apartment complex) or a building for office space, you probably have a good idea of how much property costs in your community, neighborhood or region of the state. But have you ever wondered how this value is determined? Why is a 2,000 square foot home in Santa Monica worth so much more than an equally large home in Fresno or Bakersfield? How does an appraiser know the difference between homes, or how to price them accordingly?

This chapter will introduce you to the appraisal process. The appraisal process is a detailed, data-driven process, which results in an estimated opinion. This opinion is based on all facts gathered regarding the property in question, as well as all comparable properties surrounding the property in question.

We will first describe for you an appraisal, followed by the concept of value. Following that, we will outline the different forces that determine or influence value. After you fully are exposed to value and the forces driving it, we will more closely examine the basic concept of the chapter: the appraisal process. We will discuss the steps an appraiser takes to determine a property's value, the different appraisal methods an appraiser can use, and the process an appraiser goes through when analyzing a site. Finally, you will learn the steps necessary to become an appraiser.

The appraisal process is very important for a real estate agent to understand, as clients may ask you for your opinion on a property's value. A real estate professional must understand the concepts of appraisal to give an accurate opinion, or explain how the appraiser arrived at his or her estimate of value on the property in question.

DEFINITION

Real estate appraisal is an appraiser's estimate of what a property is worth in an open market. This worth is estimated or measured based on a monetary value. This value measures the present worth of rights a homeowner may gain, as well as any future benefits that will come from ownership of the specific piece of property. It is important to understand that while there are guidelines for appraising property, the final number that the appraiser arrives at is simply an estimate, or opinion. Appraisals are also useful to determine the worth of a property for insurance or investment purposes. The appraisal can indicate a property's type and condition, its usefulness for a specific purpose, or its highest and best use.

Appraisal is the process by which an appraiser arrives at the present worth of a property. It can also be the written report the appraiser provides describing how he or she arrived at the estimated value of a property. Such a report is called an appraisal report.

The process by which the appraiser arrives at the estimate involves a series of steps. First the appraiser will inspect the property, to obtain a solid visual idea of its physical location, condition and amenities. Next, the appraiser will compile a variety of data regarding the property, its location or area, and other important data necessary to arrive at an estimate. After this, the appraiser will consider the current market forces and local market conditions which may make the property more or less desirable at a given time, given its location. Finally, the appraiser will determine the value, or estimate, of what he or she believes the appropriate property value, given the current market. The data collected and factors considered may vary, depending on the purpose(s) of the appraisal.

Appraisers are generally third parties, with no direct interest in the property. It is important for an appraiser to be unbiased in determining the value of the property, to determine its true worth. They must appraise without the emotion a seller may have, or the motivation a buyer may have, in the property. Experienced, professional appraisers are trained extensively in this process. They operate with an ethical, unbiased opinion, to correctly measure all influences determining the value of a property. Again, it is important that the appraiser be a neutral party, uninfluenced by the specific interests of either the buyer or seller.

An appraiser's final value will be a dollar value, indicating the property's market value for that specific day in that specific market. There are five main reasons for making an appraisal. Each one may arrive at different prices for the same property, even on the same day. The five reasons for obtaining an appraisal value are: to transfer property from one person to another; for financing and credit purposes; for tax reasons; for condemnation, and for insurance. When making an appraisal, it is important for the appraiser to know the specific reason the appraisal is being made, as this could drastically change the value of the appraisal.

Five reasons for an appraisal:
- Transfer property from one party to another
- Financing and credit
- Tax
- Condemnation
- Insurance

V A L U E

The price that a specific piece of real estate (whether land, house or building), or its land and all structures on it would bring in an open market where there is a willing buyer and seller is called *market value*. This figure is based on what a person is willing to pay for a specific property, given its utility or value. The market value is subjective, depending on the buyer, the purposes for which the property might be used, and other market conditions.

There are certain kinds of property or sales that do not constitute an open market value, or sale. Such sales are said to occur through default. Examples of such sales are: foreclosure; bankruptcy; divorce; death, or any other special circumstance where the sale of property is made due to a special circumstance. An appraiser would not consider the price paid for these properties (many of which may be sold at an auction or for less than the actual value of the home) a measure of market value. There are five assumptions that can be made regarding open market sales:

- The buyer and seller are willingly acting in their own interest
- The property has been on the real estate market for a reasonable length of time, given its specific property type.
- There has been full disclosure to both the buyer and seller, with a knowledgeable decision being made, taking into account the property's defects and assets
- No unusual circumstances exist
- Normal financing is available to the buyers, who qualify, and is used to purchase the property

Understanding that market value is the price that a property could bring in an open market, with both a willing buyer and seller, the market price does not necessarily mirror the accurate market value. Market price is the price at which property actually sold. So, while market price is the actual price for which the property sold, market value is the price for which it should have sold. It is important to understand that market price is not always a lower amount than market value. It is possible, in a very hot market, or in an extremely desired location, for the market price to be well above market value.

When thinking about value and cost or price, it is important for you to understand that realistic and/or humanistic factors play an important role in determining the worth of a property. For example, a home may appraise for $400,000, and could easily bring in that amount. However, the seller may be going through a bitter divorce, and needs to sell the property immediately. In this case, the seller is very motivated, and under a lot of pressure to sell the property in order to divide up marital assets. If a first-time home-buyer comes along and makes a bid of $370,000 (which is $30,000 under its market value), the bid has a good chance of being accepted, because of the seller's personal circumstances. So, the market value compared to the market price is not equal. This example serves to demonstrate that value is not always going to be the same as the cost or price of a property, although it certainly may be the same in other situations.

All properties have a utility value which is the usefulness of property for a specific purpose. A piece of farmland in California's Central Valley, hundreds of miles away from a major metropolitan city, has high utility value to a farmer, but a low utility value for a real estate developer looking to build a 60-story skyscraper for office space.

As we have seen from some of the examples given, cost is not an essential element in determining value. What one person finds valuable, another may not; still another might determine it priceless. Market value only represents the amount for which a property can be sold in the current market given all present conditions. This can be determined by data, and is thus called the *objective value*.

Value is subjective, but it is a present factor with future anticipated utility or enjoyment. There is also an anticipated profit associated with value. Price is the amount of money that is paid for an object. Cost represents the expenses that were incurred when producing an object. These costs could be in the form of labor, materials, or any other sacrifices in one area or luxury that had to be made in order to acquire another.

Remember!
- Market value is what a property should sell for in an open market
- Market price is the actual amount of money for which a property sold
- Utility value is the usefulness of a property for a specific purpose to a specific person
- Objective value is similar to market value, as it can be determined by current data
- Cost represents the amount of money it takes to produce something
- Price represents what a person paid for a good or service
- Value is defined as the present enjoyment, with consideration of future anticipated profits

There are four basic elements that must be present for an object to have value, easily remembered by the acronym DUST, which stands for: demand; utility; scarcity and transferability. A market will only exist when there is demand for a product, and the scarcer the product is, the higher the demand will be. Once a person acquires a product that is scarce, and thus holds value, it is important for this product to be transferred to someone else in exchange for money or other desired goods. Finally, utility will also determine the usefulness of a product. Utility, coupled with scarcity, will also increase the value of a product.

Four elements of value:
- Demand
- Utility
- Scarcity
- Transferability

An appraiser must take all of these elements into consideration when determining the value of a property. Is the property going to be used for its intended purpose, thus increasing its utility? Are there several similar properties in the neighborhood, or is this one unique, thus increasing the scarcity of the property? Is the title to the property clear of any encumbrances, or will the transfer of property include a long closing period, determining the ease of transferability of the property? Once each of these elements has been considered, an appropriate value can be determined for a specific property.

Just as there are elements that determine value, there are also forces and other factors that determine the value of property. There are four main forces, as well as geographical, physical and governmental sub-factors, that determine value, . The four main forces influencing value are: economic influences; social standards; environmental and physical conditions; and political regulations.

Four forces determining value:
- Economic influences
- Social standards
- Environmental and physical conditions
- Political regulations

Economic influences include factors such as: the availability of money or credit in a certain community; price levels; tax base; interest rates; and wages. Additionally, the rate of new development, building, industrial and commercial health also plays a role in economic influences. One economic influence that may not be as obvious is the amount and type of natural resources in an area. An area rich in natural resources generally has a lot of industry, tourism or other means of creating a healthy, local economy.

Social standards are less mental or behavioral characteristics, and more demographics. Some of the social standards used in determining value for an area include: marriage; birth rate; death rate; and divorce rate for a community. Population is also a factor, as the growth or decline of population in an area may be indicative of the economic health of the community.

Environmental and physical conditions are more obvious factors in determining the value of a property. In California, property tends to be more expensive if closer to water, or at a higher elevation. So, naturally ocean front property will have more value than property 50 miles inland. Property on a hill, with canyon views, will have more value than a home nestled in a valley and surrounded by other homes with no view. Other environmental factors that influence value include: climate; topography; soil type; and, as mentioned earlier in this example, proximity to mountains and oceans. Some of the other environmental or physical conditions considered when determining property values are: access to shopping; availability of public transportation; school districts; local conveniences; entertainment; and access to appropriate houses of worship.

Political regulations are the fourth and final element in determining a property's value. An example of this type of force is a community's economic base. Things like rent control, zoning regulations or building codes may also have in influence in the value of property in a community or area.

Other factors influencing value include the following:

- Shape of a lot, with irregular-shaped plots both more difficult and more expensive to develop.

- Topography of the land, which influences the cost to develop a site. Houses or buildings built on a hillside, or in the mountains, will be more expensive than those built on flat, level surfaces.

- Location is perhaps the most important factor in determining value. Is it an | oceanfront property? Does it have commanding views of the valley from atop a hill or mountain? Is it nestled next a lake or river? Or, is it located in the middle of the desert? The phrase "location, location, location" really does describe the three most important things to consider when shopping for property.

- Directional growth, which describes the direction in which a city or town is grow ing. Is the city growing to the north or south? Or, is it simply expanding all over? The new growth area of a city tends to already have a higher value or increases in value much more quickly than other areas.

- Obsolescence, which describes external influences or economic changes, which may decrease the usefulness of the property (decreasing its value).

- Utility of the property, as a property that cannot be used for its intended purchase will decrease in value. Factors affecting utility may include building restrictions or zoning ordinances.

- The business climate of an area, whether healthy or stagnant, will either increase or decrease the value of a property. If a home or business is located in a bustling area, full of shopping, office space, medical centers and wholesale and industrial areas, its value will increase.

- Corner influence, which describes the physical location of a home or business on a city block. A corner lot increases the frontage of a building. This is great for businesses who want more exposure. However, it decreases privacy for a home. Corner lots are generally larger, but can incur more maintenance costs.

- Directional exposure does not seem to be much of a condition; however, a south ern or western exposure is ideal for businesses, as those storefronts are general ly in the shade. Most consumers will walk on the shady side of the street, and the storefronts and windows will be clearly visible, without glare from the sun.

- Size of the property will obviously determine value. The larger a property, the more valuable it is in the given market.

- Through streets and width of sidewalks or streets can affect value. In a residential area, it is more desirable to live on a dead end street, or cul-de-sac, as there will be less traffic and noise. Meanwhile, a business thrives from the traffic and exposure brought by a busy street.

- Assemblage or plottage, in which plots of land are placed together to create one larger plot, owned by one single person, can create a more valuable piece of property.

Appraisers must take many factors or forces driving market value into account when arriving at their evaluation of property. It is important for an appraiser to look for all of these factors or conditions early on in the appraisal process, so they can arrive at the most accurate value figure possible. The real estate market is constantly evolving. So, an area considered desirable today may not be sought-after tomorrow. Meanwhile, an area considered run down or undesirable may provide a great opportunity for purchase property at a low price, with monies left over for renovation and creation of a very nice space. The following concepts are just a few factors that an appraiser must take into account when appraising a property.

The principle of *supply and demand* describes the availability of property to purchase, versus the number of individuals interested in purchasing that particular type of property. When there is high demand for a specific type of property or home in a certain neighborhood, and the supply of such properties is short, the property will be purchased at a premium. When the opposite happens, and there is low demand for the property, prices will drop a bit. A market in equilibrium occurs when the supply of property meets the demand for property.

A property's *highest and best use* is the best way to utilize the land. Generally, the highest and best use of land takes into account the most profitable way to utilize the land, as well as whether it is legally and physically possible to utilize the land in the desired way. When property is being redeveloped, any existing structures will also be considered. Will it be cost effective to renovate the structures? Will demolishing the property be more expensive than leaving it alone? Questions such as these must be asked when finding the land's best and most profitable use.

Keeping land in *balance* is important. Balance simply means that the land uses result in the highest profit possible for that specific use. It also can refer to the proximity of businesses, shopping and medical facilities to homes and housing developments.

The presence of similar buildings in a specific area promotes *conformity*. When each building on an industrial campus or each home in a housing development is constructed out of similar materials, with similar architecture or are of similar age, they exhibit conformity. Generally speaking, conformity in a residential neighborhood keeps property values high.

The *principle of substitution* is important to appraisers, as this is the most common way to determine value for similar properties. When a home in a particular area is put on the market for sale, an appraiser uses the principle of substitution by projecting the established property's value onto the property that has come up for sale. Of course, the appraiser will need to conduct a thorough appraisal of the new property; but having a reference point regarding where the current property market in an area is a good place to begin the appraisal process.

Most people who purchase real estate *anticipate* gaining future benefits from the property in the future. This may be as simple as expecting property values in the neighborhood to rise, anticipating the creation of equity in the home, or believing that an up and coming area will be developed as expected (creating a new hip area to live, higher property values, and high demand for property in the area).

A building's value can be affected in a positive or negative way with regards to the buildings surrounding it. This theory is described as the principle of *progression and regression*. If a nice home is situated in an area with homes of lesser value, or with homes that are not as physically appealing, the price of the nicer home will decrease to a lower level than if it were located in a different neighborhood with similar homes. This is *regression. Progression* is just the opposite; a home in a nice area, with other homes of higher value, will increase the value of that one home.

Changes, whether subtle or drastic, can raise or decrease the value of property. There are four changes, which can affect the value of property. These factors are:

- Physical
- Economic
- Social
- Political

A *physical change* could be a natural disaster, such as a land or mudslide, an earthquake or a fire. Any one of these changes could damage property, decreasing its value. A physical change can negatively impact property value; it may also increase property value. A property bordering a river or stream can benefit from the gradual building up of the land, increasing the area's land mass. *Economic forces* affecting an area could include transportation, the economy or the job market. Positive economic forces raise property value, while negative economic forces decrease its value. *Social forces* are our lifestyle and choices. The level of education in a community, the size of its families, if any, what people do in their leisure time or the general age range of a community will create a desirable or undesirable location, depending on the person seeking property. *Political forces* include zoning and building codes. If zoning codes are very restrictive, they may decrease a property's utility, thus decreasing its value.

Homeowners are constantly making improvements to their homes. The addition of a swimming pool, remodeling of a bathroom, removing of carpet and installment of hardwood floors are all improvements to a home, which may contribute to the home's value. In an appraisal, the appraiser will determine if the improvements make a **contribution** to the overall value of the home, or if such improvements raise the value of the property.

Every area will experience a very scripted, predictable *life cycle*. When an area is first being developed, it will see a growth period. New houses are being constructed in a very clean and fresh neighborhood. The growth period will naturally reach an equilibrium point when it does not see any more growth. The homes are maintained; but there is no new construction. After the equilibrium, the area will experience a decline, where properties are worth less, and may be showing their age. Eventually, there will be a revitalization stage, where new homebuyers, younger buyers or investors will purchase property to fix and either sell, or live in it. Getting new, younger buyers into an area will help revitalize it.

Competition is the theory that too much competition is not good for a property's value but a healthy level will keep value high. For example, if there are more office spaces in an area than demand, the price for which an office will be rented will be less than if there were equilibrium, or if there was more demand (renters) than supply (space).

> **Factors affecting market value**
> - Supply and demand
> - Highest and best use
> - Balance
> - Conformity
> - Substitution principle
> - Anticipation
> - Progression and regression
> - Changes
> - Contribution
> - Life cycle
> - Contribution

THE APPRAISAL PROCESS

The appraisal process is done in steps. Before the appraiser can determine the value of any property, a series of questions must be identified and then answered. The appraiser will conduct research in the following order:

1. State the problem.
2. List all data needed to solve the problem and sources from which the data can be gathered.
3. Gather and verify all necessary data.
4. Determine the highest and best use of the property.
5. Make an estimation of the value of the land itself
6. Estimate the value of the property by utilizing each of the three appraisal approaches.
7. Reconcile the estimated value of the property for a final value estimation (taken from one or a combination of more than one of the appraisal methods).
8. Create the final report of the value estimate.

The first step every appraiser must take in order to know what direction their appraisal process will take is to identify the problem or identify the property to be appraised and the purpose of the appraisal. Is the appraisal for a home currently being sold? Is it for an income property being sold and then rented? Or, is it for new construction?

Value will be determined by the rights that come with a property. If a single-family home in the middle of a neighborhood was purchased with the intent to convert it into a 6-unit apartment building, and zoning laws prohibit such a conversion, the value to the buyer will be very low. However, if a family of 6 needed a larger home, and was interested in the same property because it has 6 bedrooms and lots of space, the value to the buyer will be much higher.

> **Reasons to obtain an appraisal:**
> - Determine market value for a sale
> - Determine value for a mortgage loan
> - Determine value for condemnation purposes
> - Determine value for insurance programs or premiums
> - Determine value for inheritance
> - Determine value for property taxes
> - Determine value for the IRS

The next step an appraiser must take is to list the data needed and the sources from which this data can be obtained. Upon determining what data must be collected, the appraiser must gather the data on the highest and best use of the property. The data gathered must include more than just a visual site inspection on the home. There must be data gathered for the general region, the city and the neighborhood in which the property is located. This data is considered the general data. After the general data is gathered, the appraiser must gather specific data on the site or property itself. This data includes the location of the site, the lot on which it is located and any nearby buildings. Lastly, the appraiser needs to collect data for each individual appraisal technique. This data will include sales data for similar properties, cost data, and income and expense data for similar properties.

Data To Gather:

General Data
  • National, regional, city and neighborhood data
Specific Data
  • Site, lot and buildings or improvement data
Data for each appraisal approach
  • Sales data, cost data and income and expense data

The type of property that will be appraised will determine the different types of data to be collected. For example, if the property for sale is a single-family home, data on other homes in the area may be collected. Residential or income properties, on the other hand, would require collection and analysis of different data. The appraiser in this situation may seek out data on income or expenses of similar income properties.

Data can be easily obtained through many sources. General data can be gathered through government publications, general newspapers or magazines. Regional data, such as data for an area like the San Francisco Bay area, Central Valley, or Southern California, can be gathered from regional planning commissions, government agencies or monthly bank summaries. A major component of value, after all, is determined by demand. Subsequently, the level of income or wealth of an area will determine the consumer purchasing power. This is an important component in determining value on a regional basis. Community data can be gathered from city government agencies, the Chamber of Commerce, City Planning Commissions or banks and real estate boards. Neighborhood data is gathered by conducting personal inspections. An appraiser can also consult with local real estate agents or builders. The appraiser is looking for the age and cosmetic appearance of the neighborhoods and the proximity of the community to services (such as health providers, schools, business, transportation, recreation and houses of worship). An appraiser will also note any negative influences present (such as crime and social hazards) and any physical or social influences (such as development or the possibility of future development).

A site analysis will provide the appraiser with accurate and sufficient information regarding the condition of the lot, site and structure(s) that could not otherwise be determined by conducting a search through the MLS, Chamber of Commerce, County Recorder's office or any other agency search. The appraiser can see the lot size, shape, layout and position on the block. The appraiser can also see the type and condition of the home or structure and materials, which aids in producing a much more accurate appraisal of value.

There are six different lot types, all of which play a part in determining value. The six lot types are: cul-de-sac; corner lot' interior lot; flag lot; T-intersection, and key lot. The cul-de-sac is located at the end of what is, essentially, a dead end street. The lot is pie-shaped, with the narrow section of the lot facing the street, while the back of the lot is the wide. A corner lot has a frontage facing two streets. This can be desirable for storeowners who want maximum exposure for their business.; but this may be a deterrent for homeowners, as it reduces privacy. In addition, facing two streets increases the amount of traffic noise. An interior lot is the most common type of lot, with neighbors on each side and a frontage toward the street. The flag lot physically looks like a flag on a pole. There is no frontage to the street, except for a long, narrow drive accessing the property. There is usually another lot in front of the flag lot. A T-intersection is a lot where one street dead-ends into another. Essentially, there are two streets affecting this lot; the street that dead-ends with the oncoming headlights and the street running parallel to the lot. Finally there is the key lot, which is immediately in front of the flag lot and surrounded by several back yards. It has the least amount of privacy from neighbors.

Some of the physical factors an appraiser will inspect when conducting the site inspection include; the shape of the lot; its topography; and soil conditions; corner influence; relations of the site to other properties; landscaping and other improvements; availability of public utilities; and encroachments from neighboring properties.

Property is more valuable if it is closer to the front of the lot, close to the street than if it is to the rear of the lot. The lot is divided up into quarters, with the front quarter worth 40% of the total value; the quarter immediately behind the front is worth 30% of the total value, followed by 20% and 10% of the total values, respectively. This is sometimes referred to as the 4-3-2-1 rule. This makes it clear why commercial properties prefer corner lot properties, as the frontage of a store facing the street means it will be seen more often and first among consumers .

Now that the appraiser has gathered the data, it is time to determine which appraisal method or technique to use in appraising the property. The three different appraisal techniques that an appraiser may use: the sales comparison the cost approach; and the income capitalization approach.

> **The Three Appraisal Techniques:**
> - The sales comparison approach evaluates descriptions of recently sold comparable properties
> - The cost approach analyzes building cost data
> - The income capitalization approach requires income and expense data on both the building that may be purchased as well as other comparable properties nearby

An appraiser must determine which of the three methods to use in determining the value of a given property. Not all methods are appropriate for every appraisal; but each of the methods has an important component that adds to the final appraisal value. At the end of the appraisal process, the appraiser will weigh each of the different methods and decide which one most accurately represents the value of the property in question. The appraiser will then reconcile his or her findings in the form of a *final property value.*

Location and Types of Lots

1. Cul-de-sac

A **Cul-de-sac** is sometimes known as a dead-end street. It is a street that has only one way in and the same way out. This may be desirable because of the privacy and quiet, but the lot may be oddly pie-shaped if it is on the turn-around section of the street.

2. Corner lot

A **Corner Lot** is found at the intersection of two streets. It may be desirable because of its accessibility, but may also be noisy and expensive to maintain because of the increased frontage.

3. Key lot

A **Key Lot**, so named because it resembles a key fitting into a lock, is surrounded by the back yards of other lots. It is the least desirable because of the lack of privacy.

4. T-intersection lot

A **T-Intersection Lot** is one that is fronted head-on by a street. The noise and glare from headlights may be detractors from this type of lot.

5. Interior lot

An **Interior Lot** is one that is surrounded by other lots, with a frontage on the street. It is the most common type lot and may be desirable or not, depending on other factors.

6. Flag lot

A **Flag Lot** looks like a flag on a pole. The pole represents the access to the site, which is usually located to the rear of another lot fronting a main street.

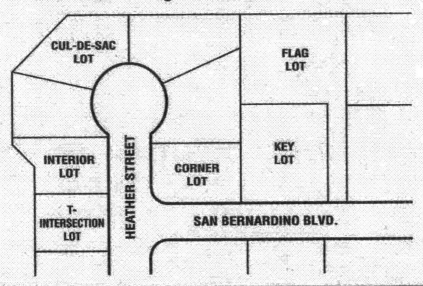

Roof Types

Dust Pan or Shed Dormer

Gable

Hip

Flat

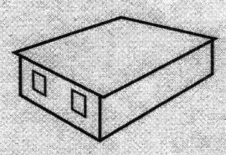

Roof Types

Single Dormers

Gambrel

Mansard

Pyramid

Cape Cod

Colonial

Contemporary

English Tudor

House Styles (continued)

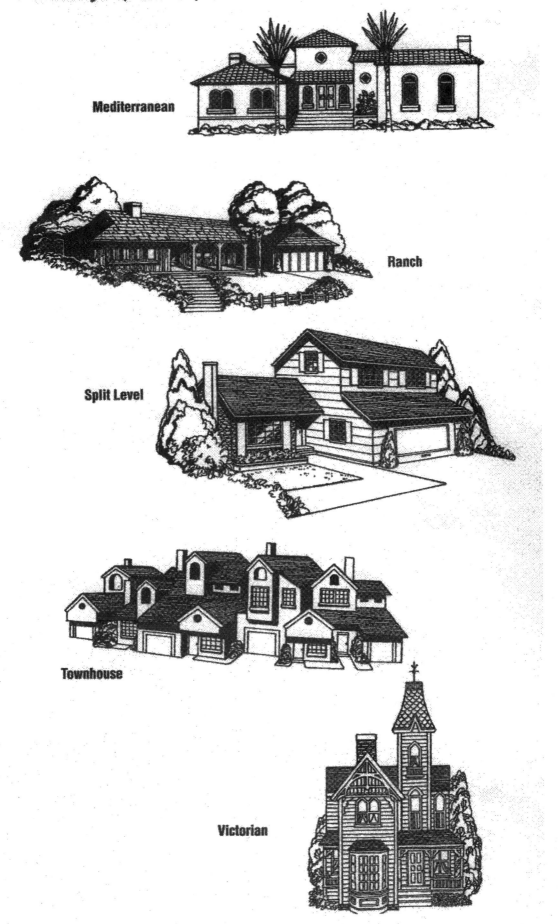

Mediterranean

Ranch

Split Level

Townhouse

Victorian

293

UNIFORM RESIDENTIAL APPRAISAL REPORT

Valuation Section   File No.

COST APPROACH

ESTIMATED SITE VALUE .... = $ 30,000

ESTIMATED REPRODUCTION COST-NEW OF IMPROVEMENTS:

Dwelling 1,950 Sq. Ft. @ $ 52 = $ 101,400

_____ Sq. Ft. @ $ =

Fence, extra insul. = 1,300

Garage/Carport 500 Sq. Ft. @ $ 15 = 7,500

Total Estimated Cost-New .... = $ 110,200

Less   Physical | Functional | External

Depreciation 10% = $ 11,020

Depreciated Value of Improvements .... = $ 99,180

"As-is" Value of Site Improvements .... = $ 3,400

INDICATED VALUE BY COST APPROACH .... = $ 132,580

Comments on Cost Approach (such as, source of cost estimate, site value, square foot calculation and, for HUD, VA and FmHA, the estimated remaining economic life of the property):

ITEM	SUBJECT	COMPARABLE NO. 1		COMPARABLE NO. 2		COMPARABLE NO. 3	
Address	4807 Catalpa	(C)		(D)		(E)	
Proximity to Subject							
Sales Price	$ N/A		$128,000		$129,500		$137,250
Price/Gross Liv. Area	$	$ 64.81		$ 66.41		$ 70.75	
Data and/or Verification Sources							
VALUE ADJUSTMENTS	DESCRIPTION	DESCRIPTION	+(-)$ Adjustment	DESCRIPTION	+(-)$ Adjustment	DESCRIPTION	+(-)$ Adjustment
Sales or Financing Concessions		Conv. mort.		Conv. mort.		Conv. mort.	
Date of Sale/Time		Current		Current		Current	
Location	Resid./Gd.	Resid./Equal		Resid./Equal		Resid./Equal	
Leasehold/Fee Simple	Fee simple	Fee simple		Fee simple		Fee simple	
Site	8,450 SF/Avg	8,450 SF/Eq		8,450 SF/Eq.		8,450 SF/Eq.	
View	Nbhd./Avg.	Nbhd./Equal		Nbhd./Equal		Nbhd./Equal	
Design and Appeal	Ranch/Good	Ranch/Equal		Ranch/Equal		Ranch/Equal	
Quality of Construction	Average	Equal		Equal		Equal	
Age	7 Yrs.	7 Yrs.		7 Yrs.		7 Yrs.	
Condition	Good	Good		Good		Good	
Above Grade Room Count	7 : 3 : 2	7 : 3 : 2		7 : 3 : 2		7 : 3 : 2	
Gross Living Area	1,950 Sq. Ft.	1,975 Sq. Ft.		1,950 Sq. Ft.		940 Sq. Ft.	
Basement & Finished Rooms Below Grade	Crawlspace	Crawlspace		Crawlspace		Finished Basement	- 7,000
Functional Utility	Good	Good		Good		Good	
Heating/Cooling	Central	Central		Central		Central	
Energy Efficient Items	Extra insul.	Extra insul.		Extra insul.		Extra insul.	
Garage/Carport	2-Car det.	2-Car det.		2-Car det.		2-car det.	
Porch, Patio, Deck, Fireplace(s), etc.	Patio, firepl.	Patio	* 2,000	Patio, firepl.		Patio, firepl.	
Fence, Pool, etc.	Fence	Fence		Fence		Fence	
Net Adj. (total)		X + - $	2,000	+ - $	-0-	+ X - $	7,000
Adjusted Sales Price of Comparable			$130,000		$129,500		$130,250

Comments on Sales Comparison (including the subject property's compatibility to the neighborhood, etc.):
The subject property conforms to the condition and quality of other property in the subject neighborhood.

ITEM	SUBJECT	COMPARABLE NO. 1	COMPARABLE NO. 2	COMPARABLE NO. 3
Date, Price and Data Source for prior sales within year of appraisal	N/A			

Analysis of any current agreement of sale, option, or listing of the subject property and analysis of any prior sales of subject and comparables within one year of the date of appraisal:

INDICATED VALUE BY SALES COMPARISON APPROACH $130,000

INDICATED VALUE BY INCOME APPROACH (If Applicable) Estimated Market Rent $ 975 /Mo. x Gross Rent Multiplier 130 = $ 126,750

This appraisal is made [X] "as is" [ ] subject to the repairs, alterations, inspections, or conditions listed below [ ] subject to completion per plans and specifications.

Conditions of Appraisal:

Final Reconciliation: Income approach value low since rents usually cover mortgage loan amount only. While reproduction cost is higher, prevailing market prices are best indicator of value.

The purpose of this appraisal is to estimate the market value of the real property that is the subject of this report, based on the above conditions and the certification, contingent and limiting conditions, and market value definition that are stated in the attached Freddie Mac Form 439/Fannie Mae Form 1004B (Revised 6/93).

I (WE) ESTIMATE THE MARKET VALUE, AS DEFINED, OF THE REAL PROPERTY THAT IS THE SUBJECT OF THIS REPORT, AS OF _____ (WHICH IS THE DATE OF INSPECTION AND THE EFFECTIVE DATE OF THIS REPORT) TO BE $ 130,000

APPRAISER:

Signature _Aria Appraiser_

Name ARIA APPRAISER

Date Report Signed 12-17-XXXX

State Certification # _____ State ____

Or State License # _____ State ____

SUPERVISORY APPRAISER (ONLY IF REQUIRED):

Signature _____

Name _____

Date Report Signed _____

State Certification # _____ State ____

Or State License # _____ State ____

[ ] Did [ ] Did Not Inspect Property

Freddie Mac Form 70   6-93   10 CH.   PAGE 2 OF 2   Fannie Mae Form 1004 6-93

U.S. Forms, Inc. 1-800-225-9583   USF# 00110

UNIFORM RESIDENTIAL APPRAISAL REPORT File No.

Property Address 4807 Catalpa Road **City** Woodview **State** CA **Zip Code** 90000
Legal Description Attached **County** Delta
Assessor's Parcel No. 6412-028-007 **Tax Year** XXXX **R.E. Taxes $** Prop. 13 **Special Assessments $** 465
Borrower **Current Owner** **Occupant** ☐ Owner ☐ Tenant ☐ Vacant
Property rights appraised ☒ Fee Simple ☐ Leasehold **Project Type** ☐ PUD ☐ Condominium (HUD/VA only) HOA$ /Mo.
Neighborhood or Project Name Forest Glen **Map Reference** **Census Tract**
Sales Price $ **Date of Sale** Description and $ amount of loan charges/concessions to be paid by seller
Lender/Client **Address**
Appraiser **Address**

Location	Urban	Suburban ☒	Rural	Predominant occupancy	Single family housing PRICE $(000) AGE (yrs)	Present land use %	Land use change
Built up	Over 75% ☒	25-75%	Under 25%	Owner ☒	90 Low 7	One family 100%	Not likely ☒ Likely
Growth rate	Rapid	Stable ☒	Slow	Tenant	120 High 7	2-4 family	In process
Property values	Increasing ☒	Stable	Declining	Vacant (0-5%)	Predominant	Multi-family	To:
Demand/supply	Shortage ☒	In balance	Over supply	Vacant (over 5%)	110 7	Commercial	
Marketing time	Under 3 mos. ☒	3-6 mos.	Over 6 mos.			( )	

Note: Race and the racial composition of the neighborhood are not appraisal factors.

Neighborhood boundaries and characteristics: The Forest Glen neighborhood is bounded on the east by the Village of Willow; south, 40th Street; west, Grand Street; north, Park District land.

Factors that affect the marketability of the properties in the neighborhood (proximity to employment and amenities, employment stability, appeal to market, etc.): The City of Woodview has remained attractive to newcomers from in-state and out-of-state because of its proximity to Bay City and diversity of employment opportunities. Houses in the price range offered by Forest Glen have benefitted from their relative affordability in the greater metropolitan area.

Market conditions in the subject neighborhood (including support for the above conclusions related to the trend of property values, demand/supply, and marketing time -- such as data on competitive properties for sale in the neighborhood, description of the prevalence of sales and financing concessions, etc.): The market is stable, with property values slowly but steadily increasing. Typical financing is the conventional mortgage, at interest rates from 7 to 8-1/4%, with as much as 95% of purchase price financed. Financing concessions are unusual.

Project Information for PUDs (if applicable) -- Is the developer/builder in control of the Home Owners' Association (HOA)? ☐ Yes ☐ No
Approximate total number of units in the subject project _____ Approximate total number of units for sale in the subject project _____
Describe common elements and recreational facilities:

Dimensions 65' x 130'	**Topography**	Level
Site area 8,450 sq. ft.	**Size**	8,450 SF/Typical
Corner Lot ☐ Yes ☒ No	**Shape**	Rectangular
Specific zoning classification and description R-2, Single-Family residential	**Drainage**	Appears adequate
Zoning compliance ☒ Legal ☐ Legal nonconforming (Grandfathered use) ☐ Illegal ☐ No zoning	**View**	Neighborhood
Highest & best use as improved ☒ Present use ☐ Other use (explain)	**Landscaping**	Average

Utilities	Public	Other	Off-site Improvements	Type	Public	Private	
Electricity	☒		Street	Asphalt	☒		Driveway Surface Asphalt
Gas	☒		Curb/gutter	Concrete	☒		Apparent easements Utilities
Water	☒		Sidewalk	Concrete	☒		FEMA Special Flood Hazard Area ☐ Yes ☒ No
Sanitary sewer	☒		Street lights		☒		FEMA Zone ___ Map Date ___
Storm sewer	☒		Alley				FEMA Map No. ___

Comments (apparent adverse easements, encroachments, special assessments, slide areas, illegal or legal nonconforming zoning use, etc.): Underground electric and telephone lines; no other easements or encroachments evident.

GENERAL DESCRIPTION	EXTERIOR DESCRIPTION	FOUNDATION	BASEMENT	INSULATION
No. of Units 1	Foundation Concrete	Slab	Area Sq. Ft.	Roof
No. of Stories 1	Exterior Walls Stucco	Crawl Space Conc. walls	% Finished	Ceiling 6" ☒
Type (Det./Att.) Detached	Roof Surface Asph. Shingle	Basement	Ceiling	Walls 6" ☒
Design (Style) Ranch	Gutters & Dwnspts. Galv./paint	Sump Pump	Walls	Floor
Existing/Proposed Existing	Window Type Aluminum	Dampness	Floor	None
Age (Yrs.) 7	Storm/Screens Aluminum	Settlement	Outside Entry	Unknown
Effective Age (Yrs.)	Manufactured House	Infestation		

ROOMS	Foyer	Living	Dining	Kitchen	Den	Family Rm.	Rec. Rm.	Bedrooms	# Baths	Laundry	Other	Area Sq. Ft.
Basement												
Level 1		1	1	1		1		3	2		6 clos	
Level 2												

Finished area above grade contains: 7 Rooms 3 Bedroom(s) 2 Bath(s) 1,950 Square Feet of Gross Living Area

INTERIOR Materials/Condition	HEATING	KITCHEN EQUIP.	ATTIC	AMENITIES	CAR STORAGE
Floors Vinyl/cpt/oak/Avg.	Type FA	Refrigerator ☒	None	Fireplace(s) # 1	None
Walls Dryw/paint/paper/Ag	Fuel Gas	Range/Oven ☒	Stairs	Patio	Garage # of cars
Trim/Finish Pine/Avg.	Condition Very good	Disposal ☒	Drop Stair ☒	Deck	Attached
Bath Floor Ceramic/Avg.	COOLING	Dishwasher ☒	Scuttle	Porch	Detached 2
Bath Wainscot Ceramic/Avg.	Central Yes	Fan/Hood ☒	Floor	Fence Rear	Built-in
Doors	Other	Microwave	Heated	Pool	Carport
	Condition Good	Washer/Dryer	Finished		Driveway Asphalt

Additional features (special energy efficient items, etc.): 6" insulation above ceiling and behind drywall

Condition of the improvements, depreciation (physical, functional, and external), repairs needed, quality of construction, remodeling/additions, etc.: The subject shows evidence of normal wear and tear only. Physical deterioration is estimated at 10%, with no sign of functional or external obsolescence. Overall property condition is good.

Adverse environmental conditions (such as, but not limited to, hazardous wastes, toxic substances, etc.) present in the improvements, on the site, or in the immediate vicinity of the subject property: No adverse conditions on or near the property were noted by the appraiser during a routine property inspection.

Freddie Mac Form 70 6-93 10-CA PAGE 1 OF 2 Fannie Mae Form 1004 6-93

Sales Comparison Approach

The sales comparison approach is not only the easiest appraisal technique; it is also the most widely used, most appropriate method for arriving at the value of residential property. The sales comparison approach is referred to as the market data approach, the market comparison approach or the paired sales approach.

The basis of the sales comparison approach is the principle of substitution. An appraiser will find several recently sold properties with comparable characteristics to the home being appraised. These homes must offer comparable amenities to the property in question and must have been sold within the past six months. Basic qualities to look for in a comparable property are: location; square footage; number of bedroom;, number of bathrooms; number of other rooms such as formal dining room or entertaining space; age of the home; its architectural style; and the financing terms of the nearby properties.

An appraiser will then analyze each of the individual sales, to determine what differences, if any, exist between the properties. The appraiser must make the necessary adjustments based on those differences. An adjustment is the addition or subtraction of value on the property being appraised. If there are similar properties that have been sold after the six months prior to the appraisal of the subject property, the appraiser may allow for an adjustment for this as well. It is important to understand when it is appropriate to add value, and when it is appropriate to subtract value. If the subject property has additional features or amenities not shared by the comparable property value must be added to the adjustment portion of the equation. If the comparable property has features or amenities not present in the subject property, value will be subtracted from the adjustments.

Once the appraiser has analyzed all of the individual comparable properties, he or she will make a determination of value of the subject property. This process if you think in terms of a mathematical equation, which would look like this:

Sales Price of Similar Properties   +/-   Adjustments   =   Subject Property Value

Example
Several properties in the Smith's neighborhood have sold within the past 3 months, and now the Smiths plan on selling their home. An appraiser has determined that the home next door is comparable to the Smith's own home. This home sold for $320,000. The Smith's home has the same number of bedrooms and bathrooms, same size entertaining space for company and is roughly the same square footage as the neighboring property. The only difference is that the Smith's home has a heated pool in the back yard, whereas the neighboring home did not. The appraiser determines that the heated pool adds an additional $11,000 to the Smith's property and determines the appropriate value for the Smith's home, using the following equation:

$320,000 + $11,000 = $331,000.

The adjusted price of the neighboring property is $331,000, which is the most accurate estimate of what the Smith's home is worth.

An appraiser is able to make adjustments for most situations. However, there is one scenario for which it is nearly impossible to make an adjustment. If the comparable home's transaction was not an arms-length transaction, it would be impossible to make an adjustment. An arms-length transaction is when the home is being sold by a willing seller, purchased by a willing buyer. If the property was sold under any other circumstances, such as a divorce or foreclosure sale, the sale price may not represent what the home could bring in an open market. Thus, an appraiser would have a hard time making an adjustment for such an issue.

As a real estate agent you have a very important tools at your disposal, your own records. No doubt, through your office, there will be a history of homes sold in the same neighborhood as one of your listings. So, a quick search of office records will give you a good place to begin an appraisal of your new listing. Additionally, if you are an independent broker and do not have records of any other properties sold in a specific neighborhood, you can always use other resources close at hand. The MLS system, for example, will provide very helpful information regarding similar properties in the same neighborhood. You may also check with the county recorder's office for any recently-recorded transactions.

Practice Problem:

You are to determine the market value of your home.
Your home is a two-story brick home with 4 bedrooms, three bathrooms, a formal living room, family room, formal dining room, eat in kitchen and detached 3-car garage. You have recently replaced all appliances but will still offer a warranty to the buyer for all major mechanical issues on these appliances. All homes to which you will compare your own are 2-story brick homes, with similar rooms and cosmetic appeal on the outside.

Differences in homes:

The dark-colored brick home only has 2.5 bathrooms.
The light-colored brick home has a fire place in the master bedroom
The grey-colored brick home is being offered without a home warranty.

It is determined that the extra half bath your home has is worth $4,300; the fireplace in the master bedroom is worth $3,300; and the home warranty is worth $750.

The dark-colored brick home sold for $300,000; the light- colored brick home sold for $315,000; and the grey-colored brick home was sold for $305,000.

Complete the chart based on the given information.

	Dark colored brick	Light colored brick	Grey colored brick
Sales Price	$300,000	$315,000	$305,000
Adjustment Variables			
Half Bath			
Fireplace			
Home Warranty			
Total Adjustments			
Adjusted Value			

Agents who are not appraisers can offer a competitive market analysis to their client in order to assist their client in selling their home. One major difference between the competitive market analysis and an appraisal is that the competitive market analysis does not include the agent's opinion of value. An agent can assist the buyer or seller in determining the fair market value of a property, but will not assign a specific value to that property *per se*. The most important source of information for a competitive market analysis is the MLS. The MLS will list properties that are currently available, properties, which have just been sold and properties that were previously listed but not sold. The MLS will also provide details such as the number of days a property has been on the market, its neighborhood, its amenities and other important features when.

A competitive market analysis will aid the seller in determining a fair asking price for the given market. An MLS history may indicate the number of days a certain priced property lasted on the market. A higher price property may take longer to sell, while a more competitively priced property may be sold in a very short amount of time. The buyer can benefit from this analysis as well, as he or she may get an idea of what price offer to make, as well as the chance of having the offer accepted.

Cost Approach

In the cost approach, the appraiser looks at two factors: the cost for reproducing the subject property; and the value of the land. When determining the final property value, the accrued depreciation must also be taken into account. The mathematical equation of the cost approach might look like this:

Cost to Build A New Structure – Accrued Depreciation + Land Value = Property Value

The cost to rebuild a new structure in the same style as the old is called the *reproduction cost*. In a reproduction cost, the builder will use the same design as well as the same materials as were used in the original structure, so, if we want to determine the cost of reproducing a 100-year old structure, the new structure must be identical to the old, and use the same materials in its build. The replacement cost is similar to the reproduction cost, except the replacement cost factors in the use of modern materials, design and building methods. The replacement structure will not have identical specifications as the one it is replacing, but will be similar.

The reproduction or replacement cost can be determined by four different methods:

- Square-foot method
- Quantity-survey method
- Unit-in-place cost method
- Index method

The *square foot method* estimates the cost of construction to replace a structure. It is the most common method used, and is simple to calculate. The square footage of the building in question will be compared to other structures with the same square footage. The cost per square foot will be used to determine the cost of the subject building. The cubic- foot method may also be used. In this method, the height of the building will also be taken into account.

The *quantity survey* method estimates all labor and materials, which go into the construction of the property. Very specific items such as overhead, insurance, contractor's profit and other direct costs will be added into the cost. This is an uncommon method in determining the replacement cost, as it is very time-consuming.

The *unit-in-place cost method* takes into account the different costs for various components of a building and then adds them all together. For example, the cost of the walls, heating or air conditioning units and flooring are all calculated on a square footage basis and added together to determine the replacement cost. This is the most detailed method of estimating value; but it is time consuming and sometimes impractical.

The *index method* is relatively simple. The appraiser takes the cost of the original building and multiplies that number by a factor that represents the increase or decrease in building expenses. This will determine the change in costs from area to area and from time period to time period.

Land value is determined through the sales comparison approach. An appraiser can consult the county recorder, to see land values for similar lots in the neighborhood.

The appraisal procedure will basically follow the equation above. First the land value will be estimated based on the comparable land sales (or the sales comparison approach). Second, the appraiser will determine the cost of existing buildings, based on a replacement or reproduction basis. After the value of the buildings has been determined if going to be rebuild, the amount of accrued depreciation will be estimated. This depreciation is taken on all improvements to the lot; the lot itself will not depreciate. Next, an appraiser subtracts the accrued depreciation from the replacement cost of the buildings to estimate the depreciated value of the structures. Finally, the estimated depreciated value for the structures is added to the land value. This number is the appraiser's opinion of the estimated value of the property.

The cost method assumes that the property is already being used for the highest and best use possible. This means that the property is very specialized, and most likely would not be considered for any other use. For example, an investor who is looking to buy property for office space would most likely not purchase a school or hospital. In the event that a school or hospital was being sold, the new owner would most likely continue using the structure in its intended manner.

Remember!
The cost method assumes that structures are already being used for the highest and best use possible, and are most likely highly specialized (or very specific purpose) buildings or properties.

Depreciation is the loss in value regardless to any cause. Depreciation can be to the result of deterioration of the structure (because the technology is old and may not be effective). It usually represents the estimate between the current cost of replacement of the entire structure and the estimated value of the existing structure. There are three main types of depreciation, which are listed and explained below:

Types of Depreciation
- Physical Depreciation may result from wear and tear or negligence. Natural factors, such as termites rot or weather may also add to the physical depreciation. This type of depreciation may or may not be correctable.
- Functional Obsolescence refers to the actual function of a structure. Poor design, style or out-of-date equipment (as well as changes of style, advancements of technology and utility demand) will con tribute to the functional obsolescence of a structure. Depending on the severity, this type of depreciation may or may not be correctable.
- Economic Obsolescence refers to depreciation due to outside forces acting on the structure. Social and economic forces can create this type of depreciation. Zoning changes, oversupply of property, decreased demand; recession or governmental restrictions will also create this type of depreciation, which is usually not correctable.

Depreciation is generally computed in one of two ways: straight-line and observed condition methods.

The straight-line depreciation method allows a certain value of depreciation to be subtracted on a yearly basis, and that number will stay constant for the life of the structure. This method is perhaps the simplest deduction of depreciation to understand.

Every building has an economic life, which is the period of time, measured in years that the building can be used for its intended purpose. The value of the building is divided by this economic life, and the resulting figure will be the amount of depreciation, which can be deducted each year. There are situations, however, where the building is maintained exceptionally well, or the technological advancements were well ahead of their time. Thus, the effective age is now longer than the estimated calendar age of the property. If the economic life is estimated at 35 years, the actual effective age may be 40 years.

Example
The effective age of a building is 35 years, while the cost to build that structure was $200,000. What is the depreciation per year on the building?

$200,000 / 35 years = $5,714.29 per year

The observed condition depreciation method requires an appraiser to deduct a loss of value for each individual depreciable item. This will not take into account those items that are curable or incurable.

Curable items are damages or problems that can be economically cured. If there is damage to a building that is not economically feasible to cure, it is considered incurable. Minor earthquake damage or other such problems, are certainly curable, while economic obsolescence is generally incurable.

An appraiser will figure the entire amount of depreciation on a building, based on three depreciation factors, and add them together. Once the physical, functional and economic obsolescence have been added together, that number is then subtracted from the reproduction cost to find the total value of the building or structure.

Income Capitalization Approach
The income capitalization approach requires the appraiser to first break down the appraisal process and determine the property's potential gross income. When determining the potential gross income of a property, the appraiser must add all sources of income for the property. For example, this income may come from rents, money collected from any vending or laundry machines, or other revenue producing sources.

Next an appraiser needs to estimate the property's market rent, which is similar to the market price of a property for sale. It represents the amount of rent the property is capable of generating in an open market. Rent received for the property is referred to as contract rent, which is usually not the same dollar amount as the market rent.

The appraiser must also figure in the vacancy and collection losses. This loss is figured because not every unit in a building is full at all times. There is also the possibility that some tenants will be late on their monthly payment. The appraiser must estimate any anticipated losses on one of these forms, and subtract this amount from the gross income to arrive at the effective gross income of the property.

Taking it one step further, operating expenses are subtracted from the effective gross income. The resulting number is the net operating income. A capitalization rate is then applied to the net operating income, to arrive at an estimate of market value for the building. The capitalization rate (cap rate) is the property owner's annual expected rate of return. This cap rate can be represented as the relationship between the net operating income from the property and the property's market value. The mathematical equation might look like this:

Net Operating Income / Value = Capitalization Rate

And

Capitalization Rate x Value = Net Operating Income

And

Net Operating Income / Capitalization Rate = Value

The income capitalization approach appears quite complicated, and certainly requires a lot of data before a property value can be estimated. There are certainly other situations where a property may not have been purchased as an income property, but ends up as such. For example, a single-family residence may have been originally purchased with the original intention of occupying a family. However, when the family learns they are being transferred to another state due to job responsibilities, they decide to remain owners of the home, and rent it out to another single family. In this case, a less complicated method (called the gross income multiplier) of determining value may be used. This value is determined by the sale prices of similar properties being rented. We divide the sales price of the similar property by the amount of rent it produces to arrive at the gross income multiplier. The mathematical equation might look like this:

Sales Price / Gross Income = Gross Income Multiplier

An appraiser should compare several properties to determine the most appropriate multiplier for the subject property. The actual property value of the subject property will be determined by multiplying the gross income multiplier by the projected income expected. That mathematical equation might look like this:

Gross Income x Gross Income Multiplier = Market Value

It is important to note that while the gross income multiplier is simple to understand and use, it fails to take into account all variables that the income capitalization rate will cover.

RECONCILIATION

The final step for in an appraisal is the appraisal report. The appraiser examines the values from each of the appraisal methods and determines which value is most appropriate for the property being appraised. Different properties benefit from different appraisal methods. To review, in general, single-family dwellings will most likely utilize the market comparison approach. New or specialized buildings will most likely use the cost approach, while rental properties (whether industrial, commercial or residential) will most likely use the income approach.

Once this value is determined, the appraiser will prepare the final report. An appraiser can report his or her opinion of value in one of three ways: through letterform; through short form; or through narrative.

The Letter form report contains: a brief description of the property in question; the type of value sought; the purpose of conducting the appraisal; the date on which the value was assigned; the final opinion of value; and the appraiser's signature. This type of report is generally used when the client is familiar with the area and does not need a lot of supporting information or data regarding the area.

A check sheet between two and eight pages is called the short form report. It is a very brief report that includes all necessary or important information regarding the property.

The narrative report is a very extensive and detailed report. All of the information included in the short form report and the letterform is included in the narrative report. This is in addition to computations, the reasons for those computations, value inclusions, maps, photographs, charts and plot plans. This type of report is prepared for those clients who are not familiar with an area or for court cases in which a detailed amount of data is required.

The appraisal report should contain the final conclusion of value, the date the value was assigned to the property, the date the report was prepared, a description of the property (whether a brief or extensive description), information on the city and neighborhood, a description of the appraisal method used to arrive at the final value, certification, and signature of the appraiser.

OBTAINING AN APPRAISAL LICENSE

Appraisers in the state of California must be licensed if they are to appraise properties that will be financed or guaranteed through federal or federally-sponsored programs. This means that persons utilizing an FHA loan, veterans using a VA or Cal-Vet loan, or persons using banks that are federally insured or backed must use a licensed appraiser when getting an appraisal on the property in which they are interested. Every licensed appraiser must take an approved, continuing education class every four years, to keep their license current and valid. It is important to note that banks require an appraisal of a property for funding purposes. So, whether an appraiser is licensed or not, an appraisal is usually necessary before a bank will fund a loan.

Appraisers may work for themselves, for an appraisal company or a bank, for a mortgage company; or for another financial institution that issues and funds loans. A fee appraiser is an appraiser who is independently employed and charges a fee to appraise a property. This appraisal amount will be the fee appraiser's opinion of the property's value. Other types of appraisers must also be licensed. An appraiser working for a bank, mortgage company, or other financial institution, will need to be licensed, as the bank will fund federally-sponsored loans or federally guaranteed loans. Appraisers working for a bank, mortgage company, financial institution, or on staff at an appraisal firm will be considered employees of those organizations, not as independently employed persons.

There are three types of appraisal licenses: a licensed appraiser; certified residential appraiser; and certified general appraiser.

A licensed appraiser can appraise a residential property consisting of one to four units up to a value of $1 million (if appraising a non-complex property) and up to $250,000 (if appraising a complex property or non-residential property).

Certified residential appraisers may also appraise residential units consisting of one to four units. However, there is no dollar value or complexity limit on the properties they can appraise. A certified residential appraiser may appraise non-residential properties valued up to $250,000.

Certified general appraisers may appraise any property, regardless of complexity, dollar amount or property type.

Three types of appraisers
- Licensed appraiser
- Certified residential appraiser
- General appraiser

More information can be obtained by visiting the website
http://howeappraisal.com/bhh2.html

S U M M A R Y

Appraisals are necessary for all real estate transactions, and it is important for the appraiser to be as accurate in their estimation as possible. Accuracy is likely when an appraiser utilizes all the tools available when analyzing a property. Appraisals are also important for other reasons, such as determining the tax base for a region, for insurance premiums or for determining the best and highest use of property.

Appraisers are in search of the market value of property. The way market value is determined is by weighing demand for the property, utility the property can provide, scarcity of the specific type of property, and transferability of the property. Appraisers can make their recommendation on a property's value on the day they inspect the property or on any day before that one. However, an appraiser cannot predict or forecast the value of a property in the future.

Appraisers have several factors or principles they must analyze, or take into account when making an appraisal. There will be several forces, constantly changing, which determine the value of a property at a given moment. Ignoring any one of these factors, or forgetting to factor it into the final equation, may yield an incorrect value estimate.

Appraisers can use the comparison approach, cost approach or income capitalization approach when determining the value of a property. Each approach is appropriate for specific appraisals. So, not all methods will work for every appraisal situation. The appraiser needs to determine the reason for the appraisal, and then utilize the necessary appraisal approach. Generally speaking, the sales comparison approach is the best method when finding the value for residential property, the cost approach is useful for new construction and the income capitalization approach is appropriate to use when determining the value of income or commercial property.

There are three different types of appraisers. Some appraisers are more restricted than others in their expertise or types of properties they are able to evaluate. Appraisers who are dealing with federally-backed or funded loans must be licensed, though this is not the case for independent appraisers who are not appraising a property for a federally backed loan.

T E R M S   A N D   P H R A S E S

Accrued – An amount that accumulates over time.

Accrued Depreciation – The difference between the cost to replace a property and that property's current appraised value.

Actual Age – The real age of a building.

Actual Depreciation – Depreciation that occurs as a result of physical, functional or economic forces

Anticipation – The principle that a property will offer future benefits, which tend to increase the present value of the property.

Appraisal – A person's opinion of how much a property is worth, supported by factual data, collected for a specific date in time.

Appraisal Report – A formal, written report, stating an appraiser's estimate of a property's value.

Appreciation – A property's increase in value over time, resulting in equity.

Balance – A principle that combines different land uses that will result in the highest overall value of a property

Book Depreciation – Accounting principle referring to an allowance a homeowner can take to recover invested capital in a home.

Book Value – The cost of a property when it was purchased plus any improvements made, minus any depreciation, which has accrued.

Capital Improvements – Improvements made to property to increase the useful life of the property or increase the property's value.

Capitalization – A process of calculating the present worth of a property on the basis of its capacity to continue to produce an income stream.

Capitalization Rate – The rate of interest considered a reasonable return on an investment, used in the process of determining value based on net operating income; the yield necessary to attract investment. Capitalization rate is also referred to as the cap rate.

Competitive Market Analysis – An informal estimate of market value, performed by a real estate agent usually for the buyer or the seller, utilizing the sales history of nearby properties and usually expressed in a range of the possible market values for the property.

Comps – A term used in the real estate profession by both appraisers and real estate agents to refer to two properties that are similar or comparable.

Conformity – A real estate principle that states that buildings or home values will be highest when all properties, buildings or homes in the area are similar in construction, age and materials used.

Contract Rent – The amount of rent agreed to by a tenant and landlord.

Contribution – A principle determining that a feature or item is valued in proportion to its total contribution to the overall value of the property, not by its cost alone.

Corner Lot – Property at the intersection of two streets with neighbors only on one or two sides of the property (versus neighbors on three or four sides of the property).

Cost – The amount of money that must be spent to obtain materials and labor; the measure of something given up or sacrificed to obtain something else.

Cost Approach – A method of appraising property in which value is assigned based on the present day cost of replacing all buildings or structures on the property, less any depreciation.

Cul-De-Sac – A name commonly referred to dead-end streets.

Deferred Maintenance – Failure of a building owner or supervisor to properly maintain the structure.

Demand – Economic concept measuring the consumer's desire to obtain goods or services.

Depreciation – Loss in value.

Economic Life – The period of time over which an improved property will yield a return on investment in the form of rent or usefulness.

Effective Age – The actual cosmetic appearance of a building or structure based on its use, rather than its actual chronological age.

Effective Gross Income – The actual income from all sources, less any collectable losses or vacancies.

External Obsolescence – A property's loss in value due to outside causes, whether economic or environmental.

Fair Market Value – The price a property would receive if it was offered in an open real estate market with both a willing buyer and seller ready to make the appropriate transaction.

Federally Related Transaction – Any transaction, loan or other financial course of action involving a bank, lending institution or other financial organization that is federally-insured or backed in some way.

Flag Lot – A lot that does not have a side facing the street (with the exception of an access drive). The lot literally looks like a flag on a pole as the narrow access drive forms the pole portion (with the flag portion representing the actual lot itself).

Front Footage – The width of a property facing the street.

Gross Rent – Income received from a rental unit before any expenses are figured or deducted from the total amount.

Highest and Best Use – The best way to use property to gain the most profit, the best legal use of property or the most physically feasible use of property to maximize its potential.

Improvements – Any fixtures, buildings or structures added to a lot.

Income Capitalization Approach – An appraisal method where the net operating income of property is divided by its expected rate of return (capitalization rate) to arrive at an estimate of market value.

Index Method – A method of estimating building reproduction costs by multiplying the original cost of the building by a factor that represents the percentage change in construction costs from the time of construction to the time of valuation.

Interior Lot – A lot surrounded by properties on both sides, with one side with its frontage to the street.

Market Rent – The amount of rent a property should bring in if being offered in an open market.

Market Value – The highest amount of money a property would bring in if being offered in an at-arms-length transaction in an open market.

Net Income – The amount of income that remains after all operating expenses have been subtracted from the gross income.

Observed Condition Method – Method whereby depreciation is calculated by estimating the loss in each individual structure

Physical Deterioration – The loss of property value by physical wear and tear on a structure.

Plottage (Assemblage) – Combining multiple plots of land, under one ownership to increase the total value of the combined lots

Potential Gross Income – The maximum amount of income a property is capable of generating

Price – The amount of money paid for a desired good or service.

Progression – The idea that a building or home of lesser value has its value increased by being near or next to a building(s) or home(s) of higher value.

Quantity Survey Method – One way of estimating building reproduction by making an accurate itemization of all construction costs through the addition of both direct costs (raw materials and labor) and indirect costs (such as permits, overhead or profits).

Reconciliation – An appraisal method analyzing the appraisal value figured by each of the three appraisal methods to arrive at the market value of a property.

Regression – The idea that a building or home's value will decline if the building(s) or home(s) around it are of lesser value.

Replacement Cost – The cost of replacing buildings using current prices, materials and labor.

Reproduction Cost – The cost of reproducing a building to make it look as it would from a previous time period, using similar building materials and methods but current prices.

Revitalization – The act of new buyers moving into a run-down or impoverished area, and fixing up homes and buildings.

Sales Comparison Approach – An appraisal method in which the sale prices of comparable structures are analyzed and adjusted to reflect differences between the comparables and the subject property. This can also be referred to as the market data approach.

Scarcity – Property that is named in a written document as collateral to secure a loan.

Site – The geographical positioning of a lot or parcel of land in a neighborhood.

Site Value – The value for a specific lot of parcel of land as it is positioned in a neighborhood.

Square Foot Method – An appraisal tool for figuring the reproduction cost of a structure by multiplying the current cost per square foot of a comparable building and comparing that to the number of square feet in the subject building.

Straight Line Method – Depreciating a building or structure at a steady rate over the life of the structure.

Substitution – The present cost of acquiring an equally valuable property compared to constructing a new building.

Supply and Demand – The economic principle outlining the amount of goods and services available compared to the consumer's desire to obtain those goods and services. Generally speaking, the scarcer a good or service, the higher the demand will be; thus dictating a higher premium or price. The opposite is true for goods or services with low scarcity.

T-Intersection – A lot that is situated at the end of a street, which will not continue as a through street. The physical shape of the two streets forms a "T". Headlights and traffic noise may become problematic for such a property location, particularly for private property, such as a home.

Transferability – The ease with which a property may be transferred from one owner to another; used to determine value. High transfer = high value

Utility Value – The usefulness of a property to a potential or current owner.

Unit-In-Place Method – A way to estimate a building's reproduction cost by adding the construction cost per unit of measure of each of the separate parts of the subject property. Adding each of the separate parts to construct yields the total unit-in-place method.

Utility Value – The usefulness of a particular property to a potential or current owner.

Vacancy Factor – The percentage of a building's square footage that remains unrented over a period of time.

Value – The amount of one good or service that must be traded to obtain another good or service of equal usefulness or benefit

C H A P T E R   Q U I Z

1. Which one of the following is not considered a reason for obtaining an appraisal of property?
    A. Taxation
    B. Insurance
    C. Financing and credit
    D. Fair market value

2. Which best describes the appraisal process?
    A. Appraisal is a mathematical science by which the appraiser determines the exact dollar amount a property is worth.
    B. Appraisal is the process by which the appraiser arrives at an estimate of the property's present worth.
    C. Appraisal is the process by which the appraiser arrives at the exact worth of a property.
    D. None of the above.

3. There are certain types of sales that would not determine, or represent, the fair market value of a property. Which one of the following is NOT one of these special circumstances?
    A. Death
    B. Divorce
    C. Cash Sale
    D. Bankruptcy

4. Which one of the following terms best describes the statement "the price a property would bring if freely offered in an open market with both a willing buyer and seller?"
    A. Market value
    B. Utility value
    C. Market price
    D. Objective value

5. The amount of money for which a property actually sold is
    A. Market value
    B. Utility value
    C. Market price
    D. Objective value

6. Which of the following is not a necessary element of value?
    A. Price
    B. Cost
    C. Both A and B
    D. Neither A nor B

7. Which one of the following is NOT one of the forces affecting value of property?
    A. Economic influences
    B. Political regulations
    C. Environmental and physical conditions
    D. Scarcity

8. The desirability of having a south or west-facing front describes which of the following factors?
    A. Exposure
    B. Corner influence
    C. Shape
    D. Location

9. A development where all homes are constructed with similar architectural style, of similar age and built from similar materials (e.g., all brick, or all adobe style) keeping the value of the homes high, best describes the principle of
    A. Contribution
    B. Conformity
    C. Balance
    D. Highest and best use

10. Which of the following characteristics does NOT determine a property's highest and best use?
    A. Most profitable use
    B. Physical possible
    C. Regression
    D. Legally permissible

11. Which one of the following factors is not a factor affecting the market value of property?
    A. Age of home
    B. Anticipation
    C. Supply and demand
    D. Conformity

12. Which of the following is NOT one of the three appraisal techniques used to determine the value of a property?
    A. Sales comparison approach
    B. Cost approach
    C. Square foot method
    D. Income capitalization approach

13. An appraiser must gather which of the following types of data when arriving at the value of a property?
   A. Regional
   B. City
   C. Neighborhood
   D. All of the above

14. An appraiser is required to take continuing education classes every
   A. 1 Year.
   B. 2 years.
   C. 3 years.
   D. 4 years.

15. The sales comparison approach is based on what factors?
   A. Sales of other homes in the neighborhood
   B. Cost of replacing the home
   C. Cost of building a new home
   D. None of these

16. Which of the following is considered physical deterioration? :
   A Termite damage
   B. Damage from severe weather
   C. Damage from normal wear and tear
   D. All of the above.

17. Which one of the following is NOT an appraisal report form?
   A. Short form
   B. Final conclusion
   C. Letter form
   D. Narrative

18. When is the cost approach most appropriately used in appraising a property's value?
   A. When determining the value of a new structure or very specialized structure, such as a church or hospital.
   B. When determining the value of a single-family dwelling.
   C. When determining the value of an income property.
   D. None of the above.

19. Of the four methods used to estimate the cost of a new building, which is the most detailed account of the value? :
   A. Square-foot method
   B. Index method
   C. Unit-in-place cost method
   D. Quantity survey method

20. What are the two methods of computing depreciation?
   A. Straight line and effective age
   B. Observed condition and economic life
   C. Economic life and straight line
   D. Straight line and observed condition.

CHAPTER

REAL ESTATE TAXATION

What you will learn in this Chapter

- Real and Personal Property Taxes

- Property Tax Collection

- Federal and State Income Taxes

- Foreign Investments in Real Property Tax Act (FIRPTA)

- Documentary Transfer Tax

- Estate, Inheritance and Gift Taxes

1. How many days after a transfer has been recorded does a person buying property have to file the Change in Ownership Statement with the county recorder or assessor?
   A. 30 days
   B. 45 days
   C. 60 days
   D. 75 days

2. Under Proposition 13, how is the new tax base established when property is transferred from the seller to the buyer?
   A. The new assessment is 2% more than the previous year's tax base.
   B. The new assessment is 1% of the sales price of the property.
   C. The new assessment will remain the same as the previous year's tax base.
   D. The new tax base will be based on the home's value from 1978.

3. Which dollar amount from the sale of a home will allow a foreign investor an exemption from the 10% federal withholding requirement?
   A. $100,000
   B. $200,000
   C. $300,000
   D. $400,000

4. How much of an exemption of taxable gain is a married couple allowed to take on the sale of their primary residence?
   A. $125,000
   B. $250,000
   C. $300,000
   D. $500,000

5. What kind of property does not qualify for a tax-deferred exchange?
   A. Personal residence
   B. Apartment complex
   C. Commercial Property
   D. Land

6. What is the documentary transfer tax rate in California?
   A. 55 cents per $500
   B. $1.10 per $1,000
   C. Both A and B
   D. Neither A nor B

7. What is the maximum amount of money a single person can gift to a donee in one year without paying taxes on it?
   A. $5,000
   B. $10,000
   C. $15,000
   D. $20,000

One of the biggest headaches when buying or selling property is determining what taxes must be paid on the property, when those taxes will be due and how to acquire the appropriate amount of money to pay those taxes on time. No doubt, property taxes are one of the biggest hurdles for people buying property, and may mean the difference between being able to afford the monthly mortgage and not being able to buy the property at all. In this chapter, we will look at the different taxes on personal and real property. We will also examine the tax rates applied to different types of property, the payment schedule for these taxes, and the withholdings, if any, that people must set aside. We will also look at exemptions, for those who qualify, and how to best use a tax exemption.

In addition to federal and state tax issues, we will examine the different requirements for foreign and domestic investors (from states outside of California). We will note the differences in withholding and any exceptions to the withholding rules for which an individual may qualify.

We will learn how taxes are assessed and also examine any special taxes people are required to pay. To wrap up the chapter, we will explore taxes on gifts or inheritances and any exemptions on such gifts.

The concept of taxation may be difficult to grasp, but it is very important for you, as a real estate professional, to protect both yourself and your client. You should also be able to aid your client in understanding the different steps required when buying or selling a home. Additionally, providing your client with information regarding the amount of property taxes required, as well as any special assessments or other issues of which they must be aware will make the buying process easier for them and allow them to gain confidence in you, as well.

PROPERTY TAX COLLECTION

All real estate investments are taxed on three different levels. The first is at the federal level, which includes income tax, estate tax and gift tax. These taxes are generally applied when the real estate has been conveyed to another person through sale or gifting.

The next level of taxation is at the state level. The state will tax a homeowner on income made from the sale (income tax) of their home. Just as with federal taxes, the state taxes from real estate profit are applied when the home is sold. Finally, there are local government taxes on real estate. These taxes are based on the property's value (sometimes referred to as *ad valorem*). Taxes assessed at the local government level are property taxes, special assessments and transfer taxes.

Ad Valorem

- A term meaning "according to value". Real estate taxation at the local government level is based on a property's value.

Taxes exist so that governments can generate funds to carry out its duties. Taxes are imposed on both real and personal property at three levels. Certain types of property are tax-exempt, but all property within the local taxing authority must also pay taxes.

Each county will elect an assessor who will be responsible for determining the assessed values of property and preparing the tax roll. Each time there is a transfer of property from one person to another, the assessor may reassess the property to get a new, more accurate assessment for tax purposes. Additionally, reassessments may occur when there has been an addition of structures, improvement or renovation on the existing structures, of when new amenities are added to a property (such as a swimming pool or tennis court). Any homeowner who disagrees with the county assessor's estimation of value may appeal the decision by contacting the assessor's office directly or by contacting the appeals board. It is important to note that there are time limits for these appeals; so, any person wishing to file an appeal must do so in a timely manner. When appealing the assessor's decision, the taxpayer must produce appraisal data, as proof that there was an erroneous assessment.

Each time a property changes owners, or property is transferred from one person to another, a change in ownership statement must be filed with the county recorder or assessor within 45 days from the date the property was recorded. If the transfer was not recorded, the change in ownership statement must be filed within 45 days from the actual change in ownership. This alerts the assessor that there maybe reason to reassess the property on a new tax basis. Any person failing to file the ownership statement will be subject to a $100 fee or 10% of the tax computed on the new basis of the property.

> **Remember!**
> Any person acquiring property (whether gift, inheritance or by purchase) must file a Change in Ownership Statement with either the recorder's office or the assessor within 45 days of the transfer, or 45 days from the recording of the change (in the event that no transfer was filed)

Taxpayers do have rights to see all documentation related to an assessor's inspection, in addition to the auditor's work papers. The Morgan Property Taxpayer's Bill of Rights requires assessors to produce this information to the property owner whose property is being assessed. For more information, you may visit the State Board of Equalization at www.boe.ca.gov.

There is a list of tasks that must be completed by all people who are a part of the assessing and tax collection process. First, the county board of supervisors determines the tax rate plus any special assessments that will be used to raise money for community purposes. The tax rate is determined by an assessor. Once this is accomplished, the city council will set the property tax rate for their city. There must be a city or, in smaller communities, a county auditor, who maintains the tax roll for all property within their jurisdiction. The city or county assessor will then examine all information regarding the properties, to establish the tax base, and send a tax bill to each property owner. This task is done on a yearly basis, to readjust the tax roll or assessment value based on improvements, renovations or additions to a property or structure. Real property is assessed at 100% of fair market value, with each property identified by a parcel number. The city or county tax collector will then decide how much tax will be paid by each property owner, based on the assessor's estimate. Land and improvements to property are assessed separately from existing structures, but are taxed at the same rate. Finally, for those property owners who disagree with their tax assessment, the county appeals board will hear any complaints regarding unfair taxation and make a determination.

REAL AND PERSONAL PROPERTY TAXES

Historically, taxes have been based on the amount of land in question, and what that land could produce. Today, taxes are still based on the amount of land, as well as what is placed on the land (such as structures). While structures can depreciate, or be built and torn down, the amount of land is a constant. In addition to land and the structures placed on it, commodities may be grown and sold on the land, with taxes paid on the income generated by those commodities.

Proposition 60

Homeowners 55 years of age or older may sell their home and transfer their current tax base to their new property. There are, however, a few limitations on this tax base transfer. The newly purchased home must be of equal or lesser value than the home being sold. This equity in value is based on the sales price of the old home, not its purchase price. The property being sold is taxed based on the property's original sale price, rather than at the price for which it was paid. So, homeowners in this age bracket will greatly benefit from this type of tax incentive. The new property must also be located in the same county as the property sold, and Proposition 60 must be recognized in that particular area, as well.

The way Proposition 60 works is that the value of the home being sold, which can be transferred as the new tax basis for the new home, is taxed at the home's value as of March 1, 1975 (or the year the property was purchased after this date). Each year, the home may see a 2% increase in its tax base, until the home is sold and replaced with another. Rather than having a new tax base on the new home at 1% of its purchase price, the tax base will be the same as the home just sold. An example will demonstrate this principal more clearly.

Example:
Andrew and Tammy purchased a home in 1978 for $100,000. The home was large enough for their 4 children who eventually left home. When their last child moved away, Andrew and Tammy decided they wanted a smaller home. Over the years, their home had appreciated to $300,000. The tax base on the home they were selling at the time of the sale was $117,500 (based on the old purchase price). Andrew and Tammy were allowed to carry this over to the new property, due to Proposition 60. The new property they purchased cost $295,000.

Tax base based carried over from sold property = $1,175
($117,500 x 1%)
Tax base on new property with no carryover = $$2,950
($295,000 x 1%)
By taking advantage of Proposition 60, Andrew and Tammy will save $1,776 in taxes.

Remember!
- Proposition 60 took effect as of March 1, 1975
- Persons 55 years or older are allowed to transfer their property tax base from one residence to another, provided the new property is worth the same or less than the amount of the property being sold
- A 2 percent increase in the tax base is assessed each year

Proposition 13

In 1978, Proposition 13 was approved as the measure of assessing property. It set a maximum annual tax on real property of no more than 1 percent of the property's base value or purchase price. Each year following this, a 2 percent increase is permissible. Each time a property is transferred from one owner to a new one, the tax base is reassessed at 1 percent of the selling price for the new owner.

Homeowners who make improvements to their property, such as adding on a new room, or putting in a pool, will be reassessed to include these improvements. However, those property owners who do not make any changes, improvements or remodels to their property will remain at a 2 percent increase per year assessment over the original tax base.

There are some special exceptions to the transfer of property and the new tax base. Under Proposition 13, a property transfer between a husband and wife will not result in a new tax assessment of 1 percent of the house's fair market value. Additionally, any principal residence transferred from a parent to a child, or the first $1 million of other real property, will be exempt from reassessment at 1 percent of its fair market value. In these two exemptions, spouses and children will continue to pay taxes at the property's original tax base, plus the 2 percent increase each year.

Remember!
- Proposition 13 took effect in 1978
- When property is transferred from one owner to another, the property is reassessed at 1 percent of the sales price or new tax base
- A 2 percent increase in the tax base is assessed per year.
- Spouses and children are exempt from a new tax base when there is a transfer of a principal residence, or other real property worth one million dollars or less

Exemptions

In general, all real and personal property is taxable, though there are a few exemptions from taxation. These exemptions are:

- An individual's personal property and home furnishings
- Property owned by non-profit organizations (such as a private school)
- Stocks and promissory notes

- Government property
- Property owned by or used for religious groups, hospitals or charitable purposes
- Some boats or ocean vessels
- Agricultural crops, fruit-bearing trees less than five years old, and grape vines less than three years old

The homeowner's exemption allows the owner to be exempt of the first $7,000 of the property's full cash value. This exemption is only allowed for primary residences, which may include townhouses, condominiums and residences. It is not available for vacation properties or income properties that are not the primary residence. The homeowner must obtain a form from the county tax assessor, and submit it by February 15 of the current tax year, to be eligible for the $7,000 exemption.

Veterans qualify for an additional exemption of $4,000 on property not already filed for exemption under the homeowner's exemption rule. So, any vacation properties or other properties not eligible for the homeowner's exemption may qualify for the veteran's exemption. There are, however, rules about which properties qualify. For example, property worth only $5,000, or property owned by a husband and wife worth $10,000 or less is ineligible for the homeowner's exemption.

Unmarried spouses as well as a pensioned father or mother of a qualified deceased veteran are eligible to receive the veteran's exemption. Any completely disabled veterans who are also eligible for an exemption of up to $100,000. This exemption may also be extended to a disabled veteran's spouse, provided the spouse remains unmarried.

Remember!
- Homestead exemption for a primary residence is $7,000
- Veterans qualify for a $4,000 exemption on property not already filed under the homestead exemption
- Disabled veterans qualify for a $100,000 exemption

Tax Year
The tax year runs from July 1 – June 30. Property taxes are payable in two installments, with one due on November 1 and the second due on February 1. For property owners who don't pay their installments at these set intervals, payment becomes delinquent as of December 10 (for the November installment) and April 10 (for the February installment). Those who make delinquent payments are charged a 10% penalty fee, which is added directly to the installment payment.

For those taxpayers who have not paid their taxes by the end of the tax year (June 30), a book sale or delinquent property sale will take place. The property owner will not lose possession or title to their property, but has only 5 years to pay the delinquent balance. If a property owner does not pay these taxes within the 5-year grace period, the state may hold a public auction to sell the property and pay for all back taxes. The highest bidder will be the new owner of the property, provided he or she is able to pay for the bid in cash. The highest bidder also receives a tax deed to the property.

Remember!
- The tax year runs from July 1 – June 30
- Installment payments are due November 1 and February 1, respectively
- Installment payments become delinquent after December 15 and April 15, respectively
- A book sale allows the property owner to remain on the property, but gives them only 5 years to pay all delinquent taxes
- An auction to sell the property occurs if the property owner does not pay his or her delinquent taxes within 5 years
- The highest bidder receives a tax deed to the property

There are a few exceptions to the tax schedule. For example, those persons 62 years of age or older, with at least 20% equity in their home and with total income less than $24,000 per year may postpone taxes or defer them. When a person takes this option, a lien is placed on the property. There is no time limit on the postponement. The state will receive its money when the home is sold, when the claimant no longer qualifies for the postponement (if his or her annual income rises above $24,000) or when the claimant no longer occupies the property. In addition to those persons 62 years or older, those who are disabled or blind may also take advantage of postponement of taxes, creating a lien on their property to the state. For more information regarding the postponement of taxes, please visit www.soo.ca.gov.

Special Assessments
Special assessments are imposed on property when a community needs to raise money for a specific purpose, such as street repairs. Special assessments will appear on the tax bill as a separate entry. Just as property taxes are based on *ad valorem*, so too are the special assessments. Special assessments are not simply charged, without the approval of the taxpayer. As long as a taxpayer exercises his or her right to vote, they will be aware of the assessment, as all special assessments must pass with a two-thirds voter majority. Special assessments may be paid in one payment, or may be spread out over several years.

Special assessments are exempt from any limitations that Proposition 13 places on property taxes. The city can sell municipal bonds and include these on the property tax bill. Additionally, any buyer who may receive a special assessment in a new development (as you will read below) must be told about the assessment. They must also be made aware that their property taxes, when paid alone, will be less than when they are included with the special assessment. Any agents who fail to disclose a special assessment when selling property may be disciplined by their real estate commission.

The Street Improvement Act of 1911 raises money in a special assessment to repair underground utilities, sewers and streets. The special assessment for the Street Improvement Act of 1911 is placed on the properties it directly affects, with payments made during the regular tax installment intervals. The Street Improvement Act of 1911 is a very specific tax, designed for special projects or repairs.

The Mello-Roos Community Facilities Act finances projects and structures such as parks, fire stations, streets, sewers, schools and other services or recreational areas found in a new development. Each lot or parcel of land in the development will have a special assessment placed on it to pay for these services. A lien is placed on the property by the developer of the property, as the developer is responsible for payment of municipal bonds for these services. The developer is responsible for payments on this municipal bond(s) until the properties are sold and special assessments are paid. Mello-Roos is a specific type of special assessment for this purpose and does not charge its improvements to property taxes.

Benefit Assessments
Benefit assessments are similar to special assessments, with one major difference. The only properties assessed for the benefit assessment are those properties that will benefit from the improvements. Benefit assessments may also be referred to as local assessments, standby availability charges or special benefit assessments.

Benefit assessments are non-deductible taxes (unlike regular taxes) used to finance maintenance. The reason benefit assessments are non-deductible is because they are used to finance property improvements. Examples include improvement of a neighborhood street, sewer line or local utility that services a specific community.

FEDERAL AND STATE INCOME TAXES

Federal income taxes are based on a person's total earnings for the year. The amount of money a person made in that year will determine their tax bracket. The more money a person earns, the higher the percentage they will pay on that money. The same is true for those persons earning less money (i.e., less money = lower percentage of taxes).

To obtain a tax shelter or tax relief, people often buy real estate. Though real estate is taxed with property taxes, there are legal reductions in tax liability for those persons who own real estate. Real estate used as the person's primary residence as well as income properties will allow a person to qualify for these tax shelters. Specific rules for the property type must be followed in order to take full advantage of these legal reductions.

Personal Residence
In the past, California allowed its residents the option to rollover some or all gains earned from the sale of a primary residence, provided the sale of the primary residence was used to purchase a new primary residence. There was a four-year grace period given to the seller to find a replacement for the primary residence. In addition to the rollover allowance, homeowners 55 years of age or over were given a once-in-a-lifetime $125,000 exemption for the sale of their principal residence.

In May 6, 1997 the old exclusions and rollover allowances were replaced by new exclusion rules for homeowners selling their primary residence. There are, however, certain circumstances where the homeowner may elect to take the old exclusions rather than the new ones. The new rules now allow a homeowner to exclude up to $250,000 of taxable income from the sale of a primary residence, while married couples may exclude up to $500,000. In order to qualify for this exemption, the homeowner must have lived in the home for the past two years. Because of this time requirement, homeowners are generally allowed to take this exemption only once every two years.

There are, however, certain circumstances, which allow a homeowner to take advantage of this exemption, even if they have not lived in the home for this two-year period. Persons who are transferred due to a job change or relocation, persons selling their home due to health reasons, or those transferring as a result of unforeseen tragedies may take advantage of this exemption.

In addition to the exemption, homeowners may take certain deductions on their home. Interest on mortgage and property taxes is deductible for both primary and secondary homes. Unfortunately a homeowner cannot deduct improvements or depreciation on the property, though improvements may be added to the cost basis when the home is sold. This aids the homeowner because the amount of taxable gain from the property at the close of sale will not be as high when the original cost basis of the home increases. If a person purchased their home for $300,000, made $75,000 of improvements, and then sold the home for $600,000, their capital gains tax will be based on a $225,000 profit. The cost of the improvements will be added to the original cost of the home, providing a break to the homeowner when they sell the property. Assuming our homeowners have been living on the property for more than 2 years, and given that the gain on the home is less than the allowable $250,000 exception, this homeowner will not have to pay capital gains taxes if they follow all necessary rules and steps when filing their taxes.

Original Purchase Price	$300,000
Improvements to the home	$75,000
Adjusted cost basis of the home	$375,000

Selling Price – Adjusted Cost Basis = Taxable Gain
$600,000 - $375,000 = $225,000

Income Property
As we have seen from the ownership of a primary residence, there are exemptions for which a homeowner may qualify if they live in the home that is being sold or certain tax deductions can be made, based on ownership of property. Income properties also have exceptions and tax benefits, though they are different from primary residence exemptions. Investors in income property can take a depreciation allowance on the property. This means that the owner of the income property can claim depreciation on the property and deduct it from the annual tax bill. As you will recall, the owner of a primary residence does not have this option.

As we learned in a previous chapter, a deduction based on depreciation may not be a physical depreciation of the structure (such as the condition of the exterior paint, or the age of the furnace). Instead, the deduction is based on the economic or useful life of the property. After a certain number of years, the building will no longer be capable of generating income, and the property owner is allowed to take a yearly depreciation on the property. Depreciation on a property such as this is generally figured using straight line depreciation, or figuring up the number of years for which a property will be useful and dividing its purchase price into this figure. The resulting number is the amount of yearly deductible from taxes, less the cost of land.

Example:
The economic life of a property is 30 years. The value of the property is $500,000, while the land value is worth $200,000. The actual value of the structure is $300,000.

$$\$300,000 / 30 \text{ years} = \$10,000$$

This investor is allowed a $10,000 tax deduction per year based on the structure's depreciation.

Other tax benefits extended to an investor include: deduction of the mortgage interest; deduction of maintenance and utilities; deduction of any loss on a sale of the property over the original or adjusted cost basis; insurance premium deduction, management fee deductions, and property tax deductions. Any profits made on the sale of an income property are deferrable (paid at a later time). This benefit is not given to owners of primary residences, , however all gain (regardless of how much or how little) on the sale of an income property is taxable.

Capital gains taxes are calculated in the same way on an income property as it is on a primary residence. There are a few additional steps to be taken when figuring the income property. The income property will begin with the purchase price, plus any improvements. Any depreciation claimed is subtracted from the amount to arrive at the adjusted cost basis. Any expenses incurred during the sale of the property, such as realtor's commission, is deducted from the sale price to arrive at the adjusted selling price.

Original Purchase Price + Improvements – Depreciation Claimed = Adjusted Cost Basis

Selling Price – Sale Expenses (Commissions) = Adjusted Selling Price

Adjusted Selling Price – Adjusted Cost Basis = Taxable Gain or Loss
(The loss is not taxable. In fact, in investor may take a tax deduction on this loss)

Installment Sale
Installment sales are used to help spread out capital gains on a property for a period of more than one year. This is done by taking several, smaller payments for the sale of property instead of one large chunk of money. A seller may also take back a note, allowing the tax payments to be deferred. When a seller takes the option of a wrap around loan, or an all-inclusive trust deed, he or she accepts monthly payments from the buyer. The seller will only be taxed on the gain earned in one year's time, which will be spread out over the term of the trust deed.

Tax-Deferred Exchanges
A tax-deferred exchange occurs when an investor exchanges property for a like property of another property of equal value, and defers any taxes until the property being exchanged is sold.

Properties must be of equal value, at least on paper. When properties are not of equal value, cash or non-like property must be added to the exchange and given to the disadvantaged property owner, to make the exchange of the two properties equal in value. This exchange is called a boot exchange. Personal residences are not allowed as inclusions in a tax-deferred exchange. Only properties such as apartment buildings, commercial buildings or land are eligible.

When the properties are sold, the cost basis of the original property being exchanged becomes the cost basis of the newly purchased property, provided the two properties are equal. If there is a boot exchange to create equality, the cost basis will change. Ultimately, the capital gain or loss is figured in the same way as it is for other income property.

Example:

Property 1

Value	$700,000
Encumbrances	$125,000
Equity	$575,000

Property 2

Value	$650,000
Encumbrances	$100,000
Equity	$550,000

In order to qualify for a tax-deferred exchange, the person owning property 2 needs to add a boot worth $25,000 to make the two properties equal. The owner of property 1 will be taxed on the $25,000 boot he or she will receive in the exchange, while the owner of property 2 will not have any taxes.

State Income Taxes

State income taxes and their brackets are different from the federal income taxes. Each person is required to file a return for both state and federal taxes.

Persons living in California for the entire year must file a tax return if they are either single or the head of a household making over $6,000 per year. They must also file if they are married with a combined income of over $12,000. All other persons who don't meet the one-year residency requirement are required to file a non-resident tax return.

FOREIGN INVESTMENT IN REAL PROPERTY TAX ACT – FIRPTA

When people outside the United States wish to invest money in property located in California, there are different tax laws for both federal and state. The Foreign Investment in Real Property Tax Act (FIRPTA) outlines the differences in the laws, as well as the requirements for the buyer. When a foreign investor wishes to make an investment, he or she is responsible for making property disclosures to the seller, so that all the necessary funds have been set aside. It is important for all real estate professionals to pay close attention to this type of transaction so that the escrow instructions are clear about the amount of funds that must be set aside for the additional taxes.

Federal income tax requirements for foreign investments require a seller who is either a non-resident of the United States or a legal alien to hold 10% of the sales price of the property, to pay any taxes from capital gains. Any property selling for less than $300,000 is exempt from this 10% requirement, and also exempt from the disclosure requirements.

Property sellers who are citizens of the United States are required to fill out a seller's affidavit of nonforeign status. This affidavit states that the seller is a citizen of the United States. A buyer must also sign a buyer's affidavit of residency, which indicates whether they are a citizen or legal resident. The buyer's affidavit also requires the person signing the statement to agree that the sale price of the property did not exceed $300,000 and that the property will be used as a residence. As long as the buyer is a resident, is purchasing the property for under $300,000, and will be living in the property as his or her primary residence, he or she will be exempt from the withholding requirement.

SELLER'S AFFIDAVIT OF NONFOREIGN STATUS AND/OR CALIFORNIA WITHHOLDING EXEMPTION

FOREIGN INVESTMENT IN REAL PROPERTY TAX ACT (FIRPTA)
AND CALIFORNIA WITHHOLDING LAW
(Use a separate form for each Transferor)
(C.A.R. Form AS, Revised 1/03)

Internal Revenue Code ("IRC") Section 1445 provides that a transferee of a U.S. real property interest must withhold tax if the transferor is a "foreign person." California Revenue and Taxation Code Section 18662 provides that a transferee of a California real property interest must withhold tax if the transferor: (i) is an individual (unless certain exemptions apply); or (ii) is any entity other than an individual ("Entity") if the transferor's proceeds will be disbursed to a financial intermediary of the transferor, or to the transferor with a last known street address outside of California. California Revenue and Taxation Code Section 18662 includes additional provisions for corporations.

I understand that this affidavit may be disclosed to the Internal Revenue Service and to the California Franchise Tax Board by the transferee, and that any false statement I have made herein (if an Entity Transferor, on behalf of the Transferor) may result in a fine, imprisonment or both.

1. **PROPERTY ADDRESS** (the address of the property being transferred):
_____

2. **TRANSFEROR'S INFORMATION:**
Full Name _____
Telephone No. _____
Address _____
(Use HOME address for individual transferors. Use OFFICE address for Entities: corporations, partnerships, limited liability companies, trusts and estates.)
Social Security No., Federal Employer Identification No., or California Corporation No. _____

3. **AUTHORITY TO SIGN:** If this document is signed on behalf of an Entity Transferor, THE UNDERSIGNED INDIVIDUAL DECLARES THAT HE/SHE HAS AUTHORITY TO SIGN THIS DOCUMENT ON BEHALF OF THE TRANSFEROR.

4. **FEDERAL LAW:** I, the undersigned individual, declare under penalty of perjury that, for the reason checked below, if any, I am exempt (or if signed on behalf of an Entity Transferor, the Entity is exempt) from the federal withholding law (FIRPTA):
   ☐ (For individual Transferors) I am not a nonresident alien for purposes of U.S. income taxation.
   ☐ (For corporation, partnership, limited liability company, trust and estate Transferors) The Transferor is not a foreign corporation, foreign partnership, foreign limited liability company, foreign trust, or foreign estate, as those term are defined in the Internal Revenue Code and Income Tax Regulations.

5. **CALIFORNIA LAW:** I, the undersigned individual, declare under penalty of perjury that, for the reason checked below, if any, I am exempt (or if signed on behalf of an Entity Transferor, the Entity is exempt) from the California withholding law:
   ☐ The total sale price for the property is $100,000 or less.
   For individual or revocable/grantor trust Transferors only:
   ☐ The property being transferred is in California and was my principal residence within the meaning of IRC Section 121.
   ☐ The property is being, or will be, exchanged for property of like kind within the meaning of IRC Section 1031.
   ☐ The property has been compulsorily or involuntarily converted (within the meaning of IRC1033) and I intend to acquire property similar or related in service or use to be eligible for non-recognition of gain for California income tax purposes under IRC Section 1033.
   ☐ The transaction will result in a loss for California income tax purposes.
   For Entity Transferors only:
   ☐ (For corporation Transferors) The Transferor is a corporation qualified to do business in California, or has a permanent place of business in California at the address shown in paragraph 2 ("Transferor's Information").
   ☐ (For limited liability company ("LLC") or partnership Transferors) The Transferor is an LLC or partnership and recorded title to the property being transferred is in the name of the LLC or partnership and the LLC or partnership will file a California tax return to report the sale and withhold on foreign and domestic nonresident partners as required.
   ☐ (For irrevocable trust Transferors) The Transferor is an irrevocable trust with at least one trustee who is a California resident and the trust will file a California tax return to report the sale and withhold when distributing California source taxable income to nonresident beneficiaries as required.
   ☐ (For estate Transferors) The Transferor is an estate of a decedent who was a California resident at the time of his/her death and the estate will file a California tax return to report the sale and withhold when distributing California source taxable income to nonresident beneficiaries as required.
   ☐ (For tax-exempt Entity and nonprofit organization Transferors) The Transferor is exempt from tax under California or federal law.

By _____ Date _____
(Transferor's Signature) (Indicate if you are signing as the grantor of a revocable/grantor trust.)

Typed or printed name _____ Title (If signed on behalf of entity Transferor) _____

SURE TRAC
The System for Success™

Published by the
California Association of REALTORS®

AS REVISED 1/03 (PAGE 1 OF 1) Print Date

Reviewed by _____ Date _____

SELLER'S AFFIDAVIT OF NONFOREIGN STATUS AND/OR CALIFORNIA WITHHOLDING EXEMPTION (AS PAGE 1 OF 1)

CALIFORNIA ASSOCIATION OF REALTORS®

BUYER'S AFFIDAVIT
That Buyer is acquiring property for use as a residence
and that sales price does not exceed $300,000.
(FOREIGN INVESTMENT IN REAL PROPERTY TAX ACT)

1. I am the transferee (buyer) of real property located at _____
_____

2. The sales price (total of all consideration in the sale) does not exceed $300,000.

3. I am acquiring the real property for use as a residence. I have definite plans that I or a member of my family will reside in it for at least 50 percent of the number of days it will be in use during each of the first two 12 month periods following the transfer of the property to me. I understand that the members of my family that are included in the last sentence are my brothers, sisters, ancestors, descendents, or spouse.

4. I am making this affidavit in order to establish an exemption from withholding a portion of the sales price of the property under Internal Revenue Code §1445.

5. I understand that if the information in this affidavit is not correct, I may be liable to the Internal Revenue Service for up to 10 percent of the sales price of the property, plus interest and penalties.

Under penalties of perjury, I declare that the statements above are true, correct and complete.

Date _____ Signature _____

Typed or Printed Name _____

Date _____ Signature _____

Typed or Printed Name _____

IMPORTANT NOTICE: An affidavit should be signed by each individual transferee to whom it applies. Before you sign, any questions relating to the legal sufficiency of this form, or to whether it applies to a particular transaction, or to the definition of any of the terms used, should be referred to an attorney, certified public accountant, other professional tax advisor, or the Internal Revenue Service.

FORM AB-11 REVISED 2/91

Remember!
- Foreign investors must set aside 10% of the sale price of a home (with the exception of homes under $300,000, which are exempt) for any capital gains
- Sellers must sign a seller's affidavit of nonforeign status, stating they are a citizen or legal resident of the U.S.
- Buyers must sign a buyer's affidavit of residency stating they are a citizen or legal resident of the U.S. and that the property was purchased for less than $300,000. They must also indicate whether the property will be used for a primary residence.

The state of California has its own tax rules and regulations regarding foreign investors, and investors from other states. A seller of property who is not a legal resident of the United States or California must withhold 3.5% of the sales price for the Franchise Tax Board, or state tax board. Buyers and real estate agents are also responsible for ensuring that this sum is withheld in the escrow instructions. There are, however, exceptions to this withholding. Any foreign investor or investor from another state is not required to withhold the 3.5% if the sales price of the property is $100,000 or less, if the home is the seller's principal residence or if the seller signs an affidavit of nonforeign status and the buyer signs an affidavit of residency for California.

Remember!
- Foreign or out-of-state property sellers must withhold 3.5% of the sales price for the state tax board
- Properties under $100,000 are exempt from withholding
- Properties being sold which were the sellers principle residence are exempt
- Persons who sign the seller's affidavit of nonforeign status or the buyer's affidavit of nonresidency for California are exempt from the withholding

DOCUMENTARTY TRANSFER TAX

A documentary transfer tax is a tax on the transfer of property from one person to another. This tax is payable to the jurisdiction in which the property is located (either the city or the county). Evidence of the tax is stated on the face of the deed or on an accompanying piece of paper.

The documentary transfer tax in California is 55 cents per $500, or $1.10 per every $1,000 of the purchase price of the property. Transactions in which the buyer is paying the full sale price of the property through a cash exchange, new loan or other method will see a documentary transfer tax on the entire purchase price. In an exchange where the buyer is assuming a current loan, and will make an additional down payment in cash to cover the selling price, the documentary transfer tax only applies to the amount of cash paid above what is owed on the assumed loan.

Example:
Amy and Sergio are purchasing a home by assuming an existing loan and paying the remaining balance of the transfer in cash. The home they are purchasing is $450,000 and they will assume an existing trust deed of $300,000. They plan on paying $150,000 in cash to cover the remaining amount of the sales price. The documentary transfer tax assessed on the transfer is:

$450,000 selling price minus $300,000 existing trust deed = $150,000 taxable amount.

$150,000 divided by $500 is $300; $300 x $0.55 = $165 documentary transfer tax.

When the documentary transfer tax has been paid, the county recorder will place a stamp on the document indicating payment. These stamps are often referred to as "doc stamps."

Remember!
A documentary transfer tax is imposed on the actual amount of money a person pays for a property. It is not applied when a buyer assumes an existing trust deed.

Some cities in California have imposed their own rate for the documentary transfer tax. Those cities and their rates are as follows:

• Culver City	$4.50
• Los Angeles	$4.50
• Pomona	$2.20
• Redondo Beach	$2.20
• Santa Monica	$3.00

ESTATE, INHERITANCE AND GIFT TAXES

California currently does not have a state tax on inheritances and gifts, as these taxes were repealed by voters on June 8, 1982. There is, however, an estate tax, which follows federal rules regarding when the tax may be assessed. These rules state that the estate tax may be assessed when the estate is worth more than $850,000. The amount will increase in the next subsequent years to $950,000 in 2005, and $1,000,000 in 2006. If an estate qualifies for the tax, the total tax amount must be paid within nine months after the death of the property owner.

Federal gift taxes are paid by persons who make more than one gift of property worth $10,000 or more in a calendar year. If a married couple wishes to make a gift, the taxable gift must be worth more than $20,000 before taxes will apply (i.e., $10,000 x 2). There are restrictions on what constitutes a gift. Tuition payments for another individual or medical care cost coverage is not considered a gift, regardless of its dollar amount. Any gift tax returns must be filed by April 15 of the year following the gift.

The person making the gift is called the *donor*. The person receiving the gift is referred to as the donee. A gift may be either real or personal property.

SUMMARY

In this chapter, you have examined what constitutes a tax, and became familiar with the several different tax laws, as well as their regulations, rules, and exemptions. Proposition 13 outlined the amount by which a property may increase per year, and how to reassess a property being transferred. Proposition 60 explains the tax benefit for homeowners 55 years or older when selling their primary residence for another property of equal or lesser value.

You now know that the tax year runs from July 1 through June 30 of the following year, with installment payments due for income taxes on November 1 and February 1, respectively. Any delinquent taxes will automatically face a lien, payable to the state. Any property sold at a property tax sale is auctioned off, with the winning bidder receiving a tax deed to the property.

Special assessments or benefit assessments may be applied to property to make improvements to utilities, streets, sewers or parks. These special assessments must be disclosed by the agent to any prospective buyer of property in an area with the assessment. Failure to do so may result in disciplinary action against the real estate agent.

There is also a documentary transfer tax, applicable when property is transferred from one person to another. This tax is only on the consideration of the sale, and is not attached to the buyer's assumption of any existing loans or trust deeds.

California has eliminated inheritance and gift taxes, though estate taxes still exist. The estate tax schedule is the same as that of the federal government. The federal government taxes gifts made from person to person but allows a yearly gift allowance of $10,000 for a single person and $20,000 for a married couple.

Homeowners may take advantage of various exemptions or tax shelters for property. Primary residences and income properties have different rules and regulations regarding what is an allowable exemption, deduction or depreciation. However, with each type of property ownership, there are certain tax advantages.

TERMS AND PHRASES

Ad Valorem – A term meaning "according to value". Real estate property taxes are based on the concept of ad valorem, (are taxed based on the value of the home).

Adjusted Cost Basis – The original cost of the structure, plus any improvements made to the structure during ownership, minus its depreciation.

Adjusted Gross Income – The total amount of income a person receives from all sources less any depreciation, tax deductions or other allowable deductions

Assessed Value – The value a county assessor places on a property or structure to determine its tax basis.

Assessment Role – The establishment of a tax base for an area or community by listing all taxable properties and showing the assessed value of each one.

Basis – Also referred to as "cost basis", it is the dollar value assigned to a property at the time of purchase. The Internal Revenue Service uses this basis to determine any gain or loss the seller may incur by selling the property to another person. The basis is also used in calculating the depreciation for income tax paid on the sale of the property. Basis is the price of the home before making an adjusted cost basis on the addition of any improvements, and deduction of all depreciation factors.

Benefit Assessment – The total amount of property owned and enhanced by any renovations, improvements or new construction.

Book Sale – The sale of real property to the state, in name only, when the property owner is delinquent on his or her property taxes.

Boot – In a property exchange, when properties are not equal, the owner or transferee of the lesser property must make up the difference by using money or offering additional property to the buyer to maintain an equal exchange.

Capital Asset – Any permanently owned asset used for producing income. Examples are machinery, land, structures or industrial equipment. Capital assets are distinctly different from inventory, as inventory is generally for sale and not permanent

Capital Gain – The amount of money earned over the amount of the adjusted cost basis for any item for sale.

Capital Improvements – Any improvements made to property.

Certificate of Redemption – A certificate issued by the county tax collector to a property owner when all money from past due taxes have been collected.

County Assessor – An elected official who determines the tax basis for each property under his or her jurisdiction.

Cost Basis – The original amount paid for property.

Deductions – Any amount of money that can be subtracted from the tax basis.

Depreciation – A decrease in value of an asset allowed in computing property value for tax purposes; or, the decrease in value of an asset due to use or other factors causing it to be worth less.

Documentary Transfer Tax – A tax on all property transfers, as stated on the deed, or any separate papers accompanying the deed.

Donee – A person receiving a gift.

Donor – A person making a gift.

Economic life – The life over which improvements to property will yield a return on the investment over returns based on land only.

Estate Tax – A federal or state tax imposed on an individual's assets inherited by heirs.

Franchise Tax – California's tax on corporations.

Fiscal Year – A year based on a business or accounting year; fiscal year may be different from the calendar year, in terms of start and end date(s)

Gift – A voluntary transfer of property form one person to another. There usually is no consideration given or taken for the transfer.

Homeowner's Exemption – California allows homeowners a $7,000 tax exemption on their principal home (not extended to vacation properties or homes)

Ordinary Income – Any income that does not qualify for capital gains tax.

Reassessment Event – An occurrence such as the sale of a property or an addition, improvement or renovation causing a re-evaluation of the property's value for tax purposes.

Recovery Property – A property that can be depreciated for income tax purposes, with the cost of the property deducted from the income over a stated period.

Special Assessment – Appropriation, in the form of a tax, on property that is enhanced by the renovation or addition of improvements (such as a new train line or other community improvement or service)

Tax Deed – The type of deed a successful bidder will receive for property gained at a tax auction.

Taxable Income – Income that is taxable from all sources, less certain payments or donations deemed untaxable (such as income placed into a retirement plan)

CHAPTER QUIZ

1. How many days after a transfer has been recorded does a person buying property have to file the Change in Ownership Statement with the county recorder or assessor?
   A. 30 days
   B. 45 days
   C. 60 days
   D. 75 days

2 Which of the following best describes the term 'ad valorem'?
   A. The amount a person is able to pay, based on their income.
   B. The amount a person is required to pay, determined by the county assessor, based on their previous year's tax returns.
   C. The amount of taxes a person is required to pay, based on the assessor's assessment of their property's value.
   D. The amount of taxes a person is required to pay, based on the assessor's assessment of their property's value plus the person's gross taxable income.

3 How old must a person be in order to take advantage of Proposition 60?
   A. 55 years old.
   B. 60 years old.
   C. 65 years old.
   D. 70 years old.

4. What is the maximum amount of increase in the tax base per year under Proposition 60?
   A. 1%
   B. 2%
   C. 3%
   D. 4%

5. How is the new tax base established when property is transferred between owners under Proposition 13?
   A. The new tax base is 2% more than the previous year's assessment.
   B. The new tax base is 1% of the sales price.
   C. The new tax base will remain the same as the previous owner's tax base
   D. The new tax base will be based of the value of the home in 1978

6. Who is exempt from the reassessment of property in terms of the tax base under proposition 13?
   A. Spouses
   B. Children
   C. Spouses and children
   D. Spouses and children, when a principal residence is transferred; or, the first million dollars of any real property transfer.

7. The homeowner's exemption for a primary residence is
   A. $4,000
   B. $7,000
   C. $10,000
   D. $100,000

8. When may a veteran take advantage of the veteran's exemption?
   A. A veteran may take the veteran's exemption on his or her principal residence, even if it is already homesteaded.
   B. If a veteran has already homesteaded his or her primary residence, he or she may take the veteran's exemption on another, separate property.
   C. A veteran may not use the veteran's exemption on any property if they have already used the homestead exemption on their primary residence.
   D. None of the above.

9. When is the beginning of the tax year?
   A. July 1
   B. June 30
   C. November 1
   D. April 15

10. When are special assessments paid?
   A. Separately, at the time the lien is placed on the property for any improvement being taken care of by the assessment.
   B. At the same time property taxes are due, but paid on a separate bill.
   C. At the same time property taxes are due, and paid on the same bill.
   D. None of the above.

11. Who gets a benefit assessment?
    A. An entire city
    B. An entire county
    C. Large portions of a city, but not the entire city.
    D. Just a small portion of a neighborhood or development.

12. Which dollar amount from the sale of a home will allow a foreign investor an exemption from the 10% federal withholding requirement?
    A. $100,000
    B. $200,000
    C. $300,000
    D. $400,000

13. What percentage from the sale of a property must a foreign investor or nonresident of California withhold for the state tax board?
    A. 2%
    B. 2.5%
    C. 3.5%
    D. 5%

14. How much of an exemption of taxable gain is a married couple allowed to take on their house?
    A. $125,000
    B. $250,000
    C. $300,000
    D. $500,000

15. What is the term used when the original purchase price of a home is altered to include the cost of improvements made to the home?
    A. Cost basis
    B. Adjusted cost basis
    C. Selling price
    D. Purchase price

16. What are two additional steps taken when determining the capital gain or loss on the sale of income property that are NOT taken when figuring out the same gain or loss on a primary residence?
    A. Depreciation deducted from basis; sale expenses deducted from selling price
    B. Depreciation deducted from selling price; sale expenses deducted from basis.
    C. Depreciation and sale expenses deducted from basis.
    D. Depreciation and sale expenses deducted from selling price.

17. What kind of property does not qualify for a tax-deferred exchange?
    A. Personal residence
    B. Apartment complex
    C. Commercial property
    D. Land

18. What is the documentary transfer tax in California?
    A. 55 cents per $500
    B. $1.10 per $1,000
    C. Both A and B
    D. Neither A nor B

19. What is the maximum amount of money a single person can gift to a donee in a single year without paying taxes on the money?
    A. $5,000
    B. $10,000
    C. $15,000
    D. $20,000

20. What is the name given to a person receiving a gift?
    A. Donee
    B. Donor
    C. Both A and B
    D. Neither A nor B

12

SUBDIVISIONS
AND
PUBLIC
CONTROLS

What you will learn in this Chapter

- Definition of a Subdivision

- Subdivision Laws and Acts

- Requirements and Government Controls of Subdivisions

- Fair Housing Laws

1. Into how many lots or parcels must land be divided before it is considered a subdivision?
    A. 3
    B. 4
    C. 5
    D. 10

2. How many lots must be included in a subdivision for the Subdivided Lands Act to apply?
    A. 3
    B. 5
    C. 8
    D. 10

3. There are three types of maps included in the Subdivision Maps Act. They are tentative, final and
    A. Parcel
    B. Plot
    C. Plat
    D. Subdivision

4. The owner of a condominium also owns which of the following?
    A. Individual unit
    B. Airspace around the unit
    C. Shared interest in common areas
    D. All of the above

5. In the Subdivided Lands Act, who releases the final report that gives developer the green light to collect deposits and contracts on lots?
    A. City and County officials
    B. Real Estate Commissioner
    C. State recorder
    D. State Legislature

6. Which state law protects citizens against discrimination when looking for a private residence, whether a single-family home or apartment?
    A. Unruh Civil Rights Act
    B. California Civil Code Section 54-55.1
    C. California Fair Employment and Housing Act
    D. Housing Financial Discrimination Act

7. Which federal law expanded the 1866 Civil Rights Act to include more than just race as a criteria protected from discrimination?
    A. Jones vs. Mayer
    B. Fair Housing Act
    C. Unruh Act
    D. Civil Rights Act of 1968 and 1988

INTRODUCTION

City growth, expansion and attrition are part of a dynamic, ongoing process. People are constantly relocating, whether to the city for a job, away from a city for affordable housing, or to a rural area for additional space and land.

Because of the rapid changes experienced in California's population, and across the nation, the government has created regulations and laws that govern how land is developed and used. This is to ensure a safe, healthy environment for all of its citizens.

The government also finds itself protecting citizens from fraud and misrepresentation from developers who may not make good on a promise. When a potential buyer is entertaining the notion of buying property in a new development, he or she can be sure that the government has ensured all claims and representation of the development are factual, even if no houses have yet been built.

Government interaction and control in the real estate industry also insures that there will be adequate public utilities, paved streets, well-planned neighborhoods and other important services that provide a high quality of life for its residents.

This chapter will introduce you to the laws and regulations placed on real estate development by the government, as well as the different types of subdivisions or property. You will also learn of the different housing laws created to keep buyers safe from discrimination and other possible fraud.

DEFINITION OF A SUBDIVISION

Subdivision is the act of dividing land into smaller parcels or lots, in an effort to sell, develop or further that division at a later time. Technically, a subdivision occurs when one larger lot of land is divided into five or more lots. Most have been subdivided at one time or another, with the possible exception of agricultural, ranch and remote, rural areas. There was a need for some type of control in the division and sale of the land to ensure that the quality of life that people were seeking was preserved; not lost through development or division.

SUBDIVISION LAWS AND ACTS

There are two basic laws, which control subdivisions in California; the Subdivided Lands Act and the Subdivision Map Act. These two laws were adopted to protect consumers by interpreting subdivision and its laws in two separate ways, both beneficial. The basic areas of jurisdiction covered by these laws are design, planning, site preparation, construction of structures, and sale of the land.

| **Laws controlling subdivisions:** |
| • Subdivided Lands Act |
| • Subdivided Map Act |

Subdivided Lands Act

The Subdivided Lands Act governs several developments and transactions between buyer and seller. First, the law outlines the different forms of ownership allowed for land that is divided up into five or more parcels, as well as land areas 160 acres or less. Lots with land masses over 160 acres are exempt from the Subdivided Lands Act, which also governs the marketing and financing of subdivisions.

The Subdivided Lands Act is administered by the real estate commissioner. It is the commissioner's responsibility to protect purchasers of property in new subdivisions from fraud, misrepresentation or other violations which may deceive the consumer into a detrimental purchase or transaction.

Any developer who wishes to create a subdivision and offer land for sale to consumers must submit all details of the subdivision plan to the real estate commissioner. Before the Commissioner gathers information on, among other things, the project's financial status and then prepares a public, subdivision report, describing the property. When consumers purchase land or homes based on the developers promise, the Commissioner's job is to ensure all promises are kept and that a final product is delivered that meets the consumer's expectations.

The subdivision report is not only issued for the sale of land in California. It is also issued for sale of land outside of California provided that the land is being marketed in the state. The report not only assures that any promises regarding structures or construction are carried out, but also that any land can be used for the intent for which it was purchased. For example, if a consumer purchased a lot with the intention of building a community gas station, the report will show the zoning laws that detail whether the zoning laws allow for this, or if the lot must be used for residential purposes only.

The developer must supply a copy of the commissioner's report to any interested buyer before a lot can be sold. The buyer must sign the commissioner's report for approval and acknowledgement. The seller must keep a copy of the signed statement for three years. The statement a buyer signs is called the receipt for public report. Public reports are valid for a period of five years, during which time amendments may be made to reflect any changes to the development.

A typical report will include the following information:

- Project name, location and size
- Subdivider's name
- Interest to be acquired by people purchasing lots or leasing space
- Procedures for handling taxes, payments and assessments
- Extraordinary expenses at the time of closing, or any anticipated expenses in the future.
- Hazardous or adverse environmental factors
- Restrictions or conditions placed on the use of the property
- Unusual easements, right-of-ways or setbacks
- Special building permits required

RESERVATION INSTRUMENT

RE 612 (Rev. 1/04)

THIS IS NOT AN OFFER OR CONTRACT TO PURCHASE OR SELL

_____ (hereinafter "Subdivider")
(Subdivider)

acknowledges receipt from _____
(Name)

(hereinafter "Potential Buyer") of _____
(Address)

of the sum of $ _____ for the reservation of _____
(Amount)   *(Lot or Unit Number)*

in _____,
(Name of Subdivision)

County of _____, State of California.
(County)

      Subdivider hereby reserves the above-identified lot or unit for Potential Buyer and represents that he will immediately place the funds and a signed copy of this document in the following escrow depository:

ESCROW NAME		STREET ADDRESS (Do not list Post Office box)	
CITY	STATE **CA**	ZIP CODE	TELEPHONE NUMBER ( )

1. This instrument does not create a contractual obligation to buy or sell on the part of either Subdivider or Potential Buyer. Either party may, at any time, cancel this reservation instrument without incurring liability to the other. In the event of cancellation by either party, all funds received towards this reservation will be returned to the potential buyer within two business days.

2. If Potential Buyer so requests by completing appropriate instructions below, subdivider will make arrangements with the escrow depository for the earning of interest on Potential Buyer's funds. $_____ will be deducted by escrow depository from interest earned as a charge for providing the service to Potential Buyer. The balance of the interest earned will be paid to Potential Buyer or credited to his/her account.

3. By initialing here _____, Potential Buyer agrees to the payment of charges as set forth above and requests that the funds be placed into an interest bearing account as follows:

NAME AS ACCOUNT IS TO BE HELD	TAXPAYER IDENTIFICATION NO. (Social Security No.)

4. CAVEAT: If the funds are to be placed into an interest bearing account:
   (a) Escrow depository will not deposit funds into the account on Potential Buyer's behalf — and therefore interest will not accrue — until escrow depository has been notified that Potential Buyer's check has cleared.
   (b) There may be a delay in returning the funds to Potential Buyer on his request.
   (c) There may be an interest penalty in the case of an early withdrawal from the account.
   (d) If after Potential Buyer has received a Final Subdivision Public Report for this subdivision, he enters into a contract with Subdivider to purchase the reserved subdivision interest, the deposit plus interest earned on the deposit, if any, may be applied toward purchase of the subdivision interest with the express authorization of Potential Buyer.

5. The price and other terms of purchase of the subdivision interest will be those set forth in a purchase contract if Potential Buyer enters into one after receiving a copy of the Final Subdivision Public Report.

NAME OF SUBDIVIDER		SIGNATURE OF POTENTIAL BUYER ▶	DATE
SIGNATURE OF AGENT ▶	DATE	SIGNATURE OF POTENTIAL BUYER ▶	DATE

LEAD-BASED PAINT AND LEAD-BASED PAINT HAZARDS DISCLOSURE, ACKNOWLEDGMENT AND ADDENDUM
For Pre-1978 Housing Sales, Leases, or Rentals
(C.A.R. Form FLD, Revised 1/03)

The following terms and conditions are hereby incorporated in and made a part of the: ☐ California Residential Purchase Agreement, ☐ Residential Lease or Month-to-Month Rental Agreement, or ☐ other; _____ _____,dated _____, on property known as: _____ ("Property") in which _____ is referred to as Buyer or Tenant and _____ is referred to as Seller or Landlord.

LEAD WARNING STATEMENT (SALE OR PURCHASE) Every purchaser of any interest in residential real property on which a residential dwelling was built prior to 1978 is notified that such property may present exposure to lead from lead-based paint that may place young children at risk of developing lead poisoning. Lead poisoning in young children may produce permanent neurological damage, including learning disabilities, reduced intelligent quotient, behavioral problems and impaired memory. Lead poisoning also poses a particular risk to pregnant women. The seller of any interest in residential real property is required to provide the buyer with any information on lead-based paint hazards from risk assessments or inspections in the seller's possession and notify the buyer of any known lead-based paint hazards. A risk assessment or inspection for possible lead-based paint hazards is recommended prior to purchase.

LEAD WARNING STATEMENT (LEASE OR RENTAL) Housing built before 1978 may contain lead-based paint. Lead from paint, paint chips and dust can pose health hazards if not managed properly. Lead exposure is especially harmful to young children and pregnant women. Before renting pre-1978 housing, lessors must disclose the presence of lead-based paint and/or lead-based paint hazards in the dwelling. Lessees must also receive federally approved pamphlet on lead poisoning prevention.

1. SELLER'S OR LANDLORD'S DISCLOSURE

I (we) have no knowledge of lead-based paint and/or lead-based paint hazards in the housing other than the following:

_____
_____
_____
_____

I (we) have no reports or records pertaining to lead-based paint and/or lead-based paint hazards in the housing other than the following, which, previously or as an attachment to this addendum have been provided to Buyer or Tenant:

_____
_____

I (we), previously or as an attachment to this addendum, have provided Buyer or Tenant with the pamphlet "Protect Your Family From Lead In Your Home" or an equivalent pamphlet approved for use in the State such as "The Homeowner's Guide to Environmental Hazards and Earthquake Safety."

For Sales Transactions Only: Buyer has 10 days, unless otherwise agreed in the real estate purchase contract, to conduct a risk assessment or inspection for the presence of lead-based paint and/or lead-based paint hazards.

I (we) have reviewed the information above and certify, to the best of my (our) knowledge, that the information provided is true and correct.

_____ Date _____
Seller or Landlord

_____ Date _____
Seller or Landlord

FLD REVISED 1/03 (PAGE 1 OF 2) Print Date

Buyer's Initials (_____)(_____)
Seller's Initials (_____)(_____)

Reviewed by _____ Date _____

EQUAL HOUSING OPPORTUNITY

LEAD-BASED PAINT AND LEAD-BASED PAINT HAZARDS DISCLOSURE (FLD-11 PAGE 1 OF 2)

Property Address: _____ Date _____

2. LISTING AGENT'S ACKNOWLEDGMENT

Agent has informed Seller or Landlord of Seller's or Landlord's obligations under §42 U.S.C. 4852d and is aware of Agent's responsibility to ensure compliance.

I have reviewed the information above and certify, to the best of my knowledge, that the information provided is true and correct.

_____ By _____
Agent (Broker representing Seller)Please Print   Associate-Licensee or Broker Signature   Date

3. BUYER'S OR TENANT'S ACKNOWLEDGMENT

I (we) have received copies of all information listed, if any, in 1 above and the pamphlet "Protect Your Family From Lead In Your Home" or an equivalent pamphlet approved for use in the State such as "The Homeowner's Guide to Environmental Hazards and Earthquake Safety." **If delivery of any of the disclosures or pamphlet referenced in paragraph 1 above occurs after Acceptance of an offer to purchase, Buyer has a right to cancel pursuant to the purchase contract. If you wish to cancel, you must act within the prescribed period.**

For Sales Transactions Only: Buyer acknowledges the right for 10 days, unless otherwise agreed in the real estate purchase contract, to conduct a risk assessment or inspection for the presence of lead-based paint and/or lead-based paint hazards; OR, (if checked) ☐ Buyer waives the right to conduct a risk assessment or inspection for the presence of lead-based paint and/or lead-based paint hazards.

I (we) have reviewed the information above and certify, to the best of my (our) knowledge, that the information provided is true and correct.

_____   _____
Buyer or Tenant   Date   Buyer or Tenant   Date

4. COOPERATING AGENT'S ACKNOWLEDGMENT

Agent has informed Seller or Landlord, through the Listing Agent if the property is listed, of Seller's or Landlord's obligations under §42 USC 4852d and is aware of Agent's responsibility to ensure compliance.

I have reviewed the information above and certify, to the best of my knowledge, that the information provided is true and correct.

_____ By _____
Agent (Broker obtaining the Offer)   Associate-Licensee or Broker Signature   Date

SURE TRAC
The System for Success™   Published by the
                                California Association of REALTORS®

FLD REVISED 1/03 (PAGE 2 OF 2)

Reviewed by _____ Date _____

LEAD-BASED PAINT AND LEAD-BASED PAINT HAZARDS DISCLOSURE (FLD-11 PAGE 2 OF 2)

NATURAL HAZARD DISCLOSURE STATEMENT

This statement applies to the following property: _____

The transferor and his or her agent(s) disclose the following information with the knowledge that even though this is not a warranty, prospective transferees may rely on this information in deciding whether and on what terms to purchase the subject property. Transferor hereby authorizes any agent(s) representing any principal(s) in this action to provide a copy of this statement to any person or entity in connection with any actual or anticipated sale of the property.

The following are representations made by the transferor and his or her agent(s) based on their knowledge and maps drawn by the state and federal governments. This information is a disclosure and is not intended to be part of any contract between the transferee and transferor.

THIS REAL PROPERTY LIES WITHIN THE FOLLOWING HAZARDOUS AREA(S): (Check the answer which applies.)

A SPECIAL FLOOD HAZARD AREA (Any type Zone "A" or "V") designated by the Federal Emergency Management Agency.

Yes _____   No _____   Do not know and information not available from local jurisdiction _____

AN AREA OF POTENTIAL FLOODING shown on a dam failure inundation map pursuant to Section 8589.5 of the Government Code.

Yes _____   No _____   Do not know and information not available from local jurisdiction _____

A VERY HIGH FIRE HAZARD SEVERITY ZONE pursuant to Section 51178 or 51179 of the Government Code. The owner of this property is subject to the maintenance requirements of Section 51182 of the Government Code.

Yes _____   No _____

A WILDLAND AREA THAT MAY CONTAIN SUBSTANTIAL FOREST FIRE RISKS AND HAZARDS pursuant to Section 4125 of the Public Resources Code. The owner of this property is subject to the maintenance requirements of Section 4291 of the Public Resources Code. Additionally, it is not the state's responsibility to provide fire protection services to any building or structure located within the wildlands unless the Department of Forestry and Fire Protection has entered into a cooperative agreement with a local agency for those purposes pursuant to Section 4142 of the Public Resources Code.

Yes _____   No _____

AN EARTHQUAKE FAULT ZONE pursuant to Section 2622 of the Public Resources Code.

Yes _____   No _____

A SEISMIC HAZARD ZONE pursuant to Section 2696 of the Public Resources Code.

Yes (Landslide Zone) _____
                                   No _____   Map not yet released by state _____
Yes (Liquefaction Zone) _____

THESE HAZARDS MAY LIMIT YOUR ABILITY TO DEVELOP THE REAL PROPERTY, TO OBTAIN INSURANCE, OR TO RECEIVE ASSISTANCE AFTER A DISASTER.

THE MAPS ON WHICH THESE DISCLOSURES ARE BASED ESTIMATE WHERE NATURAL HAZARDS EXIST. THEY ARE NOT DEFINITIVE INDICATORS OF WHETHER OR NOT A PROPERTY WILL BE AFFECTED BY A NATURAL DISASTER. TRANSFEREE(S) AND TRANSFEROR(S) MAY WISH TO OBTAIN PROFESSIONAL ADVICE REGARDING THOSE HAZARDS AND OTHER HAZARDS THAT MAY AFFECT THE PROPERTY.

The information in this box is not part of the statutory form.
☐ (if checked) The representations made in this form are based upon information provided by an independent third-party report provided as a substituted disclosure pursuant to California Civil Code §1102.4. Neither the seller nor the seller's agent (1) has independently verified the information contained in this form and the report or (2) is personally aware of any errors or inaccuracies in the information contained on this form.

Transferor represents that the information herein is true and correct to the best of the transferor's knowledge as of the date signed by the transferor.

Signature of Transferor _____ Date _____

Agent represents that the information herein is true and correct to the best of the agent's knowledge as of the date signed by the agent.

Signature of Agent _____ Date _____

Signature of Agent _____ Date _____

Transferee represents that he or she has read and understands this document.

Signature of Transferee _____ Date _____

THIS FORM HAS BEEN APPROVED BY THE CALIFORNIA ASSOCIATION OF REALTORS® (C.A.R.). NO REPRESENTATION IS MADE AS TO THE LEGAL VALIDITY OR ADEQUACY OF ANY PROVISION IN ANY SPECIFIC TRANSACTION. A REAL ESTATE BROKER IS THE PERSON QUALIFIED TO ADVISE ON REAL ESTATE TRANSACTIONS. IF YOU DESIRE LEGAL OR TAX ADVICE, CONSULT AN APPROPRIATE PROFESSIONAL.

This form is available for use by the entire real estate industry. It is not intended to identify the user as a REALTOR®. REALTOR® is a registered collective membership mark which may be used only by members of the NATIONAL ASSOCIATION OF REALTORS® who subscribe to its Code of Ethics.

The copyright laws of the United States (Title 17 U.S. Code) forbid the unauthorized reproduction of this form, or any portion thereof, by photocopy machine or any other means, including facsimile or computerized formats. Copyright © 1998-1999, CALIFORNIA ASSOCIATION OF REALTORS®, INC. ALL RIGHTS RESERVED.

Published and Distributed by:
REAL ESTATE BUSINESS SERVICES, INC.
a subsidiary of the CALIFORNIA ASSOCIATION OF REALTORS®
525 South Virgil Avenue, Los Angeles, California 90020

PRINT DATE

Page ___ of ___ Pages.
REVISED 10/99

OFFICE USE ONLY
Reviewed by Broker
or Designee _____
Date _____

FORM NHD-11

Due to the nature of land developments and subdivisions, it may take several months for a developer to get a project approved by the commissioner and receive the commissioner's report. In the time that the developer must wait for the commissioner's approval and report, the developer may begin marketing the lots or development to consumers. A preliminary report from the real estate commissioner will allow the developer to take reservations for lots for construction from consumers, however non-refundable deposits are not accepted. To accept a non-refundable deposit, the final report must be completed by the commissioner, and the buyer must sign the receipt for public report. Until that time, the buyer can fill out the reservation instrument, stating interest in the land. This is not a binding contract; but it does give the developer an idea of how many lots will potentially be sold after receiving the final report from the commissioner. This is helpful for the developer in securing construction loans or other financing for development.

Review of Subdivided Lands Act:
- Concerns subdivision containing 5 or more lots, or areas of land up to 160 acres
- Governs marketing and financing of the subdivisions
- Administered by the real estate commissioner
- Protects consumers from fraud and misrepresentation
- Commissioner will release a final report regarding the project for buyers to read
- Pertains to land within the state, as well as land sold outside of California, but marketed in the state
- Buyers must sign the receipt for public report as a sign of approval and acknowledgment of the report
- Reports may be amended when any part of the development changes
- Land may be marketed to buyers with the commissioner's preliminary report, though deposits and contracts cannot be based on this preliminary report

Subdivision Map Act

The Subdivision Map Act is concerned with the appearance of a subdivision. The specific design of the buildings, layout of the streets, size of the lots, drainage and sewage systems and impact on the environment are some specific elements looked at by city and county authorities when a developer wishes to create a subdivision. The act will also define the rules for filing maps. Whereas the Subdivided Lands Act is overseen by the Real Estate Commissioner, city and county authorities will govern the Subdivision Map Act. Specific guidelines are set, with any future improvements reviewed and approved by the same city or county board that approved the original development. The Subdivision Map Act is an enabling act, as it gives the authorization to cities and counties to establish local requirements based on local government.

The main objectives of the Subdivision Map Act are:

- To encourage an orderly community development by providing regulation and control of the design and improvement of subdivisions with consideration to its relation to the surrounding environment. This will focus on the lot's design, its size, number and character of nearby streets, drainage sewage, community patterns and other important factors, as decided by local planning authorities.

- To ensure that areas) within the subdivision dedicated to public use (such as parks or other gathering areas are properly improved or maintained by the developer, so that they will not be an issue for the community.

- To protect the public and individual transferees or buyers from fraud and misrepresentation.

Each city and county is required by the Subdivision Map Act to adopt their own laws to regulate this process. The law will regulate how the final map will look for both situations with five or more lots, as well as lot sizes of two to four lots. A map with two to four lots is called a parcel map, while a map with five or more lots is simply called a map. There are also circumstances where no map is required. In such cases, the Act allows cities and counties to adopt rules regulating subdivisions.

Before the final copy of a map is generated, a tentative map is created, to provide a legal description of the lot. This map shows the property boundaries, the widths and names of all existing streets in the development, the grade of streets and public areas, existing and proposed roads, drainage, sewers and utilities (including easements necessary for these services), the water source or supply, storm water overflow and direction of all natural flowing streams, creeks etc, as well as the purposed use of property. The final map is not necessarily based on the tentative subdivision map, though it is useful for many reasons.

The final map must include the numbered lot, each block as well as all boundaries and soil reports on public record. This map will help determine if there is any conflict with public easements or other access to pubic utilities. If there is a conflict, the public utility will be notified and given the chance to dispute the boundary conflict.

The parcel map is prepared for subdivisions containing two to four lots. Depending on local ordinances, the parcel map may not be required. If it is required, it must follow all the same requirements as the final map, as well as meet any local government requirements or regulations.

Approval of the map is left to an advisory agency, appointed by the city or county where the development will be located. The advisory agency or committee can be made up of any group of individuals, and is sometimes referred to as the planning commission. There may be a notice, hearing, limitation or other requirement for the subdivision map approval. Usually, a notice or hearing is conducted only when the subdivision will disturb a significant number of property owner's rights. However, it is usually a good idea to give notice and conduct a hearing before a subdivision is created. This will approve the tentative map and ensure all local ordinances are being observed. It will also ensure that the site is physically acceptable for such a subdivision (i.e., involves no risk to the environment or public health). A final map must be filed before the tentative map expires (which is two years following its conditional approval plus any additional time granted to the map), not to exceed a total of five years.

Review of Subdivision Map Act:

- Shows what the subdivision will physically look like on paper.
- Overseen by city or county government agency.
- Encourages orderly development and protects individuals from fraud and misrepresentation.
- Each city or county may have individual laws governing subdivision in that particular area
- A tentative map will be approved before a final map, and may exist for up to 5 years before its expiration
- Parcel maps are used for subdivisions of two to four lots.
- Final maps are used for subdivisions of five or more lots.
- A notice, hearing, limitation or other requirement may be necessary before a map will be formed.

Subdivision Classifications

We have just seen that the real estate commissioner regulates the sale of property in subdivisions, while a city- or county-appointed group regulates the actual layout of subdivisions. Compliance is required for both acts, and a full understanding of all laws, at a city, county and state level is required. Thus, it is important for developers and contractors to consult the Real Estate Commissioner when planning a new subdivision, to ensure that all laws and regulations are being followed. A developer must also understand the different classifications of subdivisions.

A *standard* classification is a land division with no common rights of ownership or land use among the owners of individual lots. An example of this is a detached, single-family home located on a private lot.

Common interest is interest in a unit that is privately-owned, with common interest or membership only in community areas of the subdivision. Common areas, shared between all members, are usually governed under a homeowner's association, which is made up of residents of the subdivision. Examples of common interest developments are condominiums, cooperatives, time-share projects and planned developments.

Common Interest Subdivisions

Planned development. An area where there are individually-owned lots as well as shared community areas. Examples of shared community areas are tennis courts, pools or clubhouses.

Community Apartment project. The owner of the apartment has exclusive rights of occupancy to the apartment, with an individual interest in the land on which the complex is built. All owners of property such as this are considered tenants in common. Tax bills, loans assumed for the project and other bills are the responsibility of all of the owners in the complex.

Condominium project. An owner of a condominium has exclusive ownership of the airspace around his or her unit, as well as ownership of the specific unit. The remaining common areas (such as hall ways, walk ways or community areas, such as club houses and exercise rooms) are community owned.

Stock cooperative project. Stock cooperatives are usually apartment buildings in which individuals share holders in a corporation, holding title to property. Individual stockholders receive exclusive occupancy in one portion of the building.

Limited equity housing cooperative. Limited equity housing cooperatives are the same as stock cooperatives, but the California Housing Finance Agency is the financier of the project, rather than the stockholders who are financing the project.

Time-share project. Time-shares are vacation properties in which the purchaser has exclusive rights to use the property during certain times of the year. Before a time-share is DRE-regulated, there must be twelve or more separate, individual interests in the property.

Time-share estate. A time-share where there is an interest in the estate, but the use is shared with other time-share holders. A time-share can be any space, from a city apartment to a campground space. Time-shares allow the investor a three-day right to rescind any offer made.

A buyer will receive *undivided interest* in a parcel of land as a tenant in common with all other tenants or owners. Each of the owners has a right to use the property when they desire. Examples of this type of undivided interest are campgrounds and recreational vehicles.

A *land project* is a subdivision made up of 50 lots or more. These subdivisions are located in an area with less then 1,500 registered voters within either the subdivision or within 2 miles from it. Buyers in a land project have 14 days to retract an offer to purchase a home and receive a full refund. This waiting period protects the buyer from any false advertisement the developer may make and gives the buyer time to investigate the subdivision, to ensure it is a place in which they want to live.

Subdivision Classifications:
- Standard
- Common Interest
- Undivided Interest
- Land Project

Subdivision Requirements and Government Controls

Environmental Impact Report (EIR)s are authorized by the California Environmental Quality Act of 1970 (CEQA) as an official report regarding the impact a new development may have on its surroundings. This report may be required before a subdivision is approved, particularly if the subdivision will have a significant impact on the environment. A significant impact on the environment is defined as "substantial environmental damage", or substantially injurious to fish, wildlife or their habitat. It is in the developer's best interest to determine whether an EIR is necessary before developing even a tentative subdivision map. If the subdivision is going to substantially injure the environment, the developer should not waste his or her time in drawing up maps for the project. If the area's environment will not be harmed, or will sustain very little damage, it is possible to have the appropriate government agency issue a negative declaration that there will be no significant damage to the environment. This enables the developer to move forward with his or her project.

Lead-hazard information must also be given to the purchaser of a home, or a renter (by the landlord). The lead-hazard information discloses possible hazards caused by lead paint or other substances that may contain lead. The disclosures must also state whether or not it is known that there was lead paint used in the construction of the property or structure. A **lead-warning statement** is included in the deposit receipt that must be signed by the buyer. In certain cases, it must also be signed by the seller as well.

Lead-Warning Statement
- Required for buyers to sign
- Included in the deposit receipt

Alquist-Priolo Special Studies Zone Act
California is famous for its earthquakes and numerous fault lines. The California Division of Mines and Geology have identified and located these fault lines and mapped them. When a buyer is looking for a home, he or she must be made aware of any fault lines by the seller or real estate agent. The Alquist-Priolo Special Studies Zone Act is a law that requires geological reports to be drawn up for projects within a quarter mile of any earthquake fault lines. Disclosures of fault activity are included in the deposit receipt when a buyer makes an offer on a property in these locations.

Zoning
Every city or county has police power, which is used to keep a community safe and healthy, as well as promote the general welfare of an area. Police power allows a city or community to adopt building codes, health codes, subdivision regulations and zoning rules and regulations.

Zoning rules and regulations dictate many physical qualities of a development, such as the lot sizes, land use, permitted structures, density and building heights. For example, in a new development, there may be a zoning law that dictates the size of each lot, with a stipulation that any lot NOT be any smaller than a certain square footage. This will keep the density in the new development down, allowing adequate space for new residents. When a community exercises its police power by creating or changing zoning ordinances, it is not necessary for the property affected by the zoning laws to be compensated for any losses they may incur.

Zoning ordinances usually allow for conditional-use permits, which allow land to be used for purposes other than those for which it was originally intended. This is called *nonconforming use*. An example of this type of use is allowing a church to be built in a residential development. Change or reclassification of a zone is referred to as rezoning.

There are different codes used to show different zoning areas. The following is a list of codes and their meaning:

- A – Agricultural
- C – Commercial
- M – Manufacturing
- P – Parking lots and Parks
- R – Homes other residences
- R1 – Single-family home
- R2 – Duplex
- R3 – Multiple-dwelling or tri-plex
- R4 – Four-plex, or high density-dwellings (such as apartment complexes)

FAIR HOUSING LAWS

Over the past 30 years, both the state and federal government have passed laws making it illegal to discriminate against people trying to purchase or rent housing. To illustrate the importance of this issue, when you renew your license, you must take a course on fair housing to ensure that you are well-versed in the laws that protect your clients. Both owners and landlords must obey all of these laws. Real estate brokers should not accept listings from sellers who discriminate against a possible buying segment of the population.

California State Law
California is famous for its progressive laws, which protect the rights of its citizens. On average, state laws are usually broader than those of the federal government laws. On a smaller scale, local governments have passed very liberal laws, aimed at protecting all citizens and providing as many housing opportunities or choices as possible.

The Unruh Civil Rights Act prohibits discrimination in business. Under the Unruh law, it is illegal for anyone to deny services to any person based on age, sex, race, ancestry, religion or national origin. This applies to real estate brokerage as well, as it is considered a service. Steering, redlining or block busting are all considered discriminatory actions on the part of real estate professionals. Steering is when a realtor only shows clients properties in certain areas, and not in others. Redlining is the act of using a property's location to ensure a client is denied financing. Block busting is a tactic used to create sales by other neighbors by telling them that an undesirable group of people are interested in other homes in the area. This causes property values to slide in that area. All of these actions are strictly prohibited.

The California Fair employment and Housing Act (formerly called the Rumford Act) prohibits discrimination in the sale or rental of property. This law also covers discrimination in financing homes. Discrimination in sale, rental or financing based on race, color, marital status, ancestry, religion, sex or national origin is strictly prohibited, and any grievances must be reported directly to the state Department of Fair Employment and Housing.

Housing Financial Discrimination Act (or the Holden Act) prohibits lenders from discriminating against a loan applicant based on the location, neighborhood or other characteristic of the property to be financed. Redlining applies here, as it prohibits a lender from denying a loan based on the aforementioned factors. The exception is if it is proven that the loan is a risky one that the bank or lender would refuse anyway. Any violations based on the Housing Financial Discrimination Act should be reported directly to the state's Secretary for Business and Transportation.

California Civil Code, Section 54-55.1 prohibits discrimination of housing to disabled persons, including those who are blind, visually-impaired, deaf, or physically disabled. Buildings with a no pet policy must also make an exception for residents who utilize a seeing eye dog.

Federal Law

The 1866 Civil Rights Act prohibits discrimination against persons based on race in any property transaction. This act was basically ignored until 1968, which saw the court case of Jones v. Mayer. United States Supreme Court Case of **Jones v. Mayer (1968)** upheld the 1866 Civil Rights Act and the 13th amendment to the United States Constitution prohibiting slavery.

The Civil Rights Act of 1968 and 1988 Amendments changed the original Civil Rights Act . The Amendment made it illegal to discriminate against people purchasing homes, or leasing property, based on race alone. It is now illegal to discriminate against a possible buyer or tenant because of their national origin, religion, age, sex, color or handicapped status.

The **Fair Housing Act** protects people from the following actions:

- Sellers refusing to sell property to qualified buyers
- Landlords refusing to rent property to qualified renters
- Landlords treating twp separate applicants differently for housing for any discriminatory reason
- Financial firms treating applicants differently in connection with rates or loan terms and conditions
- Discrimination in property advertisements
- Restricting tenants from the enjoyment or exercise of their rights under the act
- Blockbusting
- Redlining
- Brokers denying services to any group due to discrimination against race, sex, religion, color, handicap, presence of absence of children or national origin.

It is HUD's responsibility to enforce fair housing laws. If a person feels they have been discriminated against, he or she may take up their grievance with HUD, or may elect to have their case heard in a U.S. District Court. Penalties for those found guilty of discriminatory practices range from $10,000 (for the first offense), to $50,000 (for the third offense). The party discriminated against will have damages awarded, with all other monies paid to the federal government. Those who willfully fail to give information or evidence, or give false information in a fair housing investigation, will be charged with criminal penalties and a fine of up to $100,000.

Protection for People with Disabilities protects people who have a physical or mental disability that restricts one or more life activities. Handicaps include mental illness, AIDS, blindness, hearing impairment, mental retardation and mobility limitations.

Senior Citizen Exemptions

There are certain exemptions to the fair housing rules, regarding housing for senior citizens. It is allowable to discriminate against age in housing when the housing is intended for senior citizens only, provided the housing can meet the needs of the seniors living there. The following list is a list of criteria that makes senior housing exempt from the prohibition against discrimination based on familial status:

- The housing is intended for persons 62 years of age or over
- Housing provides for the social and physical needs of seniors
- Policies and procedures of the housing complex demonstrate the intent to provide housing for persons 55 years of age or over
- Housing is a federal program, designed specifically to assist senior citizens.
- Housing unit is intended and operated for persons at least 55 years of age 80% of the units are occupied by persons 55 years of age or over

Real Estate Advertising

Real estate advertising is governed by Section 804 of the Federal Fair Housing Law, which prohibits advertising from discriminating against race, color, religion, sex, handicap, familial status, or national origin. Advertising with key phrases or words which may discourage a specific group from moving into the area, or viewing the property for sale, is strictly prohibited.

All residential real estate advertisements must contain the equal opportunity logo and slogan, large enough to be read, and clearly understood. The logo features a photo of people of multiple ethnicities. When it is unclear that each of the people are of different descent, the logo is considered too small.

Advertisers of real estate need to be very careful about the images, models, photographs or drawings they use in advertisements. If the images seem exclusive, members of certain groups may feel excluded from that property or neighborhood. Images must clearly define a reasonable cross-section of all majority and minority groups, in equal social situations, using both sexes and showing families with children. The advertisements should indicate to every person that the open property is inviting to all interested buyers, and does not exclude any person based on sex, age, color, national origin, religion, race, handicap or familial status.

Word usage should not imply a preference or limitation to any group of people, based on any demographic. Catch phrases or words to be avoided are:

- Adult building
- No children
- Asian area

- Near mosque
- Ideal for physically fit
- Prefer smart, healthy person
- Restrictive
- Lutheran Church nearby
- Russian businesses in area
- Male or Female only
- Single people only
- Racially - integrated neighborhood

Words or phrases, which are acceptable, include:
- Gated
- Parks nearby
- Houses of worship nearby
- Quiet, residential area
- Close to schools

S U M M A R Y

Subdivisions are created when a developer divides land into five lots or more, with the intention to sell these lots or build homes on them for sale at a later date. Subdivisions fall under two laws: the Subdivided Lands Act and the Subdivision Map Act. These acts govern the division of the land, its use, actual plots, sizes and location of the development and public utilities and spaces. Additionally, the government will protect purchasers against fraud by ensuring the developer is delivering the promised land, lot size or home.

The Real Estate Commissioner governs the Subdivided Lands Act; ensuring consumers are protected against fraud. City or county officials govern the Subdivision Maps Act, ensuring all zoning laws are followed. This ensures the safety, public health and welfare of all citizens living in the area. Additionally, the city and county officials are in charge of accepting or rejecting a purposed map of the area before a developer can create the final map of a project.

Fair housing laws protect all people from discrimination in transactions, including the rental of property. Federal and state laws have been adopted to ensure redlining, block busting or steering does not take place by real estate professionals. These laws also prevent discrimination in selling or leasing on the seller or landlord's side. Laws have also been put in place to ensure all advertising is fair, and not specifically targeted to one group.

Now that you have been exposed to the laws and regulations of land use and subdivisions, you are better equipped to more efficiently help your clients. You are also knowledgeable of all governmental controls of which your client may need to be aware.

T E R M S   A N D   P H R A S E S

Block Busting – Causing people to move out of a neighborhood because another group of people are moving in, causing a perception of lower home values

Common Interest Subdivision – An area of land divided into separate lots but with some of the land set aside for shared ownership by all owners of the separate lots.

Community Apartment Project – A form of subdivision in which the owner has an individual interest in the land as well as exclusive right of occupancy of an apartment on the land.

Condominium Project – A subdivision providing an exclusive ownership interest in the airspace of a particular portion of real property, as well as interest in common areas of the building or complex (such as the hallways, walkways or clubhouse).

Environmental Impact Report (EIR) – A report showing the findings of a study of the impact a development will have on the environment surrounding it.

Land Projects – Subdivisions of 50 lots or more, located in sparsely-populated areas,

Manufactured Housing – Mobile homes

Police Power – The right of the state to regulate for the purpose of promoting the safety, health or welfare of a community.

Redlining – The act of denying financing to people based on the location or neighborhood of the property being purchased (done by financing firms)

Steering – Discriminatory action a realtor can take by showing properties located in only one area to a prospective client.

Subdivided Lands Act – State law protecting purchasers of property in new subdivisions from fraud in the marketing of that new subdivision. Subdivided Lands Act is also concerned with the financial aspects of a development.

Subdivision Map Act – Rules or guidelines for drawing subdivision maps to create a new subdivision. Overseen by city or county authorities concerned with the physical aspects of the development.

Subdivision – The division of land into five or more lots for the purpose of sale, lease, financing or development.

Undivided Interest Subdivision – An area of land divided into lots; each owner is a tenant in common with all other owners.

Variance – Exception to existing zoning laws.

Zoning – The act of the city or county government restricting the land use of an area for a specific purpose.

C H A P T E R   Q U I Z

1. How many lots or parcels must land be divided into before it is considered a subdivision?
   - A. 3
   - B. 4
   - C. 5
   - D. 10

2. How many lots must be included in a subdivision for the Subdivided Lands Act to apply?
    A. 3
    B. 5
    C. 8
    D. 10

3 With a preliminary report from the Real Estate Commissioner, a developer may begin doing what with a subdivision?
    A. Taking non-refundable deposits for lots from buyers.
    B. Collecting signed contracts for lots in the subdivision.
    C. The developer may not market the lots yet, the final report is required.
    D. Collecting the reservation instrument from buyers, showing their intent to pur chase a lot.

4. There are three types of maps included in the Subdivision Maps Act, they are tentative, final and
    A. Parcel
    B. Plot
    C. Plat
    D. Subdivision

5. When is a parcel map used in the Subdivision Maps Act?
    A. Always
    B With lots containing more than 160 acres
    C. With subdivisions of two to four lots
    D. With subdivisions of five or more lots

6. What are the two requirements of a land project?
    A. A subdivision with less than 50 lots and more than 1,500 registered voters.
    B. A subdivision with more than 50 lots and less than 1,500 registered voters.
    C. A subdivision with more than 50 lots and more than 1,500 registered voters
    D. A subdivision with less than 50 lots and less than 1,500 registered voters.

7. What is an example of a common interest subdivision classification?
    A. Non-joined single family residence
    B. Campground
    C. Recreational Vehicle
    D. Condominium

8. Who must sign the lead-based disclosure statement?
    A. The buyer always
    B. The seller always
    C. The buyer always; seller in certain situations
    D. The seller always; the buyer in certain situation

9. What does the code M stand for; in reference to zoning rules and regulations?
    A. Multi-family dwellings
    B. Manufacturing
    C. Milling
    D. Malls

10. The owner of a condominium also owns which of the following?
    A. Individual units
    B. Air space
    C. Shared ownership of common areas
    D. All of the above

11. What document is required of a developer to study the potential environmental hazards of a new development?
    A. Environmental Impact Report
    B. Lead Hazard Report
    C. Geologic, seismic and flood hazard report
    D. None of the above

12. In the Subdivided Lands Act, who releases the final report regarding a development that gives the developer the green light to begin collecting deposits and contracts on lots?
    A. City or county officials
    B. Real Estate Commissioner
    C. State Recorder
    D. State Legislature

13. The Aquist-Priolo Special Studies Zone Act is mostly concerned with zoning laws pertaining to what?
    A. Earthquakes
    B. Flooding
    C. Both A and B
    D. Neither A nor B

14. Which state law protects citizens against discrimination when seeking for a private residence, whether a single-family home or an apartment?
    A. Unruh Civil Rights Act
    B. California Civil Code Section 54-55.1
    C. California Fair Employment and Housing Act
    D. Housing Financial Discrimination Act

15. The act of getting people to sell their home in an area by telling them a minority group is moving in is called
    A. Steering
    B. Redlining
    C. Panic selling
    D. Block Busing

16. What federal law expanded the 1866 Civil Rights Act to include more than just discrimination against race?
    A. Jones v. Mayer
    B. Fair Housing Act
    C. Unruh Act
    D. Civil Rights Act of 1968 and 1988

17. Which of the following words or phrases would be considered discriminatory in an advertisement?
    A. Schools nearby
    B. Parks nearby
    C. Gated
    D. Lutheran church nearby

18. What actions are protected under fair housing laws?
    A. Purchase of a home
    B. Leasing an apartment
    C. Financing a home
    D. All of the above

19. A land division with no common or mutual rights of ownership or use among owners of adjoining parcels best describes which subdivision classification?
    A. Standard
    B. Undivided interest
    C. Land Project
    D. None of the above

20. What is a reservation instrument used for?
    A. Creating a contract between an interested buyer and developer.
    B. Making a reservation for a lot in a new development, with no deposit or contract signed.
    C. Making a reservation for a lot in a new development, including a deposit and contract
    D. Both A and B

13

REAL ESTATE BROKERAGE

What you will learn in this Chapter

- Ethics and Professionalism

- Regulations of the Real Estate Commissioner

- Code of Ethics

- Definition and Operations of a Real Estate Brokerage

- Requirements and Specific Disclosures of Real Estate Transactions

- Escrow and Trust Funds

1. A real estate professional found guilty of violating real estate law may face
   A. Sanctions from the Real Estate Commission
   B. Civil Punishment
   C. Criminal Punishment
   D. All of the above

2. A real estate agent is a person who holds what type of license?
   A. A broker's license
   B. A salesperson's license.
   C. Either a salesperson or broker's license
   D. A real estate agent holds an agent's license

3. Which of the following is NOT one of the five main functions of a real estate brokerage?
   A. Filling out paperwork
   B. Listing
   C. Selling
   D. Arranging or making referrals for financing

4. How many days does a broker have to deposit trust fund money into the trust account?
   A. 2
   B. 3
   C. 4
   D. 5

5. According to the Natural Hazard Disclosure Law passed in 1998, which of the following disclosures are required by law?
   A. State responsibility fire zone
   B. Seismic hazard zone
   C. Flood hazard area
   D. All of the above

6. Which one of the following hazards is NOT discussed in the environmental hazard booklet?
   A. Asbestos
   B. Lead
   C. Lead-based paint
   D. Formaldehyde

7. In a transaction between the seller and the seller's agent, when does the transaction actually begin?
   A. When the listing is received
   B. When a purchase contract is signed
   C. When escrow is opened
   D. At the close of escrow

INTRODUCTION

This book has introduced you to new concepts in real estate. The first twelve chapters have been of a very technical nature exposing you to legal, financial, economic and governmental aspects of real estate. Now, we will explore the practice of real estate and attempt to pull together what you have learned for practical application.

We will explore brokerage in this chapter, and see how a real estate brokerage works. Additionally, you will be exposed to a long list of regulations and ethics of which every realtor should be aware of as well as other application in everyday use. At the end of this chapter, you will have a better understanding of what it means to be a realtor, as well as how to pull this vast knowledge together for practical application.

ETHICS AND PROFESSIONALISM

As a real estate agent, it is challenging to remain informed of all the law changes, specific requirements of clients, disclosures for each property, and other rules and regulations you must follow as an agent. Being able to juggle several tasks at once, stay on top of all such projects and educate yourself to any changes made in your office and industry, as well as specific requirements of each one of your properties will keep you very busy. Sometimes, it is easy to get caught up in some aspects of your job, while allowing others to slide.

Your number one responsibility is to your client. However, you must also work hard, and ethically, to sell homes and earn money for yourself and your family. It seems easy to assume you will make all the right, ethically correct decisions every time; but, when dealing with difficult clients, it is sometimes easy to forget about a disclosure. You may also become so focused on your task that you simply forget some rules and regulations.

Full disclosure is one of the most important duties for you to always remember. Your broker or firm will provide you with all the necessary forms for disclosure, but it is your responsibility to remain in compliance with the law at all times. Each disclosure may require a different compliance with the law. It is also your job to fully explain what each disclosure means to your client, so that your client understands all of the disclosures they must read sign. All of the most important disclosures will be included in the deposit receipt; but that does not necessarily mean that your client understands what they are what they mean. Real estate is perhaps one of the largest investments a person will make in their lifetime; so, it is important for you to be very informative and patient.

When a real estate agent does not comply with the law, they must be prepared for civil or criminal punishment. They must also face the Real Estate Commission, where monetary penalties as well as the possibility of having their license suspended or revoked may occur. Accountability is the key. If a real estate agent fails to follow the law, a court will hold them accountable. Unfortunately, as our society becomes more and more litigious, real estate agents must become better at their job, especially regarding what to disclose, when to disclose it and to whom.

Remember!
Realtors found in violation of Real Estate Law may face:
- Criminal punishment
- Civil punishment
- Sanctions or punishment from the Real Estate Commission

Real Estate Law is found in the Business and Professional Code of the California Code of Regulations. Policing of these laws lies in the hands of the state Real Estate Commissioner. He or she may adopt regulations to enforce the Real Estate Law, as or may use the court for more serious violations. Real estate professionals need to be well-versed with the Commissioner's regulations, as they will be held accountable for them. They should also be familiar with the code of ethics to which realtors will be held accountable.

As a licensed real estate professional, you are more than a license holder; you are a resource for your clients. Because of this, it is important to be very knowledgeable about the profession itself. The following list is a good one with which to be familiar, not only for your understanding of the profession, but to prepare for the state exam. Take a moment and review the following list, to gauge your understanding of real estate topics, terms and concepts.

Property Ownership
- Classes of Property
- Land Characteristics
- Encumbrances
- Types of Ownership
- Descriptions of Property

Land Use Controls and Regulations
- Government Rights in Land
- Public Controls
- Private Controls
- Water Rights

Valuation and Market Analysis
- Value
- Methods of Estimating Value and the Appraisal Process
- Competitive Market Analysis

Financing
- General Concepts
- Types of Loans
- Sources of Funds
- Government Programs
- Deeds of Trust
- Financing and Credit Laws

Laws of Agency and Disclosure
- Law, Definition and Nature of Agency Relationships
- Types of Agencies and Agents
- Creation of Agency and Agency Agreements
- Responsibilities of Agent to Principal
- Responsibilities to Buyer and Third Parties
- Disclosure of Agency
- Disclosure of Acting as Principal or other Interest
- Termination of Agency
- Commission and Fees

Contracts
- General
- Listing Agreements
- Buyer and Broker Agreements
- Offers and Purchase Agreements
- Counteroffers and Multiple Counter-offers
- Leases as Contracts
- Options
- Rescission and Cancellation Agreements
- Broker and Salesperson Agreements

Transfer of Property
- Title Insurance
- Deeds
- Escrow
- Special Reports
- Tax Aspects
- Probate

Practice of Real Estate
- Commercial Property and Income Property
- Trust Accounts
- Fair Housing Laws
- Advertising
- Maintaining Transaction Files
- Disciplinary Actions
- Specialty Areas

So, now that you are a wealth of information and you understand the basics of the real estate business, you need to apply these basics. Study the following list and learn to perform these activities in the pursuit of your new real estate career.

Agent's Activities to Perform
- Locating and Listing Properties (MLS)
- Marketing Properties
- Negotiating Sales Contracts
- Arranging Financing, or Acting as a Referral
- Assisting with Transfer of Property
- Good Knowledge of Escrow and its Process
- Managing Property
- Educate Yourself Regarding Changes in the Industry
- Managing a Brokerage

REGULATIONS OF THE COMMISSIONER

Article 10. Discrimination and Panic Selling

2780. Discriminatory Conduct as the Basis for Disciplinary Action.
Prohibited discriminatory conduct by a real estate licensee based upon race, color, sex, religion, ancestry, physical handicap, marital status or national origin includes, but is not limited to, the following:

(a) Refusing to negotiate for the sale, rental or financing of the purchase of real property or otherwise making unavailable or denying real property to any person because of such person's race, color, sex, religion, ancestry, physical handicap, marital status or national origin.

(b) Refusing or failing to show, rent, sell or finance the purchase of real property to any person or refusing or failing to provide or volunteer information to any person about real property, or channeling or steering any person away from real property, because of that person's race, color, sex, religion, ancestry, physical handicap, marital status or national origin or because of the racial, religious, or ethnic composition of any occupants of the area in which the real property is located.

It shall not constitute discrimination under this subdivision for a real estate licensee to refuse or fail to show, rent, sell or finance the purchase of real property to any person having a physical handicap because of the presence of hazardous conditions or architectural barriers to the physically handicapped which conform to applicable state or local building codes and regulations.

(c) Discriminating because of race, color, sex, religion, ancestry, physical handicap, marital status or national origin against any person in the sale or purchase or negotiation or solicitation of the sale or purchase or the collection of payment or the performance of services in connection with contracts for the sale of real property or in connection with loans secured directly or collaterally by liens on real property or on a business opportunity.

Prohibited discriminatory conduct by a real estate licensee under this subdivision does not include acts based on a person's marital status which are reasonably taken in recognition of the community property laws of this state as to the acquiring, financing, holding or transferring of real property.

(d) Discriminating because of race, color, sex, religion, ancestry, physical handicap, marital status or national origin against any person in the terms, conditions or privileges of sale, rental or financing of the purchase of real property.

This subdivision does not prohibit the sale price, rent or terms of a housing accommodation containing facilities for the physically handicapped to differ reasonably from a housing accommodation not containing such facilities.

(e) Discriminating because of race, color, sex, religion, ancestry, physical handicap, marital status or national origin against any person in providing services or facilities in connection with the sale, rental or financing of the purchase of real property, including but not limited to: processing applications differently, referring prospects to other licensees because of the prospects' race, color, sex, religion, ancestry, physical handicap, marital status or national origin, using with discriminatory intent or effect, codes or other means of identifying minority prospects, or assigning real estate licensees on the basis of a prospective client's race, color, sex, religion, ancestry, physical handicap, marital status or national origin.

Prohibited discriminatory conduct by a real estate licensee under this subdivision does not include acts based on a person's marital status which are reasonably taken in recognition of the community property laws of this state as to the acquiring, financing, holding or transferring of real property.

(f) Representing to any person because of his or her race, color, sex, religion, ancestry, physical handicap, marital status or national origin that real property is not available for inspection, sale or rental when such real property is in fact available.

(g) Processing an application more slowly or otherwise acting to delay, hinder or avoid the sale, rental or financing of the purchase of real property on account of the race, color, sex, religion, ancestry, physical handicap, marital status or national origin of a potential owner or occupant.

(h) Making any effort to encourage discrimination against persons because of their race, color, sex, religion, ancestry, physical handicap, marital status or national origin in the showing, sale, lease or financing of the purchase of real property.

(i) Refusing or failing to cooperate with or refusing or failing to assist another real estate licensee in negotiating the sale, rental or financing of the purchase of real property because of the race, color, sex, religion, ancestry, physical handicap, marital status or national origin of any prospective purchaser or tenant.

(j) Making any effort to obstruct, retard or discourage the purchase, lease or financing of the purchase of real property by persons whose race, color, sex, religion, ancestry, physical handicap, marital status or national origin differs from that of the majority of persons presently residing in a structural improvement to real property or in an area in which the real property is located.

(k) Performing any acts, making any notation, asking any questions or making or circulating any written or oral statement which when taken in context, expresses or implies a limitation, preference or discrimination based upon race, color, sex, religion, ancestry, physical handicap, marital status or national origin; provided, however, that nothing herein shall limit the administering of forms or the making of a notation required by a federal, state or local agency for data collection or civil rights enforcement purposes; or in the case of a physically handicapped person, making notation, asking questions or circulating any written or oral statement in order to serve the needs of such a person.

(l) Making any effort to coerce, intimidate, threaten or interfere with any person in the exercise or enjoyment of, or on account of such person's having exercised or enjoyed, or on account of such person's having aided or encouraged any other person in the exercise or enjoyment of any right granted or protected by a federal or state law, including but not limited to: assisting in any effort to coerce any person because of his or her race, color, sex, religion, ancestry, physical handicap, marital status or national origin to move from, or to not move into, a particular area; punishing or penalizing real estate licensees for their refusal to discriminate in the sale or rental of housing because of the race, color, sex, religion, ancestry, physical handicap, marital status or national origin of a prospective purchaser or lessee; or evicting or taking other retaliatory action against any person for having filed a fair housing complaint or for having undertaken other lawful efforts to promote fair housing.

(m) Soliciting of sales, rentals or listings of real estate from any person, but not from another person within the same area because of differences in the race, color, sex, religion, ancestry, physical handicap, marital status or national origin of such persons.

(n) Discriminating because of race, color, sex, religion, ancestry, physical handicap, marital status or national origin in informing persons of the existence of waiting lists or other procedures with respect to the future availability of real property for purchase or lease.

(o) Making any effort to discourage or prevent the rental, sale or financing of the purchase of real property because of the presence or absence of occupants of a particular race, color, sex, religion, ancestry, physical handicap, marital status or national origin, or on the basis of the future presence or absence of a particular race, color, sex, religion, ancestry, physical handicap, marital status or national origin, whether actual, alleged or implied.

(p) Making any effort to discourage or prevent any person from renting, purchasing or financing the purchase of real property through any representations of actual or alleged community opposition based upon race, color, sex, religion, ancestry, physical handicap, marital status or national origin.

(q) Providing information or advice to any person concerning the desirability of particular real property or a particular residential area(s) which is different from information or advice given to any other person with respect to the same property or area because of differences in the race, color, sex, religion, ancestry, physical handicap, marital status or national origin of such persons.

This subdivision does not limit the giving of information or advice to physically handicapped persons for the purpose of calling to the attention of such persons the existence or absence of housing accommodation services or housing accommodations for the physically handicapped.

(r) Refusing to accept a rental or sales listing or application for financing of the purchase of real property because of the owner's race, color, sex, religion, ancestry, physical handicap, marital status or national origin or because of the race, color, sex, religion, ancestry, physical handicap, marital status or national origin of any of the occupants in the area in which the real property is located.

(s) Entering into an agreement, or carrying out any instructions of another, explicit or understood, not to show, lease, sell or finance the purchase of real property because of race, color, sex, religion, ancestry, physical handicap, marital status or national origin.

(t) Making, printing or publishing, or causing to be made, printed or published, any notice, statement or advertisement concerning the sale, rental or financing of the purchase of real property that indicates any preference, limitation or discrimination because of race, color, sex, religion, ancestry, physical handicap, marital status or national origin, or any intention to make such preference, limitation or discrimination.

This subdivision does not prohibit advertising directed to physically handicapped persons for the purpose of calling to the attention of such persons the existence or absence of housing accommodation services or housing accommodations for the physically handicapped.

(u) Using any words, phrases, sentences, descriptions or visual aids in any notice, statement or advertisement describing real property or the area in which real property is located which indicates any preference, limitation or discrimination because of race, color, sex, religion, ancestry, physical handicap, marital status or national origin.

This subdivision does not prohibit advertising directed to physically handicapped persons for the purpose of calling to the attention of such persons the existence or absence of housing accommodation services or housing accommodations for the physically handicapped.

(v) Selectively using, placing or designing any notice, statement or advertisement having to do with the sale, rental or financing of the purchase of real property in such a manner as to cause or increase discrimination by restricting or enhancing the exposure or appeal to persons of a particular race, color, sex, ancestry, physical handicap, marital status or national origin.

This subdivision does not limit in any way the use of an affirmative marketing program designed to attract persons of a particular race, color, sex, religion, ancestry, physical handicap, marital status or national origin who would not otherwise be attracted to the real property or to the area.

(w) Quoting or charging a price, rent or cleaning or security deposit for a particular real property to any person which is different from the price, rent or security deposit quoted or charged to any other person because of differences in the race, color, sex, religion, ancestry, physical handicap, marital status or national origin of such persons.

This subdivision does not prohibit the quoting or charging of a price, rent or cleaning or security deposit for a housing accommodation containing facilities for the physically handicapped to differ reasonably from a housing accommodation not containing such facilities.

(x) Discriminating against any person because of race, color, sex, religion, ancestry, physical handicap, marital status or national origin in performing any acts in connection with the making of any determination of financial ability or in the processing of any application for the financing or refinancing of real property.

Nothing herein shall limit the administering of forms or the making of a notation required by a federal, state or local agency for data collection or civil rights enforcement purposes. In any evaluation or determination as to whether, and under what terms and conditions, a particular lender or lenders would be likely to grant a loan, licensees shall proceed as though the lender or lenders are in compliance with Sections 35800 through 35833 of the California Health and Safety Code (The Housing Financial Discrimination Act of 1977).

Prohibited discriminatory conduct by a real estate licensee under this subdivision does not include acts based on a person's marital status which are reasonably taken in recognition of the community property laws of this state as to the acquiring, financing, holding or transferring of real property.

(y) Advising a person of the price or value of real property on the basis of factors related to the race, color, sex, religion, ancestry, physical handicap, marital status or national origin of residents of an area or of residents or potential residents of the area in which the property is located.

(z) Discriminating in the treatment of, or services provided to, occupants of any real property in the course of providing management services for the real property because of the race, color, sex, religion, ancestry, physical handicap, marital status or national origin of said occupants.

This subdivision does not prohibit differing treatment or services to a physically handicapped person because of the physical handicap in the course of providing management services for a housing accommodation.

(aa) Discriminating against the owners or occupants of real property because of the race, color, sex, religion, ancestry, physical, handicap, marital status or national origin of their guests, visitors or invitees.

(bb) Making any effort to instruct or encourage, expressly or impliedly, by either words or acts, licensees or their employees or other agents to engage in any discriminatory act in violation of a federal or state fair housing law.

(cc) Establishing or implementing rules that have the effect of limiting the opportunity for any person because of his or her race, color, sex, religion, ancestry, physical handicap, marital status or national origin to secure real property through a multiple listing or other real estate service.

(dd) Assisting or aiding in any way, any person in the sale, rental or financing of the purchase of real property where there are reasonable grounds to believe that such person intends to discriminate because of race, color, sex, religion, ancestry, physical handicap, marital status or national origin.

2781. Panic Selling as the Basis for Disciplinary Action.
Prohibited discriminatory conduct includes, but is not limited to, soliciting sales or rental listings, making written or oral statements creating fear or alarm, transmitting written or oral warnings or threats, or acting in any other manner so as to induce or attempt to induce the sale or lease of real property through any representation, express or implied, regarding the present or prospective entry of one or more persons of another race, color, sex, religion, ancestry, marital status or national origin into an area or neighborhood.

Code of Ethics and Standards of Practice
of the NATIONAL ASSOCIATION OF REALTORS®

Effective January 1, 2004

Where the word REALTORS® is used in this Code and Preamble, it shall be deemed to include REALTOR-ASSOCIATE®s.

While the Code of Ethics establishes obligations that may be higher than those mandated by law, in any instance where the Code of Ethics and the law conflict, the obligations of the law must take precedence.

Preamble

Under all is the land. Upon its wise utilization and widely allocated ownership depend the survival and growth of free institutions and of our civilization. REALTORS® should recognize that the interests of the nation and its citizens require the highest and best use of the land and the widest distribution of land ownership. They require the creation of adequate housing, the building of functioning cities, the development of productive industries and farms, and the preservation of a healthful environment.

Such interests impose obligations beyond those of ordinary commerce. They impose grave social responsibility and a patriotic duty to which REALTORS® should dedicate themselves, and for which they should be diligent in preparing themselves. REALTORS®, therefore, are zealous to maintain and improve the standards of their calling and share with their fellow REALTORS® a common responsibility for its integrity and honor.

In recognition and appreciation of their obligations to clients, customers, the public, and each other, REALTORS® continuously strive to become and remain informed on issues affecting real estate and, as knowledgeable professionals, they willingly share the fruit of their experience and study with others. They identify and take steps, through enforcement of this Code of Ethics and by assisting appropriate regulatory bodies, to eliminate practices which may damage the public or which might discredit or bring dishonor to the real estate profession. REALTORS® having direct personal knowledge of conduct that may violate the Code of Ethics involving misappropriation of client or customer funds or property, willful discrimination, or fraud resulting in substantial economic harm, bring such matters to the attention of the appropriate Board or Association of REALTORS®. (Amended 1/00)

Realizing that cooperation with other real estate professionals promotes the best interests of those who utilize their services, REALTORS® urge exclusive representation of clients; do not attempt to gain any unfair advantage over their competitors; and they refrain from making unsolicited comments about other practitioners. In instances where their opinion is sought, or where REALTORS® believe that comment is necessary, their opinion is offered in an objective, professional manner, uninfluenced by any personal motivation or potential advantage or gain.

The term REALTOR® has come to connote competency, fairness, and high integrity resulting from adherence to a lofty ideal of moral conduct in business relations. No inducement of profit and no instruction from clients ever can justify departure from this ideal.

In the interpretation of this obligation, REALTORS® can take no safer guide than that which has been handed down through the centuries, embodied in the Golden Rule, "Whatsoever ye would that others should do to you, do ye even so to them."

Accepting this standard as their own, REALTORS® pledge to observe its spirit in all of their activities and to conduct their business in accordance with the tenets set forth below.

Duties to Clients and Customers

Article 1

When representing a buyer, seller, landlord, tenant, or other client as an agent, REALTORS® pledge themselves to protect and promote the interests of their client. This obligation to the client is primary, but it does not relieve REALTORS® of their obligation to treat all parties honestly. When serving a buyer, seller, landlord, tenant or other party in a non-agency capacity, REALTORS® remain obligated to treat all parties honestly. (Amended 1/01)

- **Standard of Practice 1-1**
  REALTORS®, when acting as principals in a real estate transaction, remain obligated by the duties imposed by the Code of Ethics. (Amended 1/93)

- **Standard of Practice 1-2**
  The duties the Code of Ethics imposes are applicable whether REALTORS® are acting as agents or in legally recognized non-agency capacities except that any duty imposed exclusively on agents by law or regulation shall not be imposed by this Code of Ethics on REALTORS® acting in non-agency capacities.

  As used in this Code of Ethics, "client" means the person(s) or entity(ies) with whom a REALTOR® or a REALTOR®'s firm has an agency or legally recognized non-agency relationship; "customer" means a party to a real estate transaction who receives information, services, or benefits but has no contractual relationship with the REALTOR® or the REALTOR®'s firm; "prospect" means a purchaser, seller, tenant, or landlord who is not subject to a representation relationship with the REALTOR® or REALTOR®'s firm; "agent" means a real estate licensee (including brokers and sales associates) acting in an agency relationship as defined by state law or regulation; and

NATIONAL ASSOCIATION OF REALTORS®
The Voice for Real Estate®

Real Strength.
Real Advantages.

"broker" means a real estate licensee (including brokers and sales associates) acting as an agent or in a legally recognized non-agency capacity. *(Adopted 1/95, Amended 1/04)*

• **Standard of Practice 1-3**
REALTORS®, in attempting to secure a listing, shall not deliberately mislead the owner as to market value.

• **Standard of Practice 1-4**
REALTORS®, when seeking to become a buyer/tenant representative, shall not mislead buyers or tenants as to savings or other benefits that might be realized through use of the REALTOR®'s services. *(Amended 1/93)*

• **Standard of Practice 1-5**
REALTORS® may represent the seller/landlord and buyer/tenant in the same transaction only after full disclosure to and with informed consent of both parties. *(Adopted 1/93)*

• **Standard of Practice 1-6**
REALTORS® shall submit offers and counter-offers objectively and as quickly as possible. *(Adopted 1/93, Amended 1/95)*

• **Standard of Practice 1-7**
When acting as listing brokers, REALTORS® shall continue to submit to the seller/landlord all offers and counter-offers until closing or execution of a lease unless the seller/landlord has waived this obligation in writing. REALTORS® shall not be obligated to continue to market the property after an offer has been accepted by the seller/landlord. REALTORS® shall recommend that sellers/landlords obtain the advice of legal counsel prior to acceptance of a subsequent offer except where the acceptance is contingent on the termination of the pre-existing purchase contract or lease. *(Amended 1/93)*

• **Standard of Practice 1-8**
REALTORS®, acting as agents or brokers of buyers/tenants, shall submit to buyers/tenants all offers and counter-offers until acceptance but have no obligation to continue to show properties to their clients after an offer has been accepted unless otherwise agreed in writing. REALTORS®, acting as agents or brokers of buyers/tenants, shall recommend that buyers/tenants obtain the advice of legal counsel if there is a question as to whether a pre-existing contract has been terminated. *(Adopted 1/93, Amended 1/99)*

• **Standard of Practice 1-9**
The obligation of REALTORS® to preserve confidential information (as defined by state law) provided by their clients in the course of any agency relationship or non-agency relationship recognized by law continues after termination of agency relationships or any non-agency relationships recognized by law. REALTORS® shall not knowingly, during or following the termination of professional relationships with their clients:
1) reveal confidential information of clients; or
2) use confidential information of clients to the disadvantage of clients; or
3) use confidential information of clients for the REALTOR®'s advantage or the advantage of third parties unless:

a) clients consent after full disclosure; or
b) REALTORS® are required by court order; or
c) it is the intention of a client to commit a crime and the information is necessary to prevent the crime; or
d) it is necessary to defend a REALTOR® or the REALTOR®'s employees or associates against an accusation of wrongful conduct.

Information concerning latent material defects is not considered confidential information under this Code of Ethics. *(Adopted 1/93, Amended 1/01)*

• **Standard of Practice 1-10**
REALTORS® shall, consistent with the terms and conditions of their real estate licensure and their property management agreement, competently manage the property of clients with due regard for the rights, safety and health of tenants and others lawfully on the premises. *(Adopted 1/95, Amended 1/00)*

• **Standard of Practice 1-11**
REALTORS® who are employed to maintain or manage a client's property shall exercise due diligence and make reasonable efforts to protect it against reasonably foreseeable contingencies and losses. *(Adopted 1/95)*

• **Standard of Practice 1-12**
When entering into listing contracts, REALTORS® must advise sellers/landlords of:
1) the REALTOR®'s company policies regarding cooperation and the amount(s) of any compensation that will be offered to subagents, buyer/tenant agents, and/or brokers acting in legally recognized non-agency capacities;
2) the fact that buyer/tenant agents or brokers, even if compensated by listing brokers, or by sellers/landlords may represent the interests of buyers/tenants; and
3) any potential for listing brokers to act as disclosed dual agents, e.g. buyer/tenant agents. *(Adopted 1/93, Renumbered 1/98, Amended 1/03)*

• **Standard of Practice 1-13**
When entering into buyer/tenant agreements, REALTORS® must advise potential clients of:
1) the REALTOR®'s company policies regarding cooperation;
2) the amount of compensation to be paid by the client;
3) the potential for additional or offsetting compensation from other brokers, from the seller or landlord, or from other parties; and
4) any potential for the buyer/tenant representative to act as a disclosed dual agent, e.g. listing broker, subagent, landlord's agent, etc. *(Adopted 1/93, Renumbered 1/98, Amended 1/04)*

• **Standard of Practice 1-14**
Fees for preparing appraisals or other valuations shall not be contingent upon the amount of the appraisal or valuation. *(Adopted 1/02)*

• **Standard of Practice 1-15**
REALTORS®, in response to inquiries from buyers or cooperating brokers shall, with the sellers' approval, divulge the existence of offers on the property. *(Adopted 1/03)*

Article 2

REALTORS® shall avoid exaggeration, misrepresentation, or concealment of pertinent facts relating to the property or the transaction. REALTORS® shall not, however, be obligated to discover latent defects in the property, to advise on matters outside the scope of their real estate license, or to disclose facts which are confidential under the scope of agency or non-agency relationships as defined by state law. *(Amended 1/00)*

- **Standard of Practice 2-1**

  REALTORS® shall only be obligated to discover and disclose adverse factors reasonably apparent to someone with expertise in those areas required by their real estate licensing authority. Article 2 does not impose upon the REALTOR® the obligation of expertise in other professional or technical disciplines. *(Amended 1/96)*

- **Standard of Practice 2-2**

  (Renumbered as Standard of Practice 1-12 1/98)

- **Standard of Practice 2-3**

  (Renumbered as Standard of Practice 1-13 1/98)

- **Standard of Practice 2-4**

  REALTORS® shall not be parties to the naming of a false consideration in any document, unless it be the naming of an obviously nominal consideration.

- **Standard of Practice 2-5**

  Factors defined as "non-material" by law or regulation or which are expressly referenced in law or regulation as not being subject to disclosure are considered not "pertinent" for purposes of Article 2. *(Adopted 1/93)*

Article 3

REALTORS® shall cooperate with other brokers except when cooperation is not in the client's best interest. The obligation to cooperate does not include the obligation to share commissions, fees, or to otherwise compensate another broker. *(Amended 1/95)*

- **Standard of Practice 3-1**

  REALTORS®, acting as exclusive agents or brokers of sellers/landlords, establish the terms and conditions of offers to cooperate. Unless expressly indicated in offers to cooperate, cooperating brokers may not assume that the offer of cooperation includes an offer of compensation. Terms of compensation, if any, shall be ascertained by cooperating brokers before beginning efforts to accept the offer of cooperation. *(Amended 1/99)*

- **Standard of Practice 3-2**

  REALTORS® shall, with respect to offers of compensation to another REALTOR®, timely communicate any change of compensation for cooperative services to the other REALTOR® prior to the time such REALTOR® produces an offer to purchase/lease the property. *(Amended 1/94)*

- **Standard of Practice 3-3**

  Standard of Practice 3-2 does not preclude the listing broker and cooperating broker from entering into an agreement to change cooperative compensation. *(Adopted 1/94)*

- **Standard of Practice 3-4**

  REALTORS®, acting as listing brokers, have an affirmative obligation to disclose the existence of dual or variable rate commission arrangements (i.e., listings where one amount of commission is payable if the listing broker's firm is the procuring cause of sale/lease and a different amount of commission is payable if the sale/lease results through the efforts of the seller/landlord or a cooperating broker). The listing broker shall, as soon as practical, disclose the existence of such arrangements to potential cooperating brokers and shall, in response to inquiries from cooperating brokers, disclose the differential that would result in a cooperative transaction or in a sale/lease that results through the efforts of the seller/landlord. If the cooperating broker is a buyer/tenant representative, the buyer/tenant representative must disclose such information to their client before the client makes an offer to purchase or lease. *(Amended 1/02)*

- **Standard of Practice 3-5**

  It is the obligation of subagents to promptly disclose all pertinent facts to the principal's agent prior to as well as after a purchase or lease agreement is executed. *(Amended 1/93)*

- **Standard of Practice 3-6**

  REALTORS® shall disclose the existence of accepted offers, including offers with unresolved contingencies, to any broker seeking cooperation. *(Adopted 5/86, Amended 1/04)*

- **Standard of Practice 3-7**

  When seeking information from another REALTOR® concerning property under a management or listing agreement, REALTORS® shall disclose their REALTOR® status and whether their interest is personal or on behalf of a client and, if on behalf of a client, their representational status. *(Amended 1/95)*

- **Standard of Practice 3-8**

  REALTORS® shall not misrepresent the availability of access to show or inspect a listed property. *(Amended 11/87)*

Article 4

REALTORS® shall not acquire an interest in or buy or present offers from themselves, any member of their immediate families, their firms or any member thereof, or any entities in which they have any ownership interest, any real property without making their true position known to the owner or the owner's agent or broker. In selling property they own, or in which they have any interest, REALTORS® shall reveal their ownership or interest in writing to the purchaser or the purchaser's representative. *(Amended 1/00)*

- **Standard of Practice 4-1**

  For the protection of all parties, the disclosures required by Article 4 shall be in writing and provided by REALTORS® prior to the signing of any contract. *(Adopted 2/86)*

Article 5

REALTORS® shall not undertake to provide professional services concerning a property or its value where they have a present or contemplated interest unless such interest is specifically disclosed to all affected parties.

Article 6

REALTORS® shall not accept any commission, rebate, or profit on expenditures made for their client, without the client's knowledge and consent.

When recommending real estate products or services (e.g., homeowner's insurance, warranty programs, mortgage financing, title insurance, etc.), REALTORS® shall disclose to the client or customer to whom the recommendation is made any financial benefits or fees, other than real estate referral fees, the REALTOR® or REALTOR®'s firm may receive as a direct result of such recommendation. *(Amended 1/99)*

- **Standard of Practice 6-1**

  REALTORS® shall not recommend or suggest to a client or a customer the use of services of another organization or business entity in which they have a direct interest without disclosing such interest at the time of the recommendation or suggestion. *(Amended 5/88)*

Article 7

In a transaction, REALTORS® shall not accept compensation from more than one party, even if permitted by law, without disclosure to all parties and the informed consent of the REALTOR®'s client or clients. *(Amended 1/93)*

Article 8

REALTORS® shall keep in a special account in an appropriate financial institution, separated from their own funds, monies coming into their possession in trust for other persons, such as escrows, trust funds, clients' monies, and other like items.

Article 9

REALTORS®, for the protection of all parties, shall assure whenever possible that all agreements related to real estate transactions including, but not limited to, listing and representation agreements, purchase contracts, and leases are in writing in clear and understandable language expressing the specific terms, conditions, obligations and commitments of the parties. A copy of each agreement shall be furnished to each party to such agreements upon their signing or initialing. *(Amended 1/04)*

- **Standard of Practice 9-1**

  For the protection of all parties, REALTORS® shall use reasonable care to ensure that documents pertaining to the purchase, sale, or lease of real estate are kept current through the use of written extensions or amendments. *(Amended 1/93)*

Duties to the Public

Article 10

REALTORS® shall not deny equal professional services to any person for reasons of race, color, religion, sex, handicap, familial status, or national origin. REALTORS® shall not be parties to any plan or agreement to discriminate against a person or persons on the basis of race, color, religion, sex, handicap, familial status, or national origin. *(Amended 1/90)*

REALTORS®, in their real estate employment practices, shall not discriminate against any person or persons on the basis of race, color, religion, sex, handicap, familial status, or national origin. *(Amended 1/00)*

- **Standard of Practice 10-1**

  REALTORS® shall not volunteer information regarding the racial, religious or ethnic composition of any neighborhood and shall not engage in any activity which may result in panic selling. REALTORS® shall not print, display or circulate any statement or advertisement with respect to the selling or renting of a property that indicates any preference, limitations or discrimination based on race, color, religion, sex, handicap, familial status, or national origin. *(Adopted 1/94)*

- **Standard of Practice 10-2**

  As used in Article 10 "real estate employment practices" relates to employees and independent contractors providing real-estate related services and the administrative and clerical staff directly supporting those individuals. *(Adopted 1/00)*

Article 11

The services which REALTORS® provide to their clients and customers shall conform to the standards of practice and competence which are reasonably expected in the specific real estate disciplines in which they engage; specifically, residential real estate brokerage, real property management, commercial and industrial real estate brokerage, real estate appraisal, real estate counseling, real estate syndication, real estate auction, and international real estate.

REALTORS® shall not undertake to provide specialized professional services concerning a type of property or service that is outside their field of competence unless they engage the assistance of one who is competent on such types of property or service, or unless the facts are fully disclosed to the client. Any persons engaged to provide such assistance shall be so identified to the client and their contribution to the assignment should be set forth. *(Amended 1/95)*

- **Standard of Practice 11-1**

  When REALTORS® prepare opinions of real property value or price, other than in pursuit of a listing or to assist a potential purchaser in formulating a purchase offer, such opinions shall include the following:
  1) identification of the subject property
  2) date prepared
  3) defined value or price
  4) limiting conditions, including statements of purpose(s) and intended user(s)
  5) any present or contemplated interest, including the possibility of representing the seller/landlord or buyers/tenants
  6) basis for the opinion, including applicable market data
  7) if the opinion is not an appraisal, a statement to that effect
  (Amended 1/01)

- **Standard of Practice 11-2**

  The obligations of the Code of Ethics in respect of real estate disciplines other than appraisal shall be interpreted and applied in accordance with the standards of competence and practice which clients and the public reasonably require to protect their rights and interests considering the complexity of the transaction, the availability of expert assistance, and, where the REALTOR® is an agent or subagent, the obligations of a fiduciary. *(Adopted 1/95)*

- **Standard of Practice 11-3**

  When REALTORS® provide consultive services to clients which involve advice or counsel for a fee (not a commission), such advice shall be rendered in an objective manner and the fee shall not be contingent on the substance of the advice or counsel given. If brokerage or transaction services are to be provided in addition to consultive services, a separate compensation may be paid with prior agreement between the client and REALTOR®. *(Adopted 1/96)*

- **Standard of Practice 11-4**

  The competency required by Article 11 relates to services contracted for between REALTORS® and their clients or customers; the duties expressly imposed by the Code of Ethics; and the duties imposed by law or regulation. *(Adopted 1/02)*

Article 12

REALTORS® shall be careful at all times to present a true picture in their advertising and representations to the public. REALTORS® shall also ensure that their professional status (e.g., broker, appraiser, property manager, etc.) or status as REALTORS® is clearly identifiable in any such advertising. *(Amended 1/93)*

- **Standard of Practice 12-1**

  REALTORS® may use the term "free" and similar terms in their advertising and in other representations provided that all terms governing availability of the offered product or service are clearly disclosed at the same time. *(Amended 1/97)*

- **Standard of Practice 12-2**

  REALTORS® may represent their services as "free" or without cost even if they expect to receive compensation from a source other than their client provided that the potential for the REALTOR® to obtain a benefit from a third party is clearly disclosed at the same time. *(Amended 1/97)*

- **Standard of Practice 12-3**

  The offering of premiums, prizes, merchandise discounts or other inducements to list, sell, purchase, or lease is not, in itself, unethical even if receipt of the benefit is contingent on listing, selling, purchasing, or leasing through the REALTOR® making the offer. However, REALTORS® must exercise care and candor in any such advertising or other public or private representations so that any party interested in receiving or otherwise benefiting from the REALTOR®'s offer will have clear, thorough, advance understanding of all the terms and conditions of the offer. The offering of any inducements to do business is subject to the limitations and restrictions of state law and the ethical obligations established by any applicable Standard of Practice. *(Amended 1/95)*

- **Standard of Practice 12-4**

  REALTORS® shall not offer for sale/lease or advertise property without authority. When acting as listing brokers or as subagents, REALTORS® shall not quote a price different from that agreed upon with the seller/landlord. *(Amended 1/93)*

- **Standard of Practice 12-5**

  REALTORS® shall not advertise nor permit any person employed by or affiliated with them to advertise listed property without disclosing the name of the firm. *(Adopted 11/86)*

- **Standard of Practice 12-6**

  REALTORS®, when advertising unlisted real property for sale/lease in which they have an ownership interest, shall disclose their status as both owners/landlords and as REALTORS® or real estate licensees. *(Amended 1/93)*

- **Standard of Practice 12-7**

  Only REALTORS® who participated in the transaction as the listing broker or cooperating broker (selling broker) may claim to have "sold" the property. Prior to closing, a cooperating broker may post a "sold" sign only with the consent of the listing broker. *(Amended 1/96)*

Article 13

REALTORS® shall not engage in activities that constitute the unauthorized practice of law and shall recommend that legal counsel be obtained when the interest of any party to the transaction requires it.

Article 14

If charged with unethical practice or asked to present evidence or to cooperate in any other way, in any professional standards proceeding or investigation, REALTORS® shall place all pertinent facts before the proper tribunals of the Member Board or affiliated institute, society, or council in which membership is held and shall take no action to disrupt or obstruct such processes. *(Amended 1/99)*

- **Standard of Practice 14-1**

  REALTORS® shall not be subject to disciplinary proceedings in more than one Board of REALTORS® or affiliated institute, society or council in which they hold membership with respect to alleged violations of the Code of Ethics relating to the same transaction or event. *(Amended 1/95)*

- **Standard of Practice 14-2**

  REALTORS® shall not make any unauthorized disclosure or dissemination of the allegations, findings, or decision developed in connection with an ethics hearing or appeal or in connection with an arbitration hearing or procedural review. *(Amended 1/92)*

- **Standard of Practice 14-3**

  REALTORS® shall not obstruct the Board's investigative or professional standards proceedings by instituting or threatening to institute actions for libel, slander or defamation against any party to a professional standards proceeding or their witnesses based on the filing of an arbitration request, an ethics complaint, or testimony given before any tribunal. *(Adopted 11/87, Amended 1/99)*

- **Standard of Practice 14-4**

  REALTORS® shall not intentionally impede the Board's investigative or disciplinary proceedings by filing multiple ethics complaints based on the same event or transaction. *(Adopted 11/88)*

Duties to REALTORS®

Article 15

REALTORS® shall not knowingly or recklessly make false or misleading statements about competitors, their businesses, or their business practices. *(Amended 1/92)*

- **Standard of Practice 15-1**

  REALTORS® shall not knowingly or recklessly file false or unfounded ethics complaints. *(Adopted 1/00)*

Article 16

REALTORS® shall not engage in any practice or take any action inconsistent with exclusive representation or exclusive brokerage relationship agreements that other REALTORS® have with clients. *(Amended 1/04)*

- **Standard of Practice 16-1**

  Article 16 is not intended to prohibit aggressive or innovative business practices which are otherwise ethical and does not prohibit disagreements with other REALTORS® involving commission, fees, compensation or other forms of payment or expenses. *(Adopted 1/93, Amended 1/95)*

- **Standard of Practice 16-2**

  Article 16 does not preclude REALTORS® from making general announcements to prospects describing their services and the terms of their availability even though some recipients may have entered into agency agreements or other exclusive relationships with another REALTOR®. A general telephone canvass, general mailing or distribution addressed to all prospects in a given geographical area or in a given profession, business, club, or organization, or other classification or group is deemed "general" for purposes of this standard. *(Amended 1/04)*

  Article 16 is intended to recognize as unethical two basic types of solicitations:

  First, telephone or personal solicitations of property owners who have been identified by a real estate sign, multiple listing compilation, or other information service as having exclusively listed their property with another REALTOR®; and

  Second, mail or other forms of written solicitations of prospects whose properties are exclusively listed with another REALTOR® when such solicitations are not part of a general mailing but are directed specifically to property owners identified through compilations of current listings, "for sale" or "for rent" signs, or other sources of information required by Article 3 and Multiple Listing Service rules to be made available to other REALTORS® under offers of subagency or cooperation. *(Amended 1/04)*

- **Standard of Practice 16-3**

  Article 16 does not preclude REALTORS® from contacting the client of another broker for the purpose of offering to provide, or entering into a contract to provide, a different type of real estate service unrelated to the type of service currently being provided (e.g., property management as opposed to brokerage) or from offering the same type of service for property not subject to other brokers' exclusive agreements. However, information received through a Multiple Listing Service or any other offer of cooperation may not be used to target clients of other REALTORS® to whom such offers to provide services may be made. *(Amended 1/04)*

- **Standard of Practice 16-4**

  REALTORS® shall not solicit a listing which is currently listed exclusively with another broker. However, if the listing broker, when asked by the REALTOR®, refuses to disclose the expiration date and nature of such listing; i.e., an exclusive right to sell, an exclusive agency, open listing, or other form of contractual agreement between the listing broker and the client, the REALTOR® may contact the owner to secure such information and may discuss the terms upon which the REALTOR® might take a future listing or, alternatively, may take a listing to become effective upon expiration of any existing exclusive listing. *(Amended 1/94)*

- **Standard of Practice 16-5**

  REALTORS® shall not solicit buyer/tenant agreements from buyers/tenants who are subject to exclusive buyer/tenant agreements. However, if asked by a REALTOR®, the broker refuses to disclose the expiration date of the exclusive buyer/tenant agreement, the REALTOR® may contact the buyer/tenant to secure such information and may discuss the terms upon which the REALTOR® might enter into a future buyer/tenant agreement or, alternatively, may enter into a buyer/tenant agreement to become effective upon the expiration of any existing exclusive buyer/tenant agreement. *(Adopted 1/94, Amended 1/98)*

- **Standard of Practice 16-6**

  When REALTORS® are contacted by the client of another REALTOR® regarding the creation of an exclusive relationship to provide the same type of service, and REALTORS® have not directly or indirectly initiated such discussions, they may discuss the terms upon which they might enter into a future agreement or, alternatively, may enter into an agreement which becomes effective upon expiration of any existing exclusive agreement. *(Amended 1/98)*

- **Standard of Practice 16-7**

  The fact that a prospect has retained a REALTOR® as an exclusive representative or exclusive broker in one or more past transactions does not preclude other REALTORS® from seeking such prospect's future business. *(Amended 1/04)*

- **Standard of Practice 16-8**

  The fact that an exclusive agreement has been entered into with a REALTOR® shall not preclude or inhibit any other REALTOR® from entering into a similar agreement after the expiration of the prior agreement. *(Amended 1/98)*

- **Standard of Practice 16-9**

REALTORS®, prior to entering into a representation agreement, have an affirmative obligation to make reasonable efforts to determine whether the prospect is subject to a current, valid exclusive agreement to provide the same type of real estate service. *(Amended 1/04)*

- **Standard of Practice 16-10**

REALTORS®, acting as buyer or tenant representatives or brokers, shall disclose that relationship to the seller/landlord's representative or broker at first contact and shall provide written confirmation of that disclosure to the seller/landlord's representative or broker not later than execution of a purchase agreement or lease. *(Amended 1/04)*

- **Standard of Practice 16-11**

On unlisted property, REALTORS® acting as buyer/tenant representatives or brokers shall disclose that relationship to the seller/landlord at first contact for that buyer/tenant and shall provide written confirmation of such disclosure to the seller/landlord not later than execution of any purchase or lease agreement. *(Amended 1/04)*

REALTORS® shall make any request for anticipated compensation from the seller/landlord at first contact. *(Amended 1/98)*

- **Standard of Practice 16-12**

REALTORS®, acting as representatives or brokers of sellers/landlords or as subagents of listing brokers, shall disclose that relationship to buyers/tenants as soon as practicable and shall provide written confirmation of such disclosure to buyers/tenants not later than execution of any purchase or lease agreement. *(Amended 1/04)*

- **Standard of Practice 16-13**

All dealings concerning property exclusively listed, or with buyer/tenants who are subject to an exclusive agreement shall be carried on with the client's representative or broker, and not with the client, except with the consent of the client's representative or broker or except where such dealings are initiated by the client.

Before providing substantive services (such as writing a purchase offer or presenting a CMA) to prospects, REALTORS® shall ask prospects whether they are a party to any exclusive representation agreement. REALTORS® shall not knowingly provide substantive services concerning a prospective transaction to prospects who are parties to exclusive representation agreements, except with the consent of the prospects' exclusive representatives or at the direction of prospects. *(Adopted 1/93, Amended 1/04)*

- **Standard of Practice 16-14**

REALTORS® are free to enter into contractual relationships or to negotiate with sellers/landlords, buyers/tenants or others who are not subject to an exclusive agreement but shall not knowingly obligate them to pay more than one commission except with their informed consent. *(Amended 1/98)*

- **Standard of Practice 16-15**

In cooperative transactions REALTORS® shall compensate cooperating REALTORS® (principal brokers) and shall not compensate nor offer to compensate, directly or indirectly, any of the sales licensees employed by or affiliated with other REALTORS® without the prior express knowledge and consent of the cooperating broker.

- **Standard of Practice 16-16**

REALTORS®, acting as subagents or buyer/tenant representatives or brokers, shall not use the terms of an offer to purchase/lease to attempt to modify the listing broker's offer of compensation to subagents or buyer/tenant representatives or brokers nor make the submission of an executed offer to purchase/lease contingent on the listing broker's agreement to modify the offer of compensation. *(Amended 1/04)*

- **Standard of Practice 16-17**

REALTORS®, acting as subagents or as buyer/tenant representatives or brokers, shall not attempt to extend a listing broker's offer of cooperation and/or compensation to other brokers without the consent of the listing broker. *(Amended 1/04)*

- **Standard of Practice 16-18**

REALTORS® shall not use information obtained from listing brokers through offers to cooperate made through multiple listing services or through other offers of cooperation to refer listing brokers' clients to other brokers or to create buyer/tenant relationships with listing brokers' clients, unless such use is authorized by listing brokers. *(Amended 1/02)*

- **Standard of Practice 16-19**

Signs giving notice of property for sale, rent, lease, or exchange shall not be placed on property without consent of the seller/landlord. *(Amended 1/93)*

- **Standard of Practice 16-20**

REALTORS®, prior to or after terminating their relationship with their current firm, shall not induce clients of their current firm to cancel exclusive contractual agreements between the client and that firm. This does not preclude REALTORS® (principals) from establishing agreements with their associated licensees governing assignability of exclusive agreements. *(Adopted 1/98)*

Article 17

In the event of contractual disputes or specific non-contractual disputes as defined in Standard of Practice 17-4 between REALTORS® (principals) associated with different firms, arising out of their relationship as REALTORS®, the REALTORS® shall submit the dispute to arbitration in accordance with the regulations of their Board or Boards rather than litigate the matter.

In the event clients of REALTORS® wish to arbitrate contractual disputes arising out of real estate transactions, REALTORS® shall arbitrate those disputes in accordance with the regulations of their Board, provided the clients agree to be bound by the decision.

The obligation to participate in arbitration contemplated by this Article includes the obligation of REALTORS® (principals) to cause their firms to arbitrate and be bound by any award. *(Amended 1/01)*

- **Standard of Practice 17-1**
The filing of litigation and refusal to withdraw from it by REALTORS® in an arbitrable matter constitutes a refusal to arbitrate. *(Adopted 2/86)*

- **Standard of Practice 17-2**
Article 17 does not require REALTORS® to arbitrate in those circumstances when all parties to the dispute advise the Board in writing that they choose not to arbitrate before the Board. *(Amended 1/93)*

- **Standard of Practice 17-3**
REALTORS®, when acting solely as principals in a real estate transaction, are not obligated to arbitrate disputes with other REALTORS® absent a specific written agreement to the contrary. *(Adopted 1/96)*

- **Standard of Practice 17-4**
Specific non-contractual disputes that are subject to arbitration pursuant to Article 17 are:

1) Where a listing broker has compensated a cooperating broker and another cooperating broker subsequently claims to be the procuring cause of the sale or lease. In such cases the complainant may name the first cooperating broker as respondent and arbitration may proceed without the listing broker being named as a respondent. Alternatively, if the complaint is brought against the listing broker, the listing broker may name the first cooperating broker as a third-party respondent. In either instance the decision of the hearing panel as to procuring cause shall be conclusive with respect to all current or subsequent claims of the parties for compensation arising out of the underlying cooperative transaction. *(Adopted 1/97)*

2) Where a buyer or tenant representative is compensated by the seller or landlord, and not by the listing broker, and the listing broker, as a result, reduces the commission owed by the seller or landlord and, subsequent to such actions, another cooperating broker claims to be the procuring cause of sale or lease. In such cases the complainant may name the first cooperating broker as respondent and arbitration may proceed without the listing broker being named as a respondent. Alternatively, if the complaint is brought against the listing broker, the listing broker may name the first cooperating broker as a third-party respondent. In either instance the decision of the hearing panel as to procuring cause shall be conclusive with respect to all current or subsequent claims of the parties for compensation arising out of the underlying cooperative transaction. *(Adopted 1/97)*

3) Where a buyer or tenant representative is compensated by the buyer or tenant and, as a result, the listing broker reduces the commission owed by the seller or landlord and, subsequent to such actions, another cooperating broker claims to be the procuring cause of sale or lease. In such cases the complainant may name the first cooperating broker as respondent and arbitration may proceed without the listing broker being named as a respondent. Alternatively, if the complaint is brought against the listing broker, the listing broker may name the first cooperating broker as a third-party respondent. In either instance the decision of the hearing panel as to procuring cause shall be conclusive with respect to all current or subsequent claims of the parties for compensation arising out of the underlying cooperative transaction. *(Adopted 1/97)*

4) Where two or more listing brokers claim entitlement to compensation pursuant to open listings with a seller or landlord who agrees to participate in arbitration (or who requests arbitration) and who agrees to be bound by the decision. In cases where one of the listing brokers has been compensated by the seller or landlord, the other listing broker, as complainant, may name the first listing broker as respondent and arbitration may proceed between the brokers. *(Adopted 1/97)*

The Code of Ethics was adopted in 1913. Amended at the Annual Convention in 1924, 1928, 1950, 1951, 1952, 1955, 1956, 1961, 1962, 1974, 1982, 1986, 1987, 1989, 1990, 1991, 1992, 1993, 1994, 1995, 1996, 1997, 1998, 1999, 2000, 2001, 2002 and 2003.

Explanatory Notes

The reader should be aware of the following policies which have been approved by the Board of Directors of the National Association:

In filing a charge of an alleged violation of the Code of Ethics by a REALTOR®, the charge must read as an alleged violation of one or more Articles of the Code. Standards of Practice may be cited in support of the charge.

The Standards of Practice serve to clarify the ethical obligations imposed by the various Articles and supplement, and do not substitute for, the Case Interpretations in *Interpretations of the Code of Ethics*.

Modifications to existing Standards of Practice and additional new Standards of Practice are approved from time to time. Readers are cautioned to ensure that the most recent publications are utilized.

A brokerage is simply an avenue in which to sell or transfer a good or service from one person to another. The broker is the intermediary, or middleman who negotiates the transaction and ensures all technical items are both attended to and handled correctly. In our case, the brokerage is used in the transfer of real estate. The broker will negotiate the transaction on behalf of the principal, in exchange for a commission, to be paid when the transaction is completed.

All listings handled by a salesperson actually belong to the brokerage, not to the salesperson directly. The salesperson, though empowered by the broker to conduct business, is not a separate entity. The real estate broker is the only licensed real estate professional who may conduct business independently of anyone else. All salespersons conducting business must do so under a broker, and are authorized to do only what a broker allows. If a salesperson has worked on several listings, and chooses to leave the brokerage, these listings will not go with the salesperson. They will stay with the brokerage, and be handled by another salesperson, or by the broker him or herself.

A real estate brokerage is operated by a broker, who is directly responsible for the actions of any salespersons in their employ. The broker is responsible for all legal matters pertaining to the brokerage. Additionally, the broker also decides which sales people to hire and/or fire, which properties the firm will represent; and the basic guidelines and rules for all people employed. A broker is also referred to as an agent.

The salesperson is employed by a broker (in a brokerage). Salespeople cannot operate independently; they must work for a broker, until they become a broker themselves. Salespeople are directly responsible to their clients in showing homes, filling out the correct paperwork, serving as liaison between the buyer and seller, and functions as a general source of information through each step of the home buying process. Salespeople are also referred to as agents.

An agent is any person who holds a real estate license. Agents represent a principal in a real estate transaction when dealing with a third party.

Remember!

- A real estate broker is responsible for operating the brokerage, employing its salespeople and negotiating the transfer of property from one party to another
- A real estate salesperson is someone who holds a sales person's license and is able to perform the activities of a broker in the negotiation of real estate from one party to another. The salesperson must work for a broker
- A real estate agent is any person licensed by the department of real estate. An agent negotiates the transfer of property for the principal when dealing with a third party

A brokerage provides five main services to its clients. They are:

- Listing
- Selling
- Negotiating transactions
- Arranging or making referrals for financing
- Closing sales

The obvious way a salesperson receives payment is through a commission (when a transaction has gone through). Because of this incentive, there is a high degree of competition within an office and between offices, to obtain listings and ultimately move a property. With this high degree of competition comes cooperation. Salespeople who work in the same office can serve as resources for each other, by working in teams or giving referrals to one another when one is busy or not available for new listings. One salesperson, very familiar with one neighborhood or section of town may serve as a good resource to a new agent new to that area. Such a salesperson may be able to handle another agent's client questions, in the event that their agent is not in the office. Without some degree of cooperation, a brokerage will not be successful.

Even though it is not on the list above as one of the five main functions of a real estate brokerage, filling out paperwork is essential for every agent. Filling out forms, keeping track of all listings, collecting signatures for all necessary disclosures, opening and closing escrow, managing loan applications and tracking all potential clients who are looking for a very specific property or have a property that may be for sale in the near future are some of these types of paperwork. It is important for an agent to keep the door of communication open for these potential sales, or be very choosy clients to pull in more business. At the end of the day, the vast amount of paperwork that goes in each person's file is overwhelming for an unorganized agent. So, it is important, as an agent, to stay very focused and organized.

With all the responsibilities an agent must juggle, it is essential that he or she choose the appropriate brokerage for which to work. New agents may be nervous about getting started. An agent may also be new to an area and very unfamiliar with its neighborhoods. He or she may simply need good directions to find the appropriate listings. By selecting the best brokerage to fit your needs, you will have all the appropriate support, training, continuing education programs and other assistance you might need. An experienced agent may not need all the guidance, training and support that a new agent might need; so, one firm may not be right for everyone.

When selecting the right brokerage, it is important for every agent to be upfront and honest in the interview or selection process. A new agent may want to a broker to know that this is his or her first job in the industry. They might want to ensure there is sufficient training, (a mentoring program or other resources) to help them succeed for themselves and the firm. An experienced salesperson may want a very detailed support staff; capable of handling reams of paperwork in a short time, or that the brokerage has a lot of inventory to pursue.

Training is a key element in a brokerage. As mentioned in the previous paragraphs, it is one element a new salesperson must look for when choosing a brokerage for which to work. A through training program directly correlates to the success of a new agent.

A new agent may be well versed in the concepts of real estate, but much more goes into sales than just the basic concepts and law. How to interact with people, the neighborhood dynamics, as well as the firm's procedure and policy are just a few points a new agent will most likely not learn from a textbook or real estate course.

Commissions

Most brokerages will pay their salespeople on a commission basis. This means that you will earn a percentage of the commission that the brokerage receives each time you sell a property. Some brokerages have a base salary for new agents, while others use a different pay system. The vast majority of brokerages, however, operate on a commission.

Commissions in California are not set by law. The broker can charge the principal whatever amount they agree upon, though 6% is a reasonable standard. Brokerages operate on a commission split, meaning that when a property is sold, the buyer's agent and seller's agent will split the commission that the principal is obligated to pay. This commission is further split between the broker and the sales agent who worked on the property. As you can see, the more brokerages or agents involved in a transaction, the smaller each individual share in the commission.

Generally the commission split between brokerages is 50-50. Your employing broker will take 50% of the 6% commission, while your percentage of the commission will vary, depending on what agreement you have with your employing broker. For argument's sake, let's assume you will earn 50% of what your broker makes. You will earn 25% of the entire commission made from the property. This can all become very complicated when talking about percentages, commission splits and money. So, let's simplify this subject with an example.

Example:
You have just sold a property for $500,000 at 6% commission. Your brokerage receives half of this amount, while the broker who represents the buyer receives 50% of the commission You and your broker have worked out a deal where you receive half of all commissions you bring into the firm. You will make a total amount of $7,500 for your efforts.

$500,000 x .06 (6%) =
$30,000 Total commission

Now, a 50-50 split of this commission between the two brokerages
$30,000 / 2 =
$15,000 total commission for each brokerage.

You have a 50-50 split agreement with your broker, meaning you receive half of the brokerage's commission. Your commission is
$15,000 / 2 =
$7,500 total commission for you.

It is important to note that not all brokerages will provide you with a 50-50 split of the commission. Sometimes, you will receive more; at other times you will receive less. This commission is an amount you must work out with your broker.

REAL ESTATE TRANSACTION REQUIREMENTS

When we think of the beginning of a real estate transaction, we often associate this time when the purchase contract is written and escrow is opened. The transaction actually begins when a seller writes an offer. However, the real estate transaction between agent and seller actually begins when the seller enters into an agency agreement with the agent. The listing is obtained, which is usually an exclusive authorization and right to sell the property. This means that the agent will be paid a commission, regardless of who sells the home. If the buyer sells the home independent of the agent, if another agent sells the property, or the listing agent sells the property, that listing agent will receive a commission.

Once the agent finds a buyer to write an offer, there are certain steps or items that the agent must keep in mind when preparing the offer to purchase or purchase contract. The following is a checklist of the different actions a real estate agent must take in a residential transaction. Keep in mind; other transactions (such as those for agricultural, commercial, land or industrial properties) will have a different set of steps for the agent:

1. Date and place where the contract is signed by the buyer
2. The correct name and address of the buyer
3. Form of the buyer's deposit, whether in cash, check, cashiers check, promissory note, money order or other form
4. Designee to hold the deposit, whether the broker, seller, or escrow
5. Purchase price of the property
6. Terms under which the property will be purchased (whether it is to be in all cash, refinance, loan assumption or taking title subject to the existing loan)
7. Amount of time given to the seller to consider the buyer's offer to purchase the property
8. Definite termination date stated in the contract
9. Covenants, conditions and restrictions (such as easements, rights or other conditions of record) that affect the property. Will the buyer accept these conditions and move forward with the purchase contract
10. Deed of conveyance (will there be any exceptions or reservations?)
11. Are there any stipulations or agreements regarding any tenancies or rights of persons currently in possession of the property?
12. Who pays for the roof and electrical inspections?
13. Stipulations regarding common walls, encroachments or easements
14. Who will pay for the title policy, escrow services and other customary charges? Who will pay for these other, less ordinary charges?
15. Mutual agreement of the escrow holder.
16. What special documents will be required of the transaction, and who will prepare these documents?
17. On what date will the prorations be based?
18. When will possession be taken?
19. Who will pay for structural pest or other inspections?
20. Who are the other brokers involved in the transactions (include all pertinent information such as phone numbers or addresses)?
21. What is the commission, and how will it be paid?
22. Be sure all parties sign the contract
23. Every purchase contract prepared or signed by a real estate salesperson must be reviewed, initialed and dated by the salesperson's broker within five working days after preparation or signing of the salesperson, or before the close of escrow.

24. Is a financial disclosure statement required, and has it been provided by both the buyer and seller?
25. Include written disclosure statements regarding the property's condition, which may affect the value of the property.
26. A dual agent must disclose whom he or she is representing.
27. Disclosure to both the buyer and seller of any compensation received from the lender involved with the financial part of the transaction.

As soon as escrow has opened, or the purchase contract has been accepted by both parties, the seller should provide escrow with the following specifications:

1. Escrow instructions signed by all of the sellers.
2. The latest available tax information, which must be prorated through escrow
3. Seller's loan payment books and records
4. Seller's insurance policies to be transferred to the buyer
5. The current beneficiary statement regarding the amount of money owed on the property
6. Subordination or other agreements required by the purchase contract to be approved by all parties through escrow
7. Certificates or releases showing satisfaction of mechanic's liens, security agree ments, judgments or mortgages which are to be paid off through escrow.
8. List of tenant names, rent owed and the apartments they occupy, if applicable
9. Assignment to buyer of all leases affecting the property
10. Letters from the seller to the tenants, instructing them to pay all subsequent rent to the buyer, and notice of transfer of their security deposit to the buyer
11. The seller's executed and acknowledged deed of conveyance to the buyer or valid authority to execute the deed of the seller by the seller's attorney-in-fact (if the seller is acting through an agent)
12. An executed bill of sale covering any personal property to be conveyed to the buyer, together with an inventory of the items for the buyer's approval
13. A security agreement for execution by the buyer, covering any personal property included in the purchase price, but not paid by the buyer in cash.
14. The deed by which the seller acquired title to the property and the seller's policy of title insurance.
15. Any unrecorded instruments affecting the title.
16. Any other documents or instruments, which the seller is to prepare or deliver.
17. Any approvals required for documents that the seller is to receive at closing
18. Information required to be disclosed to the buyer under the seller financing disclo sure, if necessary.

Additionally, as soon as possible after the opening of escrow, the buyer should furnish the escrow holder with certain documents and information. They buyer should personally review or inspect all of the following items:

1. Escrow instructions signed by all parties in the escrow.
2. Preliminary title report and ensure there are no items of record affecting the prop erty, which have not already been approved by the buyer.
3. Conditions, covenants and restrictions affecting the property, if any.
4. Confirm the terms of any mortgages or deeds of trust to be assumed by the buyer, which will remain an encumbrance on the property
5. Beneficiary statements, fire insurance or liability policies assigned to the buyer.
6. Offset statements on loans to be assumed, or those under which the buyer is t aking title to the property, subject to existing loan terms; verify the unpaid principal

balances owed, the interest rates, dates to which interest is paid and other vital information.

7. Review structural pest reports
8. Review all loan documents prior to signing any papers
9. Compare the purchase terms to the escrow instructions; make sure there are no discrepancies.
10. If tenancies are involved: review the names, addresses and telephone numbers of tenants; the rent amounts; rent due dates; copies of rent agreements or leases; letters from the seller to the tenants verifying the terms of occupancy and notifying the tenants of change of ownership; the assignments of any unpaid rent and leases; and details on security deposits, if any.
11. Examine the bill of sale for any personal property items being conveyed to the buyer.
12. Review all prorated bills
13. Verify the proration amounts on the estimated escrow settlement sheet.
14. Make sure the property is in the same condition it was in when the buyer originally made the offer.
15. Deposit sufficient funds to cover any balance owed on the purchase contract, plus buyer's closing costs and expenses and approvals required.

SPECIFIC DISCLOSURES REQUIRED IN A REAL ESTATE TRANSACTION

One of the most important aspects of real estate is the concept of full disclosure. What used to be a relatively easy process has turned into a complex, drawn-out process. A disclosure is a statement revealing some fact regarding the real estate transaction. It could turn out that the plumbing has a leak in the guest bathroom, and that the owner is aware of it; however, the owner does not plan to make any repairs. A disclosure could also be made to a financing company, regarding the buyer and seller agreement to do a wrap around loan. Agents must disclose to clients if they have a personal interest in the property, such as if they are the buyer or seller. What is important is that the agent guides the client through all the necessary disclosures, receives all the necessary signed statements to show that the disclosure has been made, and ensured all statements made are true. If all of this is taken care of, there will be no problems. Any disclosures that go unattended may result in the loss of the sale, penalties or even criminal prosecution against the parties withholding information.

The following pages will go over all the necessary disclosures that must be made in a real estate transaction. Some have been covered in previous chapters, but this list will give you a more thorough look at these disclosures that you must cover.

Real Estate Transfer Disclosure Statement
There are many physical features or issues of a property, which a seller must disclose to a buyer. If there are too many defects in a property, a buyer may not be interested in the property, but should be made aware of these problems before making an offer. Not making these disclosures is against real estate law, as the buyer has the right to rescind out of the offer with no penalty. Any seller of a one-to-four unit home or dwelling must deliver a disclosure to potential buyers regarding the property's structure and condition. This requirement is extended to the transfer of property by sale, exchange, installment land sale contract, lease with an option to purchase, and other option to purchase, or ground lease coupled with improvements. There may be Local Opinion Transfer Disclosure Statements required or provided for neighborhoods, city or counties that would disclose special local facts regarding the property. The following

are required facts that must be disclosed to a buyer of property by the seller or the seller's agent:

- The age, condition or any defects, malfunctions or problems with the structural component of the home. This includes plumbing, electrical, heating and other mechanical components or systems of the home.
- Easements, common drives, walks or fences shared with neighbors.
- Additional rooms added to the property after it was originally built, and whether or not these rooms have the necessary building permits for construction.
- Flooding drainage or soil problems on, near or in any way affecting the property.
- Major damage to the structure or property caused from fire, earthquake or landslide.
- Whether or not the property is located within a known earthquake fault line or zone.
- Citations against the property, lawsuits against the owner affecting the transferability of the property, or other legal issues with the current owners and property.
- Homeowner's association dues and deed restrictions or common area problems, which may result in a special assessment.
- Zoning violations, such as nonconforming uses or insufficient setbacks.

Certain groups are exempt from the requirement to provide a Transfer Disclosure Statement.
- When property is transferred from one co-owner to another
- Sale by the state controller for unclaimed property
- The first sale of a residential property within a subdivision, where a copy of a public report is delivered to the buyer or where such a report is not required.
- In a foreclosure sale
- Selling to or buying from any government entity
- A court-ordered transfer by a fiduciary in the administration of a probate estate or a testamentary trust.
- Selling property to a spouse or to another related person, resulting from a judgment of dissolution of a marriage, or a legal separation, or in a property settlement agreement.
- Sale of property due to failure to pay taxes.

If a buyer does not receive the necessary disclosure document on a property in the allotted time, he or she may terminate the offer to purchase the property. The intention to terminate must be made either 3 days in person or 5 days after a deposit has been given to United States Postal Services. A written notice of termination must reach the seller or the seller's agent. The time the Transfer Disclosure Statement must be delivered varies depending on the type of transfer. If the transfer is a regular sale, then the Transfer Disclosure Statement must be delivered before the transfer of title. If the transaction was a lease option or a ground lease with improvements, the Transfer Disclosure Statement must be delivered before execution of the contract.

The seller, the seller's agent or any agent working in cooperation with the seller's agent is responsible for preparing the Transfer Disclosure Statement. This same person is in charge of delivering the disclosure to the buyer. In the event that there are multiple agents working with the seller, the agent who obtained the offer will be responsible for creating and delivering the Transfer Disclosure Statement.

Inspections may limit the liability of the seller and his or her agents. Inspections such as a land survey, pest inspection, roof inspection, plumbing inspection, geologic inspection or general contractor's opinion of the structure will give the buyer a better idea of the condition of the property. The seller's liability is limited, because any problems with the structure will be discovered in these inspections, and the buyer will not run into any surprises with the property. If there has been a violation of the law regarding the structure, it will not invalidate the property transfer. However, the seller will most likely be held responsible for fixing the problem, or may be held liable for any damages suffered by the buyer.

Transfer Disclosure Statement!
- Disclosed facts and information regarding the physical structure of the property, which is important to the potential buyer.
- Statement must be prepared and delivered by the seller, seller's agent or any agent working for the seller's agent.
- Buyers have the right to terminate any offer made if a Transfer Disclosure Statement is not received in the allotted amount of time after an offer is made.
- There are certain exemptions for which this statement does not have to be prepared.

Mello-Roos Disclosure

The Mello-Roos Community Facilities Act of 1982 authorizes communities to form facilities districts, issue bonds and levy special taxes, which finance public facilities or other services for the benefit of the public. As of July 1, 1993, the seller of a property consisting of one-to-four units, subject to the lien of a Mello-Roos community facilities district, must make a good faith effort to obtain from the district a disclosure notice concerning the special tax or levy and give the notice to a prospective buyer. Prospective buyers must be made aware of any special tax or levy that might be applied to their property so that they are aware of any additional taxes for which they might be responsible, beyond real estate taxes. Exemptions from this disclosure are listed in the Transfer Disclosure Statement.

Disclosure Regarding Lead-Based Paint Hazards

Homes that were built before 1978 fall under this disclosure. The Residential Lead-Based Paint Hazard Reduction Act of 1992, which became effective in 1996, requires owners of property with four or fewer units to offer the lead-based paint and lead-based paint hazard disclosures in a property transfer. The seller, landlord and real estate agent involved in the transfer have certain requirements under the new law. All agents must comply with the law, even if the landlord or seller fails to do so. Agents are not responsible for any information an owner or landlord conceals. The following list of requirements must be made by the specified group:

Seller and Landlord Responsibilities:

- Include standard warning language as an attachment to the contract or lease.
- Give the buyers or tenants a pamphlet called "Protect Your Family From Lead in Your Home"
- For sale transactions only, sellers must give buyers a 10 day opportunity to test the home for lead
- Disclose all known lead-based and lead-based paint hazards in the dwelling and provide the buyer or tenant with any available reports.
- Retain the signed acknowledgment for three years.
- Complete and sign statements verifying completion of requirements.

An agent must ensure that:

- Sellers and landlords are aware of their responsibilities
- Leases and sales contracts include the proper disclosure language and appropriate signatures.
- Seller and landlords disclose property information to buyers and tenants.
- Sellers give buyers the opportunity to conduct an inspection for 10 days or another mutually agreed-upon time period.

Smoke Detector Statement of Compliance

California state law requires that each living structure have a smoke detector installed in a centrally-located spot outside of the bedrooms. For two story homes with bedrooms on both floors, there are two smoke detectors required. When a property is sold, the seller must provide the buyer with a written statement, which states that the property is in compliance with this law.

New construction, whether of a completely new home or an addition onto an existing home, and improvements or remodels valued at over $1,000 have different rules. In these situations, there must be one smoke detector in each bedroom, as well as a smoke detector in a central location outside of the bedrooms. New construction requires that these smoke detectors be hardwired into the home itself, with a battery backup. In existing structures, a battery-operated smoke detector is required.

Disclosure Regarding State Responsibility Areas

State Responsibility Areas describe property that is located in a rural portion of the state, not protected at the city or federal level for fire. In these areas, if there is a large-scale wildfire, the state will be in charge of extinguishing the blaze. Whether it is a state crew fighting the fires, or just state funded firefighters, all responsibility lies with the state. Maps of these State Responsibility Areas are generated every five years, as the boundaries often change with the influx of people into or out of an area. If a seller knows that his or her property is in this State Responsibility Zone, he or she is required to disclose this information, along with the possibility of substantial fire risk at the property. In addition to these disclosures, the seller must disclose to the buyer that the land is subject to certain preventative measures.

To further blur the line of responsibility, with either the department's consent or by ordinance, a county may assume all responsibility for fires in state responsibility areas. In this situation, the seller must disclose to the buyer that the state is no longer responsible for fires in the area, but that the county, city or other district will be providing all fire protection.

Delivery of Structural Pest Control Inspection and Certification Reports

California does not require a structural pest control inspection in the transfer of real property. Financing firms or buyers, on the other hand, might require that a pest control inspection be completed before a loan can be financed, or as a condition to purchase the home. If a pest inspection is required, it must be made as soon as possible after learning that it is required. Before the title is transferred or before execution of the sales contract, the buyer must receive a copy of the pest report. The person conducting the report must also state in writing whether or not wood-destroying termites were visible. This report and written statement must be prepared by a licensed or registered structural pest-control company.

The pest inspection must be divided into two portions. The first portion will outline any existing damage or infestation, while the second portion of the report will outline the probability of other damage or infestation unseen by the inspector. The real estate agent who obtained the offer on the property is also responsible for obtaining the report and delivering it to the buyer. This occurs unless the seller has given written directions regarding the delivery of the report to another agent (such as the buyer's agent). The report may be delivered to the buyer in person or by mail, and the agent who obtains the report must keep it in his or her files for three years.

Disclosure of Geological Hazards and Special Studies Zones

The earth is a dynamic medium on which we live. Each day, there are geological changes to the surface of the earth, as well as changes happening within its core. Some of these geological changes require disclosures, while others do not. These geological changes that require disclosures are those that pose a potential, major hazard from phenomena, such as earthquakes, flooding, landslides, erosion and expansive soils. One specific condition requiring a disclosure is fault creep, or stress to the land caused by the shaking of an earthquake. Soil plays a major factor in fault creep. Softer soils or sediments, which are looser, tend to magnify an earthquake. Harder sediment, such as rock, will mask an earthquake. It is important for a new homebuyer to understand the type of soil their home sits on and the possible repercussions of this soil type during an earthquake. Also proximity to the fault line will also play a big part in what happens during an earthquake. The closer a property is to the fault line, the more severe an earthquake will be to the property. Again, this is something that must be disclosed to a homebuyer.

The State Division of Mines and Geology offers maps that show areas of the state more susceptible to fault creep. These maps may also show areas that have had landslides in the past and possible forecast to future landslides. For disclosure purposes, sellers and the agents working with them usually rely on maps offered by the state Division of Mines and Geology as the basis for the necessity of disclosure. For new construction, however, most structures designed for inhabitation are subject to the findings and recommendations of a geologic report. This report is prepared by a geologist or soils engineer registered in, or licensed by, the state of California.

Under the Alquist-Priolo Special Studies Zones Act, a seller who sells real estate, the seller's real estate agent, or any other cooperating agents must disclose the fact that a home sits in a special studies zone. This disclosure must be made on the Transfer Disclosure Statement, the Local Option Real Estate Transfer Disclosure Statement, or in the purchase agreement.

There are certain situations in which property is excluded from the requirements of the special studies zone. These circumstances are:

- Alterations worth under 50% of the total value of the structure
- Structures in existence prior to May 4, 1975
- Single-family, wood-frame or steel structures not over two stories high, provided the dwelling is not part of a development consisting of four or more dwellings.
- Single-family, wood-frame or steel-frame structures for which geologic reports have been approved, to be built in subdivisions authorized by the Subdivision Map Act.
- Conversions of existing apartments into condominiums. It must be disclosed that the property is located within a delineated special-studies zone.

An additional piece of literature for potential buyers is the Homeowner's Guide to Earthquake Safety, distributed by the Seismic Safety Commission. This is not so much a disclosure as a public brochure to encourage awareness of geologic and seismic hazards throughout the entire state of California. It outlines the related structural and nonstructural hazards, as well as recommendations for mitigating the hazards of an earthquake. The guide states that safety and damage prevention cannot be guaranteed with respect to major earthquakes; only precautions (such as retrofitting) can be undertaken to reduce the risk of damage. If a buyer of real property receives a copy of the Homeowner's guide, the seller is not required to provide any additional information regarding geologic and seismic hazards. Sellers and real estate agents must, however, disclose that the property is in a special studies zone and that there are known hazards in the area.

The delivery of the Homeowner's Guide to Earthquake Safety is required in transactions where there is a transfer of real property, those involving a residential dwelling built before January 1, 1960, and those consisting of one-to-four units (any of which are conventional, light-frame construction). It is also required in real estate transfers of any masonry building with wood-frame floors or roofs built before January 1, 1975. Exemptions to these rules apply to the same of those of the Real Estate Transfer Disclosure Statement.

The bottom line is that full disclosure is required for all material facts regarding a special studies zone, local ordinances or known structural deficiencies affecting the property. Buyers or agents may be responsible for further inquires of appropriate governmental agencies. The obligation of the buyer or the buyer's agent to make additional inquiries does not eliminate the duty of the seller's agent to make a diligent inquiry to identify the location of the real property in relationship to a defined special studies zone.

Natural Hazard Disclosure Statement
California passed the Natural Hazard Disclosure Law in 1998, which served to simplify and standardize the natural hazard disclosure requirements. As we can see from the previous disclosure requirement, there are times when disclosure is required, and times when it is not. Now, with this law, the state requires all sellers, as well as the seller's agents, to determine and disclose to prospective purchasers, whether a lot is in certain, officially-mapped natural hazard zones. It is the seller's and their agent's responsibility to do the research on this and make any necessary disclosure to the buyer.

The new law requires six disclosures in addition to informing the buyer of any other hazards of which he or she are aware. The six disclosures required by this law are: whether the property is located in a seismic hazard zone; flood hazard are;, earthquake fault zone; a state responsibility fire area; if the property is in a flood zone due to the possibility of dam failure; or, a high fire hazard severity zone. These disclosures must be made before the transfer of title, unless the purchase contract specifies that they be made earlier. If the buyer does not approve of the location of the property (due to its geographic location in a hazard zone), the buyer may rescind the offer within three days of a hand-delivered disclosure statement, or within five days of receiving the disclosure statement in the mail.

> **Natural Hazard Disclosure Statement requires six disclosures to be made**
> - Seismic hazard zone
> - Flood hazard area
> - Earthquake fault zone
> - State responsibility fire area
> - Flood zone, due to the possibility of dam failure
> - Extreme fire hazard severity zone

Secured Water Heater Law

One of the largest hazards in an earthquake is the damage to mechanical components or utilities that use electricity or gas. By damaging these lines or wires, fire is possible, which can create an even worse situation. Local requirements dictate how water heaters should be attached, strapped or anchored to the ground, so that they do not tip over in the event of an earthquake. Besides a possible fire hazard from damage to the water heater, there is the possibility of water damage to the area around the water heater. A suggested disclosure form can be found in the Homeowner's Guide to Earthquake Safety.

Disclosure of Ordnance Location

Military bases or training facilities were once scattered throughout the state, where live ammunition may still be buried. State law requires sellers of property located within one mile of these training sites to disclose to buyers that this hazard exists. The disclosure must be made to the buyer before the transfer of title. Disclosure is required only if the current seller is aware of the hazard. If the seller is not aware of the ordnance or military supplies, the disclosure is not required.

Environmental Hazard Disclosure

Sellers of property who are aware of chemical or environmental hazards are responsible to disclose this fact to a prospective buyer, under the California Real Estate Transfer Disclosure Statement. It also requires sellers to disclose the presence of asbestos, formaldehyde, radon gas, lead-based paint, fuel or chemical storage tanks, contaminated soil, water, mold or any other hazardous substances. A landlord or owner of nonresidential property must also disclose any of these hazards to tenants or a person who leases space in the building. Sellers and property owners who do not give proper disclosures will be held liable (perhaps in the form of civil penalties) for any damages caused by these hazards.

Proposition 65 states that certain businesses may not knowingly and intentionally expose any individual to a cancer-causing agent, chemical or reproductive toxin without first giving clear warning to any person present in or using the space. You will recall warning signs at filling station regarding one or more chemicals present in gas or at the filling station that may cause cancer. These signs are required to be posted by law, giving consumers proper warning to proceed at their own risk. Recent laws have also included asbestos disclosure requirements for owners of commercial buildings built before 1979.

In addition to posted signs in commercial spaces, the Department of Real Estate, in conjunction with the Office of Environmental Health Hazard Assessment, has developed a booklet to help educate and inform consumers about environmental hazards that may affect real property. The booklet explains common environmental hazards and describes the risks involved with each of the hazards. The hazards discussed in the booklet cover asbestos, radon gas, lead and formaldehyde. If a buyer has been given this booklet, the seller and the seller's agents are not required to provide any further information on such hazards. If the seller is aware that one or more of these hazardous agents are present at the time of sale, this must be disclosed.

Energy Conservation Retrofit and Thermal Insulation Disclosure
Energy conservation is a present concern for the growing population of California, due to its limited resources. State law requires a minimum energy conservation standard for all new construction. If these minimum standards are not met, a building may not receive the building permit needed to go forward with construction. Besides the state standard, local standards are imposed for further energy conservation measures on new and existing homes. By retrofitting homes before selling them, these conservation goals can be met. A seller of property must disclose to buyers the existence of state and local requirements of energy conservation. In addition to this disclosure, federal law requires sellers of new homes to disclose the type, thickness and R-value of the insulation, which has been, or will be used in each part of the house.

Special Flood Hazard Area Disclosure and Responsibilities of the Federal Emergency Management Agency (FEMA)
The Federal Emergency Management Agency (FEMA) creates flood hazard boundary maps, which identify general flood hazard zones in a community. These maps show areas of minimal risk, or areas that face risk of flooding every 500 years. There are also areas of moderate flood hazard, which has a possibility of flooding every 100 – 500 years. Special flood zones are labeled for those areas, which have to possibility of flooding every 100 years. This flood information is very useful for insurance companies when determining where more probable flood zones are located.

A seller of property within a special flood zone (or a flood hazard zone) must disclose this information to the buyer, because federal law requires the buyer to obtain flood insurance in order to secure financing for a property. The cost of flood insurance will vary, depending on the flood zone in which the property is located. So, it is important for the buyer to contact the insurance company, to determine what kind of policy is necessary for financing.

Local Requirements Resulting from City and County Ordinances
Each city, county or community has their own ordinances for land use, zoning requirements, building codes, fire, health and other safety codes and regulations. These ordinances or requirements on how to remain in compliance with the laws, as well as who these laws will affect, must be disclosed by the seller and the seller's agents to any prospective buyer of the property. Buyers may be deterred from purchasing property if its use is restricted. This is imperative for the buyer to know before the transaction is complete.

Foreign Investment in Real Property Tax

Under federal law, if a buyer purchases property from a foreign seller, the buyer must withhold and send the Internal Revenue Service (IRS) 10% of the gross sales price. As with most other disclosures, there are exemptions to this rule, as well. To be sure you are following the law correctly, it is advisable to contact the IRS and consult them regarding the transaction. Further assistance may be sought from a CPA, attorney or tax advisor.

The following exemptions are given for people investing in property sold by foreign sellers:

- Seller's non-foreign affidavit and U.S. taxpayer I.D. number
- A qualifying statement obtained through the IRS, stating that arrangements have been made for the collection of, or exemption from, the tax
- Sales price does not exceed $300,000
- Buyer intends to reside on the property as his or her main residence

Notice Regarding the Advisability of Title Insurance

In the event there is no title insurance being issued in an escrow, the buyer is required to sign the following notice as a separate document to the escrow:

Important: In a purchase or exchange of real property, it may be advisable to obtain title insurance, in connection with the close of escrow, where there may be prior recorded liens and encumbrances which affect your interest in the property being acquired. A new policy of title insurance should be obtained, in order to insure your interest in the property that you are acquiring.

The escrow holder is usually the person who will deliver this statement to the buyer, though there is no person specifically called out to do so by law. If the real estate agent is the escrow holder, the agent will be responsible for this notice.

Furnishing Controlling Documents and a Financial Statement

Any person selling a common interest development property (condominium, community apartment project, planned development or stock cooperative) must provide all prospective buyers with the following, required disclosures:

- Information on any approved change in the assessments or fees not yet due and payable as of the disclosure date (or a future date)
- A copy of the governing documents of the development such as homeowner's association rules and guidelines
- A copy of the homeowner's association's most recent financial statement
- If there is an age restriction that is not allowable by law, there must be a statement that the age restriction is only enforceable to the extent permitted by law; as well as applicable provisions of the law. This is restrictions outside of the age exemption made for seniors
- A written statement from the association specifying the amount of current regular and special assessments, as well as any unpaid assessment, late charges, interest and costs of collection which are, or may become, a lien against the property

Notice and Disclosure to Buyer of State Tax Withholding on Disposition of California Real Property

In some transactions, the State Franchise Tax Board requires the buyer to withhold 3 1/2% of the total sales price as state income tax. The escrow holder is required to notify the buyer of this responsibility. Any buyer who does not withhold this amount may be assessed a penalty; any escrow holder not informing the buyer of this obligation will see penalties assessed against the escrow holder. The following transactions are subject to this law:

- The seller shows an out-of-state address, or sales proceeds are to be disbursed to the seller's financial intermediary.
- The seller does not certify that he or she is a California resident, or that the property being conveyed is his or her personal residence.
- The sale price exceeds $100,000

ESCROW AND TRUST FUNDS

One of the job requirements you will face is collecting funds from clients for deposits or other purposes. This money is usually presented in the form of a check, to be used later in the transaction, during the disbursement process of escrow. The money you receive is called a trust fund, and real estate law is very specific on how this money should be treated. It is imperative that you be well-versed with the laws regarding how to handle these funds, as a fiduciary duty has been formed between you and the rightful owner of the money (your client). Those agents who do not perform the appropriate transaction may have their license suspended or revoked. Agents who mismanage these funds may be held financially responsible for any damages caused by such negligent actions. In certain conditions, criminal actions may be filed against the agent.

The first step in appropriately handing your client's money is identifying what is considered 'trust fund money'. Trust fund money is money collected by a real estate professional on behalf of their principal and used for a transaction in which a license is required. This kind of money is generally cash or a personal check that will be used as a deposit for the purchase of a home or a note made payable to the seller of property. Trust funds may also be items of value other than money. There is other money that an agent may collect from a principal such as commissions, which is not considered trust fund money. These funds do not belong to a third party. Thus, they are not considered trust funds. The money that does not belong to a broker (trust funds) has been given to the broker with the trust that it will be used for its intended purpose, that of purchasing property. This money MUST be accounted for separately. Accurate records are required for this money to show that all actions have been lawful, and that all accounting is up to date with the trust funds.

Trust Fund Money:
- Cash, Money or other items of value intended for use as a deposit in a real estate transaction.
- Not to be used for the purchase of property Commissions are NOT trust fund money

Once a broker or salesperson receives trust fund money from a principal, the transaction has begun. These trust funds must be placed into the escrow depository, or into a trust fund account, separate from all other accounts under the broker's control. This money must be placed in the trust fund within three business days following the receipt of funds by the broker or salesperson. An exception to the three-day rule is trust fund money received as a deposit for the offer to purchase property. This money may be held until the offer has been accepted, even if it is more than three days from receipt of the money. Once the offer has been accepted by the seller (or offeree), the check is held (and not deposited) only with written permission from the seller. Unless otherwise stated, the check must be deposited into escrow or in a trust account within three days after the acceptance. If deposited into escrow, it is deposited into a neutral depository, or into an account held by a licensed escrow holder. Before the seller accepts the funds, the buyer (or offeror) is the rightful owner of the funds. However, as soon as the offer is accepted, the seller is the owner of these funds. The funds will then be handled according to the escrow instructions (the agreed-upon instructions by both the buyer and the seller).

Remember!
- Trust funds must be deposited into escrow, or into a special account, within 3 business days following receipt of the funds.
- Money intended to be used as a deposit may be held until the offer has been accepted, even if it is held for more than three days
- With written permission from the seller, a deposit may be held longer than three days. Otherwise, the deposit must be deposited into an escrow or trust account within three days of the offer's acceptance.
- The deposit money belongs to the buyer until the point of acceptance of the offer. At that point, the money belongs to the seller

Trust Fund Accounts

A broker's trust fund account must be set up as a trust account in the name of the broker, who is the trustee of the account. All broker's trust fund accounts must be set up in the state of California with a recognized depository or bank for all transactions. Any withdrawals from this account may only be made with a signature of one or more approved persons who have access to the account. Trust fund accounts are generally not interest-bearing accounts, where written notice must be given for withdrawals. However, they can be in certain circumstances.

Anyone authorized to take money out of the account is able to make withdrawals from it. The people with this authorization are the broker (in whose name the account is maintained), any designated broker-officer (if the trust account happens to be in the name of a corporate broker) or any individuals who are authorized in writing by the broker. This person may be another broker in the firm or a salesperson working for the broker. Additionally, unlicensed employees of the broker, so long as permission is given in writing, may make withdrawals. The unlicensed employee must also be covered by a fidelity bond.

391

Persons authorized to withdraw money from a trust account:

- Trustee broker who set up the account
  Designated broker-officer of the corporate brokerage
- Salesperson or other brokers in the brokerage with written permission from the trustee's broker
- Unlicensed employee covered by a fidelity bond

Commingling

Commingling is defined as the mixing of trust funds with personal funds, and is strictly prohibited by real estate law. Any broker found to be commingling funds may be punished with suspension or revocation of his or her license. Brokers may, however, keep up to $200 of personal money in a trust account, to pay for any charges the bank may issue against the account. Commingling happens whenever any personal or company money is deposited into the trust fund bank account. The opposite is also true. If any trust money is deposited into a personal account commingling has occurred. If any commissions paid on the transaction are used from the trust account, the money must be withdrawn within 30 days. Commissions left in the account for more than 30 days are considered commingling.

Remember!
Commingling occurs when any trust fund money is mixed into a broker's personal account, or when any personal funds are placed into a trust account. There is a $200 exception, where personal funds may be deposited into a trust account for maintenance and fees that may be applied to the account.

S U M M A R Y

The ability to tie together all the technical knowledge you learned in this book and apply it to the actual practice of real estate is the key to your success as a real estate agent. This chapter will illustrate the practice of real estate, the disclosures required and the ethics and standards you will be held to as a real estate agent. It is important that you understand all the concepts used in this chapter, as they were drawn from all the previous chapters. They are presented to you in a practical application, versus a technical concept. If you take just one thing from this chapter, it is this: carefully choose the brokerage for which you will work. Choosing the best brokerage for your needs will arm you with the necessary knowledge and skills to succeed in the industry.

T E R M S   A N D   P H R A S E S

Agent – The term used for any person licensed as a real estate professional under the Department of Real Estate.

Broker – A licensed person in charge of the operations of a brokerage. Brokers are allowed to practice real estate on their own, or can operate a brokerage and hire salespersons to work for them.

Brokerage – An avenue in which to sell or transfer a good or service from one person to another. The broker is an intermediary, or middleman, negotiating the transaction and ensuring all technical items are attended to and handled correctly. In our case, the brokerage is obviously used in the transfer of real estate.

Commingling – The mixing of a broker's private funds of over $200 with other people's money, specifically client's money in the form of trust funds.

Commission Split – The agreed-upon division of money between a broker and salesperson when the brokerage has been paid a commission from a sale
Neutral Depository – An escrow business conducted by someone who is a licensed escrow holder.

Salesperson – A licensed person working for a broker in charge of the sale of homes, filling out paperwork and communication between buyer and seller. The salesperson may not work independently.

Trust Funds – Money received by a real estate broker or salesperson on behalf of the client.

C H A P T E R   Q U I Z

1. A real estate professional found guilty for violating real estate law may face
   A. Sanctions from the Real Estate Commission
   B. Civil Punishment
   C. Criminal Punishment
   D. All of the above

2. Where can real estate law be found?
   A. California Code of Regulations
   B. Business and Professional Code
   C. Both A and B
   D. Neither A nor B

3. A real estate agent is a person who holds what type of license?
   A. A real estate broker's license
   B. A real estate salesperson's license.
   C. Both a real estate salesperson's and broker's license
   D. A real estate agent's license.

4. When a real estate salesperson leaves his or her brokerage, what happens to the listings they handle?
   A. The listings go with the salesperson to his or her new brokerage
   B. The listings stay with the old brokerage
   C. The listings are canceled, and the principal must enter into a new agency agreement with a new broker
   D. None of the above.

5. Which licensee is allowed to operate independently?
   A. A broker
   B. A salesperson
   C. A salesperson, provided he or she has had 5 years of experience
   D. Any licensed agent may work independently

6. Which one of the following is NOT one of the five main functions of a real estate brokerage?
   A. Filling out paperwork
   B. Listing
   C. Selling
   D. Arranging or making referrals for financing

7. Which one of the following is an important characteristic to a salesperson when looking for a brokerage with which to work?
   A. Location of the office
   B. Size of the staff
   C. Brokerage's inventory
   D. Parking

8. When a property is sold, the two brokerages involved in the transaction generally have what kind of an arrangement when it comes to commission?
   A. The listing brokerage receives the full commission.
   B. The brokerages will do a 50-50 split of the commission
   C. The salesperson(s) will receive the entire commission, they did all the work.
   D. The brokers receive the entire commission; they will pay their salesperson a salary.

9. How many days does a broker have to deposit trust fund money into the trust fund account?
   A. 2
   B. 3
   C. 4
   D. 5

10. What kind of responsibility is placed into the hands of a broker once he or she receives funds from the principal?
    A. Fiduciary
    B. Exclusive
    C. Trustee
    D. None of the above

11. Who is allowed to withdraw funds from a trust account?
    A. Trustee broker
    B. Broker or officer in a corporate brokerage
    C. An unlicensed employee of the broker who is covered by a fidelity bond, pro vided there is written permission.
    D. All of the above

12. How much personal money is a broker allowed to keep in a trust account?
    A. None, commingling is strictly prohibited by real estate law
    B. $200
    C. $2,000
    D. $5,000

13. What will limit the responsibility of a seller regarding a Transfer Disclosure Statement delivered to a potential buyer?
    A. Inspections made to the structure and property.
    B. Verbal statement of problems.
    C. Mello-Roos Statement
    D. None of the above.

14. Homes built before which year require the lead-based paint hazard disclosure?
    A. 1996
    B. 1992
    C. 1978
    D. 1970

15. A two-story home, built in 1987, with one bedroom on the first floor and three on the second floor, requires how many smoke detectors?
    A. 1
    B. 2
    C. 3
    D. 4

16. According to the Natural Hazard Disclosure Law passed in 1998, which of the following disclosures is required?
    A. State responsibility fire area
    B. Seismic hazard zone
    C. Flood hazard area
    D. All of the above

17. Which one of the following hazards is NOT discussed in the environmental hazard booklet?
    A. Asbestos
    B. Lead
    C. Lead-based paint
    D. Formaldehyde

18. Regarding a transaction between a seller and the seller's agent, when does the transaction actually begin?
    A. When the agent receives the listing
    B. When the agent receives a purchase contract from a buyer
    C. When escrow is opened
    D. When escrow is closed.

19. What is the type of listing that guarantees the listing agent a commission, regardless of who sells the property?
    A. Open listing
    B. Net listing
    C. Exclusive authorization and right to sell listing
    D. Option listing

20. Residential offers most closely resemble that of a
    A. Commercial offer
    B. Industrial offer
    C. Agricultural offer
    D. None of the above

REAL
ESTATE
SPECIALIZATIONS

What you will learn in this Chapter

- Business Opportunity Brokerage

- Mobile Home Brokerage

- Probate Sales

1. When you purchase a business and expect the existing customer base to come | with it, this is called?
   A. Business Opportunity
   B. Goodwill
   C. Inventory
   D. Bill of Sale

2. Which of the following are elements in the sale of a business?
   A. Goodwill
   B. Inventory
   C. Lease
   D. All of the above

3. In order to complete a business opportunity transaction, what requirements must be followed?
   A. Uniform Commercial Code
   B. Bulk Transfer Act
   C. Alcohol Beverage Control Act
   D. All of the above

4. An estate worth how much money would be exempt from a probate sale?
   A. $100,000
   B. $75,000
   C. $50,000
   D. None of the above

5. What department presides over the probate court?
   A. Superior Court
   B. Regional Court
   C. State Court
   D. Supreme Court

6. A mobile home is considered real property when it is
   A. Attached to a chassis and wheels and registered with the Department of Motor Vehicles
   B. Permanently attached to a foundation and registered with the Department of Housing and Community Development
   C. Both A and B
   D. Neither A nor B

7. When may a real estate agent sell a manufactured home?
   A. Any time, as there are no restrictions
   B. Only when the mobile home is considered real property
   C. Only when the mobile home is considered personal property
   D. When the mobile home is considered real property, or if the mobile home is considered used and meets the required minimum measurements (of 8 feet wide by 30 feet long) and the real estate agent who sold the home has been licensed for one year.

INTRODUCTION

Most real estate agents are in the residential sales side of real estate. This is the most logical area of real estate to start in, as most real estate firms specialize in residential properties. Additionally, most introductory real estate educational classes and programs focus their attention on the residential side of real estate.

After agents have sold properties for some time, most decide to specialize in one aspect of the business. Residential specializations are very common (perhaps the most common); but there are other specializations into which a realtor can enter. Some of these specializations move toward the financial aspects of real estate.

In this chapter, we will discuss opportunities available to agents in business opportunity brokerage, mobile home sales and probate sales. These are just a few areas of expertise in which an agent can specialize.

BUSINESS OPPORTUNITY BROKERAGE

In real estate, the sale of a business is considered the same as the sale of a personal property. Because the sale is considered personal property, rules regarding the transfer of chattels apply. There is an expectation from the buyer that he or she is not only buying or leasing a physical space, but also buying the goodwill of a business; or the continued patronage base from the existing business. This type of transaction is sometimes referred to as a business opportunity. The buyer, seller and broker must be aware that the application of the bulk transfer laws apply in the sales of all businesses.

> **Remember!**
> Individuals buying a business acquire the following in the transaction:
> - Purchase or lease of a physical space
> - Purchase of existing inventory
> - Goodwill, or patronage

Business opportunities may be negotiated by any licensee. The agent must be aware, however, that there are certain legal issues and other demands present in this type of property transfer that will not be present in other, non-business transactions.

Elements of which an agent must be aware are the physical lease of a building or space (or the purchase of a building or space), the personal property or inventory that will come with the business, and the goodwill that comes with the business. Each of these elements has value, and each should be considered separately when selling a business.

Personal property sold with a business can range from simple inventory to complex machinery and fixtures necessary for the business to operate. For example, in a the sale of a bar, the buyer may purchase all current inventory of alcohol, glasses, dishes and flatware, keg taps, tables, chairs, and any other items you might find in a bar. All of this is fairly standard. In the sale of a brewery, a buyer may purchase all heavy equipment that goes into the production of beer, as well as any inventory (like bottles, boxes, shipping supplies etc).

Each sale of a business will be different and unique and require special knowledge from the real estate professional handling the transaction. While no two transactions are alike, there are different steps that must be taken. The following is a general list of a typical business opportunity sale. Again, please remember this is not an exclusive list; merely an idea of the process, and a good place to begin when dealing with a business opportunity transaction.

1. The business is listed for sale.
2. A business opportunity deposit receipt or offer is completed when a buyer is found to purchase the property.
3. The offer is presented to the seller by the broker or agent for the seller's approval.
4. Escrow is opened upon the acceptance of the offer.
5. All creditors of the current business are notified of the sale and a notice of intended bulk sale is published, according to the requirements of the Bulk Sales Act. To fulfill the requirements of the Uniform Commercial Code (UCC) a financing state ments is filed with the Secretary of State or the recorder's office. The financing statement is a written notice of a creditor's interests in personal property.
7. All necessary forms are filed with the Department of Alcoholic Beverage Control, if there is a liquor license involved in the transaction.
8. The landlord is contacted to reassign the lease to the buyer.
9. Copies of the seller's permit and clearance receipt are collected from the Board of Equalization to protect the buyer from any liability resulting from the unpaid sales tax that the previous owner owed.
10. Information regarding the current employee's salaries, benefits and unemployment insurance tax is noted.
11. Inventory is taken of all stock, fixtures and other personal property to be transferred in the sale of the business.
12. A bill of sale is executed, transferring ownership of all elements of the business.
13. Buyer and seller receive closing statements at the close of escrow.

Legal Requirements for the Sale of a Business
In every sale of a business, there are certain legal requirements that must be met before the transaction can go through. The requirements of the Bulk Transfer Act, Alcoholic Beverage Control Act, Uniform Commercial Code and the California sales and use tax regulations must be met for a successful sale of the business.

Bulk Transfer Act
When a business is sold, the majority of its inventory is usually sold with the business. The Uniform Commercial Code (UCC), which you will read about in the next few paragraphs, regulates the sale of this aspect of a business. The purpose of the Bulk Transfer Act is to protect the creditors from a business being sold. When a business is sold, public notice is given, so that all creditors are aware of the transfer. This is regulated under Division 6 of the UCC.

When a business is sold, the transfer and a notice of sale must be filed with the county recorder after 12 days have passes. Additionally a notice must be printed in the local newspaper where the business is being sold, as well as notice given to the county tax collector in the same twelve days before the transfer of property.

The notice to creditors will give anyone fair notice of the transfer of property, in the event the seller owes any creditors for current inventory. If a business is up for sale and a seller owes a creditor, the creditor should make sure they are paid for any servic es or goods provided before the transfer. If the business is sold without complying with the requirements of the bulk transfer law, the sale is valid between the buyer and the seller, but is considered fraudulent and void with regard to any creditors. In the event that the creditors are not notified, they may take recourse against the seller for any debt owed them, as the business was sold without the debt having been satisfied; nor was the creditor made aware of the transfer.

Alcoholic Beverage Control Act

When a business with the issue of an alcohol license is sold ,the buyer must not assume that the license will be transferred with the sale of the business. In the event that a bar, restaurant or any other establishment is sold where the buyer is interested in the alcohol license, that buyer must apply to the Department of Alcoholic Beverage Control to have the license transferred to their name. A buyer may be turned down for this license, or may be faced with a price of up to $12,000.00 for the license. Any seller who has had a license for more than two yeas may negotiate the price for the license between the buyer and seller in the sale of the business. However, if the license is sold for any time period before those two years, the buyer is subject to the price the Department of Alcoholic Beverage Control will charge for the license.

Remember!
The transfer of a business where an alcohol license is required by the Department of Alcohol and Beverage Control for businesses less than two years old charging up to $12,000 for the license, or for businesses over two years old a price agreed upon by the buyer and seller

Uniform Commercial Code

Most likely, when a business is being sold, the buyer will borrow money to purchase the business and all personal belongings to that business. In this situation, the Uniform Commercial Code, Division 9 sets the requirements for the transfer of the business and any personal property being transferred. A financing statement must be filed with the Secretary of State or the county recorder's office, giving the public notice of any security interest being created by the debt.

When a person borrows money for a real estate loan, a promissory note must be signed. The same is true for a note in the transfer of a business. A note is signed, showing the evidence of debt for the business transfer. The buyer then executes a security agreement, giving the lender an interest in the personal property and the financing statement, which will be recorded. When the financing statement is recorded, public notice is given and all parties are made aware of any interests in the property. This is much the same as a recoded trust deed, which gives public notice of a debt against real property.

California Sales and Use Tax

In the event that a business is sold, and the previous owner did not pay the necessary taxes to the state, the California Sales and Use Tax will protect the buyer from any debt owed to the State Equalization Board by the seller. All unpaid sales tax will be forgiven as far as the buyer is concerned, with the seller responsible for any dollar amount not paid to the board.

The owner of a business may obtain a seller's permit, allowing him or her to purchase goods at wholesale prices and not pay sales taxes on these products or goods. The business owner must then collect sales tax from the customers when the products are sold and give this money to the State Board of Equalization. A copy of the seller's permit and clearance receipt (stating that the business is current on sales taxes), from the State Board of Equalization should be requested by a buyer before assuming ownership of the business.

MOBILE HOME BROKERAGE

A mobile home is one of the few pieces of property a person can own that may be considered either real or personal property, depending on the terms of ownership. A mobile home is a manufactured home, built on a chassis and wheels. If the home remains on the chassis and wheels, it is moveable. Thus, it is considered personal property. If the mobile home is permanently attached to the ground, it is considered real property.

> **Remember!**
> - Mobile homes still attached to their chassis and wheels are moveable, and so are considered personal property.
> - Mobile homes that are permanently attached to a foundation are considered real property

A mobile home is commonly referred to as a trailer. Many communities have special lots that people can buy to permanently attach their home to a foundation. This creates not only a real property interest in the home, but also a community where other mobile homes can be established on lots appropriate to the size of the home. Because the housing market in California is relatively high prices, affordable housing is highly sought after. Manufactured homes are one solution to the rapidly-booming housing market and its prices.

Mobile homes are built in several widths, which defines the general size of the home. The lengths can vary as well and they may be as long as 60 feet. Standard widths are 8, 10 and 12 feet. Obviously, an object of this size is not easy to move, and so most are attached permanently to foundations once they are manufactured, and then moved to their desired location. Sometimes, two units are placed side-by-side, creating a double-wide or extra large residence. This creates a structure that is practically the same size as a traditional home, but at a much lower cost.

Simply attaching a manufactured home to a foundation will not create real property; there are four steps that must be followed. Once the structure is attached, all requirements are met for it to become real property; though the home may be moved again, if necessary. There are steps required in moving the property, as well. The four steps required to create real property from a manufactured home are:

- The manufactured home must be placed on a permanent foundation
- The residents must obtain a building permit to place the home on the foundation
- The residents must obtain a certificate of occupancy before inhabiting the home
- A document must be recorded, stating that the manufactured home has been placed on a permanent foundation.

Once a manufactured home becomes real property, it is taxable as such, and no longer requires registration from the Department of Motor Vehicles. Instead, it is registered with the county recorder as real property.

If an owner wants to move the mobile home to another community, or simply to another lot, he or she can do this. The required steps for moving a mobile home are:

- Notify the Department of Housing and Community Development 30 days before moving the mobile home
- Notify any person with interest in the property
- Notify the local tax assessor
- Obtain a new registration from the Department of Motor Vehicles or a transportation permit from the Department of Housing and Community Development.

Real estate agents may sell mobile homes as long as they are considered real property. Those manufactured homes that have been permanently attached to a foundation and sold in the current lot are under the jurisdiction of a real estate agent. A real estate agent who sells a mobile home must report the sale to the Department of Housing and Community Development within 10 calendar days from the sale of the home. Those mobile homes that are sitting on a chassis and wheels (i.e., not yet permanently attached to a foundation) can only be sold by a licensed mobile home dealer.

As with any sale of real property, the licensees involved have certain rights and actions they can perform and others they cannot. The following is a list of approved activities for licensees who are dealing with the transfer of a mobile home:

- A real estate agent may only sell manufactured homes that have been permanently attached to a foundation. In the event of attachment, the home may be listed and sold in the same manner as all other real property.
- Real estate agents must notify the Department of Housing and Community Development within 10 business days from when a mobile home has been sold.
- Used mobile homes not considered real property, but if they are at least 8 feet wide and 30 feet long they may be sold by a real estate agent who has been licensed for at least one year.
- Sales of new mobile homes may only be made by a licensed mobile home dealer.

Buyers of a mobile home are qualified for the same financing as a traditional, built-in place structure. Additionally, loans are available through government participating programs such as FHA, VA and Cal-Vet.

The Department of Housing and Community Development is the agency responsible for licensing mobile homes. Anyone acquiring or releasing an interest in a mobile home must notify the department within 20 days of a sale, so that the necessary registration card may be provided to all lien holders. A certificate of title must be signed by both the buyer and the seller. All mobile homes considered to be real property must have a tax liability clearance waver signed by the county tax collector.

Just as a condominium complex has homeowner's association rules and regulations, so too does a mobile home park. Agents must be aware of all the rules and regulations of the mobile home park before selling a home in the community, as the buyer must be informed of all rules which may result in a sale or lack of sale, depending on qualifications and rules.

Generally, in a mobile home park, the buyer of a mobile home will rent the lot from the park's owner. The homeowner will own the house itself, but not the lot to which it is attached. The buyer of the home must be approved by the owner of the mobile home park before the sale can commence. Additionally, the buyer of the home must agree to all rules and regulations of the mobile home park. A real estate agent will obtain a copy of these rules and regulations when showing a prospective buyer a home in a mobile home park, so that he or she is aware of all rules and regulations required to live there. An example of some of the rules a person might find in a mobile home park are pet policies, minimum age requirements to live there, or other rules to govern a small community.

P R O B A T E   S A L E S

A probate sale is the court-approved sale of any property of a person who is deceased. Even property that is inherited may be subject of a court's approval. All estates in California worth $60,000 or more must be approved by the probate court.

Probate courts make sure that any creditors of the estate or deceased are paid prior to the heirs inheriting the property. Once all of the creditors have been paid, and any other debts have been settled, the property may be distributed to the proper heirs or persons named in the deceased's will.

The department of the superior court presides over a probate sale. Certain procedures are followed in a probate court hearing. The following is a brief list of these procedures:

- Any offer to purchase the property must be at least 90% of the appraised value of the property.
- All buyers must petition the court for an approved sale. When the court has set a hearing to approve the sale, other persons may make bids.
- Any additional bids must be 10% of the first $10,000 of the property's value and 5% of anything over that amount.
- The court will determine which bid to accept, then confirms the sale of the property.
- At the time of sale, the court will set the amount of commission a real estate agent will receive, if there is a real estate agent involved in the transfer of the property. This amount is usually not negotiable, and is set by the court.

Once the court decides which offer it will accept, a normal escrow is opened, as defined on the terms handed down from the court.

Remember!
Any estate worth $60,000 or more is subject to probate court approval before assets can be disbursed to living heirs or according to the deceased will.

SUMMARY

Real estate is a very dynamic industry, where an agent can choose to specialize in one of a varying number of areas. This chapter has illustrated just a few different areas of expertise on which an agent can focus their talents. There are a number of other areas in which an agent can practice, such as agricultural land, commercial, industrial and land real estate sales. By understanding that there are many different possibilities available, both in residential real estate and outside of that market, you can specialize your talents and build a very lucrative practice.

TERMS AND PHRASES

Bill of Sale – The document that transfers ownership of personal property

Bulk Transfer Law – The law governing the transfer of bulk items in the sale of a business.

Business Opportunity – The sale or lease of a business

Financing Statement – The written notice, filed with the county recorder, by a creditor who has extended credit for the purchase of personal property, establishing interest in the personal property as collateral for the loan.

Goodwill – The notion that in the sale of a business, the good reputation of the business will be transferred in the sale, along with the customer base for the current business.

Manufactured Housing – Housing units constructed on a chassis and wheels, designed for permanent or semi-permanent attachment to a lot.

Probate Sale – The court-approved sale of a deceased person's property.

Sales Tax – A tax collected as a percentage of the retail sales of a product, by a retailer, and given to the State Board of Equalization.

Seller's Permit – Permit that allows a retailer to buy goods at wholesale prices without paying sales tax. The retailer must in turn collect the proper sales tax from customers and pay this sum to the State Board of Equalization.

CHAPTER QUIZ

1. When you purchase a business and expect the existing customer base to come with it, this is called?
    A. Business Opportunity
    B. Goodwill
    C. Inventory
    D. None of the above

2. Which of the following are considered elements of a business?
    A. Goodwill
    B. Inventory
    C. Lease
    D. All of the above

3. The sale of a business is considered the sale of what kind of property?
   A. Chattel real
   B. Real Property
   C. Personal Property
   D. Both A and C

4. If there will be a transfer of a liquor license in the sale of a business, what state a gency must be notified?
   A. State Board of Equalization
   B. Department of Real Estate
   C. Alcohol Beverage Control
   D. All of the above.

5. What receipt is obtained from the State Board of Equalization to release the buyer of a business from any unpaid sales taxes the seller may still owe?
   A. Clearance Receipt
   B. Bill of Sale
   C. Financing Statement
   D. None of the above

6. In order to complete a business opportunity transaction, what requirements must be followed?
   A. Uniform Commercial Code
   B. Bulk Transfer Act
   C. Alcohol Beverage Control Act
   D. All of the above.

7. In the event that a business is sold before creditors are notified, to whom can the creditors go to satisfy any current debts?
   A. Buyer
   B. Seller
   C. Both buyer and seller
   D. Neither buyer nor seller

8. In the transfer of a business, what document does a buyer sign giving the lender an interest in the personal property?
   A. Promissory note
   B. Security agreement
   C. Financing statement
   D. Trust deed

9. What protects a buyer from back sales taxes owed to the State Equalization Board?
   A. California Sales and Use Tax
   B. Uniform Commercial Code
   C. Pubic notice
   D. Seller's permit

10. An estate worth how much money would be exempt from a probate sale? (C):
   A. $100,000
   B. $75,000
   C. $50,000
   D. None of the above

11. The main function of a probate court is to ensure what?
    A. The heirs of a deceased individual get what is rightfully theirs
    B. Any creditors to whom the deceased owes money will rightfully receive payment for these debts.
    C. The deceased's will is followed exactly as he or she had intended.
    D. No main reason, it is just a formality.

12. What department presides over the probate court?
    A. Superior Court
    B. Regional Court
    C. State Court
    D. Supreme Court

13. The first bid to purchase property in a probate sale must be what total percentage of the appraised value of the property?
    A. 100%
    B. 95%
    C. 90%
    D. 85%

14. A normal escrow is opened when a bid is accepted to purchase an estate. Who defines the terms and conditions of the escrow?
    A. The will of the deceased
    B. The buyer
    C. The deceased's family
    D. The court

15. A mobile home is considered real property when it is
    A. Attached to a chassis and wheels and registered with the Department of Motor Vehicles.
    B. Permanently attached to a foundation, registered with the Department of Housing and Community Development.
    C. Both A and B
    D. Neither A nor B

16. A manufactured home referred to as a double-wide is
    A. A mobile home with a width of at least 12 feet
    B. A mobile home built to the maximum length of 60 feet
    C. A mobile home consisting of two units placed side by side, creating one large structure
    D. None of the above.

17. A manufactured home considered to be personal property must be licensed with what department?
    A. State Tax Collector
    B. County Assessor
    C. Department of Motor Vehicles
    D. County Recorder

18. When may a real estate agent sell a manufactured home?
    A. Any time, there are no restrictions
    B. Only when the mobile home is considered real property
    C. Only when the mobile home is considered personal property
    D. When the mobile home is considered real property, or if the mobile home is

considered used and meets the required minimum measurements of 8 feet wide by 30 feet long and the real estate agent who sold the mobile home has been licensed for one year.

19. Financing of mobile homes or government programs may be available through which agency?
    A. FHA
    B. VA
    C. Cal-Vet
    D. All of the above.

20. How many days is a real estate agent given to notify the Department of Housing and Consumer Development when he or she sells a mobile home? (A):
    A. 10
    B. 20
    C. 30
    D. 40

15

REAL ESTATE MATH

What you will learn in this Chapter

- Conversion factors and formulas

- Math Principles

- Investments

- Discounting Notes

- Commission

- Interest and Loan Calculations

- Cost and Selling Price

- Square Footage and Area

- Proration

- Documentary Transfer Tax

INTRODUCTION

Math is one of the largest concerns for most students studying real estate. The different computations, conversions from one value to another and other algebraic-type problems can worry students. This is especially true when it comes to the state exam. This chapter will help to calm your fears about math. You will notice that this chapter does not have a test your knowledge section. This is because this chapter will consist mainly of examples and practice problems. Remember, math is generally one problem that can be broken down into small steps to arrive at the correct answer. When a problem seems too difficult to comprehend, simplify it by asking yourself what you understand about the problem. Then, take it step-by-step.

CONVERSION FACTORS AND GENERAL FORMULAS

- 1 Acre = 43,560 square feet
- 1 mile = 5,280 feet
- 1 section of land = 640 acres
- Area of a Square = Length x Width
- Area of a Rectangle = Length x Width
- Area of a Triangle = Altitude x Base / 2
- 1 square yard = 9 square feet
- 1 square foot = 144 square inches or 12" x 12"
- 1 cubic yard = 27 cubic feet or 3' x 3' x 3'
- 1 board feet = 12" x 12" x 1" = 144 cubic inches
- The reciprocal of a number is its inverse
- The reciprocal of 8 = 1/8

MATH PRINCIPLES

Converting Percentages to Decimal Points and Decimal Points to Percentages
Many times you will have to convert a percentage to a decimal point to correctly figure a math problem. If you understand this principle, this step will be very easy for you. If this is a challenge for you, the math problem may seem impossible.

To convert a percentage to a decimal point, simply divide the percentage amount by 100. For example, 5% converted to a decimal is .05

$$5 / 100 = .05.$$

- 48% = 0.48 (48 / 100)
- 79.5% = 0.795 (79.5 / 100)
- 203% = 2.03 (203 / 100)

To convert a decimal point to a percentage, simple multiply the decimal point by 100. For example .075 converted to a percentage is 7.5%

$$0.075 \times 100 = 7.5\%$$

- 0.02 = 2% (0.02 x 100)
- 0.77 = 77% (0.77 x 100)
- 3.88 = 388% (3.88 x 100)

Addition and Subtraction of Decimal Numbers
Addition and subtraction of decimal numbers is basically the same as the adding and subtracting of whole numbers. The key difference is that the decimal points must line up, to make the problem work out accurately. You will see from the following examples what lining up the decimal points means. Remember, this operation will only work if the decimal points are lined up.

$$8.667 + 785.322 = 793.989$$

$$
\begin{array}{r}
8.667 \\
+785.322 \\
\hline
793.989
\end{array}
$$

$$679.43 - 22.55 = 656.88$$

$$
\begin{array}{r}
679.43 \\
-22.55 \\
\hline
656.88
\end{array}
$$

Multiplication of Decimals
Multiplication of decimals is the same as any other multiplication problem. Simply multiply the two numbers together to find where the decimal point goes; then add the number of decimal points of the two problems. That is the number of numbers that will be to the right of the decimal point. The example will illustrate this concept.

$$6.88 \times 32.4 = 222.912$$

$$
\begin{array}{r}
6.88 \\
\times 32.4 \\
\hline
222.912
\end{array}
$$

You will notice there are 2 decimal points in the first number, and one in the second, giving us a total of three numbers to the right of the decimal point.

Division of Decimals
To divide decimals, we create a whole number in the divisor category. To create this whole number, simply move the decimal point to the right until a whole number is created. When the decimal point is moved on the divisor, it must also be moved on the dividend.

$$0.32 / 675 = 2109.375$$

0.32 becomes 32 and 675 becomes 67500 so,

$$32 / 67500 = 2109.375$$

INVESTMENTS

All investment problems will have three variables, one of which we need to solve. The three variables are the investment (or amount invested), income (or profit earned), and rate of return (or percentage of profit). These variables are represented in the following formulas:

- To find the dollar amount invested when the income and rate of return (%) are known:

  Amount Invested = Income Earned / Rate of Return (%)

- To find the rate of return (%) when the income and the dollar amount invested are known:

  Rate of Return (%) = Income Earned / Amount Invested

- To find the income when the amount of money invested and the rate of return (%) are known:

- Income earned = Amount of money invested x Rate of return (%)

Interest rates are almost always given in terms of annual basis. If, for some reason, the interest rate is given as a monthly figure, you multiply this figure by 12 to arrive at the annual interest rate.

Example 1
Betty would like to make $200 a month in interest from her savings account. She knows the interest rate is 4%. How much money does Betty need to keep in her account to earn the money?

Amount invested = Income / rate of return

X = $2,400 / 4%
$200 / month = $2,400 year

X = $60,000

Betty must keep $60,000 in her savings account each year to make the desired $200 per month in interest.

Example 2
Adam purchased a home for $200,000, and then sold the home for $250,000. What is the rate of profit Adam made from the sale of his house?

Profit (%) = Profit made / Investment
Profit made = $250,000 - $200,000 = $50,000
Profit (%) = $50,000 / $200,000
Profit (%) = 25%

DISCOUNTING NOTES

Notes are discounted when a buyer purchases the note on the secondary mortgage market and pays less than the face amount of the note. The original owner will not make their entire investment back, but sometimes certain circumstances may dictate the early sale of a note. The buyer of the note will profit when the note is due, and when the borrower pays the entire sum of the note, plus interest. So, the buyer of the note paid less than the face amount of the note (generally in a certain percentage of the face value), but we receive the full face value of the note when it is due. Discounting notes involve three variables: the investment, the profit and the rate of return

- The investment on the note = Principal – Discount

- The profit = Interest + Discount

- Rate of Return (%) = Profit / Investment

Example:
Jamie needs to do some home repairs, and decides to take out a note for $4,000, which was to be paid off in 1 year. He owed the $4,000 plus 8% interest when the note is due. The original lender sold the note to an investor at a 20% discount. What was the rate of return invested by the investor?

Profit = Interest + Discount
$4,000 x .08 = $320 (interest due at the end of the note)
$4,000 x .20 = $800 (20% discount)
$1,120 Profit

Investment = Principal – Discount
$4,000 – ($4,000 x .20)
$4,000 - $800 =
$3,200

Rate of Return = ?

Rate of Return = Profit / Investment
Rate of Return = $1,120 / $3,200
Rate of Return = 35%

Capitalization Problems

Capitalization problems involve three variables: annual net income, capitalization rate and value of the property. These variables can be represented in formulas that look like the following:

- Net income or loss = Value of the Property x Capitalization Rate

- Value of Property = Net Income or Loss / Capitalization Rate

- Capitalization Rate = Net Income or Loss / Value of Property

Example 1
A triplex brings in $750 per unit per month. Mark is interested in buying the property as in investment and needs an investment (or capitalization) rate of a 10% return. What should Mark pay for the tri-plex?

Annual Income = 3 units x $750 per month = $2250
$2250 x 12 months = $27,000

Capitalization Rate = 10%

Value of the property = ?

Value of the Property = Net Income or Loss / Capitalization Rate
Value of the Property = $27,000 / 10%
Value of the Property = $270,000

Mark should not pay more than $270,000 for the triplex.

Example 2:
Angie paid $800,000 for a 7-unit apartment building. The gross income is $750 / month per unit, with expenses totaling $3,800 annually. What capitalization rate will Angie make on her investment? We will first need to figure up the net income, but must also know the gross income.

Gross Income = $750 x 7 units = $63,000
Expenses = $3,800
Net income = Gross income – expenses
Net Income = $63,000 - $3,800
= $59,200

Capitalization Rate = Net Income / Value of the Property

Capitalization Rate = $59,200 / $800,000
Capitalization Rate = 7.4%

C O M M I S S I O N

Commissions are based on a percentage of the selling price of real property. In some cases, there are many different people who will share in the commission. By the time it gets down to one single agent, it is less than the original commission amount. The variables used in solving commission problems are:

- Selling Price of the Property
- Amount of Commissions
- Commission Rate

The most probable equations to be used in figuring commissions look like this:

- Amount of Commission = Selling Price x Commission Rate
- Commission Rate = Amount of Commission / Selling Price
- Selling Price = Amount of Commission / Commission Rate

Example 1:
John found a buyer for his listing, a single-family home, selling for $750,000. The seller agreed to a 6% commission, which John must split 50-50 with his broker. What is the total amount of commission John will make?

Selling Price = $750,000
Commission Rate = 6%
Amount of Commission = ?

Amount of Commission = $750,000 x 6%
$750,000 x 6% = $45,000
Because John has a 50 – 50 commission split with his broker, the total amount of commission John will make will be $45,000 / 2 =
$22,500 total commission

INTEREST AND LOAN CALCULATIONS

When we borrow money, there is a charge for the use of this money, called interest. The rate charged for the interest is called the interest rate, which is a dynamic (i.e., constantly changing) figure,. Most payments toward a loan include a monthly interest payment, and a monthly principle amount in the one sum. The variables used when solving interest and loan problems are:

- Dollar amount of interest (I)
- Principal or the loan amount (P)
- Interest rate (R)
- Number of years the loan will last (length of the loan) (T)

Equations used to solve these problems look like this:

- Principal = Dollar amount of interest / (Annual interest rate x Length of the loan)
$$P = I / (R \times T)$$

- Annual Interest Rate = Dollar amount of interest / (Principal x Length of the loan)
$$R = I / (P \times T)$$

- Dollar amount of interest = Principal x Interest Rate x Length of the Loan
$$I = P \times R \times T$$

Example 1:
Andrew and Tammy borrowed $10,000 for one year, paying $900 in interest. What was the interest rate they paid?

$$P = \$10,000$$
$$I = \$900$$
$$T = 1 \text{ year}$$
$$R = ?$$

$$R = \$900 / (\$10,000 \times 1)$$

$$R = 9\%$$

Example 2:
One month interest on a five-year, straight interest-only loan is $65. If the interest rate on the note is 10% per year, what is the amount of the loan?

$$R = 10\%$$
$$I = \$65 / mo, \$780 / year$$
$$T = 1\ year$$
$$P = ?$$

$$P = I / (R \times T)$$
$$P = \$780 / (10\% \times 1)$$

$$P = \$78,000$$

COST AND SELLING PRICE

Cost and selling price problems generally deal with the amount of profit a person will make from the sale of a home. We must also be given the amount of profit a person makes and figure the cost before profit. In doing so, we work with the following three variables:

- Purchase price (original cost)
- Selling Price
- Profit (loss rate)

The equations used to find answers to these problems are:

- Selling Price = Purchase Price x Profit or Loss Rate
- Purchase Price = Selling Price / Profit or Loss Rate
- Profit or Loss Rate = Selling Price / Purchase Price

Example 1:
Jeanne sold her beach house for $700,000, which allowed her to make 15% profit. What did she pay for the property?

Purchase Price = Selling Price / Profit
Selling Price = $700,000
Profit Rate = 100% + 15% = 115%, or 1.15
Purchase Price = $700,000 / 115%
Purchase Price = $608,695

Example 2:
Emily wanted to sell her house and her real estate agent found a buyer to purchase the property. After the close of escrow, the real estate agent presented Emily with a check for $320,000, which already had the 6% commission deducted. What was the selling price on Emily's house?

Selling Price = Sellers net price / Commission rate
Sellers Net Price = $320,000
Commission Rate = 94% (100% - 6%)
Selling Price = $320,000 / 94%
Selling Price = $340,425

SQUARE FOOTAGE AND AREA

It is important to understand how to calculate square footage; this information is necessary for the cost method of appraising. It is generally a simple calculation, involving three variables. The three variables are:

- Length
- Width
- Area

The basic formulas to use in figuring area are:

- Area = Length x Width
- Length = Area / Width
- Width = Area / Length

Example 1:
James owns 2 acres of land, with a total front footage along the street of 350 feet. What is the depth of the land?

Length = Area / Width
Area = 2 acres x 43,560 square feet per acre
Area = 43,560 x 2 = 87,120 square feet
Width = 350 feet
Length = 87,120 square feet / 350 feet
Length = 248.91 feet

PRORATION

Prorating is when we find out the amount the buyer and seller will owe for expenses at the close of escrow. Certain costs are prorated, so that one party is not paying for more costs than the other. Examples of proration of expenses are income taxes or fire insurance premiums. For proration purposes, it is assumed that there are 360 days in a year and 30 days in each month. When we prorate the cost of something, there are several steps or considerations we need to make to correctly arrive at the figure we are seeking. The steps are:

- Determine the number of days the sum of money must be prorated
- Calculate the cost per day
- Multiply the number of days by the cost per day
- Decide on who will pay for this item, the seller or the buyer.

Example:
Jennifer sold her home to Kevin on September 1, 2000. Kevin assumed the existing fire insurance policy, which was paid through November 15, 2001. Jennifer originally paid $360 per year on the fire insurance policy. How much should she be credited for the unused portion of her policy at the close of escrow?

September 1, 2000 – November 15, 2001 = 435 days
$360 / 360 = $1 / day
435 days x $1 / day =$435
Jennifer should be credited with $435 of the unused portion of her fire insurance policy.

Documentary Transfer Tax

As we have learned in a previous chapter, there is a tax on the transfer of property from one person to another. This tax is called the documentary transfer tax. Certain cities will have a higher rate imposed for this tax, but for our purposes let's use the state documentary transfer tax base of $1.10 per every $1,000. This documentary transfer tax is only imposed on a cash sale, or when a buyer obtains a new loan to finance the purchase price. This tax is not imposed on assumed loans.

Example 1:
Aaron sold his house to Bernice for $400,000. Bernice was to assume Aaron's current note for $150,000 and obtain a new loan to cover the existing $250,000. What is the documentary transfer tax on this transaction?

$1.10 per $1,000 of the new loan
New loan = $250,000
$1.10 x 250 = $275.00
Documentary Transfer Tax on this transaction will be $275.00

S U M M A R Y

Real estate math does not have to be as difficult as some people imagine it to be. By understanding what is being asked for you to calculate, and breaking down the problem into what is known and what is being asked, it is easier to arrive at the correct answer. Keep in mind, the conversions you may have to make, as well as how to make these logical steps from. Also remember basic formulas and ratios; they will help solve problems much faster and easier.

T E R M S   A N D   P H R A S E S

Decimal Point – The period that sets a whole number apart from the fractional side (or portion of) that number. All numbers to the right of a decimal point are fractional numbers.

Divisor – The number by which another number is divided.

Dividend – The number into which another number is divided.

Interest – The amount of money a borrower will be charged to use another person's money.

Principal – The amount of money to be borrowed, not including the interest charge.

Proration – Process in which an escrow officer makes fair distribution of all expenses through escrow between the seller and the buyer.

Rate – The percentage of interest that will be charged on the principal amount of money borrowed.

Time – The length of the loan.

C H A P T E R   Q U I Z

1. What is .55 expressed as in a percentage?
   a. 5.5%
   b. 0.55%
   c. 55%
   d. 555%

2. What is 374% expressed as a decimal point?
   a. 0.374
   b. 3.74
   c. 37.4
   d. 374.0

3. What is 56.32 x 143.554?
   a. 8084.9612
   b. 80849.612
   c. 808.49612
   d. 808496.12

4. What is the reciprocal of 10%?
   a. 0.1
   b. 1
   c. 10
   d. 100

5. How many board feet are in a piece of lumber measuring 3 inches by 10 inches by 24 feet?
   a. 0
   b. 12
   c. 48
   d. 60

6. George has a savings account and wishes to make $120 per month off the interest. If the account is currently paying him 5% interest, how much money should Steve leave in the account?
   a. $25,800
   b. $28,800
   c. $30,800
   d. $32,800

7. Julia bought a house for $200,000 and later sold the house for $280,000. What is the rate of profit she made on this transaction?
    a. 40%
    b. 140%
    c. 71%
    d. None of the above

8. What is the name for the amount of money borrowed before interest is calculated?
    a. Usury
    b. Proration
    c. Principal
    d. Percentage

9. Amy signed a note for $10,000 payable in 12 months. The note had an interest rate of 9% when it was due. The note was later sold to a private investor at a 15% discount. What is the rate of return on the amount invested by the investor?
    a. 25.89%
    b. 28.24%
    c. 32.44%
    d. 35.47%

10. How many cubic inches are in one board foot?
    a. 12 cubic inches
    b. 2 cubic inches
    c. 48 cubic inches
    d. 144 cubic inches

11. An apartment complex brings in $800 per month per unit, with 9 units in the complex. June is interested in purchasing the property as an investment property, and needs a 9% rate of return or capitalization rate. How much money should June pay for this apartment complex?
    a. $960,000
    b. $80,000
    c. $106,667
    d. $550,000

12. How much commission will Bob make on a property sold for $300,000 at a 6% commission if he has a 50-50 split with his broker?
    a. $18,000
    b. $12,000
    c. $9,000
    d. $32,000

13. Theresa borrowed $4,000 for one year and paid $480 in interest. What was the interest rate she paid?
    a. 15%
    b. 12%
    c. 10%
    d. 9%

14. Hank sold his mountain cabin for $200,000, which gave him a 15% profit. What did he originally pay for the property?
    a. $173,913
    b. $171,856
    c. $174,857
    d. $175,237

15. Barbara was in a rush to move and had to sell her property fast. A real estate agent found a buyer immediately and presented Barbara with a check for $350,000 after the 6% commission had been taken out. What was the selling price on Barbara's house?
    a. $371,913
    b. $372,896
    c. $374,875
    d. $372,340

16. How many acres are there in 174,240 square feet?
    a. 33 Acres
    b. 25 acres
    c. 4 acres
    d. 1 acre

17. A farmer's field has a frontage stretching along 2 miles of road. How many feet is this?
    a. 5,280
    b. 10,560
    c. 5,820
    d. 11,640

18. David owns 3 acres of land with a front footage of 400 feet along the street. What is the depth of the land?
    a. 326.7 feet
    b. 39.6 feet
    c. 290 feet
    d. 3267 feet

19. A fire insurance policy was prepaid for three years. Assume it is currently September 1, 2004 and the policy will expire November 15, 2005. The policy costs $400 per year. How much of the unused portion of the policy is left?
    a. $521
    b. $501
    c. $497
    d. $483

20. Loretta sold her house to Chris for $500,000. Chris is to assume a $100,000 note and obtain a new note for $400,000 to cover the sales cost of the home. How much will the documentary transfer tax be?
    a. $550
    b. $440
    c. $110
    d. None of the above

ABATEMENT OF JUDGMENT - A document containing a condensation of the essential provisions of a court judgment.

ABATEMENT OF NUISANCE - The act of ending or terminating a nuisance; a type of legal action brought to end a nuisance.

ABSTRACT OF JUDGMENT - A summary of money judgment. The summary is usually prepared so that it may be recorded, thereby creating a (judgment) lien on real estate owned by the judgment debtor.

ABSTRACT OF TITLE - A summary of the instruments affecting title to a parcel of real property as shown by the public records.

ACCELERATE - To make a note all due and payable at one time.

ACCELERATION CLAUSE - A clause in a deed of trust or mortgage giving the lender the right to call all sums owing him or her to be immediately due and payable upon the occurrence of a certain event. It is also a clause that permits a debtor to pay off a loan before the due date.

ACCELERATION CLAUSE - A clause in a promissory note, deed of trust, or mortgage that provides that upon default of a payment or some other stated event, the entire unpaid balance becomes immediately due and payable.

ACCEPTANCE - An essential element of every contract, it is the consent to be bound by the offer. In deeds, it is the consent to accept a grant of real property.
ACCESS RIGHT - The right of an owner to go into and out of his or her property.

ACCOMMODATION PARTY - A person who, without receiving value, signs a promissory note to help another person borrow money or get credit.

ACCORD AND SATISFACTION - The discharge of an existing contract by accepting the performance under a substitute contract. Generally, consideration under the new contract is different from and of lesser value than under the original contract, and satisfaction is the performance of that contract; the combination discharges the original contract.

ACCRETION - A gradual addition to land from natural causes; for example, from gradual action of ocean or river waters.

ACCRUED DEPRECIATION
1. The difference between the cost of replacement new as of the date of the appraisal and the present appraised value.
2. The accumulated loss in value that has affected the improvements on real property

ACKNOWLEDGEMENT - A formal declaration before an officer duly authorized as a notary public by a person who has executed an instrument, stating that the execution is his or her act and deed. A formal statement (usually before a notary public) by the person signing a deed or document that the instrument was actually and freely signed.

ACOUSTICAL TILE - Blocks of fiber, mineral, or metal with small holes or a rough-textured surface to absorb sound, used as covering for interior walls and ceilings.

ACQUISITION - The act or process by which a person procures property. ACRE A measure of land equaling 160 square rods, 4840 square yards, 43,560 square feet, or a tract about 208.71 feet square.

AD VALOREM- According to value.

ADA- Refers to the Americans With Disabilities Act. The ADA applies to equal access to employment, public services, public accommodations, public transportation and telecommunications. ADA Refers to the Americans With Disabilities Act. The ADA applies to equal access to employment, public services, public accommodations, public transportation and telecommunications.

ADJACENT- Located next to or near an object or parcel of property.

ADJOINING- Located so as to touch an object or share a common property line.

ADJUSTED COST BASIS- For tax purposes it is the cost of the property plus improvements and minus depreciation, amortization, and depletion.

ADMINISTRATOR- A person appointed by the probate court to administer the estate of a deceased person. His or her duties include making an inventory of the assets, managing the property, paying the debts and expenses, filing necessary reports and tax returns, and distributing the assets as ordered by the probate court.

ADULT- Any person 18 years of age and older.

ADVERSE POSSESSION- A method of acquiring property based on open and notorious possession, under a claim of right, color of title, continuous use for five years, and the payment of taxes. A method of acquiring property through continuous use of that property while paying taxes on it.

AFFIDAVIT- A statement or declaration reduced to writing, sworn to or affirmed before some officer who has authority to administer an oath or affirmation, such as a notary public or a commanding officer in the service.

AFFIRM- To confirm, swear, ratifying, verity.

AGENCY RELATIONSHIP- A special relationship of trust by which one person (agent) is authorized to conduct business, sign papers, or otherwise act on behalf of another person (principal). This relationship may be created by expressed agreement, ratification, or estoppel.

AGENT- One who represents another called a principal and has authority to act for the principal in dealing with third parties. The relationship is referred to as an agency. Someone authorized to act for another (called the principal) in business matters.

AGREEMENT- A mutual understanding or compact between parties. Although often used a synonymous with contract, technically it denotes mutual promises that fail as a contract for lack of consideration.

AGREEMENT OF SALE - 1. A written contract between a buyer and seller setting out the terms of sale. 2. An installment sales contract covering real property, especially a long-term contract

AIDS- The seller of real property, his agents or his sub agents do not have to disclose that somebody died of AIDS or had AIDS in said property.

ALIENATION- The transferring of property to another. Conveyance or transfer of title to real estate from one person to another person.

ALIENATION CLAUSE- In a deed of trust or mortgage, a provision that if the secured property is sold or transferred, the lender has the option of accelerating the loan and declaring the entire unpaid balance immediately due and payable. Also called a "due-on-sale" clause.

ALLIGATOR- Purchasing lower priced properties will limit the appetite of the alligator. The alligator is an expensive piece of property that gobbles up all the profits. Negative cash flow on a keeper property is referred to as an alligator.

ALL-INCLUSIVE DEED OF TRUST- A financing device whereby a lender makes payments on the existing trust deeds of a borrower and takes from the borrower a junior trust deed with a face value in an amount equal to the amount outstanding on the old trust deeds and the additional amount of money borrowed.

ALLUVION (ALLUVIUM)- Soil that has been deposited by accretion on the shore of a river or body of water and that increases the real property.

ALTA POLICY- The title insurance policy issued to institutional lenders. The initials stand for American Land Title Association, an organization that regulates and standardizes the provisions within title policies.

ALTER EGO- A doctrine, which holds that a corporation is really owned by shareholders as their own property, and therefore it should not be considered as a separate entity. Usually used to try to hold shareholders liable for corporate debts.

AMBULATORY- Capable of being changed or revoked. In wills, it refers to the concept that a will may be revoked or modified at any time up to the testator's death.

AMELIORATING WASTE- Improvements to property that, while not damaging the value of the property, technically qualify as waste. For example, an apartment building constructed on property designated only for single-family structures is considered ameliorating waste.

AMENITIES- As used in the real estate business, the features that make a piece of real property, especially a home, enjoyable.

AMORTIZATION
1. The liquidation of a financial obligation on an installment basis, which includes both principal and interest.
2. Recovery of cost or value over a period of time. The method or plan for the payment of a debt, bond, deed of trust, etc., by installments or sinking fund.

ANNUAL PERCENTAGE RATE (APR)- The cost of credit as determined in accordance with Regulation Z of the Board of Governors of the Federal Reserve System for implementing the Federal Truth in Lending Act.

ANNUITY- A sum of money received or paid yearly or at other fixed periods.

ANTICIPATION- Affirms that value is created by the anticipated benefits to be derived in the future.

ANTICIPATORY BREACH- Advance notice of intention to violate the terms of a contract.

APPEAL- The review or rehearing by a higher court of a low (inferior) court's decision.

APPELLANT- The party appealing a court decision. Either party may appeal; hence, the appellant could have been either the plaintiff or the defendant in the trial court.

APPRAISAL- An estimate and opinion of value. An opinion or estimate of the fair market value of a property.

APPRAISER - One qualified by education, training, and experience, who is hired to estimate the value of real and personal property on the basis of experience, judgment, facts, and use of formal appraisal processes.

APURTENANT- Attached to or considered part of land, because of being considered necessary and incidental to the use of that land. Commonly applied to easements that are considered part of property.

ASSESSED VALUE- Value placed on property as a basis for taxation. A value used by the tax assessor before July 1978. It represented 25 percent of the assessor's fair market value. After deducting any exemptions from assessed value, one applied the tax rate to the net figure to determine annual property taxes.

ASSESSMENT- The valuation of property for the purpose of levying a tax, or the amount of tax levied.

ASSESSOR- The official who has the responsibility of determining the assessed values.

ASSIGNEE- One to whom property is assigned or transferred.

ASSIGNMENT- A transfer to another of any property or right. The transfer of one's entire interest in property. Generally, the term is limited to intangible personal property (that is, stocks, bonds, promissory notes) and to leasehold estates.

ASSIGNMENT OF RENTS CLAUSE- A clause in a deed of trust or mortgage, providing that in the event of default, all rents and income from the secured property will be paid to the lender to help reduce the outstanding loan balance.

ASSIGNMENT OF RENTS - An assignment of future rents form property as security for a debt.

ASSIGNOR- One who assigns or transfers property.

ASSUMPTION- Acceptance of personal liability for another's debt or obligation. In the case of the sale of real estate, the buyer personally accepts and promises to pay off the existing deed of trust.

ASSUMPTION OF AGREEMENT- A contract by which a person agrees to pay a debt or obligation owed by someone else.

ASSUMPTION OF MORTGAGE OR DEED OF TRUST - The taking of title to property by a grantee in which he or she assumes liability for payment of existing note secured by a mortgage or deed of trust against the property.

ATTACHMENT- Seizure of property by court order before judgment, usually done to have it available in the event a judgment is obtained in a pending law suit. The actual or constructive seizure of property by court order during a lawsuit. The usual purpose is to hold the assets as security for the satisfaction of a judgment.

ATTACHMENT LIEN- A lien on property arising because of an attachment of that property.

ATTEST
1. To affirm to be true or genuine.
2. An official act establishing authenticity.

ATTORNEY-IN-FACT- An agent authorized to perform certain acts for another under a power of attorney. (See Power of Attorney.)

AVULSION- The sudden tearing away or removal of land by the action of water flowing over or through it.

BACKFILL - The replacement of excavated earth in a hole or against the side of a structure.

BALANCE SHEET- A financial statement showing a person's assets, liabilities, and net worth.

BALLOON PAYMENT- When the final payment on a note is greater than the preceding normal installments, the final installment is termed a balloon payment. An installment promissory note providing for the last payment to be much larger than any previous payment. By statute, any payment more than twice the smallest payment is a balloon payment, although in practice generally the term refers only to the last payment.

BANKRUPTCY- Will not eliminate all loans secured by real property.

BASE AND MERIDIAN- Imaginary lines used by surveyors from which they find, measure, and describe the location of lands.

BASE MOLDING- Molding used at the top of the baseboard.

BASE SHOW- Molding used at junction of baseboard and floor, sometimes called a carpet strip.

BASEBOARD- A board that goes around the room against the wall and next to the floor.

BATTEN- Narrow strips of wood or metal used to cover joints on the interior or exterior of a building; they are also used for decorative effect.

BLOCKBUSTING- The illegal practice of trying to lower property values.

BEAM- A horizontal structural member supporting a load.

BEARING WALL OR PARTITION- A wall or partition that supports any vertical load, in addition to its own weight.

BENCH MARKS- A location indicated on a permanent marker by surveyors.

BENEFICIARY
1. One entitled to benefit from a trust.
2. The lender on the security of a note and deed of trust. The creditor (lender) under a deed of trust

BENEFICIARY STATEMENT- (See Offset Statement.)

BEQUEATH- To leave by will.

BEQUEST- Personal property that is given by the terms of a will. A gift of personal property by will.

BETTERMENT- An improvement on real property that increases the value and is considered a capital asset.

BILATERAL CONTRACT- A contract in which the consideration given by each party is a promise: that is, a promise for a promise.

BILL OF SALE- A written instrument given by the seller to the buyer to pass title to personal property.

BINDER- A written statement that binds the parties to an agreement until formal contracts can be drawn; an agreement to cover a down payment as evidence of good faith.

BLACKTOP- Asphalt paving used in streets and driveways.

BLANKET DEED OF TRUST- A deed of trust binding more than one parcel of property as security. It is frequently encountered in subdivisions, where every lot in the subdivision is bound by the same deed of trust. As the lots are sold, they are released from the deed of trust by a partial release provision.

BLANKET MORTGAGE- One mortgage or deed of trust that covers more than one piece of real property.

BLIGHTED AREA- An area in which real property is declining in value because of destructive economic forces.

BOARD FOOT- A unit of measurement for lumber: one foot wide, one foot long, one inch thick (144 cubic inches).

BONA FIDE- Good faith.

BONA FIDE PURCHASER (BFP)- A purchaser who pays fair value for property in good faith, and without notice of adverse claims.

BOND- An obligation under seal. Real estate bonds are issued on the security of a mortgage or deed of trust. A certificate representing a contract for the payment of money, often used to repay certain loans or held as security to ensure the performance of a stated act.

BOOK VALUE- An accounting term, which is the difference between cost and the total amount of depreciation that has been taken.

BRACING- Frame lumber nailed at an angle in order to provide stability to the structure.

BREACH- The breaking of or failure of duty, either by an act or omission. The violation of or failure to perform an obligation.

BREEZEWAY- A covered porch or passage, open on two ends, that connects the house and garage, or two parts of the house.

BRIDGING- Wood or metal pieces used to brace floor joists.

BROKER- An agent who earns income by arranging sales and other contracts. A real estate broker is an individual licensed by the state of California to arrange the sale or transfer of interests in real property for compensation.

BROKER'S TRUST FUND ACCOUNT- Withdrawals from this account may be made only by the broker.

BTU- British Thermal Unit; the quantity of heat required to raise the temperature of one pound of water one degree Fahrenheit.

BUILDING LINE- Often called a setback line, a building line is a line running a certain distance from the street, in front of which an owner cannot build. These lines are set by law.

BUILDING PAPER- A heavy waterproofed paper used as sheathing in exterior walls, or in roof construction as insulation and protection against moisture.

BUILT-INS- Cabinets and other features built in as a part of the house.

BUSINESS AND PROFESSIONS CODE- One of the 25 California codes containing the laws passed by the state legislature. It contains the statutes regulating the conduct of real estate brokers and establishes the Department of Real Estate.

BUSINESS OPPORTUNITY- A term used to describe a business including its stock-in-trade, fixtures, and goodwill.

C.A.R. - Abbreviation for the California Association of Realtors.

C.C. & R.- Abbreviation for covenants, conditions, and restrictions. Often used synonymously with general plan restrictions on a subdivision.

CAL-VET LOAN (CALIFORNIA VETERANS)- A program administered by the State Department of Veterans LOAN) Affairs for the direct financing of farms and homes for veterans who qualify. The funds for these loans come from the sale of state bonds.

CAPITAL ASSESTS- Assets of a permanent nature used in the production of income. Examples would include land, buildings, and equipment.

CAPITAL GAIN- The gain recognized for federal and state income tax purposes when a taxpayer disposes of a capital asset.

CAPITALIZATION- In appraising, a method of determining value of property by considering net income and a reasonable percentage of return on the investment.

CAPITALIZATION RATE- The percentage rate or rate of interest considered a reasonable return on the investment. It is used in the capitalization method of determining value based upon net return.

CARET- California Association of Real Estate Teachers; a division of the California Association of Realtors.

CARPET STRIP- (See Base Shoe.)

CASEMENT WINDOW- Windows set in frames of wood or metal that swing outward.

CASH FLOW- The new amount of cash a property produces when all cash income and other cash generated are added together and all cash expenses and other cash payments are deducted.

CAUSE OF ACTION- A legal right; facts giving rise to an enforceable claim.

CAVEAT EMPTOR- A Latin phrase meaning " let the buyer beware"; the legal maxim stating that the buyer must examine the goods or property and buy at his or her own risk.

CERTIFICATE OF REASONABLE VALUE- The Veterans Administration's written appraisal of the value (CRV) of a property.

CERTIORARI- The Supreme Court order indicating that the court has decided to exercise its discretion and accept a case offered on appeal. The court reviews only those select cases that it deems worthy of review.

CHAIN OF TITLE- A series of conveyances, encumbrances, and other instruments affecting the title from the time original patent was granted, or as far back as records are available. A history of the recorded ownership of real estate and claims against title to real estate.

CHATTEL- The old name for personal property.

CHATTEL MORTGAGE- A personal-property mortgage. (See Security Agreement.)

CHATTEL REAL- In real estate, an estate less than a freehold estate, such as a lease.

CHATTELS
1. Personal property.
2. This term is sometimes used in a law to describe any interest in real or personal property other than a freehold.

CIRCUIT BREAKER- An electrical device that automatically interrupts an electrical circuit when an overload occurs. Circuit breakers can be reset and today are used instead of fuses.

CIVIL CODE- One of the 25 California codes containing the statutes passed by the state legislature. The most important code relating to contracts and real estate, the Civil Code defines the nature and requirements for contracts and real estate transactions, among its many other provisions.

CIVIL LAW- A system of jurisprudence, sometimes called Roman law, wherein all the laws are set forth in advance to regulate conduct (as opposed to common law, where the principles of law develop on a case-by-case basis). In California the term also refers to the law relating to and between individuals, as opposed to criminal law.

CLAPBOARD- Boards that are used for siding and that are usually thicker at one edge.

CLIENT- A person represented by a broker or an attorney.

CLOUD ON TITLE- A claim or document that affects title to real estate. The actual cloud may ultimately prove invalid, but its existence mars the title.

CLTA POLICY- The title insurance policy issued to homeowners and non-institutional lenders. The initials stand for the California Land Title Association, an organization that regulates and standardizes the provisions within title policies.

CODE OF CIVIL PROCEDURE- One of the 25 California codes that contain the statutes passed by the state legislature. It contains most of the procedural requirements for enforcing rights granted by other codes, including the procedures for evictions, foreclosures, and lawsuits.

CODICIL- An amendment to a will.

COLLAR BEAM- A beam that connects the pairs of opposite roof rafters above the attic floor.

COLLATERAL- Property subject to a security interest; property used as security for a debt. (See Security Agreement.)

COLLATERAL SECURITY- The transfer of property of other valuables to ensure the performance of a principal agreement; an obligation attached to a contract to guarantee its performance.

COLLUSION- A secret agreement between two or more persons wishing to defraud another for a wrongful purpose or to obtain an object forbidden by law.

COLOR OR TITLE- That which appears to be a good title but, in fact, is not; for example, a forged deed. A document that appears to convey title, but in fact is ineffective, conveying no title at all. It is one of the requirements for adverse possession and easement by prescription.

COMBED PLAYWOOD- A grooved building material used primarily for interior finish.

COMMERCIAL ACRE- A term applied to the remainder of an acre of land after the area devoted to streets, sidewalks, curbs, and so on has been deducted from the acre.

COMMERCIAL PAPER- Negotiable instruments used in business.

COMMINGLING- The mixing of different funds so that they can no longer be distinguished. In domestic law it refers to the combination of separate property and community property, so that the separate property and community funds can no longer be distinguished; in such cases all property is considered community property. For brokers it refers to the mixing o clients' money with the broker's separate bank accounts.

COMMISSION- An agent's compensation for performing the duties of his or her agency agreement. In the real estate business, it is usually a percentage of the selling price or a percentage of the lease or rents, for example. Reduction of a real estate commission for a listing contract is considered to be unethical.

COMMISSION- A real estate broker may receive a commission from both parties.

COMMITMENT- A pledge or a promise; a firm agreement.

COMMON LAW- The body of law that grew from customs and practices developed and used in England. A body of unwritten law that developed in England from the general customs and usage. It was adopted in the United States and exercised by court decisions following the ancient English principles and the recorded law of a state.

COMMUNITY PROPERTY- All property acquired by a husband and wife living together, except separate property. (See Separate Property.) Property owned in common by a husband and wife as a kind of marital partnership.

COMPACTION- Packing or consolidation of soil. When soil is added to a lot to fill in low places or to raise the level of the lot, it is often too loose to sustain the weight of buildings. Therefore, it is necessary to compact the added soil so that it will carry the weight of the building without danger of settling or cracking.

COMPARATIVE MARKET ANALYSIS- One of three methods in the appraisal process. A means of comparing similar type properties, which have recently sold, to the subject property.

COMPETENT- Legally qualified or capable.

COMPOUND INTEREST- Interest paid on the original principal and also on the accrued and unpaid interest that has accumulated as the debt matures.

CONCLUSIVE PRESUMPTION- A legal assumption that cannot be rebutted, and is therefore accepted as true and binding on the courts.

CONDEMNATION
1. The act of taking private property for public use by a political subdivision.
2. A declaration by proper governmental authorities that a structure is unfit for use. The taking of private property for public use through the exercise of the power of eminent domain.

CONDITION
A provision in a contract stating that the contract will not go into effect or that it will terminate upon the occurrence of some specified future event.
1. A restriction added to a conveyance that, upon the occurrence or non-occurrence of some act or event, causes the estate to be defeated.
2. A contractual provision that upon the occurrence or nonoccurrence of a stated act or event, an obligation is created, destroyed, or defeated

CONDITION PRECEDENT- A condition that must occur before an estate is created or enlarged, or before some other right or obligation occurs.

CONDITION SUBSEQUENT- A condition that, upon its failure or nonperformance, causes the defeat or extinguishment of an estate, right, or obligation.

CONDITIONAL COMMITMENT- A loan commitment for a definite amount under certain terms and conditions. It is subject to an unknown purchaser's satisfactory credit rating.

CONDITIONAL SALE CONTRACT- A contract for the sale of property whereby the seller retains legal title until the conditions of the contract have been fulfilled. The buyer has an equitable interest in the property. (See Security Agreement.) A contract for the sale of property by which possession is delivered to the buyer, but title remains with the seller until full payment or the satisfaction of other stated conditions.

CONDITIONAL USE PERMIT- An exception to or relief from the application of a zoning ordinance, because of special authorization granted by the zoning authorities. The issuance rests on public policy benefits and prior authorization in the zoning ordinance.

CONDOMINUM- A system of individual ownership of units in a multifamily structure, combined with joint ownership of common areas of the structure and the land. The ownership of an individual unit in a multi-unit structure, combined with joint ownership of common walkways, land, and other portions of the property.

CONDUIT- Usually a metal pipe in which electrical wiring is installed.

CONFESSION OF JUDGMENT- Any entry of judgment upon the debtor's voluntary admission or confession.

CONFIRMATION OF SALE- A court approval of the sale of property by an executor, administrator, guardian, or conservator.

CONSIDERATION- Anything of value, or that is legally sufficient, given to induce someone to enter into a contract. The inducement for entering into a contract; usually money, services, or a promise, although it may consist of a legal benefit to the promisor or any legal detriment to the promisee.

CONSTRUCTION- The interpretation of an ambiguous term or provision in a statute or agreement.

CONSTRUCTIVE- A fiction imputed by law.

CONSTRUCTIVE EVICTION- A breach of the landlord's warranty of quiet enjoyment. Any acts by the landlord that substantially interferes with the tenant's use and enjoyment of the premises.

CONSTRUCTIVE NOTICE- Notice given by the public records; that which is considered equivalent to actual notice even though there is not actual notice.
1. Notice given by a recorded document.
2. Notice imputed by a law because a person could have discovered certain facts upon reasonable investigation, and a "reasonable man" in the same situation would have conducted such an investigation.

CONSUMER CREDIT PROTECTION ACT- A federal law that includes the truth-in-Leading Law.

CONSUMER GOODS- Goods sold or purchased primarily for personal, family, or household purposes.

CONTINGENT- Conditional, uncertain, conditioned upon the occurrence or nonoccurrence of some uncertain future event.

CONTINUATION STATEMENT- A statement filed to extend the time limit on a financing statement that had been filed earlier.

CONTRACT OF SALE- (See Conditional Sale Contract.)

CONVENANT- An agreement or a promise to do or not to do a particular act. Covenant: A contractual agreement whereby one of the parties promises to perform or to refrain from doing certain acts.

CONVENTIONAL LOAN- A loan that is made that is not federally insured or guaranteed.

CONVERSION- Is the misappropriation or misuse of trust funds.

CONVERTIBLE ADJUSTABLE RATE- Allows the borrower to adjust to a fixed interest rate.

MORTGAGE CONVERTIBLE ADJUSTABLE RATE- Allows the borrower to adjust to a fixed interest rate.

MORTGAGE CONVEYANCE
1. The transfer of the title of real property from one to another.
2. An instrument that transfers an interest in real property from one person to another. The transfer of title to real estate from one person to another.

COOPERATIVE APARTMENT- A form of ownership in which each individual apartment owner shares in a cooperative venture that entitles the owner to use, rent, or sell a specific apartment unit.

CORPORATION- A group or a body of persons recognized by law as an individual person with rights and liabilities distinct from those of the persons comprising it. Since the corporation is created by law, it may continue for any length of time that the law prescribes. An artificial entity given authority to conduct business and possess many of the rights of natural persons. One of the key characteristics is that of perpetual existence.

COST BASIS- See Adjusted Cost Basis.

CO-TENANCY- Any form of joint ownership.

COUNTERFLASHING- Flashing used on chimneys at roofline to cover shingle flashing and prevent moisture entry.

COUNTER-OFFER- The rejection of an offer by the submission of another offer, different in terms from the original offer. Any purported acceptance of an offer that introduces new terms is a rejection of that offer, and amounts to a counter-offer.

COVERSION- The wrongful appropriation of another's goods to one's own use; to change from one character or use to another.
1. In tort, an unauthorized claim of ownership over another's personal property.

2. In property, the change of character of property from real to personal, or vice versa.

CPM- Certified Property Manager; a member of the Institute of Real Estate Property management of the National Association of Realtors.

CRAWL HOLE- Exterior or interior opening permitting access underneath a building, as building codes may require.

CREDIT UNIONS- A growing source of funds for real estate loans.

CRV- These initials mean Certificate of Reasonable Value.

CURTAIL SCHEDULE- A list of the due dates and amounts by which the principal sum of an obligation will be reduced by partial payments.

DAMAGES - The indemnity recoverable by a person who has sustained an injury to either his or her person, property, or rights through the act or default of another. Compensation ordered by the courts for the loss of or injury to one's person or property.

DEALER- A person who holds property primarily for sale to his or her customers in the ordinary course of his or her business.

DEBT SERVICE- The sum of money needed each payment period to amortize the loan or loans.

DEBTOR
1. A party who "owns" the property that is subject to a security interest.
2. A person who owes a debt

DECK- Usually an open porch on the roof or another part of the structure.

DECLARATORY RELIEF- A court's decision on the rights of the parties in a question of law, without ordering anything to be done.

DEDICATION- An appropriation of land by its owner for some public use and accepted for such use by authorized public officials on behalf of the public. A gift of privately owned land to the public or for public use. It may be voluntary or involuntary.

DEED- A written instrument that when properly executed and delivered conveys title.

DEED OF TRUST- A security instrument transferring title to property to a third person (trustee) as security for a debt or other obligation.

DEFAULT
1. Failure to fulfill a duty or promise or to discharge an obligation.
2. Omission or failure to perform any act. Failure to perform a legal duty or to discharge a promise

DEFAULT JUDGMENT- A judgment obtained because the defendant failed to appear and defend his case.

DEFEASANCE CLAUSE- The clause in a mortgage or deed of trust that gives the borrower the right to redeem his or her property upon the payment of his or her property upon the payment of his or her obligations to the lender.

DEFEASIBLE- Capable of being defeated. A defeasible estate is one that has a condition attached to the title, which if broken causes the termination of that estate.

DEFENDANT- The party being sued in a lawsuit; the party against whom an action is filed.

DEFERRED MAINTENANCE- Maintenance and accumulated repairs that have been postponed.

DEFICIENCY JUDGEMENT- A judgment given for the unpaid balance of a debt remaining after the surety is sold. A court decree holding a debtor personally liable for the shortage or insufficiency realized on the sale of secured property. The debtor owes the difference between the sale price of the property and the amount of the secured debt.

DELIVERY (OF A DEED)- The unconditional, irrevocable intent of a grantor immediately to divest (give up) an interest in real estate by a deed or other instrument.

DEPOSIT- Money given to another as security to ensure the performance of a contract. The money is usually intended to be applied toward the purchase price of property, or forfeited on failure to complete the contract.

DEPOSIT RECEIPT- A contract used in the he real estate business that includes the terms of the contract and acts as a receipt for "earnest money" to bind an offer for property by the prospective purchaser. The name given to most real estate contracts containing the terms of the sale of real estate, and receipt for earnest money (deposited).

DEPRECIATION- A loss in value from any cause. This loss in value to real property may be caused by age or physical deterioration, or by functional or economic obsolescence.

DESIST AND REFRAIN ORDER- An order that the Real Estate Commissioner is empowered by law and refrain from committing an act in violation of the Real Estate Law.

DETERIORATION- The process of gradual worsening or depreciation.

DEVISE- A gift of real property by deed.

DEVISEE- One who receives real property under a will.

DICTUM- A written observation, remark, or opinion by a judge to illustrate or suggest an argument or rule of law not incidental to the case at hand, and which, therefore, although persuasive, is not binding on the judge.

DIRECTIONAL GROWTH- The direction in which the residential sections of a city seem destined or determined to grow.

DISCLOSURE STATEMENT- A statement that the Truth-in-Lending Law requires a creditor to give a debtor showing the finance charge, annual percentage rate, and other required information.

DISCOUNT- To sell a promissory note before maturity at a price less than the outstanding principal balance of the note at the time of sale. It may also be the amount deducted in advance by the lender from the face of the note.

DISCOUNT POINTS- A fee charged by the lender when making an FHA or VA loan to offset the lower interest rate the lender will receive compared with conventional loan interest rates. One point is equal to 1 percent.

DISCOUNT RATE- The interest rate that is charged on money borrowed by banks from the Federal Reserve System.

DISCOUNTED TRUST DEED- An investment in this kind of deed can be a perfect investment.

DISCRIMINATORY CONDUCT- The DRE Regulations state that discriminatory conduct is a basis for disciplinary action.

DISSOLUTION OF MARRIAGE- A divorce.

DISTRICT COURT- The main trial court in the federal court system and the lowest federal court. It has jurisdiction in civil cases where the plaintiffs and defendants are from different states (diversity of citizenship) and the amount in controversy is over $10,000, and in cases involving a federal question.

DIVESTMENT- The elimination or removal of a right or title, usually applied to the cancellation of an estate in land.

DOMICILE- A person's permanent residence.

DOMINANT TENEMENT- The tenement obtaining the benefit of an easement appurtenant. That parcel of land that benefits from an easement across another parcel of property (servient tenement).

DONEE- The person to whom a gift is made.

DONOR- The person who makes a gift.

DOUBLE ESCROW- An escrow that will close only upon the condition that a prior escrow is consummated. The second escrow is contingent upon and tied to the first escrow. While double escrow is not illegal, unless there is full and fair disclosure of the second escrow, there may be a possibility of fraud or other actionable conduct by the parties.

DOWER- The right that a wife has in her husband's estate at his death. Dower has been abolished in California.

DUE PROCESS OF LAW- A constitutional guarantee that the government will not interfere with a person's private property rights without following procedural safeguards prescribed by law.

DUE-ON-ENCUMBRANCE CLAUSE- A clause in a deed of trust or mortgage that provides that upon the execration of additional deeds of trust or other encumbrances against a secured parcel of property, the lender may declare the entire unpaid balance of principal and interest due and owing.

DUE-ON-SALE CLAUSE- An acceleration clause that grants the lender the right to demand full payment of the mortgage or deed of trust upon sale of the property. A clause in a deed of trust or mortgage that provides that if the secured property is sold or transferred, the lender may declare the entire unpaid balance immediately due and payable. Its use has been severely limited by recent court decisions. Also called an alienation clause.

DURESS- Unlawful constraint by force or fear. E.I.R. Abbreviation for Environmental Impact Report.

EARNEST MONEY DEPOSIT - A deposit of money paid by a buyer for real property as evidence of good faith. Cannot be given back to the buyer unless he obtains written permission from the seller.

EASEMENT- A right, privilege, or interest that one party has to use the land of another. Example: A right of way. A legal right to use another's land for one's benefit or the benefit of one's property (right-of-way).

EASEMENT APPURTENANT- An easement created for the benefit of a particular parcel of property. There is both a dominant and a servient estate. The easement is annexed to and part of the dominant property.

EASEMENT IN GROSS- An easement that benefits a particular individual, not a parcel of property. Involves only a servient estate. A public utility easement is an example.

EASY QUALIFIER MORTGAGE- This may be referred to as "low doc" or "no doc" loan.

EAVES- The lower projecting edge of a roof over the wall.

ECONOMIC LIFE- The remaining useful life of an improvement or structure; that period during which an improvement will yield a return on the investment.

ECONOMIC OBSOLESCENCE- The loss in value to property due to external causes such as zoning or a deteriorating neighborhood. It is also referred to as social obsolescence.

EFFECTIVE GROSS INCOME- The amount of net income that remains after the deduction from gross income of vacancy and credit losses.

EGRESS- Exit; the act or avenue or leaving property.

EMBLEMENTS- Things that grow on the land require annual planting and cultivation.

EMINENT DOMAIN- The right of the government and certain others, such as public utilities, to acquire property for public or quasi-public use by condemnation, upon payment of just compensation to the owner. The constitutional or inherent right of a government to take private property for public good upon the payment of just compensation.

ENCROACHMENT- The projection of a structure onto the land of an adjoining owner. A structure or natural object that unlawfully extends into another's property.

ENCUMBRANCE- Any claim, interest, or right improperly possessed by another that may diminish the true owner's rights or value in the estate. Examples include mortgages, easements, or restrictions of any kind. A claim, lien, or charge on property.

ENDORSEMENT- See Indorsement.

ENVIRONMENTAL IMPACT REPORT- A report that must be prepared whenever any agency or individual considers a project that may have a significant impact on the environment, as directed by the California Environmental Quality Act.

EQUAL CREDIT OPPORTUNITY ACT- Prohibits discrimination amongst lenders.

EQUAL HOUSING OPPORTUNITY- Prohibits discrimination in the listing, sale, lease, rental or financing of real property due to race, creed, religion, sex, marital status or handicap. Should apply exactly the same in all real estate

EQUAL PROTECTION- The Fourteenth Amendment to the U.S. Constitution and similar provisions in the California Constitution require each citizen to receive equal protection of the laws. There are no minimum standards of protection; all equally situated individuals must simply be treated equally. (The due process clause of the Constitution imposes certain minimum standards of protection.)

EQUITY
1. The interest or value that on owner has in real property over and above the liens against it.
2. A part of our justice system by which courts seek to supplement the strict terms of the law to fairness under the circumstances, rather than on fixed legal principles or statutes.
3. Ownership in property, determined by calculating the fair market value less the amount of liens and encumbrances.

EQUITY BUILD-UP- The increase of the owner's equity due to mortgage principal reduction and value appreciation.

EQUITY OF REDEMPTION- The right to redeem property during the foreclosure period. In California the mortgagor has the right to redeem within 12 months after the foreclosure sale.

EROSION- The wearing away of the surface of the land by the action of wind, water, and glaciers, for example.

ESCALATOR CLAUSE- A clause in a contract that provides for the upward or downward adjustment of certain items to cover the specific contingencies set forth. A clause in a promissory note, lease, or other document that provides that upon the passage of a specified time or the happening of a stated event, the interest rate shall increase.

ESCHEAT- The reversion of property to the state when there are no devisees or heirs capable of inheritance. Reversion of property to the state upon the death of an owner who has no heirs able to inherit.

ESCROW- The deposit of instruments and funds with a third neutral party with instructions to carry out the provisions of an agreement or contract. A complete or perfect escrow is one in which everything has been deposited to enable carrying out the instructions. The neutral third party (stakeholder) who holds deeds or other documents pursuant to instructions for delivery upon completion or occurrence of certain conditions.

ESTATE- The degree, quantity, nature, and extent of the interest that a person has in real property.
1. Ownership interest in real estate.
2. The quality and quantity of rights in property

ESTATE AT WILL- The occupation of real property by a tenant for an indefinite period. One or both parties may terminate it at will. A leasehold tenancy, which at common law could be terminated by either party at any time, without advance notice. Thirty days' notice is now required to terminate this type of estate in California.

ESTATE FOR LIFE- A freehold estate whose duration is measured by and limited to the life or lives of one or more persons.

ESTATE FOR PERIOD TO PERIOD- A leasehold tenancy that continues indefinitely for successive periods of time, until terminated by proper notice. When the periods are one month in duration, it is often called a month-to-month tenancy.

ESTATE FOR YEARS- A lease that will expire at a definite time or date. A leasehold tenancy of a fixed duration, being a definite and ascertainable period of a year or any fraction of multiple thereof. It has a definite beginning and ending date, and hence a known and definite duration.

ESTATE OF INHERITANCE- An estate that may go to the heirs of the deceased. All freehold estates are estates of inheritance, except life estates.

ESTOP- To ban, stop, or impede.

ESTOPPEL- A doctrine whereby one is forbidden to contradict or deny his or her own previous statement, act, or position. The doctrine that prevents a person from exercising a legal right, because that person previously acted in an inconsistent manner, so that a third person detrimentally relied on the earlier acts. An agency is created this way when an individual knowingly allows another individual to act as their agent without authorizing such acts.

ET AL- Abbreviation meaning and others (other person).

ET UX- Abbreviation meaning and wife.

ETHICS- A standard of conduct that all members of a given profession owe to the public, clients or patrons, and to other members of that profession. Refers to a branch of philosophy that deals with moral science and moral principles. It is a debatable subject and cannot be legislated. It is based on what each individual feels is good or bad.

ETHNIC- The seller of a property is not allowed to ask the buyer their ethnic background.

EVICTION- Dispossession by legal process, as in the termination of a tenant's right to possession through re-entry or other legal proceedings.

EVIDENCE- All relevant information, facts, and exhibits admissible in a trial.

EX PARTE- By only one party or side. For example, an injunction obtained by evidence presented by only one side, without notice to the other parties.

EXCEPTION- (See Reservation.)

EXCHANGE- A reciprocal transfer of properties between two or more parties.

EXCLUSIVE AGENCY- A contract hiring the broker as the exclusive agent for the seller. If anyone, except the seller, finds a buyer, the broker has earned the commission.

EXCLUSIVE AGENCY LISTING- A written agreement giving one agent the exclusive right to sell property for a specified period of time, but reserving the right of the owner to sell the property himself or herself without liability for the payment of a commission.

EXCLUSIVE RIGHT TO SELL AGENCY- A contract hiring the broker as the only person authorized to sell property. If anyone, including the seller, finds a buyer, the broker earns the commissions.

EXCLUSIVE-RIGHT-TO-SELL LISTING- A written agreement giving one agent the exclusive right to sell property for a specified period of time. The agent may collect a commission if the property is sold by anyone, including the owner, during the term of the listing agreement.

EXCULPATORY CLAUSE- A provision in leases and other instruments seeking to relieve one party of liability for his negligence and other acts. In residential leases such clauses are invalid, and in other leases the courts have limited the landlord's ability to escape liability for intentional acts, and for acts of affirmative negligence.

EXECUTE- To complete, make, perform, do or to follow out. To sign a document, intending to make it a binding instrument. The term is also used to indicate the performance of a contract.

EXECUTION LIEN- A lien arising because of an execution on property. A judgment is not self-executing; however, when a writ of execution has been obtained, the sheriff will levy (seize) property, which creates a lien on the property.

EXECUTOR- A person named by the testator of a will to carry out its provisions as to the disposition of the estate. A personal representative appointed in a will to administer a decedent's estate.

EXPANSIBLE HOUSE- A home designed for expansion and additions in the future.

EXPANSION JOINT- A fiber strip used to separate units of concrete to prevent cracking due to expansion as a result of temperature changes.

FACADE - The face of a building, especially the front face.

FAIR MARKET VALUE- The amount of money that would be paid for a property offered on the open market for a reasonable length of time with both the buyer and the seller knowing all uses to which the property could be put and with neither party being under pressure to buy or sell. See market Value.

FALSE PROMISE- A statement used to influence or persuade.

FANNY MAE- The Federal National Mortgage Association (FNMA).

FARM- It is a specific geographical location in which an agent walks every month in order to obtain listings.

FEDERAL DEPOSIT INSURANCE- A federal corporation that insures deposits in commercial CORPORATION banks (FDIC).

FEDERAL FAIR HOUSING ACT- Was established under Title VIII of the United States Civil Rights Act of 1969. It was amended in 1988. It was created to provide fair housing through out the United States.

FEDERAL HOME LOAN BANK (FHLB)- A district bank of the Federal Home Loan Bank System that lends only to savings and loan associations who are members.

FEDERAL HOME LOAN MORTGAGE CORPORATION (FHLMC)- A federal corporation that provides savings and loan associations with a secondary mortgage money market for loans. It is also known as Freddy Mac.

FEDERAL HOUSING ADMINISTRATION- An agency of the federal government that insures mortgage (FHA) loans.

FEDERAL NATIONAL MORTGAGE ASSOCIATION (FNMA)- A federal corporation that provides lenders with a secondary mortgage money market.

FEDERAL RESERVE SYSTEM- The federal banking system of the United States under the control of a central board of governors (Federal Reserve Board). It involves a central bank in each of 12 geographical districts, with broad powers in controlling credit and the amount of money in circulation.

FEDERAL SAVINGS AND LOAN INSURANCE CORPORATION (FSLIC)- A federal corporation that insures deposits in savings and loan associations.

FEE- An estate of inheritance in real property for life.

FEE SIMPLE- An estate in real property by which the owner has the greatest possible power over the title. In modern use it expressly establishes the title of real property with the owner without limitation or end. He or she may dispose of it by sale, trade, or will, as he or she chooses. In modern estates the terms "Fee" and "Fee Simple" are substantially synonymous.

FEE SIMPLE ABSOLUTE- The highest estate known at law. A freehold estate of indefinite duration, incapable of being defeated by conditions or limitations. Sometimes simply called fee or fee estate.

FEE SIMPLE DEFEASIBLE- A fee simple estate to which certain conditions or limitations attach, such that the estate may be defeated or terminated upon the happening of an act or event. Also called a fee simple subject to condition subsequent estates.

FEE SIMPLE SUBJECT TO A CONDITION SUBSEQUENT- A fee simple defeasible estate that requires the holder of the future interest to act promptly to terminate the present interest, in order for that interest to be terminated.

FHA- The FHA does not loan money. The FHA loan may be paid off at any time without a penalty. The buyer or the seller may pay discount points on a FHA loan. The down payment on a FHA loan is usually LESS than the down payment on a conventional loan.

FIDUCIARY- A person in a position of trust and confidence, as between principal and broker. A fiduciary may not make a profit from his or her position without first disclosing it to the beneficiary.

FINANCIAL FREEDOM- The freedom to make purchases with no restraint.

FINANCING STATEMENT- The instrument filed to perfect the security agreement and give constructive notice of the security interest, thereby protecting the interest of the secured parties. (See Security Agreement; Security Interest; and Secured Party.) The security interest in personal property. It is analogous to a mortgage on real property, except that it secures personal property. Under the U.C.C., it may be filed in Sacramento with the secretary of state.

FINDER'S FEE- Money paid to a person for finding someone interested in selling or buying property. To conduct any negotiations of sale terms, the finder must be a licensed broker or he violates the law.

FINISH FLOOR- The final covering on the floor, such as wood, linoleum, cork, or carpet.

FIRE STOP- A solid, tight closure of a concealed space placed to prevent the spread of fire and smoke through the space.

FIRST AMENDMENT- The constitutional amendment guaranteeing freedom of speech, press, assembly, and religion.

FIXTURE- An item of personal property that has been so attached to real property as to be considered part of that real property.

FIXTURES- Items that were originally personal property but that have become part of the real property, usually because they are attached to the real property more or less permanently. Examples: Store fixtures built into the property and plumbing fixtures.

FLASHING- Sheet metal or similar material used to protect a building from water seepage.

FLIPPER PROPERTY- Any property bought for immediate resale and profit.

FOOTING- The base or bottom of a foundation wall, pier or column.

FORCIBLE DETAINER- Wrongful retention of property by actual or constructive force.

FORCIBLE ENTRY- Entry into property without the consent of the owner, by acts that constitute more than mere trespass.

FORECLOSURE- A legal proceeding to enforce a lien on such as a mortgage or deed of trust. The process by which secured property is seized and sold to satisfy a debt. A mortgage or involuntary lien must be sold by a court-ordered sale; a sale under a deed of trust may be either by court action or through a private trustee's sale.

FOREFEITURE- Loss of a legal right, interest, or title by default.

FORMAL WILL- A will signed by the testator in the presence of two or more witnesses, who must themselves sign the will.

FOUNDATION- That part of a structure or wall wholly or partly below the surface of the ground that is the base or support, including the footings.

FOURTEENTH AMENDMENT- The constitutional amendment that directs that no state can deprive a person of life, liberty, or property without due process or equal protection of the law.

FRAUD- Deception that deprives another person of his her rights or injures him or her. False representation or concealment of material facts that induces another justifiably to rely on it to his detriment.

FREEHOLD- An estate of fee. An estate in real property that is either a life estate or an estate in fee.

FRONT FOOT- Property measurement for sale or valuation purposes. The property measurement is along the street line, and each front foot extends to the depth of the lot. It is usually used in connection with commercial property.

FROSTLINE- The depth of frost penetration in the soil.

FRUCTUS- Fruits, crops, and other plants. If the vegetation is produced by human labor, such as crops, it is called fructus industrials; vegetation growing naturally is called fructus naturales.

FURRING- Strips of wood or metal fastened to wall to even it, form air space, or to give the wall greater thickness.

FUTURE ADVANCES- Future (additional) loans made by a lender and secured under the original deed of trust. The advances may be either optional or obligatory, but the deed of trust or mortgage must provide in the security instrument that it will cover any such future advances.

FUTURE INTEREST- An estate that does not or may entitle one to possession or enjoyment until a future time.

GABLE ROOF - Pitched roof with sloping sides.

GAMBREL ROOF- A curb roof, having a steep lower slope with a flatter upper slope above.

GARNISHMENT- A legal process to seize a debtor's property or money in the possession of a third party.

GAURANTEED NOTE- A permit must be received from the real estate commissioner before being allowed to sell a guaranteed note.

GENERAL PLAN RESTRICTIONS- Covenants, conditions, and restrictions placed on a subdivision or other large tract of land, designed to benefit and burden each lot in the tract.

GIFT- A voluntary transfer of property without consideration.

GIFT DEED- A deed for which there is no material consideration.

GIRDER- A beam used to support other beams, joists, and partitions.

GOVERNMENT NATIONAL MORTGAGE- A federal corporation that assists in financing special ASSOCIATION (GNMA) assistance programs for federally aided housing. The corporation is also known as Ginny Mae.

GRADE- Ground level at the foundation.

GRADUATED LEASE- Usually a long-term lease that provides for adjustments in the rental rate on the basis of some future determination. For example, the rent may be based upon the result of appraisals to be made at predetermined times in the future.

GRANT
1. To transfer.
2. A deed.
3. When used in a deed, a technical term implying certain warranties. A transfer or conveyance of real estate.

GRANT DEED- In California, a deed in which the word grant is used as a work of conveyance and therefore by law implies certain warranties deed used to transfer property in California. By statute it impliedly contains only two limited warranties.

GRANTEE- The buyer; a person to whom a grant is made.

GRANTOR- The seller; one who signs a deed. The seller or person who executes a grant.

GRID- A chart used in rating the borrower, property, and neighborhood.

GROSS INCOME- Total income before expenses are deducted.

GROSS RENT MUTIPLIER -A number that reflects the ratio between the sales price of a property and its gross monthly rents. It is used in the income approach of appraising property.

GROUND LEASE- An agreement leasing land only, without improvements, ordinarily with the understanding that improvements will be placed on the land by the tenant.

GROUND RENT
1. Earnings from the ground only.
2. Earnings of improved property after an allowance are made for earnings of improvements.
3. A perpetual rent that a grantor in some states may reserve to himself or herself and his or her heirs when he or she conveys real property.

GROWTH EQUITY MORTGAGE- This type of mortgage will be paid back faster than the typical 30 year fully amortized mortgage.

HANDICAP - Includes but is not limited to a physical or mental impairment that substantially limits one or more of a person's major life activities.

HAZARD INSURANCE- Insurance that protects the owner and lender against physical hazards to property such as fire and windstorm damage.

HEADER- A beam placed perpendicularly to joists and to which joists are nailed in the framing of openings such as windows, doors, and stairways.

HEIRS- Persons who succeed to the estate of someone who dies intestate (without a

445

will). It sometimes indicates anyone who is entitled to inherit a decedent's property.

HEREDITAMENT- A term usually referring to real estate and all that goes with it as being incidental.

HIGHEST AND BEST USE- An appraisal phrase that means that use of real property that is most likely to produce the greatest net return on land or buildings, or both, over a given period of time.

HIP ROOF- A pitched roof with sloping sides and ends.

HOLDEN ACT- Specifically states that "redlining" is illegal in California.

HOLDER IN DUE COURSE- One who has taken a negotiable note, check, or bill of exchange in due course
1. before it was past due;
2. in good faith;
3. without knowledge that it has been previously dishonored and without notice of any defect at the time it was negotiated to him or her;
4. for value. Someone who acquires a negotiable instrument in good faith and without any actual or constructive notice of defect. The acquisition must occur before the note's maturity. Such a holder takes the note free from any personal defenses (such as failure of consideration, fraud in the inducement) that may be available against the maker

HOLOGRAPHIC WILL- A will that is entirely written, dated, and signed by the testator in the testator's handwriting. No witnesses are needed.

HOMEOWNER'S EXEMPTION- An exemption or reduction in real property taxes available to those who reside on their property as of March 1. The current amount is $70 off the normal tax bill otherwise due.

HOMESTEAD
1. A home upon which the owner or owners have recorded a Declaration of Homestead, as provided by California statutes, that protects the home against judgments up to a specified amount.
2. A probate homestead is a similarly protected home property set aside by a California probate court for a widow or minor children. A special, limited exemption against certain judgments available to qualified homeowners.

HUNDRED PERCENT LOCATION- A retail business location considered the best available for attracting business.

ILLUSORY CONTRACT - An agreement that gives the appearance of a contract, but in fact is not a contract because it lacks one of the essential elements.

IMPLIED- Not expressed by words, but presumed from facts, acts, or circumstances.

IMPOUND ACCOUNT- A trust account established by the lender to pay property taxes and hazard insurance.

INCOME APPROACH- An appraisal technique used on income producing properties. Also known as the capitalization approach.

INCOME TAX- The cost to remodel vacant property may be deducted from the income tax.

INCOMPETENT- Someone incapable of managing his or her own affairs by reason of age, disease, weakness of mind, or any other cause.

INCREMENT- Any increase.
1. A term frequently used to refer to the increased value of land because of population growth and increased wealth in the community.
2. "Unearned increment" is used in this connection since the values increased without effort on the part of the owner.

INDEBTEDNESS- A debt or obligation.

INDEMNIFICATION- Compensation to a person who has already sustained a loss. For example, insurance payment for a loss under policy.

INDIRECT LIGHTING- A method of illumination in which the light is reflected from the ceiling or other object outside the fixture.

INDORSEMENT
1. The act of signing one's name on the back of a check or a note, with or without further qualification.
2. The signature described above.

INFATIONARY HEDGE- Real estate is considered to be the best bet against inflation.

INFLATION- This is not an easy condition to eliminate.

INFLATIONARY HEDGE- Real estate is considered to be the best bet against inflation.

INGRESS- The act of or avenue for entering property.

INHERIT- To take property through a deceased's estate.

INJUNCTION- An order issued by a court to restrain one or more parties to a suit or proceeding from performing an act deemed inequitable or unjust in regard to the rights of some other party or parties in the suit or proceeding.

INJUNCTION- A court order prohibiting certain acts, or ordering specific acts.

INSTALLMENT- A partial payment of a debt due in a series of payments.

INSTALLMENT NOTE- A note that provides that payments of a certain sum or amount be paid in more than one payment on the dates specified in the instrument.

INSTALLMENT SALES CONTRACT- Also known as an agreement of sale or a land contract.

INSTALLMENT-SALE METHOD- A method of reporting capital gains by installments for successive tax years to minimize the impact of capital gains tax in the year of the sale.

INSTITUTIONAL LENDER- Lenders who make a substantial number of real estate loans, such as banks, savings and loan associations, and insurance companies.

INSTRUMENT- A written legal document created to affect the rights of the parties.

INTEREST- The charge or cost for the use of money.

INTEREST RATE- The percentage of a sum of money charged for its use.

INTEREST RATE CAP- The majority of all the mortgages do contain an interest rate cap.

INTERPLEADER- A court proceeding initiated by a stakeholder, such as a broker or escrow agent. This decides the ownership or disposition of trust funds.

INTESTATE- A person who dies without a will.

INTREST DEDUCTION- The amount of a home equity loan that qualifies for an interest deduction cannot exceed $100,000.00.

INVESTOR- A person who holds property primarily for future appreciation in value for federal and state income tax purposes.

INVITEE- A person who enters another's land because of an express or implied social invitation, such as a social guest. The term also covers certain government workers who enter someone's land, such as police officers and firefighters. Classification of such status was revoked by a recent court case.

INVOLUNTARY CONVERSION- The loss of real property due to destruction, seizure, condemnation, foreclosure sale, or tax sale.

INVOLUNTARY LIEN- Any lien imposed on property without the consent of the owner. IRREVOCABLE Incapable of being recalled or revoked; unchangeable.

IRRIGATION DISTRICTS- Quasi-political districts created under special laws to provide for water services to property-owners in the district.

JALOUSIE - A screen or shutter consisting of overlapping horizontal slats that is used on the exterior to keep out sun and rain while admitting light and air.

JAMB- The side post or lining of a doorway, window, or other opening.

JOINT- The space between the adjacent surfaces of two components joined and held together by nails, glue, or cement, for example.

JOINT NOTE- A note signed by two or more persons who have equal liability for payment.

JOINT TENANCY- Joint ownership by two or more persons with right of survivorship. Four unities must be present: time, title, interest, and possession. Property held by two or more people with right of survivorship.

JOINT VENTURE- In legal effect it is a partnership for a limited, specific business project.

JOISTS- One of a series of parallel beams to which the boards of floor and ceiling laths or plaster boards are nailed and supported in turn by larger beams, girders, or bearing walls.

JUDGMENT- A court of competent jurisdiction's final determination of a matter presented to it. The final decision by a court in a lawsuit, motion, or other matter.

JUDGMENT AFFIRMED- A decision by an appellate court reaffirming, approving, and agreeing with an inferior court's decision.

JUDGMENT DEBTOR- A person who has an unsatisfied money judgment levied against him or her.

JUDGMENT LIEN- A money judgment that, because it has been recorded, has become a lien against the judgment debtor's real property.

JUDGMENT REVERSED- A decision by an appellate court disagreeing with an inferior court's decision and modifying the decision to conform with its findings.

JUNIOR LIEN- A lien lower in priority or rank than another or other liens.

JUNIOR MORTGAGE- A mortgage second in lien to a previous mortgage.

JURISDICTION- The authority of a court to hear and decide a particular type of case. The power of a court to hear and decide a case or issue.

LACHES - Unreasonable delay in asserting one's legal rights.

LAND CONTRACT- A contract used in the sale of real property when the seller wishes to retain legal title until all or a certain part of the purchase price is paid by the buyer. It is also referred to as an installment sales contract or an agreement of sale.

LAND SALES CONTRACT- A contract for the sale of property, by which possession is delivered to the buyer, but title remains with the seller until full payment or the satisfaction of other stated conditions.

LANDLOCKED- Property totally surrounded by other property with no means of ingress or egress.

LANDLORD- The person who leases property; the owner of the property.

LANDS, TENEMENTS, AND HEREDITAMENT- Inheritable lands or interest.

LATE CHARGE- A charge made by a lender against a borrower who fails to make loan installments when due.

LATE SUPPORT- The support that the soil of an adjoining owner gives to his or her neighbor's land.

LATH- A building material of wood, metal gypsum, or insulating board fastened to the frame of a building to act as a plaster base.

LEASE- A contract between owner and tenant, setting forth conditions upon which the tenant may occupy and use the property and the term of the occupancy.

LEASEHOLD ESTATE- The estate of a tenant under a lease. (See Estate for Years.)

LEGACY- A gift of money by will.

LEGAL DESCRIPTION- A description recognized by law; a description by which property can be definitely located by reference to government surveys or approved recorded maps.

LENDER GUIDELINES- Most lenders use Fannie Mae and Freddie Mac underwriting guidelines.

LESSEE- A tenant; the person who is entitled to possession of property under a lease.

LESSOR- A landlord; the property owner who executes a lease.

LETTER OF INTENT- An expression of intent to invest, develop, or purchase without creating any firm legal obligation to do so.

LEVY- To execute upon; to seize and sell property to obtain money to satisfy a judgment.

LIABILITIES- Debts or claims that creditors have against assets.

LICENSE- Personal, non-assignable authorization to enter and perform certain acts on another's land.

LICENSEE- Under the law before 1968, which classified persons who entered upon others' land, a licensee was someone who entered upon land with the owner's express or implied permission for a business purpose.

LIEN- A lien makes the debtor's property security for the payment of a dept or the discharge of an obligation. A charge or claim against property as security for payment of a debt or obligation.

LIFE ESTATE- An estate in real property that continues for the life of a particular person. The "life" involved may be that of the owner or that of some other person. An estate in property whose duration is limited to and measured by the life of a natural person or persons.

LIGHT COLORS- Light colors make a room look larger.

LIMITED PARTNERSHIP- A partnership composed of some partners whose contribution and liability are limited. There must always be one or more general partners with unlimited liability and one or more limited partners with limited liability. A special partnership composed of limited and general partners. The general partners have unlimited liability and total management, whereas the limited partners have to voice in the management and their only financial exposure is to the extent of their investment. In some ways the limited partners' interest is similar to that of stockholders in a corporation.

LINTEL- A horizontal board that supports the load over an opening such as a door or window.

LIQUIDATED DAMAGES CLAUSE- An agreement between the parties that in the event of a breach, the amount of damages shall be liquidated (set or fixed). The amount is set before the breach, usually at the time of making the contract, on the assumption that the exact amount of damages is difficult to determine because of the nature of the contract.

LIS PENDENS- A notice of pending litigation recorded to give constructive notice of a suit that has been filed. A recorded notice that a lawsuit is pending, the outcome of which may affect title to property.

LISTING- An employment contract between a broker and his principal (client). A listing is automatically canceled upon the death of the agent (real estate broker) or the principal (owner). Another real estate broker must negotiate a new listing with the owner upon the death of the real estate broker.

LISTING AGREEMENT- An employment contract authorizing a broker to sell, lease, or exchange an owner's property.

LITIGATION- A civil lawsuit; a judicial controversy.

LOAN COMMITTEE- The committee in a lending institution that reviews and approves or disapproves the loan applications recommended by a loan officer.

LOAN CORRESPONDENT- A loan agent usually used by distant lenders to help the lender make real estate loans.

LOAN PACKAGE- A group of documents prepared along with a loan application to give the prospective lender complete details about the proposed loan.

LOAN TRUST FUND ACOUNT- (See Impound Account.)

LOAN VALUE- The lender's appraised value of the property.

LOUVER- An opening with a series of horizontal slats set at an angle to permit ventilation without admitting rain, sunlight, or vision.

LTV- These initials mean "loan to valuation"

MAI - A term that designates a person who is a member of the American Institute of Appraisers of the National Association of Realtors.

MANDAMUS- A court decree ordering a lower court judge, public official, or corporate officer to perform an act acquired of that office.

MARGIN OF SECURITY- The difference between the amount of secured loan(s) on a property and its appraised value.

MARGINAL LAND- Land which barely pays the cost of working or using it.

MARKET DATA APPROACH- (See Comparative Market Analysis.)

MARKET PRICE- The price paid regardless of pressures, motives, or intelligence.

MARKET VALUE
1. The price at which a willing seller would sell and a willing buyer would buy, neither being under abnormal pressure.
2. As defined by the courts, it is the highest price estimated in terms of money that a property would bring if exposed for sale in the open market, allowing a reasonable time to find a purchaser with knowledge of the property's use and capabilities for use.

MARKETABLE TITLE- Title free and clear of reasonable objections and doubts; also called merchantable title.

MATERIAL FACT- A fact that would be likely to affect a person's decision in determining whether to enter into a particular transaction. Any information that will influence the judgment or decision of the customer.

MECHANIC'S LIEN- A lien given by statute to persons supplying labor, materials, or other services to improve real property. Whenever a contractor, laborer, or materialman provides labor or materials to improve real property and is not paid, that person is entitled to a lien against the property as a means of securing payment. Certain statutory steps must be taken to file, record, and foreclose the lien. Memo to set: A document filed in a lawsuit which asks to be placed on the waiting list ("docket") for the next available court date.

MENACE- A threat to use duress. (See Duress.)

MERCHANTABLE TITLE- (See Marketable Title.)

MERGER OF TITLE- The combination of two estates. Also refers to the joining of one estate burdened by an encumbrance and another estate benefited by the encumbrance. Whenever a benefit and a burden are merged, the encumbrance is extinguished.

MERIDIANS- Imaginary north-south lines that intersect base lines to form a starting point for the measurement of land.

METES AND BOUNDS- Terms used to describe the boundary lines of land, setting forth all the boundary lines together with their terminal points and angles. Metes means measurements Bounds means boundaries.

MILLIONARES- Ninety percent of all millionaires become that way from owning property.

MINOR
1. A person under the age of majority.
2. In California all persons under eighteen years of age - the age of majority in California. Someone under age 18.

MINUS CASH FLOW- An event that takes place when there is not enough cash to cover expenses and service the mortgage debt.

MISREPRESENTATION- An intentional or negligent suggestion or statement of a material fact in a false manner with the intent of deceiving someone into taking a course of action he would not otherwise normally pursue. A licensee may be disciplined for misrepresentation even though the misrepresentation did not result in a loss to the principal.

MITIGATION- Facts or circumstances that tend to justify or excuse an act or course of conduct.

MOBILE HOME- A stationary, non-motorized vehicle designed and equipped for human habitation. It may be transported to a home site by special equipment.

MOLDING- Usually patterned strips used to provide ornamental variation of outline or contour, such as cornices, bases, window and doorjambs.

MONEY TO MAKE MONEY- It takes money to make money in real estate is the general belief.

MONTH-TO-MONTH TENANCY- A lease of property for a month at a time, under a periodic tenancy that continues for successive months until terminated by proper notice, usually 30 days.

MONUMENT- A fixed object and point established by surveyors or others to establish land locations.

MORATORIUM- The temporary suspension, usually by stature, of the enforcement of liability for debt.

MORTGAGE- An instrument by which property is hypothecated to secure the payment of a debt or obligation.

MORTGAGE- A contract by which property is hypothecated (pledged without delivery) for the repayment of a loan.

MORTGAGE GUARANTY INSURANCE- Insurance against financial loss available to mortgage lenders from the Mortgage Guaranty Insurance Corporation, a private company organized in 1956.

MORTGAGE LOAN BROKER- Is required to have a real estate license.

MORTGAGEE- One to whom a mortgagor gives a mortgage to secure a loan or performance of an obligation: the lender under a mortgage. (See Secured Party.) A creditor (lender) under a mortgage.

MORTGAGOR- One who gives a mortgage on his or her property to secure a loan or assure performance of an obligation; the borrower under a mortgage. (See Debtor.) A borrower (property owner) of money under a mortgage.

MULTIPLE LISTING- A listing, usually an exclusive-right-to-sell, taken by a member of an organization composed of real estate brokers with the provisions that all members will have the opportunity to find an interested client; a cooperative listing. A listing taken by a broker and shared with other brokers through a specialized distribution service, usually provided by the local real estate board. Generally, such listings are exclusive right to sell listings.

MUNICIPAL COURT- An inferior trial court having jurisdiction in cases involving up to $15,000 in money damages and in unlawful detainer actions in which the rental value is under $1,000 per month.

MUTUAL ASSENT- An agreement between the parties in a contract. The offer and acceptance of a contract.

MUTUAL WATER COMPANY- A water company organized by or for water-users in a given district, with the object of securing an ample water supply at a reasonable rate. Stock is issued to users.

NAR- National Association of Realtors.

NAREB- National Association of Real Estate Boards. This trade organization is now known as the National Association of Realtors.

NEGATIVE AMORTIZATION- Occurs when normal payments on a loan are insufficient to cover all interest then due, so that unpaid interest is added to principal. Thus, even though payments are timely made, the principal grows with each payment.

NEGATIVE AMORTIZATION- Occurs when the debt service is not sufficient to cover the interest amount of the loan. This note should only be used in area that is appreciating in value.

NEGATIVE AMORTIZATION- Occurs when the debt service is not sufficient to cover the interest amount of the loan.

NEGLIGENCE- Either the failure to act as a reasonable, prudent person, or the performance of an act that would not be done by a reasonable, prudent person.

NEGOTIABLE INSTRUMENT- A check or promissory note that meets specified statutory requirements and is therefore easily transferable in somewhat the same manner as money. The negotiable instrument can be passed by endorsement and delivery (or in some cases by mere delivery), and the transferee takes title free of certain real defenses (such as failure of consideration, fraud in the inducement) that might exist against the original maker of the negotiable instrument.

NEPA- Abbreviation for the National Environmental Protection Act, a federal statute requiring all federal agencies to prepare an Environmental Impact Statement and meet other requirements whenever a major federal action is anticipated that could significantly affect the environment.

NET LISTING- listing that provides that the agent may retain as compensation for his or her services all sums received over and above a stated net price to the owner. An employment agreement that entitles the broker to a commission only in the amount, if any that the sales price of the property exceeds the listing price.

NONFREEHOLD ESTATE- A lease tenancy. (See under Estates for the four types of leasehold estates.)

NONJUDICIAL FORECLOSURE- Foreclosure and sale of property without resort to court action, by private sale. For deeds of trust the foreclosure provisions are outlined by the statutes and the requirements in the security instrument, which include a notice of default, right to reinstate, publication of sale, and trustee's sale.

NOTARY PUBLIC- An individual licensed by the state to charge a fee for acknowledging signatures on instruments.

NOTE- A signed written instrument promising payment of a stated sum of money. Shortened name for a promissory note.

NOTICE OF COMPLETION- A notice recorded after termination of work on improvements, limiting the time in which mechanic's liens can be filed against the property.

NOTICE OF DEFAULT- A notice that is recorded in the county recorder's office stating that a trust deed is in default and that the holder has chosen to have the property sold. The trustor (property owner) has three months after the date of recording to reinstate the loan. Recorded notice that a trustor has defaulted on his secured debt.

NOTICE OF NONRESPONSIBILITY- A notice provided by law designed to relieve a property owner from responsibility for the cost of work done on the property or materials furnished for it when the work or materials were ordered by a person in possession. Notice relieving an owner from possession. Notice relieving an owner from mechanic's liens for work on property not ordered by that owner.

NOTICE TO QUIT- A notice to a tenant to vacate rented property. Also called a three-day notice. Notice given to a tenant in default of his lease terms or on his rent, which directs him either to cure the default or to vacate the premises.

NOVATION- The acceptance of a new contract in substitution for the old contract, with the intent that the new contract will extinguish the original contract. Sometimes encountered in transfers of deeds of trust, where the new owner assumes the debt and the lender, through novation, releases the former owner from any liability under the original promissory note and deed of trust.

NUISANCE- Anything that is injurious to health or indecent or offensive to the senses, or any obstruction to the free use of property so as to interfere with the comfortable enjoyment of life or property or unlawfully obstructs the free passage or use, in the customary manner, of any navigable lake or river, bay, stream, canal, or basin, or any public park, square, street, or highway. A legal wrong arising from acts or use of one's property in a way that unreasonably interferes with another's use of hid property.

OBLIGEE - A promisor; a person to whom another is bound by a promise or another obligation.

OBSOLESCENCE- Loss in value due to reduced desirability and usefulness of a structure because its design and construction become obsolete; loss because of becoming old-fashioned and not in keeping with modern needs.

OFFER- A proposal to create a contract, which signifies the present intent of the offeror to be legally bound by his proposal.

OFFEREE- A person to whom an offer is made.

OFFEROR- A person who makes an offer.

OFFSET STATEMENT- Statement by owner of a deed of trust or mortgage against the property, setting forth the present status of the debt and lien. Also called a beneficiary statement.

OPEN HOUSE- Is an opportunity for a licensee to meet potential buyers and sellers, and therefore is considered to be in the best interest of the licensee and not the seller. This is NOT the most effective way to method to advertise a piece of rental property.

OPEN LISTING- An authorization given by a property-owner to a real estate agent in which the agent is given the nonexclusive right to secure a purchaser. Open listings may be given to any number of agents without liability to compensate any except the one who first secures a buyer ready, willing, and able to meet the terms of the listing or who secures the acceptance by the seller of a satisfactory offer.

OPEN-END MORTGAGE OR DEED OF TRUST- A mortgage containing a clause that permits the mortgagor or trustor to borrow additional money without rewriting the mortgage or deed of trust.

OPTION- A right to have an act performed in the future; a right given for a consideration to purchase or lease a property upon specified terms within a specified time; a contract to keep an offer open for a particular period of time. The right of a person to buy or lease property at a set price at any time during the life of a contract.

OPTION LISTING- A listing that also includes an option, permitting the broker to buy the property at the stated price at any time during the listing period.

ORAL CONTRACT- A verbal agreement, one not reduced to writing.

ORDINANCE- A law passed by a political subdivision of the state (such as a town, city, or county).

ORIENTATION- Placement of a house on its lot with regard to its exposure to the rays of the sun, prevailing winds, privacy from the street, and protection from outside noises.

OR-MORE CLAUSE- A simple prepayment clause that permits the borrower to make a normal payment or any larger amount, up to and including the entire outstanding balance, without a prepayment penalty.

OSTENSIBLE AGENCY- An agency implied by law because the principal intentionally or inadvertently caused a third person to believe someone to be his agent, and that third person acted as if that other person was in fact the principal's agent.

OVER IMPROVEMENT- An improvement that is not the highest and best use for the site on which it is placed, by reason of excessive size or cost.

OVERAGES IN TRUST ACCOUNT- Any unexplained overages in the trust account must be held in trust by the licensee and must be maintained in a separate record.

OVERHANG- The part of the roof that extends beyond the walls and that shades buildings and covers walks.

OWNERSHIP- The right of a person to use and possess property to the exclusion of others.

PARITY WALL - A wall erected on the line between two adjoining properties that are under different ownership for the use of both owners.

PAROL- Oral or verbal.

PAROL EVIDENCE RULE- A rule of courtroom evidence that once the parties make a written contract, they may not then introduce oral agreements or statements to modify the terms of that written agreement. An exception exists for fraud or mistake, which will permit the parties to offer evidence to vary the terms of the writing.

PARQUET FLOOR- Hardwood flooring laid in squares or patterns.

PART TIME STATUS- Many real estate agents have other full-time jobs. . A part time agent cannot devote a full time effort to represent a client; therefore the failure to disclose a part time status is considered unethical real estate practice.

PARTIAL RECONVEYANCE- In a deed of trust or mortgage, a clause that permits release of a parcel or part of a parcel from the effects and lien of that security instrument. The release usually occurs upon the payment of a specified sum of money.

PARTITION ACTION- A legal action by which co-owners seek to sever their joint ownership. The physical division of property between co-owners, usually through court action.

PARTNERSHIP- An association of two or more persons to unite their property, labor or skill, or any one or combination thereof, in prosecution of some joint business, and to share the profits in certain proportions. An agreement of two or more individuals jointly to undertake a business enterprise. If it is a general partnership, all partners have unlimited liability and, absent other agreements, share equally in the management and profits of the business.

PATENT- Conveyance of title to government land.

PAYMENT CLAUSE- A provision in a promissory note, deed of trust, or mortgage, permitting the debtor to pay off the obligation before maturity.

PENNY- The term, as applied to nails, that serves as a measure of nail length and is abbreviated by the letter d.

PERCENTAGE LEASE- A lease on property, the rental for which is determined by the amount of business done by the tenant, usually a percentage of gross receipts from the business, with provision for a minimum rental.

PERIMETER HEATING- Baseboard heating or any system in which the heat registers are located along the outside walls of a room, especially under the windows.

PERIODIC TENANCY- A leasehold estate that continues indefinitely for successive periods of time, until terminated by proper notice. When the periods are one month in duration, it is often called a month-to-month lease.

PERSONAL INJURY- A term commonly used in tort (e.g. negligence cases) indicating an injury to one's being or body (for example, cuts or broken bones) as opposed to injury to his property.

PERSONAL PROPERTY- Any property that is not real property. (See Real Property.) Property that is movable, as opposed to real property, which is immovable; also includes intangible property and leasehold estates.

PETITIONER- A person who petitions the court on a special proceeding or a motion.

PIER- A column of masonry used to support other structural members.

PITCH- The incline or rise of a roof.

PLAINTIFF- The party who initiates a lawsuit; the person who sues another.

PLATE- A horizontal board placed on a wall or supported on posts or studs to carry the trusses of a roof or rafters directly; a shoe or base member, as of a partition or other frame; a small flat board placed on or in a wall to support girders and rafters, for example.

PLEDGE- Deposition of personal property by a debtor with a creditor as security for a debt or engagement.

PLEDGEE- One who is given a pledge as security. (See Security Party)

PLEDGOR- One who gives a pledge as security. (See Debtor)

PLOTTAGE INCREMENT- The appreciation in unit value created by joining smaller ownerships into one large single ownership.

PLYWOOD
1. Laminated wood made up in panels.
2. Several thickness of wood glued together with grains at different angles for strength.

POCKET LISTING- When a real estate licensee convinces a seller that he can procure a buyer for the property and wants to withhold the information from the multiple listing services. This is considered unethical.

POINTS- Points paid for refinancing must be spread out over the life of the loan to be deductible on a person's income tax.

POLICE POWER- The right of the state to enact laws and regulations and its right to enforce them for the order, safety, health, morals, and general welfare of the public. The power of the state to prohibit acts that adversely affect the public health, welfare, safety, or morals. (Zoning and building codes are examples of exercise of the police power.)

POWER OF ATTORNEY- An instrument authorizing a person to act as the agent of the person granting it. A special power of attorney limits the agent to a particular or specific act, as a landowner may grant an agent special power of attorney to convey a single and specific parcel of property. Under a general power of attorney, the agent may do almost anything for the principal that the principal could do himself or herself. A document authorizing a person (an attorney-in-fact) to act as an agent.

POWER OF TERMINATION- The future interest created whenever there is a grant of a fee simple subject to a condition subsequent estate. The future interest matures into a present interest estate only if the holder timely and properly exercises his right upon a breach by the current holder of the fee estate.

PREFABRICATED HOUSE- A house manufactured, and sometimes partly assembled, before delivery to the building site.

PREJUDGEMENT ATTACHMENT- An attachment of property made before the trial, with the intent of holding that property as security, to have an asset to sell if the court judgment is favorable to the attaching party.

PREPAYMENT PENALTY- Penalty for the payment of a note before it actually becomes due. A fee or charge imposed upon a debtor who desires to pay off his loan before its maturity. Not all prepayment clauses provide for a penalty, and in many real estate transactions the law regulates the amount of penalty that may be changed.

PRESCRIPTION- Securing of an easement by open, notorious, and uninterrupted use, adverse to the owner of the land for the period required by statute, which, in California, is five years. A method of obtaining an easement by adverse use over a prescribed period of time.

PRESENT INTEREST- An estate in land that gives the owner the right to occupy his property immediately; as opposed to a future interest, which grants only the right to occupy the premises at some future date.

PRESUMPTION- That which may be assumed without proof. A conclusion or assumption that is binding in the absence of sufficient proof to the contrary.

PRIMA FACIE
1. Presumptive on its face.
2. Assumed correct until overcome by further proof. Facts, evidence, or documents that are taken at face value and presumed to be as they appear (unless proven otherwise).

PRINCIPAL- The (client) employer of an agent. Someone who hires an agent to act on his behalf. The term also refers to the amount of an outstanding loan (exclusive of interest).

PRIORITY- That which comes first in point of time or right. Superior, higher, or preferred rank or position.

PRIVITY- Closeness or mutuality of a contractual relationship.

PROBATE- Court supervision of the collection and distribution of a deceased person's estate. This takes place in Superior Court within the county where the property is located.

PROCEDURAL LAW- The law of how to present and proceed with legal rights (for example, laws of evidence, enforcement of judgments). It is the opposite of substantive law.

PROCURING CAUSE- That event originating from another series of events that, without a break in continuity, results in an agent's producing a final buyer. Proximate cause. A broker is the procuring cause of a sale if his or her efforts set in motion an unbroken chain of events that resulted in the sale.

PROFIT A PRENDRE- An easement coupled with a power to consume resources on the burdened property.

PROMISSORY NOTE- A written promise to pay a designated sum of money at a future date.

PROPERTY- Anything that may be owned. Anything of value in which the law permits ownership.

PRORATION OF TAXES- Division of the taxes equally or proportionately between buyer and seller on the basis of time of ownership.

PUFFING- Putting things in their best perspective is not subject to disciplinary action.

PUNITIVE DAMAGES- Money awarded by the court for the sole purpose of punishing the wrongdoer, and not designed to compensate the injured party for his damages.

PURCHASE MONEY INSTRUMENT- A mortgage or deed of trust that does not permit a deficiency judgment in the event of foreclosure and sale of the secured property for less than the amount due on the promissory note. It is called purchase money since the deed of trust and mortgage was used to buy all or part of the property.

PURCHASE-MONEY MORTGAGE OR PURCHASE-MONEY DEED OF TRUST- A mortgage or deed of trust given as part or all of the consideration for the purchase of property or given as security for a loan to obtain money for all or part of the purchase price.

QUARTER ROUND - A molding whose profile resembles a quarter of a circle.

QUASI- Almost as if it were.

QUASI-CONTRACT- A contract implied by law; that is, the law will imply and consider certain relationships as if they were a contract.

QUIET ENJOYMENT- The right of an owner to the use of property without interference with his or her possession or use.

QUIET TITLE ACTION- A lawsuit designed to remove any clouds on a title to property. It forces the claimant of an adverse interest in property to prove his right to title; otherwise he will be forever barred from asserting it.

QUITCLAIM DEED- A deed to relinquish any interest in property that the grantor may have, but implying no warranties. A deed that transfers only whatever right, title, or interest, if any, the grantor owns, without implying any warranties.

QUITE TITLE- A court action brought to establish title and to remove a cloud from the title.

RADIANT HEATING - A method of heating, usually consisting of coils or pipes placed in the floor, wall, or ceiling.

RAFTER- One of a series of boards of a roof designed to support roof loads.

RANGE- A strip of land six miles wide, determined by a government survey, running in a north-south direction.

RATIFICATION- The adoption or approval of an act performed on behalf of a person without previous authorization. Approval and confirmation of a prior act performed on one's behalf by another person without previous authority.

READY, WILLING, AND ABLE BUYER- A purchaser of property, who is willing to buy on terms acceptable to the seller, and who further possesses the financial ability to consummate the sale. Producing such a buyer sometimes earns the broker a commission, even though a sale is not forthcoming.

REAL ESTATE LICENSEE- Can be a good source to find first trust deeds that can be purchased at a discount.

REAL ESTATE BOARD- An organization whose members consist primarily of real estate brokers and salespersons.

REAL ESTATE INVESTMENT TRUST- A specialized form of holding title to property that enables investors to pool their resources and purchase property, while still receiving considerable tax advantages, without being taxed as a corporation. Also known as REIT.

REAL ESTATE TRUST- A special arrangement under federal and state law whereby investors may pool funds for investments in real estate and mortgages and yet escape corporation taxes.

REAL PROPERTY- Land and anything affixed, incidental, or appurtenant to it, and anything considered immovable under the law. Land, buildings, and other immovable property permanently attached thereto.

REALTOR- A real estate broker holding active membership in a real estate board affiliated with the National Association of Realtors.

REBUTTABLE PRESUMPTION- A presumption that is not conclusive and that may be contradicted by evidence. A presumption that applies unless proven inapplicable by the introduction of contradictory evidence.

RECAPTURE
1. The rate of interest necessary to provide for the return of an investment.
2. A provision in tax laws that reduces certain benefits from claiming depreciation.

RECEIVER- A neutral third party, appointed by the court to collect the rents and profits from property, and distribute them as ordered by the court. Often used as a remedy when mere damages are inadequate.

RECONVEYANCE- A conveyance to the landowner of the legal title held by a trustee under a deed of trust. The transfer of property back from a lender who holds an interest as security for the payment of a debt. In a deed of trust, the beneficiary reconveys property upon satisfaction of the promissory note.

RECORDATION- Filing of instruments for record in the office of the county recorder. The act of having a document filed for record in the county recorder's office. Once recorded, the instrument gives constructive notice to the world.

REDEMPTION- Buying back one's property after a judicial sale. The repurchasing of one's property after a judicial sale.

REFORMATION- A legal action to correct a mistake in a deed or other document.

REINSTATEMENT- A right available to anyone under an accelerated promissory note secured by a deed of trust or mortgage on property. If a deed of trust is foreclosed by trustee's sale, the debtor may have up to three months from the recording of the notice of default to pay the amount in arrears plus interest and costs, thereby completely curing the default (reinstating) without penalty.

REJECTION- Refusal to accept an offer. Repudiation of an offer automatically terminates the offer.

RELEASE- To give up or abandon a right. The release of rights may be voluntary, as when one voluntarily discharges an obligation under a contract. The release may be involuntary, by operation of the law; for example, one's wrongful conduct may bar him from asserting his rights. In deeds of trust a partial release clause frees certain property from the security of the deed of trust upon the payment of specified sums of money.

RELEASE CLAUSE- A stipulation in a deed of trust or mortgage that upon the payment of a specific sum of money to the holder of the deed of trust or mortgage, a particular lot or area shall be removed from the blanket lien on the whole area involved.

RELICTION- The gradual lowering of water from the usual watermark.

REMAINDER- An estate that vests after the termination of the prior estate, such as after a life estate. Example: A life estate may be granted to Adams, with the remainder granted to Baker. Most commonly, an estate (future interest) that arises in favor of a third person after a life estate.

REMAND- To send back to a lower court for further action.

REMEDY- The means by which a right is enforced, preserved, or compensated. Some of the more common remedies are damages, injunctions, rescission, and specific performance.

RENT- The consideration paid by a tenant for possession of property under a lease.

RENTAL PROPERTY- Renting property to the first person that comes along can be a costly mistake.

RENTAL PROPERTY- Rental income from a smaller property may show a higher rate of profit than from a more expensive property.

RENUNCIATION- Is the cancellation of an agency relationship by the real estate agent requires written notice to the principal.

RESCISSION- The unmaking of a contract, and the restoring of each party to the same position each held before the contract arose.

RESCISSION OF CONTRACT- The canceling of a contract by either mutual consent of the parties or legal action.

RESERVATION- A right or interest retained by a grantor when conveying property; also called an exception.

RESIDUE- That portion of a person's estate that has not been specifically devised.

RESPA- Prohibits the giving and receiving of kickbacks and unearned fees.

RESPONDEAT SUPERIOR- This Latin phrase, "let the master answer," means that an employer is liable for the tortuous acts of an employee, and a principal is liable for the acts of an agent. To be liable, the acts must be within the "course and scope" of the agency or employment. For example, an employer would not be liable for the acts of an employee while at home and not doing work for the employer.

RESPONDENT- The person against whom an appeal is taken; the opposite of an appellant.

RESTRICTION- A limitation on the use of real property arising from a contract or a recorded instrument. An encumbrance on property that limits the use of it; usually a covenant or condition.

RETALIATORY EVICTION- A landlord's attempt to evict a tenant from a lease because the tenant has used the remedies available under the warranty of habitability.

REVERSION- The right a grantor keeps when he or she grants someone an estate that will or may end in the future. Examples: The interest remaining with a landlord after he or she grants a lease, or the interest an owner of land has after he or she grants someone a life estate. Any future interest (estate) left in the grantor. The residue of an estate left in the grantor after the termination of a lesser estate.

REVOCATION- Withdrawal of an offer or other right, thereby voiding and destroying that offer or right. It is a recall with intent to rescind.

RIDGE- The horizontal line at the junction of the top edges of two sloping roof surfaces. (The rafters at both slopes are nailed at the ridge.)

RIDGE BOARD- The board placed on edge at the ridge of the roof to support the upper ends of the rafters; also called rooftree, ridge piece, ridge plate, or ridgepole.

RIGHT OF SURVIVORSHIP- The right to acquire the interest of a deceased joint-owner. It is the distinguishing feature of a joint tenancy.

RIGHT OF WAY- The right to pass over a piece of real property or to have pipes, electrical lines, or the like go across it. An easement granting a person the right to pass across another's property.

RIPARIAN RIGHTS- The right of a landowner with regard to a stream crossing or adjoining his or her property.

RISER
1. The upright board at the back of each step of a stairway.
2. In heating, a riser is a duct slanted upward to carry hot air from the furnace to the room above.

RULE AGAINST PERPETUITIES- A complex set of laws designed to prevent excessive restrictions on the transferability of property. The rule holds that "no interest is good unless it must vest, if at all, not later than 21 years after some life in being at the creation of the interest."

RUMFORD ACT- Prohibits discrimination in employment and housing. Is enforced by the Department of Fair Employment and Housing.

SAFETY CLAUSE - In a listing agreement, a provision that if anyone found by the broker during his listing period purchases the property within a specified time after the expiration of the listing, the broker receives his full commission.

SALE-LEASEBACK- A situation in which the owner of a piece of property sells it and retains occupancy be leasing it from the buyer.

SALES CONTRACT- A contract between buyer and seller setting out the terms of sale.

SALESPERSON- An individual licensed to sell property, but who must at all times be under the supervision and direction of a broker.

SANDWICH LEASE - A leasehold interest that lies between the primary lease and the operating lease. Example: A leases to B; B subleases to C; C subleases to D. C's lease is a sandwich lease.

SASH- A wood or metal frame containing one or more windowpanes.

SATISFACTION- Discharge of a mortgage or deed of trust lien from the records upon payment of the secured debt. Discharge of an obligation or indebtedness by paying what is due.

SAVINGS ACCOUNT- An investor should not place money in a savings account if he wants to have financial freedom.

SEAL- An impression mark or stamp made to attest to the execution of an instrument.

SECONDARY FINANCING- A loan secured by a second mortgage or a second deed of trust.

SECONDARY MONEY MARKET- Where loans are purchased and sold.

SECTION- A square mile of land, as established by government survey, containing 640 acres.

SECURED DEBT- An obligation that includes property held as security for the payment of that debt; upon default, the property may be sold to satisfy the debt.

SECURED PARTY- The party having the security interest in personal property. The mortgagee, conditional seller, or pledgee is referred to as the secured party.

SECURITY AGREEMENT- An agreement between the secured party and the debtor that creates a security interest in personal property. It replaced such terms as chattel mortgage, pledge, trust receipt, chattel trust, equipment trust, conditional sale, and inventory lien.

SECURITY DEPOSIT- A deposit made to assure performance of an obligation, usually by a tenant. A sum of cash given as collateral to ensure faithful performance of specified obligations.

SECURITY INTEREST- A term designating the interest of a secured creditor in the personal property of the debtor.

SEIZIN- The possession of land under a claim of freehold.

SENIOR LIEN- A lien that is superior to or has priority over another lien. Also, the first deed of trust or lien on a property.

SEPARATE PROPERTY- Property that is owned by a husband or wife and that is not community property. It is property acquired by either spouse prior to marriage or by gift or inheritance after marriage; also, in California, it is the income from separate property after marriage. Property held by a married person that is not community property; it includes property owned before marriage and property acquired after marriage by gift or inheritance.

SEPTIC TANK- An underground tank in which sewage from the house is reduced to liquid by bacterial action and drained off.

SERVIENT ESTATE- That parcel of property, which is burdened by and encumbered with an easement.

SERVIENT TENEMENT- An estate burdened by an easement.

SET-BACK ORDINANCE- An ordinance prohibiting the erection of a building or structure between the curb and the set-back line. (see Building Line)

SEVERALTY- Sole ownership of property. Ownership by one person.

SEVERALTY OWNERSHIP- Ownership by only one person; sole ownership.

SHAKE- A hand-split shingle, usually edge-grained.

SHEATHING- Structural covering, such as boards, plywood, or wallboard, placed over the exterior studding or rafters of a house.

SHERIFF'S DEED- A deed given by court order in connection with the sale of property to satisfy a judgment.

SILL- The board or piece of metal forming the lower side of an opening, such as a door-sill or windowsill.

SINKING FUND
1. A fund set aside from the income from property that, with accrued interest, will eventually pay for replacement of the improvements.
2. A similar fund set aside to pay a debt.

SMALL CLAIMS COURT- A branch of the Municipal Court. The rules of this court forbid parties to be assisted by attorneys dispense with most formal rules of evidence, and have all trials heard by judges. The monetary limit of cases before the court is $1,500.

SOIL PIPE- Pipe carrying waste from the house to the main sewer line.

SOLD TO THE STATE- A bookkeeping entry on the county tax rolls indicating that the property taxes are delinquent. The entry begins the five-year redemption period, after which the property may be physically sold to the public for back taxes.

SOLE OR SOLE PLATE- A structural member, usually two-by-four, on which wall and partition studs rest.

SPAN- The distance between structural supports, such as walls, columns, piers, beams, and girders.

SPECIAL ASSESSMENT- Legal charge against real estate by a public authority to pay the cost of public improvement, as distinguished from taxes levied for the general support of government.

SPECIFIC PERFORMANCE- A legal action to compel performance of a contract; for example a contract for the sale of land. A contract remedy by which one party is ordered by the court to comply with the terms of the agreement.

SPOUSE- A person's husband or wife.

SQUARE FOOTAGE OF BUILDING- An appraiser always uses the exterior dimensions to calculate the square footage of a building.

SRA- The Society of Real Estate Appraisers.

STARE DECISIS- A fundamental principle of law, which holds that courts should follow prior decisions on a point of law. A proper decision is a binding precedent on equal or lower courts having the same facts in controversy.

STATUTE- A written law.

STATUTE OF FRAUDS- The state law that provides that certain contracts must be in writing in order to be enforceable in the courts. Examples: real property leased for more than one year or an agent's authorization to sell real estate. A law that requires certain contracts (including most real estate contracts) to be in writing to be enforceable.

STATUTE OF LIMITATIONS- A statute that requires lawsuits to be brought within a certain time to be enforceable. The basic periods are one year for personal injury, two years for oral contracts, three years for damages to real or personal property, four years for written contracts, and three years from date of discovery for fraud.

STEERING- An illegal procedure where individual buyers, who are usually minorities, are only shown properties in specific neighborhoods.

STEPPED-UP BASIS- A higher, increased tax value of property given as the result of most sales or taxable transfers. The tax basis is used in computing capital gains and losses on the transfer of property.

STOP NOTICE- A notice served on the owner of property or custodian of funds. It requests, with certain penalties for noncompliance, that any funds due to a general contractor be paid to the claimant, laborer, or materialman.

STRAIGHT MORTGAGE OR DEED OF TRUST- A mortgage or deed of trust in which there is no reduction of the principal during the term of the instrument. Payments to interest are usually made on an annual, semiannual, or quarterly basis.

STRAIGHT NOTE- A promissory note that is unamortized. The principal is paid at the end of the term of the note.

STRAIGHT-LINE DEPRECIATION- An accounting procedure that sets the rate of depreciation as a fixed percentage of the amount to be depreciated; the percentage stays the same each year.

STRING, STRINGER
1. A timber or other support for cross-members.
2. In stairs, the support on which the stair treads rest.

STUDS OR STUDDING- Vertical supporting timbers in walls and partitions.

SUBCHAPTER-S CORPORATION- A corporation that, for federal tax purposes only, is taxed similarly to a partnership. The corporate entity is disregarded for most federal tax purposes, and the shareholders are generally taxed as individual partners.

SUBJACENT SUPPORT- Support that the soil below the surface gives to the surface of the land.

SUBJECT TO
1. Burdened by and liable for an obligation.
2. A method of taking over a loan without becoming personally liable for its payment

"SUBJECT TO" MORTGAGE OR DEED OF TRUST- When a grantee takes a title to real property subject to a mortgage or deed of trust, he or she is not responsible to the holder of the promissory note for the payment of any portion of the amount due. The most that he or she can lose in the event of a foreclosure is his or her equity in the property. In neither case is the original maker of the note released from his or her responsibility. (See also Assumption of Mortgage or Deed of Trust.)

SUBLEASE- A lease given by a tenant.

SUBORDINATE- To make subject or junior to.

SUBORDINATION AGREEMENT- In a mortgage or deed of trust, a provision that a later lien shall have a priority interest over the existing lien. It makes the existing lien inferior to a later lien, in effect exchanging priorities with that later lien.

SUBORDINATION CLAUSE- Senior lien that makes it inferior to what would otherwise be a junior lien.

SUBROGATE- To substitute one person for another's legal rights to a claim or debt.

SUBROGATION- The substitution of another person in place of the creditor with regard to an obligation.

SUBSTANTATIVE LAW- The laws describing rights and duties. Differs from procedural law, which only describes how to enforce and protect rights.

SUCCESSION- The inheritance of property.

SUCCESSOR IN INTEREST- The next succeeding owner of an interest in property. The transferee or recipient of a property interest.

SUPERIOR COURT- The principal trial court of the state; a court of unlimited monetary and subject matter jurisdiction, and an appeal court for decisions of municipal courts and small claims courts.

SUPREME COURT- The highest court in the California and the federal court structure. This court is almost exclusively an appeals court, accepting (by certiorari) only those cases that, in the court's discretion, involve issues of significant magnitude and social importance.

SURETY- One who guarantees the performance by another, a guarantor.

SURVEY- The process by which a parcel of land is located on the ground and measured.

SWING LOAN- This is a short-term equity loan.

SYNDICATION- A group of individuals pooling their resources to purchase property through the holding vehicle of a partnership, corporation, or other association. Each individual owns share in the legal entity formed to acquire and hold title to the property. This is an alternative method to finance and purchase real estate. This allows an investment in real estate with out having to do any of the work.

TAX - A compulsory charge on property or individuals, the payment of which supports a government.

TAX BASIS- The tax value of property to the taxpayer. It is a figure used to compute capital gains and losses.

TAX DEED- Deed issued to the purchaser at a tax sale.

TAX SALE- Sale of property after a period of nonpayment of taxes.

TENANCY- A leasehold estate. (For specific types of leases see Estates.)

TENANCY-IN-COMMON- Ownership by two or more persons who hold an undivided interest in real property, without right of survivorship; the interests need not be equal.

TENANT- One who leases real property from the owner.

TENEMENTS- All rights in real property that pass with a conveyance of it.

TENTATIVE MAP- The Subdivision Map Act requires subdividers initially to submit a tentative map of their tract to the local planning commission for study. The approval or disapproval of the planning commission is noted on the map. Thereafter, the planning commission requests a final map of the tract embodying any changes.

TENURE IN LAND- The manner in which land is held.

TERMITE SHIELD- A shield, usually of non-corrodible metal, placed on top of the foundation wall or around pipes to prevent passage of termites.

TERMITES- Antlike insects that feed on wood.

TESTAMENT- The written declaration of one's last will.

TESTAMENTARY DISPOSITION- A gift passing by will.

TESTATE- Describes a person who dies leaving a will.

TESTATOR- A person who makes a will. Technically, a testator is a male and a testatrix is a female, although in common use testator refers to anyone who makes a will.

THE VOLUNTARY AFFIRMATIVE MARKETING AGREEMENT- Is a voluntary commitment by real estate licensees to promote fair housing by using methodology that is fairer than government regulations.

THIRTY-DAY NOTICE- A notice terminating a periodic tenancy without cause, by ending a tenancy thirty days from date of service.

THREE-DAY NOTICE- A notice giving a tenant three days in which to cure a default or quit the premises. It is the first step in an unlawful detainer action, as the means of terminating a lease for cause. When rent is delinquent, it is sometimes called a notice to quit or pay rent.

THRESHOLD- A strip of wood or metal beveled on each edge and used above the finished floor under outside doors.

"TIME IS OF THE ESSENCE"- These words, when placed in an agreement, make it necessary that all time limitations and requirements be strictly observed.

TITLE- Evidence of the owner's right or interest in property.

THE RIGHT OF OWNERSHIP- The evidence of a person's ownership or interest in property.

TITLE INSURANCE- Insurance written by a title company to protect a property-owner against loss if title is defective or not marketable. A special policy of insurance issued by a title company, insuring the owner against loss of or defects in title to the insured property. The policy may be either a CLTA policy, issued to the property owner and to non-institutional lenders, or an ALTA policy, issued to institutional lenders.

TOPOGRAPHY- Nature of the surface of the land. Topography may be level, rolling, or mountainous.

TORRENS TITLE- A title included in a state-insured title system no longer used in California.

TORT
1. A wrongful act.
2. A wrong or injury.
3. Violation of a legal right. A civil wrong, not arising from a breach of contract. Most torts lie in negligence, although they could also be intentional torts (such as assault and battery, trespass) or strict liability torts.

TORTFEASOR- A person who commits a tort.

TORTIOUS- Conduct which amounts to a tort.

TOWNSHIP- A territorial subdivision that is six miles long and six miles wide and that contains 36 sections, each one mile square.

TRADE FIXTURES- Articles of personal property that are annexed to real property but that are necessary to the carrying on of a trade and are removable by the owner. Fixtures installed to further one's trade, business, or profession. They are an exception to the general rule that fixtures are part of a building. Such fixtures installed by a tenant may be removed before the expiration of the tenancy.

TRADE-IN- Method of guaranteeing an owner a minimum amount of cash on the sale of his or her present property to permit him or her to purchase another. If the property is not sold within a specified time at the listed price, the broker agrees to arrange financing to purchase the property at an agreed-upon discount.

TRANSFER- Conveyance; passage of title.

TRANSFER DISCLOSURE STATEMENT- It is the responsibility of the seller (transferor) to issue the statement.

TRANSFEREE- The person to whom a transfer is made.

TRANSFEROR- The person who makes a transfer.

TREADS- Horizontal boards of a stairway.

TRESPASS- An invasion of an owner's rights in his or her property.
1. Unauthorized entry onto another's land.
2. Invasion of another's rights or property.

TRESPASSER- One who trespasses. The importance of this classification of individuals on property is created by the methods for removal and the liability of the property owner if the trespasser is injured on his property.

TRIM- The finish materials in a building, such as moldings applied around openings (window trim, door trim) or at the floor and ceiling (baseboard, cornice, picture molding).

TRUST- A right of property, real or personal, held by one party called the trustee for the benefit of another party called the beneficiary. Arrangement whereby one person holds property for the benefit of another under fiduciary (special confidential) relationship.

TRUST DEED- Deed given by a borrower to a trustee to be held pending fulfillment of an obligation, which is usually repayment of a loan to a beneficiary. A deed of trust. Foreclosure of this deed maybe at a foreclosure or at a trustee's sale. The lender in the trust deed is referred to as the beneficiary. Trust deed investments should be on improved property rather than on unimproved property.

TRUST FUNDS- Consists of money or property received by a real estate licensee on behalf of others. Cannot be given to the seller without the permission of the buyer. Must be in writing. These funds may not be commingled. It is against the law. Protects the money in case a legal action is taken against the broker. These records are subject to audit and examination by the D.R.E. All records and corresponding instruments must be kept for a period of (3) three years.

TRUSTEE- One who holds property in trust for another. The person who holds property in trust for another. In a deed of trust, the person who holds bare legal title in trust.

TRUSTEE'S DEED- The deed issued by the beneficiary after the foreclosure and sale under a deed of trust.

TRUSTEE'S SALE- The private sale of property held by a trustee under a deed of trust as part of the foreclosure proceedings.

TRUSTEE'S SALE- This sale must be conducted in approximately four months.

TRUSTOR
1. One who conveys his or her property to a trustee.
2. The borrower or debtor under a deed of trust.

TRUSTOR'S REINSTATEMENT RIGHTS- These rights continue for five business days prior to the date of the trustee's sale.

TRUTH IN LENDING LAW- A complex set of federal statutes designed to provide a borrower with a means of discovering and comparing the true costs of credit. Under

Regulation Z of the act, certain borrowers of property have three days after accepting a loan to rescind without cost or liability.

UNDUE INFLUENCE - A compulsory charge on property or individuals, the payment of which supports a government.

UNDUE INFLUENCE- Taking any fraudulent or unfair advantage of another's necessity or weakness of mind. Using a position of trust and confidence improperly to persuade a person to take a course of action. By relying on the trusted confidant, the decision maker fails to exercise his free will and independent judgment.

UNEARNED INCREMENT- An increase in value of real estate due to no effort on the part of the owner, often due to an increase in population.

UNENFORCEABLE- Incapable of being enforced at law. An example of an unenforceable contract is an oral listing agreement to pay a broker a commission.

UNIFORM COMMERCIAL CODE- A group of statutes establishing a unified and comprehensive scheme for regulation of security transactions in personal property and other commercial matters, superseding the existing statutes on chattel mortgages conditional sales, trust receipts, assignment of accounts receivable, and other similar matters.

UNILATERAL- One-sided, ex parte.

UNJUST ENRICHMENT- A legal doctrine that prevents a person from inequitably benefiting from another's mistake, poor judgment, or loss. In a land sales contract the vender may no longer keep both the property and the buyer's excess payments (over his damages) in the event of breach, because to do so would unjustly enrich him at the buyer's expense.

UNLAWFUL DETAINER- An action to recover possession of real property. A lawsuit designed to evict a defaulting tenant, or anyone unlawfully in possession of property, from premises. It is summary in nature, entitled to a priority court trial, and litigates only the right to possession of property (and damages resulting there from).

UNLAWFULL- Illegal.

UNRUH CIVIL RIGHTS ACT- Deals with equal rights in business establishments, prohibits age limitations in housing, and sets age limitations necessary for senior housing. It states that all persons within California are free and equal no matter what their sex, race color, ancestry, national origin or disability, they are entitled to full and equal accommodations.

UNSECURED DEBT- A debt not backed by specific property to satisfy the indebtedness in case of default.

URBAN PROPERTY- City property; closely settled property.

USURY- Claiming a rate of interest greater that that permitted by law. Charging a greater rate of interest on loans than the rate allowed by law (10 percent in many cases).

VA LOAN - This loan does not contain a "due on sale " clause.

VALID

1. Legally sufficient and authorized by law.
2. Having force or binding force. Fully effective at law; legally sufficient.

VALLEY- The internal angle formed by the junction of two sloping sides of a roof.

VALUATION
1. Estimated worth or price.
2. The act of valuing by appraisal.

VARIABLE INTEREST RATE- An interest rate that fluctuates in a set proportion to changes in an economic index, such as the cost of money. Extensive regulations cover use of VIRs in loans on residential property.

VARIANCE- An exception or departure from the general rule. An exception granted to a property owner, relieving him from obeying certain aspects of a zoning ordinance. It's granting is discretionary with the zoning authorities and is based on undue hardship suffered by the property owner because of unique circumstances affecting his property.

VENDEE- Purchaser or buyer or real property.

VENDOR- Seller of real property.

VENEER- Thin sheets of wood placed over another material.

VENT- A pipe installed to provide a flow of air to or from a drainage system or to provide a circulation of air within such system to protect trap seals from siphonage and back-pressure.

VENUE- The location in which a cause of action occurs; it determines the court having jurisdiction to hear and decide the case. For real estate, the court having proper venue is one in the county in which the property is located.

VERIFICATION- A sworn statement before a duly qualified officer as to the correctness of the contents of an instrument. Written certification under oath and/or penalty of perjury, confirming the truth of the facts in a document.

VERSUS- Against (abbreviated v. or vs.). Used in case names, with the plaintiff's name given first.

VESTED- Bestowed upon someone, such as title to property. Absolute, not contingent or subject to being defeated.

VETERAN'S EXEMPTION- A deduction from the annual property tax allowed to a qualified veteran residing on residential property. Since July 1978, it has amounted to $40 off the normal tax bill.

VOID- To have no legal force or effect; that which is unenforceable. Unenforceable, null, having no legal effect.

VOIDABLE- An instrument that appears to be valid and enforceable on its face but is, in fact, lacking some essential requirement. May be declared void, but is valid unless and until declared void.

VOLUNTARY LIEN- Any lien placed on property with the consent of the owner or as a result of the voluntary act of the owner.

WAIVE - To give up a right.

WAIVER- Giving up of certain rights or privileges. The relinquishment may be voluntary and knowing, or it may occur involuntarily through action of the parties. The action resulting in the waiver is unilateral, and requires no action or reliance by the other party.

WARRANTY- An absolute undertaking or promise that certain facts are as represented. Occasionally used interchangeably with guarantee.

WARRANTY DEED- A deed that is used to convey real property and that contains warranties of title and quiet possession; the grantor the lawful claims thus agrees to defend the premises against of third persons. It is commonly used in other states, but in California the grant deed has replaced it. Used predominantly in states that do not have title insurance companies. This deed contains six full warranties of protection to the buyer, including warranties that the seller owns the property, that it is unencumbered, and that the seller will defend title against any defects.

WARRANTY OF HABITABILITY- Implied warranty in residential leases. The landlord covenants by implication that the premises are suitable for human occupancy. The implied warranties are found in the statutes and implied by common law.

WASTE- The destruction, or material alteration of or injury to premises by a tenant-for-life, or tenant, or tenant-for-years. Example: a tenant cutting down trees or mining coal. The destruction, injury, material alteration, or abusive use of property by a person rightfully in possession, but who does not own the fee or entire estate (for example, by a lessee or life tenant).

WATER TABLE- Distance from the surface of the ground to a depth at which natural groundwater is found.

WILL- A document that directs the disposition of one's property after death.

WITNESSED WILL- A formal will, signed by the testator in the presence of two or more witnesses, each of whom must also sign the will.

WRAP AROUND MORTGAGE (DEED OF (See All-Inclusive Deed of Trust.) TRUST) WRAP-AROUND DEED OF TRUST- A sophisticated financing package that permits the seller to sell his property without paying off the outstanding deed of trust. The buyer's larger loan, which is used to purchase the property, includes provisions for paying off the seller's existing loan.

WRIT- A process of the court under which property may be seized. An order from the court to the sheriff or other law enforcement officer directing and authorizing a specific act.

WRIT OF ATTACHMENT- A writ authorizing and directing the physical attachment (seizure) of property.

WRIT OF EXECUTION- An order directing the sheriff to seize property to satisfy a judgment.

WRIT OF IMMEDIATE POSSESSION- An order authorizing a landlord to obtain immediate possession of a tenant's premises, pending the outcome of an unlawful detainer action or other court proceeding.

ZONE - The area set off by the proper authorities in which the real property can be used for only specific purposes.

ZONING- Act of city or county authorities specifying the type of use to which property may be put in specific areas. A government's division of a city or other geographic area into districts, and the regulation of property uses within each district.

Index

154

Broker's license 4, 10, 11, 12, 14, 102, 358, 395

Bundle of Rights 3, 25, 26, 27, 28, 30, 31, 39, 40, 42, 43, 181

Business Opportunity 7, 6, 15, 397, 398, 399, 400, 405, 406, 429

C

California Association of Realtors 2, 3, 20, 23, 24, 165, 429

California Land Title Association 70, 71, 430

Cal-Vet 250, 263, 266, 267, 268, 274, 302, 403, 408, 429

Cancellation 4, 109, 112, 121, 143, 211, 361, 436, 458

Capital Gain 323, 330, 333, 429

Capitalization Rate 301, 304, 306, 413, 414, 420, 429

Caveat Emptor 429

Certificate of Title 46, 69, 75, 174, 403

Chain of title 69, 70, 71, 162, 174, 430

Change of Ownership 69, 381

Civil Law 46, 47, 48, 73, 430

Cloud on the Title 55, 69, 163, 164

Color of Title 156, 424

Commercial Banks 250, 251, 255, 273

Commission 7, 2, 5, 6, 14, 15, 22, PB 24, 48, 79, 104, 105, 108, 109, 113, 114, 115, 117, 122, 123, 124, 125, 126, 127, 136, 138, 139, 140, 142, 143, 144, 145, 146, 148, 150, 152, 154, 167, 169, 171, 177, 262, 263, 274, 320, 323, 344, 358, 359, 361, 376, 377, 378, 379, 380, 386, 394, PB 395, 404, 409, 414, 415, 416, 420, 421, 431, 439, 451, 457, 459, 463, 466

Common Areas 194, 336, 345, 346, 352, 354, 432

Common Law 3, 46, 47, 48, 73, 83, 163, 430, 431, 438, 468

Community Apartment Project 346, 352, 390

Community Property 46, 47, 48, 50, 52, 53, 54, 69, 73, 74, 155, 164, 431, 460

Compensation 5, 6, 10, 15, 83, 84, 102, 104, 105, 107, 113, 115, 123, 126, 137, 142, 145, 146, 147, 148, 380, 428, 431, 434, 437, 444, 451

Concurrent Ownership 50, 71, 73

Condemnation 280, 286, 431, 437, 446

Condition 16, 17, 28, 40, 41, 68, 71, 107, 111, 113, 114, 117, 135, 143, 144, 147, 170, 174, 184, 194, 197, 202, 203, 240, 265, 272, 279, 283, 287, 300, 306, 310, 322, 380, 381, 382, 383, 385, 386, 432, 434, 436, 440, 445, 455, 458

Condition Subsequent 28, 40, 68, 71, 432, 440, 455

Conditional Delivery 165, 174

Condominium 32, 67, 264, 336, 346, 352, 353, 354, 390, 403, 471

Conflict of Interest 112, 139, 144, 145

Consideration 31, 34, 40, 43, 50, 78, 81, 83, 110, 112, 113, 114, 115, 118, 161, 162, 163, 175, 180, 181, 183, 192, 201, 202, 204, 258, 281, 282, 329, 331, 344, 423, 424, 428, 432, 442, 444, 451, 452, 456, 458

Construction Costs 306, 307

Contract 4, 10, 14, 15, 22, PB 24, 31, 33, 41, 43, 66, 70, 74, 77, 78, 79, 80, 81, 82, 83, 84, 85, 86, 101, 102, 103, 104, 106, 107, 108, 110, 111, 112, 113, 114, 115, 116, 117, 118, 122, 123, 124, 125, 126, 127, 128, 135, 140, 141, 142

Conventional Loan 433, 435, 441

Cooperating Broker 124, 136, 137, 144, 145, 146

Corporation 6, 10, 20, 22, PB 24, 50, 102, 252, 253, 257, 258, 273,   346, 425, 433, 440, 442, 448, 450, 457, 462, 463

Cost Approach 278, 288, 298, 301, 303, 305, 309, 310, 471

Cost Basis 322, 323, 329, 330, 333, 424, 433

Costa-Hawkins Rental Housing Act 205

Counteroffer 111

County Assessor 316, 329, 330, 331, 407

Covenant 67, 68, 114, 117, 180, 193, 200, 202, 433, 458

Covenants, Conditions and Restrictions 67, 379

Creative Financing 42

Credit Unions 6, 250, 251, 255, 272, 273, 434

Creditor 54, 269, 270, 275, 400, 401, 405, 427, 435, 450, 454, 460, 463, 472

D

Declaration of Default 214

476

Chapter 1

Test Your Knowledge: 1-A, 2-D, 3-C, 4-C, 5-C, 6-B, 7-D
Chapter Quiz: 1-B, 2-C, 3-D, 4-C, 5-D, 6-C, 7-C, 8-C, 9-B, 10-B, 11-B, 12-A, 13-A,
14-A, 15-D, 16-C, 17-C, 18-D, 19-B, 20-D

Chapter 2

Test Your Knowledge: 1-B, 2-A, 3-D, 4-C, 5-B, 6-A, 7-D
Chapter Quiz: 1-B, 2-D, 3-C, 4-A, 5-D, 6-B, 7-A, 8-C, 9-B, 10-D, 11-C, 12-D, 13-A,
14-A, 15-B, 16-B, 17-A, 18-D, 19-A, 20-D

Chapter 3

Test Your Knowledge: 1-C, 2-A, 3-D, 4-C, 5-A, 6-D, 7-C
Chapter Quiz: 1-C, 2-A, 3-C, 4-D, 5-A, 6-C, 7-D, 8-B, 9-C, 10-A, 11-C, 12-B, 13-D,
14-C, 15-A, 16-B, 17-A, 18-D, 19-C, 20-D

Chapter 4

Test Your Knowledge: 1-B, 2-C, 3-D, 4-C, 5-B, 6-A, 7-D
Chapter Quiz: 1-C, 2-B, 3-A, 4-A, 5-D, 6-C, 7-D, 8-D, 9-C, 10-A, 11-B, 12-C, 13-D,
14-C, 15-B, 16-A, 17-D, 18-B, 19-C, 20-D

Chapter 5

Test Your Knowledge: 1-A, 2-B, 3-C, 4-B, 5-B, 6-D, 7-C
Chapter Quiz: 1-A, 2-D, 3-A, 4-C, 5-C, 6-B, 7-C, 8-A, 9-B, 10-D, 11-A, 12-B, 13-B,
14-A, 15-D, 16-C, 17-D, 18-A, 19-C, 20-C

Chapter 6

Test Your Knowledge: 1-B, 2-A, 3-C, 4-D, 5-C, 6-D, 7-D
Chapter Quiz: 1-B, 2-C, 3-A, 4-A, 5-D, 6-C, 7-B, 8-D, 9-C, 10-D, 11-D, 12-D, 13-B,
14-D, 15-B, 16-C, 17-A, 18-C, 19-A, 20-B

Chapter 7

Test Your Knowledge: 1-D, 2-A, 3-B, 4-B, 5-D, 6-D, 7-D
Chapter Quiz: 1-D, 2-A, 3-D, 4-C, 5-D, 6-A, 7-B, 8-D, 9-C, 10-A, 11-C, 12-B, 13-C,
14-B, 15-B, 16-D, 17-D, 18-D, 19-D, 20-B

Chapter 8

Test Your Knowledge: 1-A, 2-C, 3-B, 4-A, 5-D, 6-C, 7-B
Chapter Quiz: 1-D, 2-B, 3-A, 4-B, 5-C, 6-C, 7-C, 8-A, 9-B, 10-D, 11-A, 12-D, 13-A,
14-D, 15-C, 16-C, 17-B, 18-A, 19-D, 20-A

Chapter 9

Test Your Knowledge: 1-C, 2-D, 3-C, 4-A, 5-B, 6-D, 7-B
Chapter Quiz: 1-B, 2-C, 3-D, 4-C, 5-A, 6-A, 7-D, 8-A, 9-B, 10-C, 11-B, 12-A, 13-D,
14-B, 15-B, 16-D, 17-A, 18-B, 19-A, 20-D

Chapter 10

Test Your Knowledge: 1-D, 2-A, 3-B, 4-C, 5-D, 6-D, 7-B
Chapter Quiz: 1-D, 2-B, 3-C, 4-A, 5-C, 6-B, 7-D, 8-A, 9-B, 10-C, 11-A, 12-C, 13-D, 14-D, 15-A, 16-D, 17-B, 18-A, 19-C, 20-D

Chapter 11

Test Your Knowledge: 1-B, 2-B, 3-C, 4-D, 5-A, 6-C, 7-B
Chapter Quiz: 1-B, 2-C, 3-A, 4-B, 5-B, 6-D, 7-B, 8-B, 9-A, 10-C, 11-D, 12-C, 13-C, 14-D, 15-B, 16-A, 17-A, 18-C, 19-B, 20-A

Chapter 12

Test Your Knowledge: 1-C, 2-B, 3-A, 4-D, 5-B, 6-C, 7-D
Chapter Quiz: 1-C, 2-B, 3-D, 4-A, 5-C, 6-B, 7-D, 8-C, 9-B, 10-D, 11-A, 12-B, 13-C, 14-C, 15-D, 16-D, 17-D, 18-D, 19-A, 20-B

Chapter 13

Test Your Knowledge: 1-D, 2-C, 3-A, 4-B, 5-D, 6-C, 7-A
Chapter Quiz: 1-D, 2-B, 3-C, 4-B, 5-A, 6-A, 7-C, 8-B, 9-B, 10-A, 11-D, 12-B, 13-A, 14-C, 15-B, 16-D, 17-C, 18-A, 19-C, 20-D

Chapter 14

Test Your Knowledge: 1-B, 2-D, 3-D, 4-C, 5-A, 6-A, 7-D
Chapter Quiz: 1-B, 2-D, 3-D, 4-C, 5-A, 6-D, 7-B, 8-B, 9-A, 10-C, 11-B, 12-A, 13-C, 14-D, 15-B, 16-C, 17-C, 18-D, 19-D, 20-A

Chapter 15

Chapter Quiz: 1-C, 2-B, 3-A, 4-C, 5-D, 6-B, 7-A, 8-C, 9-B, 10-D, 11-A, 12-C, 13-B, 14-A, 15-D, 16-C, 17-B, 18-A, 19-D, 20-B